48: *American Poets, 1880-1945,* Second Series, edited by Peter Quartermain (1986)

49: *American Literary Publishing Houses, 1638-1899,* 2 parts, edited by Peter Dzwonkoski (1986)

50: *Afro-American Writers Before the Harlem Renaissance,* edited by Trudier Harris (1986)

51: *Afro-American Writers from the Harlem Renaissance to 1940,* edited by Trudier Harris (1987)

52: *American Writers for Children Since 1960: Fiction,* edited by Glenn E. Estes (1986)

53: *Canadian Writers Since 1960,* First Series, edited by W. H. New (1986)

54: *American Poets, 1880-1945,* Third Series, 2 parts, edited by Peter Quartermain (1987)

55: *Victorian Prose Writers Before 1867,* edited by William B. Thesing (1987)

56: *German Fiction Writers, 1914-1945,* edited by James Hardin (1987)

57: *Victorian Prose Writers After 1867,* edited by William B. Thesing (1987)

58: *Jacobean and Caroline Dramatists,* edited by Fredson Bowers (1987)

59: *American Literary Critics and Scholars, 1800-1850,* edited by John W. Rathbun and Monica M. Grecu (1987)

60: *Canadian Writers Since 1960,* Second Series, edited by W. H. New (1987)

61: *American Writers for Children Since 1960: Poets, Illustrators, and Nonfiction Authors,* edited by Glenn E. Estes (1987)

62: *Elizabethan Dramatists,* edited by Fredson Bowers (1987)

63: *Modern American Critics, 1920-1955,* edited by Gregory S. Jay (1988)

64: *American Literary Critics and Scholars, 1850-1880,* edited by John W. Rathbun and Monica M. Grecu (1988)

65: *French Novelists, 1900-1930,* edited by Catharine Savage Brosman (1988)

66: *German Fiction Writers, 1885-1913,* 2 parts, edited by James Hardin (1988)

67: *Modern American Critics Since 1955,* edited by Gregory S. Jay (1988)

68: *Canadian Writers, 1920-1959,* First Series, edited by W. H. New (1988)

69: *Contemporary German Fiction Writers,* First Series, edited by Wolfgang D. Elfe and James Hardin (1988)

70: *British Mystery Writers, 1860-1919,* edited by Bernard Benstock and Thomas F. Staley (1988)

71: *American Literary Critics and Scholars, 1880-1900,* edited by John W. Rathbun and Monica M. Grecu (1988)

72: *French Novelists, 1930-1960,* edited by Catharine Savage Brosman (1988)

Documentary Series

1: *Sherwood Anderson, Willa Cather, John Dos Passos, Theodore Dreiser, F. Scott Fitzgerald, Ernest Hemingway, Sinclair Lewis,* edited by Margaret A. Van Antwerp (1982)

2: *James Gould Cozzens, James T. Farrell, William Faulkner, John O'Hara, John Steinbeck, Thomas Wolfe, Richard Wright,* edited by Margaret A. Van Antwerp (1982)

3: *Saul Bellow, Jack Kerouac, Norman Mailer, Vladimir Nabokov, John Updike, Kurt Vonnegut,* edited by Mary Bruccoli (1983)

4: *Tennessee Williams,* edited by Margaret A. Van Antwerp and Sally Johns (1984)

5: *American Transcendentalists,* edited by Joel Myerson (1988)

Yearbooks

1980, edited by Karen L. Rood, Jean W. Ross, and Richard Ziegfeld (1981)

1981, edited by Karen L. Rood, Jean W. Ross, and Richard Ziegfeld (1982)

1982, edited by Richard Ziegfeld; associate editors: Jean W. Ross and Lynne C. Zeigler (1983)

1983, edited by Mary Bruccoli and Jean W. Ross; associate editor: Richard Ziegfeld (1984)

1984, edited by Jean W. Ross (1985)

1985, edited by Jean W. Ross (1986)

1986, edited by J. M. Brook (1987)

1987, edited by J. M. Brook (1988)

Concise Series

The New Consciousness, 1941-1968 (1987)

Colonization to the American Renaissance, 1640-1865 (1988)

Realism, Naturalism, and Local Color, 1865-1917 (1988)

French Novelists, 1930-1960

Dictionary of Literary Biography • Volume Seventy-two

French Novelists, 1930-1960

7585

Edited by
Catharine Savage Brosman
Tulane University

A Bruccoli Clark Layman Book
Gale Research Inc. • Book Tower • Detroit, Michigan 48226

Manufactured by Edwards Brothers, Inc.
Ann Arbor, Michigan
Printed in the United States of America

Library of Congress Cataloging-in-Publication Data

French novelists, 1930-1960/edited by Catharine Savage
    Brosman.
        p.   cm.—(Dictionary of literary biography; v. 72)
    "A Bruccoli Clark Layman book."
    Includes index.
    ISBN 0-8103-4550-1
    1. French fiction—20th century—History and criti-
cism. 2. French fiction—20th century—Bio-bibliography.
3. Novelists, French—20th century—Biography—Dic-
tionaries. I. Brosman, Catharine Savage, 1934-   . II. Series.
PQ671.F68 1988
843'.912'09—dc19   88-16462
[B]   CIP

In Memory: Paul Victor Hill and Della Stanforth Hill

Contents

Plan of the Series ix

Foreword xi

Acknowledgments xv

Louis Aragon (Louis Andrieux) (1897-1982) 3
  Rima Drell Reck

Marcel Arland (1899-1986) 26
  Alain D. Ranwez

Marcel Aymé (1902-1967) 32
  Dorothy Brodin

Simone de Beauvoir (1908-1986) 42
  Elaine Marks

Georges Bernanos (1888-1948) 58
  William Bush

Maurice Blanchot (1907-   ) 77
  Jeffrey Mehlman

Henri Bosco (1888-1976) 83
  Arlette M. Smith

Joë Bousquet (1897-1950) 99
  Joseph Brami

Emmanuel Bove (1898-1945) 106
  F. C. St. Aubyn

Albert Camus (1913-1960) 110
  Raymond Gay-Crosier

Louis-Ferdinand Céline (Louis-Ferdinand
  Destouches) (1894-1961) 136
  David O'Connell

Pierre Drieu La Rochelle (1893-1945) 148
  Rima Drell Reck

Jean Genet (1910-1986) 170
  Joseph H. McMahon and Megan Conway

Jean Giono (1895-1970) 187
  Walter Redfern

Julien Green (1900-   ) 209
  John M. Dunaway

Louis Guilloux (1899-1980) 220
  Walter Redfern

Joseph Kessel (1898-1979) 231
  Alain D. Ranwez

André Malraux (1901-1976) 237
  Robert S. Thornberry

Henry de Montherlant (1896-1972) 273
  John Fletcher

Paul Nizan (1905-1940) 288
  Walter Redfern

Raymond Queneau (1903-1976) 300
  Vivian Kogan

Antoine de Saint-Exupéry (1900-1944) 314
  Catharine Savage Brosman

Jean-Paul Sartre (1905-1980) 331
  Catharine Savage Brosman

Georges Simenon (1903-   ) 357
  Catharine Savage Brosman

Elsa Triolet (1896-1970) 377
  Konrad Bieber

Boris Vian (1920-1959) 384
  Zvjezdana Rudelic

Marguerite Yourcenar (1903-1987) 397
  C. Frederick Farrell, Jr., and Edith R. Farrell

Books for Further Reading 411

Contributors 415

Cumulative Index 419

Plan of the Series

. . . Almost the most prodigious asset of a country, and perhaps its most precious possession, is its native literary product—when that product is fine and noble and enduring.

Mark Twain*

The advisory board, the editors, and the publisher of the *Dictionary of Literary Biography* are joined in endorsing Mark Twain's declaration. The literature of a nation provides an inexhaustible resource of permanent worth. We intend to make literature and its creators better understood and more accessible to students and the reading public, while satisfying the standards of teachers and scholars.

To meet these requirements, *literary biography* has been construed in terms of the author's achievement. The most important thing about a writer is his writing. Accordingly, the entries in *DLB* are career biographies, tracing the development of the author's canon and the evolution of his reputation.

The purpose of *DLB* is not only to provide reliable information in a convenient format but also to place the figures in the larger perspective of literary history and to offer appraisals of their accomplishments by qualified scholars.

The publication plan for *DLB* resulted from two years of preparation. The project was proposed to Bruccoli Clark by Frederick G. Ruffner, president of the Gale Research Company, in November 1975. After specimen entries were prepared and typeset, an advisory board was formed to refine the entry format and develop the series rationale. In meetings held during 1976, the publisher, series editors, and advisory board approved the scheme for a comprehensive biographical dictionary of persons who contributed to North American literature. Editorial work on the first volume began in January 1977, and it was published in 1978. In order to make *DLB* more than a reference tool and to compile volumes that individually have claim to status as literary history, it was decided to organize volumes by topic, period, or genre. Each of these freestanding volumes provides a biographical-bibliographical guide and overview for a particular area of literature. We are convinced that this organization—as opposed to a single alphabet method—constitutes a valuable innovation in the presentation of reference material. The volume plan necessarily requires many decisions for the placement and treatment of authors who might properly be included in two or three volumes. In some instances a major figure will be included in separate volumes, but with different entries emphasizing the aspect of his career appropriate to each volume. Ernest Hemingway, for example, is represented in *American Writers in Paris, 1920-1939* by an entry focusing on his expatriate apprenticeship; he is also in *American Novelists, 1910-1945* with an entry surveying his entire career. Each volume includes a cumulative index of subject authors and articles. Comprehensive indexes to the entire series are planned.

With volume ten in 1982 it was decided to enlarge the scope of *DLB*. By the end of 1986 twenty-one volumes treating British literature had been published, and volumes for Commonwealth and Modern European literature were in progress. The series has been further augmented by the *DLB Yearbooks* (since 1981) which update published entries and add new entries to keep the *DLB* current with contemporary activity. There have also been *DLB Documentary Series* volumes which provide biographical and critical source materials for figures whose work is judged to have particular interest for students. One of these companion volumes is entirely devoted to Tennessee Williams.

We define literature as the *intellectual commerce of a nation:* not merely as belles lettres but as that ample and complex process by which ideas are generated, shaped, and transmitted. *DLB* entries are not limited to "creative writers" but extend to other figures who in their time and in their way influenced the mind of a people. Thus the series encompasses historians, journalists, publishers, and screenwriters. By this means readers of *DLB* may be aided to perceive litera-

*From an unpublished section of Mark Twain's autobiography, copyright © by the Mark Twain Company.

ture not as cult scripture in the keeping of intellectual high priests but firmly positioned at the center of a nation's life.

DLB includes the major writers appropriate to each volume and those standing in the ranks immediately behind them. Scholarly and critical counsel has been sought in deciding which minor figures to include and how full their entries should be. Wherever possible, useful references are made to figures who do not warrant separate entries.

Each *DLB* volume has a volume editor responsible for planning the volume, selecting the figures for inclusion, and assigning the entries. Volume editors are also responsible for preparing, where appropriate, appendices surveying the major periodicals and literary and intellectual movements for their volumes, as well as lists of further readings. Work on the series as a whole is coordinated at the Bruccoli Clark Layman editorial center in Columbia, South Carolina, where the editorial staff is responsible for accuracy of the published volumes.

One feature that distinguishes *DLB* is the illustration policy–its concern with the iconography of literature. Just as an author is influenced by his surroundings, so is the reader's understanding of the author enhanced by a knowledge of his environment. Therefore *DLB* volumes include not only drawings, paintings, and photographs of authors, often depicting them at various stages in their careers, but also illustrations of their families and places where they lived. Title pages are regularly reproduced in facsimile along with dust jackets for modern authors. The dust jackets are a special feature of *DLB* because they often document better than anything else the way in which an author's work was perceived in its own time. Specimens of the writers' manuscripts are included when feasible.

Samuel Johnson rightly decreed that "The chief glory of every people arises from its authors." The purpose of the *Dictionary of Literary Biography* is to compile literary history in the surest way available to us–by accurate and comprehensive treatment of the lives and work of those who contributed to it.

The *DLB* Advisory Board

Foreword

DLB 72: French Novelists, 1930-1960 is the second of three volumes in the *DLB* series devoted to French fiction writers of the present century. The first volume, *DLB 65: French Novelists, 1900-1930,* treats novelists whose principal production appeared either before World War I or in the ten years or so following the war and who are thus associated chiefly with the early decades of the century, even if, like Roger Martin du Gard and François Mauriac, they continued publishing well after 1930. The third volume will feature authors whose careers were established around 1960 or later, or whose most characteristic or most significant works date from this period. Among them are the New Novelists, whose remarkable literary innovations began to attract widespread attention in the late 1950s and 1960s, although in some cases their first work appeared earlier.

This chronological grouping of novelists whose careers often spanned more than one period was made on practical grounds more than on critical ones, and like other such classifications is somewhat arbitrary and inevitably produces some overlapping. The arrangement is not to be taken as an attempt to define literary schools and generations, although to some degree the authors classed together share aesthetic and other concerns, and among their works there are similarities characteristic of their historical periods.

This is particularly true of *DLB 72,* which spans the second decade of the interwar period, World War II, and the following fifteen years and deals with what can accurately be called the generation of committed literature and French existentialism. In many ways 1930 marks a literary watershed in France, as it marks a political watershed. The major literary monuments of early twentieth-century aesthetic experimentation, notably the works of André Gide and Marcel Proust, had appeared, and, while they proved to be very influential on later generations, including the New Novelists, there was a sense that they could not, and doubtless should not, be rewritten, and that their aesthetic was perhaps no longer appropriate for the time. Surrealism had not run its course, but the finest days of the movement were over, and former surrealists such as Louis Ara-

gon were becoming involved in politics and moving in new literary directions. The 1920s climate, which now appears to have been one of a vitalistic iconoclasm and relative optimism, even ebullience, was replaced by an atmosphere of tension that many observers recognized as the forerunner of another European conflict. On the political scene, the precarious situation and then dissolution of the Weimar Republic in neighboring Germany, the consolidation of fascism in Italy, the failure of the League of Nations, and political extremism and growing social unrest in France were signs that European peace, which the treaties of 1919 were to have assured, was far from stable. The crash of the American stock market had shown by its European repercussions how interdependent and vulnerable were the capitalistic economies of the Western powers. After mid decade, the continued military buildup and persecutions under Hitler, the Spanish civil war and fall of the young republic, the erosion of the accomplishments of the French Popular Front government, the annexation of Austria by Germany, the Munich agreement, and the invasion of Czechoslovakia signaled increasing unrest in Europe, which ultimately led to the declaration of war in September 1939, plunging Europe into days even darker than those of what had been called the Great War.

While not all the novelists in this volume responded identically to the events of the 1930s, and some were not yet publishing, as a generation they were marked by the sense of the inadequacy, even the failure of European democracy and by forebodings of conflict that would surpass what they had known before. They were also heirs to what Marcel Arland had termed in 1924 "un nouveau mal du siècle"–a sense of futility and malaise that doubtless reflected the horrors of World War I. As the poet Paul Valéry wrote in 1919 in "La Crise de l'esprit," "Nous autres, civilisations, nous savons maintenant que nous sommes mortelles" (We civilizations now know that we are mortal). It is no surprise then that, as a whole, the work of these novelists reflects both metaphysical disquiet and social and political concerns. Their political allegiances varied widely, of course, from the fascism of Pierre Drieu La Rochelle and the anti-Semitism of Louis-Ferdinand Céline, to the Christian monarchism of Georges Bernanos and the communism of Paul Nizan, and this is visible in their work, both fictional and polemic. But in having concluded from the darkening years prior to 1939 that radical social changes were both inevitable and desirable, and having made social criticism central in their fiction these writers are generally alike. They have also tended to distance themselves from what they considered an absurd world and adopt positions that approached nihilism. Even an author such as Jean Giono, whose work remained outside literary trends, revealed how his age impinged upon him when he adopted the pacifism that is visible in his work.

As for World War II itself, it marked French literature in ways that cannot be fully assessed. A number of seasoned writers disappeared in its course, including Nizan and Antoine de Saint-Exupéry; the deaths of others, some doubtless on the thresholds of their careers, extinguished much literary talent. Drieu La Rochelle died by his own hand, partly as a result of the events of the Occupation; the course of Céline's career was changed forever by his exile and postwar imprisonment in Denmark. The work of Jean Cayrol, who will appear in the third volume, was profoundly marked by his years in a concentration camp. Other writers, not included in these volumes, such as Robert Brasillach, executed for collaboration, had their careers ended as a result of the conflict.

Moreover, there were many interruptions in the careers of writers who did survive, and some found writing impossible, while others were able to compose and publish work of high quality, such as *La Reine morte* (*Queen After Death*) by Henry de Montherlant, Albert Camus's *L'Etranger* (*The Stranger*) and *Le Mythe de Sisyphe* (*The Myth of Sisyphus*), all published in 1942, and Jean-Paul Sartre's *Huis clos* (*No Exit*), published in 1945. Some authors lost partly finished manuscripts that were never recovered. At the war's end, many intellectuals shared a sense that there should be radical changes in French and European society, and that their writings should serve as a foundation for these changes. That there were deep disagreements on what should be done, in a nation that was characterized by widely diverging political beliefs and had gone through a traumatic Occupation, became clear all too shortly but did not immediately undermine the impulse toward change. The careers of many

of the novelists included here, such as Aragon, Simone de Beauvoir, Montherlant, and Sartre, were shaped in the postwar years by their desire to make their writing serve through underscoring the weaknesses and needs of contemporary France. For most of them this concern lasted past mid century and continued to characterize their work, even as younger writers and those who had come later to literary maturity were exploring other directions in fiction.

It would be erroneous to suppose that the social and political concerns that mark much of the fiction of the thirty years covered by this volume stifled writers' imaginations and produced chiefly tedious *romans à thèse* and undistinguished social criticism masking as fiction. A number of novels now recognized as masterpieces of the twentieth century, such as Céline's *Voyage au bout de la nuit* (*Journey to the End of the Night*), André Malraux's *La Condition humaine* (*Man's Fate*), Bernanos's *Journal d'un curé de campagne* (*Diary of a Country Priest*), Sartre's *La Nausée* (*Nausea*), and Camus's *L'Etranger*, belong to the period. Although some writers continued to cultivate the traditional short story, psychological novel, and novel of manners, others were led to formal innovations. Malraux rejected traditional psychological portraiture and used such techniques as clipped notations, multiple plot lines, and rapid, almost cinematographic switching between scenes to convey such events as the Shanghai uprisings of the 1920s and the Spanish civil war. In "Qu'est-ce que la littérature?" (*What Is Literature?*, 1947) Sartre, the very model of the committed writer, called for a new fiction to fit the postwar understanding of social and psychological man and had already displayed his own innovations in *Le Sursis* (*The Reprieve*) in 1945.

These examples illustrate how what Sartre saw as the acceleration of the pace of the historical process in the twentieth century has had as its parallel the rapid evolution of fictional form, as writers search for the new, or at least attempt to shape old forms to changing realities. This is one of the hallmarks of modern French fiction. Yet few critics in 1900 could have conceived of the variety and richness that the novel would display in France well before the end of the new century. A form that had been preeminently associated with the mimetic intentions of romanticism and realism—although certain of the symbolists had also adapted it to their ends—was to undergo, by mid century or shortly thereafter, modifications so sweeping and numerous as to test its identity, eroding its generic distinctiveness and making it, in the term of more than one critic, an *anti-roman*. By interior ironies, redefinition of its contours, and restatement of its subject matter, the novel form has been called into question and has taken on alternately the features of poetry, criticism, drama, autobiography, essay, history, and film. It has thus shown more of the remarkable resilience that had already made it the preferred genre of postclassical France. In the early decades of the century, even as Valéry was writing that he would not compose a novel, because of the arbitrariness of the genre–that is, he could not deign to write a sentence such as "The marquise ordered her carriage and went out at five o'clock"–Proust, Gide, and others were demonstrating how fictional structure could be like that of a great poem, or a great cathedral, or a piece of music, a puzzle, or a mathematical formula, with internal rigor and coherence as well as ornamental beauty. From the *roman*–the medieval term meaning a narrative, whether in prose or verse, in the vulgar or Romance tongue–through its late medieval, Renaissance, and numerous modern avatars, the romance or novel has proved itself to be both attractive to popular audiences and suitable for some of the loftiest and most ingenious expressions of sentiment and ideas of which the Western mind has proved itself capable. It is as if the very concept of story, with its linear structure corresponding to the temporal dimension of human experience, were singularly fitting for the rendering of this experience; even later fictions that are deliberately nonlinear and atemporal draw their identities from reference to the basic journey pattern that they seek to overturn.

Nor has any literary genre been more sensitive to the tremendous developments in the sciences as well as to the profound social and historical changes of the century. Even if analogies, such as that which critics once sought to establish between Albert Einstein and Proust–to take but one example–have proved shaky, post-Newtonian physics and its vast technological consequences have affected, it would seem, the contents of fiction and its form alike. Certain writers have refused to give their work a sense of closure, seeking instead the impression of expansion, as well as nonlinearity, distortions brought about by observers, and other parallels to physical phenomena. Mathematics itself is reflected in certain fictional undertakings, as the essays on Raymond Queneau in the present

volume and Georges Perec in the third volume reveal. Philosophy, linguistics, and the social sciences have had an even greater impact; not only have individual writers been influenced by such figures as Friedrich Nietzsche, Sigmund Freud, Edmund Husserl, Henri Bergson, and, more recently, Ferdinand de Saussure, Claude Levi-Strauss, and Jacques Lacan: twentieth-century psychology, psychiatry, anthropology, and sociology have claimed the novel as one of their fields of investigation as well as a privileged form of expression. Such characteristics as fictional polyvalence and ambiguity, multiple plots and narrators, and competing levels of reality within the text mirror the multiplication of modes of knowledge in the twentieth century. Most of all, the modern French novel has shared with the sciences an epistemological function, calling into question previous modes of knowledge, proposing new ones, and questioning, by its ironic self-interrogation, the very possibility and value of knowledge. As for the great historical upheavals of the twentieth century–wars, economic crises, revolutions, colonial uprisings–there is no need to dwell further here on their reflections in French fiction, since they are more striking and widespread in the period treated in this volume than in any other.

The desire to show the widest possible range of fictional types and experimentation, while giving full treatment to those authors who are now considered the greatest modern French novelists, is the principle underlying these volumes. Both historical importance and what now seems like lasting value have been weighed. Currents such as the poetic novel, the working-class novel, the feminist novel, the ideological novel, and the experimental novel occupy an important place in the selection. In this context the term *experimental* is not intended to denote any particular technique or content but merely a departure from previous norms; as Alain Robbe-Grillet rightly observed, Gustave Flaubert wrote the "new novel" of 1857, Marcel Proust that of 1913. In addition, these volumes treat numerous other figures, whose production does not fit entirely into the rough categories just mentioned. There is a wide range of aesthetic, ideological, and behavioral opposites: innovators and traditionalists, Communists and royalists, Catholics and atheists, feminists and misogynists, working-class writers and aristocrats, partisans of thought and partisans of action, activists and recluses, practitioners of the *roman-fleuve* and those of the terse narrative.

Readers will note, however, the predominant movement toward formal and ideological liberalism–that is, a loosening of forms and an ideological drift away from authoritarian nineteenth-century structures and standards toward a questioning of all inherited values. That these phenomena do not always appear together does not detract from their forcefulness in the modern French novel, which, it can be argued, has played more than once the role of an instrument of social change, while also reacting to change. On the one hand, for instance, a great literary innovator such as Proust is in most respects a social conservative; on the other, a literary traditionalist such as Martin du Gard questions profoundly the society that preceded World War I.

Readers will observe also the significant place occupied by foreign literary influences, particularly American writers and such novelists as Fyodor Dostoyevski and Franz Kafka, and by other arts–painting, the cinema–whose aesthetic principles often underlie the fictional experimentation reflected here. It is more than a curiosity, furthermore, that many French novelists have traveled widely or lived abroad; there are also a number of foreigners who have made French their literary language, although they were born to others. This literary cosmopolitanism has been a major influence in the development of the modern French novel.

A further phenomenon to be noted is the importance of magazines, schools, literary friendships, and other connections between French novelists; despite, on the part of some, tendencies to iconoclasm and independence, occasionally to isolation, many, like their counterparts in previous centuries, played important roles in literary groups, notably those of the *Nouvelle Revue Française* and, later, of *Tel Quel.* Literary friendships have been strikingly important, as the essays on Gide and Martin du Gard in *DLB 65* illustrate. Taken as a whole, the modern French novel demonstrates in several ways what Julia Kristeva terms intertextuality–strictly speaking, the presence of one text in another, for instance, by allusion or quotation; more loosely construed, any reference of a text (thematic or formal) to previous ones. For these novelists have been voracious readers as well as writers, and they have written for those who know the canon, even when they have rejected it: Nathalie Sarraute's no-

tion of character cannot be understood without reference to Honoré de Balzac. Reflected in these essays, moreover, is a web of personal relationships among authors, not just the friendships referred to above but also marriages and love affairs between writers that were central to their development; the most striking illustration is furnished by two authors in this volume, Aragon and Elsa Triolet, in the joint publication of their *Œuvres romanesques croisées* (1964-1974).

One further observation to be made on French literary life concerns the numerous and prestigious prizes for fiction, prizes that are mentioned time and again in the *DLB* essays. The announcements of the Goncourt, Médicis, Fémina, Renaudot, Interallié, and Académie Française awards are always major events of the literary year. A number of novelists treated in these three volumes won the Nobel Prize for Literature: Romain Rolland (1915), Roger Martin du Gard (1937), André Gide (1947), François Mauriac (1952), Albert Camus (1957), Jean-Paul Sartre (who rejected the 1964 prize), Claude Simon (1985). The Irish novelist Samuel Beckett, who wrote a large part of his work in French and was the Nobel laureate in 1969, is treated in volumes 13 and 15 of the *DLB.*

Three practical observations need to be added. First, the French novelist *DLB* volumes do not include essays on writers whose work belongs to a Francophone literature outside of France; the development of fiction in Black Africa, North Africa, and the Antilles is separate and significant enough to deserve treatment by itself, and Quebec novelists are treated in the *DLB* volumes on Canadian writers. Nor are novelists dealt with here who are considered Swiss or Belgian. Second, the claim is not being made that these three *DLB*s are exhaustive. There are other novelists in France in this century who, it might be argued, deserve a place in one of these three volumes. While some were omitted for practical reasons, others were excluded because, in one way or another, their work did not seem as representative or as significant as that of others. Such decisions inevitably reflect editorial preferences. Third, the lists of references following each essay do not include several major general bibliographies; along with suggestions for further reading, these are given at the end of each volume.

–Catharine Savage Brosman

Acknowledgments

This book was produced by Bruccoli Clark Layman, Inc. Karen L. Rood is senior editor for the *Dictionary of Literary Biography* series. Margaret A. Van Antwerp was the in-house editor.

Production coordinator is Kimberly Casey. Art supervisor is Cheryl Crombie. Copyediting supervisor is Joan M. Prince. Typesetting supervisor is Kathleen M. Flanagan. Laura Ingram and Michael D. Senecal are editorial associates. The production staff includes Rowena Betts, Charles D. Brower, Joseph Matthew Bruccoli, Patricia Coate, Mary Colborn, Mary S. Dye, Sarah A. Estes, Cynthia Hallman, Judith K. Ingle, Maria Ling, Warren McInnis, Kathy S. Merlette, Sheri Neal, Virginia Smith, and Jack Turner. Jean W. Ross is permissions editor. Joseph Caldwell, photography editor, and Penney Haughton did photographic copy work for the volume.

Walter W. Ross and Rhonda Marshall did the library research with the assistance of the staff at the Thomas Cooper Library of the University of South Carolina: Daniel Boice, Cathy Eckman, Gary Geer, Cathie Gottlieb, David L. Haggard, Jens Holley, Dennis Isbell, Jackie Kinder, Marcia Martin, Jean Rhyne, Beverly Steele, Ellen Tillett, Carol Tobin, and Virginia Weathers.

French Novelists, 1930-1960

Dictionary of Literary Biography

Louis Aragon
(Louis Andrieux)
(3 October 1897-24 December 1982)

Rima Drell Reck
University of New Orleans

SELECTED BOOKS: *Feu de joie* (Paris: Sans Pareil, 1920);

Anicet ou Le Panorama (Paris: Gallimard, 1921);

Les Aventures de Télémaque (Paris: Gallimard, 1922);

Les Plaisirs de la capitale (Berlin, 1923);

Le Libertinage (Paris: Gallimard, 1924);

Le Mouvement perpétuel (Paris: Gallimard, 1926);

Le Paysan de Paris (Paris: Gallimard, 1926); translated by Frederick Brown as *Nightwalker* (Englewood Cliffs, N.J.: Prentice-Hall, 1970); translated by Simon Watson Taylor as *Paris Peasant* (London: Cape, 1971);

Traité du style (Paris: Gallimard, 1928);

La Grande Gaîté (Paris: Gallimard, 1929);

Persécuté persécuteur (Paris: Editions Surréalistes, 1931);

Les Cloches de Bâle (Paris: Denoël & Steele, 1934); translated by Haakon M. Chevalier as *The Bells of Basel* (New York: Harcourt, Brace, 1936; London: Peter Davies/Lovat Dickson, 1937);

Hourra l'Oural (Paris: Denoël & Steele, 1934);

Pour un réalisme socialiste (Paris: Denoël & Steele, 1935);

Les Beaux Quartiers (Paris: Denoël & Steele, 1936); translated by Chevalier as *Residential Quarter* (New York: Harcourt, Brace, 1938);

Le Crève-cœur (Paris: Gallimard, 1941);

The Century Was Young, translated by Hannah Josephson (New York: Duell, Sloan & Pearce, 1941); French version published as *Les Voyageurs de l'impériale* (Paris: Gallimard, 1942);

Louis Aragon (photograph copyright © Jerry Bauer)

Josephson's translation republished as *Passengers of Destiny* (London: Pilot Press, 1947); definitive French-language edition (Paris: Gallimard, 1947);

Les Yeux d'Elsa (Neuchâtel: Editions de la Baconnière, 1942);

Cantique à Elsa (Algiers: Fontaine, 1942);

Brocéliande (Neuchâtel: Editions de la Baconnière, 1942);

Le Témoin des martyrs (Paris: clandestine edition, 1942);

Le Crime contre l'esprit, par le témoin des martyrs (Paris: clandestine edition, Bibliothèque Française, 1942);

Les Bons Voisins, as Arnaud de Saint Roman (Paris: Editions de Minuit, 1942);

En français dans le texte (Neuchâtel: Ides et Calendes, 1943);

Matisse-en-France (Paris: Martin Fabiani, 1943);

Le Musée Grévin, as François la Colère (Paris: Bibliothèque Française, 1943);

France, écoute (Algiers: Fontaine, 1944);

Aurélien (2 volumes, Fribourg: Librairie de l'Université Egloff, 1944; 1 volume, Paris: Gallimard, 1944); translated by Eithne Wilkins (London: Pilot Press, 1946; New York: Duell, Sloan & Pearce, 1947);

Neuf Chansons interdites, 1942-44, as François La Colère (N.p.: Bibliothèque Française, 1944);

La Diane française (Paris: Seghers, 1945);

En étrange pays dans mon pays lui-même; En français dans le texte; précédés de De l'exactitude historique en poésie (Monaco: A la Voile Latine, 1945);

Servitude et grandeur des Français: Scènes des années terribles (Paris: Bibliothèque Française, 1945);

Aragon, Poet of the French Resistance, translated by Rolfe Humphries, Hannah Josephson, Malcolm Cowley and others, edited by Josephson and Cowley (New York: Duell, Sloan & Pearce, 1945); republished as *Aragon, Poet of Resurgent France* (London: Pilot Press, 1946);

Saint-Pol-Roux, ou l'espoir (Paris: Seghers, 1945);

Le Musée Grévin. Les Poissons noirs et quelques poèmes inédits (Paris: Editions de Minuit, 1946);

L'Enseigne de Gersaint (Neuchâtel & Paris: Ides et Calendes, 1946);

L'Homme communiste, 2 volumes (Paris: Gallimard, 1946, 1953);

Apologie du luxe (Geneva: Skira, 1946);

Chroniques du bel canto (Geneva: Skira, 1947);

La Culture et les hommes (Paris: Editions Sociales, 1947);

Le Nouveau Crève-cœur (Paris: Gallimard, 1948);

Les Communistes, 6 volumes (Paris: Bibliothèque Française, 1949-1951); revised in *Œuvres romanesques croisées d'Elsa Triolet et Aragon* (1964-1974);

La Lumière et la paix (Paris: Lettres Françaises, 1950);

Hugo, poète réaliste (Paris: Editions Sociales, 1952);

L'Exemple de Courbet (Paris: Editions Cercle d'Art, 1952);

La Vraie Liberté de la culture, réduire notre train de mort pour accroître notre train de vie (Paris: Lettres Françaises, 1952);

Les Egmont d'aujourd'hui s'appellent André Stil (Paris: Lettres Françaises, 1952);

Le Neveu de Monsieur Duval, suivi d'une lettre d'icelui à l'auteur de ce livre (Paris: Editeurs Français Réunis, 1953);

Mes Caravanes et autres poèmes (1948-1954) (Paris: Seghers, 1954);

La Lumière de Stendhal (Paris: Denoël, 1954);

Journal d'une poésie nationale (Lyon: Armand Le Henneuse-Ecrivains Réunis, 1954);

Les Yeux et la mémoire (Paris: Gallimard, 1954);

Littératures soviétiques (Paris: Denoël, 1955);

Le Roman inachevé (Paris: Gallimard, 1956);

Entretiens sur le Musée de Dresde, by Aragon and Jean Cocteau (Paris: Editions Cercle d'Art, 1957);

La Semaine sainte (Paris: Gallimard, 1958); translated by Chevalier as *Holy Week* (New York: Putnam's, 1961; London: Hamilton, 1961);

Elsa (Paris: Gallimard, 1959);

Choix de poèmes (Moscow: Editions en Langues Etrangères, 1959);

J'abats mon jeu (Paris: Editeurs Français Réunis, 1959);

Poésies: Anthologie 1917-60 (Paris: Club du Meilleur Livre, 1960);

Les Poètes (Paris: Gallimard, 1960; revised, 1969);

Histoire parallèle des Etats-Unis et de l'U.R.S.S., 4 volumes, by Aragon and André Maurois (Paris: Presses de la Cité, 1962); revised and enlarged as *Les Deux Géants: Histoire des Etats-Unis et de l'U.R.S.S., de 1917 à nos jours*, 5 volumes (Paris: Editions du Pont Royal, 1962-1964); volumes 1 and 2 of *Histoire parallèle* translated by Patrick O'Brien as *A History of the USSR from Lenin to Khrushchev* (New York: McKay, 1961; London: Weidenfeld & Nicolson, 1964);

Le Fou d'Elsa (Paris: Gallimard, 1963);

Il ne m'est Paris que d'Elsa (Paris: Laffont, 1964);

Le Voyage de Hollande (Paris: Seghers, 1964);

Entretiens avec Francis Crémieux (Paris: Gallimard, 1964);

Les Collages (Paris: Hermann, 1965);

La Mise à mort (Paris: Gallimard, 1965);

Shakespeare, illustrated by Picasso (Paris: Editions Cercle d'Art, 1965); translated by Bernard Frechtman (New York: Abrams, 1965);

Elégie à Pablo Neruda (Paris: Gallimard, 1966);

Blanche ou l'oubli (Paris: Gallimard, 1967);

Irène, as Albert de Routisie (Paris: Or du Temps, 1968);

Les Chambres, poème du temps qui ne passe pas (Paris: Editeurs Français Réunis, 1969);

Je n'ai jamais appris à écrire ou Les Incipit (Geneva: Skira, 1969);

Henri Matisse, roman, 2 volumes (Paris: Gallimard, 1971); translated by Jean Stewart as *Henri Matisse: A Novel*, 2 volumes (London: Collins, 1972; New York: Harcourt Brace Jovanovich, 1972);

Théâtre/Roman (Paris: Gallimard, 1974);

Le Mentir-vrai (Paris: Gallimard, 1980);

Ecrits sur l'art moderne, edited by Jean Ristat (Paris: Flammarion, 1981);

La Défense de l'infini (Paris: Gallimard, 1986).

Collections: *Œuvres romanesques croisées d'Elsa Triolet et Aragon*, 42 volumes (Paris: Laffont, 1964-1974);

Œuvre poétique, 15 volumes (Paris: Livre Club Diderot, 1974-1981).

OTHER: Lewis Carroll, *La Chasse au snark—une agonie en huit crises*, translated by Aragon (Paris: Hours Press, 1928);

"La Peinture au défi" (preface), in *Exposition de collages—Arp, Braque, Dali, Derain, Duchamp, Ernst, Lissitsky, Magritte, Man-Ray, Miró, Picabia, Rodtchenko, Tanguy* (Paris: José Corti, 1930);

Cinq Sonnets de Pétrarque avec une eau-forte de Picasso et les explications du traducteur, translated by Aragon (Paris: A la Fontaine de Vaucluse, 1947);

Avez-vous lu Victor Hugo?, edited by Aragon (Paris: Editeurs Français Réunis, 1952);

Introduction aux littératures soviétiques, edited, with a preface, by Aragon (Paris: Gallimard, 1956);

Tchinghiz Aitmatov, *Djamilia*, translated by Aragon and A. Dimitriev, preface by Aragon (Paris: Editeurs Français Réunis, 1959);

Elsa Triolet choisie par Aragon, edited, with an introduction, by Aragon (Paris: Gallimard, 1960);

L'Armoire à glace un beau soir (from *Le Libertinage*, 1924), translated by Michael Benedikt as *The Mirror-Wardrobe One Fine Evening*, in *Modern French Theater*, edited by Benedikt and George E. Wellwarth (New York: Dutton, 1964), pp. 177-195.

PERIODICAL PUBLICATION: "Une Vague de rêves," *Commerce*, 2 (Autumn 1924): 89-122.

Louis Aragon, who died in 1982 at the age of eighty-five, was a quintessential twentieth-century French writer, involved in literature, politics, and painting to a degree rivaled only by Jean-Paul Sartre and André Malraux. Lacking Sartre's towering intellect and Malraux's visionary aesthetic detachment, Aragon was gifted with extraordinary talent for both poetry and fiction, a pure and vivid sense of the French language, and a remarkable capacity for work and for ideological optimism verging on bad taste. Like his great nineteenth-century predecessors Victor Hugo and Honoré de Balzac, Aragon was oceanic, flawed, and ubiquitous. His opus—which includes poetry, fiction, autobiography, art criticism, literary theory, journalism, polemics, and history—forms a vast illustrated album of his time. World War I, the 1920s of Dada and surrealism, the rise of international communism and the doctrine of socialist realism, the advent of Hitler, the Spanish civil war, World War II and the fall of France, the Occupation and Resistance, the literary-political battles of liberated France, the Paris revolution of May 1968, the Soviet occupation of Prague and the demise of communist romanticism, the rise of structuralism and the crisis in critical thought—all these nightmares, romances, and disappointments were part of Aragon's lifetime and were reflected in his work.

Aragon became well known in the 1920s as a poet and cofounder with André Breton of the surrealist movement. Following his political conversion in the early 1930s, for some thirty-five years Aragon the Communist writer dominated leftist literature in France. In this most long-lasting of his incarnations he was guided by his muse Elsa Triolet, the Russian-born writer he met in 1928. In his last fifteen years Aragon haunted the French artistic scene as a literary elder statesman, publishing puzzling experimental novels, overseeing new comprehensive editions of his and Elsa Triolet's works, and reshaping his literary past in a series of still unevaluated autobiographical and critical texts. As the living man—attractive, flamboyant, irritating, sentimental, pedantic, self-indulgent, intoxicated with words—recedes from center stage, a more complex figure begins to emerge: the self-created, acutely deliberate professional man of letters–in the twentieth-century active style. Aragon's mode of life and work, while the opposite of Joyce's or Flaubert's, is no less typical of the modernist adventure.

Aragon's consciousness of his historical role in the literature of the twentieth century made him artistically canny to a degree remarkable even among French writers. Except for one early unfinished novel, he published or scrupulously saved everything he wrote. In the 1920s, as adviser to Paris couturier Jacques Doucet, Aragon helped establish the Fonds Doucet, a collection of documents on modern literature now housed in the Bibliothèque Sainte-Geneviève in Paris. He also wrote for inclusion in the archives detailed accounts of contemporary literary events he considered historically significant. Some fifty years later, in 1977, Aragon donated his personal hoard of unpublished manuscripts to the Centre National de la Recherche Scientifique in Paris, with a presentation speech urging researchers to develop a genetic criticism concerned with the evolution of texts through all phases of their production. It now appears that Aragon considered himself to be the principal archivist of French literary history in the twentieth century and that he wrote the texts or provided the raw materials for many of its most important primary sources.

Aragon's thirteen novels fall into three major periods. The first period coincides with the height of the surrealist movement and includes three experimental prose works: *Anicet ou Le Panorama* (Anicet or The Panorama, 1921); *Les Aventures de Télémaque* (Telemachus' Adventures, 1922); and *Le Paysan de Paris* (1926). Only the last has been translated into English, as *Nightwalker* (1970) in the United States and as *Paris Peasant* (1971) in England. The second, socialist realist period includes the six novels Aragon grouped under the cyclical heading *Le Monde réel* (The Real World): *Les Cloches de Bâle* (1934; translated as *The Bells of Basel*, 1936); *Les Beaux Quartiers* (1936; translated as *Residential Quarter*, 1938); *Les Voyageurs de l'impériale* (1942; published in the United States as *The Century Was Young* the year before its appearance in France and republished in England as *Passengers of Destiny*, 1947); *Aurélien* (1944; translated, 1946); *Les Communistes* (six volumes, 1949-1951); and *La Semaine sainte* (1958; translated as *Holy Week*, 1961). Except for *Les Communistes* these essentially realistic works have reached a wide audience both in French and in

translation. The last period includes four novels, all strongly poetic, painterly, or theatrical in technique and fairly difficult of access: *La Mise à mort* (The Execution, 1965); *Blanche ou l'oubli* (Blanche or Forgetting, 1967); *Henri Matisse, roman* (1971); and *Théâtre/Roman* (Theater/Novel, 1974). Only *Henri Matisse* has been translated into English, in 1972, as *Henri Matisse: A Novel*.

Aragon's poetry–distinguished by striking lyric-colloquial diction, extensive metric experimentation, and an extraordinary mastery of the history of poetry and in several languages–is among the most highly regarded and best known of twentieth-century French verse. His poetic range includes the audacious aural and calligraphic games of the early works; the flood of emotionally charged traditional lyrics inspired by the fall of France that made Aragon's poetic voice the symbol of his embattled nation and his Elsa the Beatrice of World War II; in the later years the extended poetic autobiography, mature love poetry, and scholarly epic verse. The inclusion of poetry in the later novels echoed the theme of aesthetic collage that dominated his increasingly synesthetic theoretical and confessional writings, while Aragon's evolving mastery of poetic forms was paralleled by a growing conviction that fiction is the more challenging and elusive literary genre because it reconstructs the discrete particles of lived, imagined, and historical experience that constitute reality.

Aragon's earliest years were colored by lived and written fictions. His mother, Marguerite Toucas, was twenty-four when he was born Louis Andrieux in 1897, the illegitimate son of a married man of fifty-six (also named Louis Andrieux). Brought up to believe his mother was his sister, his maternal grandmother his legal guardian, and his natural father his *précepteur* (tutor), Aragon later recollected all his childhood relationships with adults as cast in a light of mystery and uncertainty. Only in 1917, when he was called up for military service, did Aragon's mother tell him the truth. The web of false family identities and the cast of inevitably shifting background characters at the pension the family ran in the sixteenth arrondissement of Paris (one of the "beaux quartiers," or beautiful quarters, evoked in Aragon's 1936 novel) reinforced his love of storytelling; it also shaped his later attraction to ideological "families" and to strong individuals (Breton, Elsa Triolet, Nancy Cunard) who personally and artistically took him in hand.

Aragon as an army auxiliary doctor in 1918

Vingt-cinq Années de vie littéraire (Twenty-five Years of Literary Life, 1908), a volume of selections from the work of Maurice Barrès won as an academic prize at age eleven, first aroused Aragon's fascination with the figure of the professional writer and the power of printed words, "ces pauvres mots merveilleux laissés dans notre nuit par quelques hommes que je n'ai pas connus" (those few marvelous words scattered across our night by some men I've never met). Through Barrès he also discovered the writings of Stendhal, another subtle prophet of the cult of self. Aragon's mother, herself a translator (and possibly an author) of novels, shared with him her love of the great nineteenth-century Russian novelists, and a young Georgian woman at the pension lent him fiction by the twentieth-century Russian writer Maksim Gorky. Aragon's early admiration for the strange, subversive power of writing led to a lifelong habit of relentless reading. He often remarked that had he not spent half his life reading, he would never have become a writer. In one of his most striking late autobiographical-theoretical texts, *Je n'ai jamais appris à écrire ou Les Incipit* (I Never Learned to

Write, or The Beginnings, 1969), Aragon interpreted his early slowness in learning to write as a creative rebellion against the purely denotative use of words. With the realization that putting words on paper could be a form of discovery, he was instantly transformed into a writing machine. Aragon's text, reminiscent of Joyce's *A Portrait of the Artist as a Young Man* (1916), illuminates the obsession of the storyteller, raptly *listening* to himself write. Brilliant experimental prose and hopelessly long-winded panoramic novels both sprang from this breathless enchantment with putting words on paper.

In 1916, after completing his secondary studies, Aragon enrolled in the preparatory year for medicine, studying anatomy while soldiers were dying on the front, as he later noted in *Le Roman inachevé* (The Unfinished Novel, 1956), a book-length autobiographical poem. He also wrote poetry and frequented Adrienne Monnier's avant-garde bookstore, becoming acquainted with the works of Apollinaire and Lautréamont and learning of the cubist painters and their revolt against traditional representational art. In 1917 he was mobilized into the army, where, at the Val-de-Grâce medical facility, he met André Breton, who became his friend, mentor, and fellow high-wire walker in the artistic revolutions of the Dada and surrealist years. Aragon's war experience was relatively brief, respectably served (he received a Croix de Guerre for service as an auxiliary doctor in the infantry), and somehow curiously remote, by his own account. He participated in the 1919 occupation of the Saar and the Rhineland, where his infantry battalion was ordered to shoot striking miners who were refusing to descend to their work because of dangerous conditions. According to a passage in *La Semaine sainte*, his brief, intense sympathy with the miners was the first stirring of social conscience, subsequently buried for some dozen years.

The most significant events of the war and immediate postwar years for Aragon were expressions of revolt against traditional society. In the army Aragon and Breton read Lautréamont aloud to one another at Val-de-Grâce and pinned a photograph of a Matisse painting on the wall of their room. In 1917 Lenin traveled from Zurich to Germany to the Finland Station in Russia, as Tristan Tzara, Picabia, and others founded the Dadaist movement in Zurich. Sigmund Freud's work on dreams and the unconscious began to be known in France, and Albert Einstein's discoveries radically altered ways of thinking about time and space. The young writers of Paris went to the movies, followed newspaper accounts of daring crime escapades, and reveled in small acts of literary terrorism expressing the frenetic, unstable, revolutionary spirit of the time. In June 1917 Apollinaire's *Les Mamelles de Tirésias, drame surréaliste* (Tiresias's Breasts, A Surrealist Play) had a single performance in Paris. In November 1917 the October Revolution broke out in Russia, and in Paris Apollinaire delivered his lecture "L'Esprit nouveau et les poètes" (The New Spirit and the Poets) at the Théâtre du Vieux-Colombier. Poet Paul Eluard joined Breton, Aragon, and Philippe Soupault in what would be the nucleus of the surrealist group. Late in 1918 Apollinaire died; he was buried on Armistice Day, a month before his essay on "the new spirit" appeared in *Le Mercure de France*.

In September 1918 Aragon's first significant article, "Du décor" (On Settings), on the evocative power of objects and signs in movie sets, appeared in the magazine *Le Film*. In 1919 Aragon, Breton, and Soupault started a review, *Littérature,* devoted to avant-garde poetry, where some of Aragon's first poems appeared. Painters continued to lead the way for the Paris avant-garde, and jazz music imported from the United States became the rage. Out of the army Aragon wrote poetry and prose and temporarily resumed his medical studies. In 1920 *Feu de joie* (Fire of Joy), Aragon's first volume of poetry, with a drawing by Pablo Picasso, was published, revealing the influence of cubism, an intense physical awareness of the city of Paris, and considerable Dadaist negativism. Dada continued to flourish, while Breton published an article in which for the first time he used the term *surréaliste*. Aragon and Breton, tiring of Dada, began to define a more constructive form of countercultural rebellion, emphasizing novelty, the unexpected, and the suprarational, thus laying the foundations for the surrealist movement. The novel, identified with traditional forms and a dying bourgeois society, was regarded as inimical to the new artistic spirit and effectively banned by the surrealist group.

Unable to resist storytelling, Aragon continued to experiment with narrative and in 1921 published his first novel, *Anicet ou Le Panorama,* an unusual fiction of just under two hundred pages. Narrated in a deliberately literary, slightly stilted prose style, the novel opens with a pastiche of Voltaire's philosophical tale *Candide:* "Anicet n'avait retenu de ses études secondaires que la règle des trois unités, la relativité du temps et de l'espace; là se bornaient ses connaissances de l'art et de la vie" (Anicet had retained from his secondary education only the concept of the three unities and the relativity of time and space; those were the limits of his knowledge of art and of life). Realizing from his indiscreet public behavior that their son is a poet, his parents throw him out of the house. Borrowing elements from the Gidean *sotie* or satiric morality tale, crime novels, the films of Charlie Chaplin, Pearl White serials, and the older traditions of the epic quest, chivalric romance, and picaresque novel, Aragon follows his hero through a series of symbolic encounters. Two major literary standard-bearers frame the tale. Arthur (Rimbaud), the first stranger Anicet meets, appears as a somewhat stuffy, outmoded romantic figure tending his private search for beauty. Lautréamont and his radical reinterpretation of traditional aesthetic categories illuminate the novel's final pages, where Anicet goes to prison as a fall guy. At an inn Anicet meets a group of masked figures representing (according to Aragon's "Clef à *Anicet*" [key to *Anicet*] deposited in the Fonds Doucet) Charlie Chaplin, Jean Cocteau, Max Jacob, Paul Valéry, Pablo Picasso, and André Breton. All are members of a secret society devoted to the adoration of Mirabelle, a woman symbolizing beauty and living like a harlot with a series of lovers.

Anicet ou Le Panorama is a revolution within a revolution, a work of protest against the Dadaist movement to which it belongs. The apparently lighthearted, rather loosely constructed tale conceals a complex critical spirit that finds its most apt embodiment in a scene where Anicet, carrying out one of the challenges he must fulfill in order to be admitted to the cult of Mirabelle, burns a huge pile of traditional paintings at the top of the Arc de Triomphe. Aragon's descriptive gifts illuminate Anicet's walk through the Passage des Cosmoramas, where familiar objects in shop windows take on a life of their own–artificial limbs move like snakes in a jungle, wax dummies spirit Anicet into a furious dance. The novel has obvious weaknesses: frequently tiresome dialogues between Anicet and his many would-be mentors; excessively self-conscious sensuality and sexual double entendres in the carnivalesque scenes. But the total effect is dazzling–a catalog of artistic protest, an illustrated album of popular and elite art forms of the period. In the July 1921 *Nouvelle Revue Française,* Pierre Drieu La Rochelle praised *Anicet ou Le Panorama* for its refreshing sexual frankness and daring literary of-

[142] où je lève les yeux vers le plus noir du ciel, enfin n'importe, que les dévastations déchirent le terrain des routes, que mon cœur... je puis donc prononcer le nom misérable de mon cœur ? Perdu à tout jamais sous la nuée, je rêve, et rien n'arrêtera ce songe vers la mort.

(Le manuscrit s'arrête ici. Il devait contenir encore quelques feuillets, comme l'attestent les restes d'une dizaine de pages arrachées. Celui qui l'a oublié voulait-il détruire ces dix pages ou ne conserver qu'elles, et détruire ce qui précède ? Il n'en sait probablement rien lui-même, étant comme on a pu comprendre un de ces hommes qui ne croient pas qu'on puisse jamais rien détruire, bien que ce ne soit pas l'envie qui en manque, mais qui savent ~~au moins~~ que l'on peut toujours séparer .)

Aragon.

Paris, le 28 Janvier 1930

Final page from a later draft of "Le Cahier Noir," a section from Aragon's novel La Défense de l'infini *(courtesy of Fonds Doucet, Bibliothèque Sainte-Geneviève, Paris)* fensive, suggesting prophetically that Aragon's first prose work was already "les Mémoires de sa vieillesse" (the Memoirs of his final years). Indeed, the burlesque of progress in art, the lyrical evocations of walks through Paris, the serial inquiries about beauty and reality, the central character's ultimate defeat would remain deep-seated thematic patterns of Aragon's fiction over the years, finding their ultimate form in his last novel, *Théâtre/Roman*.

Aragon's second novel, *Les Aventures de Télémaque,* is a pastiche of a pastiche, a rewriting of Fénelon's *Télémaque* (1699), itself a didactic quest narrative based on the fourth section of Homer's *Odyssey*. With characteristic brashness and inventiveness Aragon depicts Télémaque and his guide Mentor traveling through an incoherent world governed by the space-time relativism of Einstein. Borrowing elements from Rabelais (the storm at sea), Poe (horror), and Alfred Jarry (the absurd word and the nihilistic gesture), Aragon attacks the growing sterility of the Dadaist movement. Lavish theatrical settings and painterly decors replace Fénelon's lush natural scenery. Odd linguistic experiments and word games, symbolized by cryptograms in bottles, satirize the taste for nonsense that was one of Dada's hallmarks. Much in the manner of Marcel Duchamp, who was putting his signature on all manner of "objets trouvés" (found art), Aragon uses anything he happens to find–plagiarism, parody, verbal collage–in his tale. *Les Aventures de Télémaque* is far less successful than *Anicet ou Le Panorama,* lacking the earlier novel's lyricism and minimal character development. Télémaque's metaphysical suicide from the top of a cliff (an echo of the suicides of several of Aragon's contemporaries) comes across as a tiresomely clever reaction to the jumbled pseudoscientific world and bad advice the hero discovered on his travels. In later years Aragon reclassified *Les Aventures de Télémaque* and included it among his poetic works, an unsatisfactory solution to the literary problems it failed to resolve.

In the years between *Les Aventures de Télémaque* and his next novel, Aragon continued to experiment with fiction. In *Le Libertinage* (Libertinism, 1924), a collection containing ten stories, a play (published in translation in Michael Benedikt and George Wellwarth's *Modern French Theater,* 1964), and an epistolary novella, each narrative piece is a parody or, when successful, a reinvention of the characteristic style of its dedicatee. Scattered sequences evoke the Paris glimpsed in *Anicet ou Le Panorama,* here seen in a nocturnal and somewhat malevolent light. Despite the pronounced element of story, because *Le Libertinage* was not a novel, Breton could refer indulgently and affectionately to "les terribles histoires d'Aragon" (Aragon's terrible tales).

Le Paysan de Paris, Aragon's major early novel, has achieved the status of a literary myth. Its brilliant prose and varied aesthetic techniques convey his unique surrealist vision–the real world of Paris in the mid 1920s transmuted into the "urban marvelous," a domain between dream and waking, between revelation and history–and highlight his persistent attraction to a fluid form of the novel. The thematically related major narratives, "Le Passage de l'Opéra" (The Passage [or Street] of the Opéra) and "Le Sentiment de la nature aux Buttes-Chaumont" (A Feeling for Nature in the Buttes-Chaumont Park), are framed by two shorter, abstract sections, "Préface à une mythologie moderne" (Preface to a Modern Mythology) and "Le Songe du Paysan" (The Peasant's Dream). The narrative perspective is that of an invisible author-narrator who undertakes an exploration of the unfamiliar or untranslated aspects of experience. In the framing sections he briefly emerges as a strong dramatic voice rejecting the solutions offered to the troubled young men of Aragon's generation by traditional philosophy and proposing instead the exploration of love, the poetic life, and realism-materialism.

The underlying theme of the first narrative, "Le Passage de l'Opéra," is the loss of poetry in modern life, symbolized by the incursion of urban demolition into one of the covered streets that were being demolished to make way for Baron Eugène-Georges Haussmann's grand plan for the Opéra section of the city. About to fall under the pickaxes was this marvelous place in which to walk and to dream, filled with shops, cafés, hairdressers, a shoe-shine parlor, several brothels, a striptease theater, a transients' hotel–a separate, enclosed world with strange aquarium-like light filtering down through its glass skylight. The Paris peasant strolls through the Passage, lingering over sights and niches that will soon disappear in the path of progress. He observes the shoppers, strollers, prostitutes, and would-be lovers, listens to the complaints of merchants forced to move or go out of business, examines the geometry of chair arrangement and the drink menu at the Café Certâ, a traditional Dada-surrealist hangout, and moves on, inspired by what he has seen and saddened by its imminent disappearance (another meaning, in French, of *passage*).

In the second narrative, "Le Sentiment de la nature aux Buttes-Chaumont," Aragon, Breton, and Marcel Noll—three young men with little to do, longing for love and the ideal woman—pay an evening visit to a park in one of the city's grubbiest and least "marvelous" neighborhoods. The themes of modern love and the difficult search for beauty are satirically developed through interlocking styles. Lyrical passages describe pairs of lovers of diverse amorous tastes tucked into corners of the park's landscaping. A dry, bookish voice reads the posted lists of architects, builders, and public figures responsible for the park's undistinguished monuments. The narrative eye, following instructions on geographical plaques affixed to the park's statues, meticulously measures off distances to points of greater touristic interest elsewhere in the city. The long roll call of "credits" for poor urban design and the recognizable style of touristic guidebooks recall the tone of Flaubert's *Dictionnaire des idées reçues* (Dictionary of Received Ideas), from the 1881 novel *Bouvard et Pécuchet*. Lyrical description and official style are set off against invocations to classical and impromptu deities representing love, history, travel, dream, and chance. The young urban explorers yearn to find "une femme de propos délibéré, une femme ayant de la vie un sens si large, une femme si vraiment prête à tout, qu'elle vaille enfin la peine de bouleverser l'univers" (a woman with clear ideas, with such a broad sense of life, so ready for anything, that she is worth changing the world for) to come into their lives. When the park is locked up for the night with the visitors still inside, darkness confers on it the heroic dimension of a Greek temple of love.

Le Paysan de Paris boldly uses painting, printing, and film techniques for its mythological exploration of contemporary Paris. The signs, placards, and menus reproduced in the pages of "Le Passage de l'Opéra" create the effect of a theater program or illustrated album and make the text itself a printed souvenir of a now extinct part of the city. The cubist geometry, meticulous cartography, and stagy lighting effects of "Le Sentiment de la nature aux Buttes-Chaumont" endow an unpromising urban site with intense theatricality. The witty ironic contrasts between the guidebook pastiche of "Le Sentiment de la nature aux Buttes-Chaumont" and the sensual urban lyricism of "Le Passage de l'Opéra," between the lecture tone of the preface and the

dreamy accents of the peasant's closing peroration reinforce the structural unity of the diverse parts. To paraphrase Aragon on Matisse, *Le Paysan de Paris* is a striking literary collage that focuses as much on the differences between things as on the things themselves. A veritable encyclopedia of the myths, life-style, and artistic techniques of surrealism, Aragon's masterpiece has had significant, still unexamined influence on other writers. Céline's *Voyage au bout de la nuit* (*Journey to the End of the Night*, 1932), Sartre's *La Nausée* (*Nausea*, 1938), the novels and plays of Beckett, and Joyce's *Finnegans Wake* (1939) all bear its imprint. Ironically, at the time of its publication, the primary significance of *Le Paysan de Paris* was negative: it was "the work of the break," the first gesture of Aragon's farewell to surrealism.

The reception of *Le Paysan de Paris* precipitated a crisis in Aragon's life. Critics almost totally ignored it, while Breton, supporting theoretical surrealism which favored the landscape of the unseen and the unconscious, disapproved of the novel's intense preoccupation with the visible world. For several decades after its publication Aragon avoided references to the novel, instead citing *Anicet ou Le Panorama* as his major early work of fiction. An intense love affair with Nancy Cunard, the beautiful, stylish heiress best known from her 1927 photographic portrait by Man Ray, distracted Aragon from the total dejection that threatened to submerge him and delayed his decision to join the Communist party, which had seemed to many of the surrealists a viable expression of political protest against French military intervention in Morocco in 1925. He continued to publish poetry (*Le Mouvement perpétuel* [Perpetual Motion], 1926; *La Grande Gaîté* [Great Joy], 1929), but his artistic elan was dwindling. The unpublished novel "La Défense de l'infini" (Defense of the Infinite), described by Aragon as a huge, infernal narrative of multiple parallel destinies, a fragment of which had appeared in *La Revue Européenne*, was going nowhere. While on a holiday in Madrid with Nancy Cunard in 1927, Aragon burned the manuscript; in the same year he joined the French Communist party. *Traité du style* (Treatise on Style, 1928), a raging work of literary theory and personal analysis, expresses a growing dissatisfaction with surrealism and its failure to offer any positive rallying point for writers. In Venice, further discouraged by his own poverty and by Cunard's flamboyant wealth and involvement with another man, Aragon attempted suicide.

The meeting with Elsa Triolet in November 1928 at the café La Coupole in Paris marked a decisive turn in Aragon's career. According to Pierre Daix, Aragon's biographer, Triolet, who had fallen in love with the author of *Le Paysan de Paris,* initiated the encounter. In Aragon's literary call for "a woman with clear ideas" she saw revealed the major role she could play in his life. (Aragon at first suspected the Russian-Jewish émigrée of being a spy.) The couple took up life together late in 1928 and, faced with separation in the war, married in 1939. For Aragon, Triolet was identified with literary Russia: she knew Gorky; her sister Lili Brik was the mistress of the revolutionary Russian futurist poet Mayakovski. Triolet's toughness of character, her intense commitment to channeling Aragon's energies, and her own literary talent (in the 1940s she became a French novelist of some distinction) enabled her to become the legendary companion in a long personal, creative, and political alliance terminated only by her death in 1970. Her initial tasks were to lead Aragon to discover Russia and the dream of human perfectibility and to separate him from the surrealists.

Aragon and Triolet's visit to Russia in 1930 was one of the earliest writers' pilgrimages of the period. In Kharkov the Second International Congress of Revolutionary Writers nourished Aragon's taste for group activities, polemics, and politics, while the publication of "La Peinture au défi" (Painting Takes Up the Challenge, 1930) as the preface to the exhibition catalog *Exposition de collages,* reflected his continuing attachment to surrealist aesthetics and to the plastic arts; this work on collage was the first of Aragon's extraordinary studies of modern painting that culminated in 1971 with *Henri Matisse, roman.* The poems of *Persécuté persécuteur* (Persecutor Persecuted, 1931) mixed surrealism with new political elements. Inspired by the example of Mayakovski, Aragon opened the volume with "Front rouge" (Red Front), a rather poor poem that attracted a great deal of attention. For advocating open violence against the authorities in France, he was convicted of inciting soldiers to mutiny and of provocation to murder and given a suspended five-year prison sentence. Breton drafted a petition in Aragon's defense, claiming that poets should be protected from judicial proceedings purely in the name of poetry and also noting that Aragon's poem was a piece of occasional verse ("poésie de circonstance") that did not represent the true direction of poetry. Publicly disavow-

ing the surrealist defense, Aragon consummated his break with Breton and with the movement that had sheltered his early career. In 1933 Triolet translated Céline's *Voyage au bout de la nuit* (considered a great proletarian novel by Leon Trotsky) into Russian, and Aragon, now free to write fiction, began to work on the first novel of the cycle he would call *Le Monde réel* to distinguish his world from that of the surrealists.

In 1933 Aragon became a literary and political journalist—a métier that would provide his principal livelihood until the international success of *La Semaine sainte* in 1958—as joint editor with Jean-Richard Bloch of *Commune,* a major leftist magazine of the 1930s and 1940s, and as a reporter with *L'Humanité,* the official newspaper of the French Communist party. In 1934 Aragon and André Malraux attended the Congress of the Union of Soviet Writers in Moscow at which Andrey Zhdanov elaborated the literary doctrine of socialist realism, which demanded that artists be realists in the service of the historical dialectic and depict man as he ought to be. For Aragon this theory shed new light on the writings of Tolstoy, Stendhal, and Hugo and justified his own evolving conception of prose fiction. Aragon's new base in communism appeared to offer strong artistic advantages—an identifiable audience for his writings, the challenge of mastering a new literary approach, and a revolutionary involvement to replace the fervor of surrealism.

The first novel of the cycle *Le Monde réel* is *Les Cloches de Bâle,* a disjointed assemblage of three parts and an epilogue portraying, with varying levels of density and detail, three women who represent the evolutionary phases of female consciousness in the years prior to World War I. As the instances accumulate, the novel's simple message emerges: capitalism, which deforms human lives and leads to the historical catastrophe of war, must be replaced by revolutionary socialism. In this novel, written some fifteen years after his experience in the army, Aragon at last allows World War I to intrude into his fictional world, where it will recur as the massive, unassimilable evil that closes the first three volumes of the cycle. (World War II closes the next two.) In *Les Cloches de Bâle* the war serves to justify the novel's unintegrated structure and weaves the simplistic social and political messages symbolized by the characters' lives into an implied meaningful whole. Aragon's first assay into the literature of conviction prefigures many of the difficulties he will meet on the road to a Marxist *Comédie*

Aragon with Elsa Triolet, André Breton, Paul Eluard, and Nusch Eluard in 1931, the year Aragon broke with the surrealists (collection René Char)

humaine. In his dual role as prophet of a revealed truth and artistic chronicler of the random beauty, terror, and complexity of human life, Aragon faces the essential dilemma of ideological fiction: to create the impression of life itself out of abstract ideas.

Courtesan Diane de Nettencourt's liaisons with industrial magnate Wisner (who reappears in *Les Communistes*) and with the wealthy speculator Brunel, last glimpsed standing in a crowd planning to assassinate the Socialist leader Jean Jaurès, demonstrate the horror of male-female relationships based solely upon money. The young Georgian Catherine Simonidzé, a densely portrayed, often moving character, represents a transitional phase of feminine articulation. Her ultimate inability to take the definitive step into communism, explained implicitly as the fault of the world in which she lives, allows Aragon to include in the chronicle of her unsuccessful odyssey scenes portraying the working class. Aragon's depiction of life at an anarchist newspaper and his rendering of the Paris taxi strike of 1912 are both failed exercises in imaginative construction. Victor, the stereotypical "good Communist worker" of Soviet films of the 1920s and 1930s, is no more than an abstraction dressed up with a body and a face, as Aragon later admitted in *J'abats mon jeu* (I Lay My Cards on the Table, 1959). The epilogue introduces Clara Zetkine, the elderly, unattractive German Communist "new woman" who attends the Socialist Congress at Basel on the eve of the war; based on a figure Aragon saw in a newspaper photo taken at the 1920 French Socialist Congress at Tours (transposed to the novel's 1912 Socialist Congress in Basel), Clara functions as the historical figure intended to give the novel its positive social meaning.

An easy colloquial style, a tapestrylike historical backdrop that makes use of real names and dates, and some notable descriptive passages point the way to Aragon's later historical fiction. Critical reaction to *Les Cloches de Bâle*, considered Aragon's first novel by most critics, was mixed. Surprised leftist reviewers in France and the United States welcomed a novel on the class struggle by a noted poet but deplored its programmatic structure and sketchy characterization. Philip Rahv's comment in the *Nation* was typical: "Aragon's problem . . . is to overcome the tendency of his sociological facts to become the limbo of his imagination."

Aragon's immersion in international literary politics and in realistic writing reached a high point in the mid 1930s. He joined with other Western writers troubled by the worldwide depression, the rise of fascism, and scattered armed political battles such as the Paris riots of February 1934 to organize in defense of "culture," a vague term inconsistently used, as Roger Shattuck has noted in *The Innocent Eye* (1984). As a French representative to the first World Congress of the International Association of Writers for the Defense of Culture, held in Paris in 1935, Aragon was joined by Bloch, Malraux, and André Chamson. Attending writers from other nations included Aldous Huxley, E. M. Forster, Robert Musil, and Bertolt Brecht. In 1935 Aragon published the theoretical work *Pour un réalisme socialiste* (Toward a Socialist Realism), a discussion of realism in the novels of Hugo and Zola and in the poetry of Rimbaud and Apollinaire in which he defined writers as engineers of the soul who must be willing to move like sand in the wind of history. This was the first of a series of critical studies that would later extend to Hugo's poetry, Stendhal's novels, and the work of the painters Watteau, Courbet, and Matisse. The Second International Congress of Writers for the Defense of Culture, held in Spain in 1936 with Aragon, Malraux, Pablo Neruda, John Dos Passos, Arthur Koestler, George Orwell, and Ernest Hemingway in attendance, showed increasing militancy. Malraux and Hemingway stayed on to fight on the Republican side in the Spanish civil war, while Aragon and Triolet took a ship from London to Russia to visit the dying Maksim Gorky. During the voyage Aragon completed *Les Beaux Quartiers*, his second realistic novel.

Les Beaux Quartiers is the most neatly integrated of Aragon's historical novels. Concentrating on two central characters who represent the broad lines of the class struggle, it works by a careful series of vivid antitheses to illustrate the ills of French capitalist society and to suggest ways of curing them. The afterword, officially announcing the cycle *Le Monde réel* retroactive to *Les Cloches de Bâle*, situates the novel within a series that looks to the future, "où des livres s'écriront pour des hommes pacifiques et maîtres de leur destin" (when books will be written for men who are at peace and masters of their own destiny), and underlines Aragon's definitive separation from surrealism and his undirected past, "cette œuvre de nuages que je laisse derrière moi" (that world of clouds I leave behind me). The narrative follows brothers Edmond and Armand Barbentane, sons of a wealthy and influential doctor, from their youth in the French provincial town of Sérianne-le-Vieux to diverging destinies in Paris in the period leading up to World War I. Edmond, attracted by wealth and comfort and moved by a desire to manipulate women, climbs in society through a series of advantageous love affairs, while Armand breaks radically with his bourgeois past and his dream of going into the theater to live a "real," difficult life as a self-chosen member of the Paris working class. In a narrative of considerable sensual density and old-fashioned reading appeal, Aragon skillfully manipulates ironic contrasts between upper Sérianne, where the poor live in dramatic despair and violence, and the center of town, where the privileged doctors, tradesmen, and politicians feed off the less fortunate; between Armand's grungy Paris Left Bank and the "beautiful quarters" on the Right Bank where "des statues aux yeux blancs rêvent sur les places" (eyeless statues dream over the squares).

Aragon's debt to the realistic tradition of Hugo and Stendhal is at times overly obvious, and his purposive reinterpretation of Stendhal's definition of the realistic novel as "un miroir qu'on promène le long d'un chemin" (a mirror carried along a roadway) produces mirror angles whose social intention is often obtrusive. However, Aragon's eyes and ears frequently prevail over his political conscience, creating striking visual, aural, and spatial effects that bring startling life and texture to scenes of French life. An election Sunday in the provinces combines the striking detail and color of nineteenth-century realist painting with political satire. A walk through the butchers' section of Les Halles gives intense, cruel poetic life to the details of feeding the inhabitants of a large city. At times, in effects reminiscent of Tolstoy's *War and Peace* (1864-1869), fictional and historical figures appear in the same scene, as when Armand stands in a crowd listening to Jaurès speak. The factual backdrop, awkwardly integrated into the narrative, makes the reader aware of Aragon's serious effort to make a social statement. He would later use this technique more knowingly and to considerably better effect in *La Semaine sainte*.

Characterization is the novel's outstanding weakness. While bourgeois figures are relatively convincing, members of the working class, about whom Aragon obviously knew very little, remain wooden. A few characters fortunately transcend their ideological conception and achieve a density having little to do with the author's social intentions. Carlotta, the poor, beautiful young Italian girl who becomes part of Edmond's road to wealth, illustrates nothing; her sensual appeal and psychological density spring most of all from Aragon's personal fascination with her. His passion for some of his characters and for the visible world raises the novel well above the ranks of most socialist-realist writing of the period. Critical reaction to *Les Beaux Quartiers* was generally favorable, despite reservations over its old-fashioned manner, excessive length, and inordinate fascination with violent emotions such as lust, greed, hysteria, and hatred. The novel was awarded the Prix Théophraste Renaudot for 1936.

The troubled publishing history of *Les Voyageurs de l'impériale*, Aragon's third realistic novel, completed in 1939 and published three years later, is an accurate reflection of the rhythms of his life in the late 1930s and early 1940s. In 1937 he traveled to Spain to meet with Republican intellectuals, became codirector of the communist weekly *Ce Soir*, and began work on a long novel based on the life of his grandfather. Aragon's editorial expressing the French Communists' support of the Russo-German pact of August 1939 led to the suspension of *Ce Soir*. In the fall as the French government intensified efforts to identify and isolate the Communists in a special army regi-

Aragon and Triolet with publisher Pierre Seghers at Villeneuve-lès-Avignon in 1941 (collection Pierre Seghers)

ment, Aragon took shelter at the Chilean embassy in Paris in order to complete his novel. The manuscript of *Les Voyageurs de l'impériale* was sent to his American publisher and Aragon was mobilized into the workers' unit. Evacuated from Dunkirk in June 1940, he returned to Paris just before the French government abandoned the capital to the Germans on 11 June. The novel first saw print in English translation in 1941; the money from the American edition, bartered for francs at an enormous profit according to Triolet's biographer Dominique Desanti, was spent during the four years Aragon and Triolet lived in hiding in the south of France. By the time *Les Voyageurs de l'impériale* came out in France in 1942 in incomplete censored form, Aragon had substantially completed *Aurélien*. The postwar, complete edition of *Les Voyageurs de l'impériale* in 1947 stirred up all the partisans: Communists approved it as a dissection of asocial individualism; anticommunists found it excessively long and tiresome. It remains highly problematic, a work with a dual existence much like Aragon's own as a literary double agent within the realistic tradition.

Pierre Mercadier, the central character of *Les Voyageurs de l'impériale*, is a teacher of history, a secretive financial speculator, and a sometime collector of paintings whose search for individual fulfillment spans a twenty-five-year period from the Paris Exposition of 1889 to his death on the eve of World War I. The novel's historical frame includes the collapse of Ferdinand de Lesseps's Panama Canal venture, the Dreyfus Affair, and the French political and economic background to the war. Aragon's often riveting narrations of intimate personal experiences–Pierre's realization of estrangement from his wife, his son Pascal's childhood dreams of love and glory during summers in Provence, Pierre's years abroad pursuing his illusions, and his final days in the Paris *banlieue* (suburbs) as the love object of the elderly brothel owner Dora Tavernier–irresistible for the first ten or twenty pages, lose the reader's interest over forty or more. Lengthy excerpts from Mercadier's notes for his never-to-be-completed biography of Scottish economist John Law, the inventor of paper money, useful as illustrations of the destructive force of economic abstractions, quickly grow wearisome.

Aragon's most successful techniques in *Les Voyageurs de l'impériale* are illustrative and satirical. Picture-postcard scenes at the 1889 Exposition (initial reactions to the Eiffel Tower), glowingly painted landscapes of Provence à la Zola, Pierre's sojourn in Venice as a study in illustrated clichés and counterclichés (Venice in cold, rainy weather), Dora's tavern-and-brothel, and the unbearably detailed depiction of Pierre's physical deterioration after his stroke–all belong to the realm of book illustrations and satirical cartoons. Aragon interestingly represents time and change by concrete objects, by a sequence of knickknacks, vignettes, monuments, costumes–history viewed as a collage of visual experience, a stereopticon display of individual scenes animated by satire, irony, and the grotesque in the manner of Hugo.

The theme of alienation, symbolized by the image of the double-decker bus and its *impériale* (top deck) from which passengers see only what their physical position and social class permit, is developed in striking depictions of characters almost abstractly framed by their milieus that suggest the "estrangement effects," the dramatic simplifications of Brecht's plays, but lack their arresting starkness. The self-conscious narrative intrusions of the two earlier realistic novels are largely absent; only the epilogue showing Pierre's son Pascal going to war to spare his own son from ever having to fight has the recognizable treatise tone. *Les Voyageurs de l'impériale* most of all lacks a sense of effective proportion. Considerably cut and edited, it could have been a successful generational novel at the level of Thomas Mann's *Buddenbrooks* (1901). As published, it is an occasionally captivating and frequently tiresome fiction in which Aragon's greatest natural talents as a novelist are buried by his excessive facility with words and a total lack of self-criticism.

During the Occupation Aragon returned to poetry after a hiatus of seven years, and in a series of simple, easily remembered lyrics about separated lovers and the fallen nation, he spoke to occupied France. Madeleine Renaud recited "Le Temps des mots-croisés" (The Time of Crossword Puzzles) at the Comédie-Française, while the collection *Le Crève-cœur* (Heartbreak, 1941) sold widely throughout France and copies appeared in London, New York, Montreal, and Beirut. From their scattered hiding places the French Communists, their national legitimacy restored by the end of the Russo-German pact in June 1941, became active in the nascent Resistance movement, whose heroes they would be, for a brief time, after the war. The underground literature flourished, establishing poetry reviews such as *Poésie 40*, clandestine publishing houses such as the Editions de Minuit and Editions Seghers, and the literary weekly *Les Lettres Françaises*. Aragon and Triolet lived in the South, arranged their lives around the practical and political necessities of the time, with Jean Paulhan formed the Comité National des Ecrivains (the CNE that would lead the *épuration* or settling of accounts after the Liberation), and devoted long, quiet hours to their writing. As he put his public energies into the poems and pamphlets of the new literary revolution–the Resistance–in imagination Aragon turned to the past and to the city he now rarely saw.

Aurélien, completed in 1942 and published in 1944, is the simplest, most intense, and most haunting novel of *Le Monde réel*. Aurélien Leurtillois, a veteran of World War I unable to find his emotional bearings in civilian life, falls in love with Bérénice Morel, a married woman from the provinces visiting Paris and her cousin Edmond Barbentane (of *Les Beaux Quartiers*) for the 1921 Christmas holidays. Aragon's tale of Aurélien and Bérénice's unconsummated romance, set in the Paris of the 1920s and taking place over a brief time span, is distinguished by an extraordinarily complex network of literary, visual, and linguistic references that reflect the unusually focused intensity of its composition period.

Aurélien has three major characters: the title figure, Bérénice, and the city of Paris. Paris, a physical and emotional presence, symbol of a world threatened with disintegration, forms the backdrop of the novel. Unlike the broad historical frames of the earlier realistic novels, Paris represents no moral lesson, no social insight. It is at once the mirror of Aurélien's search for wholeness and a separate world governed by its own poetic necessities. The oddly beautiful Bérénice is at once a real, passionate woman who fears losing Aurélien if she becomes involved with him and a strange death-mask figure who stands always just beyond his reach. Her name, with its echoes of Racine and Barrès, becomes a poetic leitmotif variously embroidered in the course of the narrative. The touching, confused hero Aurélien–a hybrid of the youthful Aragon and Pierre Drieu La Rochelle, his close friend in the 1920s–assumes an intense fictional existence that dominates the visual and psychological fields of the novel. Aurélien's relationship to the war, about which he rarely thinks directly, is the central fact of his life. With just enough of an inherited income to allow him not to work, out of touch with the strange rhythms of the avant-garde artistic life he tries to live, Aurélien is a piece of the war's debris drifting toward an undefined stopping place. His intensely literary imagination transforms the world he stumbles through into a multistoried corridor of references and allusions that resembles the process of writing a novel. Aragon would later identify this form of concrete-abstract prose as "le roman de parenthèse" (the novel of parenthesis), a work reflecting the creative process itself, which slips in among the standard fictional elements and subtly becomes the text itself.

The epilogue, largely unjustified by what precedes it, shows Aurélien and Bérénice meeting again in 1940, when he is a married officer now in the army and she a strange "new woman" in the process of formation. They reminisce briefly about the images of their love each has sheltered over the years; then Bérénice is killed by a stray German bullet. Her real death mask fuses with the luminescent passionate visage Aurélien had watched over in his apartment on the Ile-

Saint-Louis in 1921, as Aragon hastily ties up the impossibly dangling threads of his novel with the opening lines for a classical funeral cortege. This striking novel of crossed, random destinies appeared to most readers in occupied France as an elaborate waste of time, a sign that Aragon had worn out his inspiration as a novelist.

After the Liberation, Triolet won the Prix Goncourt (awarded in 1945 for 1944) for a collection of short stories, while Aragon was consecrated as one of France's leading poets (along with Paul Eluard) when a selection of his poems was published in 1945 as the second volume of the new series Poètes d'aujourd'hui. Aragon and Triolet's brief period as the leading literary couple of Paris ended, however, with the rapid ascension of the new leaders of French intellectual life, Jean-Paul Sartre and Simone de Beauvoir. Considered a failure as a writer of fiction and rapidly losing his clout as a hero of France, Aragon energetically immersed himself in the communist movement and returned to his theoretical writings on realism, expanding their scope in 1946 with *L'Enseigne de Gersaint* (Gersaint's Shop Sign, titled for a painting by Watteau), a lavishly produced art book on the eighteenth-century French painter Watteau as a symbol of French nationalism and its role in the history of art. As director of the revived *Ce Soir* and of Editeurs Français Réunis, a communist publishing house he had started during the war, Aragon became the Party's cultural and intellectual luminary. He collected his wartime pamphlets and poems into volumes, began a novel set during World War II, and in 1948 wrote an editorial against the government that led to his being deprived of civil rights (the right to vote, to serve on juries, to bear witness, and so on) for ten years.

The six-volume *Les Communistes*, a thesis novel intended to explain the Party's policy shift on Germany, its persecution by the French government, and its role in the defense of France, is Aragon's weakest work of fiction; it is also the one on which he lavished the greatest attention. This epic of dissidence–which opens in February 1939 with the defeat of the Spanish republicans by Francisco Franco and ends with the fall of France in 1940 (considerably short of the originally planned five-year span)–involved five years of work and extensive historical research and served as training ground for the historical labors that would inform *La Semaine sainte* and the epic poem *Le Fou d'Elsa* (Elsa's Madman, 1963). In 1966 Aragon radically rewrote *Les Communistes*

Aragon in 1945

for the *Œuvres romanesques croisées d'Elsa Triolet et Aragon* (Crossed [or Mixed] Fictional Works of Elsa Triolet and Aragon, 1964-1974), recasting it into five volumes, attempting to minimize its programmatics, removing some of the most dated references to the 1939 political scene, and restructuring elements to reflect the new light of post-Stalinism. However, no degree of labor could salvage a novel that, as Catharine Savage Brosman has shown in *Malraux, Sartre, and Aragon as Political Novelists* (1964), lacks most of the essentials for fiction. The reader's interest in Cécile Wisner, wife of a wealthy, sexually ambiguous industrialist, and Jean de Moncey, the young student with whom she falls in love, remains minimal as the narrative overwhelms their human relationship with facts, generals, politicians, and communist tracts, and a deliberately simple, dreary prose style designed to appeal to the masses. Unsurprisingly, the only novel of *Le Monde réel* with a contemporary setting has had a severely limited audience. Aragon's next novel, a wily historical costume drama set in the early nineteenth century, at last brought him the wide recognition as a novelist that he had long sought.

La Semaine sainte, the best known and most widely acclaimed of his novels, signals the perfec-

tion and closure of a period of Aragon's life. For despite the author's disclaimer on its opening page, this immense novel–the final installment of *Le Monde réel*–is, in fact, at once historical and intensely political. Examining the relationship between personal experience and the tide of historical events in the week that initiated Napoleon's brief return to power in 1815 and saw the flight of Louis XVIII and his troops from Paris, *La Semaine sainte* demonstrates Aragon's ultimate absorption into the realistic tradition and marks the outer limits of his involvement with it.

The novel was conceived, researched, and completed during the apogee of Aragon's career as "l'homme communiste" (the Communist Man, the designation used as the title of two volumes of his collected political writings published in 1946 and 1953). He became director of *Les Lettres Françaises* in 1953; he wrote on the relationship between painting and French history; he was elected a permanent member of the Central Committee of the French Communist party in 1954. The essay collection *La Lumière de Stendhal* (The Light of Stendhal, 1954) emphasized the central role of the *political* view in realistic fiction. The revelations of Stalin's atrocities that became public in 1956 shook Aragon, but publicly he remained

Aragon (right) with Pablo Picasso on the speaker's platform at a 1949 May Day rally (photo Roger-Viollet)

loyal to the dream of the Soviet utopia; he was rewarded with the Lenin Peace Price in 1957. However, at the moment of his fullest acceptance as a loyal soldier in the service of the revolution, Aragon was beginning to question the artistic results of the long years of political commitment. Once again, as he had done in the late 1920s and early 1930s, he was gradually breaking away from a family. This time, however, no heavily populated shelter awaited him. The hard-won acceptance of his past signaled by the autobiographical poem *Le Roman inachevé,* the deepening sense that Triolet's fiction was more daring and perhaps more significant than his own, and the darkening shadow of old age were pushing Aragon to a confrontation with himself that would in the 1960s initiate a new cycle of novels.

La Semaine sainte, while shaped by the insights of socialist realism, works in the opposite direction from the early volumes of *Le Monde réel,* using a technique Aragon called "la stéréoscopie" to read the past in order to shed light on the present. Aragon assembles the elements of a colorful moment in French history in a series of sixteen chapters or tableaux, arranging the characters at varying levels of visual relief. The monarchist officers who accompany the king on his gradually disintegrating retreat form the novel's secondary plane; they are portrayed as a strong corps of bodies, voices, and personal dramas. The meticulous re-creation of costuming and of physical setting serves to validate the research and to set off the novel's primary figures–History, France, and the painter Théodore Géricault. History, as lived, remembered, and reinterpreted, and France, as represented by the crowds of people who gather, watch, and wait as their future is shaped by armed men and by events they cannot comprehend, form the canvas against which Géricault discovers–through his contact with the people and a growing disaffection with the cause at stake–that the truth of his experience is elsewhere, in the future, in the paintings he has not yet conceived. Through Géricault's realization that history subsumes individual destinies, Aragon addresses that movement of history whose direction socialist realism seeks to determine and appears to suggest that while big solutions can be found, they have yet to be defined.

The novel relies on a curious amalgam of broad effects involving great crowds of people and hallucinatingly precise minor details. Narrative techniques are distractingly varied: traditional exposition; extensive dialogue; cinematic re-creations of mass movements such as long cavalry rides; colorful crowd scenes; authorial intrusions commenting on the significance of the events depicted and speaking of the author's life one hundred years after the action of the novel. Aragon's authorial reminiscences and speculations weave in and out of the chronologically arranged but discrete particles of the week-long tale to form an overlayer of literary commentary, a scattered essay on the nature and meaning of historical fiction as practiced by Hugo, Stendhal, Tolstoy, and Zola.

Critical reaction to *La Semaine sainte* was enthusiastic, although a few critics complained about the excessive use of detail, tiresome fragmentation, and overpowering self-absorption of the authorial intrusions. Several perceived that the theme of the artist involved in war referred not only to Aragon's two stints in the army but also to the ongoing Algerian conflict. The novel's colorful historical flavor, rather than its complex literary historicism, made it a great financial success in France and in numerous translations.

With his new fame as a novelist and his first real financial independence from the tasks of journalism, Aragon at last faced his smoldering jealousy of Triolet's reputation as a writer of fiction. Now resigned to her status as a significant writer, he prepared *Elsa Triolet choisie par Aragon* (Elsa Triolet [as] Chosen by Aragon, 1960), a volume of selections from her work with a long critical introduction. While researching the background for his great epic poem on the fall of Granada, *Le Fou d'Elsa,* he also witnessed, in 1960 and

1961, the publication of three book-length studies (by Hubert Juin, Pierre Lescure, and Roger Garaudy)–to be followed by many more–of his opus. Aragon the older writer, still a rebellion-seeker, began to move into his third career as a novelist. To pave the way, he conceived what may well stand as one of the most intriguing instances of intertextuality in late-twentieth-century literature, the *Œuvres romanesques croisées d'Elsa Triolet et Aragon,* which would ultimately comprise forty-two volumes. The texts, lavishly produced and accompanied by numerous full-color plates, include a series of critical prefaces by Triolet and Aragon addressing each other's work and commenting on the accompanying texts and on the interrelationship of their work over the years.

La Mise à mort, Aragon's 1965 novel, is the complex, deliberately dispersed account of a man who has lost his image in the mirror and whose three faces–indifferent blue-eyed Christian Fustel-Schmidt, famous writer Anthoine Célèbre, narrator Alfred-Louis–represent Aragon's fictional and psychological odyssey from surrealism to socialist realism to the moment of reassessment he had reached. Fougère-Ingeborg Usher (and, by extension, Elsa Triolet) has loved the indifferent young man, chosen to change him into the public Anthoine she now no longer cares for, and appears largely unmoved by his present dilemma. Fougère the muse, now Ingeborg the famous singer, at last is forced to face the new Anthoine-Alfred, turned by his loving her "à la folie" (to the point of madness, a reference both to Aragon's twenty-year-long public cult of Elsa and to the epic poem *Le Fou d'Elsa*) into an old man with "les yeux quelque peu bleus" (somewhat blue eyes), like Christian, and white hair. Aragon's hall-of-mirrors examination of the problems of authorship and writing, of political faith and loss of faith, and of the tangled relationships between men and women has moments of intense emotional and visual resonance: the author's repudiation of his former blind acceptance of Soviet propaganda, his pain at seeing Elsa slip beyond his reach into her private self and her work, a striking use of lavishly decorated period mirrors on café walls and dressing tables and ceilings, and a deeply felt anguish over the distances between his several former selves and the unfamiliar figure he is becoming in his own eyes.

The knowing use of a huge network of literary sources (the German romantics, Edgar Allan Poe, Robert Louis Stevenson, Lewis Carroll, James Joyce, Gottfried Benn, Robert Musil)

makes reading *La Mise à mort* an adventure in literary source-hunting. The speed with which critics picked up Aragon's devilishly fashionable suggestion that he was elaborating "une nouvelle science du roman" (a new science of the novel) demonstrated his persistent ability to confuse commentators and to divert their attention from his more obvious aims. The central questions Aragon raises about realism in fiction and in political journalism combine with an imitation/pastiche of the then highly regarded *nouveau roman* to make *La Mise à mort* a recognizably ironic, unintegrated literary manifesto in the manner of *Anicet ou Le Panorama*. In his novel Aragon challenges famous dead writers and newly acclaimed young novelists to witness an execution/resurrection in the literary arena of Paris. The phrase *la mise à mort* connotes, among other things, the moment when the bullfighter finishes off the bull in a stylized gesture that is a form of ritual mercy and renewal.

Predictably, this tale of the writer consumed by his public image, of the lover destroyed by his muse, of man as the plaything of history invited endless critical exegesis and biographical speculation, thus ensuring precisely the kind of close textual attention most of Aragon's realistic novels had tended to deflect. The year *La Mise à mort* was published Aragon received an honorary doctorate from the University of Moscow, and in 1966, fortified by his new success as a nontraditional novelist and no longer able to ignore the revelations from behind the Iron Curtain, he wrote an editorial in *L'Humanité* attacking the Soviets for sentencing writers Andrei Sinyavksy and Yuly Daniel that marked the French Communist party's first break with Moscow's party line.

The 1967 novel *Blanche ou l'oubli* employs multiple points of view and time frames to examine the relation between fiction and scientific or historical interpretations of human experience. The meditations on language and signs that arise naturally out of the central narrator's profession as a linguist reflect Aragon's intense awareness of the *nouveau roman* and of the structuralist controversy that was beginning to dominate French letters. Geoffrey Gaiffier is trying to understand why his wife Blanche deserted him some eighteen years ago. He undertakes to write a novel about a character named Marie-Noire, a young woman of the contemporary generation, in order to penetrate the depths of feminine psychology. Gaiffier's premise that the novel is not a form of science or of history but an account of what might be, a tool for *reading* life, is a refinement

of Aragon's methodology in *La Semaine sainte*. As Gaiffier meditates on meanings and change as reflected in language, Aragon develops his central ideas: that the words a novelist uses partake of "le royaume de la disponibilité" (the reign of availability), when everything can happen this way or that, and that fiction can thus create meaning where none existed before.

Gaiffier has not reckoned, however, with the intense reality fictional characters can assume. Marie-Noire steps out of the tale he is constructing and begins to narrate *him*. She undertakes her own fiction about Blanche, eluding her creator and reenacting the ritual of separation whose reality Gaiffier has been unable to comprehend over the years. *Blanche ou l'oubli* displays many of Aragon's characteristic preferences in the novel: extreme length, overwhelming accumulation of detail, brilliantly illustrated but often overly extended parallels and references. However, with less anecdotal dispersion than *La Mise à mort*, a better integrated use of imagery and dialogue, and some hilarious linguistic meditations at once acknowledging and parodying the "new science" of semiotics (the symbols used in the *Guide Michelin* as a future form of hieroglyph), *Blanche ou l'oubli* demonstrates a ripeness of experimental vision and a new ease in handling biographical and historical detail that mark a high point in Aragon's third career as a novelist.

Now accepted as a mainstream French writer, Aragon was elected to the Académie Goncourt in 1967; however, with a characteristic flair for publicity, he resigned noisily the next year in a dispute over a candidate he proposed. In May 1968 the Paris student revolution threw the city into turmoil. Ridiculed in the streets of the Latin Quarter for his white hair by the young revolutionaries, his sympathetic articles in *Les Lettres Françaises* ignored, Aragon returned to a long-term project first conceived during the Occupation, a novel about Henri Matisse. As the young bourgeois revolutionaries occupied the citadels of traditional French culture (the Sorbonne, the Comédie-Française) and brought Paris to an eerie standstill, he also put the finishing touches on a brief, iconographic text on the genesis of his novels–*Je n'ai jamais appris à écrire ou Les Incipit*. In August 1968 Soviet troops invaded Prague, further reviving Aragon's sense of living on the edge of historic catastrophe. The expulsion of Aleksandr Solzhenitsyn from the Soviet Writers Union in 1969 loosened the last threads of Aragon's attachment to the dream of Soviet per-

Triolet and Aragon, 1967 (photo Benichou)

fectibility. His fundamental "deferred optimism"–a belief in a better future for coming generations–remained intact, but Triolet's declining health threw a cloud over his creative horizon. As she became increasingly confined but labored to finish her last works, Aragon tried to bring together the parts of his continually expanding book on Matisse. Triolet died in June 1970, the year before Aragon's book at last appeared in print.

The two-volume *Henri Matisse, roman* is the most complex, meditative, and joyous of Aragon's works after *Le Paysan de Paris,* whose linguistic ease, texture of invention, and creativity of form it shares. This collection of texts on Matisse written between 1941 and 1970–brilliantly interwoven with photographs and color plates tracing the evolution of Matisse's work and studded with Aragon's multilayered dated commentaries on the texts–traces the tale of how Aragon could not write his planned novel about Matisse in the early 1940s because of the fall of France, poetry, clandestinity, and the Resistance and carries the

principles of intertextuality in literature and art forms to what may well be the highest plane they have reached in the twentieth century. As a direct challenge to Malraux's *Les Voix du silence* (*The Voices of Silence,* 1951), Aragon records not the epic tale of the role of art in human existence but the unique personal dramas of two artists–Matisse and Aragon–who lived directly the patient, difficult, endlessly repetitive, and constantly renewed task of distilling into works of art a personal vision of the world.

Aragon characterizes Matisse through his works, through photographs of the painter at his easel, through sketches and photographs of the familiar objects that appear in the paintings, and through Matisse's words–in letters, written in the margins of his books, spoken aloud–commenting on his own oeuvre and also on Aragon's developing text which began with their first meeting in the south of France during the early years of the Occupation. Aragon's self-portrait, as memorable as his portrait of Matisse, is traced by bold strokes, sudden retreats, revisions and commentar-

Title page by Aragon for his 1969 discussion of the genesis of his novels

ies and footnotes, in a startling, rhythmic text that brings together his theories on the novel, on the aesthetics of books, and on the relationships between themes and variations in art.

Henri Matisse, roman is a highly original novel about art and artistic vision, but, predictably, critical reaction was puzzled and frequently circumscribed by unfamiliarity with the evolution of Aragon's fiction or with the history of modern painting. Pierre de Boisdeffre, recalling the music of Aragon's war poetry and relating Aragon's depiction of Matisse painting in the south of France under the Occupation to the renaissance in French letters between 1940 and 1944, read *Henri Matisse* as a novel about the survival of the French spirit (*Revue des Deux Mondes*, February 1972). Peter Brooks, in a review of the English translation, elaborated on Aragon's challenging discussion of signs in literature and painting (*New Republic*, 16 December 1972). Nowhere more clearly than in *Henri Matisse* does Aragon define and describe his preference for the big novel, the work with many levels and multiple degrees of relief. In the text entitled "L'Homme fait parenthèse" (Man Makes a Parenthesis), written in 1968 and forming part of the second volume of *Henri Matisse*, Aragon writes: "Je vois bien que les romanciers au fur et à mesure tombés dans le raffinement, en sont arrivés à nous donner pour roman *une seule parenthèse*, une pauvre petite parenthèse.... Pour ma part, je nomme roman une machinerie, un machin ... un peu plus compliqué, complet, complexe ... un truc comploté, mijoté, composite pour parler architecture ..." (I know that novelists as they have become more refined have gotten to the point that they give us as a novel *one single parenthesis,* one poor little parenthesis.... As for me, I give the name novel to a machine, a thing that's a bit more complicated ... a tangled, stirred, composite thing to use an architectural term ...).

Aragon's last novel, *Théâtre/Roman,* published in 1974 when he was seventy-seven years old, is his darkest, most abstract fiction, a novel-collage that evokes the author's *theater,* that interior space where his dreams and his lies reside. Strikingly aural in quality–a departure from Aragon's traditional preference for pictures–the novel includes three characters, Romain Raphaël the actor, Daniel the director, and the Old Man who follows Romain around. The numerous brief segments composing the novel's two principal subdivisions are arranged in arbitrary order, with fragments of letters, poems, and deliberately confusing footnotes scattered throughout. Echoes of *King Lear,* of Beckett, of Dante, Lewis Carroll, and of Aragon himself make this novel the artistically disordered, printed script of an old man's world, a drafty corridor where memory, absence, and language merge in a threnody on the writer as an actor-in-history and history as acted through him. The rare visual sequences abandon the bright, sun- and sky-colored images of Matisse's paintings for the demonic, tangled faces and forms of Hieronymous Bosch. The poem "Où rien n'a qu'un œil" (Where everything has only one eye), set in the land of profiles, captures the failing rhythms of wheezing lungs and the fading vision of old eyes. Aragon's farewell to the novel is an extraordinary performance, achieving an architectonics of sound that subsumes fiction, biography, and meditation into a slow thrust-and-parry rhythm reminiscent of the later Beckett. Aragon becomes his own ghost, the writer disembodied and *disponsible* (free-floating), recording his vision of an empty space where Utopia used to be.

In Aragon's last years he oversaw the collection of his short stories (*Le Mentir-vrai,* Lying Like the Truth, 1980), the publication of the fifteenth and final volume of his complete poetic works, and the gathering of his scattered pieces on twentieth-century painting into *Écrits sur l'art moderne* (Writings on Modern Art, 1981), preparing for posterity the opus he would leave behind. Perhaps more intensely than any French writer of this century, Aragon faced the great temptation of the era for a creative writer–the temptation of politics–and succumbed to it often to the detriment of his art. But he had sufficient talent, longevity, and self-regenerative powers to survive historical upheavals, political disillusionment, and changes of literary fashion and to create in the novel, which he loved perhaps better than he did poetry–above all in *Le Paysan de Paris, Aurélien, Blanche ou l'oubli,* and *Henri Matisse, roman*–lasting works that illuminate the relationship, in an unforgiving century, between human experience and literary form.

Bibliographies:

Crispin Geoghegan, *Louis Aragon: Essai de bibliographie. Œuvres d'Aragon,* 2 volumes (London: Grant & Cutler, 1979, 1980);

Marie Lemaître, *Louis Aragon: Bibliographie analytique* (Paris: Centre National de Documentation Pédagogique, 1983).

Biography:

Pierre Daix, *Aragon, une vie à changer* (Paris: Seuil, 1975).

References:

Dominique Arban, *Aragon parle avec Dominique Arban* (Paris: Seghers, 1968);

Anna Balakian, "*Anicet,* or The Pursuit of Pulchérie," in *Symbolism and Modern Literature: Studies in Honor of Wallace Fowlie,* edited by Marcel Tétel (Durham: Duke University Press, 1978), pp. 237-247;

Marie Bancquart, *Paris des surréalistes* (Paris: Seghers, 1972);

Michel Beaujour, "The Surrealist Map of Love," *Yale French Studies,* no. 32 (1964): 124-132;

Lucille F. Becker, *Louis Aragon* (New York: Twayne, 1971);

Catharine Savage [Brosman], "Aragon and the Marxist Novel," in her *Malraux, Sartre, and Aragon as Political Novelists* (Gainesville: University of Florida Press, 1964), pp. 43-60;

William Calin, "The Poet's Poet: Intertextuality in Louis Aragon," *Symposium,* 40 (Spring 1986): 3-15;

Lionel Follet, *Aragon, le fantasme et l'histoire. Incipit et production textuelle dans "Aurélien"* (Paris: Editeurs Français Réunis, 1980);

Roger Garaudy, *Itinéraire d'Aragon* (Paris: Gallimard, 1961);

Yvette Gendine, *Aragon, prosateur surréaliste* (Geneva: Droz, 1966);

Mary Gutermuth, "Triangular Schizophrenia and the *Execution* of Aragon," *Kentucky Romance Quarterly,* 14, no. 4 (1967): 379-392;

Charles Haroche, "Relecture des *Communistes* d'Aragon," *Cahiers du Communisme,* 9 (September 1982): 102-111;

Hubert Juin, *Aragon* (Paris: Gallimard, 1960);

Doris Kadish, "L'Ironie et le roman engagé. 'Les Beaux Quartiers' de Louis Aragon," *French Review,* 45 (February 1972): 596-609;

Bernard Lecherbonnier, *Aragon* (Paris & Montreal: Bordas, 1971);

Pierre Lescure, *Aragon romancier* (Paris: Gallimard, 1960);

Georges Raillard, *Aragon* (Paris: Editions Universitaires, 1964);

Rima Drell Reck, "Marxism, History, and Fiction," in her *Literature and Responsibility: The French Novelist in the Twentieth Century* (Baton Rouge: Louisiana State University Press, 1969), pp. 216-256.

Papers:

The largest collection of Aragon's early manuscripts is in the Fonds Doucet at the Bibliothèque Sainte-Geneviève, Paris; these include "Clef à Anicet," some unpublished extracts of "Le Cahier noir," and several chapters of "Projet d'histoire littéraire contemporaine," as well as extensive correspondence with Jean Cocteau, Max Jacob, Jacques Doucet, André Gide, Jean Paulhan, Paul Valéry, and others. Most of Aragon's later manuscripts are housed at the Centre National de la Recherche Scientifique in Paris.

Marcel Arland
(5 July 1899-12 January 1986)

Alain D. Ranwez
Metropolitan State College

BOOKS: *Terres étrangères* (Paris: Gallimard, 1923);
Etienne (Paris: Gallimard, 1924);
La Route obscure (Paris: Gallimard, 1924);
Maternité (Paris: Sans Pareil, 1926);
Monique, Précédé de Terres étrangères (Paris: Gallimard, 1926);
Les Ames en peine (Paris: Gallimard, 1927);
Etapes (Paris: Gallimard, 1927);
Où le cœur se partage (Paris: Gallimard, 1927);
Edith (Paris: Gallimard, 1929);
L'Ordre (Paris: Gallimard, 1929);
Une Epoque (Paris: Corrêa, 1930);
Carnets de Gilbert (Paris: Gallimard, 1931);
Essais critiques (Paris: Gallimard, 1931);
Antarès (Paris: Gallimard, 1932);
Les Vivants (Paris: Gallimard, 1934);
La Vigie (Paris: Gallimard, 1935);
Les plus beaux de nos jours (Paris: Gallimard, 1937);
Terre natale (Paris: Gallimard, 1938);
La Grâce (Paris: Gallimard, 1941);
Sur une terre menacée (Paris: Stock, Delamain & Boutelleau, 1941);
Cinq contes (Brussels: Editions Lumière, 1944);
Le Promeneur (Paris: Editions du Pavois, 1944);
Zélie dans le désert (Paris: Gallimard, 1944);
Avec Pascal (Paris: Editions du Salon Carré, 1946);
Les Echanges (Paris: Gallimard, 1946);
Il faut de tout pour faire un monde (Paris: Gallimard, 1947);
Faire le point (Paris: Cayla, 1948);
Chronique de la peinture moderne (Paris: Corrêa, 1949);
Sidobre (Paris: Editions de Minuit, 1949);
Marivaux (Paris: Gallimard, 1950);
Lettres de France (Paris: Albin Michel, 1951);
La Consolation du voyageur (Paris: Stock, Delamain & Boutelleau, 1952);
Essais & Nouveaux Essais critiques (Paris: Gallimard, 1952);
Nouvelles Lettres de France (Paris: Albin Michel, 1954);
La Grâce d'écrire (Paris: Gallimard, 1955);

Marcel Arland

L'Eau et le feu (Paris: Gallimard, 1956);
Je vous écris (Paris: Grasset, 1960);
A perdre haleine (Paris: Gallimard, 1960);
Les Nuits et les souris (Paris: Gallimard, 1963);
Le Temps de Kerlo (Paris: Mercure de France, 1964);
Le Grand Pardon (Paris: Gallimard, 1965);
Carnets de Gilbert, suivis de Carnets d'un personnage, Qui parle? et J'écoute (Paris: Gallimard, 1966);
La Musique des anges (Paris: Gallimard, 1967);

Discours de réception de Marcel Arland à l'Académie Française et réponse de Jean Mistler, by Arland and Jean Mistler (Paris: Gallimard, 1969);

Attendez l'aube (Paris: Gallimard, 1970);

Proche du silence (Paris: Gallimard, 1973);

Avons-nous vécu? (Paris: Gallimard, 1977);

Ce fut ainsi (Paris: Gallimard, 1979);

Dans l'amitié de la peinture (Paris: Luyeau Ascot, 1980);

Mais enfin qui êtes-vous? (Paris: Gallimard, 1981);

Lire Guillevic (Lyons: Presses Universitaires de Lyon, 1983);

Lumière du soir (Paris: Gallimard, 1983).

OTHER: *Anthologie de la poésie française,* edited by Arland (Paris: Stock, Delamain & Boutelleau, 1941; revised and enlarged, 1947, 1956, 1960);

Le Paysan français à travers la littérature, edited by Arland (Paris: Stock, Delamain & Boutelleau, 1941);

La Prose française: Anthologie, histoire, et critique d'un art, edited by Arland (Paris: Stock, Delamain & Boutelleau, 1951);

Georges Rouault and André Suarès, *Correspondance,* edited, with an introduction, by Arland (Paris: Gallimard, 1960); translated and edited by Alice Low-Beer as *Correspondence, 1911-1939,* introduction by Arland (Ilfracombe, U. K.: A. H. Stockwell, 1983);

Entretiens sur André Gide, edited by Arland and Jean Mouton (Paris: Mouton, 1967).

Marcel Arland was a literary and intellectual leader in France from the 1920s to the late 1970s. Although an established novelist, he is best known for his short stories, which demonstrate his affinity with the American short story at the turn of the twentieth century. His criticism ranged from art to literature and covered artists and writers of several centuries. He was also respected for the encouragement he gave new writers in his position as editor of the prestigious *Nouvelle Revue Française* from 1953 to 1977 and for his interest in preserving the artistic values that literary review represented.

Arland was born 5 July 1899 in Varennes-sur-Amance in Haute-Marne, roughly halfway between Paris and the eastern French border. It is a sylvan setting of hills and sloping valleys that often appears, in Arland's fictional world, most specifically in his 1938 narrative, *Terre natale* (Native Land). His father, Victor Arland, died when Arland was three years old, and he and his older brother were brought up in a religiously constrained environment by their unyielding mother, Noémie Vincent Arland, whose Sunday visits to the cemetery became ritualistic. These childhood memories are relived vividly in Arland's *Antarès* (1932), a novel in which death is powerfully present. Arland was painfully influenced by these early years. His attempts to escape the stifling atmosphere created by his mother and both maternal and paternal grandparents often led him to the old books he found in the attic or into a world of reverie in the surrounding Varennes woods. His solitary tendencies were further accentuated by the relationship he had with his more serious and socially adept brother; they were able to form a fraternal bond only years after adolescence.

In 1911 Arland moved to Langres, a town in his native region, where his mother had settled so that her older son could attend school there. Arland became a student at the local Collège Diderot and received his *baccalauréat* in 1918. It was during these formative years that Arland discovered the French authors who were to have an impact on him, most notably Stendhal and Baudelaire; the former would furnish a fictional model for Arland's 1929 novel *L'Ordre* (Order) and the latter a taste for syntactic discipline. In 1919 he went to Paris, took courses at the Sorbonne, and frequented Parisian literary circles, through which he met Marcel Proust, Jean Giraudoux, François Mauriac, Roger Vitrac, and Blaise Cendrars. Arland became impatient with university classes, however, gave up his academic pursuits after receiving a *licence-ès-lettres,* and initiated a fervent reading of the works of Dostoyevski, Nietzsche, and André Gide. Entranced by the prospect of a literary career, Arland became editor for the literary section of the review *L'Université de Paris* in 1919. He also joined the army for a short period of military service, which he performed halfheartedly, spending more time with his literary associates in Paris than in the barracks. The following year, in connection with the Dada movement, he founded the avant-garde review *Aventure.* Arland had been attracted by the movement's desire to create a sense of novelty in a static social and artistic milieu. Only three issues of the review appeared, because of difficulties Arland had with André Breton's segment of the Dada group. Arland chose to separate himself from that publication and created another, which he called *Dés* (Dice).

In 1921 Arland met André Malraux, who would achieve international recognition with the publication of *La Condition humaine* (*Man's Fate*) in 1933. They became close friends and saw each other on a daily basis until the latter's departure for Indochina to study Asian art. Arland and Malraux shared the same beliefs concerning the meaning of individual independence and responsibility, held the same youthful disdain for cloistered literary groups, and had a common appreciation for painting. Both published critical works on art later in their professional lives. Their friendship lasted until Malraux's death in 1976.

It was also during the early 1920s that Arland formulated the concept that writing was not a simple intellectual exercise but an act of personal realization. Literature became, for him, a form of salvation which demanded not only an aesthetic quality but an ethical value as well. Many experiences, both ethical and philosophical, from Arland's formative years helped shape his novels *L'Ordre* and *Les Ames en peine* (Souls in Purgatory, 1927) and his first essay, *La Route obscure* (The Obscure Road, 1924), in which the essayist relinquishes preestablished doctrines in favor of a personal ethos formed through the equal consideration of individual moral needs and the solicitations of the world. This ethical way can be chosen only by following an obscure path, without preexisting values. Arland's premise foreshadowed that of Sartrean existentialism, which flourished in France during the years immediately following World War II.

Arland published his first fictional work in 1923. Rather than calling *Terres étrangères* (Foreign Lands) a novel, he chose to label it a *récit* (narrative), borrowing André Gide's designation for a short work of moral inclination. The title refers to the passion and tragedy belonging to the world of Arland's childhood. Gide acclaimed Arland's *récit* and Valery Larbaud praised it in the *Nouvelle Revue Française*. This initial success brought Arland and the review's leaders together, and through the group he met Jean Paulhan, a critic and *moraliste* with classical leanings with whom he would retain a lifelong friendship and professional connection. This contact with the *Nouvelle Revue Française* also initiated some of Arland's most important critical contributions to the review he would codirect with Paulhan beginning in the early 1950s. Arland's editorship of the *Nouvelle Revue Française* lasted until June 1977, when he retired from both editing and writing.

Arland's first article, published in 1924, was entitled "Sur un nouveau mal du siècle" (On a New Malaise). In the article, titled for Chateaubriand's phrase describing the existential malaise of the post-French Revolution generation, Arland denounces the general atmosphere of the post-World War I years as well as the literature fostered by dadaism and surrealism which he thought was comprised of attitudes, gestures, and fantasies with no meaningful premises. He aimed at bringing young authors back to a sincere and individual type of literature, away from facile conventions. Arland reinforced that literary concept in fictional form with the publication of his first full-length novel, *L'Ordre*, based in part on his recollections of his own relationship with his brother. Gilbert Villars, the novel's young hero, is the spiritual son of Stendhal's Julien Sorel in *Le Rouge et le noir* (*The Red and the Black*, 1830) and Balzac's Rastignac in *Le Père Goriot* (*Father Goriot*, 1834); he is in perpetual conflict with society's mediocrity, and in the end finds solace in his reconciliation with others but not with himself. Villars is an individual intent upon using his arrogance to secure a place outside tradition, and he reflects well the existential concerns of Arland's generation. The novel, in which Arland played out his own obsession with death through the hero's revolt, was named winner of the 1929 Prix Goncourt.

The following year, Arland's life turned around; from a life of anxieties seemingly without aim, he found peace in his marriage to Janine Bérand, with whom he had a daughter, Dominique, in 1930. The Prix Goncourt and marriage liberated him, and he left Paris in favor of Port-Cros in the French countryside, where only his close friends came to visit, among them Paulhan, Jacques Chardonne, and the artist Georges Rouault. During this period he began to favor the short story for its rhythm reminiscent of life and rigorous form.

The years preceding World War II proved to be productive for Arland. His work reflected an internal metamorphosis perhaps best exemplified in his 1935 *récit*, *La Vigie* (The Lookout). The destructive instinct which overpowered Gilbert Villars in *L'Ordre* is not lacking in *La Vigie*, but in the later work happiness does win over the hero's tendencies to bow to nihilism. *La Vigie* is an ethical book depicting man's perpetual combat with his dark forces. The experiences of Arland's own youth are a strong influence in this work, as well as in other publications of this period. *Terre natale* is a

Arland with André Malraux, Jules Supervielle, Jean Paulhan, and Paul Valéry at the Nouvelle Revue Française *(Archives André Malraux)*

confession full of childhood memories and an attempt on the author's part to come to grips with his life and with the internal process by which he came to be a writer. The story collection *Les Vivants* (The Living, 1934) takes Arland back to his native Varennes, where man is a perpetual prisoner of his past. This sense of entanglement is even more acute in Arland's 1937 collection of short stories, ironically entitled *Les plus beaux de nos jours* (Our Finest Days). This collection, also set in Varennes, depicts a humble people, their rough language, and their daily struggles. There is a strong feeling of dignity in their partaking of the earth with all of their senses, but their actions are carried out with fear and ultimately fail to improve their lot.

Drafted at the outbreak of World War II, Arland was stationed first at Langres and then at Nantes, as chief sergeant. He also served a short term in Algeria before returning to occupied Paris in October 1940. In November of that same year he met with Pierre Drieu La Rochelle, who wanted to revive the *Nouvelle Revue Française*. Its editor before the Occupation, Jean Paulhan, had refused to continue publication under German authority and would not declare the review bankrupt as requested. Consequently, the German-controlled Vichy government handed the review over to Drieu La Rochelle. Although Arland did cooperate with Drieu on a few numbers of the review, Drieu's right-wing political views and affinity with Nazi doctrine and the New Order soon prompted Arland to quit the project. Arland recorded his personal and professional judgment of Drieu in *La Grâce d'écrire* (The Gift of Writing), an essay collection published in 1955.

This collection continues what Arland had initiated in 1946 with the publication of *Les Echanges* (Exchanges). Like *La Grâce d'écrire, Les Echanges* is a collection of critical essays dealing with the process of literary creation and with the psyche behind the work as well. In both volumes Arland's aim is to discover the personal gift of each writer he discusses, the talent without which that person could not have become an artist. In the first collection Arland considers Racine, Fénelon, Mme de La Fayette, Marivaux, Choderlos de Laclos, and Benjamin Constant, while in the second he deals more with his contemporaries: Drieu La Rochelle, Saint-Exupéry, Radiguet, and Bernanos. Arland's approach is noteworthy in that he conducts imagined interviews with his subjects in order to illustrate how writers obtain their gifts, their saving grace. In short, in these two works Arland attempts a psychology of literary creation.

Besides writing critical works and editing the review *Comœdia*, during the Occupation Arland worked on a *récit* entitled *Zélie dans le désert* (Zelie in the Desert, 1944), which recalls the Varennes woods of Arland's childhood and continues to explore the emotional territory the author had delineated in his first *récit, Terres étrangères*. After the war Arland spent more time on his critical essays: *Avec Pascal* (With Pascal, 1946), in which he seeks to understand the internal forces which had shaped the seventeenth-century thinker; *Lettres de France* (Letters from France, 1951), a collection of articles he had written for *La Gazette de Lausanne* and an important work for the study of French literary life in the 1950s; *Marivaux* (1950), a book-length study in which Arland considers the eighteenth-century writer's work as a long confession on life, love, and happiness; and a long meditation on the creation of life, *La Consolation du voyageur* (The Consolation of the Traveler, 1952), which he dedicated to his wife.

In the years after the war Arland also began to nurture a more tragic vision of life. His collection of stories entitled *L'Eau et le feu* (Water and Fire, 1956) presents a microcosm of solitude and anguish in which the characters seem devoured by an internal rage. *A perdre haleine* (Out of Breath, 1960) is probably his most tragic work

Arland in 1952 (photo Laure Albin-Guillot–Viollet)

and is considered by many reviewers to be his fictional masterpiece. Arland's world in this story collection is void of hope as man appears to be crushed by an invisible force. Also in 1960 Arland published *Je vous écris* (I Write to You). It is an intimate essay, a collection of imaginary letters written during the composition of *A perdre haleine*. This meditation focuses on Arland's creative experience, and although the feeling of anguish is not absent from the text, there is also a sense of serenity, as if the author were finding a harmony between his world and his creative genius.

The *Nouvelle Revue Française* ceased publication for the second time in June 1943, under the directorship of Drieu La Rochelle. Because of the shameful reputation the journal had acquired under Drieu it was difficult to revive it immediately after the Liberation. It was, however, reestablished in 1953 under the name *Nouvelle Nouvelle Revue Française,* thanks in part to the efforts of Gaston Gallimard of the Parisian publishing company where the offices of the review had always been housed. (It returned to its prewar title in 1959.) The directorship was offered to Arland and his lifelong friend Paulhan. Together they shared the review's editorial responsibilities until Paulhan's death in 1968. Arland stayed on alone at the urging of Gallimard; his final article as editor appeared in the June 1977 issue. The book that Arland claimed would be his last also appeared that year: *Avons-nous vécu?* (Have We Lived?) is a collection of personal and philosophical memoirs.

It is difficult to think about the *NRF* today without thinking of Marcel Arland, whose artistic leadership and intensity helped make the journal the best of its kind. He brought to the *NRF* the experience he had amassed through his contributions and editorial work for *Hommes et Mondes, Contemporains, La Gazette de Lausanne, La Table Ronde,* and *Combat,* edited by Albert Camus, the young author of *L'Etranger* (*The Stranger*, 1942), during the German occupation.

Arland also directed the first French colloquium of writers after the war. It was held in 1948 at Royaumont and brought together three generations of writers and a variety of political factions. Arland continued to organize this annual event, eventually moving it to Cerizay. In 1952 Arland received the Grand Prix de Littérature from the Académie Française, and in 1960 he was awarded the Grand Prix National des Lettres. Arland was elected in 1968 as one of the Académie's forty immortals (or living members) assuming the seat left vacant by the death of André Maurois. He was also named Grand Officier de la Légion d'Honneur.

Arland began his career as a writer within the realm of revolt. Confronted with a Europe shaken by World War I, he wrote to contest static society and art. At first attracted to dadaism and surrealism in his search for something new, he later condemned the movements for their lack of individualism and authenticity. Constantly torn between order and anarchy, destruction and the desire for harmony, Arland's literary work is both modern and classical. He preferred the form of the *récit,* which usually concentrates on few characters and only one or two problems, to that of the novel, more fully developed and complex. The *récit* was a better means of expressing inner conflicts and displaying his gift for psychological analysis. Arland died of a heart attack at his country home at Brinville, near Fontainebleau, in January 1986. He was eighty-six.

References:

Jean Duvignaud, *Arland* (Paris: Gallimard, 1962);

Alvin Allen Eustis, *Marcel Arland, Benjamin Crémieux, Ramon Fernandez: Trois Critiques de "La Nouvelle Revue Française"* (Paris: Nouvelles Editions Debresse, 1961).

Marcel Aymé

(29 March 1902-14 October 1967)

Dorothy Brodin

Herbert H. Lehman College, City University of New York

SELECTED BOOKS: *Brûlebois* (Poitiers: Cahiers de France, 1926);

Aller retour (Paris: Gallimard, 1927);

Les Jumeaux du diable (Paris: Gallimard, 1928);

La Table-aux-Crevés (Paris: Gallimard, 1929); translated by Helen Waddell as *The Hollow Field* (London: Constable, 1933; New York: Dodd, Mead, 1933);

La Rue sans nom (Paris: Gallimard, 1930);

Le Vaurien (Paris: Gallimard, 1931);

Le Puits aux images (Paris: Gallimard, 1932);

La Jument verte (Paris: Gallimard, 1933); translated by Norman Denny as *The Green Mare* (London: Bodley Head, 1955; New York: Harper, 1955);

Les Contes du Chat perché (Paris: Gallimard, 1934);

Le Nain (Paris: Gallimard, 1934);

Maison basse (Paris: Gallimard, 1935); translated by Denny as *The House of Men* (London: Bodley Head, 1952);

Le Moulin de la Sourdine (Paris: Gallimard, 1936); translated by Denny as *The Secret Stream* (London: Bodley Head, 1953; New York: Harper, 1953);

Gustalin (Paris: Gallimard, 1937);

Derrière chez Martin (Paris: Gallimard, 1938);

Silhouette du scandale (Paris: Sagittaire, 1938);

Le Bœuf clandestin (Paris: Gallimard, 1939);

La Belle Image (Paris: Gallimard, 1941); translated by Denny as *The Second Face* (London: Bodley Head, 1951; New York: Harper, 1951); republished as *The Grand Seduction* (Greenwich, Conn.: Fawcett, 1958; London: Sphere, 1969);

Travelingue (Paris: Gallimard, 1941); translated by Eric Sutton as *The Miraculous Barber* (London: Bodley Head, 1950; New York: Harper, 1951);

Le Passe-muraille (Paris: Gallimard, 1943);

La Vouivre (Paris: Gallimard, 1943); translated by Sutton as *The Fable and the Flesh* (London: Bodley Head, 1949);

Vogue la galère (Paris: Grasset, 1944);

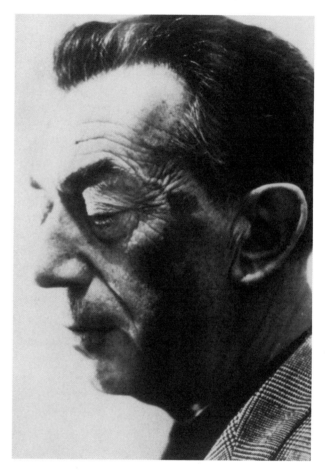

Marcel Aymé (photo N. Treatt)

Le Chemin des écoliers (Paris: Gallimard, 1946); translated by Sutton as *The Transient Hour* (London: Bodley Head, 1948; New York: A. A. Wyn, 1948);

Lucienne et le boucher (Paris: Grasset, 1947);

Le Vin de Paris (Paris: Gallimard, 1947);

Uranus (Paris: Gallimard, 1948); translated by Denny as *The Barkeep of Blémont* (New York: Harper, 1950); republished as *Fanfare in Blémont* (London: Bodley Head, 1950);

Le Confort intellectuel (Paris: Flammarion, 1949);

Across Paris and Other Stories, translated by Denny (New York: Harper, 1950); republished as

The Walker-Through-Walls and Other Stories (New York: Berkeley, 1950);

Autres Contes du Chat perché (Paris: Gallimard, 1950);

Clérambard (Paris: Grasset, 1950); translated by Denny (London: Bodley Head, 1952);

En arrière (Paris: Gallimard, 1950);

The Wonderful Farm, translated by Denny (New York: Harper, 1951; London: Bodley Head, 1952);

La Tête des autres (Paris: Grasset, 1952);

The Magic Pictures: More About the Wonderful Farm, translated by Denny (New York: Harper, 1954);

Les Quatre Vérités (Paris: Grasset, 1954);

Return to the Wonderful Farm, translated by Denny (London: Bodley Head, 1954);

Les Sorcières de Salem, adapted by Aymé from Arthur Miller's *The Crucible* (Paris: Grasset, 1955);

Paris que j'aime, by Aymé, Antoine Blondin, and Jean-Paul Clébert (Paris: Editions Sun, 1956); translated by Clébert as *The Paris I Love* (N.p.: Tudor, 1963);

Les Oiseaux de lune (Paris: Gallimard, 1956);

La Mouche bleue (Paris: Gallimard, 1957);

Derniers Contes du Chat perché (Paris: Gallimard, 1958);

Soties de la ville et des champs (Paris: Club de Libraires de France, 1958);

Vu du pont, adapted by Aymé from Miller's *A View from the Bridge*, *Avant-scène*, no. 204 (1959);

Les Tiroirs de l'inconnu (Paris: Gallimard, 1960); translated by Denny as *The Conscience of Love* (London: Bodley Head, 1962; New York: Atheneum, 1962);

Louisiane (Paris: Gallimard, 1961);

Oscar et Erick (Paris: Gautier-Languereau, 1961);

The Proverb, and Other Stories, translated by Denny (London: Bodley Head, 1961; New York: Atheneum, 1961);

Les Maxibules (Paris: Gallimard, 1962);

Enjambées (Paris: Gallimard, 1967);

Le Minotaure, précédé de La Convention Belzébir et de Consommation (Paris: Gallimard, 1967);

The Walker-Through-Walls and Other Stories, translated by Denny (London: Bodley Head, 1972);

L'Etrange, le merveilleux et le fantastique, 2 volumes (Le Havre: Société des Amis de Marcel Aymé, 1983-1984);

La Fille du shérif (Paris: Gallimard, 1987).

Collection: *Œuvres romanesques*, 6 volumes (Paris: Flammarion, 1977).

PLAY PRODUCTIONS: *Vogue la galère*, Paris, Théâtre du Vieux-Colombier, April 1948;

Clérambard, Paris, Comédie des Champs-Elysées, 1950;

La Tête des autres, Paris, Théâtre de l'Atelier, 15 February 1952;

Les Quatre Vérités, Paris, Théâtre de l'Atelier, 23 January 1954;

Les Oiseaux de lune, Paris, Théâtre de l'Atelier, 15 December 1955;

La Mouche bleue, Paris, Comédie des Champs-Elysées, 20 October 1957;

Louisiane, Paris, Théâtre de la Renaissance, 18 September 1961;

Les Maxibules, Paris, Théâtre des Bouffes Parisiens, 21 November 1961;

Le Minotaure, Paris, Théâtre de l'Athénée, 20 November 1966;

La Convention Belzébir, Paris, 1966.

OTHER: *Désert vivant: Images et couleurs de Walt Disney*, adapted by Aymé, Louis Bromfield, Albert Camus, Julian Huxley, François Mauriac, André Maurois, and Henry de Montherlant (Paris: Société Française du Livre, 1954);

Leo Tolstoy, *L'Enfance et l'adolescence*, preface by Aymé (Paris: Livre de Poche, 1961);

Georges Simenon, *Le Chien jaune*, preface by Aymé (Paris: Livre de Poche, 1962);

Rabelais, *Les Cinq Livres de Rabelais*, preface by Aymé (Paris: Magnard, 1964);

Charles Perrault, *Contes*, preface by Aymé (Paris: Club des Libraires de France, 1965);

Jean de la Bruyère, *Les Caractères*, preface by Aymé (Paris: Club des Classiques, 1968).

Marcel Aymé was a protean writer whose work cannot be classified by genre, "ism," or mood. Nor does Aymé's career resemble that of the typical French author. He was not shaped by classical and humanistic disciplines or fashioned in the usual university mold. He was always a nonconformist, rejecting political and literary labels and steadfastly refusing to be considered an intellectual. His experience of the world and his transposition of that experience were essentially pragmatic and individualistic. Consequently he has appealed to many audiences. Some have seen in Aymé an amusing author of improbable and risqué tales; others have described him as an indul-

Aymé in Paris, 1945 (photo Lipnitzki)

gent moralist whose work is a mixture of irony and tenderness; still others have considered him a bitter spectator of the human comedy whose caustic humor spares neither men nor institutions, however sacred. His vivid and unusual style, the unexpected quality of his vision, his facility with words, and his talent for making the most baroque situations credible have led readers to compare him in turn with Rabelais, Molière, Voltaire, Balzac, Maupassant, Queneau, Lewis Carroll, Faulkner, and others. There is a measure of validity in all these comparisons as they relate to particular facets of Aymé's work, but the truth is at once more complex and simpler: his experience of life was rich and varied, his imagination fertile, his sensitivity to his surroundings acute, and he wrote according to the inspiration of the moment, each succeeding moment having its own specific characteristics.

Marcel Aymé, the youngest of six children, was born on 29 March 1902 in Joigny, where his father, Joseph Aymé, worked as a blacksmith. His mother, Emma Monamy Aymé, died when he was two years old, and his father placed him in the care of her parents in Villers-Robert, a village where he spent the next eight years and which he used, under the name of Claquebue, as the background for the 1933 novel *La Jument verte* (translated as *The Green Mare*, 1955). He

then went to live with an aunt, spending most of his youth in and near Dole, a small city of the Franche-Comté region. He completed his studies at the local lycée, showing more talent for mathematics than for literature.

After serving as a soldier in the artillery, Aymé traveled and tried his hand at various trades and professions. He did a stint on a newspaper and discovered that he enjoyed writing but that he was probably too outspoken for a career as a reporter. Later, while convalescing from an illness, he wrote his first novel, *Brûlebois* (1926), which, like his other early works, was based largely on childhood memories. *Brûlebois* (so titled for its protagonist) has a small town as its setting and challenges traditional middle-class priorities. In 1929 Aymé's fourth novel, *La Table-aux-Crevés* (translated as *The Hollow Field*, 1933), received the Prix Théophraste Renaudot and brought the author to the attention of the reading public. This work portrays lusty peasants in realistic terms and underlines the absurdities which human beings can impose on a neutral, if not benevolent, world.

In 1933, the year after his marriage to Marie-Antoinette Arnaud, *La Jument verte*, perhaps Aymé's masterpiece, earned him an international reputation. Its immense success made it possible for him to devote all of his time to writing novels, short stories, plays, and essays. He made Paris his home and there became a recognized member of the literary scene and a well-known figure in Montmartre.

Of the early novels, *La Jument verte* is undoubtedly the most important. This bawdy Rabelaisian tale pictures the life and politics of a village where personal, social, and partisan conflicts take on epic proportions. Conservatives and liberals, republican militants and staunch defenders of the status quo clash and finally engage in a mock-heroic test of the power exercised by their respective deities. In the microcosm represented by the small town of Claquebue and the two feuding families, the Malorets and the Haudoins, children, adults, civil servants, local dignitaries, and clerics continually fight to defend or impose their ideas. It is characteristic of Aymé that the story is told by an unusual witness, in this case a mare portrayed in brilliant green who is a figure in a painting on the wall. The "propos de la jument" (the mare's comments) punctuate the tale as the horse plays a part like that of a Greek chorus.

In 1935, with *Maison basse* (translated as *The House of Men*, 1952), Aymé began to write more frequently about those who lived in cities, although he always retained something of the Franc-Comtois peasant, closely in touch with those who tilled the soil, whose lives unfolded according to the rhythm of the seasons.

As he began to deal with the bourgeoisie, he became more caustic, but unlike Maupassant, who also satirized both peasants and city-dwellers, Aymé did not develop a cohesive outlook based on a naturalistic point of view. He simply described the people he remembered. *Le Moulin de la Sourdine* (1936; translated as *The Secret Stream*, 1953), which some might consider a parody of a detective story, is basically a tale of prejudice and hypocrisy told with a strong measure of black humor. A murder has been committed in a town where nothing is what it seems and truth is a secondary concern. Respectability is the only important consideration. Everyone in the town is ready to believe in the guilt of Troussequin, who, like Victor Hugo's hunchback Quasimodo, is poor, simpleminded, and, worst of all, monstrously ugly. When the real murderer, in his contempt for his fellow citizens, confesses his crime, no one believes him, for he is a pillar of society.

In Aymé's writings the pretentious and self-righteous are constantly satirized. His treatment of naive and honest country people, of hard-working postmen, gendarmes, and clerics, is always kind, albeit amusing. Toward hypocrites, smug and pompous bourgeois professionals, social climbers, and misers he is less indulgent. The 1937 novel *Gustalin* is, by Aymé's account, a fable of field mice and city mice in which the latter wreak havoc in the lives of the former, to whom they bring their false values. *Travelingue*, published in 1941, is clear-cut sociopolitical satire that reflects Aymé's long-standing interest in motion pictures. Whereas the French title is taken from cinema jargon, describing a shot in which a camera, mounted on tracks or on a dolly, moves to follow the action, the 1950 English translation bears the title *The Miraculous Barber*. Both are accurate. The novel deals in part with the influence of motion pictures on young people and presents a set of characters whose lives are devoted to ridiculous aspirations, posturing, and "arty" conversations. One of the most memorable characters is a barber who makes grandiose, cliché-ridden philosophical speeches that offer simplistic solutions to all kinds of problems. The more superficial and silly his pronouncements seem, the more power the barber wields. Without ever being elected to office he calls cabinet meetings, distributes decorations and rewards, and virtually runs the country. This caricature of loquacious hairdressers many readers have known becomes, in Aymé's hands, a symbol of the occult and often senseless forces at work in society.

In 1943, with *La Vouivre* (translated as *The Fable and the Flesh*, 1949), Aymé returned to the novel of the countryside and its earthy denizens. This novel, like the earlier *La Jument verte*, features a bitter vendetta engaged in by two families. There is no ideology involved in this quarrel between the Mindeur and Muselier clans, although everyone expends untold energy on unimportant matters and inane village politics. Other battles rage, including those between men and women and between the supernatural and the everyday world. The title character, La Vouivre, is an attractive woodland divinity who walks about accompanied by her attendant snakes, stops in a café for refreshment, and makes love to Arsène, a young peasant who does not believe in the supernatural.

Perhaps Aymé wrote *La Vouivre* in an attempt to escape from daily reality during the years of World War II and the Occupation, which he wrote about later in short stories, some serious, realistic, and at times bitter, others amusing, satirical, or even belonging to the realm of science fiction. The novels *Le Chemin des écoliers* (1946; translated as *The Transient Hour*, 1948) and *Uranus* (1948; translated as *The Barkeep of Blémont*, 1950) are set during those times as well, and the author's bitterness is evident on almost every page. He was deeply wounded by the events of those years. He hated the erosion of morality which accompanied the Occupation and the savagery of that period and its aftermath. After the Liberation the effort to seek out and punish those who were guilty of collaboration with the Germans led to fear, denunciations, and lynchings. Aymé, who had continued to publish during the Occupation, was not prosecuted, but several writers had to face trials because of their publications. Aymé did not hide his indignation, stating that he found it nauseating that a writer could be arrested for his opinions.

Le Chemin des écoliers and *Uranus* were widely read at the time of their publication and continue to afford interesting reading for anyone interested in what was happening in France in 1945. The title of the first novel recalls a popular

Manuscript page from act 3 of Aymé's Clérambard, *reproduced in the program for the 12 September 1986 revival of the play*

A scene from the first production of Clérambard *at the Comédie des Champs-Elysées, 1950 (photo Harlingue)*

*Jean-Pierre Marielle as Comte Hector de Clérambard and Nadia Barentin as La Langouste in the 1986 revival
(Reportage François Darras)*

expression. "Prendre le chemin des écoliers" (to take the schoolboys' route) means to take a long, meandering way to one's destination. It is an indication of the path followed by fundamentally "normal" young people who are perverted by the times in which they live, by the basic immorality of their superficially respectable environment, and by the economic disarray and rampant black market operations of the postwar period in France. Michaud and Lolivier, average schoolteachers, see their students become increasingly estranged and aware of their parents' mediocrity. Aymé's account creates a sense of terrible malaise as the young settle into a cynical acceptance of compromise and evil. The disturbing story of the main plot is underscored by Aymé's use of footnotes to relate details of his characters' personal lives. In these brief, paratextual additions, the author acquaints the reader with the dreadful conditions of that era–a time of mob violence, savagery, and cowardice. Still, there is an indication of hope in the novel's title. Aymé did not give up on humanity and the hope that the meandering would eventually reach a good and humane end.

Uranus is no less satirical, no less cruel a depiction of the postwar period. Before the war Blémont had been a civilized town, but in the aftermath of the conflict the varnish of civilization has disappeared and the town has reverted to barbarism. Fear is the moving force; corruption is rampant. Profiteers amass fortunes, collaborate with the Germans, and play both ends against the middle. They use any means to satisfy their lust for power as the historical period in which they live brings out the basic flaws in their characters. They are products of their era. Yet, in a sense, *Uranus* emphasizes the glimmer of hope suggested by the title *Le Chemin des écoliers*. There is in *Uranus*, despite the horrors it recounts, a strong current of optimism and a statement of Aymé's faith in mankind's ability to survive with honor intact. Professor Watrin, a character whose ideas reflect those of the author, asserts that the world is marvelously built and that man is the masterpiece. He is an optimist who may appear naive but, like the Haudoins in *La Jument verte,* he represents the people Aymé admires most, the simple, sincere men and women who may appear comical at times but whose fundamental decency can triumph over evil.

Aymé's last novel, *Les Tiroirs de l'inconnu* (1960; translated as *The Conscience of Love,* 1962, although perhaps the title is best translated as Se-

cret Drawers or Secret Hiding Places), is a strange satirical commentary on the absurdity of the world and has been compared to Camus's *L'Etranger (The Stranger,* 1942). At the end of the novel, a minor character, Jean Bouvillon, philosopher and author, having found absolute proof of the existence of God, burns the manuscript he has been working on because he believes that religion should remain an adventure.

Aymé's numerous short stories are perhaps better known than his longer works and contain some of his best and certainly most imaginative writing. In them realistic people and animals are found side by side with centaurs, educated oxen, and fictional characters who step out of the books in which they figure and attend literary cocktail parties. The world described may be intensely real, as is the case of Paris during the Occupation years in "La Traversée de Paris" ("Across Paris"), or it may be a world in which natural laws are suspended. In "Le Passe-Muraille" ("The Walker-Through-Walls") the main character possesses the ability to pass through walls. The boy of "Les Bottes de sept lieues" ("The Seven-League Boots") dons seven-league boots (à la Brothers Grimm) and brings home a bouquet of early-morning sunbeams for his mother. At times Aymé's world is that of science fiction, in which realistic laws and decrees are shown in nonrealistic situations. "La Carte" ("The Life Ration"), for instance, is a tale of wartime shortages and rationing, which lead to the distribution of "life cards" for the number of days of life per month a citizen is allowed according to his usefulness in the eyes of the bureaucracy. As each citizen jealously defends his right to a privileged status, the situation gets out of hand with the organization of a black market, allowing some to live fifty or sixty days a month. Although the story is extremely funny, it is also serious social satire. Like "La Carte," many of Aymé's stories function as a kind of literary shock treatment which tears off the masks people wear and at the same time focuses attention on the meaning and possible consequences of human actions.

Among the best and most popular of Aymé's short stories are those developed in one of his favorite rural settings, the farm. *Les Contes du Chat perché* (1934) and its sequels, *Autres Contes du Chat perché* (1950) and *Derniers Contes du Chat perché* (1958) (the titles combine the idea of an animal, *le chat,* or cat, with that of a children's game of tag, *le chat-perché*), were, in Aymé's words, written for children from "4 to 75." They feature two bright little girls, Delphine and Marinette, their solid, stolid, unimaginative farmer parents, and a collection of barnyard fowls, pigs, peacocks, and other animals. The animals talk and behave as stupidly as mere human beings, whereas the girls, with the best of intentions, cause trouble because they do not fully understand the long-term results of their interference with the laws of nature. In "Les Bœufs" (The Oxen), for example, they decide to educate the oxen because they have heard a speech on the value of education and do not realize that what might be good for a future engineer is useless or perhaps dangerous for an ox. They teach the animals to read, and one of them becomes so proficient that he spends all his time with books and is no longer of any use on a farm. Good intentions are not enough; they must be grounded in good sense. These tales are an excellent example of Aymé's humor as well as a summary of his tolerant and compassionate attitude toward people.

Aymé has often been called a fabulist, a designation which certainly applies in his animal stories and also throughout his work, with its plots and situations that take on abstract and universal meanings. His personal experience is often the basis of his writings, and miracles are by no means excluded by this anticlerical freethinker. Some of them are spurious, like the "resurrection" in *La Jument verte*, which takes place when Messelon, the old republican mayor, who has been proclaimed officially "dead," is kissed by the statue of Marianne, symbol of the French Republic. In contrast, the miracle that occurs in "Les Bottes de sept lieues" is real and comes as an unexpected conclusion to an otherwise realistic story. Another kind of miracle occurs in "Le Paon" (The Peacock), when Delphine and Marinette, in order to keep their pig from dying of anorexia in his attempt to be as beautiful as the peacock, tell him that he has achieved his goal. The pig makes a supreme effort to look over his shoulder, and, at that very moment, a rainbow crosses the sky and casts its colors on the creature's back, giving him the beauty he sought. This is a miracle born of human kindness.

Aymé had an acute ear for the spoken word, which is perhaps what led him to write for the stage. It was not until 1944 that his first play, *Vogue la galère*, was published, a work more literary than truly theatrical, a kind of parable concerning the dangers of unrealistic idealism. Its title can be translated in two ways: literally, "let the galley sail on," and the action does involve a mutiny

Aymé near the end of his life (photograph copyright © Jerry Bauer)

of galley slaves; or "let the chips fall where they may," an interpretation that points up the irresponsibility of the mutiny's leader.

With *Clérambard*, published in 1950 and presented that year at the Comédie des Champs-Elysées, Aymé hit his stride as a playwright. The play scandalized many people, who saw in it an attack on religion and on the very foundation of a stable society. The Clérambard family members live miserably in the ruins of their ancestral castle and work like slaves to raise enough money for repairs. The situation is turned upside down when Saint Francis appears to the Comte de Clérambard and effects the nobleman's conversion by performing a miracle. Clérambard, who remains as much of a hotheaded tyrant after his conversion as before, plunges into his new obsession and forcibly attempts to convert those around him. As the play ends, everyone, with the notable exception of the village priest, sees the vision of Saint Francis.

Like Molière, Aymé achieved fame and notoriety with plays which scandalized many spectators and critics. After *Clérambard*, *La Tête des autres* (Other People's Heads), produced and published in 1952, provoked violent reactions. It is one of the most vitriolic of his works, a satire of the legal profession and of what passes for justice in a society motivated by greed, ruthless struggles for power, and insensitivity to the rights and feelings of individuals. The play portrays a murder trial in which lawyers engage in a rhetorical contest for a "trophy"–which happens to be the life of the defendant. The family and friends of the lawyers follow the proceedings as if they were attending a sporting event, and when the prosecutor's children hear that the accused has been sentenced to death, they cheer. The prosecutor Maillard sees the episode as a personal victory which had almost escaped him but which he finally achieved. Aymé treated the themes of law and order, justice, and honor in many other works, including *Le Moulin de la Sourdine, Silhouette du scandale* (Silhouette of Scandal, 1938), and *Vogue la galère*, but *La Tête des autres* contains his most dramatic and bitter satire of those responsible for administering justice.

The next two plays are of a very different nature. The first, *Les Quatre Vérités* (The Four Truths, or, in more colloquial speech, Straight Talk, 1954), is an exploration of prevarication and truth set in a pseudoscientific atmosphere, as though truthfulness, especially between a man and a woman, were a quality that can be scientifically verified. The play was moderately successful with audiences, though its humor is a bit labored.

The second, *Les Oiseaux de lune* (Moonbirds, 1956), is comedy, science fiction, and pure fantasy. A young man discovers a substance that can turn people into birds, loses control of his discovery, and transforms people in increasing numbers. He rationalizes his actions, stating that his victims are happier as birds because they no longer have to think. In the preface to an edition of the published play, Aymé writes, "C'est généralement ce que disent les hommes disposant du pouvoir absolu" (Generally, that is what men say when they wield absolute power). *Les Oiseaux de lune* is occasionally revived by amateur companies and might well attract the interest of a modern audience.

In 1950 *Collier's* magazine invited Aymé to spend a few months writing articles in the United States. Although he found much to admire in America, he felt uncomfortable in a country and culture so different from his own. The ambience of the McCarthy era as well as the atmosphere of stress generated by the business world was antago-

nistic to his nature. He felt that the United States was too "modern" for him and facetiously remarked that he would never be able to understand a nation that had once forbidden the drinking of wine.

His 1957 play, *La Mouche bleue* (The Blue Fly), marks a return to caustic satire, focusing on life in the United States. With devastating irony it paints a terrifying portrait of a man haunted by the notion of efficiency and living in fear (of which the blue fly is the symbol) in an atmosphere of inane conversation and the middle-class need to keep up with the Joneses. Discussing this play in a 28 August 1957 *Arts* interview, Aymé commented: "Il m'a semblé amusant d'imaginer ce que pourrait être l'âme de ces américains qui dominent le monde, envoient des fusées dans la lune et dépassent la vitesse du son. Ils n'ont pu inventer le bonheur" (I thought it might be fun to picture the soul of those Americans who dominate the world, send rockets to the moon, and travel faster than sound. They have been unable to invent happiness).

Before *La Mouche bleue* the only original writing Aymé had published after his trip to the United States had been "Le Mendiant" (The Beggar), included in *En arrière* (Backwards), a collection of short stories published in 1950. Drawing on the Bible, the epic of the Mormons, and the lives of American evangelists, he described, in this irreverent parody of the Christmas story, the founding of a new religion whose supreme being is "le Grand Moteur" (the Great Motor). Aspects of American life are also featured in *Louisiane*, a well-constructed drama on the subjects of racism, prejudice, and expedient justice, which was produced and published in 1961.

When Aymé was asked about his feelings with respect to the United States, he wrote in a letter to Dorothy Brodin dated 15 May 1962 that he felt neither contempt nor hostility for any foreign country and that it was only in the southern United States that he had been shocked by anything he had seen. He added that although he felt rather separated from the American style of life, which, incidentally, was obviously modifying habits and institutions in his own country, he could probably adopt it comfortably if he were thirty or forty years younger. He added that he admired many things in America and had met many cordial and likable people there.

Aymé at this time seemed to feel increasingly out of step with the brave new world of technology, machines, and scientific research. His last plays point to this. *La Convention Belzébir*, produced in 1966 and published, with *Le Minotaure*, the following year, shows a future world in which a rich man can buy a license allowing him to hunt and kill another person according to strictly mandated rules and regulations. A subversive group finds this custom abhorrent and plans to overthrow the government, but there is no need for plots or revolutions: matters work out nicely when war is declared and everyone, rich or poor, man or woman, can (and must) engage in killing.

Aymé's last years were spent writing short stories and plays. In spite of his growing reputation, he steadfastly shunned honors and remained unassuming and rather shy. He died in October 1967. During his forty-year career several of his works were adapted for the screen, and he collaborated in writing the French script for Walt Disney's *The Living Desert* (1954).

Aymé was a fundamentally French writer who might at times seem desperately cynical, or, on the contrary, too conservative, unless one realizes that his roots run deep in the French skeptical and humanistic tradition, the tradition of Rabelais, La Fontaine, Molière, and the eighteenth-century philosophers. Like them, Aymé was irreverent and quick to challenge heavy-handed or senseless authority. He detested posturing and sham but was ever kind in his treatment of simple and sincere creatures. His sensible and straightforward philosophy of life is apparent in many of his works, but perhaps especially in his long essay *Le Confort intellectuel* (Intellectual Comfort), published in 1949.

Marcel Aymé has always been popular, especially for his short stories, which are staples of the pocket-book sales. His works have been translated into many languages, and recently there has been a renewal of interest in his writings. In 1982 the Association des Amis de Marcel Aymé was created for the purpose of promoting knowledge of the author and his works. In September 1986 *Clérambard* was revived on the stage where it had first been seen thirty-six years earlier. With Jean-Pierre Marielle in the leading role, this production was, for many critics, the revelation of a strange and fascinating play. It was acted in a lusty, vigorous style which would have been impossible in Aymé's time. The play, which had shocked audiences in 1950, today seems rather to emphasize the power of faith and love and to embody Aymé's basic beliefs.

References:

Dorothy Brodin, *The Comic World of Marcel Aymé* (Paris: Debresse, 1964);

Jean Cathelin, *Marcel Aymé ou le paysan de Paris* (Paris: Debresse, 1958);

Jean-Louis Dumont, *Marcel Aymé et le merveilleux* (Paris: Debresse, 1970);

Graham Lord, *The Short Stories of Marcel Aymé* (Nedlands, Perth: University of Western Australia Press, 1980);

Georges Robert and André Lioret, *Marcel Aymé insolite* (Paris: Revue Indépendante, 1958);

Hélène Scriabine, *Les Faux Dieux* (Paris: Mercure de France, 1963);

Pol Vandromme, *Introduction à Aymé* (Paris: Gallimard, 1960).

Simone de Beauvoir

(9 January 1908-14 April 1986)

Elaine Marks
University of Wisconsin-Madison

See also the Beauvoir obituary in *DLB Yearbook: 1986.*

BOOKS: *L'Invitée* (Paris: Gallimard, 1943); translated by Yvonne Moyse and Roger Senhouse as *She Came to Stay* (London: Secker & Warburg/ Lindsay Drummond, 1949; Cleveland: World, 1954);

Pyrrhus et Cinéas (Paris: Gallimard, 1944);

Le Sang des autres (Paris: Gallimard, 1945); translated by Moyse and Senhouse as *The Blood of Others* (London: Secker & Warburg/ Lindsay Drummond, 1948; New York: Knopf, 1948);

Les Bouches inutiles (Paris: Gallimard, 1945); translated by Claude Francis and Fernande Gontier as *Who Shall Die?* (Florissant, Mo.: River Press, 1983);

Tous les hommes sont mortels (Paris: Gallimard, 1946); translated by Leonard M. Friedman as *All Men Are Mortal* (Cleveland: World, 1956);

Pour une morale de l'ambiguïté (Paris: Gallimard, 1947); translated by Bernard Frechtman as *The Ethics of Ambiguity* (New York: Philosophical Library, 1948);

L'Amérique au jour le jour (Paris: Morihien, 1948); translated by Patrick Dudley as *America Day by Day* (London: Duckworth, 1952; New York: Grove Press, 1953);

L'Existentialisme et la sagesse des nations (Paris: Nagel, 1948);

Le Deuxième Sexe, 2 volumes (Paris: Gallimard, 1949); translated by H. M. Parshley as *The Second Sex* (New York: Knopf, 1953; London: Cape, 1953);

Must We Burn Sade?, translated by Annette Michelson (London: Nevill, 1953); republished in *The Marquis de Sade*, edited by Paul Dinnage (New York: Grove Press, 1953);

Les Mandarins (Paris: Gallimard, 1954); translated by Friedman as *The Mandarins* (Cleveland: World, 1956; London: Collins, 1957);

Simone de Beauvoir (photograph copyright © Jerry Bauer)

Privilèges (Paris: Gallimard, 1955);

La Longue Marche: Essai sur la Chine (Paris: Gallimard, 1957); translated by Austryn Wainhouse as *The Long March* (London: Deutsch, 1958; Cleveland: World, 1958);

Mémoires d'une jeune fille rangée (Paris: Gallimard, 1958); translated by James Kirkup as *Memoirs of a Dutiful Daughter* (London: Deutsch/Weidenfeld & Nicolson, 1959; Cleveland: World, 1959);

Brigitte Bardot and the Lolita Syndrome, translated by Frechtman (London: Deutsch/Weidenfeld & Nicolson, 1960; New York: Reynal, 1960);

La Force de l'âge (Paris: Gallimard, 1960); translated by Peter Green as *The Prime of Life* (Cleveland: World, 1962; London: Deutsch/ Weidenfeld & Nicolson, 1963);

La Force des choses (Paris: Gallimard, 1963); translated by Richard Howard as *Force of Circumstance* (London: Deutsch, 1965; New York: Putnam's, 1965);

Une Mort très douce (Paris: Gallimard, 1964); translated by Patrick O'Brian as *A Very Easy Death* (London: Deutsch/Weidenfeld & Nicolson, 1966; New York: Putnam's, 1966);

Les Belles Images (Paris: Gallimard, 1966); translated by O'Brian (London: Collins, 1968; New York: Putnam's, 1968);

La Femme rompue. L'Age de discrétion. Monologue (Paris: Gallimard, 1968); *La Femme rompue* translated by O'Brian as *The Woman Destroyed* (London: Collins, 1969; New York: Putnam's, 1969);

La Vieillesse (Paris: Gallimard, 1970); translated by O'Brian as *Old Age* (London: Deutsch/ Weidenfeld & Nicolson, 1970); O'Brian's translation republished as *The Coming of Age* (New York: Putnam's, 1972);

Tout compte fait (Paris: Gallimard, 1972); translated by O'Brian as *All Said and Done* (London: Deutsch/Weidenfeld & Nicolson, 1974; New York: Putnam's, 1974);

Quand prime le spirituel (Paris: Gallimard, 1979); translated by O'Brian as *When Things of the Spirit Come First* (New York: Pantheon, 1982);

La Cérémonie des adieux, suivi de Entretiens avec Jean-Paul Sartre (Paris: Gallimard, 1981); translated by O'Brian as *Adieux: A Farewell to Sartre* (New York: Pantheon, 1984).

OTHER: *Djamila Boupacha*, edited by Beauvoir and Gisèle Halimi, preface by Beauvoir (Paris: Gallimard, 1962); translated by Peter Green (London: Deutsch, 1962; New York: Macmillan, 1962);

Violette Leduc, *La Bâtarde*, preface by Beauvoir (Paris: Gallimard, 1964);

Que peut la littérature?, (Paris: Union Générale d'Editions, 1965)–comprises contributions by Beauvoir, Jean-Paul Sartre, Jean-Pierre Faye, and others;

Claire Cayron, *Divorce en France*, preface by Beauvoir (Paris: Denoël-Gontier, 1974);

Anne Tristan and Annie de Pisan, *Histoires du M. L. F.*, preface by Beauvoir (Paris: Calmann-Lévy, 1977);

Claude Lanzmann, *Shoah*, preface by Beauvoir (Paris: Fayard, 1985); translated (New York: Pantheon, 1985).

Teacher, philosopher, political activist, and writer; autobiographer, essayist, journalist, novelist, and playwright; atheist, existentialist, and feminist, Simone de Beauvoir is one of the best-known French writers and thinkers of the twentieth century. The number of languages into which many of her books have been translated and the attention she received in the media during the last fifteen years of her life suggest that she may be the best-known woman writer of all times.

Simone de Beauvoir died in a Paris hospital of pneumonia on 14 April 1986. She was buried in the Montparnasse cemetery in the same grave with Jean-Paul Sartre's ashes. Five thousand men, women, and children attended the funeral. More than sixty bouquets and wreaths of flowers, sent by women's organizations around the world, decorated the tomb.

She was born in Paris in 1908 into an upper-middle-class but impoverished family whose religious and social values she rejected at an early age. Her father, Georges Bertrand de Beauvoir, a lawyer from a respectable, upper-middle-class family, had little personal ambition and preferred to spend his time and limited resources pursuing the pleasures of the age, especially amateur theatricals and the racetrack. Her mother, Françoise Brasseur de Beauvoir, came from a hardworking family that had been prosperous until the family bank failed in 1909. There was considerable conflict in the Beauvoir marriage, which the straitened circumstances only increased. Yet Beauvoir's childhood, as she described it retrospectively in *Mémoires d'une jeune fille rangée* (1958; translated as *Memoirs of a Dutiful Daughter*, 1959), was a happy one. In spite of the personal and ideological tensions between her parents, Beauvoir and her younger sister, Hélène de Beauvoir, called Poupette, who became a painter, developed a passion for living and an insatiable curiosity about the world. Beauvoir attributed her becoming an intellectual to the discrepancy between her mother's piety and her father's disbelief coupled with his admiration for certain French writers.

Mémoires d'une jeune fille rangée traces her development from an adored baby in love with her mother to a child who began at an early age to rebel against the order imposed by her mother, particularly in religious matters. In this work, one follows Beauvoir as she becomes an avid reader of fiction, a devotee of Louisa May Alcott and George Eliot, and a precocious writer. She wrote her first story, "Les Malheurs de Marguerite" (The Misfortunes of Marguerite), at the age of eight. It was a patriotic story about a young and heroic Alsatian orphan who attempted to cross over into France with her brothers and sisters.

Beauvoir portrays herself as a dutiful daughter and a brilliant student, first at the Catholic Cours Désir, then at the Sorbonne. At the age of nine she met Elisabeth Mabille (Zaza), who was to inspire the first significant passion of her life outside the family circle. Their friendship lasted until Zaza's death in 1929. Her death was due perhaps to meningitis but occurred after she had fallen in love with a fellow student and realized that her parents would never approve of her marriage to him or to anyone else whom they had not selected. She died, according to Beauvoir's interpretation, a victim of Monsieur and Madame Mabille's Catholic prejudices and their convictions about appropriate behavior for young Catholic women from good families. This death, the first of many that Beauvoir was to report on both clinically and dramatically, seems to have reinforced her sense of writing as a mission, the obligation to communicate with her readers by revealing the discrepancies between ideological constructs and the ambiguities of human existence. It also seems to have reinforced her hostile attitude toward the bourgeoisie and toward marriage and motherhood as institutions.

This same year, 1929, she met Jean-Paul Sartre, a student at the prestigious Ecole Normale Supérieure, who was preparing, as she was, for the *agrégation de philosophie*. They studied for the examination together and also spent considerable time with a group of friends, all witty and brilliant; it was this group who gave her her nickname Castor (French for *beaver*). Sartre and she remained intimate friends and intellectual companions from that initial collaboration until his death in 1980. They were lovers but not monogamous by any means. Once, she said, they briefly considered marriage—when there was some possibility that Sartre would go to Japan in the 1930s. But when that eventuality did not materialize and she realized that they did not want to have children, they resolved to maintain their free union, which would not exclude what they called

"contingent" loves, some of which became important in their lives.

Having successfully passed the examination, placing second (to Sartre's first place), Beauvoir taught philosophy in French lycées at Marseilles, Rouen, and Paris from 1931 to 1943. In the 1930s her life was essentially that of a provincial professor with intellectual leanings, a wide circle of friends and acquaintances (some of them writers) and a somewhat bohemian life-style. She and Sartre were antiestablishment and prosocialist but played no political roles until after World War II. It was then that she became one of the outspoken atheistic, left-wing intellectuals who exerted a strong influence on the beliefs and opinions of readers both in France and abroad.

When Sartre was called for military service in September 1939 after war was declared, Beauvoir and he were separated for weeks on end for the first time since they had met. His voluminous correspondence, *Lettres au Castor et à quelques autres* (Letters to Castor and a Few Others, 1983), which dates chiefly from the early war years, is a record of her life as well as his because he discusses with her in detail what she writes about her life in Paris. Against the regulations she managed to visit him at his post in eastern France. The separation was prolonged during the months, beginning in June 1940, that Sartre spent as a prisoner of war. When he returned in 1941, they resumed their life together as intellectuals in Paris. They were, however, determined to become more involved in public life, especially politically. Both abandoned their teaching to devote themselves to writing and often to political activism.

Beauvoir's biography from that time on is the story of her writing, her contacts with other writers and people from the theater and the graphic arts, and her personal relationships. Her devotion to Sartre and sense of their common intellectual life did not waver. However, both had important love affairs with others. During a trip to the United States in 1947 she fell in love with the writer Nelson Algren. Their liaison proved difficult, doubtless partly because of the distance that separated them most of the time. After several transatlantic visits it ended in 1950. Some two years later she began a relationship with the writer and filmmaker Claude Lanzmann, many years her junior; it lasted during most of the 1950s. Neither of these liaisons seems to have threatened Sartre, although Beauvoir had been apprehensive when Sartre's affair with an Ameri-

Beauvoir in the café de Flore on the boulevard Saint-Germain, where she did much of her early writing (photo Doisneau-Rapho)

can resident seemed to be assuming a great deal of importance for him, and she probably suffered also from his attachment to other women, including Olga Kosakievicz, with whom she and Sartre had formed a "trio" in the late 1930s, and Arlette Elkaïm, his last such companion. Throughout their decades together, Sartre and Beauvoir engaged in common causes, such as protests against the war in Algeria, and supported each other's undertakings. They also traveled widely together. She was one of those who furnished companionship to him in his last years and helped take care of him. Their dialogue is recorded partially in *La Cérémonie des adieux, suivi de Entretiens avec Jean-Paul Sartre* (1981; translated as *Adieux: A Farewell to Sartre,* 1984), which consists of her account of his last months and lengthy recorded conversations between them.

To observe that Beauvoir's philosophical

and aesthetic ideas as well as her literary production parallel those of Sartre and owe a great deal to them is not to deprecate her, for they developed their thought together to a considerable extent. It would be impossible to understand her fiction, drama, and other writings without reference to such basic concepts of Sartrean existentialism as freedom, commitment, bad faith, and the role of the Other, some of which appear in her own philosophical work, *Pour une morale de l'ambiguïté* (1947; translated as *The Ethics of Ambiguity,* 1948). Although she less frequently uses a technical philosophical vocabulary, Beauvoir agrees with Sartre that human beings are free, without a God to give meaning or purpose to their lives, and in a world without preordained values. This freedom leads to anguish, because human beings must rely wholly on themselves and are thus responsible for everything that happens to them, including their own failures; circumstances and situations are givens, but the individual is entirely responsible for dealing with them and making something of the freedom they possess to act within them. To work toward the creation of values, especially those that enhance freedom in political and social terms, is to commit oneself to an authentic human enterprise. To deny freedom, to fall back on historical or ethical or religious givens or to blame the circumstances is to act in bad faith.

The existence of other human beings, or what in existentialist terminology is called the Other, poses a special problem, since the freedom of others seems to pose limits to one's own. This dilemma is central to Beauvoir's writing. The reaction to the Other is often sadistic–the desire to harm or remove this rival, both a threat and a mirror for the self. Or it can be masochistic–the assumption of inferiority in front of the Other. Such reactions are inauthentic and are a variety of bad faith. A genuinely free human relationship, as Sartre and Beauvoir were to understand it later, especially as he expounded it in his *Critique de la raison dialectique* (1960; partially translated as *Critique of Dialectical Reason*, 1961), would not be a subject-object or master-slave relationship but a true community achieved through common action in view of a common goal in the world.

The details and the main events of Beauvoir's life, as she selected and interpreted them, are recorded in her four lengthy volumes of memoirs: *Mémoires d'une jeune fille rangée* was followed in 1960 by *La Force de l'âge* (translated as *The Prime of Life*, 1962), in 1963 by *La Force des choses* (translated as *Force of Circumstance*, 1965), and in 1972 by *Tout compte fait* (translated as *All Said and Done*, 1974). These volumes are invaluable documents for following the development of her career as a writer: why and when she began to work on her novels and nonfictional texts; the importance of her diary and of her conversations with Sartre; what she was reading at different periods in her life; the impact of the sociopolitical scene on her writing; the relationship among her love affairs, her friendships, and her productivity; an account of how her published books were received by the critics and by the general public. Although some schools of critical thought that have denounced the intentional fallacy would hold that statements of intention such as those Beauvoir makes concerning her writing are be-

side the point or invalid, her own aesthetics, which emphasizes a literature of ideas if not the *roman à thèse*, holds that fiction is shaped by the writer's purpose and related to that purpose; one cannot ignore, therefore, what she indicates about the genesis and her own understanding of her works.

Since 1973, when Beauvoir publicly declared herself to be a feminist and joined feminist groups in Paris, lending her name to journals, organizations, public meetings, and petitions, her novels have tended to receive less critical attention than her nonfiction. *Le Deuxième Sexe* (1949; translated as *The Second Sex*, 1953), *La Vieillesse* (1970; translated as *Old Age*, 1970), and her book on the death of her mother, *Une Mort très douce* (1964; translated as *A Very Easy Death*, 1966), along with her memoirs, became the focus of scholarly and public attention. The emphasis was on Beauvoir's pronouncements about women and the elderly and how these pronouncements corresponded to the ways in which she lived her life: her relationship with Sartre; her decision not to marry or to have children; her attitudes toward homosexuality and lesbianism; her attitudes toward psychoanalysis and poststructuralism. An interest in Beauvoir as a feminist thinker and writer seems to have obliterated any concern for Beauvoir as an existentialist thinker who wrote novels. If the novels were examined, it was with the avowed purpose of analyzing the ways in which female characters were represented. It is also true that since the late 1960s the traditional novel, with its claims to present the human world through characters and story, has fallen into disrepute within the ruling intellectual communities in Paris. The lack of interest in Beauvoir's novels is, thus, doubly, a sign of the times.

But Beauvoir is, first and foremost, a novelist. The case could be made that the memoirs and the texts on the death of her mother and the death of Sartre are novels. At the very least they are narratives in which the autobiographical and the fictional are constantly intertwined. In a similar vein all her novels and short stories contain autobiographical elements. Beauvoir's narratives subvert boundaries and make the distinction between the case history and the invented story clearly ambiguous.

In the essay "Littérature et métaphysique" (Literature and Metaphysics), published in *Les Temps Modernes* in April 1946 and included in the volume *L'Existentialisme et la sagesse des nations* (Existentialism and Ordinary Wisdom, 1948), Beauvoir makes explicit the importance of the novel as a privileged form that allows the writer "d'évoquer dans sa vérité complète, singulière, temporelle, le jaillissement originel de l'existence" (to evoke in its complete, unique, and temporal truth, the original bursting forth of existence). For Beauvoir the novel has the power of making metaphysical experiences concrete, of allowing the reader to communicate with a subjectivity in a manner that no other literary genre can provide. Nineteen years after "Littérature et métaphysique," in her contribution to the volume *Que peut la littérature?* (What Can Literature Do?, 1965), she again makes explicit her conception of literature. She insists on the notion that literature is an activity undertaken by human beings for human beings with the goal of unveiling the world for them. But in order for this unveiling to take place, there must be identification between the reader and the writer. The reader must enter into a world that becomes his or her own. The ultimate mission of the literary work is "nous rendre transparents les uns aux autres dans ce qu'elle a de plus opaque" (to make us transparent to each other through what is most opaque in the literary work). What has not changed in the period that separates the two texts is that for Beauvoir literature, and particularly the novel, is a unique means of communication with transforming powers; the novel produces effects. Language for Beauvoir has an important referential dimension. It is not a closed system referring only to itself. Nor is it primarily symptomatic of the unconscious. It does not create barriers; it removes them.

Between her first novel, *L'Invitée* (1943; translated as *She Came to Stay*, 1949), and the novella collection *La Femme rompue. L'Age de discrétion. Monologue* (1968; translated as *The Woman Destroyed*, 1969), Beauvoir's fictional writing comprises four novels: *Le Sang des autres* (1945; translated as *The Blood of Others*, 1948), *Tous les hommes sont mortels* (1946; translated as *All Men Are Mortal*, 1956), *Les Mandarins* (1954; translated as *The Mandarins*, 1956), and *Les Belles Images* (1966; translated as *Les Belles Images*, 1968). The fiction illustrates in concrete terms the major themes of her philosophical essays. But whereas the essays tend to have a positive, authoritarian tone, the fiction is suffused with ambiguity. Whereas the themes of commitment and solidarity seem to emerge triumphant in the essays, in the fiction anguish at the absurdity of the

mortal predicament of human beings seems to dominate.

Written between 1943 and 1968 Beauvoir's major fiction presents a detailed tableau of a Parisian artistic and intellectual milieu before, during, and after World War II. The situations in which the characters find themselves are historically recognizable, and the problems raised by these situations are the very problems passionately discussed by French intellectuals of the period. Each of Beauvoir's fictional works focuses on relationships between characters who are obliged to make weighty decisions that involve themselves and others: questions of life and death, of psychic pain and loss, of the continuity or the decline of a human community.

L'Invitée was published during the war. This work, whose original title was "Légitime Défense," was begun in the fall of 1937 and completed during the summer of 1941. In *La Force de l'âge* Beauvoir describes her struggles with the craft of fiction, her inability to find a subject that she could successfully treat. *La Force de l'âge* also provides the autobiographical elements that gave rise to her desire to write this particular novel: the triangular relationship in which she, Sartre, and Olga were involved. She discusses the difficulties of shaping autobiographical material, the influence of John Dos Passos and Ernest Hemingway on her choice of novelistic techniques, and the criticism she received from Sartre, who was always her first reader, as she was his.

L'Invitée is, on one level, the story of an impossible ménage à trois that ends with one of the characters, Françoise, killing another character, the other, younger woman, Xavière. More important, it is a relentless description of how the familiar becomes strange, how the appearances of an ordered universe are brutally unmasked. The epigraph from Hegel, "Chaque conscience poursuit la mort de l'autre" (Each consciousness pursues the death of the other), underlines the fundamental impossibility of reciprocity in human relationships. In this novel the statement made in the epigraph is carried out in the plot.

The setting for *L'Invitée* is Paris in 1938-1939. Pierre Labrousse, an actor and director, and Françoise Miquel, a writer, have been lovers and coworkers for ten years. They pride themselves on having created a perfect love. They are not married, and the question of marriage is never raised between them. The social problems that agitate bourgeois society have little

Beauvoir with Jean-Paul Sartre at a Paris kiosk (photo Walter)

meaning in the milieu in which Françoise and Pierre live. The problems that they face are metaphysical rather than social in nature.

In the first part of *L'Invitée* the presence of Xavière, whom Françoise and Pierre have invited to come to Paris, begins to undermine the structure and the quality of their lives. Françoise becomes jealous of Xavière, and Pierre begins to question his work and his life. Xavière has the power to make people uneasy. She does not work, and she scorns any form of routine. The closer Pierre moves toward Xavière, the more morbid Françoise becomes. Finally, she falls ill and enters the hospital. During her illness Françoise becomes the stranger, the other.

The second part of the novel opens with Françoise's release from the hospital, the establishment of the trio, and the pressing menace of war. Slowly, but surely, Xavière begins to destroy everything that surrounds her. Her hatred and jealousy of Françoise and Pierre as a couple increase, and the more Xavière asserts herself, the stronger Françoise's revolt becomes: "à travers la jouissance maniaque de Xavière, à travers sa haine et sa jalousie, le scandale éclatait, aussi monstrueux, aussi définitif que la mort; en face de Françoise, et cependant sans elle, quelque chose existait comme une condamnation sans

recours: libre, absolue, irréductible, une conscience étrangère se dressait" (through Xavière's maniacal pleasure, through her hatred and her jealousy, the scandal erupted, as monstrous, as definitive as death; facing Françoise and yet without Françoise, something existed like a condemnation without appeal: free, absolute, irreducible, an alien consciousness rose up). Françoise has felt both physically and psychically the presence of the other, and her own existence is threatened by this presence. The only thing that she can do is to get rid of it.

When the war breaks out Pierre is mobilized and Françoise and Xavière take an apartment together in Paris. Xavière, like the war, continues to represent an enemy presence, a scandalous presence that Françoise can no longer bear. Xavière constructs an image of Françoise as a jealous, hypocritical woman who erroneously believes herself to be loved by her young lover Gerbert and by Pierre. When she tries to impose this image on Françoise, Françoise kills her. There is in the character of Françoise, along with her annoying nobility and her ambiguous sensuality, a profound inhumanity.

It would be difficult not to make a comparison between *L'Invitée* and Sartre's play *Huis-clos* (*No Exit*) written in 1944. In both texts there are three main characters, two women and a man. Although the two situations represented are different, the fundamental theme is the same: hell is the way in which others would have us see ourselves.

The most significant technical aspect of the novel is the point of view. During most of the novel the reader is given Françoise's point of view and is a witness to the way in which the world is felt and perceived by her. Two other characters, Elisabeth, Françoise's sister-in-law, and Gerbert, provide an outsider's point of view on the main action of the novel.

L'Invitée is an impressive first novel. It succeeds in conveying to the reader both a sense of place in time, Paris in the year preceding World War II, and the combined psychological and philosophical anguish of a triangular amorous configuration. *L'Invitée* was a success with readers and critics. In *La Force de l'âge* Beauvoir enumerates the reviews and unabashedly comments on her pleasure at being taken seriously as a novelist. During the first six months following publication the novel sold twenty-two-thousand copies. Since 1943 it has been translated into ten languages.

Le Sang des autres, written during the German occupation, deals with specific problems raised by the pre-World War II period and by the Occupation. The theme, however, has more than political ramifications. To what extent is one responsible for the lives of others? This problem haunts Jean Blomart in his personal as well as in his political life. The quotation from Dostoyevski that is used as an epigraph proposes an overwhelming answer: "Chacun est responsable de tout devant tous" (Each human being is responsible for everything to everyone).

Le Sang des autres is divided into thirteen chapters and composed of a series of flashbacks. Seven chapters are narrated by Jean, an active member of the Resistance, who broke with his bourgeois milieu before the war and became a member of the Communist party. He recounts these experiences: the death of Louise's baby (Louise was his family's impoverished maid); the death of Jacques, a friend's brother, for which he feels responsible; and his subsequent involvement in trade union movements followed by Resistance activity after the defeat of France. The other chapters are told from the point of view of Hélène Bertrand, whom he has loved and who is now dying. Anxious to determine the degree of his responsibility, he delves into his past and relives relevant scenes of his life from his childhood to the present. In all the situations he remembers the same desperate question forms: what is his responsibility for the death of Hélène, whom he has sent on a mission, and for the death of Jacques, whom he had convinced to work for the revolutionary cause?

Before World War II Hélène was a girl interested only in her own happiness. When the war breaks out and Jean goes into the army she wants him to come back to Paris. He refuses to accept an assignment that would keep him away from the front. France is conquered and Hélène dances with the Germans, but she discovers that she cannot bring herself to accept the offer of a rich German to take her to Berlin. This marks a change in her attitude toward the situation in France. Its tragedy is revealed to her when she attempts to hide a Jewish friend. Similarly, at the Place de la Contrescarpe she sees a mother running after a bus that is carrying her child away. When the mother cries out the child's name, Hélène is suddenly overcome by the same feeling that had seized Jean when Louise's baby died: she feels responsible, as Jean had. She contacts Jean, who is now head of a group of Resistance fighters. During the brief period in which Hélène works with Jean in carrying out anti-German activities, she comes to know the joys of love and fraternity. She is mortally wounded in the course of a mission, but before she dies she absolves Jean of any responsibility for her death. Like Françoise Miquel, Hélène has chosen for herself. The moral that Jean draws from this death is that fighting for freedom is worth the weight of crime and remorse.

Le Sang des autres resolves to a certain extent the problems of responsibility and action, but it must be noted that the characters cannot find an equilibrium in times of peace. It is only in a time of crisis, faced with extreme situations, when good and evil have acceptable meanings, that Jean and Hélène succeed in living a moral life. In *Les Mandarins* one finds similar characters living in the postwar period when the equilibrium furnished by the values created during the Occupation no longer exists.

Le Sang des autres was well received by the critics in 1945. It was the first French novel to speak openly about the Resistance movement. From 1945 to 1947 it had thirty-two printings, and it has been translated into twelve languages. In *La Force des choses* Beauvoir is critical of this novel, as she is of a play that she wrote in 1945, *Les Bouches inutiles* (translated as *Who Shall Die?*,

Beauvoir and Sartre during a weekly radio broadcast of "La Tribune des Temps modernes*" (photo Doisneau-Rapho)*

1983). She insists that in both works the characters are reduced to ethical attitudes, and that as a result both the novel and the play suffer from didacticism and idealism.

Tous les hommes sont mortels is dedicated to Sartre. The novel demonstrates that the meaning of a human life depends on the condition of mortality. Fosca, an immortal, finds it impossible to live in his own time. A mortal can be committed to the point of death; he engages his freedom in a cause, thereby creating a value, and, if need be, his death authenticates his commitment. For an immortal such commitment has no meaning. An immortal is, moreover, incapable of understanding joy and anguish since they are the inevitable accompaniment of the mortality that defines the human predicament.

Against the background of a vast historical panorama that extends from the thirteenth century to the twentieth, the novel relates the adventures of Prince Fosca. The five parts of the novel follow the five stages of his career. Tyrant of the Italian city of Carmona, Fosca drinks, despite the pleas of his wife, an elixir offered to him by a beggar. He falls asleep for forty days, and when he awakes he is immortal. Fosca then attempts to direct the fate of others, to make himself necessary as an agent of destiny. He fails on both the historical and the personal planes. By making himself immortal, he has removed himself irremediably

from the world of men. He can no longer understand them.

For two hundred years, beginning in the early fourteenth century, Fosca fights for Carmona. When he sees that his dream of uniting the world, his dream of the absolute, is not possible in Italy, he joins first the Holy Roman Emperor Maximilian I and then his successor Charles V, whose faithful counselor he becomes. He advises the emperor on political and social issues, such as the nascent Reformation and the rise in prices because of the influx of gold. He would like to create a world of justice, stability, and peace, but this goal is impossible. Fosca next goes to the New World with the Spanish and later meets Carlier, an explorer (who resembles Jacques Cartier). He returns to Europe in the eighteenth century and, since France was at that time the center of Europe, it is in France that the reader finds him. He works to found an academy of science, and he remarries. In the fifth part of the novel, Fosca is still in France. It is the period of the July revolution of 1830. Fosca becomes a worker-revolutionary; he is put into prison and freed after the revolution of 1848. He goes to sleep for sixty years, and when he awakens he is put into a home for the insane. This terminal point of his story is the beginning of the novel, which opens in the contemporary world and proceeds by flashbacks, as he tells his story to

Régine, a member of a Parisian acting company performing in Rouen. One of the stars of the troupe, she is haunted by dreams of fame and immortality. Dreams are transformed into reality as she finds herself face to face with an immortal. The story of Fosca's life reveals the difficulties inherent in being immortal in a mortal world: no adventure, no cause can really be his own. Régine understands his terrible solitude, the horror of being immortal. But the anguish of her own mortality has not been dissipated by his story.

Tous les hommes sont mortels glorifies the greatness of mortal men. Martin Luther is the best example of this glorification. At the moment when Fosca dreams of uniting the world, Luther arrives on the world stage. Fosca, at the Diet of Worms, understands that Luther is his most formidable enemy. Luther incarnates for Fosca human pride; he represents the man who obeys only his conscience, the part of man that the immortal Fosca cannot make submit to his will. Luther represents a committed individual, *l'homme engagé*. Fosca, immortal, is by definition a man who cannot be committed. He will always be alive; in other words, he will never be *en situation*, or in those situations in which existentialists see human responsibility dramatized. Fosca exhibits the sense of the absurd and the deadly ennui that permeate the image of human beings in the literature of the 1930s and the 1940s in France. For Beauvoir commitment is a means of escaping from the absurdity of the human predicament.

Although *Tous les hommes sont mortels* was translated into eleven languages, it was not well received in France. It has quite consistently had negative reviews. It is, nonetheless, Beauvoir's most audacious attempt to dramatize the ambiguous metaphysical situation in which human beings find themselves.

Les Mandarins won the Prix Goncourt for the outstanding French novel of 1954. It has been translated into fifteen languages. In this work once again the author portrays a milieu composed of French intellectuals, this time during the period immediately following the Liberation of Paris. Beauvoir attempts to expose the political, intellectual, and personal problems that beset a small group at the center of this intellectual world and which are to be taken as representative of many of the choices facing intellectuals and activists in the immediate postwar period. Interwoven with these dramas are several love affairs, of which the most important takes place between Anne Dubreuil, a psychoanalyst, and

Beauvoir in the 1950s (photo Gisèle Freund)

Lewis Brogan, an American writer, who is clearly based on Nelson Algren. (Algren was not pleased with Beauvoir's transposition of their affair.) Although Beauvoir insists in *La Force des choses* that *Les Mandarins* is not a roman à clef, it is impossible not to see reflected also in the novel the relationships between Albert Camus and his wife, Francine Faure Camus, both of whom Sartre and Beauvoir saw frequently in the postwar years. Further parallels can be distinguished between certain characters and other well-known intellectuals, such as Arthur Koestler.

Anne Dubreuil and Henri Perron, a writer and journalist who resembles Camus in many respects, are the two central figures in the novel. Beauvoir indicates in *La Force des choses* that they are the same character, or rather that they represent a double projection of their creator. Anne, although an intellectual, lives to a considerable degree for her husband and daughter; she often expresses the feminine point of view. Henri and the other male characters are more involved in politics. But what both Anne and Henri have in common is the personal quest for happiness in the midst of collective struggles. Through Anne the reader meets her husband, Robert, their daughter Nadine, and Lewis Brogan. Through Henri Perron, Paule and a middle-class milieu and Josette and a theatrical milieu are introduced. The other characters in the novel, Lambert, Vincent, Scriassine, and Lenoir, are writers, journalists, and political figures.

Henri Perron and Robert Dubreuil find themselves in a difficult situation after the Liberation. During the war they found a meaning to their lives through the Resistance movement. The war and particularly the Occupation provided them with a code of ethics, based on the obvious priority of liberating France; but with the end of hostilities this moral code no longer seems operative. Ideologically, they find themselves squeezed between the political right and left, between the United States and the Soviet Union. By not choosing either of these two alternatives, they feel condemned to inaction. As a solution they attempt to do the impossible: to create a noncommunist leftist party composed of workers and intellectuals.

Robert's political party works with the communists on most issues but refuses to adhere to the party dogma. Henri meanwhile directs a left-wing paper, *L'Espoir*. But on certain issues, such as revelations about Soviet labor camps, they do not agree, Robert wishing to avoid any revelations that would jeopardize the standing of the socialist movement and bring grist to the mill of the Americans (Sartre's position frequently), Henri insisting that a journalist must do everything in his power to campaign against the camps. Their disagreement ends in a rupture. The Mandarins no longer agree among themselves, and unity and solidarity become increasingly difficult to maintain. The men who are associated with Robert and Henri before and after this rupture represent almost all the political attitudes of the period: Vincent is a terrorist; Scriassine hates the Soviet Union; Lenoir belongs to the Communist Party; Lambert is revolted by politics; Trarieux is an opportunist.

Anne Dubreuil, whom the reader follows in her melancholy, in her daily preoccupations, and in her love affair with Lewis Brogan, is the character whose point of view is most frequently presented. Often she speaks in the first person, thus creating moments of stasis and meditation within the structure of the novel. Anne is also the figure with whom the novel ends. When her love affair

Beauvoir with Claude Lanzmann and Sartre in Giza, Egypt, 1967

with Brogan is over she feels that she has had her last chance for personal happiness, and she decides to kill herself. But the voices of her family, of those who would have to live her death, call her back to life. "Qui sait? Peut-être un jour serai-je de nouveau heureuse. Qui sait?" (Who knows? Perhaps one day I will be happy again. Who knows?) The question marks stand for the fundamental ambiguity of the entire novel.

Although Paris is the geographical center of the action, the novel records several voyages: Nadine and Henri go to Portugal; Anne, Robert, and Henri take a bicycle trip in France; Anne makes three trips to the United States. These travels remove the characters from the agitation of Paris and shed considerable light on the depth of their human and political commitments.

Les Mandarins is composed of numerous juxtaposed scenes which are almost entirely in the form of dialogue. The Mandarins speak a great deal and almost always about the same problems.

The reader may have the impression of reading a conversation already read. These conversations and discussions, many of which reappear in *La Force des choses,* are a further indication of the extent to which Beauvoir drew much of her fiction directly from her own experience.

In 1954 the novel was well received by the communist and by the "bourgeois" press. Both groups sensed in the novel a severe critique of the other. In the first month after publication *Les Mandarins* sold forty thousand copies. Sales soared after Beauvoir won the Goncourt prize, and, as she notes with pleasure in *La Force des choses,* with fame came an enormous number of letters from her readers.

In Beauvoir's first four novels the characters are not explained in terms of traditional psychological motivation. When one encounters Xavière and Hélène, one knows nothing of their childhoods or of their families. They appear *en situation,* and their actions, their ways of doing or not doing, define them. These characters are determined neither by heredity nor by childhood experiences. To the contrary, they are free at each moment of their existences to choose themselves. But they must recognize that they are free. Rather than a psychological and relative explanation of their acts, Beauvoir gives them an existential dimension. One of the best examples of this is in *L'Invitée.* A novelist working within the tradition of the psychological novel might have analyzed the uneasiness aroused in Françoise by the presence of Xavière in terms of jealousy or latent homosexuality. However, Xavière represents for Françoise neither a desired child nor an unexamined pre-Oedipal attachment to her mother; she represents the Other.

The danger of this perspective, Beauvoir herself notes in her memoirs, is that the characters tend to become abstractions. This is indeed what often happens in her novels. Only Xavière and Hélène manage to escape from and transcend the author's grid. These two young women, so different from each other, are the most successful of Beauvoir's fictional creations. Xavière's "non serviam" and Hélène's "serviam" are equally convincing.

There is a strong link among the characters who appear in Beauvoir's first four novels. Indeed, from novel to novel the same men and women, particularly the same couple, reappear under different names. Like other novelists Beauvoir has her own stock characters who play similar roles from novel to novel. The milieu in which the characters are situated is always the same: a group of Parisian intellectuals, artists, and revolutionaries living in Paris on the Left Bank. With the exception of *Tous les hommes sont mortels,* these early novels are set in the 1930s, 1940s, or 1950s.

The couple whom one meets in *L'Invitée* reappears in other novels. Françoise is the neither young nor middle-aged woman, between thirty and forty, beautiful but without knowing it, intellectual, and attached to a man with whom she rarely or never sleeps. Françoise is Régine of *Tous les hommes sont mortels* and Anne of *Les Mandarins.* For those readers who are familiar with Beauvoir's memoirs, Françoise-Régine-Anne is a transparently transposed version of the narrator-character Simone de Beauvoir. Pierre reappears even more frequently. He is Jean in *Le Sang des autres,* Fosca in *Tous les hommes sont mortels,* and Robert in *Les Mandarins.* He is represented as intellectual and perhaps impotent. We are told that Pierre has mistresses. But in the 418 pages of *L'Invitée* he remains chaste. Anne and Robert in *Les Mandarins* no longer sleep together. Robert, it is stated, is too old. Jean sleeps with Hélène but without enthusiasm and primarily to make her happy. Fosca, the immortal, is rarely sexually aroused. In her novels Beauvoir has created a couple that maintains an exemplary equilibrium in the absence of sexual passion.

Still another character who is present in each of the novels is the unloved woman: Elisabeth in *L'Invitée,* who is in love with Claude; Marianne in *Tous les hommes sont mortels,* who is in love with Fosca; Hélène in *Le Sang des autres,* who is in love with Jean; and Paule in *Les Mandarins,* who is in love with Henri. Unlike Françoise-Régine-Anne, Elisabeth-Marianne-Hélène-Paule would abdicate her freedom to possess the man she loves. She represents, in Beauvoir's fictional world, those members of the second sex who accept the image imposed on them by society. They are each portrayed as acting in bad faith because they try to deny their freedom to do otherwise. They can be related to the figures of the narcissist, the woman in love, and the mystic described in the second of the two volumes that make up *Le Deuxième Sexe,* and they prefigure the unmitigated tale of woe recited by the hysterical narrator of "Monologue" in *La Femme rompue.*

Finally, there are the girls: Xavière, Béatrice, Hélène, and Nadine. These young women emerging from adolescence are the most complex of Beauvoir's characters. Both sensual and revolted by overt manifestations of sexuality, they succeed in upsetting the lives of those adults with whom they come into contact. They are charming, ambiguous, disquieting, and subversive. It seems clear that the model for Xavière, like the model for Sartre's Ivich in *L'Age de raison* (1945; translated as *The Age of Reason*, 1947), is Olga Kosakievicz, who plays such a prominent role in the lives of Beauvoir and Sartre in *La Force de l'âge*, and who had been Beauvoir's pupil in Rouen. She was, according to an arrangement with her parents, to take a philosophy degree under Beauvoir's tutelage, but the course of studies was soon abandoned, and she pursued, in Rouen and later in Paris, a life of utter indolence, marked by temper tantrums alternating with euphoria. Beauvoir was her protector; Sartre was in love with her. The experiment of the trio finally failed, under pressures from within and from without; Olga fell in love with someone else, and Sartre began to take an interest in her younger sister, Wanda. But the relationship had been important to all three and is reflected in the works of both Beauvoir and Sartre.

There is an evolution in Beauvoir's first four novels. In all of them Beauvoir is primarily interested in human beings *en situation* with other human beings. The individual is never alone in Beauvoir's fictional world. The problem of the Other, of the relationships between characters, is a fundamental theme of her writing. In *L'Invitée* the problem is explored in relation to a trio; in *Le Sang des autres* the problem is developed with relation to a larger human community during a war. In *Tous les hommes sont mortels* Fosca is the other for all mortals, and all mortals are the other for Fosca. In trying to direct their lives, Fosca realizes that they are the center of their own worlds.

With *Les Mandarins* a significant change is perceptible. What was in Beauvoir's novels a metaphysical experience carefully rendered concrete has become a projection of the confusion of the intellectuals in the postwar period. The problem of the other still exists in the domain of love relationships in *Les Mandarins*. But historical events have invaded daily life with such force that they have shattered the emphasis on metaphysical theories and made them appear obsolete.

During the years between 1954 and the publication of her last two fictional works, *Les Belles Images* in 1966 and *La Femme rompue* in 1967, Beauvoir wrote and published the first three volumes of her memoirs and *Une Mort très douce*. Her last two volumes of fiction differ from the four preceding ones. They are shorter in length—one novel of 250 pages and three short narratives—and they are less ambitious in scope. The protagonists of *Les Belles Images* and *La Femme rompue* are all lonely women, complicitous victims in a society that uses women for its own ends and discards them after a certain age.

Les Belles Images was one of the most successful of Beauvoir's novels. It was on the best-seller list in France for twelve weeks and sold, during that time, about 120,000 copies. It has been translated into eighteen languages. In the fourth volume of her memoirs, *Tout compte fait*, Beauvoir explains her intentions. She was attempting to reproduce the "discours" (discourse) of an affluent group of Parisians in the "société technocratique" (technocratic society) of the 1960s. Unlike the milieus described in the four earlier novels, the world represented in *Les Belles Images* is one to which Beauvoir is hostile. Aside from the protagonist Laurence's ten-year-old daughter, Catherine, Catherine's Jewish friend, Brigitte, and, to a lesser degree, Laurence, there are no characters in the novel for whom the narrator displays any sympathy.

Laurence works for an advertising company and is a producer of *belles images* (advertisements and, by extension, false material values). She is so afraid of relapsing into her nervous breakdown of five years before that she plays the game of covering up, that is, of creating *images* or appearances and trying to believe in them: she plays it with her husband, her lover, her divorced parents, and her children. The reader feels that the novel has been constructed as a demonstration in which the characters act out certain attitudes of their class: Laurence's father is nostalgic for old, lost values and is incapable of living in the present; her husband, Jean-Charles, thinks only of the technological wonders of the future; Laurence's mother, Dominique, is a successful career woman terrified of the social stigma of being a woman without a man. All the characters have their own discourse and their individual set of *belles images*. These *belles images* mask what in Beauvoir's fictional universe constitutes the human condition: metaphysical anguish, psychological malaise, and social and political injustice.

Laurence's own facade is shattered by the questions of her daughter about human existence and human suffering. Laurence is unable to cope with her daughter, and the social group in which she lives refuses to confront such questions. The only possible solution offered is psychotherapy, as if concern over the meaning of life and the poverty and hunger of a considerable part of the planet could only be a neurotic symptom. Laurence's final refusal to continue to send her daughter to a psychiatrist and her insistence that Catherine be allowed to spend her vacation with Brigitte are, within the context of this novel, positive political gestures. They represent a momentary, if precarious, victory.

La Femme rompue is a collection of three short narratives: "L'Age de discrétion," "Monologue," and "La Femme rompue." Like most of Beauvoir's fictional works, *La Femme rompue* was commercially successful and was translated into numerous languages. The critics, however, were as severe in their judgment of this volume as they had been of *Les Belles Images*. Feminist critics were particularly offended by the portrayal of women who seemed to conform to and reproduce the worst stereotypes of feminine dependency, bad faith, narcissism, and failure.

The protagonists of the three narratives are all women of a similar age, wives and mothers, whose lives, and the *belles images* they have constructed in order to control them, have been shattered. There are, however, important differences in the attitudes of the three women, differences that relate to their milieu and their lucidity. The narrator in "L'Age de discrétion" is a wife, a mother, and a writer. She is a member of the left-wing bourgeois intelligentsia who, at the age of sixty, has alienated her husband and her son and feels she can no longer write. Her husband, André, is also having difficulties adjusting to growing old. He is a scientist who can no longer keep up with his field. Their son Philippe abandons their left-wing political principles, agrees to work for the conservative government, and plans to marry a woman whose family can help him further his career. André accepts Philippe's decision and refuses to break with him, whereas the narrator rejects her son. "L'Age de discrétion" is about the difficulties of aging in a world whose values have radically changed. But a visit to André's octogenarian mother, a militant member of the Communist party who lives in the south of France, and the occasion to spend some time alone with her husband away from Paris soften the narrator's intransigence. This is the only one of the three narratives in which dialogue between husband and wife is reestablished at the end.

The narrator of "Monologue" is a woman of forty-three, alone in her apartment on New Year's eve. The narrator rants and raves about her life, accusing others of being responsible for her misfortunes, wallowing in bad faith, and returning over and over again to the suicide of her daughter, Sylvie. The monologue suggests that she feels responsible for her daughter's death. She deals with this feeling by refusing to accept it and by seeking verbal vengeance on other members of her absent family. The narrator of "Monologue" is a prime example of bad faith.

In the third narrative, "La Femme rompue," the narrator, Monique, discovers that her husband, a successful Parisian doctor, is having an affair with another woman. The banal scenario of infidelity in middle-aged couples is faithfully followed. Monique has devoted herself exclusively to her husband, has not had a career of her own, and has not been particularly involved in her husband's work. The woman for whom he will leave her is a lawyer with a life of her own. Monique's diary reveals her double role as victim and accomplice and suggests once again that dependency, as opposed to autonomy and reciprocity, leads inevitably to bad faith.

Except for *Quand prime le spirituel* (1979; translated as *When Things of the Spirit Come First*, 1982), five early stories dealing with female characters (some of whom are clearly based on herself and Zaza), *La Femme rompue* is Beauvoir's last published work of fiction. Nonfictional narratives dominate her last period: *La Vieillesse*, *Tout compte fait*, and *La Cérémonie des adieux*.

La Cérémonie des adieux was reviewed with praise and with dismay by the critics, praise for the sobriety of tone maintained throughout the text and dismay at the exposure of Sartre's physical and mental decrepitude. In *La Cérémonie des adieux* the narrator, Beauvoir herself, returns to many of the themes that were developed in *La Femme rompue*, but the bad faith of the female protagonists has been replaced in this text by a poignant and sustained lucidity. The interviews between Sartre and Beauvoir that conclude this volume, done in 1974, are a rich source of information on both of them and a touching reflection of their mutual devotion.

Simone de Beauvoir, as a writer and a thinker, belongs to a double tradition: to the group of French existentialists who lived and wrote in Paris in the 1940s and 1950s and to the longer tradition of French women writers who, from Christine de Pizan to Colette, have produced works of literature at whose center one finds woman as the subject of discourse. With the

Beauvoir during the International Abortion March in Paris, November 1971 (Magnum)

death of Beauvoir and the distance from the living woman that death inevitably brings, it may be easier for critics to read her work in a multiplicity of contexts and to recognize her novels and her existentialist perspective as having a relevance equal to her essays, her memoirs, and her feminism.

Bibliography:

Claude Francis and Fernande Gontier, *Les Ecrits de Simone de Beauvoir* (Paris: Gallimard, 1979).

Biography:

Claude Francis and Fernande Gontier, *Simone de Beauvoir* (Paris: Perrin, 1985); translated by Lisa Nesselson as *Simone de Beauvoir: A*

Life . . . A Love Story (New York: St. Martin's, 1987).

References:

Arc: Simone de Beauvoir et la lutte des femmes, special issue on Beauvoir, no. 61 (1975);

Daniel Armogathe, *"Le Deuxième Sexe." Simone de Beauvoir: Analyse Critique* (Paris: Hatier, 1977);

Carol Ascher, *Simone de Beauvoir: A Life of Freedom* (Boston: Beacon, 1981);

Jean-Raymond Audet, *Simone de Beauvoir face à la mort* (Lausanne: Age d'homme, 1979);

Hazel E. Barnes, *The Literature of Possibility* (Lincoln: University of Nebraska Press, 1959);

Christian Louis van der Berghe, *Dictionnaire des idées: Simone de Beauvoir* (Paris & The Hague: Mouton, 1966);

Konrad Bieber, *Simone de Beauvoir* (Boston: Twayne, 1979);

Claire Cayron, *La Nature chez Simone de Beauvoir* (Paris: Gallimard, 1973);

Robert D. Cottrell, *Simone de Beauvoir* (New York: Ungar, 1975);

Madeleine Descubes, *Connaître Simone de Beauvoir* (Paris: Editions Resma, 1974);

Mary Evans, *Simone de Beauvoir: A Feminist Mandarin* (London: Tavistock, 1985);

Claude Francis, ed., *Simone de Beauvoir et le cours du monde* (Paris: Klincksieck, 1978);

Donald Hatcher, *Understanding "The Second Sex"* (New York, Bern & Frankfurt am Main: Peter Lang, 1984);

Francis Jeanson, *Simone de Beauvoir ou l'entreprise de vivre* (Paris: Seuil, 1966);

Terry Keefe, *Simone de Beauvoir: A Study of Her Writings* (Totowa, N. J.: Barnes & Noble, 1983);

Jean Leighton, *Simone de Beauvoir on Woman* (Rutherford, N. J.: Fairleigh Dickinson University Press, 1975);

Axel Madsen, *Hearts and Minds: The Common Journey of Simone de Beauvoir and Sartre* (New York: Morrow, 1977);

Elaine Marks, *Simone de Beauvoir: Encounters with Death* (New Brunswick: Rutgers University Press, 1973);

Marks, ed., *Critical Essays on Simone de Beauvoir* (Boston: G. K. Hall, 1987);

Chantal Moubachir, *Simone de Beauvoir* (Paris: Seghers, 1972);

Judith Okley, *Simone de Beauvoir* (New York: Pantheon, 1986);

Alice Schwarzer, *Simone de Beauvoir Today: Conversations 1972-1982,* translated by Marianne Howarth (London: Chatto & Windus, 1984); also published as *After The Second Sex* (New York: Pantheon, 1984);

Simone de Beauvoir. Un film de Josée Dayan et Malka Ribowska (Paris: Gallimard, 1979);

Simone de Beauvoir Society Newsletter, edited by Yolanda Paterson (Menlo Park, Cal.: Simone de Beauvoir Society, 1983-   );

Simone de Beauvoir Studies, edited by Paterson (Menlo Park, Cal.: Simone de Beauvoir Society, 1983-   );

Anne Whitmarsh, *Simone de Beauvoir and the Limits of Commitment* (London & New York: Cambridge University Press, 1981);

Yale French Studies: Simone de Beauvoir; Witness to a Century, special issue on Beauvoir, edited by Hélène V. Wenzel, no. 72 (1987);

Jacques J. Zéphir, *Le Néo-féminisme de Simone de Beauvoir* (Paris: Denoël/Gonthier, 1982).

Georges Bernanos

(20 February 1888-5 July 1948)

William Bush
University of Western Ontario

BOOKS: *Sous le soleil de Satan* (Paris: Plon-Nourrit, 1926); translated by Veronica Lucas as *The Star of Satan* (London: John Lane, 1927); translated by Pamela Morris (London: John Lane/Bodley Head, 1940; New York: Macmillan, 1940); revised and enlarged edition, edited by William Bush (Paris: Plon, 1982);

L'Imposture (Paris: Plon, 1927);

Madame Dargent (Paris: Cahiers Libres, 1928);

Saint Dominique (Limited edition, Paris: Tour d'Ivoire, 1928; trade edition, Paris: Gallimard, 1939);

Une Nuit (Paris: Cité des Livres, 1928);

Dialogue d'ombres (Paris: Cité des Livres, 1928);

La Joie (Paris: Plon, 1929); translated by Louise Varèse as *Joy* (New York: Pantheon, 1946; London: Bodley Head, 1948); revised and enlarged edition, edited by Albert Béguin (Paris: Club du Meilleur Livre, 1954);

La Grande Peur des bien-pensants: Edouard Drumont (Paris: Grasset, 1931);

Jeanne, relapse et sainte (Paris: Plon, 1934); translated by R. Batchelor as *Sanctity Will Out: An Essay on St. Joan* (New York: Sheed & Ward, 1947; London: Sheed & Ward, 1947);

Un Crime (Paris: Plon, 1935); translated by Anne Green as *The Crime* (New York: Dutton, 1936); translation republished as *A Crime* (London: Museum Press, 1946);

Journal d'un curé de campagne (Paris: Plon, 1936); translated by Morris as *The Diary of a Country Priest* (New York: Macmillan, 1937; London: Boriswood, 1937);

Nouvelle Histoire de Mouchette (Paris: Plon, 1937); translated by J. C. Whitehouse as *Mouchette* (New York: Holt, Rinehart & Winston, 1966; London: Bodley Head, 1966);

Les Grands Cimetières sous la lune (Paris: Plon, 1938); translated by Morris as *A Diary of My Times* (London: Boriswood, 1938; New York: Macmillan, 1938);

Scandale de la vérité (Paris: Gallimard, 1939);

Nous autres Français (Paris: Gallimard, 1939);

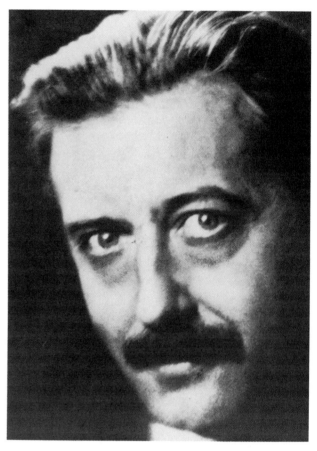

Georges Bernanos (photo Laure Albin-Guillot)

Lettre aux Anglais (Rio de Janeiro: Atlantica, 1942); translated by Harry Lorin Binsse as *Plea for Liberty* (New York: Pantheon, 1944); translated by Binsse and Ruth Bethell (London: Dobson, 1945); French version republished (Paris: Gallimard, 1946);

Monsieur Ouine (Rio de Janeiro: Atlantica, 1943); translated by Geoffrey Dunlop as *The Open Mind* (London: John Lane, 1945); French version republished (Paris: Plon, 1946); revised and enlarged edition, edited by Béguin (Paris: Club des Libraires de France, 1955);

Le Chemin de la Croix-des-Ames (4 volumes, Rio de Janeiro: Atlantica, 1943-1945; 1 volume, Paris: Gallimard, 1948);

La France contre les robots (Rio de Janeiro: Editions de la France Libre, 1944; Paris: Robert Laffont, 1947); translated as *Tradition of Freedom* (London: Dobson, 1950; New York: Roy, 1950); revised and enlarged French-language edition, edited by Béguin (Paris: Club Français du Livre, 1955); enlarged again, edited by Jean-Loup Bernanos (Paris: Plon, 1970);

Dialogues des Carmélites (Neuchâtel: La Baconnière, 1949; Paris: Seuil, 1949); translated by Michel Legat as *The Fearless Heart* (London: Bodley Head, 1952; Westminster, Md.: Newman Press, 1952);

Les Enfants humiliés, journal 1939-1940 (Paris: Gallimard, 1949);

Un Mauvais Rêve, suivi de notes et variantes . . . et de vingt-sept lettres de G. Bernanos, edited by Béguin (Paris: Plon, 1950); *Un Mauvais Rêve* translated by W. J. Strachan as *Night Is Darkest* (London: Bodley Head, 1953);

La Liberté, pour quoi faire? (Paris: Gallimard, 1953); translated by Joan and Barry Ulanov as *Last Essays* (Chicago: Regnery, 1955); republished as *The Last Essays of Georges Bernanos* (New York: Greenwood Press, 1968);

Le Crépuscule des vieux (Paris: Gallimard, 1956);

Français, si vous saviez, 1945-1948 (Paris: Gallimard, 1961);

Le Lendemain c'est vous (Paris: Plon, 1969);

Essais et écrits de combat, edited by Yves Bridel, Jacques Charbot, and Joseph Jart (Paris: Gallimard, 1971);

La Vocation spirituelle de la France (Paris: Plon, 1975);

Les Prédestinés (Paris: Seuil, 1983).

Collections: *Œuvres*, 6 volumes (Paris: Plon, 1947);

Œuvres romanesques, suivies de Dialogues des Carmélites, edited by Michel Estève (Paris: Gallimard, 1961).

Georges Bernanos's life of sixty years was no less paradoxical than his work. His first novel, *Sous le soleil de Satan* (1926; translated as *The Star of Satan*, 1927), was an immediate best-seller when he was thirty-eight; his third novel, *La Joie* (1929; translated as *Joy*, 1946), received the Prix Fémina when he was forty; and his famed *Journal d'un curé de campagne* (1936; translated as *The Diary of a Country Priest*, 1937) won the Grand Prix du Roman from the Académie Française when he was forty-eight. Yet in 1926, 1937, 1940, and 1946 he refused the Légion d'Honneur. The last time the offer came from Charles de Gaulle, he who once called *Journal d'un curé de campagne* "le plus grand roman français" (the greatest French novel). Similarly, in March 1946, when François Mauriac let Bernanos know that the Académie was ready to welcome him, he politely declined the honor. Yet his large family was often in dire financial straits and prevented from starving for extended periods of time only by his churning out pages of manuscript to send to his publishers for advances on royalties. The nightmare of waking up each morning to the familiar family refrain of "Tes pages! Tes pages!" (Your pages! Your pages!) haunted him on his deathbed at the American Hospital at Neuilly, where he died of cancer of the liver on 5 July 1948, worrying how the night nurse would be paid.

A quarter century after Bernanos's death, André Malraux called him "le plus grand romancier de son temps" (the greatest novelist of his time), an arresting statement since Bernanos's time had also been Malraux's, roughly that quarter century extending from 1925 to 1950. Bernanos's fairly modest corpus of fiction (eight novels, one play, and three major short stories) is classical in tone; in fact, he is one of the twentieth-century writers most often quoted in the *Robert* dictionary, and the standard volume on French style, Maurice Grévisse's *Le Bon Usage*, cites him as a great stylist. Although Léon Daudet likened Bernanos's genius to that of Proust when *Sous le soleil de Satan* appeared in 1926, boldly proclaiming, "Une étoile est apparue au firmament littéraire . . ." (a star has appeared in the literary heavens. . .), as a novelist Bernanos is more like Dostoyevski in that both regard man's soul as a battlefield where good and evil are at war. A sense of urgency in discovering hidden motives characterizes Bernanos's writing, in which a breathtaking, almost hallucinatory deployment of images reveals the unseen warfare taking place within the major characters.

Nothing in Bernanos's immediate family background would give reason to suspect his considerable literary gifts. From his birth above his father's interior decorator's shop, in Paris at 23 rue Joubert on 20 February 1888, he was the object of solicitude on the part of his pious, strong-willed peasant mother. Baptized in the neighboring parish church of St. Louis d'Antin, he was a sickly child who nearly died at the age of eighteen months, his survival being attributed to the intercession of the Holy Virgin. Throughout his sixty years Bernanos would be as haunted by the specter of death's inevitability as by a mysterious hatred of self rooted in nostalgia for lost childhood's purity. His constant preoccupation with death may be an echo of his mother's trauma as a parent in losing her firstborn, a three-year-old daughter. Bernanos's only surviving sibling was a sister five years his senior. He was thus the object of maternal indulgence as the last-born and only male child. The debt he owed his mother was great in that the only theology Bernanos said he knew was his catechism, learned at her knee.

Born Marie-Clémence Moreau and called Hermance, Bernanos's mother came from the isolated country village of Pellevoisin (Indre). Though transplanted from Pellevoisin to Paris as maid to the Countess de la Rochefoucauld, she would never lose the accent of her native region. Her marriage in the capital to Jean-François ("Emile") Bernanos was favored by the countess, who offered a handsome dowry enabling the groom to go into business for himself.

The family origins of Emile Bernanos were no less modest than those of his bride. Though there were claims of distant ties with a seventeenth-century Basque adventurer who had helped secure Santo Domingo for Louis XIV, Emile Bernanos's family had been in Lorraine for generations. His father had been a cobbler who left Lorraine with his Alsatian wife to seek his fortune in mid-nineteenth-century Paris, where he was working as a day laborer when his son was born. Emile Bernanos, aided by the dowry of his wife, hard work, talent, and taste, became financially successful prior to World War I. The ideals he passed on to his son, however, were far from materialistic; Emile Bernanos was both a Catholic and a royalist, ideals to which the writer would hold fast to the end.

When Georges Bernanos was eight years of age his family acquired a large country house—locally referred to as "le château"—in the northern village of Fressin (Pas-de-Calais); there the growing boy spent his summers and holidays, liberated from the confines of boarding school and city apartment. Childhood memories of Fressin provided Bernanos with a rich store of memories of the Artois region, not only of the physical and geographic settings but also of the values, which were those of a rural, premechanized France. The most important of Bernanos's eight novels (*Sous le soleil de Satan, Journal d'un curé de campagne, Nouvelle Histoire de Mouchette* [1937; translated as *Mouchette*, 1966], and *Monsieur Ouine* [1943; translated as *The Open Mind*, 1945]), are set in fictionalized villages resembling Fressin. Bernanos's skill in evoking the sea winds and smell of decaying leaves, as well as in depicting the old ways of the locals, sipping gin-laced bowls of coffee through sugar cubes clenched firmly in their teeth, speaks of his deep empathy for this region. Yet, once his parents, struck by a reversal of fortune during World War I, were forced to sell the chateau in 1925, he never revisited it again.

Emile Bernanos's financial success also allowed him to put his son in one of the best schools in Paris, the Jesuit school at 391 rue de Vaugirard. The boy entered as a day student in 1898 at age ten and remained three years, a schoolmate of the sons of the aristocracy, including Charles de Gaulle. Bernanos's first communion at the Jesuit school on 11 May 1899 was still fresh in his memory as he lay dying half a century later. He was so profoundly moved when the moment came to approach the altar rail with the others to receive the Holy Sacrament that he could not do so. For on that day he felt illumined by the light of God and prayed for one thing only: the grace to be a missionary. From the time he composed his first novel, he insisted that his writing was a vocation and not a career, as well as that all vocations lead to Calvary. In the meantime, however, he had to work his way through adolescence, that painfully duplicitous stage that he saw as the time when death's substance suddenly pollutes the very flow of human blood.

From 1901 to 1903 Bernanos became a boarding student at the preseminary school of Notre-Dame-des-Champs in Paris. Extremely unhappy, he was in the lowest group of his class both years. His mother entrusted him to two young priest-schoolmasters from her native region who were returning from studies in Paris to teach at the Collège Saint-Célestin in Bourges. One of these, the abbé Lagrange, was the boy's professor of rhetoric in 1903-1904 and awakened in him a sense of pride in his ability for French composition. Although he remained unsuccessful in mathematics and Greek and, at the end of the year, failed his first *baccalauréat*, the future author of *Journal d'un curé de campagne* did receive the prize for French composition. At the second sitting for the *baccalauréat* he failed again, and his parents brought him back to Pas-de-Calais to the Collège Sainte-Marie at Aire-sur-la-Lys; there, in

Bernanos, circa 1904, while he was a student at the Collège Saint-Célestin in Bourges

1905, he finally passed the first *baccalauréat*, and, in 1906, with no difficulty, he passed the second, preuniversity *baccalauréat*, in philosophy, thus completing his secondary studies.

The letters Bernanos sent to the abbé Lagrange during those two years at Aire-sur-la-Lys reveal the youth's rejection of facility and romanticism, his seeking of his Christian vocation outside the priesthood, and his conscious effort to see God in everything in order to escape his fear of death. While the abbé Lagrange showed a penchant for the Christian Democratic movement of Marc Sangnier's Sillon movement, his young correspondent opted for the right-wing Action Française group. The young Bernanos rejected the Christian Democrats since they believed in the perfectability of man and were incapable of taking in what he called "la commune détresse" (the common dilemma) of man's mortality.

In the fall of 1906 Bernanos began studies at the Faculté de Droit at the Université de Paris, much to the disappointment of his parents, who had hoped he would show more interest in commercial studies. Over the next three years Berna-

nos completed his licence in law as well as in literature with courses at the Institut Catholique. It was during these years that the Action Française under Charles Maurras became highly visible with its daily newspaper. In the wake of the Dreyfus affair and the laws putting religious orders under the control of the state and then forbidding them from teaching, a largely Catholic following flocked to Maurras's monarchist movement with its highly nationalistic aim: "La France aux Français!" (France for the French!) Protestants, Jews, Freemasons, and foreigners residing in France were excluded. Bernanos's friends from the Jesuit school and from Notre-Dame-des-Champs recognized him as their natural leader and formed a team around him, calling themselves the "les hommes de guerre" (Men of War). As members of the Action Française youth guard, Les Camelots du Roi, they participated in the frequently violent demonstrations staged by Maurras's men. Bernanos and his friends were more than once listed on the Action Française honor roll of wounded and imprisoned fighters. Important also during this period was that, as early as 1907, Bernanos found an outlet for his attempts at short stories in royalist publications.

These beginnings of his career as a writer were interrupted in 1909 when Bernanos, his studies completed, was called up for obligatory military service. The shock of relentless training broke his health, and he was released in 1910 to recuperate at Fressin before returning to Paris with its political and journalistic ferment. Regrouping his Men of War, he joined in a 1912 attempt to restore the monarchy in Portugal, much to the horror of the leaders of Action Française, who did not consider their royalist program international. One of the leaders, Léon Daudet, suggested that Bernanos be sent to the provinces to use his energies to edit a royalist weekly at Rouen called *L'Avant-garde de Normandie*. Bernanos began in October 1913, and, in addition to his own polemical articles–including a series of gratuitous attacks on the philosopher Alain (Emile Chartier), then lycée professor in Rouen–he published some of his own short stories. At *L'Avant-garde* he worked with one of his men of war, Ernest de Malibran, who shortly joined two others of their group in a youthful adventure in Paraguay, where they dreamed of setting up a French colony imbued with the ideas of Christian chivalry. The outbreak of war in August 1914 brought them back to France, just as it cut short Bernanos's career as a newspaper editor.

Rouen marked him for life, for there he met his future wife, Jehanne Pauline Marie Talbert d'Arc, who spelled her first name exactly as her ancestor's famous martyred sister did. They were married on 14 May 1917, at Vincennes (where her parents resided), by Dom J-M Léon Besse, a royalist Benedictine from the Abbey of Liguge and a writer whom Bernanos had taken as his spiritual director. Léon Daudet was best man. Bernanos had been back in uniform since August 1914, having found a sympathetic officer who got him reinstated in his old unit, the sixth Dragoons. He never rose above the rank of corporal, but he was wounded and decorated. More important for his writing, however, was that he knew trench warfare in all its horror. He was still in the army at the birth of his first child, Chantal, on 25 April 1918 and was not discharged until 10 July 1919, eight months following the armistice and very shortly before the birth of Yves, his first son, on 16 August 1919.

Moving in with the Talbert d'Arcs at Vincennes, the returning veteran and his expectant wife joined his sister and her husband at the seaside at Berck after his discharge, and it was here that he began, with no delay, what was to become his first and most sensational novel, *Sous le soleil de Satan.* Seven years later it would catapult him to glory.

In his prewar attempts at the short story Bernanos had either idealized fidelity to the monarchy with dramatic acts of heroism and sacrifice on the battlefield or shown a keen psychological analysis of characters who preferred a career or abstract idea to life itself. In contrast, he wished his first novel to bear witness to what he had learned while facing mutilation and death in the trenches: the implacable power of the demonic in the affairs of men. This ambitious program led him to produce a novel whose three parts might be compared to the panels of a triptych, a novel which, interestingly, has no mention of the war.

The left panel presents Mouchette, a sixteen-year-old girl who is pregnant by the local marquis. She kills him when she realizes he is less noble than her ideal of him. Her second lover, the local doctor and representative to the Assemblée Nationale, proves no more worthy of her romantic dream. The right panel of the triptych describes the last day in the life of the old saint of Lumbres, reputed to be a second curé of Ars. (The historical curé of Ars, St. Jean Baptiste

Marie Vianney [1786-1859], was much talked about at the time Bernanos was working on the novel; Vianney was canonized by Pius XI in April 1925.) Like the first curé, Bernanos's saint can read souls, and he attracts pilgrims who come daily in great numbers to confess to him. On this last day, even as he is dying, he is pushed into trying to raise a dead child but realizes that he has blasphemed in asking for the miracle in the name of man's justice and not out of love for God.

Uniting these two seemingly unrelated parts is the dominant central panel presenting the early formation of the saint of Lumbres as the young abbé Donissan, an awkward junior priest in his first parish. His superior, upon discovering on Christmas morning that Donissan wears a hair shirt and instruments of penance, tells him he is called to be a saint and that he must either rise to the calling or be lost. Plunged into despair at such a thought, the young priest flagellates himself to unconsciousness, believing he must eradicate any joy he might feel in his experience of God. One night the young priest meets a horsetrader who turns out to be Satan. This powerful scene of spiritual seduction shows the young cleric finally being kissed by his companion, who then bestows upon him the gift of reading souls. The most disturbing feature of the encounter is that the hero, when he looks into the face of his much-desired companion, sees only his own face looking back.

The three threads of the plot are fully united when the abbé Donissan meets the half-crazed Mouchette whose despair is equal to his own. Rejecting his compassion, she returns home, slits her throat, and then indicates she wants the abbé Donissan to carry her to the church to die.

This strange novel, haunting in its power yet mysterious in its shape, was completed in 1925. While Bernanos did the writing, a second daughter, Claude, was born 31 January 1921, and a second son, Michel, arrived 20 January 1923. Unemployed until February 1922, when he found a job as a traveling insurance agent in the east of France, the veteran and his family lived first with his wife's parents in Paris; at the beginning of 1922 they joined his parents at Fressin. In April of 1923 Bernanos fell gravely ill. This experience, too, was connected to his first novel, for as he later remarked in an interview, in that illness he had felt the solicitation of death but had

Bernanos and Jehanne Pauline Marie Talbert d'Arc shortly before their marriage on 14 May 1917

not wanted to die without first having *witnessed,* referring to his novel *Sous le soleil de Satan.*

To be nearer his work in the east of France, the family moved to Bar-le-Duc in the fall of 1923 and resided there until after the sensational launching of *Sous le soleil de Satan* in 1926. The author's constant travels meant that much of *Sous le soleil de Satan* was written in railway cars, modest hotels, and cafés. The novel also owed much to Robert Vallery-Radot, a friend introduced to Bernanos by Dom Besse in 1919, after Bernanos's discharge from the service. As an established writer, Vallery-Radot in 1922 got Bernanos's

short story "Madame Dargent" published in *La Revue Hebdomadaire,* and it was he who recognized the genius of Bernanos when he read the last part of the novel in order of composition, that is, the central panel of the triptych. Vallery-Radot passed the manuscript to Henri Massis, a literary advisor at Plon publishers, who was collaborating with Jacques Maritain and Stanislas Fumet in launching Plon's new spiritually oriented collection, Le Roseau d'Or. As founder of this collection, Maritain felt responsible for theological and philosophical questions treated in it and thus exacted many changes and suppressions in the text, seriously altering Bernanos's basic vision, before the novel's publication in March 1926. Nonetheless, within three months it had sold more than fifty-eight thousand copies and was being translated into five European languages.

In the euphoria of success and wishing to devote himself fully to his second novel, *L'Imposture* (The Imposture, 1927), already under way, Bernanos decided to give up his job on 1 July. The winter had been marked by family illnesses, particularly affecting his wife. A stay in the Pyrenees was suggested, and they moved to the mountains with Bernanos's parents. There Emile Bernanos died in January of cancer of the liver, and his son wrote that he felt he was watching his own death. *L'Imposture* was completed by March when Bernanos moved his family back north, moving in temporarily with the Talbert d'Arcs in Amiens.

At this point, a year after the success of *Sous le soleil de Satan*, Bernanos spoke to Plon's director, Maurice Bourdel, about returning to a steady job to assure family security but was told that he was of great value to the publisher and should not have to worry about finances. Bourdel offered him a monthly income of five thousand francs and, when Bernanos spoke of wanting to buy a home, gave him an additional fifty thousand francs. That every franc offered Bernanos would one day have to be accounted for, once his reserves were exhausted, did not enter the author's mind.

The family moved into their new home at Clermont (Oise) in August. Bernanos was already busy writing the sequel to *L'Imposture*. The sequel, *La Joie*, was finished in a state of panic in December of 1928. Not only had the birth of the fifth child and third daughter, Dominique, on 1 November 1928, interrupted the household, but as of October of that year, Massis, in order to prod Bernanos into completing the sequel, had started serializing *La Joie* in *La Revue Universelle* even though the conclusion had not yet been written. The memory of this episode stayed with Bernanos, who afterward said that had he had time he might have made these two novels into another sensational single volume.

Both *L'Imposture* and *La Joie* deal with the same impostor priest, the abbé Cénabre, an erudite member of the Académie Française who writes on mystics and saints. In *L'Imposture* Bernanos probes the priest's loss of faith while satirizing the Catholic literary milieu of Paris. At the end of the novel Cénabre is left alone with his se-

cret. The abbé Chevance, the old priest to whom he had confided it but refused to confess it as a sin, dies from uremic poisoning, attended only by his spiritual daughter, Chantal de Clergerie, the heroine of *La Joie*. She will continue Chevance's mission to the impostor.

Chantal de Clergerie's spirituality was a conscious effort on Bernanos's part to incarnate in a fictional character the mysterious yet down-to-earth spirituality of Thérèse of Lisieux, who, like the curé of Ars, was canonized by Pius XI in April 1925. Chantal's widowed father entrusts her with running his strange household, which includes not only his own mad mother but also a drug-addicted Russian chauffeur who, by the novel's end, has killed Chantal even though he venerates her as a saint. Clergerie's houseguests are little better; the strange assembly includes his psychiatrist friend, Dr. Lapérouse, a secret acquaintance of the Russian's, and the abbé Cénabre, whom Clergerie wants Chantal to take as her confessor to replace the deceased abbé Chevance. Thinking that Chevance must have confided his secret to Chantal as he was dying, Cénabre himself confesses it to her. At the end of the novel, when he beholds her slain virginal body beside that of the Russian, dead by his own hand, he finally prays and then falls senseless; he dies later in a hospital without having regained consciousness.

In spite of its somber tone, *La Joie*, published in June of 1929, won the Prix Fémina in December, crowning what was for Bernanos a very successful year. Though he had not published more short stories as he had done in 1928 when "Dialogue d'ombres" (Dialogues of Shadows) and "Une Nuit" (One Night) had appeared (first in periodicals and then in a book), he had boldly used an article on Joan of Arc to attack the hierarchy of the Church, which, two years before, had officially condemned the Action Française. Bernanos had taken delight in pointing out that the ecclesiastical condemnation of the Maid of Orleans was legal but was still wrong since she had been proclaimed a saint by the same church which had condemned her. Published in book form in English as *Sanctity Will Out* (1947), the article first appeared in French in *La Revue Hebdomadaire* and then as a book; the title, *Jeanne, relapse et sainte* (1934), implies that an officially recognized relapsed heretic was, in the end, actually holy.

In 1929 Bernanos had also begun his personal homage to Edouard Drumont, publisher of *La Libre Parole*, a newspaper taken by Bernanos's father when Bernanos was a boy. *La Libre Parole* denounced the subversion of the glory and honor of France by the power of the rich, and Drumont, author of *La France juive*, placed the lion's share of the blame on the Jews. Though presented in the guise of a biography, the title of Bernanos's homage clearly implies that it was a polemical volume dealing with Drumont's period: *La Grande Peur des bien-pensants* (The Great Fear of Those who Think Properly, 1931). A searing indictment of the political and religious conflicts in Drumont's lifetime, it was published by Grasset. The fact that Bernanos wrote this tribute to Drumont for having taught him at his father's breakfast table what injustice was has often caused Bernanos to be dismissed as an anti-Semite–a superficial judgment that ignores his position in more mature writings.

With the Prix Fémina in hand and another volume under way, it must have come as a rude shock to Bernanos to be informed by Bourdel, Plon's director, that his reserves were exhausted and that all monthly advances would cease until his large debt to Plon was settled. Bernanos thus found himself at the beginning of 1930 with his wife and family of five children cut off from the regular income he had naively come to think his due as a writer of great commercial value. He was now dependent on Grasset's advances on his book on Drumont, though there were occasional lecture fees. To make matters worse, Hermance Bernanos died in March. The timing could not have been worse, and her only son suffered atrociously with crises of night anguish. He was dispatched for the summer for a rest cure in the Alps where his family joined him until September. They decided to return to Clermont in October, sell the house, and move to the southern coast.

In November, accompanied by the Talbert d'Arcs, they settled into a villa in Toulon. Bernanos corrected proofs for the book on Drumont. It came out in February 1931, and that month the author, within the space of two weeks, began first one, then a second novel. The first, which he said disgusted him, eventually became *Un Mauvais Rêve* (1950; translated as *Night is Darkest*, 1953), while the second, the one he called his great novel, *Monsieur Ouine* (1943), was completed in 1940.

In the spring they moved once again before finally settling for three years at the villa Le Fenouillet in La Bayorre, near Hyères. This villa, with its high terrace and alleys of palms, was open to visitors, some of whom came away with tales of family turbulence. While Bernanos struggled to write his "great novel," *Monsieur Ouine*, financial disaster was threatening. Vallery-Radot, now literary director of *Le Figaro*, engaged Bernanos to write regular articles in that venerable daily, recently acquired by the perfume manufacturer François Coty. Coty was a self-made man and had acquired potential for political power through his purchase of newspapers. His isolation appealed to Bernanos. But the Action Française, which Bernanos had so selflessly defended after its condemnation by the Church in 1927, now attacked him. They were at war with Coty. Maurras bade Bernanos adieu in a public letter and Bernanos replied. Then, in June, he ceased his collaboration with *Le Figaro* until the end of 1932, when he made a brief return there from October to December.

At the beginning of 1933, with no prospects of income in sight, Bernanos resolved that he must finish *Monsieur Ouine*. He allowed a public subscription to be launched for a special deluxe edition, expecting to finish the novel forthwith. In April, however, while riding his motorcycle, he lost three chapters, two of which he could never bring himself to rewrite. Then in July, again on his motorcycle, he was injured when he was struck by a car. The accident left him with an infirm leg, and he was able to walk thereafter only when assisted by two canes. Suffering terribly from his injured leg and, once again, by crises of anguish at night, he dragged himself with difficulty to the church for the baptism of his sixth child and third son, Jean-Loup, born at La Bayorre on 30 September 1933.

As pressures mounted, he borrowed from Plon on what he hoped to receive for damages from the accident. In 1934 he needed a solution that would keep his family from starving, and he agreed in July with Plon that for every page of manuscript sent to them he would receive a sixty-franc advance on royalties. Given the urgency of the situation–the rent was overdue–he decided to drop *Monsieur Ouine* and dash off a detective story. The first part of *Un Crime* (1935; translated as *The Crime*, 1936), consisting of one hundred pages, was written in August. In September, however, Bernanos thought he could take advantage of the five scenes left from the unfinished novel he had set aside in order to begin *Monsieur Ouine* in February 1931. The mysterious, drug-addicted, and suspect female secretary of the aging writer described in the first of the

Bernanos in 1930 at the offices of Plon, publisher of his novel La Joie, *which won the 1929 Prix Fémina*

five scenes of that novel became the murderess in his new detective story.

The first part of *Un Crime* describes the arrival, in a hamlet in the Alps, of the new village priest the morning after two murders have taken place: first that of Madame Beauchamp, the elderly lady of the local chateau, and second, that of an unknown young man, shot and found dying in the chateau park. No one realizes that the dying young man is the real priest, who had the misfortune of encountering the woman responsible for the murder in the chateau as she was fleeing. She shoots him, strips off his cassock, and passes herself off as the new priest for twenty-four hours before disappearing. In its final form,

Un Mauvais Rêve would end with the murder by which *Un Crime* begins, that of the old lady in the chateau. In *Un Mauvais Rêve* the murderess stops short of killing the priest, and one is left with the impression that she might even repent. In *Un Crime* the murderess is motivated by more sensational elements—by love for her female recluse companion and by her own origins. She is, in fact, the child of a nun, now defrocked, who had been another companion to the old lady and who commits suicide after the old lady's murder, adding to the confusion. Her father may even have been a priest.

But all of this was not to be written at the villa at La Bayorre. Rent had not been paid, the

Bernanos in September 1931, photographed by his friend Jean Tenant (Editions du Centurion)

bailiff arrived, and, as in a pathetic scene from one of his novels, Bernanos and his wife and children, leaving everything behind, bravely descended the alleys of palms, carrying only their suitcases. They took only his motorcycle with them as they boarded the boat for the Spanish island of Majorca. There living was cheaper, he had been told. Their belongings were sold at auction to pay the rent. Excepting the four years in the early 1940s at Barbecena in Brazil, they were never again housed in anything resembling their own home.

In spite of many moves from one furnished house to another, the two and a half years in Majorca were a fecund period for Bernanos as he sent pages of his novels to Plon, pleading, always pleading that the money be sent by wire, deducting expenses. Thinking he had completed his detective story by 18 December 1934, he received from Plon twenty-five thousand francs for the family's first Christmas abroad. This Christmas also saw the birth of that novel which, above all others, has assured Bernanos's status as a writer, the classic *Journal d'un curé de campagne*. Indeed, he had strong premonitions that this novel was one of his best works, as attested in his letters from that time.

Disaster struck on 15 January 1935, however. A letter from Plon announced that the second and third parts of *Un Crime* (those into which he had incorporated material from the novel begun earlier) simply would not do. They were far too literary for a detective story, and no review would accept his mystery novel as it stood for prepublication in serial form–a financial concern of mutual interest to Bernanos and Plon. Already paid advances for these pages, Bernanos dared not suggest that he be compensated to rewrite them. He did propose that Plon send the offending second and third parts back to him so that, after having completely rewritten them, he might incorporate them into yet another novel. Plon accepted, and the author, abandoning *Journal d'un curé de campagne*, rewrote *Un Crime* until May 1935, then reshaped *Un Mauvais Rêve* until August, when he returned to his abandoned story of a young priest serving in his first parish who is struck down by cancer.

Bernanos's premonitions concerning *Journal d'un curé de campagne* proved to be justified. Honored with the Grand Prix du Roman de l'Académie Française, it was widely praised and, in the judgments of many readers, is his finest work. It is the story of a young, idealistic priest in his first parish, a dreary village and its environs. His diary is the reflection of his struggle to bring faith to others and keep his own. From the beginning, his attempts to bring the Gospel to his parishioners and to assist them meet with failure. His efforts to create a club for the village youth are in vain; his catechism classes are the source of problems; the gentry of the village attend divine services but believe that religion, and the priest, should keep their place. The priest has further difficulties with his housekeeper, the grocer's wife, and some of his superiors. As if that were not enough, he is not physically strong. Yet it is clear that, despite failure and weakness, he is endowed with a powerful spiritual life, which he himself no doubt understands poorly. His very presence seems to call up people's darkest secrets, and soon, despite or perhaps because of his innocence, he discovers sordid dramas in the village and at the chateau of the count and countess.

The central conflict arises from his own spiritual struggle and his relationships with his parishioners, and the two are not unrelated. As he sinks into self-doubt, he also becomes, despite himself, more involved in others' dramas. He discovers the adultery of the count with his daughter's

governess. Without the overt intervention of any element of the supernatural, and in a strictly secular setting, he brings the daughter to confess her utter desperation, brought about by seeing her beloved father betray her thus. For Bernanos, the despair of children was one of the great tragedies and to drive them to despair, a heinous crime. Her confession is almost like an exorcism. In a powerful subsequent scene, the priest leads the countess to confess the resentment and spiritual despair in which she has lived since the death of her infant son; from the depths of his own spiritual misery and doubt, he is able to find the means to reconcile her with God. Her death from a heart attack the ensuing night is attributed by gossipmongers and even by his superiors to his having threatened her; in fact, at the very last moment, when her eternal destiny was at stake, he saved her.

Nowhere else does Bernanos show so clearly that the ways of the world contradict divine ways and that spiritual truths cannot be judged by appearances. The curé is a failure and a source of dissension. He is nearly forsaken: only an older priest and a young soldier from the Foreign Legion on furlough show him any understanding. Signs that pages have been torn from his diary point to his struggle. He meets with a doctor who is a drug addict and who kills himself and discovers that a seminary classmate is now defrocked and living with a charwoman. The worst discovery is that he himself has inoperable cancer. Yet it brings about his enlightenment, as he realizes that his ineptitude is unimportant, since he is not called to hold a parish for more than a few months anyway; his destiny lies elsewhere. Although his death may be seen as compromised by the fact that it takes place in the apartment of his defrocked friend, who had left the church through what he called his intellectual evolution, he dies breathing the words of Thérèse de Lisieux, "Tout est grâce" (Everything is grace, an utterance unfortunately rendered in Pamela Morris's 1937 English translation as "Grace is everywhere").

Bernanos's next novel, *Nouvelle Histoire de Mouchette*, is his short stylistic masterpiece. He began it in March 1936, soon after completing his story of the country priest, and finished it the following July. The Mouchette of this novel has nothing in common with the Mouchette of *Sous le soleil de Satan* except for the despair in which she dies. In this novel the fourteen-year-old daughter of a smuggler on the Belgian border is followed through her last twenty-four hours as she flees school to avoid ridicule, is caught in a storm, and rescued by a poacher friend of her father's who rapes her. She returns home at dawn to find her mother dying. The old lady who shrouds the dead makes her a present of a beautiful white dress. Mouchette dons it and drowns herself. Bernanos insisted that Mouchette was a little heroine, struggling nobly to the end, like an animal caught in a trap or a bull in the bullring, dying only because there is no escape.

Just as *Nouvelle Histoire de Mouchette* was completed, the Spanish civil war reached the island of Majorca. From June 1936 to February 1937 Bernanos sent articles to the Dominican review *Sept*, published in Paris. These articles inspired his book on the Spanish conflict, *Les Grands Cimetières sous la lune* (literally The Great Moonlit Cemeteries but translated in 1938 by Pamela Morris as *A Diary of My Times*, with a considerable blunting of Bernanos's trenchant prose). The poetic title reflects the author's attempt to preserve the memory of a hideous experience he had one night when he was out riding his motorcycle. Noticing clouds of stinking black smoke billowing from a country cemetery, he stopped to investigate. There he discovered great piles of corpses, all victims of execution, doused with gasoline and set aflame.

With autumn 1936 approaching, Chantal, Claude, and Michel were dispatched for schooling in France while the sixteen-year-old Yves held a lieutenant's commission in Francisco Franco's forces. Soon unable to stomach the executions, he deserted and had to be smuggled off the island to mainland Spain, later to be repatriated. Bernanos, however, felt he must stay as a witness to denounce, as a Christian, what was being done in the name of Christianity and even termed a crusade against the godless by the hierarchy of the Church. Two attempts on his life finally persuaded him to return to France at the end of March 1937 with his wife and two youngest children.

At the end of April they returned to Toulon, where Bernanos wrote his volume on the conflict that he and others considered a dress rehearsal for the war that was about to sweep all of Europe. The following year, in April 1938, *Les Grands Cimetières sous la lune* was published by Plon, winning Bernanos a new wave of admirers. Simone Weil, disillusioned by her experience in fighting on the Communist side in Spain, wrote him a long and impassioned letter saying that he

alone had told the truth. Another new admirer who instantly recognized in this passionate volume the marks of a literary genius was Gaston Gallimard. The Paris publisher unabashedly wooed Bernanos, proposing that he sign a contract and waving aside all objections that Bernanos owed books to other publishers.

Although flattered, Bernanos was preoccupied with that old dream he had shared before World War I with his men of war: to establish a French colony in Paraguay. As he had proven, he could write his books anywhere and under any circumstances, but the children, he thought, must be situated in a place where they could grow their own food. To help with this plan his nephew, Guy Hattu, would join them in December once they were installed. Money from his spate of recent publications, plus an advance from Gallimard on the contract which he did sign just prior to departure, would make this new endeavor possible. Even his misgiving about lacking a French doctor abroad was taken care of: a young royalist disciple, Dr. Jean Bénier, his wife, and their two young children, were joining them.

They set sail on the *Florida* from Marseilles to Buenos Aires on 20 July 1938, seen off by a few friends. Prominent among them was a young Dominican priest, Father Raymond Bruckberger, whom Bernanos had met through Jacques Maritain and who, as the boat reached open water, raised his hand in blessing. Dropping anchor in the harbor of Rio de Janeiro on the evening of 4 August, the writer and his wife were greeted by some of Brazil's most distinguished men of letters, who invited them to dine with them and even tried to dissuade Bernanos from going on to Paraguay, where they assured him life would prove impossible for them. The author, however, had not come this close to the Eden of his old dream to abandon it now.

Upon disembarkation in Buenos Aires he was more formally received. Maritain had alerted the Argentinians, for whom Bernanos gave two lectures before boarding the paddle-wheeler which would take the party up the river passage to Asunción, the capital of Paraguay. Five days were enough for Bernanos to realize that living there was three times as expensive as it had been in Toulon, and Dr. Bénier discovered he could not practice medicine in Paraguay.

They returned to Rio and were housed in a hotel when news of what Bernanos considered the English and French capitulation at Munich

Page from Bernanos's draft for a dedication to Nous autres Français *(courtesy of Fonds Georges Bernanos, Bibliothèque Nationale, Paris). The publisher, Gallimard, refused to print it.*

reached them. Bernanos began *Nous autres Français* (We French, 1939), trying to articulate what French honor should be, for he agreed with Winston Churchill that in choosing dishonor instead of war, the allies would inevitably have both dishonor and war. While awaiting the arrival of his nephew, in November the family found temporary quarters at Itaïpava, where the children could have horses; in December they moved farther away from Rio to Juiz de Fora for two months. Bernanos interrupted *Nous autres Français,* to write a denunciation of Charles Maurras. His old master had been elected to the Académie Française, and the reception was scheduled to take place in June 1939. Though the text was intended as a preface to an anthology of texts by Drumont that Father Bruckberger was preparing, Bruckberger had it published by Gallimard as a separate volume in time to denounce Maurras before his entry into the Académie. Bruckberger titled the volume *Scandale de la vérité* (Scandal of Truth, 1939), for Maurras had favored Munich, and Bernanos viewed his entry into the Académie as an official approval of Maurras's pro-Munich stand.

From February through June 1939 Bernanos resided at Vassouras, where he completed *Nous autres Français,* his last volume to reach Gallimard before the outbreak of war. Plans were afoot to launch the family's great agricultural installation. Encouraged by Vergilio de Mello Franco, son of an ambassador and an important man in the Brazilian state of Minas Gerais, Bernanos moved to a large *fazenda,* or ranch of seven thousand hectares with 280 head of cattle, far inland at Pirapora, more than six hundred kilometers from Rio, and at the end of the railway line. As Mello Franco's shipping line controlled the traffic along the São Francisco River, cattle, having been bought cheaply and fattened, could be taken to market with no difficulty. Bernanos was assured by his Brazilian friends that in five years his financial worries would be over. While waiting in Pirapora for the ranch to be made habitable, the family camped in a house with no running water. It was here that news of the declaration of war was received. Bernanos reacted by writing one of his most beautiful volumes of nonfiction, which he called a "war diary," published after the war in 1949 as *Les Enfants humiliés, journal 1939-1940* (The Humiliated Children: Journal 1939-1940). Simultaneously he found that he could at last write an episode that had given him great difficulty: the death of Mon-

sieur Ouine. This episode constitutes the book's most extraordinary chapter, finished, according to Bernanos, the same day that the Germans unleashed their forces to crush France: 10 May 1940.

The coincidence seems strangely appropriate, for *Monsieur Ouine* is perhaps best read as an allegory. The professor-hero's name implies that he always manages to say "yes" and "no" at the same time, representing in a sense modern civilization. The fourteen-year-old boy called Steeny whom Monsieur Ouine seduces can be seen as representative of Bernanos himself, seduced by his own civilization. Monsieur Ouine has lived for some time at the disintegrating chateau of the local aristocrat and his suspect wife. The aristocrat is dying, and Ouine, a retired professor, seems to preside perniciously over all that transpires in the nearby village of Fenouille, where Steeny lives with his mother, widowed during the war, and her English companion, Daisy, who was sexually abused as an orphaned child and is now intent upon suspect games she tries to play with Steeny. The night of the seduction a young cowherd is murdered, and the discovery of his nude body turns the whole village inside out. The mayor goes mad, the poacher accused of the murder commits suicide along with his young wife, and, at the funeral, the aristocrat's wife is lynched. An exchange between the priest and the village doctor offers some of Bernanos's most disturbing (and prophetic) insights into the future of the human race and leads the reader to Monsieur Ouine's death. The long last chapter stands as a memorial to Bernanos's short sojourn at Pirapora in Brazil's hinterland where Bernanos metamorphosed Hitler's conquest of Europe into the old professor's death, finishing the novel that had cost him nine years of work.

Apart from Bernanos's success in completing *Monsieur Ouine,* the venture at Pirapora was ill-fated. The house was habitable by November 1939, but with Dr. Bénier and Bernanos's nephew called up for repatriation and military service in February 1940, they were shorthanded after just three months. Bernanos's son Yves, recently recovered from malaria after an adventure into the interior to contact hostile Indians with a Lazarist missionary, was called up for repatriation in June, leaving only the seventeen-year-old Michel to oversee the workers living on the *fazenda.*

Another dream was abandoned. Bernanos moved back nearer civilization to Barbecena, buying a house with three acres. It was called Cruz das Almas (Cross of Souls) after a cross erected there in memory of early martyrs. During their four years there it came to resemble a French country residence. Here the author undertook a series of letters to the English, *Lettre aux Anglais* (1942; translated as *Plea for Liberty*, 1944) giving his readers yet another volume explaining what it means to be French. The idea had come to him as he answered a request from the *Dublin Review* to submit a text on French honor. A Swiss-German publisher, Charles Ofaire, brought out this wartime volume at his Atlantica press in Rio. Ofaire published the first editions of *Lettre aux Anglais*, *Monsieur Ouine* (Atlantica's 1943 edition was highly faulty and incomplete), and, in four volumes, published, respectively, in 1943 (I), 1944 (II and III), and 1945 (IV), Bernanos's newspaper articles collected under a title which was borrowed from the name of his residence at Barbecena: *Le Chemin de la Croix-des-Ames* (The Way of the Cross of Souls). A French-language edition of *Journal d'un curé de campagne* was published by Ofaire in 1944.

The articles written from 1942 to 1945, assembled in a one-volume edition of *Le Chemin de la Croix-des-Ames* published by Gallimard after the war, are many. Together with the volume of postwar articles entitled *Français, si vous saviez, 1945-1948* (Frenchmen, If You Knew, 1945-1948, published in 1961), they bear witness not only to the tremendous efforts the novelist made to support his family by journalism but also to the consistency of his thought concerning French honor, for him rooted in Christianity. Some elements of the Resistance movement, morally sustained by his wartime writings, considered him their conscience.

As the war dragged on, Yves returned from England in 1942 with tuberculosis, and Michel flew off to join the Free French navy, participating in the Normandy landings in 1944. In 1943, when Madame Bernanos was asked to christen the Brazilian aircraft the *Joan of Arc*, Bernanos was the speaker, giving a seminal address on Joan of Arc and Thérèse of Lisieux. During the summer of December 1943 to February 1944, wealthy Brazilian friends–of whom there were many–arranged for a Bernanos family holiday on the Isle of Paqueta in Rio's harbor, where Yves met Elza, a Portuguese woman who would become his wife.

A telegram from the office of Gen. Charles de Gaulle to the French ambassador in Rio in Sep-

tember 1944 requested that Bernanos be told that the general would be happy to see him in newly liberated Paris. In December the embassy sent word that Bernanos was planning to return, but it was not until he received a telegram from de Gaulle himself that he made up his mind. "Votre place est parmi nous" (Your place is here with us), the cable of 16 February 1945 read.

To the dismay of the children, the house at Barbecena was sold, and on 2 June on an old banana boat, it was once again a family of six who set out to sea. Yves's young wife and their daughter replaced Chantal, married in Belo Horizonte, and Michel. At the moment of departure Bernanos's Brazilian friends noticed that his face was bathed in a cold sweat as he embraced them. No priest blessed this departure. Instead, as the old vessel bore them away, it was Bernanos who bestowed a blessing on the Brazilians and their country.

Docking in Liverpool on 26 June after a three-week crossing, they arrived in France on the evening of the twenty-ninth, first landing at Dieppe, where the harbor was littered with capsized, rusting boats, then arriving at the Saint-Lazare railway station in a Paris without streetlights. They settled in August in a primitive chateau in Briasq, near Sisteron, in the Alps, with neither gas, electricity, nor running water, circumstances typifying the moral and physical destitution of their return home. With no heating but open fireplaces, they left this dwelling in December, moving south to the sea at Bandol.

Though Bernanos, whose reputation had never been higher, was offered attractive arrangements with certain important newspapers which proposed such amenities as a regular salary in exchange for one article per week and even an apartment in Paris, he consistently answered negatively, clinging tenaciously to his absolute freedom, just as he had done in Brazil when papers had wanted to claim him as their own. The difference was that Bernanos's journalism in Brazil was often surreptitiously subsidized by wealthy friends, who instructed editors to pay him double the normal fee. In France such lucrative journalism was not to be found. He contributed to a variety of publications, including Albert Camus's *Combat*, as well as *La Bataille, Carrefour, Le Figaro*, and *L'Intransigeant*, among others. In March of 1946 Plon published *Monsieur Ouine*, reproducing the faulty Rio edition even though the manuscript lay in their archives. It would be discovered only by Albert Béguin when he prepared a new edition in 1955 for Club des Libraires de France, giving Bernanos's complete text.

Bernanos was now much in demand as a lecturer, notably in North Africa, Switzerland, and Belgium. In September 1946 he was one of the distinguished speakers at the Rencontres Internationales of Geneva, speaking on the subject of the European mind. In this lecture entitled "L'Esprit européen" and collected in *La Liberté, pour quoi faire?* (1953; translated as *Last Essays,* 1955), he evokes the hallucinatory experience of having just crossed a devastated Germany. The hideousness of the desolation was a true image of the final fate awaiting Europe's old Christendom if free men did not try to save it, he maintained.

Moving from Bandol to Thoisy near La Chapelle-Vendômoise (Loir-et-Cher) to be nearer Paris, Bernanos lectured in Belgium in November. The postwar bloodletting disturbed him, and he pleaded for several of those tried and executed for collaboration with the Germans. *La France contre les robots* (published in Brazil in 1944) was published by Robert Laffont in Paris in 1947. Lectures in Switzerland in February 1947 were followed the same month by his well-known lecture "Révolution et liberté" ("Revolution and Freedom," collected in *La Liberté, pour quoi faire?*) in the grand amphitheater of the Sorbonne. In March of that year Bernanos was invited to undertake a lecture tour in North Africa. He decided the family should join him and his wife there, for Yves was permanently hospitalized with tuberculosis, and the young man's wife and two small daughters added three more dependents to the family which still included the two youngest Bernanos children, Dominique and Jean-Loup. Michel had gone back to Brazil, but Claude would be joining them in August.

It was in Tunis that Bernanos gave what turned out to be his last lecture, on 4 April 1947. He entitled it "Nos Amis les saints" ("Our Friends, the Saints"), and it is one of his most important texts, included as the final piece in *La Liberté, pour quoi faire?*. In it is found an explicit articulation of the special frame of reference used by Bernanos when he speaks of sanctity. Indeed, any reader of his *Journal d'un curé de campagne* will find the great scene between the young curé and the countess considerably illuminated by this text. Man's participation in the life of Christ in the world, Bernanos maintains, comes when one does the impossible, such as accepting the death of one's child and saying "yes" to God because God is God. This acquiescence is what sanctity is,

for in saying "yes" one accepts the risk of loving God, of being human to the fullest. And by using one's freedom to love God one is filled with the charity of Christ, and becomes, in that moment, at least, a saint.

Bernanos continued to work on lectures and newspaper articles. The family took a villa furnished only with camp cots, a few chairs and stools, and two tables (one reserved for the writer), in an orange grove in Hammamet, overlooking the sea. Bernanos had acquired a second-hand motorcycle and, once he managed to get on, felt young again, like his declining hero in *Journal d'un curé de campagne*. But death was near. On 4 August 1947, the ninth anniversary of the family's arrival in the harbor at Rio, Yves's thirteen-month-old daughter, Sabine, died. She was buried in Hammamet.

Father Bruckberger arrived in October to get Bernanos to sign a contract to write the dialogues for a film scenario adapting Gertrud von Le Fort's *Die Letzte am Schafott* (The Song from the Scaffold, 1931). In this novel the fictional heroine, daughter of a marquis, joined the Carmelite convent at Compiègne just before the Revolution and was caught up in the drama of the historic guillotining of the sixteen nuns of that community on 17 July 1794. Starting work on the scenario just seven months before his death, Bernanos wrote the dialogues as his own health declined, achieving his greatest heights for limpid, classical language and wisdom, probing the great mysteries of life and death, love and sacrifice, strength and weakness. He sensitively follows Blanche, the heroine of these dialogues, as she flees the convent after taking a vow of martyrdom with the other nuns of the community. Eventually the Carmelites are condemned to die, and Blanche overcomes her fears to emerge luminously from the crowd at the scaffold and follow the last of her singing sisters up the guillotine steps. Although not used for Bruckberger's film, Bernanos's dialogues were published in 1949 as a drama, *Dialogues des Carmélites* and translated as *The Fearless Heart* (1952). Adapted for the stage, the dialogues became, with minimal cuts, the libretto for Francis Poulenc's 1957 opera of the same title.

Only Bernanos's last illness kept him from yet another migration, this time to Italy, with the thought of perhaps returning to South America from there. Before leaving Hammamet in January to move to a hotel in Gabès, Bernanos finished yet another important text in the form of a

Bernanos with one of his granddaughters

letter-preface addressed to Gaston Gallimard which would serve as the introduction to the French edition of *Le Chemin de la Croix-des-Ames.* In it he termed both collaboration and the Resistance "lies." In 1948 when the book appeared, wounds were still too fresh in France for Bernanos to be forgiven this lack of tact, in spite of visionary insights.

In his hotel in Gabès in January Bernanos worked on the dialogues. He celebrated his sixtieth birthday in February. A diary kept over these final months gives a terse but remarkable insight into the workings of his interior life in God as he tried to cope with the implacable forces governing his exterior life: family, health, money, and

his work. At the end of January his condition had worsened considerably, and as the months passed the possibility of an operation was discussed. An uneasy note to a friend from Brazil, Henri Jacques, a businessman, brought a plane to fly Bernanos and his wife to Paris on 21 May. He was first in a clinic, then transferred to the American Hospital on 1 June.

The young priest who attended Bernanos at the end, the future Monseigneur Daniel Pezeril, assured him prior to the operation that his work would intercede for him, but Bernanos, citing the case of the woman healed by power received from touching the garment of Jesus Christ, surprisingly replied that the same power was the source of his own work, emphasizing, "Je ne suis pas responsable de ce que j'ai créé" (I'm not responsible for what I've created). He added: "Je suis responsable de ce que je n'ai pas été" (I am responsible for what I have not been).

He survived the operation and, as he had been determined as a young veteran in 1919 to bear witness in his first novel to his wartime experience of the power of the demonic in the affairs of men, so now was he determined that his writing remain an extension of his life. He said that if indeed God did grant him life, he would set aside everything and write only the life of Jesus with which he had tantalized his publishers for years but of which he had never composed more than a few pages.

This decision would have been one of Bernanos's last, were it not for the crucial question of naming his literary executor. This problem was solved when Henri Jacques, Bernanos's executor, pleaded ignorance in literary matters and persuaded the dying author to assign the task to Albert Béguin, the Swiss critic who visited the hospital daily and who venerated Bernanos as a great prophet as well as a master novelist.

Twice on the afternoon of 4 July Bernanos said to his wife that he was caught up in the Holy Agony. He thus indicated that he knew the hour had come for him to live that mystery around which he had so carefully constructed both *Dialogues des Carmélites* and *La Joie:* the agony of Jesus Christ in the garden when facing His passion and death. Earlier that year Bernanos had written in his diary as he meditated on death, "notre mort est d'ailleurs La Sienne" (our death is really His).

He survived until dawn and received a last kiss from those present: Claude, Michel, Dominique, Guy Hattu, and the abbé Pezeril. Then, holding his wife's head to himself as she recited the Lord's Prayer and the Hail Mary, he died, repeating her name, an extraordinary beauty in death transfiguring his tortured face. He was buried in the family vault in his mother's native village of Pellevoisin.

Over the next nine years Béguin would try to bring order to one of the century's most important, yet most dispersed literary heritages, gathering Bernanos's writings from sources on both sides of the Atlantic. He moved swiftly to prepare a valuable volume of personal recollections published in 1949 to benefit the widow and children: *Georges Bernanos. Essais et témoignages* (Georges Bernanos: Essays and Personal Recollec-

tions). These recollections start with those of the abbé Lagrange and Bernanos's men of war and conclude with the narration of Bernanos's death by Daniel Pezeril, writing while he was still under the impact of the author's powerful personality.

Béguin also edited for publication *Dialogues des Carmélites,* which in subsequent years became the subject of continuing lawsuits between Father Bruckberger and the Bernanos heirs. He also published *Les Enfants humiliés,* lost during the war. The novel Bernanos had never been able to publish (he had received advances for it from both Plon and Gallimard) was edited for publication in 1950 by Béguin. This book was that ill-fated work begun in February 1931, abandoned for *Monsieur Ouine,* abortively incorporated into *Un Crime* in 1934, and, in 1935, reworked to stand on its own: *Un Mauvais Rêve.* Three years later Bernanos's postwar lectures were assembled by Béguin in *La Liberté, pour quoi faire?.*

The first complete and accurate text for *Monsieur Ouine,* edited by Béguin, was published in 1955, replacing the faulty Rio text of 1943 (which was the basis of the first English translation, *The Open Mind,* in 1945). In 1956 Béguin edited a volume of Bernanos's texts under the title *Le Crépuscule des vieux* (The Twilight of the Old Men), covering the period from 1909 to his arrival in Brazil in 1938. Béguin's untimely death in 1957 prevented him from bringing to fruition his work of collecting and editing Bernanos's correspondence. The correspondence did not appear until 1971 when the volume Béguin had begun was completed by Jean Murray. Another volume of letters, prepared by Jean-Loup Bernanos, appeared in 1983.

The last surviving son of the author has also prepared three volumes of his father's writings, some of them previously published but generally difficult to find: *Le Lendemain c'est vous* (Tomorrow Is Yours) in 1969; an edition of *La France coutre les robots,* containing important unpublished or little-known texts from Brazil, in 1970; *La Vocation spirituelle de la France* (France's Spiritual Vocation) in 1975; and *Les Prédestinés* (The Predestined Ones) in 1983. The last presents in one small volume Bernanos's essays on St. Dominic, Joan of Arc, and Martin Luther, as well as his last lecture, "Nos Amis les saints."

In 1982 a new, uncut edition of Bernanos's *Sous le soleil de Satan,* based on the original manuscript and edited by William Bush, was published by Plon, revealing, after fifty-six years, that the fullness of Bernanos's vision of the solidarity between saint and sinner existed in 1926 but had been edited out by Maritain. Finally, the volume entitled *Georges Bernanos à la merci des passants* (Georges Bernanos at the Mercy of Those Passing By) and published in 1986, a compendium of important previously published material and biographical precisions, edited by Jean-Loup Bernanos, should be mentioned as essential to understanding the literary biography of Bernanos, as is the still useful *Bernanos par lui-même* by Albert Béguin. Two volumes in Gallimard's Pléiade collection have, as it were, consecrated Bernanos: *Œuvres romanesques* (Fictional Work), published in 1961 in a volume that also includes *Dialogues des Carmélites;* and *Essais et écrits de combat* (Essays and Polemics), the first of two projected Pléiade volumes devoted to Bernanos's nonfiction, published in 1971.

Letters:

Correspondance, edited by Albert Béguin and Jean Murray, O.P., 2 volumes (Paris: Plon, 1971);

Lettres retrouvées, 1904-1948. Correspondance inédite, edited by Jean-Loup Bernanos (Paris: Plon, 1983).

Biographies:

Robert Speaight, *Georges Bernanos: A Study of the Man and the Writer* (London: Collins & Harvill, 1973);

Jean-Loup Bernanos, *Georges Bernanos à la merci des passants* (Paris: Plon, 1986).

References:

Hans Aaraas, *Georges Bernanos. Bind 1, 1888-1935* (Oslo: Gyldendal Norsk, 1959);

Hans Urs von Balthasar, *Bernanos* (Cologne & Olten: Jakob Hegner, 1954); translated by Maurice de Gandillac as *Le Chrétien Bernanos* (Paris: Seuil, 1956);

Albert Béguin, *Bernanos par lui-même* (Paris: Seuil, 1954);

Béguin, ed., *Georges Bernanos. Essais et témoignages* (Neuchâtel: La Baconnière/Paris: Seuil, 1949);

Gerda Blumenthal, *The Poetic Imagination of Georges Bernanos* (Baltimore: Johns Hopkins University Press, 1956);

Bulletin de la Société des Amis de Georges Bernanos (Paris: Société des Amis de Georges Bernanos, 1949-1969);

William Bush, *Georges Bernanos* (New York: Twayne, 1969);

Luc Estang, *Présence de Bernanos, précédé de "Dans l'amitié de Léon Bloy" de Georges Bernanos* (Paris: Plon, 1947);

Michel Estève, *Bernanos* (Paris: Gallimard, 1965);

Estève, *Georges Bernanos: Un Triple Itinéraire* (Paris: Hachette, 1981);

Jean de Fabrègues, *Bernanos tel qu'il était* (Paris: Mame, 1963);

Guy Gaucher, *Georges Bernanos ou l'invincible espérance* (Paris: Plon, 1962);

Paulus Gordon, *Freundschaft mit Bernanos* (Cologne & Olten: Jakob Hegner, 1959);

Henri Guillemin, *Regards sur Bernanos* (Paris: Gallimard, 1976);

Peter Hebblethwaite, *Bernanos: An Introduction* (London: Bowes & Bowes, 1965);

Henri Jamet, *Un Autre Bernanos* (Paris: Vitte, 1959);

Joseph Jurt, *Les Attitudes politiques de Georges Bernanos jusqu'en 1931* (Fribourg: Editions Universitaires, 1968);

Jurt, *George Bernanos. Essai de bibliographie des études en langue française consacrées à Georges Bernanos,* 3 volumes (Paris: Lettres Modernes/Minard, 1972-1975);

Max Milner, *Georges Bernanos* (Paris: Desclée & Brouwer, 1967);

Thomas Molnar, *Bernanos: His Political Thought and Prophecy* (New York: Sheed & Ward, 1960);

Hubert Sarrazin, ed., *Bernanos no Brasil* (Petropólis, Brazil: Vozes, 1968).

Papers:

The Fonds Georges Bernanos are at the Bibliothèque Nationale, Paris. The D. B. Weldon Library at the University of Western Ontario in London, Ontario, has Hubert Sarrazin's photocopies of materials from Bernanos's Brazilian period.

Maurice Blanchot

(22 September 1907-)

Jeffrey Mehlman
Boston University

BOOKS: *Thomas l'Obscur* [novel] (Paris: Gallimard, 1941);

Aminadab (Paris: Gallimard, 1942);

Comment la littérature est-elle possible? (Paris: José Corti, 1942);

Faux Pas (Paris: Gallimard, 1943);

L'Arrêt de mort (Paris: Gallimard, 1948); translated by Lydia Davis as *Death Sentence* (Barrytown, N.Y.: Station Hill, 1981);

Le Très-Haut (Paris: Gallimard, 1948);

La Part du feu (Paris: Gallimard, 1948);

Lautréamont et Sade (Paris: Editions de Minuit, 1949);

Thomas l'Obscur [récit] (Paris: Gallimard, 1950);

Au moment voulu (Paris: Gallimard, 1951); translated by Davis as *When the Time Comes* (Barrytown, N.Y.: Station Hill, 1985);

Le Ressassement éternel (Paris: Editions de Minuit, 1952); translated by Paul Auster as *Vicious Circles* (Barrytown, N.Y.: Station Hill, 1983);

Celui qui ne m'accompagnait pas (Paris: Gallimard, 1953);

L'Espace littéraire (Paris: Gallimard, 1955); translated by Ann Smock as *The Space of Literature* (Omaha: University of Nebraska Press, 1985);

Le Dernier Homme (Paris: Gallimard, 1957);

La Bête de Lascaux (Paris: G.L.M., 1958; enlarged edition, Montpellier: Fata Morgana, 1982);

Le Livre à venir (Paris: Gallimard, 1959);

L'Attente, l'oubli (Paris: Gallimard, 1962);

L'Entretien infini (Paris: Gallimard, 1969);

L'Amitié (Paris: Gallimard, 1971);

Le Pas au-delà (Paris: Gallimard, 1973);

La Folie du jour (Montpellier: Fata Morgana, 1973); translated by Davis as *The Madness of the Day* (Barrytown, N.Y.: Station Hill, 1981);

L'Ecriture du désastre (Paris: Gallimard, 1980); translated by Ann Smock as *The Writing of Disaster* (Omaha: University of Nebraska Press, 1985);

The Gaze of Orpheus, and Other Literary Essays, translated by Davis, edited by P. Adams Sitney (Barrytown, N.Y.: Station Hill, 1981);

De Kafka à Kafka (Paris: Gallimard, 1981);

The Sirens' Song: Selected Essays of Maurice Blanchot, translated by Sacha Rabinovitch, edited by Gabriel Josipovici (Bloomington: Indiana University Press, 1982; Brighton: Harvester, 1982);

Après coup, précédé de Le Ressassement éternel (Paris: Editions de Minuit, 1983);

La Communauté inavouable (Paris: Minuit, 1985);

Michel Foucault tel que je l'imagine (Montpellier: Fata Morgana, 1986); translated by Jeffrey Mehlman as *Michel Foucault as I Imagine Him* (New York: Zone Editions, 1987).

In both his fiction and criticism Maurice Blanchot, since the 1940s, has figured as one of the great austere voices of French letters. In works that have done more than any others to render in French prose a sensibility that might be described as late Heideggerian, he has made of his writing a meditation on the problematic being–or nonbeing–of language, its ultimate incompatibility with self-consciousness, the exhilarating havoc it wreaks on any claim to either objective or subjective identity. The myth that precariously presides over his work is that of Orpheus: not the poet who conquers death, but he who through art loses both the world (Eurydice) and himself (through dismemberment) in an expenditure without end. To have evoked that myth–and the self-effacing austerity with which Blanchot, to all (public) appearances, has disappeared into his work–is to hint at the specific difficulties facing his would-be literary biographer. For at one level his writing is a sustained implicit critique of the possibility of both biography and autobiography: to write, for Blanchot, is to enter into a realm whose most adequate metaphorical equivalent is death. His fiction, in particular, has tended less toward autobiography than toward what Jacques Derrida, writing of Blanchot, has called "heterothanatography": its most recurrent subject is the unsettling entry into alterity itself, the experience of the death of the *other*. In one of the author's most succinct formulations: *"Noli me legere"*: the one thing beyond any possibility of retrieval from literature is the experience of an ego—and, least of all, Blanchot's own.

The impediment on principle to any literary biography of Blanchot is further complicated by a crucial empirical obstacle: the effective obliteration from his bibliography of a considerable number of texts from the 1930s. Those articles, written (for such overtly Fascist journals as *L'Insurgé* and *Combat*) from a perspective that at least one leading scholar of the period, Zeer Sternhell, has found exemplary in its fascism, form a body of political writing so inherently scandalous in its anti-Semitism and calls to violence, and so remarkably different in tenor from both the philo-Semitism that has been a hallmark of Blanchot's critical writing and the espousal of passivity that has characterized his literary stance in general, as to constitute a stumbling block for any attempt to gauge the enigma of Blanchot's career in its entirety. It is as though the point of departure for a comprehension of the conditions of Blanchot's oeuvre lay in thinking through the articulation between the 1930s sympathizer with Charles Maurras's Royalist movement Action Française and the subsequent ideologue/practitioner of literature as "une passivité au-delà de toute passivité" (a passivity beyond all passivity). But then that point of departure, it may already be anticipated, may prove to be far more—as though the evanescence of the writing subject as conceived by Blanchot might be decisively illuminated by a strong reading of the term *rien* in Bernanos's line: "Qui a été maurrassien, et ne l'est plus, risque de n'être plus rien" (Whoever has been a Maurrassian, and no longer is one, runs the risk of no longer being anything at all).

One crucial term binding (and dividing) the two incarnations of Blanchot is *terrorisme*. Illustrative of the first is the July 1936 article "Le Terrorisme, méthode de salut public," which, in its call to acts of terror against the Blum Popular Front government, is characteristic of the texts Blanchot published in *Combat*. As a group those articles delineate the Third Republic as an infernal machine, emptying France of its reality, reducing it to a paralysis from which liberation is to be sought principally through acts of violence. The first separately published work on literature by Blanchot, *Comment la littérature est-elle possible?* (How Is Literature Possible?, 1942), presents the author's thought in the form of a discussion of Jean Paulhan's *Les Fleurs de Tarbes ou la terreur*

dans les lettres (Flowers of Tarbes or Terror in Literature, 1941). In it Terror becomes a metaphor for that literary will to virginal perception that has writers decrying "flowers" of rhetoric and clichés insofar as they are degraded forms of repetition. Blanchot's argument consists in developing the paradoxical position that Terror, thus understood, is an illusory or deluded wish engendered and enabled by an aggravation of the very linguistic forms it prides itself on being pitted against. From politics to literature, that is, terrorism has gone from being a political option to a metaphorical (antimetaphorical) impossibility.

But what interpretation ought that evolution to receive? For Blanchot, who was a Fascist out of French nationalism and who was consequently active during World War II in the orbit of the anti-German (Communist) Resistance, one can only speculate, given the author's silence, on the excruciating strain of attempting to remain faithful to both Fascist ideology and the anti-German imperative of French patriotism. Under the pressures of historical circumstance, it was his commitment to (Fascist) terrorism that was sacrificed, and the muted pain of that sacrifice (as well as the subsequent realization of how close his 1930s commitment brought him to the most disastrous of human and political commitments) has continued to resonate through the disorienting topography of "l'espace littéraire" (the space of literature). If literature, for the later Blanchot, is the realm of primordial error and unspeakability, one is hard put not to hypothesize its essential links to that original (political) error on which both he and his most lucid commentators have maintained the strictest silence.

Further light is cast on these beginnings by Blanchot's first work of fiction, "L'Idylle" (written in 1935, published in the 1952 volume *Le Ressassement éternel*, translated as *Vicious Circles* in 1983). It is in many ways the work of a young man. A "stranger" is admitted into the most sinister of institutions, a "hospice" prominently featuring a vast shower room. The colony, much touted for its totalitarian mix of kindness and severity, is obsessed by the question of whether or not its director and his wife love (as they claim) or detest each other. The sole possibility of escape for an inmate lies in marriage, a solution that ends particularly disastrously for Blanchot's protagonist. The tale, in brief, can be read as a quasi-Kafkaesque fantasy of the impasses of family life in bourgeois society. In a 1983 volume Blanchot published "L'Idylle" with a postface,

"Après coup" (Afterwards), which, because it serves as the book's title piece, is accorded more importance than the fiction itself. In that text Blanchot views the totalitarian hospice as a premonition of Auschwitz and speaks of his text as being to that extent particularly "unfortunate." And yet, however innocent of what was to follow, the text, for Blanchot, was also marked by a strange aesthetic bliss: "heureux dans l'infortune qu'il laisse pressentir et qu'il risque sans cesse de changer en attrait" (happy in the misfortune it anticipates and which it constantly runs the risk of changing into an attraction), as though it were of the essence of art to be at some level affirmative of what it relates. As he approaches the end of his career, Blanchot thus invents an imaginary relation to Fascist totalitarianism in his first piece of fiction, all the better to avoid acknowledging the far more direct relation between his own anti-Semitic texts of the same period and the fate that was later to befall the Jews during the war. What remains is the reference to Auschwitz as an absolute before which coherent narrative fails: "Récit d'avant Auschwitz. A quelque date qu'il puisse être écrit, tout récit désormais sera d'avant Auschwitz" (A tale from before Auschwitz. At whatever date it be written, every tale henceforth shall be from before Auschwitz). The imperative of fragmentation–"plus jamais de récit" (no more narratives)–which characterizes such later fictions of Blanchot as *La Folie du jour* (1973; translated as *The Madness of the Day*, 1981) here is grounded in the unspeakability of a primal reality and related to the inception of Blanchot's career as a writer of fiction. What it displaces, however, is the historical reality in which Blanchot was deeply engaged during the very years "L'Idylle" was being composed.

A bafflingly totalitarian institution, of the sort that had Blanchot, in his comments on "L'Idylle," talking of Auschwitz, is at the center of Blanchot's novel of 1942, *Aminadab*. Thomas, its protagonist, is inadvertently drawn by what he takes to be a gesture of invitation into a rooming house whose denizens are all subject to an unknown but ineluctable law imposed from the upper reaches of the house. The house proves a labyrinth in which Thomas wanders from room to room in search of the law, negotiates confusions arising from the infiltration of servants and tenants of the house into each other's ranks, comes to know a companion or doppelgänger who ends up depriving him of his very words, and finally is told that the imperative to enter

the house was not at all directed at him and that his presence there is surely an error. The novel, written in deliberately flattened prose, was the subject of an essay that Jean-Paul Sartre later incorporated in the first volume of *Situations* (1947). Sartre analyzed the work critically, accusing Blanchot of having succeeded in turning the novelistic vision of Kafka into a series of clichés. Curiously enough, the one episode Sartre qualified as "excellent" is that in which Thomas discovers that without knowing it he has been fulfilling the role of house executioner. That nightmarish revelation is of a piece with the relations sketched above: to have been an anti-Semitic journalist in the France of the 1930s meant inevitably to have a share of responsibility, however unintended, in the misfortune that was subsequently to overcome the Jews–to find oneself, in spite of oneself, executioner in the labyrinthine inferno of *Aminadab*.

In 1948 Blanchot published *Le Très-Haut* (The Most High), a novel that in its concern with the dissimulation of the Law is something of a companion volume to *Aminadab*. The book's protagonist and narrator is Henri Sorge, whose last name derives from the Heideggerian term for solicitude. He is a minor functionary whose situation is modeled on that of the Greek Orestes: a father who disappears suddenly under suspicious circumstances; a threatening but ludicrous mother known ironically as the queen; her precipitous remarriage to one of the father's colleagues; a sister obsessed with mourning and the dream of future vengeance, and so on. What is most odd about this Orestes, as Michel Foucault has pointed out, is the extent of his submissiveness. Given the violence, suffering, and epidemic illness the populace endures under a rotten regime, nothing could be more eerie than Sorge's repeated admonitions to the revolutionary Bouxx that the latter's madness casts him in the service of those he condemns, that the Law in its ruses will contrive to turn to its advantage every attack levied against it. It is as though Sorge, who speaks as a first-person narrator of the book, were disseminating the lesson inflicted on Thomas, in his estrangement, in *Aminadab*. But that lesson–of the uselessness of rebellion, of terror–is precisely the substance (or tutelary metaphor) of Blanchot's reading of Paulhan in *Comment la littérature est-elle possible?*: terror always already vitiated by its constitutional dependence on the very reality it would seek to destroy. What is oddest in the novel is that the polemic against terror is issued from within the totalitarian nightmare that was in effect, for Blanchot, its consequence. The world of the State is the last of those sinister institutions in Blanchot's fiction whose (deferred) prototype, according to the author, was Auschwitz. There is thus a particular poignancy attached to the community of survivors fixated to the painful memories which had, all the same, come to dominate their lives, the almost "liturgical" rehearsal of past suffering, and the narrator's role in it all: "Mon rôle était d'intervenir dans le récit à titre d'auditeur perpétuellement absent, mais toujours impliqué.... Pendant les psalmodies solennelles, au cours desquelles se répétait, comme s'il se fût agi d'une souffrance présente, le souvenir des jours de détresse, chacun sans doute prêtait l'oreille, mais quelqu'un de très haut écoutait aussi, quelqu'un qui par son attention donnait à ces ruminations lamentables un caractère d'espérance et de beauté" (My role was to intervene in the narrative as a perpetually absent–but implicated–listener.... During the solemn psalmodizing, in the course of which was repeated, as though a present suffering, the memory of the days of distress, each lent his ear, but someone most high also listened, someone whose attention bestowed on the lamentable ruminations a character of hope and beauty). Aesthetic passivity–or redemptive silence–here is the attribute of the witness-interlocutor of tales of institutional suffering one is hard put not to associate with the survivors of concentration camps. It is, moreover, the one episode in which the book's title appears. The new dispensation would have Blanchot make of his texts mute testimony to the shattering experience of the camps, a move whereby the author's new philo-Semitic stance is consolidated.

The year 1948, in which *Le Très-Haut* was published, was also the year in which Blanchot abandoned the novel for the genre of the shorter narrative, the *récit*. The first of these is *L'Arrêt de mort* (translated as *Death Sentence*, 1981), something of a metaphysical ghost story in which the narrator, in the work's first part, finds himself witness to (and participant in) the dying of a young woman friend, J., whose doctor has given her three weeks to live. The second part finds the narrator some years later eerily overcome by the devastating realization that Nathalie, the object of his current liaison, may indeed be J. come back from the dead. Foucault, in his consideration of the *récit*, invokes the myth of Orpheus, whose most radical implications Blanchot would later develop

in *L'Espace littéraire* (1955; translated as *The Space of Literature*, 1985). Derrida, attracted by the Mallarméan resonances of a death sentence (*arrêt*) that might impede (*arrêter*) itself, offers the hypothesis that the two women might be accomplices in the discomfiture of the male narrator (as though Blanchot had rewritten Mallarmé's *L'Après-midi d'un faune* [*The Afternoon of a Faun*, 1876]). In either case, with *L'Arrêt de mort*, Blanchot's fiction, having abandoned a phantasmagoria of the Law, would appear to have found its principal aesthetic mode: the death of the other as allegory of the writer's own otherness to himself, the dissolution of plot in a radicalized experience of repetition.

And yet *L'Arrêt de mort* contains several links with *Le Très-Haut* which modify that understanding considerably. J., for instance, the woman dying in *L'Arrêt de mort*, is described as having a sister, Louise. And Louise is the name of the Electra figure of *Le Très-Haut*. In *both* works Louise's–and J.'s–mother is referred to ironically as the "queen mother." Louise, that is, is the same in both. But if J. is Electra's sister, she must at some level be Iphigenia–sentenced to death. Once that is established, the dating of the events in part 1 of the *récit* takes on importance. J. dies in October 1938 during the most somber days of the Munich crisis–with the French army (like Agamemnon's) mobilized to no avail for an undesired war. Even (or above all) the bipartite structure of the *récit* confirms the pertinence of the Iphigenia reference. For in Euripides' *Iphigenia Among the Taurians*, Orestes is astonished to discover that the sacrificed heroine of *Iphigenia at Aulis* had in fact been saved. But 1938 was the time of the break in Blanchot's career, the liquidation of his Fascist past. It is as though in order to get on with the French nationalist cause and fight the anti-German war it had become painfully necessary to forswear his own investment in fascism–or Iphigenia. As for the allegorical sense of the second Iphigenia (Nathalie), one is tempted to see in it an anticipation of Blanchot's surprisingly vigorous participation, thirty years later, in the "events" (the student riots) of May 1968, something of a reverse return of the (political) repressed. A reading of the political tracts authored by Blanchot in 1968, and an understanding of just how much the (rightist) anti-Republican riots of February 1934 and the (leftist) ones of May 1968 had in common, go far to sustain the supposition.

The choice between Iphigenia and Orpheus, the political and the aesthetic, is also that between the (auto)biographical and the (hetero)thanatographical. Thereafter, in such *récits* as *Thomas l'Obscur* (adapted in 1950 from the novelistic version of 1941) and *Le Dernier Homme* (The Last Man, 1957), Blanchot went on to consolidate his aesthetics of the death of the other. As though a radical otherness had shattered any possibility of self-consciousness or self-expression, the very coherence of a first-person voice becomes the ultimate casualty of the strange and brilliant seizures of an intensity unto death that his works relate. In *Thomas l'Obscur* the words "il" (he) and "je" (I) enter into a relation described as "carnage." "Qui parle?" (Who is speaking?) is the opening refrain of *L'Attente, l'oubli* (Waiting, Forgetting, 1962). In *Celui qui ne m'accompagnait pas* (The One Who Didn't Accompany Me, 1953) its equivalent is: "Ecrivez-vous? écrivez-vous en ce moment?" (Are you writing? are you writing now?). In each case, as Eurydice blots out Iphigenia—and Orpheus, by implication, Agamemnon—the myth of the poet's dismemberment implicitly serves to render every attempt at literary biography hopelessly beside the point.

And yet consider what has been lost in an understanding of the texts in the process. *Au moment voulu* (translated as *When the Time Comes*, 1985), for instance, the *récit* that followed *L'Arrêt de mort* in 1951, transposes the temporal sequence of the earlier narrative to space. A narrator is undone, reduced to an "image errante" (errant image) by his oddly uneventful stay in the apartment shared by Judith, whom he once knew, and Claudia, her (Slavic) friend. Judith, that is, replaces J. (Iphigenia), and Claudia, the (Slavic) Nathalie. To the extent that the narrator is referred to by Claudia as the "ennemi" (enemy), the 1951 fiction seems better suited to Derrida's analysis of *L'Arrêt de mort* than *L'Arrêt de mort* itself. Indeed references to the two women combing—each lost in the hair of the other—and the devastating effect of the "cruel interval" between the two seem almost deliberately allusive to Mallarmé's *L'Après-midi d'un faune*. Foucault, for his part, evokes Claudia's strangely "neutral, indifferent" singing voice, "bereft of itself," in order to center his reading of the *récit* on the myth of the Sirens (to which Blanchot would devote an eloquent chapter of *Le Livre à venir* [The Future Book, 1959]): the Sirens would be to the 1951 text what Eurydice had been to the author's first *récit* in 1948.

The narrative—typically—moves toward a devastating climax, ever more abstract, ever more violent, ever more caught up in pressing its abstractions to further extremes of self-cancellation. Now that climax is accorded an odd frame by Blanchot. It is preceded by the narrator staring at length at the bombed-out facade of a synagogue: truth, he comments, does not perish easily. And toward the book's end Judith's fate is compared to that of Abraham, who, upon descending from Mount Moriah, was incapable of seeing anything but the freshly sacrificed ram in the features of his son Isaac. Those references—both contemporary and biblical—to traumatic episodes in Jewish history seem odd indeed given the aesthetic context evoked for the tale: what link might there be between the myth of the Sirens and the (near) sacrifice of Isaac? An answer may be broached by suggesting that if *Au moment voulu* is indeed a spatial transposition of the temporal sequence related in *L'Arrêt de mort*, it is fitting that a common myth—of the (near) sacrifice of the child: Isaac, Iphigenia—should inform each: Iphigenia behind Eurydice, then, and the binding of Isaac behind the Sirens. Now if the sacrifice of the 1948 text at some level relates the liquidation of Blanchot's investment in a Fascist future for France, that of the 1951 text, with its bombed-out synagogue, plainly alludes to the near-destruction of the Jews. But with the Jewish victim (Isaac) in the position of the Fascist (Iphigenia), things begin to revolve into their opposites. J.—Iphigenia herself—may be Judith, but Judith, according to the narrative, is already Abraham (Agamemnon). The configuration is that of "l'étrange roue ardente privée de centre" (the strange ardent wheel deprived of a center) which transfixes the narrator toward the end of *Au moment voulu*.

Iphigenia and Isaac; the Fascist and the Jew: to imagine the members of each of those antithetical pairs revolving into each other in a mad spin would be, perhaps, to accede to that realm of the "neutral"—neither one nor the other, but the return of their difference as the same—whose unthinkability at the core of literature Blanchot has sought, in both his fiction and criticism, to affirm. That that affirmation has, on the whole, been sustained in terms indebted to Nietzsche's eternal return has been in part responsible for its role in separating all consideration of the work from the life of its author—a life which by definition would be "human, all too human." And yet surely there is no *difference* inscribed in the work more radical than the one that has seen the

1930s anti-Semite become, for instance, a writer whose work has been received not merely as philo-Semitic but as importantly Jewish as well. The key connection here is Blanchot's association with the philosopher Emmanuel Levinas, who in his volume *Sur Maurice Blanchot* (On Maurice Blanchot, 1975) has insisted on the role of the "nomadic" in Blanchot as a means of moving beyond what remains hopelessly seigneurial and closed to the ethical in the otherwise insuperable philosophy of Heidegger. Blanchot, that is, in Levinas's reading, would allow for a Jewish critique of Heidegger. And he himself, in his numerous references to Levinas's work (in *L'Ecriture du désastre*, [1980; translated as *The Writing of Disaster*, 1985], for example) seems tacitly to have agreed.

To have forgotten the roots of such "Jewish" thought in 1930s French anti-Semitism (and the trauma it presumably underwent during the war and its aftermath) has no doubt facilitated the obliteration of the politicoethical enigma constituted by Blanchot's career in its entirety. And to that extent it has helped consolidate the hold that Orpheus–in opposition to Iphigenia–has continued to maintain on his work. Yet the work, in spite of itself, continues to allude to its own most troubling antecedents. *La Communauté inavouable* (The Unavowable Community, 1985) ultimately grounds the notion of "community" in the unspeakability of the death of the other, but the very title seems to speak of a political community–say, the 1930s contributors to *Combat*–so "unavowable" as to be beyond mention. In a moment of displaced *dis*avowal, Blanchot, in an essay on Jean-Denis Bredin's *L'Affaire* (1983; translated as *The Affair: The Case of Alfred Dreyfus*), isolates the revelation of the young Paul Valéry's

anti-Dreyfusard stance as a key moment in the book. The autobiographical import of the remark seems almost embarrassingly clear. Finally, in *L'Ecriture du désastre*, what had earlier, in *L'Espace littéraire*, been isolated as death at its most irretrievably undialectical–the dismemberment of Orpheus–finds its emblem in the para-Freudian fantasy: "On tue un enfant" (A child is being killed). For that limit-configuration–death at its most unthinkable–to have strayed (back) from the orbit of Orpheus to that of Iphigenia (and/or Isaac) is a move toward confrontation with what within the work remains most hauntingly unassimilable. All open prospects (of an explicit account of the rift in Blanchot's career around 1938) which seem endlessly intriguing, but will in all probability never materialize. For it is unclear, to revert to the Orphic paradigm, just how much of Blanchot's *art*, among the most important to have appeared in France since the war, has been written under the express condition that such confrontation at all costs be avoided.

References:

Françoise Collin, *Maurice Blanchot et la question de l'écriture* (Paris: Gallimard, 1971);

Jacques Derrida, *Parages* (Paris: Galilée, 1986);

Michel Foucault, *La Pensée du dehors* (Montpellier: Fata Morgana, 1986);

Emmanuel Levinas, *Sur Maurice Blanchot* (Montpellier: Fata Morgana, 1975);

Jeffrey Mehlman, *Legacies of Anti-Semitism in France* (Minneapolis: University of Minnesota Press, 1983);

Zeev Sternhell, *Ni droite ni gauche: l'idéologie fasciste en France* (Paris: Seuil, 1982).

Henri Bosco

(16 November 1888-4 May 1976)

Arlette M. Smith
Temple University

BOOKS: *Pierre Lampédouze* (Paris: Georges Crès, 1924);

Irénée (Paris: Gallimard, 1928);

Le Quartier de Sagesse (Paris: Gallimard, 1929);

Le Sanglier (Paris: Gallimard, 1932);

Le Trestoulas (Paris: Gallimard, 1935);

L'Ane Culotte (Paris: Gallimard, 1937); translated by Sister Mary Theresa McCarthy as *Culotte the Donkey* (Oxford: Oxford University Press, 1978);

Hyacinthe (Paris: Gallimard, 1940);

Le Jardin d'Hyacinthe (Geneva: Cheval Ailé, 1945; Paris: Gallimard, 1946);

Le Mas Théotime (Algiers: Charlot, 1945; Geneva: C. Grasset, 1946; Paris: Charlot, 1946); translated by Mervyn Savill as *The Farm Théotime* (London: Aldor, 1946); republished as *Farm in Provence* (Garden City: Doubleday, 1947);

L'Enfant et la rivière (Algiers: Charlot, 1945; Paris: Gallimard, 1953); translated by Gerard Hopkins as *The Boy and the River* (London: Oxford University Press, 1956; New York: Pantheon, 1956);

Monsieur Carre-Benoît à la campagne (Paris: Charlot, 1947); translated by Savill as *Monsieur Carre-Benoît in the Country* (London: Staples Press, 1956);

Sylvius (Paris: Gallimard, 1948);

Malicroix (Paris: Gallimard, 1948);

Le Roseau et la source (Paris: Gallimard, 1949);

Un Rameau de la nuit (Paris: Flammarion, 1950); translated by Savill as *The Dark Bough* (London: Staples Press, 1955);

Des sables à la mer: Pages marocaines (Paris: Gallimard, 1950);

Sites et mirages (Paris: Gallimard, 1951);

Antonin (Paris: Gallimard, 1952);

L'Antiquaire (Paris: Gallimard, 1954);

Les Balesta (Paris: Gallimard, 1955);

Le Renard dans l'île (Paris: Gallimard, 1956); translated by Hopkins as *The Fox in the Island* (London: Oxford University Press, 1958);

Barboche (Paris: Gallimard, 1957); translated by Hopkins (London: Oxford University Press 1959); French version republished as *Le Chien Barboche* (Paris: Gallimard, 1966); Hopkins's translation republished as *The Adventures of Pascalet* (London: Oxford University Press, 1976);

Sabinus (Paris: Gallimard, 1957);

Bargabot, suivi de Pascalet (Paris: Gallimard, 1958);

Saint Jean Bosco (Paris: Gallimard, 1959);

Un Oubli moins profond (Paris: Gallimard, 1961);

Le Chemin de Monclar (Paris: Gallimard, 1962);

L'Epervier (Paris: Gallimard, 1963);

Don Bosco (Paris: Spes, 1964); translated from the Italian by John Bennett (New York: Universe Books, 1967);

Le Jardin des Trinitaires (Paris: Gallimard, 1966);

Mon Compagnon de songes (Paris: Gallimard, 1967);

Le Récif (Paris: Gallimard, 1971);

Tante Martine (Paris: Gallimard, 1972);

Une Ombre (Paris: Gallimard, 1978).

OTHER: Jean-Cléo Godin, *Henri Bosco: Une Poétique du mystère*, preface by Bosco (Montreal: Presses de l'Université de Montréal, 1968).

Henri Bosco, primarily known as a novelist although he also produced poetry and some musical compositions, characterized himself aptly by stating that, as a writer, he did not belong to his generation. Indeed, his inspiration, his concerns, and the texture of his writings are different from those of most twentieth-century French writers who have won wide public attention and whose innovative techniques, ideological statements, and rhetorical strategies have mobilized the interest of the critics. His career spanned a period in the course of which surrealism, existentialism, structuralism, the *nouveau roman,* and other new perspectives created ferment by questioning traditional literary norms, redefining them, and opening the way to experimentation. Bosco, however, deliberately stayed away from the new trends, and in a century when such writers as

Henri Bosco (photograph by René Isner, by permission of Marseille)

André Breton, Jean-Paul Sartre, Albert Camus, Samuel Beckett, Michel Butor, Alain Robbe-Grillet, and others were blazing new trails thematically and formally, he cultivated a personal mode of writing and dealt with subjects more akin to the classical tradition.

Bosco's writings can be described as mainly introspective. He is essentially concerned with the exploration of the self, particularly when its complex and secret manifestations challenge and threaten the will and the rational faculties of the mind. His conception of the human psyche is antithetically structured: the latter is depicted as a maze of obscure, compulsive, and often destructive tendencies, feelings, and aspirations in conflict with the positive notions of lucidity, balance, and order. Bosco's predilection for the description of the inner world does not preclude a profound love of nature and a permanent sense of wonder at its creations. In his works nature is not perceived uniquely in its material presence, as an inanimate object; it is also seen as an almost sentient reality with a diffuse and mysterious ability to interact with human beings. As a result of his interest in the arcane areas of the mind, his sensitive approach to the natural world, and his thoroughly religious personality, he deals frequently with the realms of the unexplained and the unpredictable, which accounts for the importance of mystery as one of his recurrent themes.

Henri Bosco, an only child, was born in Avignon on 16 November 1888 to a family whose ancestors had emigrated from Italy earlier in the nineteenth century. He was strongly marked by the physical and human environment of his native Provence, which is represented in most of his novels by settings, characters, sayings, beliefs, and myths typical of that geographical area. His father, Louis Bosco, was an opera singer of some renown. The author describes him as a reflective and withdrawn man who found great pleasure in singing, playing the guitar, and doing delicately finished carpentry. In contrast, his mother, Louise Falena Bosco, was vivacious and excitable. She had lost four children before Henri was born and was overprotective of her son. Bosco's parents had envisaged a musical career for him, wishing him to be a conductor, and he received serious training in composition. He was distantly related to Don Bosco, an Italian saint whose biography he produced in 1959 under the title *Saint Jean Bosco.*

At the lycée of Avignon he received an excellent education in the classics and became a distinguished Latinist and Hellenist. The intellectual discipline associated with the acquisition of a classical training left a durable imprint on his literary personality. The powerfully imaginative yet controlled quality of his creative works attests to his constant regard for moderation and self-imposed limits. In the same vein the linguistic richness of his writing and the wide scope of his imagery reflect the virtuosity of his creative genius, as well as the care he exercised in keeping his talents within the bounds of good taste.

Pursuing his classical studies, he graduated from the University of Grenoble in 1909. He then attended the French Institute in Florence, Italy, where he obtained the *agrégation* degree in Italian in 1912. After teaching Italian for a year at the lycée in Avignon he was assigned, in 1913, as a teacher of French, Latin, and Greek, to a post in Philippeville, Algeria.

During World War I his military duties in the French army took him for a time to Greece, a fact which probably deepened his interest in that country whose literary tradition he already knew well. Greece was to become for him a significant source of inspiration; in 1971, for example, he published *Le Récif* (The Reef), a novel concerning an adventure which takes place on the island of Paros.

For ten years (1920-1930) he taught at the French Institute in Naples, and there he became interested in the mystery cults of antiquity and particularly in their initiation rites. The knowledge he thus acquired was to have a lasting effect on his aesthetics and on his personal philosophy. Indeed, most of his novels, *Malicroix* (1948) and *L'Antiquaire* (The Antique Dealer, 1954), among others, are structured on the model of the quest undertaken by mystagogues who, in search of knowledge or spiritual perfection, undergo a series of trials and acts of self-renunciation until they have reached the final stage of illumination and fulfillment. Self-knowledge, awareness of the divine, and the value of solitude for heightened spiritual receptivity are notions common to Bosco's philosophical views and to the traditions of esoteric religions. In 1930, upon his return to France from Naples, he married Madeleine Rhodes.

Bosco started his literary career as a poet; his earliest poetry, composed during his adolescence and which has now disappeared, was inspired by Dante and Petrarch, and it expressed philosophical concerns. Through his twenties he continued to write poems, mostly in a picturesque vein, which were a depiction of Provençal scenes. They were published in local journals such as *Les Terrasses de Lourmarin, Les Cahiers de la Collette,* and *Le Feu,* the last under the direction of Joseph d'Arbaud, a writer who was a major force in the promotion of the Provençal dialect as a vehicle of literary expression. "Les Poètes," "Eglogues de la mer" (Poems from the Sea), and "Devant le mur de pierre" (In Front of the Stone Wall) are typical of his poetry, some of which he put to music.

Finding the poetic mode unsatisfactory in conveying the depth and range of his inspiration, he turned to fiction, confessing that his poetic temperament had failed to fulfill itself completely through poetry. *Pierre Lampédouze* (1924) and *Irénée* (1928) were his first prose works to be published; neither of them, however, is representative of the profound metaphysical vein which characterizes his major work. On the contrary, they appear as stylistic experimentations, pastiches of current literary fads, witty pieces written with a humorous intention.

Pierre Lampédouze was summarized by Bosco as "l'histoire d'un homme qui part de l'artificiel et va au vrai" (the story of a man who goes from the artificial to the authentic). Pierre, the hero, who lives in Paris, at first responds wholeheartedly to the literary fads of the early 1920s, admiring such writers as Jean Cocteau, Blaise Cendrars, and Max Jacob. Then, disenchanted with the artificiality of the literary scene, he returns to his native Provence, where the slower pace of life and the respect for traditions create a climate propitious to the deepening of his inner life and to the awakening of a new concept of beauty. He ridicules the values and aesthetics which he had formerly made his own, and he expresses his denunciation through satire, irony, and incisive pastiches.

Pierre Lampédouze is also the narrator in *Irénée,* a love story written in a whimsical, humorous, and slightly affected tone: it re-creates the elegant and carefree atmosphere enjoyed by the wealthy in such Mediterranean resorts as Capri, Naples, and Ravello. The book can be categorized as a light *roman de mœurs,* a type of novel which pictures the way of life of a particular social group in a specific historical context. It does not aim at depth; rather its objective is to entertain, which it does successfully.

Bosco's next teaching assignment was Rabat, in Morocco, where he remained for twenty-four years and wrote some of his most acclaimed novels. He arrived there in 1931, and in 1932 he published *Le Sanglier* (The Wild Boar). While it may not be his most praised work, it can be considered one of the most significant because it marks a turning point in his inspiration. The nature of the topics treated, the concerns of the protago-

NEKUOMANTÉIA

ἔνθα δέ πολλαί
ψυχαὶ ἐλεύσονται νεκύων κατατεθνηώτων
ΟΔΥΣΣΕΙΑ-Χ.

Ils montent.
Longues, lentes, très douloureuses,
nos Implorations les domptent.
Ils soulèvent leurs têtes creuses.
Ils montent de la terre, ils montent,
ils montent. Rien ne brûle aux trous de leurs mémoires.
Les lamentations, hélas! les thrènes
ont écarté les mouches noires.
Ils montent tout le long des pentes souterraines.
Ce ne sont que songes sans formes.
Ils montent lentement. Ils dorment.
Une forêt immense les brise.
Ils semblent soulevés par une corde. Ils glissent
immobiles le long des Évocations.
Ce sont les morts, immense et faible nation
les morts peuple sans joie et sans mélancolie!
les morts dogues de l'âme où fleurit la lumière,
les morts aux langues abolies,
les morts tout ruisselants de nos prières,
les morts inhabités, les morts vides, si creux
qu'ils cèdent sous le poids de la Terre où soupirent
les nouvelles des vents inutilement bleus,
les morts qui nous aimaient et que l'oubli retire
du cours habituel de nos paroles, ceux
qui ne peuvent trouver de solitude pire,
les morts frêles, troués jusqu'au fond de leurs yeux,
et sur qui, éveilleur de Puissances inertes
j'ai prononcé a Chant funèbre, en suppliant
avec de faibles mots de pitié le Néant
de rendre leur tendresse à ma Ville déserte.

12. Mai 1925

Henri Bosco

Fair copy of the 1925 poem Bosco wrote in memory of his friend Robert Laurent-Vibert (courtesy of Fonds de Documentation Henri Bosco, Université de Nice). The Greek title means "Evocation of the Dead."

nists, and the tone of the narrative are all elements which inaugurate the author's new and mature concept of the art and craft of novel writing. The setting of the story is a rural area of Provence, a backdrop which will reappear in several later works. It is narrated in the first person, another standard feature of Bosco's novels, and it deals with some of his major and most persistent themes. The compulsive power of instincts, the dangerous effects of unrestrained imagination, the perception of the natural environment as a focus of active forces capable of influencing human behavior, such are the main motifs of *Le Sanglier*.

The main character, René, tells of his return to his village located at the foot of the Lubéron mountain and of a sequence of ghastly events in which he is both participant and witness. Endowed with a prolific and bizarre imagination, engrossed with his monstrous phantasms, he wishes secretly that they might become part of reality. His wish seems to materialize when he takes part in the pursuit of a group of gypsy murderers hidden in the remote recesses of the mountain. He is awestruck at the sight of a gigantic and mysterious mountain dweller accompanied by a boar of enormous size. In the course of the chase he witnesses violence and death. This accumulation of horrible events assumes a metaphorical significance, depicting the savage instincts latent in René's subconsciousness; they are a projection of the obscure and unavowed tendencies and feelings which foster his imagination. *Le Sanglier* illustrates Bosco's preoccupation with the polarity of the human psyche, especially stressing the ravages resulting from the failure of reason to assert itself as a regulating power. One should note the importance of the Lubéron, which, in this book as well as in several others, is not merely perceived as an element of the scenery; it is also felt by the author as a presence with a soul, a presence which stirs in him an aesthetic and almost sacred emotion and plays a significant role in his inspiration.

Montagne du Lubéron is the setting of Bosco's 1935 novel, *Le Trestoulas*. It deals with the theme of communication and harmony between human beings and nature and with mankind's duty to develop an attitude of conciliation toward the natural world rather than one of domination and arrogance. This short novel is the account of a sharp division between two groups of villagers about the fate of a water fount. Some want to get rid of it by filling it in; others protest against

such an interference with the natural order and insist that it be allowed to run. At the height of the controversy all water sources mysteriously dry up, making life in the village impossible and causing the inhabitants to depart. Soon afterward, however, the water starts flowing again abundantly, and nature prevails. *Le Trestoulas* has merits other than its unequivocal symbolism; it is also a dramatic depiction of village life and a vivid portrayal of the human types associated with a rural environment.

The three novels that follow *Le Trestoulas*, *L'Ane Culotte* (1937; translated as *Culotte the Donkey*, 1978), *Hyacinthe* (1940), and *Le Jardin d'Hyacinthe* (Hyacinthe's Garden, 1945) deal with the different stages of the same story and have main characters in common. Constantin Gloriot, the narrator of *L'Ane Culotte*, tells of his childhood in the village of Peïrouré, where he lives a sheltered and happy life with his grandparents, who also raise a young orphan girl, Hyacinthe. The charm, peacefulness, and innocence of country living are effectively conveyed. However, this bucolic setting is the theater of the disturbing and secret activities of Cyprien, a magician and worshiper of telluric deities who believes that happiness derives entirely from the total enjoyment of the natural and material world. He uses his powers to create a luxuriant garden, "Fleuriade," which he considers a replica of the Garden of Eden and to which he attracts many animals, holding them under his spell. The prosperity of Fleuriade rests exclusively on the strength of his knowledge of magic. Unknowingly, Constantin causes the annihilation of Cyprien's earthly paradise by breaking a branch of almond blossoms, thus exercising his free will, a forbidden act in the magician's totally subjugated universe. The story ends on a note of tragic suspense with the disappearance of Hyacinthe, who, so Constantin presumes, has been put under a spell by Cyprien and taken away by him.

Bosco wrote a very early version of *L'Ane Culotte* for a class of young students at the beginning of his career as a teacher of French. Although this novel may be read as a story for children and an imaginative treatment of the biblical myth of the lost garden, it articulates one of the basic concepts expressed in Bosco's works: the preeminence of rational and spiritual values over material phenomena. Two antinomic visions of the world are at the heart of *L'Ane Culotte*: one, symbolized by the idyllic and harmonious existence in Peïrouré, is based on a sensible appreciation for the bounties of nature; the other, represented by Fleuriade, is an expression of an excessive reverence for the dynamism of the natural world and of a surrender to its dominion.

It appears that the book was not an immediate success and was not widely known until a few years after its publication. André Gide is credited for having "discovered" it in 1945 and for having called attention to its merits. Bosco himself rated it as one of his best pieces of writing for its poetical quality and philosophical message.

Hyacinthe differs markedly from *L'Ane Culotte* in setting and in tone as well as structurally and stylistically. It is the account of the events which follow the disappearance of Hyacinthe by an unidentified narrator whose anguished mind is a web of tenuous, elusive, and indistinct feelings over which he has practically no grasp. Through him Bosco portrays the extreme metaphysical distress experienced by someone unable to discover any transcendent meaning to life, one who has lost all sense of cohesion with the world around him. The story possesses the hallucinatory quality of a dream because of the fleetingness of the narrator's state of consciousness: the events and characters give the impression of being hazy visions. Owing to his sensitive use of words and images and to the musical quality of his prose, Bosco succeeds in giving a representation of mental turmoil which is both evocative and artistic. Stressing the uniqueness of his book, he once said, "*Hyacinthe* est un livre à part, qui ne ressemble à rien. . . . La musique d'*Hyacinthe* est magique; c'est une incantation, avec une mélopée" (*Hyacinthe* is a book set apart, which resembles nothing. The music of *Hyacinthe* is magical; it is an incantation, with melopoeia).

Narrative perspective is subtly used to create uncertainty in the reader's mind as to whether the narrator's story is factual or imagined. By the narrator's account, Hyacinthe has been stolen by Cyprien, aided by a tribe of nomads, and the magician, undaunted by the failure of his first magic garden, attempts to create another one. Inspired by his demiurgic ambitions, he wants his creation to respond to his sole domination and to be free from any mental or spiritual influence except his own. To that effect he annihilates Hyacinthe's mind, and she grows up with no memory of her past, living only on the physical level. The narrator, however, claims to have been visited by her, mistakenly, as she was seeking Constantin Gloriot, after her escape from Le Domaine, Cyprien's second garden. Con-

stantin, the narrator's only neighbor across a bleak snow-covered plain, had been waiting for her return. Waiting and hope are symbolized by the light of the lamp in his window. This unusual novel ends on a note of discovery and triumph, as the words of a prayer to the Holy Spirit surge from Constantin's subconsciousness and thus signal to him the revelation of divine transcendence; Hyacinthe's search also comes to an end when she is finally reunited with Constantin, guided by the lamp which he keeps burning until she finds him. The themes of enlightenment and self-revelation give unity to this work, and the symbolism of the lamp emphasizes their importance.

The philosopher and critic Gaston Bachelard, who studied the activities of the imagination, praised Bosco and mentioned his works in several treatises. One of them, *La Flamme d'une chandelle* (A Candle's Flame, 1961), was dedicated to Bosco and deals partially with the importance of the symbolism of the lamp in *Hyacinthe*. The publication of Bosco's novel coincided with the start of World War II; partly for that reason and partly, perhaps, because its narrative form and style may have seemed disconcerting to some readers, it did not win immediate recognition.

Contrary to what one might expect, *Le Jardin d'Hyacinthe* is not a temporal sequence to *Hyacinthe*, telling Hyacinthe's story after her reunion with Constantin. It is a continuation of *L'Ane Culotte*, and it recounts, from the point of view of a different narrator, the events of the girl's life after she has been taken away by Cyprien. Méjean de Mégremut is a gentleman farmer living in the vicinity of the Lubéron mountain. In his preliminary comments he states that his purpose in telling the story is to correct the inaccuracies and the exaggerations which he had found in *Hyacinthe*. He characterizes *Hyacinthe* as bizarre and irrational and its narrator as a contemplative man so thoroughly engaged in self-exploration that he was unable to discriminate between facts and illusions. He, in turn, asserts the veracity of his own account, having known and partly raised Hyacinthe after Cyprien's nomad accomplices abandoned her. His story differs from that of the narrator in *Hyacinthe* in that he provides precise details about the different episodes of her life and about her mental condition. He tells of the failure of Cyprien's second garden, which is a metaphoric parallel to his inability to shape Hyacinthe's mind anew according to his own will. He describes the child as mentally inert throughout her adolescence until, one day,

Le Bastidon, Bosco's home at Lourmarin

Constantin, on a visit to Mégremut, recognizes her and, by calling her name, revives her memory and awakens her mental life.

Water symbolism is used predominantly, as in several of Bosco's novels. Here its importance is brought out by a secondary episode in which the flowing of water in a previously drought-stricken hamlet coincides with the revival of Hyacinthe's consciousness. This poetic tale illustrates a concept that forms part of Bosco's philosophical views, according to which the full achievement of the self can be attained only if the cerebral and spiritual activities are left unhampered, for a subjugated mind is doomed to sterility. The narrative pattern in *Le Jardin d'Hyacinthe* is the same as that in the two preceding novels: although the stories are told in the first person, singleness of perspective is avoided by the introduction of Cyprien's diary, which reveals his own outlook on the events presented previously by the narrator.

Le Mas Théotime (1945; translated as *The Farm Théotime*, 1946) introduced Bosco to a wide public and won him two literary prizes, the Prix Théophraste Renaudot (1945) and the Prix Louis Barthou de l'Académie Française (1947). Like water in *Le Jardin d'Hyacinthe*, earth is endowed with emblematic significance in *Le Mas Théotime*,

in which it has a central function in articulating the author's belief in the superiority of thought over instincts. Pascal, the protagonist-narrator, is a landowner who manages his fields with care, sensitivity, and a constant awareness of his human duty as a farmer to tame the wilderness of nature, to transform its incoherent activity into disciplined productivity. However, he does not exert a subjugating power over the soil because his authority is tempered with the intuitive conviction that nature must be wisely controlled but not annihilated. Conversely, Clodius, his cousin, yields to the fascination of the uncultivated land; he avoids all agricultural activity and encourages the spread of the wilderness, thus abdicating his human prerogative over the land, that is, taming the exuberance of the natural world. Bosco portrays this confrontation between the peasant and his land as a mythical struggle between the human species and telluric forces, bringing out the tension between man's nobler aspirations and the appeals of his physical nature. This same tension underlies Pascal's sentimental life. He rejects the deep mutual love existing between his cousin Geneviève and himself because her unrestrained and emotional temperament would weaken his effort to achieve the moderation and stability which he considers the cardinal virtues of life.

The theme of self-discipline is further stressed and assumes an extreme form when Geneviève, after a period of intense soul-searching, decides to renounce worldly life and take religious vows.

Bosco considered *Le Mas Théotime* the only geniune novel he had written because it conforms more strictly to the criteria of the genre: a plot with chronological continuity built around a crisis and displaying lifelike characters. It is, indeed, a multifaceted work in which suspense, psychological interest, and philosophical concerns fuse into a harmonious balance.

The year 1945 marked an increase in Bosco's literary productivity, since, in addition to *Le Jardin d'Hyacinthe* and *Le Mas Théotime*, he produced *L'Enfant et la rivière* (translated as *The Boy and the River*, 1956). That year he retired from the teaching profession, which allowed him to devote the last thirty years of his life exclusively to literary activities. Instead of returning to France, he chose to spend ten more years in Morocco. *L'Enfant et la rivière* is a treatment of the rediscovery of childhood, and without being an actual autobiography, it contains some of the memories, dreams, and longings of the author's early years, when he was living in the countryside of Avignon, in Provence. According to Jean-Cléo Godin in *Henri Bosco: Une Poétique du mystère* (1968), the river which plays such an important part in the book is modeled on the Durance, which inspired the young Bosco with a feeling of fascination and awe the first time he saw it. The novel is written in simple, poetic prose, and the author succeeds in conveying the sense of wonder, the freshness of vision of a child attentive to the sights, sounds, and smells of outdoor life in the country. The charm of *L'Enfant et la rivière* resides in the poetic descriptions, as well as in the subtle evocation of the awakening of a child's aesthetic sensitivity. Bosco gives an implicit treatment of the Paradise motif, which is recurrent in his works. Two children, Pascalet and Gatzo, embark upon a trip on the river, and, during their escapade, they live in a world which they perceive as new because they see it for the first time in its authenticity, from a perspective that is neither utilitarian nor human-centered. The pristine quality of the universe thus revealed to them identifies it with the Garden of Eden. Water symbolism here has a dual significance: it represents the object of Pascalet's yearnings, that river he had longed to see but could not because it was flowing beyond his sight, in the distance; it also signifies the culmination of joy and freedom, when the two boys, let-

ting their boat wander at leisure, gaze at the beauty of the surrounding scenery.

Childhood is one of Bosco's favorite themes, and it is the subject of *Le Renard dans l'île* (1956; translated as *The Fox in the Island*, 1958), *Barboche* (1957; translated, 1959), and *Bargabot* (1958), three novels related to *L'Enfant et la rivière;* they are sometimes referred to as the Pascalet cycle. All drawing on the same inspiration, they are reminiscent of the places and people familiar to the author in his early youth.

Monsieur Carre-Benoît à la campagne (1947; translated as *Monsieur Carre-Benoît in the Country*, 1956) revealed a new facet of the author's creative talent: a vein of light satire directed at the world of business, financial speculation, and bureaucracy. It is the story of the corruption and deterioration of a small rural community when it falls prey to the dishonest commercial tactics of Bourmadier, a liquor manufacturer from the city. Monsieur Carre-Benoît, a recently retired bureaucrat portrayed as a literal-minded man of limited intelligence, assists Bourmadier in his plans and, without being aware of the fraud in which he is involved, helps bring about the ruin of the villagers. The whole enterprise ultimately fails, however, owing to the secret maneuvers of the village lawyer, Monsieur Ratou, who makes it his duty to preserve the integrity of solid mores and rural values. From a thematic point of view, *Monsieur Carre-Benoît à la campagne* deviates from the author's aesthetic principles according to which social and political concerns are not proper literary topics because they are incompatible with artistic intents. Bosco's novel, however, is not a *roman à thèse;* the derisive tone which pervades it and the one-dimensionality of the characters provoke amused disbelief rather than serious reflection.

Sylvius (1948) deals with the recurring theme of the journey as a metaphor for the fulfillment of a yearning which the conventions and routine of daily life render impossible. In the tradition of Constantin in *L'Ane Culotte* and Pascalet in *L'Enfant et la rivière*, who yield to the temptation to see beyond the boundaries of their familiar horizon, Sylvius Mégremut, an elderly farmer of sedentary habits, decides to join a group of migrant comedians. His family sets out to look for him and finds him living happily among the comedians and displaying a genuine musical talent which had been unsuspected previously. According to a mutual agreement, he is to spend half of the year with his family in their native village and the other half traveling with his new friends. But unexpectedly, after fulfilling the first part of the pact, as he is about to join the actors, he becomes sick and dies. The quest pattern which underlies many of Bosco's novels is recognizable here, as is the theme of self-revelation, achieved by the hero after he has put aside accepted imperatives and customs of his current life. In this novel Bosco expresses a philosophical concern which relates to the process of the discovery of the authentic self deeply hidden in the depths of the psyche. In Sylvius's case, his musical sensitivity represents the most genuine aspect of his personality, which had been stifled by the pragmatism which he had demonstrated for most of his life.

Malicroix, also published in 1948, offers some similarities with *Sylvius* structurally and thematically. Bosco considered *Malicroix* his best piece of fiction and ranked it his favorite. It was enthusiastically received by the public and won the Prix des Ambassadeurs. It remains one of the author's most widely read works. He called it a poem, specifying that the only generically authentic novel he had written was *Le Mas Théotime.* It may be argued, however, that *Malicroix* is also a novel, for, in addition to its remarkable poetic merits, its rich and evocative prose provides a strongly structured and captivating plot. It contains some of the author's persistent themes: solitude, introspection, the antinomic duality of the self, and acquisition of self-knowledge viewed as an initiation process.

Martial de Mégremut, the protagonist, is the last descendant of two families characterized by the antithetic nature of their temperaments: the Malicroix, rugged, independent, intransigent; and the Mégremuts, gentle, accommodating, and endowed with an indefectible sense of family solidarity. At the start of the story Martial, the narrator, learns of the death of his great-uncle, Cornélius Malicroix, who has named him his heir. Martial decides to undertake the journey to La Redousse, the inhospitable, weather-beaten island in the Rhône river where Cornélius had lived in almost complete solitude. As a typical, sedentary, quiet Mégremut, he is fearful of the unexpected and feels unprepared for the circumstances which lie ahead of him. His stay on the island proves, indeed, to be trying; it assumes the significance of a religious initiation, as he overcomes successive challenges which test his patience, his fortitude, his self-confidence. He endures successfully atmospheric disturbances of major proportions, isolation, danger, and hostil-

ity from those who covet his inheritance, and he realizes in the process that he possesses all the strong virtues associated with the Malicroix, virtues which had remained latent in him so far. "La goutte de sang Malicroix" (the drop of the Malicroix blood) running through his veins, which allows him to surmount those threatening situations, manifests its power. He becomes aware of his true nature which, contrary to his own self-perception, is daring and heroic.

Following *Malicroix,* in 1949 a collection of Bosco's poetry, *Le Roseau et la source* (The Reed and the Spring), appeared. It contains poems which had been published previously in various literary reviews, as well as new ones. Most of them follow the same thematic traditions as his major novels, re-creating such Provençal sites as the Lubéron, while others, reflecting a mystical inspiration, evoke the familiar notion of the spiritual pilgrimage toward enlightenment. Some poems echo personal feelings, such as the mourning of a friend. The simplicity and directness of Bosco's poetic diction, suited to the feelings expressed, are among the merits of the work.

The relationship between identity and duality constitutes the central theme of the quasi-fantastic *Un Rameau de la nuit* (1950; translated as *The Dark Bough,* 1955). The hero, Frédéric Meyrel, experiences a gradual change of identity and assumes mysteriously the personality and feelings of a man unknown to him, Bernard Dumontel, who has been dead for several years. Bernard and his niece Clotilde had fallen in love with each other, but, in order to avoid an incestuous relationship, he had gone away, dying while he was abroad. Like most of Bosco's heroes, Frédéric is engaged in an inner conflict which opposes the two aspects of his personality, for, in this case, Bernard is actually a metaphoric representation of a level of the self attempting to rise above the other and to overshadow it. Bernard symbolizes the illicit and deeply repressed human tendencies endeavoring to surface and to dominate. Indeed, as Bernard progressively takes possession of Frédéric's mind, he also transfers to him his love for Clotilde so that its consummation might be effected through his alter ego, Frédéric. *Un Rameau de la nuit* is one of Bosco's most somber novels, for it portrays a hero almost totally overpowered by adverse forces. Frédéric is agonizingly torn between his concern to remain himself and the powerful sensual attraction exerted on him by Clotilde, and which, should he surrender to it, would mean a complete abdica-

Bosco's study at Le Bastidon

tion of his identity in favor of Bernard's. The book does not, however, end with a defeat but, as is often the case with Bosco, with the implication that the protagonist has succeeded in casting away the obscure and evil forces at work against him and that he is progressing toward enlightenment. Frédéric recognizes that he has gone through a period of aberration which almost cost him his mental equilibrium, but he also understands that by telling his story he has exorcised his demons. Having recovered his wholeness and reconciled the bewildering tensions which had polarized his self-perception, he yearns to discover the unity of the divine presence. To that effect, his final wish is to return to the village church in search of the holy man, Elzéar, whose simple and serene faith in God he longs to experience.

Un Rameau de la nuit is a rich and complex book; the metaphysical and psychological notions expressed are skillfully integrated into the narrative and do not overshadow its artistic merits: its suspense, mystery, and poetry. As usual in Bosco's work, the role of nature is significant, and the description of its different aspects is used to connote metonymic relations between the mental states, moral qualities, and emotional conditions of the protagonists and their environment. The lush and oppressive Loselée forest,

for example, conveys Frédéric's sexual obsession and his helplessness to combat it.

The two works that followed *Un Rameau de la nuit*, *Des sables à la mer: Pages marocaines* (Between Sand and Sea: Moroccan Pages, 1950) and *Sites et mirages* (1951), mark a departure from the rest of the author's work with their settings which are Morocco and Algeria respectively. Morocco, where Bosco spent twenty-four years, was his second home. In addition to his teaching duties and to the writing of his works, he was president of the cultural association L'Alliance Française and founder of a journal, *Aguedal;* he also contributed articles to publications both in France and North Africa. His interest in philosophical and religious matters led him to acquaint himself with the Islamic faith with the assistance of some of his friends, among whom were the novelist François Bonjean and Dr. Joseph Mardrus, who translated the *Arabian Nights* and had a profound knowledge of Arab mysticism and of Sufism. His metaphysical preoccupations were echoed, and probably heightened, by his contact with the teachings of Islam and by the spiritual vision of its thinkers.

Des sables à la mer and *Sites et mirages* deal with topics related to realities of North Africa. Both works were written at the request of Bosco's publisher. *Des sables à la mer* reflects the descriptive talents of the author as well as his contemplative temperament. The Moroccan cities, countryside, and holy places are presented in their tangible reality, but, more important, the sight of them inspires the author to dream, to meditate, or to ponder. As a result the interest of the work rests less on its picturesque aspect and more on its conceptual value as the author reflects on such themes as the divine presence, the life of the soul, and solitude.

Sites et mirages was first written to serve as a commentary for an illustrated book which was published in a limited edition with a series of Algerian scenes by the artist Albert Maquet. But such were the literary merits of Bosco's text that it was published separately in 1951 without the visual component which had first motivated its writing. *Sites et mirages* consists mainly of the author's memories of Algeria, his reactions to the Algerian scene, and his musings. The book is striking in its diversity: it contains elements of a travel diary and also some aspects of the essay, occasionally interspersed with short passages of poetry. In addition it reproduces the lyrics and music of a song celebrating the intrepidity of the pirate Thomas Bosco, the author's legendary ancestor believed to have defeated many a Turkish corsair along the Barbary Coast.

Antonin (1952) indicates Bosco's return to some of his more familiar topics, the privileged world of childhood and the quest for Paradise as metaphors of perfect innocence and happiness. The work contains events and situations fictionalized from the author's childhood. Young Antonin is entrusted to the care of friends during his parents' prolonged absence; young Henri Bosco had also been deprived of his parents' presence as a result of his father's artistic engagements, which kept the couple away from home for weeks at a time. The feeling of loneliness experienced by Antonin and his propensity to daydream are certainly reminiscences of Bosco's early youth. Antonin, an imaginative boy, transfigures the elements of his daily life, which is spent in the Avignon countryside. Some characters, such as Cassius and Barnabé, the hunchback owners of the grocery store, fill him with terror, and in the child's consciousness they assume the dimension of demonic figures. In contrast, his friendship with his playmate Marie, who shares his poetic and idyllic vision of life, personifies beauty, innocence, and happiness. The myth of the Garden of Eden underlies the development of events. Evil, brought out by the maliciousness

of the hunchbacks, causes the departure of Marie and, consequently, the separation of the children, an episode which can be read as the loss of Paradise. Lonely and dejected, Antonin is determined to find Marie, and he undertakes a journey to Almuradiel, a place totally unknown to him, where he is convinced he will find her. When he reaches his destination, he discovers an enclosed garden of extraordinary peace and beauty and experiences a feeling of bliss approaching ecstasy, which he interprets as the imminence of Marie's coming. The recovery of Paradise after a life marked by loneliness and trials is strongly connoted by Antonin's arrival in Almuradiel, the place of total fulfillment. Bosco's preoccupation with good, evil, the misfortunes of life, the definition of guilt, and other such profound concerns form the thematic core of this work. However, despite the sternness of those notions, the story retains a quality of serenity, purity, and simplicity because of the author's ability to write from the children's point of view and to render the authenticity of their vision.

Bosco's period of intense literary activity continued with the publication of *L'Antiquaire*, which is regarded as one of his most hermetic novels, a judgment shared by the author himself. The plot and characterization, as well as Bosco's concepts, are conveyed through a complicated symbolism often related to astrology and to some of the mystery cults of antiquity. Consequently, the significance of the book depends, to a certain extent, on the reader's familiarity with the symbolic representations used.

One of the main themes is metaphysical isolation. The spiritual void experienced by Baroudiel, the narrator, is the central notion of this novel and its strongest organizing feature. Neither the pleasures of the mind nor those of the senses have helped Baroudiel find any meaning to life or discover any profound truth about himself. Like the mystagogue figures frequently found in Bosco's works, he is confronted with temptations, challenges, and trials typical of a spiritual pilgrimage, and he finally reaches "la Voie" (the Way), the rewarding outcome of his search. After refusing to be subjugated by the powers which rule world of matter and rejecting the hegemony of the intellect, he disappears, thus leaving the impression that his quest has ended in failure. In his works Bosco usually avoids any clear-cut denouement, preferring only to suggest the conclusion. So it is with *L'Antiquaire:* no explicit detail is given about Baroudiel's final fate,

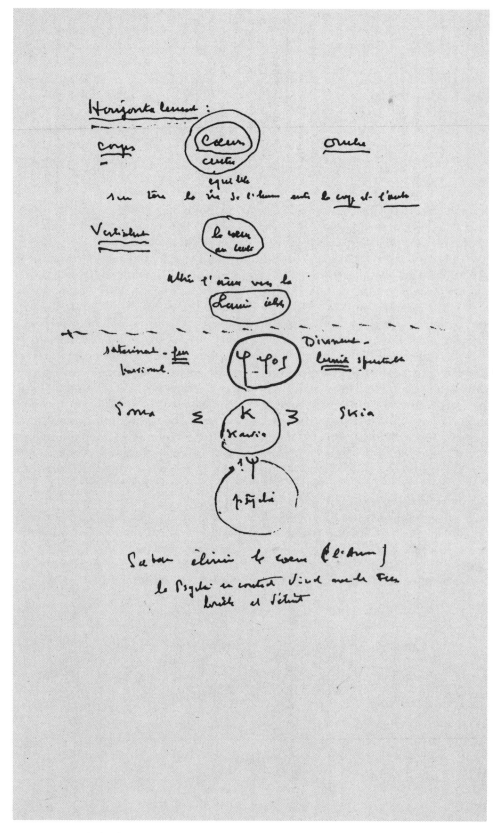

Page from the notes Bosco attached to his manuscript for Une Ombre, *the unfinished novel posthumously published in 1978 (by permission of Prof. L. Van Bogaert)*

yet it is implied that his search comes to an end after he discovers that only faith in divine transcendence can bring an end to his anguish.

The complexity of *L'Antiquaire* does not limit its undeniable merits. The novel contains, indeed, some of the most compelling imaginary and symbolic settings ever created by the author. The description of the subterranean abode of the Sourbidouze brothers, worshipers of the Earth deity, and the representation of the room-size aquarium in which an ever-changing display of colors, forms, and motion suggests the futility of the world of appearances are endowed with a strong power of suggestion. Bosco's technique in *L'Antiquaire* conveys the concerns of a thinker, reveals the narrative skill of a novelist, and, finally, communicates the vision of a poet.

In 1955 Bosco left Morocco definitively and returned to Provence. He settled in Nice in a house which became known as La Maison Rose (The Pink House) and continued to live an active and diverse life. He went on with his creative work, delivered lectures, and was appointed a member of the Conseil de l'Université de Nice or university board of trustees. Several times he was called upon to preside over literary juries. He spent his time either in Nice or in Lourmarin, a community at the foot of the Lubéron mountain, where he owned a country home. During the war he had made the acquaintance of Robert Laurent-Vibert, a scholar of classical literature and arts who was the proprietor of a chateau in Lourmarin. A lasting friendship developed between the two men. Laurent-Vibert undertook to turn his chateau into a cultural foundation with the help of Bosco, who, after Laurent-Vibert's death, continued working on the project, brought it to completion, and became one of the foundation's board members.

Les Balesta (The Balestas, 1955) is the first in a trilogy of novels comprising the chronicle of a closely knit family whose story presents some similarities with the author's. Like the Boscos, the Balestas' ancestors emigrate from Italy in the late nineteenth century and settle in Provence, where they have some of the experiences the Bosco family had during the early stages of their life there. The other novels of the trilogy are *Sabinus* (1957) and *L'Epervier* (The Hawk, 1963).

The trilogy can be read as a treatment of the problem of evil: its ambiguity, the fatality of its occurrence, its control over human beings, and the different strategies used in order to escape it or to minimize its effects. Joachim

Balesta, the narrator of the trilogy, re-creates events in the life of his family who lived in the previous century and participated in events that transpire in *L'Epervier*. Joachim's purpose is to elucidate a strange belief held by the Balestas. According to family rumors handed down, the Balestas, admired for their congeniality and their generosity, are said to be the recipients of a mysterious gift referred to as "le don," which, quite independently from their will, exerts the most severe revenge against anyone who causes them harm. The power of "le don" is dreaded by the Balestas, who are naturally forgiving, and, deploring the implacability of the avenging force, they try to prevent its intervention by behaving in exemplary fashion, so as to discourage the neighbors' hostility and ill-treatment.

Les Balesta is a statement on the unpredictability of evil. The story centers on the life of Melchior Balesta, a peaceful craftsman who spends his time making small wooden Christmas figurines known as *santons* and playing the harp. He is twice the victim of an act of calculated malice. In his youth he suffers a broken heart when he is separated from Elodie, the girl he loves, as the result of the machinations of Justine, a jealous young woman; soon afterward Justine becomes incurably insane, which is regarded as the retaliatory action of "le don." As a middle-aged man he falls prey to the wiles of Ameline-Amelande, a seductive and demonic woman whom he takes as his wife. She succeeds in alienating him from his family and in causing their financial ruin. When, as a sick and dying man, he finally realizes the depth of his wife's malice, he escapes from their home and returns to his family, from whom he begs forgiveness. No harm, however, comes to Ameline-Amelande in spite of her wrongdoings. The two major events in Melchior's life illustrate the inconsistency of evil and the erratic character of its manifestations. Thus, the very essence of evil is called into question, because it is shown to partake of two contradictory concepts: it is sometimes an instrument of justice and at other times a condoner of wrongdoing.

The resigned and fearful attitude of the Balestas in relation to "le don" assumes thematic significance in both *Sabinus* and *L'Epervier*, in which the problem of finding an appropriate response to adversity and to evildoers becomes the main preoccupation of the protagonists. Sabinus, the central character in the second novel of the trilogy, a Balesta from the sailors' branch of the family, holds that there is no validity to the existence of "le don," which he considers the creation of superstitious minds. He further believes that the only way to counter evil is to fight it with all possible means. Bosco seems to have used his legendary ancestor Thomas Bosco as a model for Sabinus. The seafaring Sabinus undertakes to take revenge on Ameline-Amelande for her malicious deeds against his family, and, through a series of stratagems, he succeeds in defeating her, thus restoring the Balestas to their former position and status in the village. Bosco's predilection for antinomic patterns is reflected by the contrasts between Sabinus and his rural cousins. His feisty and self-assured temperament and his incredulity concerning "le don" are in direct contradiction with the rest of the family's conciliatory and sometimes fearful nature.

This opposition between the two branches of the Balesta family becomes the thematic focus of the last novel of the cycle, *L'Epervier*, as Joachim Balesta, the last descendant of the family, inherits the contradictory character traits of both branches of his ascendancy. As a typical Bosco protagonist, he strives to define his own personality and to find out which of its two aspects is more deeply entrenched in him. In the course of a visit to Pierrelousse, his ancestral village, prompted by a sentimental need to view this special place, he becomes embroiled in a network of intrigues and is the victim of the pettiness and malice of its inhabitants. Having to choose between forgiveness or retaliation, he decides in favor of revenge, inspired by his admiration for Sabinus. His identification with the latter is also expressed metonymically by his growing fascination with the sea.

In the trilogy, as in most of Bosco's writings, the plot and the characters operate on several levels of signification. In *Sabinus* the complexities created by a dual and conflicting heredity are images used to concretize two conceptions of life: one, action-oriented, stresses pragmatism, while the other, more meditative, is open to mystery and faith. *Sabinus* does not provide an answer to the perplexities caused by the manifestations of evil, and, in this respect, it does not offer a solution to the problems examined throughout the trilogy. Neither does Joachim's choice to challenge evil and to defend himself from its effects reflect any rhetorical intent from Bosco, who, in fact, condemned didactic fiction. The Balesta chronicle is in essence another of Bosco's treatments of evil which reveals the great extent to which the author was concerned with the metaphysical dimension of human existence.

As he was completing *Sabinus*, Bosco remarked that while he was working on the novel he had been writing down some childhood memories as a diversion from the difficulties involved in bringing the Balesta cycle to a satisfactory end. In the 1960s three books of memoirs were then published: *Un Oubli moins profond* (Saved From Total Oblivion, 1961), *Le Chemin de Monclar* (The Monclar Road, 1962), and *Le Jardin des Trinitaires* (The Trinitarian Garden, 1966). In these works Bosco describes himself as a lonely, observant, and imaginative child, receptive to the mystery he perceived in the surrounding countryside. He emerges as the prototype of Antonin, Pascalet, and Constantin Gloriot, the child protagonists in his novels. One of his last works dealing with his childhood years is *Mon Compagnon de songes* (My Fellow Dreamer, 1967). Although it contains identifiable autobiographical elements, it is generally distinct from the previous childhood memoirs, having undergone fictionalization to a degree which places it in the category of Bosco's novels.

Bosco's meditation on the duality of the human psyche and on the dynamics created by the pull of antithetic tendencies informed his fictional work until his death. *Le Récif*, one of his last novels, is a dramatization of the opposition between positive and negative values which compete for a man's allegiance. A distinctive feature of this work is that one of its settings is the sea, which also functions symbolically as a perfidious and demonic force.

The author makes use of two narrative voices. Jérome Moneval-Yssel is the main narrator who, after reading the diary of his cousin Markos, whose disappearance during a trip to Greece remains a mystery, decides to follow Markos's itinerary in order to discover the circumstances of this strange event. As the main narrator, he provides the information necessary to situate the plot, and his introduction is followed by the diary of Markos, who thus becomes the second narrator. Jérome picks up the narration to describe his own experiences in Greece as he tries to reconstruct the events which led Markos to his fate. The novel can be read as a mythological allegory in which the characters function as representations of moral and metaphysical notions rather than as individuals with distinctive psychological traits.

Markos, an imaginative man, receptive to mystery, had been asked by his friend Manoulakis to go to Greece on an exorcism mission: a Christian sanctuary located on the top of a reef was about to fall under the domination of the pagan deities who had been forced to retreat to the bottom of the sea at the advent of Christianity. In this drama of mythical dimension Markos embodies the defense of the good, and as such, his role is to keep the lamps of the sanctuary burning in order to prevent the intrusion of the pagan gods, symbols of demonic powers. Markos's flaw is his excessive imagination which, in his case, opens the way to temptation by the pagan deities, who attract him to their abode in the depths of the sea. His immersion signals the loss of saving grace and the failure of his mission. Indelibly marked by his contact with the world of evil, he finds no satisfaction after his return home, and he disappears definitively during a second trip to Greece, presumably having joined the pagan gods forever. Markos's doom, however, does not signify the final defeat of good, for in spite of his defection, the lamps in the sanctuary are kept burning by Diakos, a young boy who assumes a sacrificial and redeeming role. When Jérome goes to Greece he undergoes the same trials as Markos, but he does not fall prey to the phantasms of imagination, and he maintains an indefectible faith in the Christian God. Owing to his steadfast religious beliefs and to the sincerity of his prayers, the sanctuary is exorcised.

Although the pseudomythological setting may represent a new aspect of Bosco's fictional work, the familiar notion is articulated concerning the role of the rational faculties as agents of moderation and order as well as a source of inner strength. In *Le Récif* there is an evident syntagmatic connection between evil, the hegemony of the imagination, on the one hand, and, on the other, the search for God, the virtues of self-knowledge and self-control. By the contrast it provides, the technique of a dual narrative perspective gives greater scope to the subject by showing how and why Markos and Jérome respond so differently to the same situation. Jérome's vigilant faith is brought into sharper contrast by Markos's vulnerability to temptation.

In *Le Récif* Bosco's religious concerns are more explicit, and they are explored in greater depth than in the rest of his fiction: the themes of prayer, of the relationship to God, of salvation and doom are strongly stressed. Although elsewhere his conceptions of the spiritual quest, of purification, and of the exploration of the self are undoubtedly linked to the notion of divine transcendence, they are not as obviously related to any specific religious tradition as they are in this novel, in which the Christian God and the deities of the pagan world are explicitly mentioned. In *Le Récif* the perennial conflict between good and evil is metaphorically represented within the context of two definite religious systems.

Tante Martine (Aunt Martine, 1972) is the last of Bosco's works devoted to fictionalized childhood memories. The main character, Martine, has a real model: she was Bosco's favorite aunt. She is presented as a loving, wise old woman whose occasional grumpiness and habitual scoldings are a mask for her great sensitivity and for her affection for her nephew, placed in her charge during his parents' frequent trips. The atmosphere re-created by the author is a blend of factual description of rural life with episodes that are striking in their eeriness and legendlike quality, such as the story about the mysterious trees which retain the souls of the dead captive under their bark. Bosco was eighty-four when he wrote *Tante Martine*, yet the memory of his early years seems to have remained fresh and emotionally rich.

Shortly after completing *Tante Martine*, the author began writing what was to be his last work, *Une Ombre* (A Shadow, 1978). It is an unfinished novel, interrupted by his death, which occurred in May 1976. Bosco had, however, proofread the manuscript and remarked that he had approximately fifty pages to write in order to finish the novel. There is similarity between the narrative pattern of *Une Ombre* and that of *Le Récif:* one narrator tells his story, and some fifty years later one of his descendants comments on it. The substance of the work revolves around the tenuous distinction between dream and reality. The reader is left wondering whether the first man was telling a dream or an actual event and whether the second man's comments are the elucidation of a factual episode or simply phantasms. This theme is represented symbolically by the recurring apparition of a shadow who causes the narrator to wonder constantly about the notions of substance and appearance. One of the merits of the book is the highly poetic quality of the language, which possesses a richness and a subtleness worthy of Bosco's best writings.

Henri Bosco's reputation rests on the qualities which define his originality with regard to other twentieth-century writers. He remains known for his poetic language and for the spiritual dimension of his works, his conception of life as a search for the divine and as a process of mortification and purification leading to deeper insight into the self. His freedom from generic constraints is another feature of his aesthetics that retains the attention of readers: his works defy attempts at rigid classification, partaking of autobiography, the tale, the diary form, allegory, the detective story, and other genres. His multifaceted creativity is one of the elements which has brought him recognition. His preoccupation with the dynamics of imagination imparts a distinctive cachet to his works.

Bosco's admirers founded the Fonds de Documentation Henri Bosco, a resource center containing his manuscripts, correspondence, and other material relating to his life and works. It is located at the library of the Université de Nice and is open to the growing circle of Bosco scholars. Three years before his death L'Amitié Henri Bosco was created. An association whose purpose is to maintain and develop interest in the author, it publishes *Cahiers Bosco*.

During his long career Bosco received several honors: the Grand Prix de la Méditerranée in 1965, the Grand Prix de l'Académie de Vaucluse in 1967, and the Grand Prix du Roman de l'Académie Française in 1968. In addition he was made Commandeur de la Légion d'Honneur. He had also received several military decorations during World War I.

References:

L'Art de Henri Bosco, papers from the third Henri Bosco colloquium, Nice, May 1979 (Paris: José Corti, 1981);

Gaston Bachelard, *La Flamme d'une chandelle* (Paris: Presses Universitaires de France, 1961);

Bachelard, *La Poétique de l'espace* (Paris: Presses Universitaires de France, 1957);

Michel Barbier, *Symbolisme de la maison dans l'œuvre d'Henri Bosco* (Aix-en-Provence: Faculté de Lettres, 1966);

Germaine Brée and Margaret Guiton, *An Age of Fiction: The French Novel from Gide to Camus* (New Brunswick: Rutgers University Press, 1955), pp. 105-107;

Bulletin Henri Bosco, 1 volume (Nice: Université de Nice, 1972); continues as *Cahiers de l'Amitie Henri Bosco*, 19 volumes (1973-1980); continues as *Cahiers Bosco* (Nice: L'Amitie Henri Bosco, 1981-);

Jean-Pierre Cauvin, *Henri Bosco et la poétique du sacré* (Paris: Klincksieck, 1974);

Claude Girault, *Regard sur l'œuvre d'Henri Bosco* (Lyons: Audin, 1966);

Jean-Cléo Godin, *Henri Bosco: Une Poétique du mystère* (Montreal: Presses de l'Université de Montréal, 1968);

Michel Guiomar, *Miroir des ténèbres: Images et reflets du double démoniaque*, volumes 1 and 3 (Paris: José Corti, 1984);

Simone Hilling, "Henri Bosco: Vérité biographique et création romanesque," *French Review*, 38 (January 1965): 362-370;

Jean Lambert, *Un Voyageur des deux mondes* (Paris: Gallimard, 1951);

Jacqueline Michel, *Liturgie de la lumière nocturne dans les récits de Henri Bosco* (Paris: Lettres Modernes, 1982);

Lionel Poitras, *Henri Bosco et la participation au monde* (Fribourg: Editions Universitaires, 1971);

John Prince, "New Light on the Origins and Symbolism of *Malicroix*," *French Review*, 47 (March 1974): 773-782;

Le Réel et l'imaginaire dans d'l'œuvre de Henri Bosco, papers from the second Henri Bosco colloquium, Nice, March 1975 (Paris: José Corti, 1976);

Arlette Smith, "Les Gens de la terre dans l'œuvré romanesque d'Henri Bosco," *French Review*, 59 (October 1985): 65-73;

Jean Susini, *Henri Bosco, explorateur de l'Invisible* (Alès: Editions Brabo, 1959);

William Van Grit, "Interview avec Henri Bosco," *French Review*, 47 (April 1974): 882-888.

Papers:

Bosco's papers, including manuscripts and correspondence, are in the Fonds de Documentation Henri Bosco at the Université de Nice.

Joë Bousquet

(19 March 1897-28 September 1950)

Joseph Brami
Massachusetts Institute of Technology

BOOKS: *Il ne fait pas assez noir* (Paris: Debresse, 1932);

Le Rendez-vous d'un soir d'hiver (Paris: Debresse, 1933);

Une Passante bleue et blonde (Paris: Debresse, 1934);

La Tisane de sarments (Paris: Denoël & Steele, 1936);

Le Mal d'enfance (Paris: Denoël, 1939);

Traduit du silence (Brussels: Cahiers du "Journal des Poètes," 1939; revised edition, Paris: Gallimard, 1941);

Le Passeur s'est endormi (Paris: Denoël, 1939);

Iris et Petite Fumée (Paris: G.L.M., 1939);

Le Médisant par bonté: Histoire d'avares, de fols, de peulucres, contarailles et contaraignes, complétées par une note de Frérot sur la médisance (Paris: Gallimard, 1945);

La Connaissance du soir (Paris: Editions du Raisin, 1945; revised edition, Paris: Gallimard, 1947);

Le Meneur de lune (Paris: J.-B. Janin, 1946); revised in *Œuvre romanesque complète*, volume 2 (1982);

La Neige d'un autre âge (Paris: Cercle du Livre, 1952); revised in *Œuvre romanesque complète*, volume 2 (1982);

Les Capitales; ou, De Jean Duns Scot à Jean Paulhan (Paris: Cercle du Livre, 1955);

Langage entier (Limoges: Rougerie, 1966);

Notes d'inconnaissance (Limoges: Rougerie, 1967);

Le Sème-chemins (Limoges: Rougerie, 1968);

Le Pays des armes rouillées (Limoges: Rougerie, 1969);

D'une autre vie (Limoges: Rougerie, 1970);

Mystique (Paris: Gallimard, 1973);

L'Homme dont je mourrai (Limoges: Rougerie, 1974);

La Romance du seuil, suivi de Poésie (Limoges: Rougerie, 1976);

Le Bréviaire bleu (Limoges: Rougerie, 1977);

Le Roi du sel: roman, suivi de Le Conte de sept robes (Paris: Albin Michel, 1977);

Isel (Mortemart: Rougerie, 1979);

Joë Bousquet

Papillon de neige (Lagrasse: Editions Verdier, 1980);

D'un regard l'autre: 1948-1949 (Lagrasse: Editions Verdier, 1982);

Note-book, suivi de D'une autre vie (Mortemart: Rougerie, 1982).

Collection: *Œuvre romanesque complète*, 4 volumes to date, volumes 1-3 edited by René Nelli, volume 4 edited by Christine Michel (Paris: Albin Michel, 1979-   ).

OTHER: "Tristan l'Hermite," in *Tableau de la littérature française*, volume 1 (Paris: Gallimard, 1939), pp. 567-582.

PERIODICAL PUBLICATIONS: "A propos des 'Fleurs de Tarbes,'" *Cahiers du Sud,* no. 215 (April 1939);
"La Terreur dans les lettres," *Cahiers du Sud,* no. 244 (March 1942);
"Jean Giradoux," *Confluences,* special issue on the novel (1943);
"Mallarmé le sorcier," *Lettres,* third year (1948);
"L'Esprit de la parole," *Empédocle,* 6 (December 1949).

Joë Bousquet was born in 1897 in Narbonne, a small town in southwest France. Both his parents belonged to families rooted in the region. A few years after Bousquet's birth his father, who had been until then a military doctor, left the army and opened a private practice in the neighboring Carcassonne. There, Bousquet was to grow up and spend most of his life. After finishing high school Bousquet went to Paris to study at the Ecole des Hautes Etudes Commerciales, the most prestigious French business school. These studies were interrupted, however, by World War I. Bousquet enlisted in the army and became an intrepid and distinguished officer, often leading assaults against the enemy. One of these assaults determined the course of his remaining life. In 1918 the twenty-one-year-old Bousquet was wounded at Vailly (Aisne). His spine was damaged badly, and he remained paraplegic and impotent. Brought back to his parents' house at Carcassonne, Bousquet spent almost all the rest of his life shut away in his room, enduring mental and physical pain.

However, in the midst of this ordeal, Bousquet reacted. An inactive long period followed the tragedy, about ten years of what Bousquet called his "restauration" phase. But with the passing of time, he surrounded himself with friends, including the philosophers Claude Estève and Ferdinand Alquié and the poet René Nelli. Bousquet also began to write–letters, diaries, articles, and books.

A ladies' man before he was wounded–he had been considered a local Don Juan–Bousquet continued after he was bedridden to start new love affairs. Three volumes of his love letters–*Lettres à Poisson d'Or* (1967), *Lettres à Marthe* (1978), and *Lettres à Ginette* (1980)–have been published. Critics have praised their literary quality, and one can presume that these are just part of a much richer secret mine.

Gradually Bousquet's literary relations extended well beyond Carcassonne. He became one of the driving forces of the literary journal *Cahiers du Sud.* He established contacts with the surrealists and began to be known in select intellectual circles. Writers of such stature as Paul Valéry, André Gide, Paul Eluard, Louis Aragon, and Jean Paulhan, and such painters as Max Ernst and Hans Bellmer paid Bousquet visits at Carcassonne, interested both in his personality and in his writings. Bousquet swiftly became a character on the French literary scene, where he was known as the wounded, bedridden writer. Aragon, who wrote one of the first major articles on Bousquet in 1941, entitled it "Introduction à la vie héroïque de Joë Bousquet" (Introduction to the Heroic Life of Joë Bousquet).

This recognition by his peers did not, however, help Bousquet develop a large readership during his life. Even during the first years following his death, in spite of the fact that substantial essays appeared by, among others, René Nelli, Ferdinand Alquié, Hubert Juin, and Alain Robbe-Grillet, Bousquet's literary reputation slowly began to fade. His work remained forgotten until relatively recently, when major efforts were undertaken by several publishers to reintroduce his writings. Four volumes of his *Œuvre romanesque complète* have been published by Albin Michel; several hitherto unknown manuscripts have appeared under the Rougerie imprint; and Gallimard, Rougerie, Albin Michel, and others have brought out volumes of correspondence. In the last ten years or so colloquia and special issues of literary journals have been devoted to Bousquet.

Presenting Bousquet's work is a ticklish enterprise. He is looked upon as a mystic by many, as a true believer by some, and as a man animated by a Luciferian spirit by others. As much has been said about his stoicism as about his careful cultivation of suffering. It has been suggested that his work develops both materialistic and idealistic reflections, that it contains and blends surrealism, platonism, and existentialism. Numerous labels have been given to his work, and future readers will undoubtedly find new ones. Paradoxically, all these labels are both justified and contradicted by Bousquet's work.

As his friend the philosopher Ferdinand Alquié put it, Bousquet's language is indeterminable: "Il se situe en dehors de toute catégorie" (It is set outside all categories). As a dynamic principle, Bousquet's poetic language seems to govern infinite channels of contradictions. His work illustrates a compelling effort to struggle against any

Bousquet in 1916

attempt at systematization. If his work shows coherence, it is through its very incoherence.

Bousquet's writings include prose fiction, for example, *Il ne fait pas assez noir* (It Is Not Dark Enough, 1932), *Une Passante bleue et blonde* (A Woman Passing By, Blue and Blonde, 1934), *La Tisane de sarments* (Vine-branch Tea, 1936), *Traduit du silence* (Translated from Silence, 1939), and *Le Meneur de lune* (The Moon Driver, 1946); poems, some of which were collected in *La Connaissance du soir* (Knowledge of the Evening, 1945); articles and reviews regularly contributed by Bousquet to different periodicals and journals, especially to *Cahiers du Sud;* and an extraordinary essay, *Les Capitales* (1955), in which Bousquet develops reflections on poetic language and to which he devoted the last ten years of his life.

These generic distinctions, although useful, do not give a true understanding of the special nature of Bousquet's work. All of his writings derive from a series of private diaries, which Bousquet entitled "Cahier noir" (Black Notebook), "Cahier vert" (Green Notebook), "Cahier saumon" (Salmon Notebook), and so forth.

Bousquet draws on passages from the diaries and sometimes uses parts of the same entry in different books. Thus an uninterrupted flow of language and thought runs through his entire oeuvre.

One of the most significant aspects of Bousquet's contribution to twentieth-century French literature is his radical questioning of the subject's identity. This puts him at the heart of so-called *modernité*, a notion that has varied and often antithetical literary and philosophical connotations. With respect to writers of Bousquet's generation, *modernité* embraces surrealist poetics, the fiction and reflection on literary language developed by Jean Paulhan and by Maurice Blanchot, and the novelistic and dramatic universe of Samuel Beckett. With respect to following generations, one can add to the list the attempt to question literature led by the authors of the *nouveau roman* and those of the *Tel Quel* group, the *Logique du sens* of Gilles Deleuze (1969), and the notion of *écriture* as developed by Jacques Derrida. It is not surprising that Bousquet's work has drawn the attention of Eluard, Aragon, Paulhan, and Blanchot, as well as that of Deleuze and Robbe-Grillet.

Bousquet poses the problem of identity through his focus on the difficulties of poetic invention, its disorders, its disturbances, its conflicts, and its embarrassments. These difficulties are those that occur in the writer's mind during the process of writing. They are also the source of the writer's inventive play with complex poetic effects that seduce and entrap the reader. To say that reading Bousquet's work is a difficult task is an understatement.

Throughout his fiction Bousquet presents a poetic "I" whose function is to serve as a narrative voice. Most often, this character is sick, disabled, and shut away in his room. Writing is his main occupation. This consistent feature induces the reader to see in this character a fictionalized portrait of Bousquet himself, especially when one knows that most of Bousquet's books are composed of fragments taken out of notebooks in which he jotted down daily impressions and thoughts. However, the purpose of this disguised self-portrait, transposed from one book to the other, does not rest on the evocation of life's daily problems, nor in the story of the disabled man's torments, nor in the search for coherence and meaning in his existence. The purpose of the representation is to call into question conventional mental categories and the systems that

Bousquet with his friends (left to right) Gaston Massat, Jean Ballard, and Léo Matarasso, Villalier, 1931

help them function. In Bousquet's work the self-portrait becomes a writing practice that transforms literature into an instrument for demonstrating the total dispossession of the self.

The journal fragments composing Bousquet's books are of varied length. They extend from a few lines, as is most often the case, to a few pages, which happens rarely. Most of the books are divided into two or three parts, with each part subdivided into sections. In spite of this meticulous organization, one typically barely discerns why one fragment comes before another or why one section is placed before the other. There are here and there in Bousquet's books

some recognizable accounts of events in his life or of remembrances. For example, in some texts there is a vague love story which seems to develop between the writer character and one, two, or three women; once these indefinite feminine presences appear, they seem to be sent back to the very evanescence from which the writer character has conjured them. It is impossible to ascertain whether these presences are alive, dead, or resurrected; whether they refer to past, present time, and so forth. In fact, there is no chronology whatsoever in Bousquet's books. One might better consider them as attempts at verbal spatial arrangements, which Bousquet himself empha-

Bousquet, circa 1940

sizes when he often puts a "preface" at the end of a work, an "epilogue" at the beginning, and vice versa.

The seemingly arbitrary nature of gathering together fragments is intensified by the fact that the fragments are most often made up of heterogeneous and intricate entanglements of dreams, meditations, remembrances, and descriptions. In a single fragment or paragraph, or even in a single sentence, Bousquet's flow drifts from a love dream, from the description of a landscape or of a movement of light in the foliage to an apparent philosophical meditation about space and time, about literary language and poetic invention, or about the sodomitic nature of an erotic act, and then back again.

This feature of Bousquet's discourse has two facets which reflect one another as in a mir-

ror. One concerns the writer; the other, the reader. Bousquet's discourse mediates the mode of strangeness in which the writer character perceives his relation to the world surrounding him. It is not a strangeness determined by oddness, by the fantastic, or even by nonsense; it is not a feeling of indifference or an intimate feeling of being a stranger to the world. On the contrary, one might say that the character's desire is for total adhesion to things and beings. But it is precisely this desire that creates strangeness. From one book to the other the character's reflections tell of a rush to follow a course in a world where sense seems to abound, although the character can grasp it only in a fragmented and intermittent fashion. The relation of the character to his universe–to the evanescent figures, for example, who come and go around him–is lived in a mode

Bousquet in 1949 recording a talk for radio

of light contact, not in one of successful adhesion.

Through this experience of light contact, the character constitutes himself as a subject becoming aware at each moment of an essential lack, as a subject dispossessed of his world and of himself, one constantly separated, "fantôme sans avoir et sans identité" (a ghost with neither possession nor identity), as Bousquet notes in one work. Strangeness relates specifically to this condition of ambivalent and simultaneous movements between a desire to belong and an awareness of separation. This strangeness leads the character to an experience and expression of radical doubt about himself.

Perhaps the principal interest of Bousquet's books lies in this experience of radical doubt and the manner in which it is conveyed to the reader, for Bousquet pushes his reader, too, to question his identity as a subject. The heterogeneous character of Bousquet's discourse triggers in the reader effects determined by a fundamental paradox. To describe this paradox, one might have recourse to psychologist Gregory Bateson's concept of "double bind": a notion which refers to a situation in which two contradicting orders are given at the same time, leaving the person who receives them in a blocked and therefore untenable posi-

tion. It is a kind of Batesonian paradox which governs the process of communication between the writer character and his reader.

For the writer character, literature is communication. He speaks, he writes, and he wants the reader to do the same. For, as he puts it, "l'acte d'écrire est invention d'un interlocuteur" (the act of writing is the invention of an interlocutor). But he gives contradictory signals. At first, the communication seems smooth. There is a whole lyrical movement, and the reader is seduced by the beauty of the language and of the images. But, at the same time, because the text is composed of reflections, the reader is incited to try to understand what he reads. He is pushed to make an effort of reasoning. And because of an endless process of contradictions, the reader is led to realize that although he thought he had understood, he did not comprehend what he read.

From the point of view of communication—which in Bousquet's words is the essential part of literary process—when Bousquet incites the reader to understand, he gives him an opportunity to react, that is to say, to comment on the text. But when, at the same time, he makes the reader realize that he does not understand, he blocks the reader's speech and his commentary. Most important, Bousquet forces the reader to go through the experience of confronting contradictions while commenting. And thus, as the reader comments upon the texts, he must first address that experience of contradiction. In a sense, there is nothing that can be asserted about Bousquet's books which cannot be immediately contradicted by another reader. This essentially paradoxical literary communication is determined by Bousquet's theoretical background and, more specifically, by the way Bousquet conceives of the act of criticism.

Bousquet's theoretical background was nurtured in part by the German romantic notion of criticism. Bousquet defines the act of criticism as an insurmountable experience of doubt. Thus, when he pushes the reader to reason and at the same time to realize that he is wrong, he makes the reader doubt his own abilities to understand. The experience of reading Bousquet is, in and of itself, a radical critique of reason. This critique leads to the notion that it is impossible for anyone to define or even to assert oneself as a subject. Bousquet places his conception of the act of criticism in opposition to an interpretation he gives of the Cartesian ego, summarized by the well-known dictum *cogito, ergo sum* (I think, therefore I am). Contrary to Descartes's experience, there is, for Bousquet, no assertion of the self once doubt is resolved, but, paradoxically, the assertion is contemporary with the doubt. This is so because, for Bousquet, knowledge cannot be distinguished from language. Consequently, if the experience of language, of which the act of criticism is a privileged instance, leads to unresolved doubt, how can the reader as a critic assert himself as a subject?

Bousquet is among those whose writings have pushed the question of identity to what seems to be its current limits. Those who read Bousquet's books discover the extent to which their own relationship to literature changes. It simply cannot be the same as it was because when readers are made aware of the radical experience of doubt that literature finally reveals itself to be, they can no longer approach it from any other point of view. If Bousquet's goal was to bring his readers to such a point of uncertainty and reassessment concerning the reader-text relationship, then there can be no doubt that he succeeded admirably in achieving it.

Letters:

Lettres à Poisson d'Or (Paris: Gallimard, 1967);

Correspondance, edited by Suzanne André (Paris: Gallimard, 1969);

Lettres à Jean Cassou (Limoges: Rougerie, 1970);

Lettres à Carlos Suarès (Limoges: Rougerie, 1973);

Lettres à Stéphane et à Jean (Paris: Albin Michel, 1975);

Lettres à Marthe: 1919-1937 (Paris: Gallimard, 1978);

Lettres à Ginette (Paris: Albin Michel, 1980);

A Max-Philippe Delatte/Joë Bousquet. Précédé de Petite Histoire de "Critique 38," by Delatte (Mortemart: Rougerie, 1981);

Correspondance/Simone Weil, Joë Bousquet (Lausanne: Age d'Homme, 1982);

Un Amour couleur de thé: Correspondance (Lagrasse: Verdier, 1984).

References:

Suzanne André, Hubert Juin, and Gaston Massat, *Joë Bousquet: Trois Etudes* (Paris: Seghers, 1958);

Maurice Blanchot, "Traduit du silence," in his *Faux Pas* (Paris: Gallimard, 1943);

René Nelli, *Joë Bousquet, sa vie, son œuvre* (Paris: Albin Michel, 1975);

Alain Robbe-Grillet, "Joë Bousquet le rêveur," *Critique*, 77 (October 1953); revised in Robbe-Grillet's *Pour un nouveau roman* (Paris: Gallimard, 1963);

Gabriel Sarraute, *La Contrition de Joë Bousquet* (Mortemart: Rougerie, 1981).

Emmanuel Bove

(20 April 1898-13 July 1945)

F. C. St. Aubyn
University of Pittsburgh

BOOKS: *Mes Amis* (Paris: Ferenczi, 1924); translated by Janet Louth as *My Friends* (Manchester, U.K.: Carcanet, 1986);
Visite d'un soir (Paris: Emile-Paul, 1925);
Armand (Paris: Emile-Paul, 1927); translated by Louth (Manchester, U.K.: Carcanet, 1987);
Bécon-les-Bruyères (Paris: Emile-Paul, 1927);
Le Crime d'une nuit (Paris: Emile-Paul, 1927);
Un Soir chez Blutel (Paris: Editions Kra, 1927);
Un Père et sa fille (Paris: Sans Pareil, 1928);
Une Fugue (Paris: Editions de la Belle Page, 1928);
La Coalition (Paris: Emile-Paul, 1928);
Cœurs et visages (Paris: Editions de France, 1928);
Henri Duchemin et ses ombres (Paris: Emile-Paul, 1928);
La Mort de Dinah (Paris: Editions des Portiques, 1928);
L'Amour de Pierre Neuhart (Paris: Emile-Paul, 1929);
Journal écrit en hiver (Paris: Emile-Paul, 1931);
Un Célibataire (Paris: Calmann-Lévy, 1932);
Deux Jeunes Filles (Paris: Emile-Paul, 1932);
Un Raskolnikoff (Paris: Plon, 1932);
Le Meurtre de Suzy Pommier (Paris: Emile-Paul, 1933); translated by Warre B. Wells as *The Murder of Suzy Pommier* (Boston: Little, Brown, 1934);
Le Beau-fils (Paris: Grasset, 1934);
Le Pressentiment (Paris: Gallimard, 1935);
Adieu Fombonne (Paris: Gallimard, 1937);
La Dernière Nuit (Paris: Gallimard, 1939);
Départ dans la Nuit (Paris: Charlot, 1945);
Le Piège (Paris: Trémois, 1945);
Non-lieu (Paris: Robert Laffont, 1946);
Un Homme qui savait (Paris: Table Ronde, 1985);
Mémoires d'un homme singulier (Paris: Calmann-Lévy, 1987).

Emmanuel Bove, August 1930 (courtesy of Madame Nota ae Meyenburg-Bove)

In spite of efforts by the French publisher Flammarion to make some of Emmanuel Bove's works available to the reading public in the 1970s and 1980s, his place in French literature remains uncertain. That his novels should have lan-guished in almost total obscurity for some fifty years is difficult to understand when one considers that it was the established writer Colette who urged the firm of Ferenczi to publish his first novel. Rainer Maria Rilke, perhaps the greatest German poet of the twentieth century, was so impressed by Bove's first novel, *Mes Amis* (1924; translated as *My Friends*, 1986), that he made a point of meeting the author in Paris. The well-known French poet Max Jacob wrote to Bove in 1928 saying that Bove's novel *Un Père et sa fille* (A Father and His Daughter, 1928) was one of the most beautiful books he had ever read. When the novelist and dramatist Samuel Beckett was asked shortly after World War II for the name of the unrecognized writer whom he would most recommend reading, he answered, "Emmanuel

Bove: Il a, comme personne, le sens du détail touchant" (He has like no one else a feel for the touching detail). With such noteworthy recommendations, seconded by modern critics who often cite Bove as a precursor of the New Novelists, an attempt should be made to assess Bove's accomplishments anew to determine if they do indeed live up to their notices.

Bove was born in Paris in 1898. His father, Emmanuel Bobovnikoff, a Jewish émigré from Kiev, Russia, was a nihilist and something of a womanizer. Bove's mother, a chambermaid in the hotel where his father lived, came from Luxembourg. (The couple never married.) Bove's only claim to a literary heritage was the fact that his father had published a dictionary for rich Russian tourists who attended the 1900 world's fair in Paris. Bove's younger brother, Léon, was born in 1902, but the fact that he had two sons did not prevent Bobovnikoff from allying himself with a wealthy English woman by the name of Emily Overweg, by whom he had a son, Victor. Overweg took an interest in Bove and sent him to the Ecole Alsacienne, one of the best private schools in Paris. When his father and Overweg moved to Geneva, he accompanied them. But he also spent some time with his mother and Léon, in far more modest circumstances. After the outbreak of World War I Overweg sent him to boarding school in England. When he returned to Paris at the age of eighteen, after his father's death and Overweg's loss of income through wartime devaluation, he was forced to earn his living, according to one source, as a train conductor, taxi driver, dishwasher, and unskilled laborer in the Renault plant. He spent a short time as a writer of pulp fiction, turning out a book every week and a half. He used the family name of his wife, Suzanne Vallois, a teacher whom he had married in 1921, as his nom de plume. The marriage did not last; the couple had two children, a daughter, Nora, and a son, Michel, whom Bove never saw again because their mother opposed his attempts to visit.

Bove lived in Vienna in 1921 and 1922. His first short story was published the following year. During 1926 and 1927 he lived with Henriette de Swetschine near the suburban rail station Bécon-les-Bruyères, which later became the subject of one of his works. Suddenly, in about sixteen months in 1927 and 1928, he wrote ten books and became something of a celebrity who knew many of the literary luminaries on the Left Bank in Paris. His first book, *Mes Amis,* was

awarded the Prix Figuière. In all he produced more than twenty-five works, not including three unpublished novels and a dozen short stories. During the 1930s Bove contributed to two left-wing publications, *Marianne* and *Vendredi.*

In 1928 he met the woman who would become his second wife, Louise Ottensvoser, a sculptress of modest talent who was both rich and a communist. Wishing to marry her, he asked Suzanne for a divorce, which was granted in 1930. His new wife came from a prosperous Jewish banking family. When France fell to the Germans in 1940, he moved Louise to Lyons in the unoccupied zone. In 1942, after the Germans overran the free zone, living in Lyons became dangerous for a Jew who was also a communist; the couple fled to Algiers, where they encountered many other writers in exile, including André Gide, and also met such writers as Antoine de Saint-Exupéry and Emmanuel Roblès. Already at that time Bove's health was failing, most people thought from tuberculosis. He also contracted malaria. In 1944 he and his wife returned to Paris and settled in the apartment of Bove's half-brother, Victor, where Bove remained until his death in 1945. The cause of death was listed as cardiac arrest after an attack of malaria.

During his lifetime Bove experienced abrupt switches from comfort to poverty and from obscurity to celebrity; these, plus his frequent displacements from France, first to Switzerland, then to England, Austria, and Algeria, and his several liaisons suffice to explain something about this enigmatic man who never really communicated with others outside his immediate family except through his novels. A final irony is that the bohemian and peripatetic Bove was buried in the very proper mausoleum of the Ottensvoser family in the Jewish section of the Montparnasse cemetery. His second wife died in 1977, the year Flammarion began to republish some of his works.

Bove's greatest talent lay in his ability to create character. One has only to think of the types whose names head the central chapters in the novel *Mes Amis* or the more than twenty-five personalities quickly and deftly sketched in *Journal écrit en hiver* (Journal Written in Winter, 1931) to appreciate his ability.

In *Mes Amis* the brief introduction and conclusion are separated by five chapters, each carrying the name of a friend of the narrator: Lucie Dunois, Henri Billard, the sailor Neveu, Monsieur Lacaze, and Blanche. The narrator's name is Victor Bâton. One wonders if Bove was flattering or insulting his half brother by giving the name Victor to his miserable hero, a veteran of World War I who lives on his meager fifty percent disability pension in a wretched room in the working-class suburb Montrouge, south of Paris, where Bove himself once resided. Bâton illustrates to some degree the feelings of maladjustment and futility that characterized those who returned from the trenches. He awakens and takes the inventory of his dilapidated surroundings. Before making his desultory ablutions he also takes an inventory of his immediate neighbors, among them a girl living next door who only laughed at him when he told her he loved her. Another neighbor is a little old man who is gravely ill. His situation resembles Balzac's Père Goriot in that his elegantly dressed daughter arrives by taxi every Sunday to visit but does nothing to relieve her father's misery. The Lecoin family lives on the same landing. The husband dislikes Bâton because he gets up late and does not need to work, a foreshadowing of the catastrophes to come. Upon leaving his apartment Bâton takes the inventory of his street: the café next door where he has his morning coffee; the grocery store whose owner no longer speaks to him because he refused to help him carry a crate for fear of getting a hernia; the butcher shop; the bakery; and so forth. These inventories remind the reader of the narrator's in Robert Pinget's *L'Inquisitoire* (The Inquisitory, 1962), but the reader realizes that Bâton is searching for something quite different from Pinget's narrator.

What Bâton is really seeking is a true friend. He sleeps with Lucie Dunois, a fat widow who operates a saloon on the Rue de Seine, but after their night together she never acknowledges that anything has happened between them. He then thinks he has found a friend in Henri Billard, whom he encounters in the street. In the end Billard plays with Bâton as if he were a ball in a game of billiards. Bâton loans Billard and his girlfriend Nina fifty francs, but when he goes back to visit them they have disappeared. On the banks of the Seine he encounters the sailor Neveu. Bâton appears so sad the sailor thinks he wants to commit suicide. Neveu also wants to commit suicide and fills his pockets with rocks in order to sink more quickly when he jumps in the water. Bâton, who recognizes in Neveu a possible friend, saves them both with the revelation that he has a little money. They have a good meal; Bâton pays. They get drunk and Neveu takes

him to a whorehouse, where he immediately forgets Bâton. He is unaware that Bâton's heart is full of tenderness. Another friendship has failed. The pattern continues as Bâton encounters the rich industrialist Monsieur Lacaze and, finally, a woman named Blanche, whom he picks up on the street. After spending the night with Blanche, Bâton makes no attempt to see her again. He has lost his spirit, given up all hope of making contact with others.

Bâton's saga ends when the owner of his apartment house orders him to move. The other tenants have complained because he does not work; they also say he is dirty (which is true) and has female visitors (which is false). In Bâton's view they cannot forgive him because he is free. Personal freedom thus becomes one of the recurrent themes in Bove's works. Bâton has to sell his furniture and live in a hotel room, reduced to solitude; a beautiful thing, he says, when it is chosen, a sad thing when it is imposed.

Raymond Cousse in his preface to *Un Soir chez Blutel* (An Evening at Blutel's, 1927) quotes from Bove's journal: "Il n'y a pas de sujet, il n'y a que ce qu'on éprouve. J'éprouve avec force par exemple l'inaction, ce sera une action dans mon livre" (There is no subject, there is only what one experiences. I experience strongly, for example, inaction, that will be an action in my book). Bâton is the personification of that dictum. This naive, harmless wanderer with a childish faith in his capacity for friendship who roams the streets of Paris in search of a friend becomes in the eyes of others a menace to society. Bove's achievement is to make his hero's experiences convey the existential tragedy of man's solitude.

In the short novel *Un Soir chez Blutel* a young man named Maxime Corton is returning to Paris from Vienna, where (like Bove himself) he had been unable to find work. He picks up a girl, Madeleine, and spends the night with her, an action that is characteristic of Bove's narrators. He then calls a friend, André Blutel, and attends a party Blutel and his mistress are giving. The longest part of the novel consists of a series of brilliant character sketches of the host, his mistress, and their five guests. Corton asks Blutel to intervene for him with his friends to help him find a job. Nothing happens, and the long set pieces merely follow one another with little interaction among the characters so carefully delineated. Corton recounts his life, which sounds very much like Bove's own. The story ends when he thinks that with Madeleine he will find a few hours or a few days of peace. He has not been reduced to the dire circumstances of Bâton, but he would seem to be headed for the same fate. Corton elicits little sympathy or even interest, certainly less than Bâton. In some ways the work does suggest developments of the *nouveau roman* but without the technical innovations which make the later works new departures in contemporary French literature.

Among the works that Bove published in 1928 are *Un Père et sa fille* and *Une Fugue* (A Flight or An Escape). In the long story *Un Père et sa fille* he utilizes to good effect the kind of touching detail mentioned by Beckett. The father, Jean-Antoine About, almost achieves the success for which he had worked hard, but when he realizes that his is not a great achievement, he gives up completely and comes to resemble Bâton. But in this case, in contrast to Bâton's story, the author explains the circumstances which lead to his resignation. These include the desertion of About's wife and his alienation from his beloved daughter. When an attempted reconciliation fails, his lot seems decided forever. Bove shows how such a tragedy can take place, how sensitivity and madness are only a breath apart. He avoids the sentimental in this father-daughter relationship, revealing how they both understand and misunderstand one another and return to their individual solitude.

The long story *Une Fugue* is one of Bove's most satisfying works psychologically. It deals again with a daughter's problems, this time with both her parents. Sent from father to mother and back, Louise runs away from home. The rest of the plot consists of the complications that ensue when she tells one person after another a story, totally fabricated, about having been caught for stealing a fur in a department store. A family friend and a lawyer are drawn into the plot, as well as one of Louise's own friends and a café waiter with whom she sets up a rendezvous at the dingy hotel where she is staying. Attempts to find her and get her back to her parents are finally successful, after she has feigned suicide and just as the waiter arrives for his tryst. The studious and reserved Louise has at last gotten the attention she desired and played a trick on her

negligent parents. The story would make an entertaining film.

Journal écrit en hiver (1931) teems with characters who are rapidly and skillfully delineated. Louis Grandeville, who keeps the journal for the four months from 7 October to 2 February, obviously belongs to the upper bourgeoisie. His obsessive love for his wife reminds one of the infatuation of Proust's narrator with Albertine in *A la recherche du temps perdu* (*Remembrance of Things Past*, 1913-1927). Grandeville eventually drives away his wife. Unfortunately, she is a less sympathetic character than Albertine and, while Bove's portrayal of the psychology of the husband so obsessed by his beloved is convincing, he too is not a very congenial character. The reader in the end cares little about the hero or the heroine. This demonstration of Oscar Wilde's remark that each man kills the thing he loves is occasionally interesting but not movingly so.

Thus, while Bove has created an interesting array of characters in these and other works, one has to agree with Jane Kramer when she writes in a 1985 article for the *New Yorker* that "it is unlikely that people are going to stay passionate about Emmanuel Bove" and that in the end "the great pleasure was in the discovery." Nevertheless, he deserves a place in the history of twentieth-century French literature for the use he makes of nondescript and "outsider" characters, his treatment of plot, and his existential themes.

References:
Bernard Alliot, "Tentative de biographie d'un fantôme," *Monde*, 4 March 1983, pp. 15, 18;
Raymond Cousse, "Boviens de tous pays," *Magazine Littéraire*, no. 193 (March 1983): 54-56;
Cousse, ed., *Emmanuel Bove* (Paris: Flammarion, 1983);
Yves-Alain Favre, "Découvrir Emmanuel Bove," *Revue Universelle des Faits et des Idées*, no. 94 (1983): 52-55;
Jane Kramer, "Letter from Europe," *New Yorker*, 61 (20 May 1985): 102-117;
Paul Morelle, "Avez-vous lu Bove?," *Monde*, 3 December 1977, p. 19;
Morelle, "Le Retour d'Emmanuel Bove: Un Romancier de la solitude et du dénuement," *Monde*, 4 March 1983, pp. 15, 18.

Albert Camus
(7 November 1913-4 January 1960)

Raymond Gay-Crosier
University of Florida

BOOKS: *Révolte dans les Asturies,* by Camus and others (Algiers: Charlot, 1936);

L'Envers et l'endroit (Algiers: Charlot, 1937); translated as "Betwixt and Between" in *Lyrical and Critical* (1967); translated as "The Wrong Side and the Right Side" in *Lyrical and Critical Essays* (1968);

Noces (Algiers: Charlot, 1939); translated as "Nuptials" in *Lyrical and Critical* (1967) and in *Lyrical and Critical Essays* (1968);

L'Etranger (Paris: Gallimard, 1942); translated by Stuart Gilbert as *The Outsider* (London: Hamilton, 1946); republished as *The Stranger* (New York: Knopf, 1946); translated by Matthew Ward as *The Stranger* (New York: Knopf, 1988);

Le Mythe de Sisyphe (Paris: Gallimard, 1942); translated by Justin O'Brien as *The Myth of Sisyphus* (London: Hamilton, 1955) and in *The Myth of Sisyphus and Other Essays* (1955);

Le Malentendu suivi de Caligula (Paris: Gallimard, 1944); translated by Gilbert as *Caligula and Cross Purpose* (New York: New Directions, 1947; London: Hamilton, 1947);

Lettres à un ami allemand (Paris: Gallimard, 1945); translated as "Letters to a German Friend" in *Resistance, Rebellion and Death* (1961);

La Peste (Paris: Gallimard, 1947); translated by Gilbert as *The Plague* (New York: Knopf, 1948; London: Hamilton, 1948);

L'Etat de siège (Paris: Gallimard, 1948); translated as *State of Siege* in *Caligula and Three Other Plays* (1958);

Actuelles: Chroniques 1944-1948 (Paris: Gallimard, 1950); translated in part in *Resistance, Rebellion and Death* (1961);

Les Justes (Paris: Gallimard, 1950); translated as *The Just Assassins* in *Caligula and Three Other Plays* (1958);

L'Homme révolté (Paris: Gallimard, 1951); translated by Anthony Bower as *The Rebel* (London: Hamilton, 1953; New York: Knopf, 1954);

Actuelles II: Chroniques 1948-1953 (Paris: Gallimard, 1953); translated in part in *The Myth of Sisyphus and Other Essays* (1955) and in *Resistance, Rebellion and Death* (1961);

Les Esprits, adapted from Pierre de Larivey's play (Paris: Gallimard, 1953);

L'Eté (Paris: Gallimard, 1954); translated as "Summer" in *Lyrical and Critical* (1967);

The Myth of Sisyphus and Other Essays, translated by O'Brien (New York: Knopf, 1955);

Requiem pour une nonne, adapted from William Faulkner's novel (Paris: Gallimard, 1956);

La Chute (Paris: Gallimard, 1956); translated by O'Brien as *The Fall* (London: Hamilton, 1956; New York: Knopf, 1957);

L'Exil et le royaume (Paris: Gallimard, 1957); translated by O'Brien as *Exile and the Kingdom* (London: Hamilton, 1958; New York: Knopf, 1958);

Réflexions sur la peine capitale, by Camus and Arthur Koestler (Paris: Calmann-Lévy, 1957); Camus's contribution translated by Richard Howard as *Reflections on the Guillotine; An Essay on Capital Punishment* (Michigan City, Ind.: Fridtjof-Karla, 1959);

Actuelles III: Chronique algérienne 1939-1958 (Paris: Gallimard, 1958); translated in part in *Resistance, Rebellion and Death* (1961);

Caligula and Three Other Plays, translated by Gilbert (New York: Knopf, 1958)—comprises *Caligula, Le Malentendu, L'Etat de siège,* and *Les Justes;*

Discours de Suède (Paris: Gallimard, 1958); translated by O'Brien as *Speech of Acceptance upon the Award of the Nobel Prize for Literature, Delivered in Stockholm on the Tenth of December, Nineteen Hundred and Fifty-seven* (New York: Knopf, 1958);

Les Possédés, adapted from Fyodor Dostoyevski's novel (Paris: Gallimard, 1959); translated by O'Brien as *The Possessed* (London: Hamilton, 1960; New York: Knopf, 1960);

Resistance, Rebellion and Death, translated by O'Brien (London: Hamilton, 1961; New

Albert Camus (photo Laty; collection of Mme Catherine Camus)

York: Knopf, 1961)–comprises *Lettres à un ami allemand;* excerpts from *Actuelles: Chroniques 1944-1948, Actuelles II: Chroniques 1948-1953, Actuelles III: Chronique algérienne 1938-1958;* and other essays;

Carnets, mai 1935-février 1942 (Paris: Gallimard, 1962); translated by Philip Thody as *Carnets* (London: Hamilton, 1963); republished as *Notebooks, 1935-1942* (New York: Knopf, 1963);

Théâtre, récits, nouvelles (Paris: Gallimard, 1962);

Carnets, janvier 1942-mars 1951 (Paris: Gallimard, 1964); translated by O'Brien as *Notebooks, 1942-1951* (New York: Knopf, 1965); translated by Thody as *Carnets, 1942-1951* (London: Hamilton, 1966);

Essais (Paris: Gallimard, 1965);

Lyrical and Critical, edited and translated by Thody (London: Hamilton, 1967)–comprises *L'Envers et l'endroit, Noces, L'Eté,* and other essays;

Lyrical and Critical Essays, edited by Thody, translated by Ellen Conroy Kennedy (New York: Knopf, 1968)–comprises *L'Envers et l'endroit, Noces, L'Eté,* and other essays;

La Mort heureuse, Cahiers Albert Camus, no. 1 (Paris: Gallimard, 1971); translated by Howard as *A Happy Death* (London: Hamilton, 1972; New York: Knopf, 1972);

Le Premier Camus, suivi de Ecrits de jeunesse d'Albert Camus, Cahiers Albert Camus, no. 2 (Paris: Gallimard, 1973); translated by Kennedy as *Youthful Writings* (New York: Knopf, 1976; London: Hamilton, 1977);

Fragments d'un combat: 1938-1940, Alger Républicain, Le Soir Républicain,, edited by Jacqueline Lévi Valensi and André Abbou, 2 volumes (Paris: Gallimard, 1978);

Journaux de Voyage (Paris: Gallimard, 1978);

Caligula, version de 1941, suivi de La Poétique du premier Caligula, edited by A. James Arnold (Paris: Gallimard, 1984).

Camus (kneeling at front, in black apron) at his uncle's cooperage, 1920

Collection: *Œuvres complètes d'Albert Camus*, 5 volumes (Paris: Club de l'Honnête Homme, 1983).

PLAY PRODUCTIONS: *Le Malentendu*, Paris, Théâtre des Mathurins, 24 August 1944;
Caligula, Paris, Théâtre Hébertot, 26 September 1945;
L'Etat de siège, Paris, Théâtre Marigny, 27 October 1948;
Les Justes, Paris, Théâtre Hébertot, 15 December 1949;
Les Esprits, adapted from Pierre de Larivey's play, Angers, Festival d'Art Dramatique, 16 June 1953;
Requiem pour une nonne, adapted from William Faulkner's novel, Paris, Théâtre des Mathurins, 22 September 1956;
Les Possédés, adapted from Fyodor Dostoyevski's novel, Paris, Théâtre Antoine, 30 January 1959.

OTHER: Nicholas-Sébastien Roch [de] Chamfort, *Maximes et anecdotes*, preface by Camus (Monaco: Dac, 1944);
André Salvet, *Le Combat silencieux*, preface by Camus (Paris: Portulan, 1945);

Jean Camp and others, *L'Espagne libre*, preface by Camus (Paris: Calmann-Lévy, 1946);
Pierre-Eugène Clairin, *Dix Estampes originales*, introduction by Camus (Paris: Rombaldi, 1946);
Jacques Méry, *Laissez passer mon peuple*, preface by Camus (Paris: Seuil, 1947);
Jeanne Héon-Canone, *Devant la mort*, preface by Camus (Angers: Siraudeau, 1951);
"Herman Melville," in *Les Ecrivains célèbres*, volume 3 (Paris: Mazenod, 1952);
Daniel Mauroc, *Contre-Amour*, preface by Camus (Paris: Minuit, 1952);
A. Rosmer, *Moscou sous Lénine—Les origines du communisme*, preface by Camus (Paris: Editions de Flore, 1953);
Désert vivant: Images et couleurs de Walt Disney, adapted by Camus, Marcel Aymé, Louis Bromfield, Julian Huxley, François Mauriac, André Maurois, and Henry de Montherlant (Paris: Société Française du Livre, 1954);
Konrad Bieber, *L'Allemagne vue par les écrivains de la Résistance française*, preface by Camus (Geneva: Droz, 1954);
"L'Enchantement de Cordes," in *Cordes-en-Albigeois*, edited by C. Targuebayre (Toulouse: Privat, 1954);

Oscar Wilde, *Ballade de la geôle de Reading*, preface by Camus (Paris: Falaize, 1954);

Roger Martin du Gard, *Œuvres complètes*, 2 volumes, preface by Camus (Paris: Gallimard, 1955);

La Vérité sur l'affaire Nagy, preface by Camus (Paris: Plon, 1958);

Henriette Grindat, *La Postérité du soleil*, text by Camus (Geneva: Engelberts, 1965).

TRANSLATIONS: James Thurber, *La Dernière Fleur* (Paris: Gallimard, 1952);

Pedro Calderón de la Barca, *La Dévotion à la croix* (Paris: Gallimard, 1953);

Dino Buzzati, *Un Cas intéressant*, Avant-Scène, no. 105 (1955): 1-25;

Félix Lope de Vega Carpio, *Le Chevalier d'Olmedo* (Paris: Gallimard, 1957).

Albert Camus is one of the best-known twentieth-century French authors. Born and raised in North Africa, after the beginning of World War II he moved to Paris where he intended to pursue his career as a journalist and aspiring writer. In 1942, with the publication of *L'Etranger* (translated in England as *The Outsider* and in the United States as *The Stranger*, 1946) and *Le Mythe de Sisyphe* (translated as *The Myth of Sisyphus*, 1955), he found instant fame and was widely and wrongly considered a major representative of the emerging existentialist movement. As an influential editorialist of *Combat*, France's leading daily in the immediate post-World War II period, he became a highly public figure and was perceived for a while, in international opinion, as the conscience of his nation. His instinctual rejection of ideologies and the carefully nurtured ambiguity which informs all his works and, in the eyes of several critics, some of his positions are some of the reasons for the increasingly ambivalent reception his work has received in France. From the cold war period through the Algerian struggle for independence and into the 1960s, reaction to both the man and his work often turned to hostility and ridicule, especially among left-wing intellectuals in France who thought that he had betrayed them. Outside of France, where Camus has been the subject of more detached critical inquiry, his reputation has continued to grow. The flow of criticism on Camus is matched only by the perennially high sales figures of his major works, both in French and in translation. Camus remains a popular but controversial writer whose importance and influence are undeniable. To understand the ongoing controversy, his thought and work must be seen in the decisive contexts of his formative years in North Africa and his self-imposed "exile" in Paris during and after World War II.

The younger of two brothers, Albert Camus was born on 7 November 1913 in Mondovi (named after a Napoleonic victory) in Algeria, which remained a French colony until its independence in 1962. His father, Lucien Auguste Camus (1885-1914), who lived most of his adult life in Algiers where he worked for a wine distributor, had taken the family to Mondovi shortly before Camus's birth. As Herbert R. Lottman has demonstrated in his amply documented *Albert Camus: A Biography* (1979), the paternal side of the family was neither of Alsatian descent nor from Lorraine, as Camus himself believed. Rather, archival evidence indicates that the Camus family can be traced to Bordeaux and that the paternal grandmother's Cormery family originated in Ardèche in south-central France. Albert Camus's frequently displayed hispanophilia is attributed to his mother's and grandmother's Spanish ancestry. His mother, Catherine Sintès Camus (1882-1960), and his grandmother, Catherine Marie Sintès (1857-1931; her maiden name was Cardona) were descendants of emigrants from Majorca, one of the Balearic islands which Camus visited in 1935 and described in "Amour de vivre" (Love of Life), a chapter of *L'Envers et l'endroit* (1937; translated as "Betwixt and Between" in *Lyrical and Critical*, 1967, and as "The Wrong Side and the Right Side" in *Lyrical and Critical Essays*, 1968). Neither Camus nor his mother or grandmother spoke Spanish. The little Spanish he knew later on he picked up on his own.

Lucien Auguste Camus grew up fatherless. He was the youngest of five children and never forgave his mother and family for placing him in a Protestant orphanage. After his obligatory military service (1906-1908), he was taken in by the family of his future in-laws who never talked to the Camus clan because of what they had done to Lucien. In 1914 he was called into service again and injured at the battle of the Marne. He died in a military hospital on 11 October 1914 from his wounds and was buried in Saint-Brieuc. Thus, like his father before him, Albert Camus knew his father only through his family's memories. The absent father would haunt him all his life, and by the time he died in an automobile accident in 1960, he was working on what was intended to be the novel of his literary maturity,

Camus with poet René Char (collection of Mme Catherine Camus)

"Le Premier Homme" (The First Man), a family epic in which he intended to retrace, albeit in fiction, his French-Algerian father's dual European and North African roots.

While Lucien Camus was moderately literate, his wife Catherine was illiterate. Upon the news of his death this shy and submissive woman withdrew even more into her own world of stubborn silence. Back in Algiers, the widow lived with her two sons, Albert and Lucien (1910-1983); her brother, Etienne Sintès; and her mother. They occupied a three-room apartment without electricity in the lower-working-class Belcourt district. Sustenance came from the mod-

est income of her brother and her own work as a cleaning woman. The reverence for his mother which pervades Camus's writings must be seen in the context of her unassuming yet heroic devotion and sense of duty. She was unable to show tenderness or affection. A stubborn yet telling silence constituted the only link between an inhibited mother and a son who was not only in permanent search of his father but always longing for his mother.

In many ways Camus the writer derived his ethics and aesthetics from the lessons he learned in Belcourt and from team sports, especially soccer. These lessons included particularly a simple but strictly observed honor code predicated on a strong sense of duty, which to Camus's mind helped compensate for external signs of motherly love: "On ne 'manque' pas à sa mère" (You don't "fail" your mother) is one of the canons which he summarized in *Noces* (1939; translated as "Nuptials" in *Lyrical and Critical*, 1967). And on the occasion of his 1957 Nobel Prize speech he startled the world with a surprisingly emotional opinion which underscored the importance and strength of his roots: "Je crois à la justice, mais je défendrai ma mère avant la justice" (I believe in justice, but I shall defend my mother above justice). His difficult relationship with his mother is a dominant theme in *L'Etranger, Le Malentendu* (1944; translated as *Cross Purpose*, 1947), *La Peste* (1947; translated as *The Plague*, 1948), *La Mort heureuse* (1971; translated as *A Happy Death*, 1972), and numerous shorter pieces. The very first entry in his *Carnets, mai 1935-février 1942* (1962; translated as *Notebooks, 1935-1942*, 1963) focuses in a penetrating and surprisingly candid manner on the determining aspect of his childhood memories: "Le sentiment bizarre que le fils porte à la mère constitue *toute sa sensibilité*. Les manifestations de cette sensibilité dans les domaines les plus divers s'expliquent suffisamment par le souvenir latent, matériel de son enfance (une glu qui s'accroche à l'âme)" (the strange feeling which the son has for his mother constitutes *his whole sensibility*. The latent material memory which he has of his childhood [a glue that has stuck to the soul] explains why this way of feeling shows itself in the most widely differing fields).

Several family incidents left deep marks on the young boy and future writer. One of them involved his father, who one day came home sick after witnessing the public execution by guillotine of a criminal. The story, transmitted as one of the few paternal legacies by Camus's mother, reappears in *L'Etranger* and *La Peste*. Two key incidents involved the mother. At some point the widow took a lover in spite of her brother's violent disapproval. This situation led to an altercation between the two men in which her older son, Lucien, came to his mother's defense. Another time his mother was attacked in the apartment by an intruder who was suspected to be an Arab. Fictional accounts of these events can be found in "Voix du quartier pauvre" in *Le Premier Camus, suivi de Ecrits de jeunesse d'Albert Camus* (1973; translated as "Voices from the Poor Quarter" in *Youthful Writings*, 1976) and *La Mort*

Camus at the offices of Combat, *1944 (collection of Mme Catherine Camus)*

heureuse. By far the strongest and most objectionable character in the household was grandmother Sintès, whose domineering attitude, aggressive hypocrisy, and hypochondria led to strong literary scenes in *L'Envers et l'endroit*.

Although the family lived in poverty, along with the other residents of the Belcourt district, Camus, by his own account, did not really suffer in his childhood from the restrictive living conditions. Belcourt, in the words of Herbert Lottman, "was the district of Algiers' deserving poor, those who worked hard for low wages in the small factories and harbor installations, or for themselves as independent craftsmen." Camus found the traditional escape through education. After learning to read and to write at the kindergarten in the Allée des Mûriers, Camus was enrolled in the *école communale* on the Rue Aumerat. The books he read in the school library were complemented by detective and cloak-and-dagger novels borrowed from the municipal library. As a *pupille de la Nation*, a child of a fallen French soldier, he received a modest allocation for school supplies and free hospital care. Former classmates remember him as a somewhat aloof and distant child who avoided rough games. Louis Germain, the stern but perspicacious fifth-grade teacher to whom Camus later dedicated his Nobel Prize acceptance speech, recognized his pupil's unusual talents. Germain coached Camus by making him work after hours so he could apply for competitive grants which would enable him to pursue his secondary studies at the highly selective Lycée Bugeaud, called the Grand Lycée. The elementary schoolteacher even helped overcome the family's resistance. The grandmother especially thought that Camus, like his brother, Lucien, should secure a remunerative position as soon as possible. Once he was enrolled in the Grand Lycée, Camus was automatically scheduled to pursue a curriculum leading to the French *baccalauréat*, the highly competitive exit examination which remains the standard prerequisite for admission to any French university.

Historically the formative years spent in the lycée, especially the last one in which the subject of philosophy played a central role, provided students with stimulating intellectual contacts. Camus was no exception to this pattern. His major influence was his philosophy teacher whom he encountered first in his last year at the lycée and then again at the University of Algiers: Jean Grenier. A peripatetic essayist and decidedly independent thinker who had good connections with the publishing house Gallimard, Grenier was then a man in his early thirties just about to begin a long and mostly underrated writing career. Among other essays, he would publish *Les Iles* (The Islands, 1933) and *Essai sur l'esprit d'orthodoxie* (Essay on the Orthodox Spirit, 1938), both, like his other writings, highly unorthodox works which Camus found seminal for the development of his own style and thought, first in his lyrical essay *Noces*, later in his major philosophical essays *Le Mythe de Sisyphe* and *L'Homme révolté* (1951; translated as *The Rebel*, 1953).

Camus wrote the preface for the 1959 edition of *Les Iles*. While comparing the influence of *Les Iles* on his generation with the impact of André Gide's *Les Nourritures terrestres* (The Fruits of the Earth, 1897), he felt that Gide's invocations "venaient trop tard, avec leur invitation au bonheur. Le bonheur, nous en faisions profession, avec insolence" (came too late with their invitation to happiness. We were professing happiness with insolence). His debt to Grenier is more of a methodological than of a substantive nature: "Ainsi, je ne dois pas à Grenier des certitudes qu'il ne pouvait ni ne voulait donner. Mais je lui

dois, au contraire, un doute, qui n'en finira pas et qui m'a empêché, par exemple, d'être un humaniste au sens où on l'entend aujourd'hui, je veux dire un homme aveuglé par de courtes certitudes (Thus, I do not owe certainties to Grenier which he neither could nor would provide. Rather, I owe him a doubt which will never end and which prevented me, for example, from being a humanist in today's sense, that is a man blinded by shortsighted certainties).

Perhaps the best assessment of this singular relationship in twentieth-century French letters between a respectfully shy student and a reserved and evasive but well-meaning professor is their correspondence, published in 1981, which spans the years 1932 to 1960. From the correspondence one can infer the range of mutual understanding, misunderstanding, and compassion that marked the longstanding relationship during which they taught each other lessons of proximity and distance. Until 1942 (if not beyond), the year in which *L'Etranger* and *Le Mythe de Sisyphe* launched Camus in Paris literary circles, he remained the respectful former student. Gradually, and especially after his 1957 Nobel Prize, the roles of the correspondents would shift but not reverse, for Camus never forgot the influence his former philosophy professor had on him. It may have been Gide, André Malraux, Henri de Montherlant, and other authors associated with the then avant-garde *Nouvelle Revue Française* who helped Camus shape his style and focus. But it was Grenier who opened for him the doors to the pre-Socratics, Saint Augustine, the Eastern and Western mystics, Pascal, Kierkegaard, Schopenhauer, and Nietzsche. It was Grenier who, from the beginning, made his student reflect on commitment and indifference and who, above all, acted as an exemplary practitioner of productive ambiguity, discreet irony, and noncorrosive skepticism. It was also Grenier who gave the young Camus André de Richaud's *La Douleur* (Sorrow), a love story between a young French widow and a German soldier, set during World War I, and keenly observed by the woman's young son. It was impossible for Camus not to relate this story to his own situation as a war orphan. Grenier cannot be summed up by a simple label, but it would do him no injustice to call his thought and expression, as well as his life-style, quintessentially ambiguous. It is no accident that Grenier's reading list of the late 1920s and early 1930s prefigured by several decades the standard curriculum of the post-World War II generation.

Camus with his children, twins Jean and Catherine, at Chambon-sur-Lignon, 1946

Paradoxically, the noncommittal Grenier, for whom life itself was the ultimate paradox, encouraged Camus to join the Communist party. Although the choice turned out to be a wrong one which resulted in Camus's expulsion from that organization, it provided the aspiring writer with an experience which decisively shaped his political philosophy. Finally, it was Grenier who opened the way for Camus's first publications in his own cultural monthly *Sud.* Written first as school assignments, these early essays have been collected in *Ecrits de jeunesse d'Albert Camus* (1973; translated in *Youthful Writings,* 1976).

In 1929, when he was sixteen, Camus experienced his initial contact with Gide's *Les Nourritures terrestres.* One of his uncles, Gustave Acault, a widely read butcher whose anarchistic tendencies impressed his nephew, gave him the book. Gide's poetic invocations, which had gone almost unnoticed when the work was published in 1897, had become a primer for young intellectuals of the generation after World War I. This early encounter with the romantic temperament and classical style of one of the major names in French letters, who as a cofounder was also a power broker in the circles of the *Nouvelle Revue Française,* left Camus cool. He returned the book to his uncle and later wrote in his 1951 "Hommage à Gide" (published in *Nouvelle Revue Française* in November 1951) that "Le rendez-vous était manqué" (It was a missed rendez-vous). In the same text Camus acknowledges, however, that a second reading jolted him. Gide seemed to him "le modèle de l'artiste, le gardien,

Director Jean-Louis Barrault, composer Arthur Honegger, and Camus (at front); with Barrault's company at the staging of
L'Etat de siège *in Marigny, 1948 (photo Lipnitzki)*

fils de roi, qui veillait aux portes d'un jardin où je voulais vivre" (the model of an artist, the guardian, son of the king, who kept the gates of a garden in which I wanted to live). When Gide's 1947 Nobel Prize generated a host of criticisms that his ideas were outdated, Camus applied to him criteria which clearly had become his own: "Les plus grandes philosophies peuvent vieillir; mais le style demeure" (The greatest philosophies may age; but style remains).

The monotonous life-style of the city of Algiers, as described in *L'Etranger,* was interrupted by occasional visits to the movies, sports, and by outdoor activities. Camus was an avid soccer player, a goalkeeper, who would find in his team, the Racing Universitaire Algérois, the communication and social contacts which he lacked in the taciturn environment of his family. He recognized early, and often repeated, that team sports taught him the most important moral lessons, that what he knew about morality and duty he owed to sports and learned in the RUA.

In 1930, at seventeen, Camus was diagnosed as having tuberculosis. Its physical and emotional effects, in fact the illness itself, remained with him for the rest of his life. Suddenly this sports-minded youth was condemned to a sedentary life-style to which he only fully acquiesced during relapses. Before he had tasted life, the adolescent was made to confront the possibility of imminent death, a theme that is reflected in *La Mort heureuse, Le Mythe de Sisyphe, L'Etranger*, and later works. For his convalescence the doctor recommended that he stay with his uncle Acault who had the resources and the red meat—thought to help the cure—necessary to provide Camus with a healthier environment and more wholesome nutrition. Acault not only gave Camus a better home but also money to buy clothes and books. Above all, he acted as an example of how to develop a life-style mixing work and pleasure. A butcher in the morning, he spent his afternoons in cafés blending into the Algiers intelligentsia. However, in spite of his aspirations he never became a surrogate father to the sick boy whose independence was already too advanced by the time his uncle took him in. Thanks to Acault's material assistance, Camus, who always dressed neatly, took on dandylike dressing habits with a distinct preference for all-white attire. His literary imagination was running wild, and some of his friends saw in him Lafcadio, the hero of Gide's *Les Caves du Vatican* (*Lafcadio's Adventures*, 1914). One of them, Max-Pol Fouchet, who was also stricken by tuberculosis, later broke with him because Camus won from him Simone Hié (1914-1970), the "Siren of Algiers," who became the future author's first wife in 1934.

Camus's literary and philosophical apprenticeship, the intensive readings which his condition encouraged and which the rigorous curriculum of his lycée required, made him read the stoics and Pascal with a more mature understanding. Once he became a philosophy student, he constructed a highly personal frame of reference consisting mainly of the pre-Socratics, the stoics, the church fathers, Kierkegaard, Schopenhauer, and Nietzsche. It was not pessimism that he learned from them but the art of ironic distance. His reading background prior to his formal university studies was enhanced by a year relatively free of pressure immediately following his *baccalauréat*. It was part of a two-year curriculum preparing students for the *grandes écoles* such as the Ecole Normale Supérieure. Because only the first year was available in Algiers and a move to Paris was out of the question, Camus was able to devote considerable time to extracurricular activities.

In the fall of 1933 he began his philosophy studies at the University of Algiers. By then his uncle Acault no longer supported him because he did not approve of his nephew's affair with Simone Hié, an exotic beauty with a drug problem who flaunted her liberated behavior and shocked the Algiers bourgeoisie. Modest financial assistance came from the future mother-in-law, an understanding ophthalmologist. The couple married on 16 June 1934 but continued to shun conventional behavior. Taking their cue from literary models, Simone and Albert Camus never used the familiar *tu* but always *vous* in addressing each other. Even with most of his friends, who recognized his natural leadership, Camus kept his distance by insisting on the formal *vous*. Obviously, this did not sit well with everybody and contributed to the reputation of his haughtiness. At the university his main professor was René Poirier. Jean Grenier, an *agrégé* like Poirier, also taught courses at the university and thus was able to continue the intellectual mentorship of Camus begun at the lycée. His third major professor was Jacques Heurgon, who taught Latin and provided an additional link with metropolitan intellectual circles. While Poirier lectured on subjects of the traditional philosophy curriculum in French universities, but also on Kierkegaard, Husserl, and Heidegger, Grenier included in his courses less orthodox topics such as Taoism, Hindu philosophy, and Chekhov. The erudite Poirier immediately recognized that Camus's strength was not school philosophy but the free expression of seminal ideas in essay form, that the promising student had more talent as an artist than as a philosopher. Under Poirier's direction Camus wrote his thesis for the third year of his curriculum which led to the *diplôme d'études supérieures* and a potential teaching career. The subject allowed Camus to intellectualize theological and philosophical issues and some of his own metaphysical concerns by examining an epochal encounter of ideas through Plotinus and Saint Augustine.

His thesis was submitted in 1936 but not published until 1965, when it appeared in Camus's *Essais* (Essays) under the title "Métaphysique chrétienne et néoplatonisme" (Christian Metaphysics and Neoplatonism). It is a typical academic exercise with a heavy, although not always pertinent, apparatus. But as a valuable early document of sustained reflection it mirrors many personal preoccupations which Camus projects into the texts he interprets. Its strength lies in the precocious quality of the synthesis, in numerous intuitions and flashes prefiguring themes which would form the core of Camus's later works. Its

Camus in the typesetting room of the weekly L'Express

weaknesses are the analysis of complex philosophical and theological arguments, a tendency to generalization, and borrowing too liberally from sources without proper reference. Of Hellenistic culture, for which he would sustain his admiration, Camus writes that "Ses temples sont construits à sa mesure. En un certain sens les Grecs acceptaient une justification sportive et esthétique de l'existence" (Its temples are built to its size. In a certain way, the Greeks accepted a sporting and aesthetic justification of existence). The first part deals with the relationship of the Incarnation to pessimism and hope in the New Testament; the second focuses on the Gnostics who attempted to reconcile knowledge and salvation. In the more widely known second half Camus develops his cherished notion of the confluence of two cultures in the Mediterranean basin: the ahistorical Greek and the eschatological Christian. Thus the third and fourth parts are devoted to Plotinus, the artist philosopher, and to Saint Augustine, the converted sensualist who roots his faith in the discovery of evil and grace. While Camus writes approvingly of Saint Augustine's methodical limitation of the range of purely philo-

sophical reflection, he disapproves implicitly of Saint Augustine's "la damnation des enfants morts sans baptême" (damnation of the children who die unbaptized). In spite of his admiration for the fellow North African, in subsequent works, Camus repeatedly presents the dogmatic position of the bishop of Hippo as scandalous, and he uses the issue as a theme as late as *La Peste.*

The years from 1934 to 1937 were marked by Camus's increasing political involvement and related cultural activities, his travels to the Balearic islands and to central Europe, the rapid deterioration of his marriage and eventual separation from Simone Hié, whose drug addiction and related extramarital escapades became unbearable. Camus continued to lend her support even after the divorce, which occurred belatedly in 1940, and never tolerated open criticism of his former wife. To survive he worked at several odd jobs, including a clerkship at the Algiers *préfecture* from which he was fired for his inability to master the bureaucratic style. His studies ended with the *diplôme d'études supérieures* granted in May 1936. For health reasons he was prevented from submit-

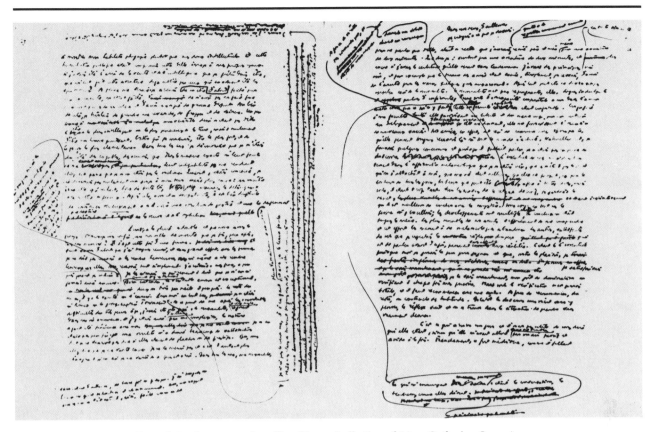

Pages from the manuscript of La Chute *(collection of Mme Catherine Camus)*

ting himself to the rigors of the *agrégation,* a grueling national competition for teaching positions at the upper lycée level. In fact, he shied away from seeking a teaching position altogether. After standing on the sidelines for a while—for too long in the eyes of some of his companions—he joined the Communist party in 1935, informing Grenier but few of his other friends.

On behalf of the party he worked on several fronts, but above all his politically motivated activities were cultural. He cofounded and codirected the party's Maison de la Culture and performed duties at the Collège du Travail, a kind of workers' college. Among the main tasks of the Maison de la Culture was the exposure of major metropolitan artists to the local public and the dissemination of indigenous and Mediterranean art and civilization. With a few friends he formed a theater group called Théâtre du Travail (Labor Theater) whose ambitious program included production of an adaptation by Camus of André Malraux's *Le Temps du mépris* (*Days of Wrath,* 1935). The text of this adaptation has been lost. But in spite of the lack of professional training, the work on the text, the casting and directing (shortly thereafter Camus would also ap-

pear in roles acting for the itinerant theatrical group of Radio-Algiers) revealed theater to him as a total art soliciting mind and body and fostering companionship. For the rest of his life Camus declared that theater was his preferred genre.

The emphasis on the collective enterprise found its dramatically and politically most direct expression in *Révolte dans les Asturies* (Revolt in Asturias, 1936), the plot of which was based on a Spanish miners' strike in 1934. The highly charged political situation in Algiers and Camus's emotional ties to Spain, which was then on the verge of its civil war, clearly made the subject matter attractive. Cowritten by Camus and his fellow students and comrades Anne Sicard, Alfred Poignant, and Yves Bourgeois, the propagandistic play was rehearsed and publicly announced, but it could not be performed because the mayor of Algiers banned it. It was printed in a small edition by a friend and beginning publisher, Edmond Charlot. An extract of the play was performed twice at the Maison, under the title *Espagne 34* (Spain 34) in April 1937. In May 1937 Charlot brought out Camus's first book, *L'Envers et l'endroit,* and in 1939 he published *Noces.* Both are volumes of essays. The same year ideological differences with his cell led to Camus's expulsion from the Communist party, an event which prompted him to change the name of his theater group to Théâtre de l'Equipe (Team Theater). The process of artistic and intellectual maturation that Camus was undergoing can be clearly observed by comparing *La Mort heureuse,* on which he worked from 1936 to 1938, *L'Envers et l'endroit,* and *Noces.*

In 1936, when his marital situation deteriorated beyond repair, Camus rented a house overlooking the bay at Algiers. He was able to do so because three student friends of his, Jeanne Sicard, Marguerite Dobrenn (who would later edit the Camus-Grenier correspondence), and Christiane Galindo, joined him in what became a playful adventure of communal living. The Maison Fichu, as it had been called after the owner, became the Maison devant le Monde (House above the World). Its features and surroundings are painstakingly described in the first novel Camus wrote, whose publication he never permitted in his lifetime.

Written in 1937 from a distinctly Nietzschean perspective, *La Mort heureuse,* by its very title and content, signals from the outset of Camus's career as a fiction writer the subdued yet pervasive presence of irony. Although he would later say in his notebooks that all his work was ironical and complain that humor in his writings was not appreciated enough, he considered *La Mort heureuse* an artistic failure. A vague predecessor of Meursault, the protagonist of *L'Etranger,* the main character in *La Mort heureuse,* Patrice Mersault–the name is a combination of *mer* and *soleil,* sea and sun–seeks advice for his pursuit of happiness from a crippled rich man named Zagreus whose presence evokes the many-faced Dionysus whose excesses, sacrifice, and rebirth make him a cornerstone of Nietzsche's concept of the tragic. This wheelchair-bound pre-Beckettian figure without legs convinces Mersault that money is capable of buying freedom and happiness, both of which he, Zagreus, can never enjoy because of his physical impairment. Professing a doctrine of will-to-happiness, Zagreus convinces his docile pupil that the realization of happiness can and must be achieved by any means. Zagreus's mentoring and semimythical status recall Ménalque (in Gide's *L'Immoraliste,* 1902), who exercises a similar subversive influence upon the protagonist Michel's dream of self-fulfillment. True to his mentor's insistent advice, he kills Zagreus in a mutually prear-

ranged way to make his murder look like suicide. With his friend's stolen fortune he sets out to live a life free of work. But he catches what appears to be a cold and is soon forced to return home to the sun of North Africa from a trip to rainy and foggy Europe. In Algiers he lives with three like-minded women above the bay in the House above the World. But Mersault soon tires of the communal life and seeks happiness in solitude in an isolated house at Chenoua. His search for communion with the sun and the sea ends in ultimate solitude which he finds by dying a "happy death" as a result of his sickness, which turns out to be pleurisy. The symptoms and course of the pleurisy, the life-style and aspirations refer quite overtly to Camus's own health and state of mind at the time.

It was not only the transparency of autobiographical elements (including the pilgrimage to Europe) and the formal as well as structural deficiencies that induced Camus not to publish *La Mort heureuse.* Mersault's egotistic drive for absolute happiness and the containing forces of relativism posed a conflict for which Camus soon found more adept representatives in Meursault of *L'Etranger,* the antihero of the relative, and the Roman emperor Caligula, the hero of the absolute and title character of Camus's 1944 play. Meursault and Caligula live and die for a believable cause, no matter what moral objections the reader might have to it. Patrice Mersault, in contrast, is unable to separate self-fulfillment from self-gratification convincingly. Thus he dies neither a hero nor a champion or antihero but a somewhat hypocritical *raisonneur* lacking redeeming–that is, aesthetic–value. Mersault, Meursault, and Caligula face, each in his own way, the central question on which Camus will focus his attention in *L'Homme révolté* and which he will clearly answer negatively: Does the end ever justify the means? In the light of his war experience, the strong Nietzschean overtones which characterize Camus's early writings, his own propensity to nothingness, to being "stone among stones," do not disappear but find a more successful form of artistic transformation which avoids transparent autobiography and ideology through sustained ambiguity.

Until it was republished by Gallimard in 1958, *L'Envers et l'endroit* existed only in the 1937 Charlot edition of a few hundred copies. Not surprisingly, this first book was dedicated to Jean Grenier. Although Camus once asserted that in his twenties an aspiring writer hardly knows how to write, some Camus scholars consider it a key text. In many ways the five essays describe the enriching qualities of the poverty which Camus endured but from which he never suffered. "La pauvreté, d'abord, n'a jamais été un malheur pour moi: la lumière y répandait ses richesses. Même mes révoltes en ont été éclairées" (First, poverty has never meant misfortune to me: light spread its riches. Even my rebellions have been enlightened by it). "L'Ironie" ("Irony"), the opening essay of the five pieces, gives the young narrator's perspective on old people awaiting their deaths, one of whom is clearly Camus's tyrannical grandmother. "Entre oui et non" ("Between Yes and No") describes life in the Belcourt district and a child facing the obstinate silence of his mother: "Elle ne l'a jamais caressé puisqu'elle ne saurait pas" (She never caressed him since she would not know how). Mother and son live "une solitude à deux" (solitude for two), and the young narrator finds the room in which his mother lives a summary of "toute *l'absurde* simplicité du monde" (all the *absurd* simplicity of the world). "La Mort dans l'âme" (Death in the Soul) is an account of his trip to somber Prague and the return to North Africa via Italy. Attempting to escape his anguish through visiting art sites, "je voulais," he writes, "résoudre ma révolte en mélancolie" (I attempted to resolve my revolt in melancholy). The burnt landscape of Italy reveals to him a Gidean lesson of *dénuement*, or willful destitution, "une forme dépouillée et sans attraits de ce goût du néant que je portais en moi" (a stripped and unattractive form of this taste for nothingness which I harbored). A trip to the Balearics yields the essay "Amour de vivre" ("Love of Life") in which, once more, the narrator notices "ce Nada qui n'a pu naître que devant des paysages écrasés de soleil" (this nothingness which could only arise before landscapes which were crushed by the sun). The title essay, "L'Envers et l'endroit," placed last in the volume, relates the story of an old woman who invested an inheritance that came to her late in life in her own small mausoleum. Consciousness and not happiness is what the narrator seeks now. Once more, irony teaches him how to balance love and despair. "Vivez comme si . . ." (Live as if . . .)– Ivan Karamazov's adage constitutes for him "toute ma science" (all my science). Dostoyevski and, especially, Karamazov's "as if" continue to figure prominently in Camus's thought and art. In 1938 the Théâtre de l'Equipe performed,

under Camus's direction, Jacques Copeau's adaptation of *The Brothers Karamazov*.

Camus felt that the literature of his time did not pay enough attention to landscapes. It might have been for this reason that both essay volumes, but especially *Noces*, place landscapes in the center of attention. The four lyrical essays in *Noces*, organized along the alternate themes of life and death, nature and culture, can be considered prose poems. "Noces à Tipasa" ("Nuptials at Tipasa"), "Le Vent à Djémila" ("The Wind in Djemila"), L'Eté à Alger" ("Summer in Algiers"), and "Le Désert" ("The Desert") praise the marriage of man, time, and space. No matter how fragile happiness is, the small port city of Tipasa with its Roman ruins incites its visitor to risk a hymn to life. A "dead town," Djemila bathes in relentless sun and wind, a splendidly vulgar landscape forcing its visitor to a "lucidité aride" (arid lucidity). While he is constantly reminded of death, he finds in the stones the telling silence and indifference of beauty. The monotony of Algiers is especially visible in August, but the people's simple desires and fast pace of life teach him that "une seule chose est plus tragique que la souffrance et c'est la vie d'un homme heureux" (one thing only is more tragic than suffering and it is the life of a happy man). In contrast, the mineral grandeur of desertscapes is reflected on the faces of many Mediterraneans whose lives and characters have been shaped by indifference and placidity. The narrator's memories of Italy and Spain, where nature and culture form a perfect union, make him discover that "le bonheur naît de l'absence d'espoir; . . . l'esprit trouve sa raison dans le corps" (happiness is born from the absence of hope; . . . mind finds its reason in the body). Like *L'Envers et l'endroit*, *Noces* contains the nucleus of most key thoughts which Camus developed in his later works. Chief among them is the notion of measure which *Le Mythe de Sisyphe* informally and *L'Homme révolté* formally link to "affirmative negation": Florence, Pisa, and, especially, the ethereal painted faces of Piero della Francesca reveal to him once and forever that "S'il est vrai que toute vérité porte en elle son amertume, il est aussi vrai que toute négation contient une floraison de 'oui'" (If it is true that every truth contains its own bitterness, it is also true that every negation contains a blossoming of "yes").

From 1938 to the outbreak of World War II Camus worked as a journalist for *Alger Républicain*. This new daily was financed by a cooperative of politically like-minded friends. Its editor in chief, Pascal Pia, who came from Paris, turned out to be one of Camus's most important links to the metropolis before he became an adversary. An aggressive opposition paper, *Alger Républicain* soon reflected pacifist and protoanarchistic tendencies. A convinced pacifist himself, Camus was responsible for the city desk, court reporting, and an occasional book review. He also had investigative reporting assignments. Representative segments of his important series on poverty in Kabylia were later included in *Actuelles III: Chronique algérienne 1939-1958* (1958). Periodically he used his forum to indict the right-wing policies of Algiers mayor Augustin Rozis. To overcome the paper's steadily mounting financial troubles, an evening edition named *Le Soir Républicain* was added. After September 1939 the censors made publishing the papers impossible. Both Pia and Camus had to give up their ambitious venture and transfer to the politically more tolerant Paris.

The transfer was to be Camus's most important change in his career as a writer, which, thus far, had been centered on Algiers and the Mediterranean basin. While Pia was able to secure Camus a job with the large daily *Paris-Soir*, the war forced the paper's staff to retreat, first to Clermont-Ferrand, then to Lyons. In this city Camus married, in December 1940, Oran-born Francine Faure (1914-1979), and soon thereafter he lost his job on account of paper shortages and reduction of personnel. The couple returned to Oran where Camus had a hard time finding employment; he did teach in a couple of private schools and renew his contacts with the remainder of his group in Algiers. Thanks to their contacts, Pia and Grenier were able to secure the help of influential readers and intermediaries in Paris, such as Francis Ponge, Marcel Arland, Jean Paulhan, and André Malraux. As a result, two of the three volumes of the "cycle of the absurd," *L'Etranger* and *Le Mythe de Sisyphe*, were published by Gallimard in 1942. *Caligula* followed in 1944 together in a single volume with another play, *Le Malentendu* (translated as *Cross Purpose*, 1947). In spite of his absence Camus now had a firm foothold in the metropolis. Above all, he had access to one of France's premier publishing houses. His deteriorating health forced him to seek refuge from the humid climate in Oran. He obtained a medical pass and in August 1942 the couple settled for what they thought would be a few weeks enjoying the mountain air in a friend's boardinghouse near Chambon-sur-Lignon (Mas-

sif Central). To seek employment Francine Camus returned to Algiers before her husband. Camus, who had already booked his passage, was caught by surprise by the 7 November 1942 landing of the Allies in North Africa. The couple remained separated until the liberation of Paris in 1944.

As early as 1938 Camus had begun to focus on what would become his triptych of the absurd: the *récit L'Etranger;* the philosophical essay *Le Mythe de Sisyphe;* and the play *Caligula*. This three-genre approach to a common theme was a pattern later reflected in, among other works by Camus, the triad on revolt: *La Peste* (narrative), *Les Justes* (play) (1950; translated as *The Just Assassins* in *Caligula and Three Other Plays*, 1958), and *L'Homme révolté* (essay). But while the themes of the absurd and of revolt are at the core of the two cycles respectively, they constitute from the beginning inseparable entities. Thus, at first sight *L'Etranger* appears to be a fictional account of Meursault, the protagonist, caught in the web of absurdity. But his way of recognizing and coping with the absurd makes absurdity a stepping-stone for his rejection of the beliefs and the life-style which society attempts to impose on him. Meursault's initially instinctual refusal becomes a lucid revolt. Thus he is able to look toward his execution not as a victim but as an antihero capable of remaining faithful to himself.

Upon learning that his mother has died, Meursault is forced to review his relationship with her and with life. A taciturn but understanding clerk with no career ambitions, he is not bothered by his mother's death and accepts the monotony of his life-style, quickly taking up a moviegoing habit again and resuming a carefree love affair. He befriends Raymond, a pimp who mistreated an Arab woman and is pursued by her relatives. During a seemingly harmless weekend on the beach with Raymond and a couple, the men are involved in a brawl with two Arabs who have followed them. Raymond is cut. Later Meursault returns to the beach and, blinded by the glare of the sun and the blade of the Arab's knife, he shoots and kills the Arab. The second part of the *récit* shows Meursault's imprisonment and trial in which he is pitted against the representatives of the legal, social, and religious authorities. He is sentenced to death and finds solace in the "tendre indifférence du monde" (his tender indifference to the world). "L'Indifférent" (The Indifferent) was, at one time, a title Camus had planned to use for this, his first major piece of fiction.

Published in one of the darkest years of modern French history, 1942, *L'Etranger* was immediately recognized for its innovative narrative techniques. As early as 1937 the major theme of *L'Etranger* appears in the *Carnets:* "Récit–l'homme qui ne veut pas se justifier. L'idée qu'on se fait de lui lui est préférée. Il meurt, seul à garder conscience de cette vérité–" (Story–the man who refuses to justify himself. Other people prefer their idea of him. He dies, alone in his awareness of what he really is–). Psychological depth, an established parameter of quality in the traditional French novel, was for Camus a concession to the need for continuity and transparency. As an admirer of the ahistorical perspective of the pre-Socratic thinkers, he discovered, as he wrote in *Carnets,* an "Erreur d'une psychologie de détail.... La psychologie est action, non réflexion sur soi-même" (Mistake of a psychology which concentrates on details.... Psychology is action, not thinking about oneself). By the time he was working on *L'Etranger* his search for his own style had been informed by such writers as Kierkegaard, Nietzsche, Kafka, Dostoyevski, and Gide. But another major impact would come from the New World: the American novel of the 1930s and 1940s which "prétend trouver son unité en réduisant l'homme, soit à l'élémentaire, soit à ses réactions extérieures et à son comportement" (claims to find its unity by reducing man either to the elementary or to his reactions and to his behavior).

Stylistically the telegram which announces Meursault's mother's death seems to infuse the rest of the text, which is composed of short, chopped sentences, most of them main clauses. Thus Meursault's deceptive simple-mindedness is directly reflected in a discourse whose stylized orality is underlined by the repetition of key phrases ("Cela ne veut rien dire" [This means nothing]) and the almost exclusive use of the present and perfect tenses. With the ascent of the New Novel and the increasing attention given to narrative techniques, critics have made of this *récit* one of the parameters of modern fiction which may represent anything from "blank writing" (Roland Barthes, *Le Degré zéro de l'ecriture,* 1953) to interior monologue (Robert Champigny, *A Pagan Hero,* 1969), autoreferential text, and "hermeneutic paradigm" (Brian T. Fitch, *The Narcissistic Text,* 1982). Sustained ambiguity makes it impossible for the reader to determine conclu-

sively at which time the narrative was articulated and by whom it was "written." Both deductive and inductive logic will involve the reader avid for "truth" in the same quagmire into which the defense attorney, the prosecutor, and the priest throw Meursault in the pursuit of their truth. The only plausibility that can be found, then, is on the fictional, or aesthetic, level.

Not surprisingly, many interpreters jumped to the conclusion that Meursault professes moral bankruptcy and nihilism, a condemnation which echoes the first impressions Gide's *L'Immoraliste* made on his public. Paradoxically, Meursault's crime and "fall" induce the rise of his consciousness. The entire second part of the *récit* shows him no longer as a primal creature indifferent to human relations and equating all his experiences without distinction but as an increasingly self-aware observer and implicit critic of the world. Refusing the recourse to hope, he is capable of transforming his indifference and detachment into lucidity. Above all, Meursault discovers that absurdity, once recognized and defined as the absence of answers to vital questions, can lead to conscious affirmation of life, to happiness; that death cannot kill the desire for life in this world at this moment. While the prosecutor's arguments and the death penalty leave no doubt as to how Meursault's contemporaries judged him, it remains up to each generation's readers to decide the meaning of his "guilt." One possible reading of *L'Etranger* is that it is an ironical presentation, a fictional deconstruction of the seemingly austere theory of the absurd presented in *Le Mythe de Sisyphe.*

Simply put, *Le Mythe de Sisyphe* argues that the innate meaninglessness of the world, the absurd, must first be recognized and then protested. The founding paradox is that man cannot cease to yearn for answers which cannot be found. But if life has no preordained meaning, is suicide, Camus asks, a logical conclusion? His answer is a resounding *no.* Absurdity does not mean resignation but rather the beginning of rebellion against it. The recourse to any transhuman help (God, metaphysical hope, transcendence, the supernatural, and so on) is a mere escape which Camus calls "le suicide philosophique" (philosophical suicide). Life is a struggle in which individuals shape and define themselves and their values by rebelling against the absurd. The legendary Sisyphus, condemned by the gods to roll a boulder up a hill, only to have it roll down again each time, thus becomes a para-

Francine and Albert Camus in Stockholm, at the time he was awarded the Nobel Prize (collection of Mme Catherine Camus)

digm for the individual who finds his fulfillment in persisting in his rebellion. He turns the gods' punishment against them by finding happiness in rolling the boulder uphill.

The referential framework of Camus's first major philosophical essay points to the authors he read as a philosophy student. A new outbreak of tuberculosis which affected the second lung sharpened his already keen preoccupation with sickness, death, and suicide. Although *Le Mythe de Sisyphe* has all the trappings of a treatise, its value lies less in the arguments proper than in the manner in which Camus arranged them and, especially, in the abstract articulation of the

major themes of his theatrical and fictional works. In *Le Mythe de Sisyphe* he develops a rather egocentric ethic of quantity of which Don Juan, the actor, and the conqueror are prime practitioners. In many ways these three are ironic actors on the stage of life. They act as if the world had an established meaning, fully knowing that this is not the case. But while revolt is an important ingredient in *Le Mythe de Sisyphe*, it is too open-ended; it does not yet have a tangible value-oriented direction. Values, for Camus, have validity only if they are rooted in the individual's experience. His involuntary exile in occupied France after 1942 and his subsequent involvement in the Resistance provided that experience and enabled him to give his rebellion a more authentic moral dimension.

Thus, separation and exile, two major themes of *La Peste*, must be directly linked to Camus's war experiences. In a 1943 text entitled "Les Exilés dans la peste" (collected in *Théâtre, récits, nouvelles*, 1962) he treats these themes in an analytical manner. From the fall of 1942, when Camus found himself unexpectedly separated from his wife and his home city because of the Allied invasion of North Africa, he could no longer look at European history from the North African vantage point which had enabled him to maintain a pacifistic position. The new situation gave him an opportunity to become involved in the growing resistance movement. His actions were limited to clandestine journalism and communications, but soon he played a leading role in a paper whose very name meant struggle. *Combat*, which began as an underground pamphlet, moved from the province to Paris and, with Camus as editor in chief, became indisputably the leading newspaper in Paris after the Germans were driven from the city in August 1944. Although some of today's readers find his editorials "unreadable," "simplistic and dogmatic," in the words of his recent biographer Patrick McCarthy, Camus's leadership, his persistent appeal for placing politics in an ethical perspective and for building a new society, made *Combat* the moral conscience of post-Liberation France. He never liked to talk about the Resistance because he felt uncomfortable with the nostalgia of war veterans.

In November 1943 he accepted a position as *lecteur*, or reader of manuscripts, at Gallimard, a position which provided regular contacts with the literary lions, including Jean Paulhan, the *éminence grise* of the publishing house, who occasionally would utter biting comments on Camus's style. Trapped in France, he concentrated on his work on *La Peste* and also witnessed the public's reaction to *L'Etranger* and *Le Mythe de Sisyphe*. For the first time he met as a fellow writer his admired colleagues Jean-Paul Sartre, Simone de Beauvoir (both of whom contributed to *Combat*), André Malraux, and Louis Aragon; a little later he made the acquaintance of Maurice Merleau-Ponty, Boris Vian, Raymond Queneau, Michel Leiris, and others. It was the beginning of the existentialist era which saw Left-Bank intellectuals regularly gather in the Saint-Germain neighborhood in cafés such as the Flore. At ease at first in these trendy circles, Camus soon developed the same re-

calcitrance vis-à-vis orthodox Marxism, which his companions rarely questioned at the time, and the dominant ideology of "self-respecting" intellectuals. In May 1945 he was at Gide's side when the armistice was declared. He was also reunited with his old friend Pascal Pia, now *directeur* of *Combat*. However, their different political leanings and views on how and whether to continue the financially floundering paper, and possibly also some envy on Pia's part, eventually led to their parting. But for a short while Camus, Sartre, and other intellectuals were united in a common political and intellectual enterprise which they saw as one of the highest forms of *engagement*, or commitment in the existentialist sense.

As he had done in Algiers, Camus operated concurrently on several levels. Apart from his editorial activities, which gave him high visibility, he finished a second play, *Le Malentendu*, in which he renews the legend of the son who returns home incognito and is murdered by his own mother and sister. It was performed in August 1944, more than a year before *Caligula*. Its somber character further strengthened the view, long held thereafter, that Camus was prone to nihilism. Jolted by the horrors of the German war machine and genocidal atrocities, he published his *Lettres à un ami allemand* (1945; translated as "Letters to a German Friend" in *Resistance, Rebellion and Death*, 1961). The first two had been published separately in journals in 1943 and 1944; four letters comprise the single volume of 1945. In these letters he rejects the German way of dealing with absurdity which led this nation to equate nihilism and annihilation. The letters constitute the most telling documents showing Camus's switch from moral revolt to active resistance. They also sharply reject any philosophy which justifies the means by the end and associate rebellion with moderation and distributive justice, main themes of his later editorials in *Combat* and of *L'Homme révolté*. His major energies were devoted to what, in the popular view at least, would be his "war novel." At a time when, because of superficial interpretations of his essay on the absurd, he was widely heralded as a champion of despair, he pursued the completion of the "cycle of revolt" composed of *La Peste*, *Les Justes*, and *L'Homme révolté*. To finish his second novel Camus took a leave from *Combat;* he resigned in 1947 over sharp ideological and managerial differences and because, in his view, the paper had ceased to be a trendsetting voice.

While in Oran before *L'Etranger* was published, Camus had already begun his work on *La Peste*. With an eye on Cervantes, Defoe, and Melville, he was looking for a modern version of the battle against absurdity in which man has no recourse to God and victory will be temporary only. In "Présentation d'Herman Melville," published in *Essais* (1965), he writes that *Moby-Dick* is "l'un des mythes les plus bouleversants qu'on ait jamais imaginés sur le combat de l'homme contre le mal et sur l'irrésistible logique qui finit par dresser l'homme juste contre la création et le créateur d'abord, puis contre ses semblables et contre lui-même" (one of the most moving myths ever imagined on man's fight against evil and on the irresistible logic which ends up by pitting the just man first against creation and the creator and later against his equals and against himself). When in a February 1955 issue of *Club* he answered Roland Barthes's criticism of the ahistorical character of *La Peste,* Camus compared it to *L'Etranger* and stressed that it marked "le passage d'une attitude de révolte solitaire à la reconnaissance d'une communauté dont il faut partager les luttes" (the passage from an attitude of solitary revolt to the recognition of a community whose struggles must be shared).

Presented as a "chronicle," *La Peste* is seemingly the result of detached observations written by a narrator who, toward the end of the book, reveals himself to be one of the main characters, Dr. Rieux. It depicts the reaction to an imagined plague befalling Oran by individuals who, like the doctor, are trapped in the city and attempt to cope with the situation. They include Tarrou, an idealist of "sainteté sans Dieu" (sanctity without God); Rambert, a journalist who seeks to escape the city and rejoin the woman he loves but renounces his project when the opportunity occurs; Father Paneloux, a Jesuit priest who is Rieux's spiritual opponent and whose heart, but not faith, is shaken when he witnesses the agony of a child; Grand, an insignificant and suicidal clerk who is also an aspiring writer; and Cottard, a suspected criminal who is killed by the police. The struggle of Oran's citizens against the plague as an agent of absurdity and evil was perceived by the contemporary readers primarily as a thinly disguised allegory of the German occupation. Among the variety of human reactions to oppression two stand out: one can fight the plague with human means, which is what the doctor does, or one can seek recourse in transhuman help, which is what Father Paneloux proposes. In spite of its tempo-

rary character, the medical victory over the plague is a valuable community effort and as such preferable to moral or theological rationalization. *La Peste* was Camus's first large-scale popular success partly because it follows more traditional narrative patterns than *L'Etranger* and partly because of its topicality. Only later would *L'Etranger* replace *La Peste* as one of Gallimard's perennial best-sellers. The latter was also the basis of a stage version of the theme. Directed by Jean-Louis Barrault and entitled *L'Etat de siège* (1948; translated as *State of Siege* in *Caligula and Three Others Plays,* 1958), this play, produced in October 1948, turned out to be an artistic failure.

Seeing in Kafka's fiction the art of capturing the banality of the tragic, in *La Peste* Camus creates with Oran the setting of an utterly banal city. Its people live a life of routine, boredom, and insignificance. Pestilence will force some of the citizens to come to grips with themselves and the others to fight a deadly evil by shaping a difficult solidarity under the most adverse circumstances. The focus is on Rieux's relationships and on the mode of action and interaction of pairs composed of himself and the others. Neither hero nor saint, he practices the revolt of a common man, while Tarrou, the idealist, dreams of a sainthood without God. If the situation required it, Tarrou would consent, like Kaliayev, the hero of *Les Justes,* to be a "meurtrier innocent" (an innocent murderer) because his duty is to "limiter les dégâts," or contain the damages. Four years before *L'Homme révolté* pleads the case of antitotalitarianism explicitly, *La Peste* does so implicitly, especially through the spiritual conflict which opposes Rieux and Paneloux. The doctor proposes limited solutions for the present; his is a concrete set of relative values. Paneloux, the compassionate but faithful Jesuit for whom Rieux has considerable understanding, seeks final solutions in a distant future, a salvation that for Rieux belongs to the abstract world of the absolute. Grand's insignificance is paradigmatic of the general theme of the novel but also of the act of writing since he spends his free moments rewriting the opening sentence of a book in search of perfection.

As a chronicler, Rieux shows a constant concern for his means of expression and search for objectivity. This hands-on doctor and scrupulous writer pursues an aesthetic tainted with irony when he proclaims, speaking of himself, "Il n'a presque rien voulu modifier par les effets de l'art" (He wanted to change almost nothing by artistic effects). The important part of this statement, of course, is the modifier *almost*. The variety of levels of reading, writing, and discourse points far beyond the return to the "traditional" (supposedly realistic or naturalistic) novel with which a majority of readers associated *La Peste*. Until the late 1960s scores of interpreters assessed it mainly from an ethical vantage point and saw it as a stage in the author's evolution from moral relativism to value-founded solidarity, as a shift from individual to collective revolt. More recently, however, narrative techniques, especially the status of the text of *La Peste* and its relationship to the rest of Camus's fiction rather than the narrative's plot, characters, and moral lessons, have come under rigorous scrutiny. In spite of the illusion of realism which *La Peste* creates, close examination of the text shows that its surface referential function is matched by its ability to produce a language which draws attention to itself.

The turbulent postwar years were marked for Camus by a trip to the United States in early 1946, the political and ideological repercussions of the cold war, which led to his increasing disenchantment with his intellectual peer group, his break with Merleau-Ponty (1947), and, after an acrimonious polemic centered on *L'Homme révolté*, with Sartre (1952). These years were also marked by the birth of his twins, Jean and Catherine (5 September 1945), and by his moderate success as a playwright. While *Le Malentendu* had met with a cool reception, *Caligula* generated enthusiastic reviews and launched the career of one of France's leading actors of the 1950s, Gérard Philipe, who played the Roman emperor. *L'Etat de siège* was a failure and *Les Justes*, a play about the internal and external conflicts of a group of Russian terrorists, was only a partial success. The title of the play helped perpetuate the myth of Camus as a champion of justice, as a living model of what Rieux, in *La Peste*, calls "sainteté laïque" (holiness without God). In 1950 he produced *Actuelles: Chroniques 1944-1948* (translated in part in *Resistance, Rebellion, and Death*, 1961) a cross section of his editorials in *Combat* to which he added a series of stirring articles entitled "Ni victimes ni bourreaux" ("Neither Victims nor Executioners"), first published in *Caliban* (1947) and translated in *Adelphi* (1948). But his main attention in the late 1940s was devoted to reflections on historical configurations of revolt and revolution at a time when a chorus of ideologists was calling for radi-

cal changes. This resulted in his second major philosophical essay, *L'Homme révolté*.

The main parts of the essay are entitled "Metaphysical Revolt," "Historical Revolt," "Revolt and Art," and "Thought at the Meridian." Beyond the individual and communal ethic outlined in previous works, *L'Homme révolté* is an attempt systematically to apply ethical principles to politics and history. "Metaphysical Revolt" is a critical examination of types who represent absolute negation (Sade, for example, and the dandy) and affirmation (Nietzsche) and poetic revolt (Lautréamont and surrealism). "Historical Revolt" focuses on regicides, deicides, individual, rational, and irrational state terrorism. One of the best chapters, "Revolt and Art," amounts to a poetics of revolt and offers some of Camus's most penetrating pages on the art of the novel. Apart from the methodology Camus used, it was the metaphorical conclusion of "Thought at the Meridian" which generated the ire of many commentators, especially the team of *Les Temps Modernes*, Francis Jeanson, Simone de Beauvoir, and Jean-Paul Sartre. In this section he argued that revolutionary ideology based on historical effectiveness, which he associated with Northern Europe, particularly the Germans, always goes, by its very essence, beyond human and natural limits and turns back on itself, becoming limitless servitude–in opposition to the Mediterranean spirit, "la pensée solaire" (solar thought), which acknowledges the limits of man and stresses measure and balance between man and nature. Camus's discourse on revolt was meant to be a passionate exposure of the totalitarian foundation of several collectivist ideologies, including Marxism and fascism, and their devastating effect on the individual as well as on communities. As in his thesis "Christian Metaphysics and Neoplatonism" and in *Le Mythe de Sisyphe*, his philosophical arguments are often based on secondhand material. His historical analyses are validated by broad generalizations and omissions. But such imperfections were not the primary reason why the "Gauche engagée" (committed Left) decried him as a traitor. Rather, it was his daring juxtaposition of two contemporary forms of totalitarianism, fascism and communism, which was declared anathema. His allegedly vague and ethnocentric referral to the balanced form of Mediterranean thought culminating in its exemplary practice of measure was considered by critics from the Right and the Left a naive and irresponsible form of escapism. Recent French intellectual history, including the "new philosophers" in the 1970s and widely practiced questioning and occasional rejection of absolutist ideologies of any kind, has placed Camus's controversial essay in a new and more favorable light.

After the controversy that surrounded *L'Homme révolté* Camus was caught, in the last decade of his life, in the cross fire of the Algerian struggle for independence and the mounting criticism of his ambiguous position as a *pied noir*, or Algerian-born Frenchman, then living in France. Eventually he resorted to silence rather than fuel a debate which appeared to him fruitless, a silence for which he was much criticized. A long-standing liaison with actress Maria Casarès (who had played leading roles in three of his four plays) led to serious marital difficulties. Continued health problems further aggravated his general tiredness which led to a writing block, especially in the second half of the 1950s. But he lapsed into his "silence" only when he felt that several attempts to propose a compromise solution had failed. Worse yet, his numerous appeals to reason and support of a federalist solution in Algeria precipitated his political isolation. He was, in Patrick McCarthy's words, "a pied-noir at bay" whose intellectual and especially political sanity was openly and derisively questioned. It was fashionable in "progressive" circles to characterize him as a puppet of capitalism, as a careerist who had sold out his earlier convictions to the bourgeoisie eager to buy his books.

Never a partisan of regimented *engagement*, a leftist who strongly criticized communism (especially its orthodox Bolshevik configuration which some of his former friends publicly espoused), Camus neither sought nor found an escape from political harassment in his creative work. The only time he left his self-imposed political exile was to make two speeches, both in 1956. The first speech was an ill-fated attempt to propose, in Algiers facing a hostile crowd, a civilian truce; the second one was part of the uproar in the West that followed the Russian invasion in Hungary. In his attempt to overcome his writing difficulties, he returned to the theater and even sought, through Malraux, who in his Gaullist days was suspicious of leftist artists, the directorship of a state theater. Despite his problems he did manage to continue his work in the by now familiar three areas of theater, fiction, and essay. He produced a half dozen theatrical adaptations (the best known are his stage versions of William Faulkner's *Requiem for a Nun*, produced and pub-

lished in 1956, and Dostoyevski's *The Possessed*, produced and published in 1959). He also completed *Actuelles II: Chroniques 1948-1953* (translated in part in *The Myth of Sisyphus and Other Essays*, 1955, and in *Resistance, Rebellion and Death*, 1961), in which the concluding piece, "L'Artiste et son temps" ("The Artist and his Time"), is an attempt to answer and counteract some of the criticism he had received; *L'Eté* (1954; translated as "Summer" in *Lyrical and Critical*, 1967), a collection of Mediterranean essays; and *Actuelles III: Chronique algérienne 1939-1958* (1958; translated in part in *Resistance, Rebellion and Death*), in which he retraces his position on the Algerian problems and appeals for a civilian truce.

From June 1955 to February 1956 he resumed his journalistic activities by writing for the magazine *L'Express*, now collected in *Albert Camus editorialiste à "L'Express"* (1988), hoping to find a forum for his solitary solidarity with his time and his views on the Algerian problem and also to generate support for Pierre Mendès-France's return to power as premier (his cabinet fell in 1955 on the issue of his liberal North Africa policy). Teaming up with Arthur Koestler, he once more expressed the moral foundation of his opposition to the death penalty in "Réflexions sur la guillotine" in *Réflexions sur la peine capitale*, published in 1957 with an introduction and study by Jean Bloch-Michel (translated as *Reflections on the Guillotine*, 1959). But his most significant creative works of that period were his last novel, *La Chute* (1956; translated as *The Fall*, 1956), and a collection of short stories, *L'Exil et le royaume* (1957; translated as *Exile and the Kingdom*, 1958). In 1957 Camus was awarded the Nobel Prize which made him, at forty-three, the youngest author after Rudyard Kipling to receive this honor. The prize allowed him to buy a house in Lourmarin where he hoped to find the necessary calm to pursue his writing and to complete "Le Premier Homme." Many of his critics remarked that the Nobel Prize merely confirmed the finished character of his work and predicted that it would soon be forgotten, a prediction which persistently strong sales figures and sustained critical interest have proven wrong.

The cold war period, which began in France in 1947, not only brought about a hardening of political positions but also induced Sartre and others, especially after the "betrayal" of *L'Homme révolté*, to cover Camus's "donquichottisme moral" (moral Don Quixotism) with fashionable ridicule. He, in turn, displayed his share of intransigence in editorials and other public statements. Simone de Beauvoir's *Les Mandarins* (1954), although presented as fiction, included a thinly disguised portrait of Camus that would further disseminate his image as a nice guy but an ideologically naive and bumbling pontificator. After *La Peste* and *L'Eté* seemed to indicate that he was giving up the search for new fictional forms and returning to more established patterns of expression, the public at large, but particularly Camus's former comrades, were stunned by the unfamiliar style and tone of *La Chute*. As they had earlier, events in his life, particularly his tribulations with ideologues and experience with the metropolitan intelligentsia and politicians, furnished the background for his third major piece of fiction. At the height of his polemic with *Les Temps Modernes* he scorned the "parvenus de l'esprit révolutionnaire, nouveaux riches et pharisiens de la justice" (the parvenus of the revolutionary spirit, the newly rich and Pharisees of justice).

His last novel, however, is not simply a thematic treatment of autobiographical elements nor, as some critics prematurely indicated, a *règlement de comptes* (settlement of old scores) with the existentialist and communist coteries. Rather, *La Chute* engages both the protagonist, Jean-Baptiste Clamence, and the reader in an endless moral and intellectual spiral which subverts all systems of thought and expression, including the ability to distinguish truth and falsehood. Not only are there direct and indirect intertextual allusions to the philosophical (not to say pseudotheological) battles fought by Left Bank café intellectuals of the first half of the 1950s, but Clamence's masterful mixture of mockery, irony, and sarcasm is also, and unmistakably, directed against Camus's own strength and weakness. Clamence's brilliant success as a trial lawyer in Paris, where he is at ease in the best social circles and collects women like butterflies, is a caricaturesque reminder of Camus's own meteoric literary and social career in the metropolis. Beyond the rise and the fall of a star, Clamence depicts, in his corrosively autocritical discourse, the extreme and grotesque consequences of self-righteousness, methodical doubt, and intellectualized eroticism. His is the tale of one man in two cities, Paris and Amsterdam, who, driven by the revolutionary zeal to change the world after he renounces his hollow triumphs in Paris, transforms once and for all the reality that surrounds him and, as Adele King put it in *Albert Camus* (1964), "creates his own Hell." Bent on converting the world, as his biblical ancestor John the Baptist had set out to do as "vox clamantis in deserto," Clamence finds for his congenial and contagious duplicity a name which he elevates to a profession: "judge-penitent." Two key episodes, which he reveals in reverse order, induced his fall from Eden which he intends to transform into a rise: a barely noticed leap from a bridge by a suicidal woman whom he decided not to save and a haunting laugh of derision which he hears later when he crosses the bridge or looks into a mirror. In fact, the mirror becomes a preferred weapon in his campaign. While the silent interlocutor of his mono-dialogue, whose role the reader assumes inevitably, listens to Clamence's relentless self-analysis and self-deprecation, both the interlocutor and the reader are gradually forced to hold up their own mirrors of self-revelations.

Just when the public was finally accepting and admiring Camus's "evolution" from Meursault's self-centeredness to Rieux's relativist yet constructive ethics, Clamence signaled a mocking and shocking return to the metaphysical doubts which poisoned Caligula's mind. For Clamence is a tamed Caligula, caught, like his imperial predecessor, in the endless struggle between the absolute and the relative. He turns the tables by declaring not only the others but himself first and above all absolutely guilty. He transforms his rhetorical brilliance, which made him a winning trial lawyer, into dialectical artistry, which borders on exhibitionist sophistry, and involves the reader in a captivating mirror game of delusions. Whatever Clamence undertakes or says, he cannot hide the motivation of his actions: an insatiable *libido dominandi* which he expresses, for instance, in his preference for Archimedean vantage points such as balconies and summits.

As was the case in *L'Etranger* and *La Peste,* in *La Chute* Camus integrates landscape into the structure of his novel. Thus the cityscape of Paris with its high-culture and high-society symbols is contrasted with the cityscape of Amsterdam with its fog, doves, low-class people of the harbor district (especially in the Mexico-City, the bar that is Clamence's headquarters), and concentric rings of canals. Clamence's increasingly feverish point of view and accelerated pace of discourse throw the reader into an endless spiral of duplicity, duplicity within duplicity, confession and false confession, lies, half-truths, and verbal mirror effects. There is no end to the verbal tumble, no exit from this hell. "Puis-je, monsieur, vous proposer mes services, sans risquer d'être importun?" (May I, *monsieur,* offer my services without running the risk of intruding?) is the insinuation with which Clamence opens his discourse. Raising in his final statement the rhetorical question of what he would do if given a second chance to save the woman, he bristles: "Il faudrait s'exécuter. Brr...! l'eau est si froide. Mais rassurons-nous! Il est trop tard, maintenant, il sera toujours trop tard. Heureusement!" (We would have to go through with it. Brr...! The water is so cold! But let's not worry! It's too late now. It will always be too late. Fortunately!).

With this last strike against any notion of hope Clamence ends his sermon, but the reader's imagination cannot turn off the dizzying spiral. Because of Clamence's obsession with guilt, *La Chute* not only increased Camus's theologically minded readership but also induced several critics to predict the author's imminent conversion to Christianity. More recently criticism has turned attention to Clamence's verbal and Camus's textual virtuosity which subtly solicit the complicity of the reader to whom a high degree of intelligence and understanding is granted in advance. Ultimately the rhetorical and narrative techniques of *La Chute* call upon and into question the imaginary capacity of the reader as much as they call into question the reader's moral fiber. Meursault, Rieux, and Clamence, Camus's three narrators, are characterized by, depending on the point of view, an attractive or repulsive evasiveness which they cultivate. To the sophisticated reader they are less characters than, in Brian T. Fitch's words from *The Narcissistic Text* (1982), thematic "variations on a common theme: ostensibly of masks and men, of stories and storytellers . . . , of mirrors and mirages. Characters who refuse to identify themselves are produced by texts that never stop doing so."

For a long time the story collection *L'Exil et le royaume* did not receive the critical attention it deserves. Selected stories in translation appeared in popular American magazines or remained mainstays of college textbooks (for example, "L'Hôte" or "The Guest"). Beyond the formal similarities there is a thematic coherence underpinning *L'Exil et le royaume.* As English Showalter, Jr., has pointed out in *Exiles and Strangers* (1984), these themes have a past as well as contemporary relevance: "women's liberation, labor relations, terrorism, privacy, and modernization."

In spite of its title "La Femme adultère" ("The Adulterous Woman") does not relate an ex-

tramarital affair but the escape of Janine trapped in the boring routine of her husband who is a traveling salesman. In an old desert fort the woman has a kind of telluric experience leading to a mystical union with the sky and the stars. After her epiphanic adventure in the kingdom of nature, Janine returns to the inescapable exile of her and her husband's culture. But she takes along the self-awareness which she gained at the climax of her nocturnal experience. As in *L'Etranger,* Camus focuses on an unremarkable individual whose transgression leads to an emotional and intellectual breakthrough. And like the novels and several other short stories, "La Femme adultère" ends in intriguing ambiguity. As Showalter states, Janine and other protagonists in the short stories (Daru ["L'Hôte"], the Renegade ["Le Renégat"], the Silent Men ["Les Muets"]) "all embody aspects of the failures of language and the temptations of silence."

The discursive challenges posed by "Le Renégat" ("The Renegade") are unique in Camus's work. A former missionary, who in his zeal is a sort of brother-gone-mad to Jean-Baptiste Clamence, is held prisoner by the cruel people of Taghâsa, the city of salt. Having been forced to abjure his cultural and religious identity and to worship the local fetish, he tells of his task to kill the new missionary in a desert ambush. The Renegade's narration, an interior monologue made more dramatic by the fact that his tongue has been cut out by his torturers, constitutes a transfer of his former obsessions to his new goals. He appears to be as much a prisoner of his solitude and pervasive absolutism as a slave of his tormentors. The calculated madness of his jumble paradoxically contributes to the structural coherence of the story which the reader cannot overlook. The former voice of a European city has become a silent scream in the African desert.

By contrast, "Les Muets" ("The Silent Men") seem to speak of a simple world of artisans whose trade is on its way to obsolescence. The social conflict pits a group of barrel makers and their spokesman, Yvars, returning from a strike against Lasalle, an understanding cooper for whom they work. Lasalle's daughter is stricken by a mysterious illness. In spite of their sympathy for his situation, the workers do not offer him comfort but remain silent in the face of his predicament. A simple social conflict shows how easily solidarity is eclipsed by solitude. What links this story to the others is the common root of "exile" which, ultimately, can be found in the isolation

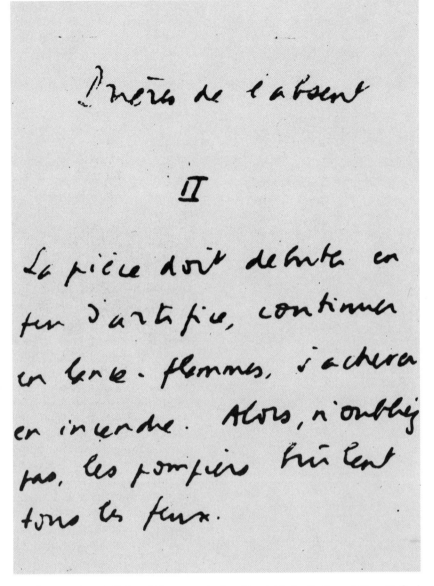

Camus's note about "Prière de l'absent" for actors in Les Possédés *(collection of Mme Catherine Camus)*

of the self caused by imposed or self-imposed language barriers.

The short story best known in the United States, "L'Hôte," is also set in North Africa. Already isolated geographically, a French-Algerian schoolteacher finds death threats written on his blackboard after he has supposedly guided an Arab prisoner accused of murder to the jail at the request of the local gendarme. Actually he left the prisoner at a crossroads, giving him a choice between going to town to surrender to the authorities and returning to his people and "freedom." The prisoner chooses to surrender. Beyond the surface conflict, which refers to Algeria's growing struggle for independence and the dilemma in which second- and third-generation colonists found themselves, "L'Hôte" raises an existential and metaphysical question which is inscribed in the barren mountainscape: will justice and freedom, solitude and solidarity ever be compatible?

Most interpreters see in "Jonas ou l'artiste au travail" ("Jonas or The Artist at Work") an autobiographical description of Camus's creative difficulties. Gilbert Jonas is a painter who discovered his artistic vocation late in life. The combination of sudden fame, family obligations, and social success hampers him in his creative endeavor. He promises his wife to resume his work but retreats to a loft where he spends his time meditating.

One day he is found in front of a canvas on which he scribbled a word which can be deciphered either as "solitary" or "solidary." While the obvious autobiographical elements are stressed in most readings, there are several textual levels that might be considered: the Bible (Jonah), comedy and satire, irony, intra-intertextuality (especially comparison with Clamence), the relationship of art and reality, social criticism, communication or the lack thereof, narrative technique, the relationship between writing/painting as production and text/picture as product, and so forth. Not only is the undecipherable word painting "solitary/solidary" ambiguous, but all "messages" emanating from the muddled communications of the characters as well as those between the text and the reader remain confused. This pervasive ambiguity makes it impossible to determine whether Jonas, who falls ill, will regain his creative power or continue his retreat from art and humanity. A topically related dramatic version entitled *La Vie d'artiste: Mimodrame en deux parties* (The Artist's Life: Mimodrama in Two Parts) was published in 1953 in *Simoun,* a journal in Oran.

"La Pierre qui pousse" (The Growing Stone) takes place in Iguape, an isolated town in Brazil where d'Arrast, a French engineer, has to build a flood-control dike. After meeting a cross section of the town's people and notables, d'Arrast befriends a man called the Cook. The latter introduces him to the exotic local mixture of religious and social customs. The town possesses an enshrined stone which supposedly grows miraculously. When the Cook, who has made a vow to carry a large stone in a procession to the church, is too weak to do so, because he spent the previous night at a Macumba dance, d'Arrast relieves him of this task by carrying the stone himself. However, he deposits it not at the church but in the center of the Cook's hut where he is welcomed by the family. Like Rieux in *La Peste,* d'Arrast believes in the relative and seeks temporary solutions to problems by assuming a hands-on posture and by displaying a high degree of genuine curiosity and tolerance. The townspeople teach him lessons of modesty and open his eyes to a new concept of faith and civilization which he does not espouse but respects. The mark of his heroism is, in Showalter's words, "that he accepts the challenge of communication at all levels." The desert stone which in other works either reminds man of his absurd and solitary condition or generates his desire for nothing-

ness becomes an agent of socialization in the last short story of *L'Exil et le royaume.* But it is the Cook's boulder and not the miracle stone enshrined by the church which is the focus of the attention of the modern-day Sisyphus. Some elements of the story are based on impressions Camus gathered during a trip to South America in June, July, and August of 1949.

With each story in *L'Exil et le royaume* Camus shows to what extent the never-ending circle of absurdity and revolt remains his epistemological grounding. But just as revolt cannot yield definitive "solutions" to the problem of the absurd, fiction and art in general do not, in Camus's perspective, produce clear "answers" but lead instead to open-endedness and ambiguity. The pervasive presence of ambiguity in Camus's art and thought is at the root of the often hostile reactions he provoked, especially in political circles. Not surprisingly, however, it is also responsible for the sustained interest in his work and for many of the most innovative readings of the last decade. As the criticism of his work and its contradictory history amply exemplify, neither adulation nor condemnation is the proper reaction to Camus because both are the result of the same kind of blindness. Irony, ambiguity, paradox, proximity, distance, and indifference, which mark his best fictional works, may be interpreted as strategies of evasiveness. In aesthetic terms they constitute the very foundation of his art and thought. Rather than descriptive or even prescriptive—as some of his editorials may be regarded—*L'Etranger, La Peste, La Chute,* and *L'Exil et le royaume* are open invitations to an ever renewable interpretive game which becomes more captivating the more its rules change.

When Albert Camus died on 4 January 1960 on his way to Paris from his vacation home in Lourmarin, in a car driven by Michel Gallimard, he had in his briefcase the manuscript of the beginning of "Le Premier Homme," his next novel.

Letters:

Albert Camus, Jean Grenier: Correspondance: 1932-1960, edited by Marguerite Dobrenn (Paris: Gallimard, 1981).

Interview:

Robert Donald Spector, "A Final Interview," *Venture,* 3-4 (20 December 1959).

Bibliographies:

Maurice Beebe, "Criticism of Albert Camus: A Selected Checklist of Studies in English," *Mod-*

ern Fiction Studies, 10 (Autumn 1964): 303-314;

Peter C. Hoy, *Camus in English* (Wymondham, U.K.: Brewhouse Press, 1968);

Robert F. Roeming, *Camus: A Bibliography* (Madison: University of Wisconsin Press, 1968);

Brian T. Fitch and Hoy, *Essai de bibliographie des études en langue française consacrées à Albert Camus (1937-1967)* (Paris: Minard, 1969);

Francesco de Pilla, *Albert Camus e la critica. Bibliografia internazionale (1937-1971)* (Leece: Milella, 1973);

Raymond Gay-Crosier, *Camus* (Darmstadt: Wissenschaftliche Buchgesellschaft, 1976).

Biographies:

Philip Thody, *Albert Camus: A Study of His Work* (New York: Grove Press, 1959);

Herbert R. Lottman, *Albert Camus: A Biography* (Garden City: Doubleday, 1979);

Patrick McCarthy, *Camus* (New York: Random House, 1982).

References:

Alex Argyros, *Crimes of Narration: Camus' "La Chute"* (Toronto: Paratexte, 1985);

Germaine Brée, *Camus* (New Brunswick: Rutgers University Press, 1959);

Brée, *Camus and Sartre. Crisis and Commitment* (New York: Delta, 1972);

Brée, ed., *Camus. A Collection of Critical Essays* (Englewood Cliffs, N.J.: Prentice-Hall, 1962);

Cahiers Albert Camus (Paris: Gallimard, 1971-   );

Robert Champigny, *A Pagan Hero: An Interpretation of Meursault in Camus' "The Stranger"* (Philadelphia: University of Pennsylvania Press, 1970);

John Cruickshank, *Albert Camus and the Literature of Revolt* (London: Oxford University Press, 1959);

Peter Cryle, "Routine Elevation: *Le Mythe de Sisyphe, La Peste, L'Exil et le royaume, La Chute,*" in his *The Thematics of Commitment: The Tower and the Plain* (Princeton: Princeton University Press, 1985);

Brian T. Fitch, *The Narcissistic Text. A Reading of Camus' Fiction* (Toronto: University of Toronto Press, 1982);

Edward Freeman, *The Theater of Albert Camus. A Critical Study* (London: Methuen, 1971);

Raymond Gay-Crosier, *Albert Camus 1980* (Gainesville: University Presses of Florida, 1980);

Thomas Hanna, *The Thought and Art of Albert Camus* (Chicago: Regnery, 1958);

Rosemarie Jones, *Camus' "L'Etranger" and "La Chute"* (London: Grant & Cutler, 1980);

Adele King, *Albert Camus* (New York: Grove Press, 1964);

Donald Lazere, *The Unique Creation of Albert Camus* (New Haven: Yale University Press, 1973);

Connor Cruise O'Brien, *Albert Camus of Europe and Africa* (New York: Viking Press, 1970);

Jean Onimus, *Albert Camus and Christianity* (University: University of Alabama Press, 1970);

Emmett Parker, *Albert Camus, the Artist in the Arena* (Madison: University of Wisconsin Press, 1965);

Leo Pollmann, *Sartre and Camus. The Literature of Existence* (New York: Ungar, 1970);

Phillip H. Rhein, *Albert Camus* (New York: Twayne, 1969);

Anthony Rizzuto, *Camus' Imperial Vision* (Carbondale: Southern Illinois University Press, 1981);

Rizzuto, ed., *Albert Camus' "L'Exil et le royaume": the Third Decade* (Toronto: Paratexte, forthcoming);

English Showalter, Jr., *Exiles and Strangers: A Reading of Camus's "Exile and the Kingdom"* (Columbus: Ohio State University Press, 1984);

Susan Tarrow, *Exile and the Kingdom: A Political Rereading of Albert Camus* (University: University of Alabama Press, 1985);

Fred H. Willhoite, *Beyond Nihilism: Albert Camus's Contribution to Political Thought* (Baton Rouge: Louisiana State University Press, 1968);

Mary Ann Frese Witt, *Existential Prisons: Captivity in Mid-Twentieth-Century French Literature* (Durham: Duke University Press, 1985).

Papers:

Although many of Camus's papers are deposited at the Bibliothèque Nationale in Paris, the bulk of the writer's estate remains with the family.

Louis-Ferdinand Céline
(Louis-Ferdinand Destouches)
(27 May 1894-1 July 1961)

David O'Connell
Georgia State University

BOOKS: *La Vie et l'œuvre de Philippe-Ignace Semmelweis (1818-1865)* (Rennes: Simon, 1924); translated by Robert Allerton Parker in *Mea culpa & The Life and Work of Semmelweis . . .* (Boston: Little, Brown, 1937; London: Allen, 1937);

Voyage au bout de la nuit (Paris: Denoël & Steele, 1932); translated by John H. P. Marks as *Journey to the End of the Night* (Boston: Little, Brown, 1934; London: Chatto & Windus, 1934);

L'Eglise (Paris: Denoël & Steele, 1933);

Mort à crédit (Paris: Denoël & Steele, 1936); translated by Marks as *Death on the Installment Plan* (Boston: Little, Brown, 1938; London: Chatto & Windus, 1938);

Mea culpa, suivi de La Vie et l'œuvre . . . (Paris: Denoël & Steele, 1936); translated by Parker as *Mea Culpa & The Life and Work of Semmelweis . . .* (Boston: Little, Brown, 1937; London: Allen, 1937);

Bagatelles pour un massacre (Paris: Denoël & Steele, 1937);

Van Bagaden (Paris: Denoël & Steele, 1937);

L'Ecole des cadavres (Paris: Denoël & Steele, 1938);

Les Beaux Draps (Paris: Nouvelles Editions Françaises, 1941);

Guignol's Band, volume 1 (Paris: Denoël, 1944); translated by Bernard Frechtman and Jack T. Nile (New York: New Directions, 1954; London: Vision, 1954);

Foudres et flèches (Paris: C. de Jonquières, 1948);

Casse-pipe (Paris: Chambriand, 1949);

Scandale aux abysses (Paris: Chambriand, 1950);

Féerie pour une autre fois 2 volumes (Paris: Gallimard, 1952);

Normance, volume 2 of *Féerie pour une autre fois* (Paris: Gallimard, 1954);

Entretiens avec le professeur Y (Paris: Gallimard, 1955); translated by Stanford Luce in *Conversations with Professor Y.*, bilingual edition

Louis-Ferdinand Céline

(Hanover: University Press of New England, 1986);

D'un château l'autre (Paris: Gallimard, 1957); translated by Ralph Manheim as *Castle to Castle* (New York: Delacorte, 1968; London: Blond, 1969);

Ballets sans musique, sans personne, sans rien (Paris: Gallimard, 1959);

La Naissance d'une fée (Paris: Gallimard, 1959);

Voyou Paul, pauvre Virginie (Paris: Gallimard, 1959);

Nord (Paris: Gallimard, 1960; definitive edition, 1964); translated by Manheim as *North* (New York: Delacorte, 1972; London: Bodley Head, 1972);

Le Pont de Londres, volume 2 of *Guignol's Band* (Paris: Gallimard, 1964);

Rigodon (Paris: Gallimard, 1969); translated by Manheim (New York: Delacorte, 1974);

Casse-pipe, suivi du Carnet du cuirassier (Paris: Gallimard, 1970);

Semmelweis et autres écrits médicaux, edited by Jean-Pierre Dauphin and Henri Godard (Paris: Gallimard, 1977);

Progrès (Paris: Mercure de France, 1978);

Chansons, edited by Frédéric Monnier (Paris: Flûte de Pan, 1981).

Collections: *Œuvres complètes,* 5 volumes, edited by John A. Ducourneau (Paris: André Balland, 1966-1969);

Romans, edited by Henri Godard (2 volumes, Paris: Gallimard, 1973-1974; revised edition, 1 volume, 1981);

Œuvres de Céline, 9 volumes to date, edited by Frédéric Vitoux (Paris: Club de l'Honnête Homme, 1981-).

In the last twenty years Louis-Ferdinand Céline has emerged, in the opinion of many critics, as one of the most important French novelists of the twentieth century. This turnaround in his literary fortunes is one of the most interesting stories in modern literature and is understandable if one remembers that Céline's work was the object of what amounts to a conspiracy of silence by French (mostly leftist) intellectuals from the end of World War II until about the mid 1960s. Having been accused of collaborating with the Nazis during the war, he was for a long time treated as a persona non grata; it took almost twenty years for his name to be cleared. Once it became apparent that despite his vocal anti-Semitism of the late 1930s he had not been a Nazi collaborator during the Occupation, younger Frenchmen were at last able to read Céline and to know more about his life and work.

Louis-Ferdinand Destouches, who took his pseudonym Céline from his maternal grandmother's given name, was born on 27 May 1894 in Courbevoie, a suburb of Paris. His father, Ferdinand-Auguste Destouches, worked for an insurance company, and his mother, Marguerite-Louise Guillou Destouches, to make ends meet, ran her own retail establishment, a soft goods store in the Passage de Choiseul near the Place de l'Opéra on the Parisian Right Bank. Beginning in 1899, the family lived at the same address as Mme Destouches's store, and young Louis, an only child, attended local schools be-

fore being sent off by his parents in the years 1907-1909 for protracted stays in both Germany and England in order to learn the languages of the two countries. In his mother's thinking, such knowledge would eventually come in handy in the lace business. This early exposure to foreign languages and cultures was unusual for a young French boy of this period, especially for one from his less-than-privileged petit bourgeois social class.

After his return from abroad, he took odd jobs in the period 1909-1912, working for various small businesses in his neighborhood. Although he later claimed that the desire to study medicine had come to him early in life, he did not attend school throughout these adolescent years. Not long after reaching the age of eighteen in 1912, he joined a cavalry regiment and had attained a rank equivalent to that of sergeant by the time World War I began. He was seriously wounded in the arm while carrying out his duties at the front in Flanders and was operated on shortly thereafter. Fearful that army doctors would take the easy way out and remove his arm, he insisted on being treated without anesthesia. Thus, he kept his arm, the loss of which would have impeded his later medical career. Awarded a citation and the Médaille Militaire for his bravery, he was sent back to Paris to recuperate. His disability for the arm injury and for damage to his eardrums was rated at seventy-five percent, so there was no question of his being sent home rather than back to the front.

The next year, 1915, after his return to Paris, he was sent to the French Consulate General in London, where he worked in the passport office. During the year that he spent there, he married Suzanne Nebout, a French bar girl working in one of the local nightclubs that he frequented. The marriage was never declared to the French consulate and thus not registered by the French administration. When Céline left London in 1916, having been definitively released from military service, in the eyes of the French authorities it was as though his marriage had never taken place. He left his wife behind, and, in search of adventure, he spent the next year in West Africa working as a trader in the bush for a French forestry company. His stay in the Cameroons was shortened when, because of ill health caused by the harsh climate, he had to return home. Back home in France in May 1917, he seemed ready to settle down. Taking accelerated course work, he took his *baccalauréat* degree in 1919. Enrolling at

Céline (standing at left) with members of his cavalry unit (collection particulière, photo R. Laffont)

the medical school of the University of Rennes in that same year, he completed his medical degree in 1924 and, in the process, married Edith Follet, the daughter of his school's director.

His doctoral dissertation, entitled *La Vie et l'œuvre de Philippe-Ignace Semmelweis (1818-1865)*, was published by the medical school in 1924 (and translated as *The Life and Work of Semmelweis . . .* , 1937); this, and good connections in the medical profession thanks to his marriage, seemed to promise a bright professional future for Céline. But this very perspective, a bourgeois life of privilege, did not appeal to him. On the contrary, he felt restricted by it. For this reason, he left his wife and daughter in 1925 to take a job as a doctor with the League of Nations. Thanks to this post, he was able to travel to Geneva and Liverpool and back to West Africa. He also made a trip to the United States, Canada, and Cuba that lasted more than two months in 1925 and that took him to several cities in the eastern and the southern United States as well as to Detroit, where he took a particular interest in the social, psychological, and medical problems of assembly-line workers in the Ford plant there. These wanderings continued until 1928, when he finally settled down in Clichy, a dreary working-class suburb of Paris. Divorced since 1926, he spent the next ten years there, the first three in private practice and then, beginning in 1931, as an employee of the local clinic.

It was in the 1920s, when Céline was about thirty-two, that he began to write. He devoted most of his free time during a four-year period to the composition of his first novel, *Voyage au bout de la nuit* (1932; translated as *Journey to the End of the Night*, 1934). Its publication was by far the major literary event of 1932. As Leon Trotsky, a great admirer of the book, if not of Céline himself, put it: "Louis-Ferdinand Céline est entré dans la grande littérature comme d'autres pénètrent dans leurs propres maisons" (Louis-Ferdinand Céline walked into great literature the way other people walk into their own homes). The novel is a startling one, and its bitter pessimism continues to affect readers in a powerful way more than a half century after publication. It is impossible to be indifferent to *Voyage au bout de la nuit* and, by extension, to its author.

Léon Daudet, a member of the Goncourt jury and an ardent admirer of the novel, sought to have *Voyage au bout de la nuit* awarded the prestigious Prix Goncourt for 1932. The other members of the jury were frightened, however, by the idea of giving the prize to such a bitterly pessimistic work. Thus, as a matter of simple politics, the award went to the now-forgotten writer Guy Mazeline for his novel *Les Loups* (The Wolves). Instead, and as a kind of consolation prize, Céline's first novel was awarded the Prix Théophraste Renaudot.

Céline, 1934

Voyage au bout de la nuit opens with young Ferdinand Bardamu talking with his friend and fellow medical student Arthur Ganate. The point of view of the novel, from the very beginning, is that of a first-person narrator. Bardamu sees a parade passing by and, in a fit of patriotism, decides to join the army. From here one follows him through World War I, to the front, and then back to Paris, where he convalesces. This section of the novel contains some of the strongest antiwar passages ever written. It attacks the stupidity of professional military men, the cupidity and mendacity of politicians, the plundering and exploitation of civilians behind the front lines, and the docility with which the average citizen accepts his fate. After the war Bardamu goes to Africa, where he works in the bush for a French company. Here the reader sees colonialism at work,

as the black natives are systematically exploited by the whites as well as by each other. Although the narrator clearly feels that the natives are inferior to whites, he displays sympathy for their woes and for the fact that the white colonials are creating more problems for them. At the end of this section, as in the previous section, the hero lapses into a state of delirium brought on by the stress of living. Delirium to Céline is an escape from the stressful reality of modern life, and it is only through delirium that Bardamu escapes from Africa.

When he awakens he is in New York, and from there his travels take him to Detroit, where he falls in love with Molly, a local whore, and gets a job in a Ford factory. While in the United States he comes in contact with unrestrained capitalism and the worship of money and material comfort as reflected in modern American life. At the same time he sees how people at the bottom of the social ladder live in comparison to the rich. In Detroit he meets again a certain Léon Robinson, his alter ego, whom he had already encountered in other stressful situations—at the front in France, in Paris, and even in Africa. Partly in order to get away from Robinson and partly to put his own life in order, Bardamu leaves the United States and returns to France, where he decides to study medicine.

Here, about a third of the way through this five-hundred-page novel, begins what can be called the second part of the work. Now, instead of running away from reality, he vows to attempt to meet it head on. First, his life as a doctor in the working-class suburb of Rancy is chronicled. Caring for the sickest and least educated segment of society, Bardamu descends into the lowest circles of the hell of modern life. Predictably, he again runs into Robinson, who is living in the neighborhood. When Robinson tells him that he has been hired to assassinate a neighbor, Old Lady Henrouille, who has become a nuisance to her son and daughter-in-law, Bardamu tries to stay out of it. As Robinson is setting the bomb that he hopes will kill the old lady, it suddenly goes off in his face, blinding him. At this point Bardamu gets involved with the Henrouilles and helps them arrange for both the old lady and Robinson to work in the crypt of a church in Toulouse, where they will serve as guides for tourists interested in seeing the mummies preserved there. Finally, after the trip to Toulouse, Bardamu returns to Paris where he works in a privately run mental institution. There, he seems to

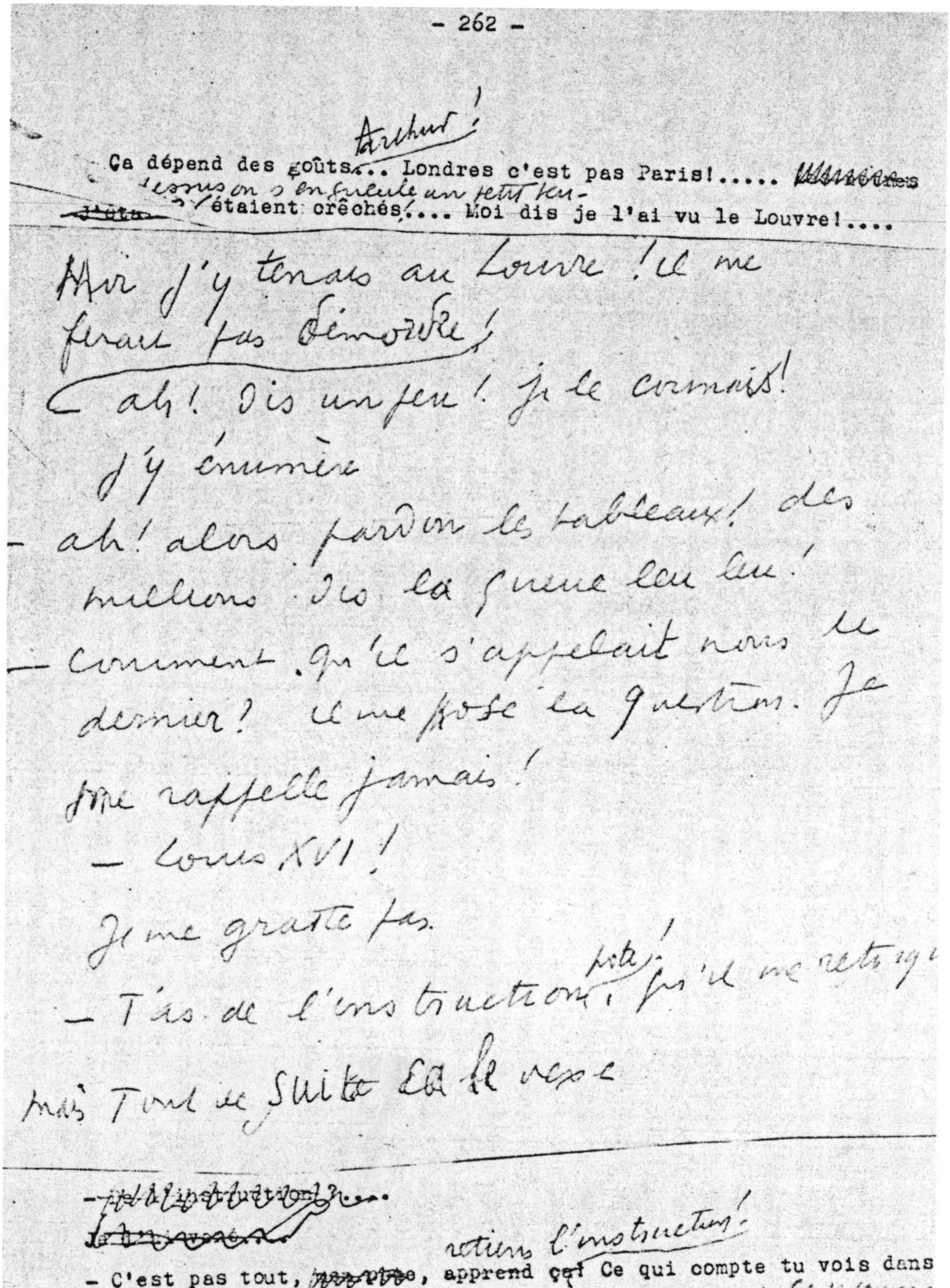

- 262 -

Ça dépend des goûts... Londres c'est pas Paris!..... Arthur!

étaient crêchés!... Moi dis je l'ai vu le Louvre!....

Moi j'y tenais au Louvre! il me ferait pas démordre!

— ah! dis un peu! je le connais!

j'y énumère

— ah! alors pardon les tableaux! des millions dis la queue leu leu!

— comment qu'il s'appelait nous le dernier? il me pose la question. Je me rappelle jamais!

— Louis XVI!

Je me gratte pas.

— T'as de l'instruction, pote! qu'il me rétorque

mais tout de suite ça le vexe

retiens l'instruction!

- C'est pas tout, apprend ça! Ce qui compte tu vois dans la vie c'est l'intelligence naturelle!...Moi j'en ai, voilà le

... qui savaient des cinq

Corrected page from the typescript for Guignol's Band *(Erika Ostrovsky,* Voyeur Voyant, *Random House, 1972)*

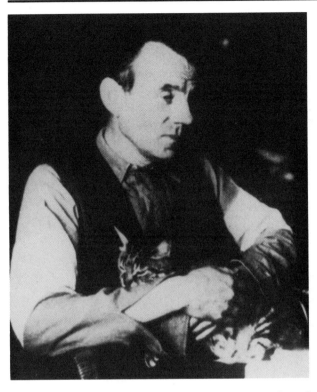

Céline in Copenhagen after his release from Vesterfangsel prison in 1947 (collection of L. Destouches)

conclude at the end of the novel, he will be safe from man, the most dangerous predator in the universe. Living among the insane, he has finally found his place in the world.

This second part of the novel, which some critics have found slower-paced than the first part, is highlighted by the author's strong social protest against poverty and ignorance as well as against some of the tools which, in his view, society uses to maintain the status quo: alcohol, the press, and the cinema. The overriding concern of Céline in *Voyage au bout de la nuit* is to depict the conditions of modern life. The words of the great Catholic novelist of the interwar years Georges Bernanos still apply to *Voyage au bout de la nuit*: "Pour nous la question n'est pas de savoir si la peinture de M. Céline est atroce, nous demandons si elle est vraie. Elle l'est" (For us the question is not to decide if Céline's view of life is horrible, but whether it is true. It is).

As the first part of the novel is characterized by flight and a search for self and for meaning to existence, the second part is static and shows the hero willing to stay in place, to compromise if necessary, while awaiting death and attempting to find out what meaning he should eventually assign to that event. Living and work-

ing among the poor, Bardamu, like Céline himself, comes to the realization that life for most people in modern consumer societies is humdrum and boring. The major difference between the rich and the poor is that the former have the means to buy forgetfulness, while the poor, whom Céline knew all too well, do not have any such opportunity. Much has also been written about the Bardamu/Robinson relationship, but Merlin Thomas's assessment in *Louis-Ferdinand Céline* (1979) is probably the most sensible. To him, each of these characters represents a different view of death. Bardamu, who has a role to play in life, struggles to go on living. Robinson, however, who has no role to play, is happy to have his life ended. Murdered by a girlfriend whom he scorned, he has, in Thomas's words, "decided upon his own death: he could have avoided it. . . . It all amounts to a question of ultimate acceptance of the lot of humanity." As the novel ends, Bardamu has clearly decided to go on living. He knows that death is what awaits him at the end of the night, but his time has not yet come.

Voyage au bout de la nuit caused an enormous stir. More than one hundred reviews were published in five months, and there were aftershocks in the daily press, in political and academic circles, and among members of the Académie Française. There were even legal ramifications: the novel was at the center of two lawsuits. Those who had voted against awarding Céline the Prix Goncourt felt obliged to justify their vote. Other critics hailed the novel as a totally new departure in French fiction. Louis Aragon, Marcel Arland, Claude Lévi-Strauss, and Raymond Queneau are among those who praised it and perceptively identified aspects of its originality. Others condemned it as crude, shocking, pessimistic, and formless; the French Communist press was generally not favorable to it. Its influence was immediate: Henry Miller acknowledged Céline's crucial importance for his *Tropic of Cancer* (1934); and for many French writers of the 1930s and later, including Jean-Paul Sartre, Céline was the author who had, at one blow, felled the spirit of academicism and the idols of classical proportions and fine style, and thus had freed literary language from its fetters.

Céline's next novel, *Mort à crédit*, was published in 1936 (and translated as *Death on the Installment Plan* in 1938). Like *Voyage au bout de la nuit*–and the novels that would follow–this book is based on the author's experience. It goes back

Céline during his exile in Denmark

in time to the period that precedes the action recounted in *Voyage au bout de la nuit*, to Céline's childhood and adolescence.

Although he enjoyed publicly poking fun at Marcel Proust, Céline nonetheless admired Proust's ability to fashion an imposing multivolume novel out of the stuff of memory. As if to mimic Proust and his *A la recherche du temps perdu* (*Remembrance of Things Past*, 1913-1927), Céline begins *Mort à crédit* by showing a mature character, Ferdinand, at work as both a doctor and a writer. Ferdinand's lapses into a state of delirium brought on by both an attack of malaria contracted in Africa and a recurrence of dizziness caused by war wounds recall the situation of Proust's supine, sleepless narrator at the beginning of *A la recherche du temps perdu*, and his excursions into childhood memory as he lies ill in bed recall Proust's privileged moments, such as the one provoked by the dipping of the famous *madeleine* into a cup of linden tea—an action that brings understanding of past events through the process of involuntary memory. Soon, however, striking differences between Proust and Céline become obvious. Whereas the former wrote in long, highly stylized periodic sentences about upper-bourgeois and aristocratic characters, Céline uses this fit of delirium to summon up recollections of

his working-class past and express them in a slang style that is even more daring than the one with which he experimented in *Voyage au bout de la nuit*. In *Mort à crédit* Céline begins to rely more on what he would later call his "style télégraphique," little bits of sentences separated from one another and punctuated by three or more suspension points. The reason for using this technique, he claimed, was that in order to achieve the emotional effect he sought, he had to write the way people talk so that the reader would have the impression of hearing genuine working-class speech. In *Mort à crédit*, beginning with his childhood in the fictional Passage des Bérésinas, the Passage de Choiseul of Céline's youth, the first-person narrator, Ferdinand, paints a bleak picture. His father, a loser stuck in a dead-end job, takes out his frustrations by beating his son. His mother fixes noodles for most of the family's meals because she is afraid that anything else will leave odors in the lacework that she has for sale. The relatives are just as bad, with the exception of Ferdinand's grandmother, Caroline (a transposed version of his beloved grandmother Céline), who dies in due course, and his uncle, Edouard, who understands, helps, and consoles him.

Leaving school in his early teens, long before finishing his *baccalauréat* degree, he works at two different jobs and ends up being fired from each one. His Uncle Edouard intervenes and suggests that the boy be sent to England for language study. Enrolling in Meanwell College in England for a year, Ferdinand eventually has an affair with the headmaster's young wife, Nora, and returns home. Like Molly of *Voyage au bout de la nuit*, Nora is treated with sensitivity and warmth and stands out in Céline's fiction for this reason. When Ferdinand is back in France, Uncle Edouard again comes to the rescue and introduces him to an inventor and con man, Courtial des Pereires. Just as Robinson had slowly assumed increasing importance in *Voyage au bout de la nuit*, now Courtial, with his quacky experiments and projects, becomes a major character as *Mort à crédit* progresses. But when he finally commits suicide near the end of the novel because his idealistic vision cannot be achieved (just as Robinson was killed off by his creator because there was no place for him in life), Ferdinand realizes that, like Bardamu in *Voyage au bout de la nuit*, he will have to go ahead on his own and make some sense out of life. Returning to Paris from the experimental farm that Courtial had organized, he decides that he will have to get away from his family and seek true independence. Ironically, he seizes upon joining the army as the means of making this fresh start in life, and it is with this goal in mind that he takes leave of the reader at the end of the novel.

Mort à crédit did not achieve the critical and popular success of *Voyage au bout de la nuit*. It did, however, solidify Céline's reputation as a pessimistic writer with a negative view of family and social relationships. Despite the sympathetic feelings that the narrator expresses for Uncle Edouard (and some of the warmest pages that Céline ever wrote concern this character), it is difficult to disagree with this assessment. Like *Voyage au bout de la nuit*, *Mort à crédit* was immediately translated into the major European languages, and it kept Céline's name before the public as that of an important author (seemingly, but not really, of the Left) in a world about to go to war.

Céline's royalties from the publication of *Voyage au bout de la nuit* were substantial. He used them to buy a house in Saint-Malo, but he still continued to live in his shabby Paris apartment and never stopped working among the poor and dispossessed. The translation of his work into Russian resulted in the accumulation of a vast sum of money held in his account in the Soviet Union. Since the Soviets would not send him the money, he accepted an invitation in 1936 to visit the country that the French Left held to be the workers' paradise. As a result of that trip, Céline published the first of four polemical political works that appeared during the period 1936-1941. *Mea culpa* (published in 1936 in a volume that included Céline's work on Semmelweis) attacked the Soviet Union as a brutal dictatorship organized on the philosophical basis of materialism. Its citizens, he announced, lived in filth and depravation and were exploited by a new ruling class—the Party. The significance of the work's title is obvious: Céline repented for having allowed people to believe that he was sympathetic to the organized political Left in France.

The following year his next polemic, *Bagatelles pour un massacre* (Trifles for a Massacre), exploded on the political scene. In this work Céline's political consciousness, comparatively subdued in his two novels, in which he makes extensive use of understatement, and only beginning to show itself in *Mea culpa*, directs itself to a frontal assault on international Jewry. Claiming that the Jews in France, with their brothers in London and New York, are planning another war in which they intend to wipe out the Aryans, he calls for the neutralizing of Jewish power in France. Reaction to the work, which was extensive, was mixed in France, and in fact many intellectuals, including André Gide, the reigning pontiff of French letters, thought that Céline was joking, that the anti-Semitic tone was so exaggerated that it must be ironic. When, in the following year, 1938, Céline published another political text, *L'Ecole des cadavres*, that picked up where *Bagatelles pour un massacre* left off, going so far as to propose a Franco-German alliance against the Soviet Union and the Jews as the only way for Europe's Aryans to survive, there could be no doubt about his intentions. As a result of these publications, Céline found himself politically isolated from both the Left and the Right, and he would remain in this state for the rest of his life. The last of the four works, *Les Beaux Draps* (A Nice Mess), which was published during the Occupation in 1941, castigates the French army for running away from the Germans. The basic proposition of the work is that France ought to institute what for Céline was a true form of communism, in which everyone would receive the same salary no matter what form of work he did. In this book he drops the anti-Semitism of the years

Céline with his wife Lucette and their Great Dane Bonzo in 1952, after their return from Denmark

1937-1938 and presents himself as a patriot and a decorated hero of the Great War. In fact, after the outbreak of World War II, Céline had served on board a French vessel in the Mediterranean that was shelled by the German navy. Although he had openly called for a Franco-German alliance in 1938 to counter what he took to be Soviet, British, and Jewish attempts to start a new war, he rallied to the defense of his country once the Germans attacked.

Céline's major literary projects during the Occupation were his two-volume novel *Guignol's Band* (1944, 1964; volume 1 translated into English, 1954) and the ambitious but never com-pleted novel that was published in 1949 under the title *Casse-pipe* (War). The word *guignol* in French refers to a kind of marionette show, the Grand Guignol, which was popular as a children's entertainment and marked by extreme contrasts of good and evil human behavior. The word also refers to the chief character, and by extension to a human being who is comic and ridiculous, and it is this meaning that attaches to Céline's old narrator, again named Ferdinand, who reflects on the foolish and laughable youth that he once was and on the "band" of characters that he knew while residing in London for a year during World War I.

144

The first volume of *Guignol's Band* portrays the underworld characters, pimps, prostitutes, and the like, that Céline frequented during his year in London. Various adventures culminate in Ferdinand's flight to the French Consulate, where he demands to rejoin the French army, since he has concluded that service at the front cannot be more dangerous than life in the London underworld. There, however, he meets Sosthène de Rodiencourt, a would-be magus who seeks access to the fourth dimension of existence. Ferdinand falls under his spell, in much the same way as the Ferdinand of *Mort à crédit* had been bemused by Courtial. As volume 1 ends, they go off together in search of adventure. In the second volume of the novel, entitled *Le Pont de Londres* (London Bridge), lost in manuscript for years and published in 1964 two years after Céline's secretary had accidentally come upon it, the quack inventor Col. J. F. C. O'Calloghan, who is working on a new type of gas mask, and his lovely niece Virginia become major characters. As in the first part of the novel, unbelievable and farfetched events take place throughout this second part, which culminates with Ferdinand's symbolic crossing of London Bridge in order to leave these characters behind and seek adventures elsewhere. The plot line of the two parts is generally incoherent, and most critics have found that the novel fails for this reason. However, in *The Inner Dream: Céline as Novelist* (1978), J. H. Matthews contends that his "failure" was a deliberate strategy on the part of Céline. In this novel plot is downgraded, he claims, so that readers will not concentrate upon narrative incident so much as on the manner in which Ferdinand gives an account of events. This might well be the case, but it does not make this tedious novel easier to read.

Casse-pipe, preserved only in fragments that constitute less than two hundred pages of text, is centered on barracks life in the cavalry during the period 1912-1914. Chronologically, it draws on experiences from Céline's life not previously covered in *Mort à crédit* or *Voyage au bout de la nuit*. The published sections of the novel are all that are known to exist, although additional fragments may well be discovered in the future.

After the Allied landings in Normandy in June 1944, Céline decided that he should leave Paris, for he supposed that it would be liberated shortly and that he would then be arrested, be denied a fair trial, and quite possibly be executed on charges of collaboration with the enemy (such

charges would have been based on his anti-Semitism and hostility to communism, expressed at length in his prewar political texts). In July 1944 he left Paris with his wife Lucette Almanzor, a former ballet dancer whom he had married the year before, his friend the actor Le Vigan, and his cat, Bébert. After his departure his apartment was ransacked and his library and papers, including sections of *Casse-pipe*, were destroyed. After a short stay in Baden-Baden, he made a trip to Berlin to visit hospitals and then remained for several months in Kränzlin, in Brandenburg, northwest of Berlin. When the Vichy government, by now in exile, retreated to Sigmaringen, Céline moved there and joined the French colony in November 1944. He stayed on as a house physician until March 1945. At that time, allegedly to recover money which he had hidden in a friend's backyard in Copenhagen before the war, he left for Denmark. He arrived there three weeks later.

Féerie pour une autre fois (Fairy Tale for Another Time) and *Normance*, volume 2 of this work, published in 1952 and 1954 respectively, are generally considered Céline's weakest works of fiction. Written for the most part during his exile in Denmark, these two books are best considered as transitional works that show Céline moving from the transformation of his lived experiences into novels to, in his last three books, chronicles in which the first-person narrator is Céline himself. In the opening pages of *Féerie pour une autre fois* the embittered narrator is in Paris, but throughout most of the book he is in prison in Copenhagen lamenting his fate, pointing out, among other things, that there are plenty of real collaborators freely walking the streets of Paris while he is in prison in exile. Volume 2, *Normance*, written before the first part of the novel but published after it, is set in Paris and revolves around an Allied air raid on the French capital. The word *féerie*, which denotes a form of entertainment that includes an element of magic and the supernatural, indicates here essentially Céline's ironic fantasy about himself. The importance of this narrative lies in the fact that it points the way to Céline's last three works, hailed as masterpieces by critics.

The events of the nine-month period beginning in July 1944 with Céline's departure from Paris provided the subject matter for his last three works: *D'un château l'autre* (1957; translated as *Castle to Castle*, 1968), *Nord* (1960; translated as *North*, 1972), and *Rigodon* (1969; translated,

1974), which he completed the morning of the day he died, 1 July 1961. In these three volumes, which he referred to as the work of a "mémorialiste" (writer of memoirs), the author abandons the pretense of fiction and writes in his own name about his experiences in the declining months of the war and the postwar years. He does, however, use invented names for some of his acquaintances, and instead of recounting events in order and adhering strictly to fact, he arranges his material impressionistically and combines fantasy, accusations, and ravings with reminiscences of his experiences and observations. The end result is over a thousand pages that describe life in the closing days of the Third Reich. The Allied bombardments, as well as the reactions of the French puppets to their inevitable fate and of the German population to the realization that their cities will soon be overrun by the enemy, are vividly recounted.

These three books are remarkable in that they reflect Céline's contempt for the Germans. The same man who had sought a Franco-German alliance in 1938 now scoffs at the German people and their leaders. Another recurrent theme is that of the corruption of leadership, for the masters in the Third Reich never seem to lack the creature comforts so absent from the lives of ordinary citizens. A third continuing theme is that of the collapse of Germany, the confusion and disintegration of a whole society. Finally, what is perhaps the most important theme of the three works, one which ties these late narratives to *Voyage au bout de la nuit,* is that of sheer survival. Céline will do anything, flatter any person, do whatever is asked to go on living. Both the fright and desperation that he experienced and the cunning required to overcome them are described by Céline in his usual self-deprecating way. Convinced of his political innocence, for which he argues throughout these pages, he also strikes a note for the poor and dispossessed, with whom now more than ever he identifies.

In April 1945 a French court issued a warrant for Céline's arrest as a collaborator, and it was eight months later that French officials in Copenhagen demanded his immediate extradition. The Danes responded by imprisoning both Céline (for fourteen months) and his wife (for two months). In February 1947 Céline's ill health caused him to be hospitalized. After another four months, his health restored, he was allowed to go free on condition that he not leave Denmark. He remained in that country until he was granted am-

nesty in April 1951. The last ten years of his life were lived in quiet and seclusion on the outskirts of Paris where he earned his living by practicing medicine.

Céline's reputation as a major novelist seems secure. He had the ability to create striking characters and put them in situations that, while sometimes extreme, still carry a sense of reality and speak to the reader. His ability to handle language, especially a crude slang that had scarcely found its way into print before him, led to a wide range of tones and voices in his texts, including the voice of speaker-protagonists who address themselves or the reader in broken, but continuing, outbursts. His images pile up torrentially, and his best work, especially *Voyage au bout de la nuit,* is visionary. His influence was felt, and sometimes acknowledged, by writers of his own generation such as Samuel Beckett, Queneau, and Sartre; later writers, especially Americans, including Joseph Heller, Jack Kerouac, and William Burroughs, also acknowledged their debt to him.

While often compared to the nineteenth-century realists and naturalists, he denies the standards of realism–that is, the faithful depiction of a group of characters or a class–for to adhere to them would be to subscribe to middle-class values. He rejects the search for transcendence through religion, art, or thought that marks the works of André Malraux, Georges Bernanos, and Albert Camus. He also stands opposite Gide, Proust, and other great French aesthetes, for whom literary art, especially when couched in a balanced or metaphorically rich style, is the supreme achievement; for Céline's is an antistyle, a language that denies the values of beauty, harmony, balance, and abstract thinking in favor of popular and crude words that convey an explosion of spontaneous reactions and physical sensations. This stylistic reaction is part of a deep-seated rebellion against French values as they had been defended, ostensibly, in World War I and were expressed in institutions (government, literature, and the press) in the first half of the twentieth century. Indeed, in Céline's work a whole civilization is judged deficient, as is perhaps even mankind itself. Such an accusatory image remains popular, generation after generation; despite tremendous social changes in Europe and the rest of the world, present readers can find in Céline outbursts of sarcasm and anger against individuals and institutions that seem timely today.

Letters:

Milton Hindus, *Louis-Ferdinand Céline tel que je l'ai vu*, includes letters by Céline and Hindus (Paris: L'Herne, 1969); Céline-Hindus letters edited and translated in Hindus's *The Crippled Giant: A Literary Relationship with Louis-Ferdinand Céline* (Hanover & London: University Press of New England, 1986);

Choix de lettres de l'hiver 1949-1950, edited by J.-P. Louis, special issue of *Lérot Rêveur*, 23 (1978);

Lettres et premiers écrits d'Afrique, 1916-1917, edited by Jean-Pierre Dauphin (Paris: Gallimard, 1978);

Pierre Monnier, *Ferdinand Furieux, avec trois cent treize lettres de Louis-Ferdinand Céline* (Lausanne: L'Age d'Homme, 1979);

Lettres à des amis, edited by Colin W. Nettelbeck (Paris: Gallimard, 1979);

Lettres à son avocat: 118 Lettres inédites à maître Albert Naud, edited by Frédéric Monnier (Paris: Flûte de Pan, 1984);

Lettres à Tixier: 44 Lettres inédites à maître Tixier-Vignancourt, edited by Monnier (Paris: Flûte de Pan, 1985).

Bibliography:

Stanford L. Luce and William K. Buckley, *A Half Century of Céline: An Annotated Bibliography 1932-1982* (New York & London: Garland, 1983).

Biographies:

Erika Ostrovsky, *Voyeur Voyant: A Portrait of Louis-Ferdinand Céline* (New York: Random House, 1971);

Patrick McCarthy, *Céline: A Biography* (New York: Viking, 1975);

François Gibault, *Céline*, 3 volumes (Paris: Mercure de France, 1977-1985).

References:

Maurice Bardèche, *Louis-Ferdinand Céline* (Paris: Table Ronde, 1986);

James Flynn and C. K. Mertz, *Understanding Céline* (Seattle: Genitron, 1984);

Bettina L. Knapp, *Céline: Man of Hate* (University: University of Alabama Press, 1974);

J. H. Matthews, *The Inner Dream: Céline as Novelist* (Syracuse: Syracuse University Press, 1978);

David O'Connell, *Louis-Ferdinand Céline* (Boston: Twayne, 1976);

Erika Ostrovsky, *Céline and His Vision* (New York: New York University Press, 1967);

Allen Thiher, *Céline: The Novel as Delirium* (New Brunswick: Rutgers University Press, 1972);

Merlin Thomas, *Louis-Ferdinand Céline* (New York: New Directions, 1979).

Pierre Drieu La Rochelle

(3 January 1893-16 March 1945)

Rima Drell Reck
University of New Orleans

BOOKS: *Interrogation* (Paris: Nouvelle Revue Française, 1917);

Fond de cantine (Paris: Gallimard, 1920);

Etat civil (Paris: Gallimard, 1921);

Mesure de la France (Paris: Grasset, 1922);

Plainte contre inconnu (Paris: Gallimard, 1924);

L'Homme couvert de femmes (Paris: Gallimard, 1925);

La Suite dans les idées (Paris: Sans Pareil, 1927);

Le Jeune Européen (Paris: Gallimard, 1927);

Blèche (Paris: Gallimard, 1928);

Genève ou Moscou (Paris: Gallimard, 1928);

La Voix (Paris: Edouard Champion, 1928);

Une Femme à sa fenêtre (Paris: Gallimard, 1929); translated by Patrick Kirwan as *Hotel Acropolis* (London: Nash & Grayson, 1931);

L'Europe contre les patries (Paris: Gallimard, 1931);

Le Feu follet (Paris: Gallimard, 1931); translated by Richard Howard as *The Fire Within* (New York: Knopf, 1965); translated by Martin Robinson as *Will o' the Wisp* (London: Calder & Boyars, 1966);

L'Eau fraîche, Cahiers de Bravo, 18 (supplement for August 1931);

Drôle de voyage (Paris: Gallimard, 1933);

Journal d'un homme trompé (Paris: Gallimard, 1934); definitive edition, including "Le Mannequin" (Paris: Gallimard, 1978);

La Comédie de Charleroi (Paris: Gallimard, 1934); translated by Douglas Gallagher as *The Comedy of Charleroi and Other Stories* (Cambridge, U.K.: Rivers Press, 1973); translated by Thomas M. Hines (Columbia, S.C.: French Literature Publications, 1979);

Socialisme fasciste (Paris: Gallimard, 1934);

Beloukia (Paris: Gallimard, 1936);

Doriot ou la vie d'un ouvrier français (Saint-Denis: Les Editions Populaires Françaises, 1936);

Rêveuse Bourgeoisie (Paris: Gallimard, 1937);

Avec Doriot (Paris: Gallimard, 1937);

Gilles (expurgated edition, Paris: Gallimard, 1939; complete edition, Paris: Gallimard, 1942);

Ecrits de jeunesse (Paris: Gallimard, 1941)–comprises *Interrogation, Fond de cantine, La Suite dans les idées, Le Jeune Européen, "Défense de sortir"*;

Ne plus attendre (notes à leur date) (Paris: Grasset, 1941);

Notes pour comprendre le siècle (Paris: Gallimard, 1941);

Chronique politique 1934-1942 (Paris: Gallimard, 1943);

L'Homme à cheval (Paris: Gallimard, 1943); translated by Hines as *The Man on Horseback* (Columbia, S.C.: French Literature Publications, 1978);

Charlotte Corday; Le Chef (Paris: Gallimard, 1944);

Le Français d'Europe (Paris: Editions Balzac, 1944);

Les Chiens de paille (Paris: Gallimard, 1944);

Plaintes contre inconnue (Paris: Frédéric Chambriand, 1951);

Récit secret, limited edition (Paris: A. M. G., 1951);

Récit secret, suivi du Journal 1944-1945 et d'Exorde (Paris: Gallimard, 1961); translated by Alastair Hamilton as *Secret Journal and Other Writings* (Cambridge, U.K.: Rivers Press, 1973; New York: Fertig, 1973);

Le Feu follet, suivi de Adieu à Gonzague (Paris: Gallimard, 1963);

Histoires déplaisantes (Paris: Gallimard, 1963);

Sur les écrivains, edited by Frédéric Grover (Paris: Gallimard, 1964);

Mesure de la France, suivi de Ecrits, 1939-1940 (Paris: Grasset, 1964);

Mémoires de Dirk Raspe (Paris: Gallimard, 1966);

Les Derniers Jours (periodical written and edited with Emmanuel Berl in 1927, facsimile reprint, Paris: Editions Jean-Michel Place, 1979);

Fragment de memoires, 1940-1941 (Paris: Gallimard, 1982).

OTHER: J.-L. Le Marois, *L'Ode aux voiles du Nord*, preface by Drieu La Rochelle (Paris: Henri Jonquières, 1928);

Pierre Drieu La Rochelle (photo Harlingue-Viollet)

Maria Czapska, *La Vie de Mickiewicz,* preface by
   Drieu La Rochelle (Paris: Plon, 1931);
Ernest Hemingway, *L'Adieu aux armes,* preface by
   Drieu La Rochelle (Paris: Gallimard, 1931);
D. H. Lawrence, *L'Homme qui était mort,* translated
   by Drieu La Rochelle and Jacqueline Dal-
   sace, preface by Drieu La Rochelle (Paris: Gallimard, 1934);
"Diderot," in *Tableau de la littérature française de Corneille à Chénier* (Paris: Gallimard, 1939), pp.
   303-313.

PLAY PRODUCTIONS: *L'Eau fraîche,* Paris, Co-
   médie des Champs-Elysées, 20 May 1931;
Le Chef, Paris, Théâtre des Mathurins, 14 Novem-
   ber 1934;
Charlotte Corday, Lyon, Théâtre des Célestins, 20
   January 1942.

   Pierre Drieu La Rochelle was one of the
most original and influential writers of the
French interwar generation. As novelist, poet,
short-story writer, playwright, political essayist,
and critic of literature and painting, Drieu participated in the principal historic and artistic upheav-

als of his time–World War I, surrealism, literary
cubism, the political watershed of the thirties,
World War II in occupied France–and was an
early champion of Aragon, Malraux, Céline, Hemingway, Lawrence, Huxley, Picasso, and Matisse.
His choice of a utopian "socialisme fasciste" in
the mid 1930s and his editorship of the *Nouvelle
Revue Française* for three years under the German occupation led, after his suicide in 1945, to
the immediate decline of his literary reputation.
However, the persistent fascination of Drieu's artistic vision, in particular of his ill-timed epic
novel *Gilles* (1939), has spurred a gradual
reappraisal of his work. Unfortunately this posthumous literary revival, often shaped by ideological
and psychological concerns, has been skewed by
distortions of emphasis and of fact. Drieu's principal biographers have relied very heavily on his fiction and artistically crafted late memoirs to
record a life that *reads* like a Drieu novel. The as-
sorted critical portraits of Drieu–an intellectual
gone politically wrong, a ruthless seducer of
women, an accidental novelist unable to find his
true voice, a pathetic clown, a dilettante more interested in appearances than in art, a tragic hero–

Drieu La Rochelle (at foot of ladder) with (top to bottom) Colette Jeramec, André Jeramec, and an unidentified woman, at Charleroi, 1914 (Photo X)

have obscured the essential coherence of his life as a writer.

Drieu was a post-World War I romantic, a participant in the French *années folles* (mad years) and contemporary of the American lost generation, a modernist whose apocalyptic view of Europe in the 1920s resembled the world of Eliot's *The Waste Land,* of Joyce's *Ulysses,* of Picasso's barbaric forms in *Les Demoiselles d'Avignon.* Like Aragon and Malraux, Drieu was a writer whose work bridged several genres and art forms. His percep-

tions of the theatrical interplay of human desires, actions, and social structures with the visible world of nature and art are expressed in a series of works whose central motif is what he called "la comédie de formes." Drieu's artistic and spiritual patron saints point to the key elements of his own work: in literature Stendhal, Baudelaire, and Flaubert; in painting Watteau, Daumier, Manet, and the cubist, futurist, and expressionist artists of his own time. The best of Drieu's novels—*L'Homme couvert de femmes* (The Man Covered

Drieu La Rochelle (seated at center) recovering from his wounds at a hospital in Toulouse, 1915 (courtesy of Jean Drieu La Rochelle)

with Women, 1925), *Blèche* (1928), *Le Feu follet* (1931; translated as *The Fire Within*, 1965), *Drôle de voyage* (Strange Journey, 1933), *La Comédie de Charleroi* (1934; translated as *The Comedy of Charleroi and Other Stories*, 1973); *Gilles* (1939), and *Mémoires de Dirk Raspe* (Memoirs of Dirk Raspe, 1966)–are complex pictorial fictions that successfully fuse the French romantic and realist traditions with a strikingly fractionalized and spare modernist vision.

Paternal great-grandfather Jacques Drieu, *dit La Rochelle* (called La Rochelle), wounded in and pensioned from the Napoleonic army, left to the petit bourgeois family its noble-sounding name. Pierre Drieu La Rochelle was born in Paris on 3 January 1893 to Emmanuel Drieu La Rochelle, a lawyer, and Eugénie-Marie Lefèvre, daughter of an architect. The childhood he fictionalized in *Etat civil* (Vital Statistics, 1921, an autobiographical memoir), in *Rêveuse Bourgeoisie* (Dreamy Bourgeoisie, 1937, a novel of the middle period), and in the unpublished late memoirs highlights the motifs of family pretense, emotional and sexual conflict between mother and father, youthful literary daydreaming, physical weakness, streaks of sadism, and the intertwining

of family and national history. The accounts of early education at a Marist private school, the influence of a loving and strong-willed maternal grandmother and a fearful, dominated grandfather, and two early visits to England follow the pattern of the traditional French memoir of self-explanation. Strains of Rousseau, Constant, Barrès, Carlyle, Kipling, Whitman, Turgenev, Tolstoy, Dostoyevski, and Nietzsche all blend into a carefully structured literary portrait of the artist as a young Frenchman at the turn of the century. From his visits there in 1908 and 1909, England would remain Drieu's imaginary land of refinement, spiritual liberation, dazzling museums (the Tate Gallery with its Turners), and tasteful male dress.

In October 1910 Drieu entered the prestigious Ecole Libre des Sciences Politiques in Paris. In this austere *grande école*, which was to prepare him for a diplomatic or bureaucratic career, Drieu absorbed traditional French literary criticism and read enormous quantities of history; he also discovered the vast distance between his own background and the world of his wealthy schoolmates. Several close friends at Sciences Politiques would contribute directly to his still-undiscovered

Drieu La Rochelle, Maurice Martin du Gard, and André Germain, 1921 (courtesy of Jean Drieu La Rochelle)

literary vocation. Raymond Lefebvre, a subscriber to the avant-garde *Nouvelle Revue Française*, introduced Drieu to the poetry of Francis Jammes and Paul Claudel, to the writings of Italian futurist Filippo Tommaso Marinetti, and to a Goyaesque direct experience of police violence in a Paris street riot. Lefebvre's 1920 drowning at sea returning from a Communist meeting in Russia would represent for Drieu the first "destin politique" among his early friends. Young dandy Raoul Dumas, a devotee of Parnassian poetry, counseled Drieu on writing sonnets. Visits with the wealthy Jewish family of André Jeramec,

whose sister Colette later became Drieu's first wife, forced him to compare the Jeramecs' handsomely appointed, book-filled Paris apartment, dinner table conversations on art and literature, and connections in Paris society to the mean-spirited Drieu household, with its tasteless mass-produced furniture, endless quarrels over money, violent marital rancors, and querulous political rightism. Drieu's father, sharing what Pierre Andreu has called the strong family resemblance to "les pères d'avant 1914" (the fathers of before 1914) of Drieu's and Céline's novels, was loudly and impotently proroyalist, anti-Dreyfusard and anti-Semitic, and impatient with the Third Republic's perceived softness on socialism. While a student at Sciences Politiques Drieu gave a talk on the origins of the legend of France as a victim of history and as a country of defeat.

In 1913 Drieu managed, after being near the top of his class for three years, to fail dramatically the final examination that would have earned him a degree. (The recently uncovered examination bears a curious comment by an examiner: "On ne déforme pas l'histoire pour prouver une théorie" [One does not distort history just to prove a theory].) Persuading André Jeramec to join him, in the fall of 1913 Drieu entered the army to serve his compulsory three years of military service. Stationed in Paris, with the Opéra, the Ballets Russes, and Henri Bergson's courses all so near and yet out of reach, Drieu became acquainted with the unfamiliar layers of French society represented by the peasants and workers in his infantry division. In the nine months preceding World War I he survived the boredom of the barracks and was promoted to corporal. On a trip to Munich in April 1914, while recovering from jaundice, he admired the disciplined marching of German soldiers and noted that the Munich museum would make a fine setting for a scene in a novel. After the assassination of Archduke Ferdinand on 28 June 1914, patriotic fervor rolled through Europe. At the announcement of the general mobilization on 1 August, as Paris crowds pillaged shops that carried German or German-sounding foodstuffs, Drieu's company was sent onto the boulevards to maintain order.

On 6 August Drieu's regiment left Paris, cheered on by flag-waving crowds; he carried with him a well-worn copy of Nietzsche's *Thus Spake Zarathustra*. The batallion of thirty-five hundred men, of whom half would die within two months, traveled by train to Amagne, then between 15 and 18 August completed a forced march over the Belgian border, arriving on the nineteenth at Charleroi. The battle of Charleroi would be the basis for Drieu's 1934 novella, *La Comédie de Charleroi*. His initial experience of this major conflict was a jumble of blood, noise, fragmentary exhilaration, waves of depression, and horror on learning that André Jeramec, whose group was moved to a less protected position, had been killed. A minor shrapnel wound in the head reinforced Drieu's sense of a formless conflict that little matched the glorious battles in his childhood books. In the hospital at Deauville in August he began to compose his first war poems.

In October 1914 Drieu, now a sergeant, rejoined his regiment in Champagne, where he spent ten days in the trenches, received a slight wound in the left arm, and witnessed corpses being shelled out of their graves in a country graveyard. As he recuperated in the hospital, a bout of venereal disease further depressed him. In 1915, now officially engaged to Colette Jeramec, Drieu visited Paris, where he found the world of women and of civilians largely alien. In a fit of despair, he volunteered for a division being sent to fight in the Dardenelles. After a wild spree in Marseilles prior to what he saw as certain death in Turkey, Drieu reached his destination. There in 1915 he spent the most depressing months of his army career, largely inactive and living in a trench, acutely ill with dysentery, surrounded by decaying bodies, and plagued by oppressive heat and a growing conviction that the horror of war had at last submerged any of its redeeming literary associations. Removed to a hospital in Toulon, Drieu read Claudel, wrote some new poems with freer rhythms and stronger images than his earlier ones, and meditated on the fact that he no longer loved Colette. In January 1916 he was attached to a shock regiment and sent to Verdun where, late in February, after three days of inaction in the snow and ruins, he sustained his last and most serious battle injury, a deep wound in the left arm that would require several operations and would leave the arm partially immobile. Drieu's vision of soldiers walking over his prone body at Verdun remained in his memory, along with the terrible cry of fear and pain he slowly recognized as his own.

After a hospital stay in Paris and reclassification to auxiliary service, Drieu began his literary career with the publication in August 1916 of his first poem in *SIC* (Son, Image, Couleur; that is, Sound, Image, and Color). The cubist and futurist paintings Drieu saw in Paris were plastic representations of the disintegration and reintegration of forms he had experienced at Charleroi, Champagne, the Dardenelles, and Verdun between 1914 and 1916. In the winter of 1916-1917 Colette Jeramec, now studying medicine, introduced Drieu to fellow student Louis Aragon; the two young men formed an intense friendship that would endure until the political quarrels of the late 1920s. (The hero of *Aurélien*, the most luminous of Aragon's realist novels, written in the

Drieu La Rochelle and his second wife, Alexandra Sienkiewicz, with (at right) Mr. and Mrs. Jean Bernier, 1929 (courtesy of Jean Drieu La Rochelle)

early 1940s, is a composite of the two young writers in their immediate postwar years; Drieu read the novel in proof a few days before his death.) As Aragon and Drieu shared their love of poetry and painting, of obsessive conversation, of endless tours of Paris streets, cafés, and brothels, Colette arranged for Drieu to read several of his poems aloud at avant-garde salons. She also showed them to Léon-Paul Fargue (one of the forces behind Sylvia Beach's publication of Joyce's *Ulysses* in 1922), who admired their originality and encouraged Drieu to assemble a volume for publication.

In August 1917 Drieu and Colette were married. To ensure Drieu's literary independence Colette settled on him a sum of five hundred thousand francs (worth $86,750 in 1917). After problems with the wartime censors over two poems sympathetic to the Germans, *Interrogation*, a slim volume of seventeen poems, appeared quietly with Editions de la Nouvelle Revue Française in an edition of 150 copies. Drieu was compared to Whitman and Rimbaud. This volume by a mem-

ber of "la génération sacrifiée" (the sacrificed generation) seemed living proof that not all the literary talent of France was being destroyed on the battlefields. His new literary celebrity did not prevent Drieu from finding life away from the war paler than the remembered hours in battle. In July 1918 he resumed active duty and became an interpreter for an American division stationed near the Swiss frontier, where he studied the mythical Americans at close range and reflected on the imminent fate of Europe. In February 1919 he wrote to Colette, "Notre siècle est de fer et nos vies seront dramatiques" (We live in an iron century, and our lives will be dramatic). In March 1919 Drieu was at last demobilized; a few months later he was awarded the Croix de Guerre, which he refused to wear except for a few weeks in 1940, just before the new declaration of war.

In the early 1920s Drieu published poems, dialogues, and odd essays in avant-garde magazines, and a second collection of poetry, *Fond de cantine* (From the Bottom of My Footlocker,

Drieu La Rochelle, 1936 (photo Keystone)

1920). He loved the theater and attended the Comédie-Française, the newest plays on the boulevards, and the music halls and circuses the surrealists favored. A brief but intense love affair with an older woman, constant brothel trips with Aragon, and steadily disintegrating relations with Colette, whose furniture and wallpaper he claimed to find execrable, made the marriage intolerable. Drieu and Colette separated in 1920, divorced in 1921, and remained friends. "Le riche Drieu" acquired some fine English clothes, spent heavily on his friends, participated in Dadaist demonstrations and literary surveys, and contributed regularly to *Littérature,* the magazine founded by Aragon, André Breton, and Philippe Soupault. He also published in the *Nouvelle Revue Française,* where André Gide admired his work.

Etat civil, Drieu's first prose work, appeared in 1921. Best described as an essay-memoir, it sketches the psychological and intellectual biography of Drieu's first sixteen years, introducing several recurrent themes of the later essays: the sorry moral and physical state of France, the dangers of excessive psychological self-analysis (a startling jab at Gide), the role of *le mal du siècle* in the development of his literary imagination. Cogle, the persona of the child Drieu, is treated gently but ironically, reflecting the influence of Joyce's *A Portrait of the Artist as a Young Man.* Despite its many flaws–an oddly fluctuating tone, periodic passages of declamatory prose, a maze of unintegrated characters and observations–*Etat civil* reveals considerable literary talent and an original approach to the French memorial tradition. Critic Marcel Arland, writing in the *NRF*, saw it as a brilliant promise of more interesting works to come. In 1921 Drieu's review in the *NRF* of Aragon's first novel, *Anicet ou le panorama* (Anicet or the Panorama), revealed extraordinary critical gifts. He noted the novel's refreshing sexual frankness, its slightly quaint Voltairean form, and predicted accurately the full curve of Aragon's lengthy career as a novelist. The year 1921 also saw a rush of surrealist activities–literary parades and demonstrations, the mock trial of Maurice Barrès, a dramatic reading of an apology for suicide by Jacques Rigaut. (Rigaut, who killed himself in 1929, served as the model for Gonzague, the hero of Drieu's 1924 short story "La Valise vide" [The Empty Suitcase], and for Alain of *Le Feu follet* in 1931.)

Mesure de la France (The Measure of France, 1922), Drieu's first book-length political essay, added to his growing reputation. This sweeping analysis of postwar France's declining moral and physical strength–based on an odd fusion of historical analysis and personal experience–calls for an alliance of European nations to counter the growing power of the United States and Russia. Drieu extended his critique of contemporary French society to the arts with a series of reviews of theater, music hall, and circus performances ("Chroniques des spectacles," *NRF*, November 1923-March 1924) that extended the traditions of Baudelaire's writings on art and urban life and Daumier's satirical cartoons of the Parisian theater public. Drieu's first collection of short stories, *Plainte contre inconnu* (Complaint against a Person Unknown), published in 1924, depicts the disoriented youth of the postwar generation at their hollow games of sex and money. The spare, flat dialogue of these tales resembles Hemingway's, while the abstract passages of psychological analysis reflect unsuccessfully the methods of seventeenth-century French fiction. Drieu's last peaceful years with his surrealist friends included renting a villa in the south, to which flocked Aragon and scores of other friends; buying a yellow roadster he drove badly; having a stormy love affair with a married American woman; and financing a surrealist pamphlet attacking Anatole France, whose recent national funeral symbolized for avant-garde writers the glorification of defunct literary values.

L'Homme couvert de femmes (1925), Drieu's first novel, dedicated to Aragon, recounts the visit of twenty-seven-year-old Gille Gambier to the country estate of friend Luc and his sister,

Finette, a wealthy widow. Attracted by Finette's obvious interest, Gille nevertheless begins his stay with sexual encounters with three of the female guests; then, depressed by their shallow sensuality, he escapes for a few days to Paris for a frantic tour of bars and brothels. On his return, Gille begins a liaison with Finette that offers physical pleasure and financial security, but communicates a frightening sense of emotional void. Luc, a fitfully frenetic homosexual, suggests to Gille that they both are looking for an impossible perfect union. Finette's guarded involvement with Gille (she is older and fears becoming emotionally dependent) precipitates a long, meditative despair that finally leads him to flee in search of an ideal love elsewhere.

The novel's simple lines are unbalanced by Gille's long bouts of self-analysis and by unconvincing shifts into the minds of several of the women. However, the opening scene, composed of unidentified lines of dialogue as Finette and her guests discuss the newly arrived Gille approaching them across the lawn, has both the look (on the printed page) and the sound of some of Hemingway's dialogues, no mean feat in French. The sexual encounters, vivid without being prurient, are tersely and cinematically narrated, filled with unspoken tensions. The novel's sexual boldness assumes its most imaginative dimensions in the long chapter devoted to Gille's interim fling in Paris. The sensual rhythms of his idle Paris life, his openness to glimpsed faces that seem to break over him in waves, his journey to "la rue des prostituées" where the women look like forms in a cubist painting, his sexual encounter with a huge woman he perceives as a surrealist dummy, the dazzling scene in a visual garden of women at the second brothel of the day–all point to the aesthetic center of Drieu's sensibility and to the painterly significance of the novel's title. Not surprisingly, Drieu's first novel was considered more a *succès de scandale* than an artistic triumph, and admirers continued to wait for the real Drieu to emerge. A collection of odd stories and poems, *La Suite dans les idées* (The Flow of Ideas, 1927), did little to satisfy them. Discouraged by the reception of his novel, Drieu began to doubt that he had in him "ces personnages robustes fondés dans des vies vigoureuses" (those robust characters based on vigorous lives) he identified with successful traditional novels. Privately, he found the novels of Balzac and Zola overlong and boring, and preferred the ironic method of Stendhal and the beautiful, distanced novels of

Drieu La Rochelle in Majorca at the time of his second divorce (photo Gisèle Freund)

Flaubert. However, apart from Gide's *Les Faux-Monnayeurs* (The Counterfeiters), published in 1925, French fiction and criticism of the 1920s offered Drieu's quest for new narrative methodologies no encouragement.

In 1925, outraged by the surrealists' attack on ambassador-poet Paul Claudel for supporting French colonial policy in Morocco and their declaration of sympathy with the Communists, Drieu published an open letter in the *NRF* that condemned Aragon and Breton's betrayal of art's independence from political issues. This quarrel would escalate into an open break with Aragon a few years later. Moved by the dazzling originality of Aragon's surrealist novel, *Le Paysan de Paris* (The Paris Peasant, 1926), Drieu deplored publicly its incredibly poor critical reception and worried increasingly about his own literary future.

Drieu's sense of literary alienation deepened in 1927 with the negative reception of *Le Jeune Européen* (The Young European), a prose work that defies easy classification. Originally conceived as a novel, the text uses a life story loosely resembling Drieu's own up to 1927 as a literary myth. In the opening section the young European recounts his basic biography: he is a modern version of Chateaubriand's René who has survived the war, traveled through the world, made some money, and returned disillusioned to live in Paris. The second part traces his choice between "le sang et l'encre" (blood and ink) and the difficult birth of a literary vocation. This section's intensely personal, self-critical tone discomfited Drieu's contemporary critics and continues to mislead interpreters who read a sincere confession into a carefully managed parody of romanticism. The brilliant final section, "Le Music-Hall," bearing an epigraph from Aragon's *Le Paysan de Paris*, dramatizes Drieu's critique of contemporary French society through an imagined visit to the Casino de Paris, where the narrator meditates on the myths that animate Frenchmen in the 1920s. *Le Jeune Européen* bears many resemblances to Malraux's "D'une jeunesse européenne" (On European Youth, 1926, itself influenced by Drieu's earlier *Mesure de la France*), while its opening biographical summary reads like an outline of Céline's 1932 *Voyage au bout de la nuit* (*Journey to the End of the Night*). Drieu's tone and methodology prefigure Malraux's *Antimémoires* (*Anti-Memoirs*, 1967) and paranovels such as Norman Mailer's *The Armies of the Night* (1968). Reviewers were thrown totally off balance by what Benjamin Crémieux, in the November 1927 *NRF*, described as Drieu's unacceptable mix of analysis of the self and analysis of the world and by his progressive movement away from literary creation. In *Les Derniers Jours* (The Last Days), a short-lived political magazine he founded and wrote in collaboration with Emmanuel Berl in 1927, Drieu published his second and third letters to the surrealists, underlining the depth of his disillusionment with the movement and his mounting aversion to communism as an answer to the ills of Europe. Another political essay, *Genève ou Moscou* (Geneva or Moscow, 1928), jumbles history, prophecy, and literary commentary in a plea for a union of European states to create the stable peace that 1918 had failed to bring.

Drieu's second marriage in 1927, to Alexandra Sienkiewicz, daughter of a Parisian banker, provided barely six months of surcease from his alternating fear of and pursuit of solitude; he began consciously to realize that he worked best when alone, preferably while writing letters to a loved woman about his current literary projects. Early in 1928 he made a solitary trip to Greece and was struck by the Parthenon's pink beauty, by the hopelessly American Athenian suburbs, and by the decor of his hotel, which looked like a setting for a movie or a novel. Drieu's literary reputation continued to grow. Quite tall, slim, fair-haired, with blue eyes and a sensual mouth, Drieu was–despite his rapidly thinning hair–oddly handsome. His striking personal presence, described not without a touch of malice by Clara Malraux as a combination of affected boredom, slightly old-fashioned grandeur, and Baudelairean spleen, endeared him instantly to the young André Malraux, whom he met in 1927 and who shared his passion for art and for sweeping historical generalization. In 1928 Drieu met Argentine writer, intellectual, and literary-magazine editor Victoria Ocampo, noted for her beauty, wealth, independence of mind, and collection of famous lovers. Drieu's affair with her overshadowed completely his fitful attachment to his new wife. Over the years many of Drieu's most revealing literary letters, analyzing his reactions to contemporary writers such as Lawrence, Céline, Huxley, and Virginia Woolf, would be written to Ocampo, the only woman in his life who was his intellectual peer.

Blèche, Drieu's second novel, appeared in 1928. An exquisitely executed portrait of *le salaud* (the Sartrean man of bad faith), the novel dissects the structure of self-deception that Blaquans, an influential journalist in the conserva-

tive Catholic press, has created for himself. Although married and the father of three children, Blaquans lives and writes in a sparely appointed bachelor apartment just behind Notre Dame cathedral, occasionally visiting his wife Marie-Laure, an unseen Madonna-like figure with a harelip. When a pair of expensive earrings Marie-Laure has given him to finance a trip to America and Russia disappears, Blaquans's world comes apart. He suspects his maid Amélie and his young secretary Blèche. While trying to discover the thief, Blaquans begins to face himself. His relationship with Blèche twists into a cruel game of suspicion and seduction, after which Blèche attempts suicide, quits her job, and ultimately leaves for a job in New York.

The carefully modulated style of Blaquans's first-person narration is a triumph of narrative subversion. Blaquans's role as a political writer has allowed for no perception of individuals; he has lived in a world of phantoms whom he has either totally assimilated (Marie-Laure) or addressed from his smug journalistic pulpit. He sees Blèche sitting behind her typewriter putting his words on paper as a Delphic priestess transmitting the truth. However, as Blaquans observes her more closely, she changes into a contemporary siren with cropped hair, blue-shadowed eyelids, and endless cigarettes. Glowingly redheaded, Blèche appears as a striking oil portrait with green facets in her blindingly white skin, a terrifying "other" whose existence apart from Blaquans's work threatens his sense of himself. The extraordinary vegetal quality of the seduction scene bears a striking resemblance to surrealist paintings of man-eating female monsters. A striking modernist variation on the traditional French novel of analysis, *Blèche* was fairly well received. Novelist Colette, who disliked Drieu personally, called it "une manière de chef-d'œuvre" (a kind of masterpiece), and Ramon Fernandez, in the December 1928 *NRF,* grudgingly hailed Drieu's newfound order, clarity, and unity.

Une Femme à sa fenêtre (A Woman at her Window, 1929; translated as *Hotel Acropolis,* 1931), one of Drieu's weaker novels, is set in Greece in 1924. Margot Santorini, wife of a handsome Italian diplomat, becomes emotionally involved with Michel Boutros, a determined young bourgeois-turned-Communist who takes refuge in her Athens hotel room one night when fleeing the police. Margot's life with largely effeminate international expatriates, an idly philandering husband, and a reserved middle-aged French busi-

Page from Drieu La Rochelle's secret journal, containing material which appeared in a section of the posthumously published
Récit secret (photo Flammarion)

nessman suitor has been one of unarticulated desperation. Boutros represents action, choice, and the possibility of devoting herself to potentially transcendent goals. She instinctively assumes the risk of hiding him and setting up his escape from Athens, then engages in a night of Lawrentian mystical sexual union. Margot's ultimate decision to give up her wealth and rejoin Boutros for a new and difficult life ends the novel on an uncertain vista. Symbolic, at times clumsily cinematic in conception, *Une Femme à sa fenêtre* incorporates several of Drieu's theoretical preoccupations with politics and male-female relationships into a mildly exotic tale lacking the visual and aural density of his novels set in France. Its critical reception was less than lukewarm.

Continuing his exploration of Europe and of the evolving contours of contemporary literature, in 1930 Drieu visited Germany and published major critical articles on Malraux and Huxley. In 1931 the rising tempo of his writing included the preface to the French translation of Hemingway's *A Farewell to Arms,* a new political essay (*L'Europe contre les patries* [Europe Against Nations]), admired by Thomas Mann, Bertrand Russell, and Benedetto Croce, and a play (*L'Eau fraîche* [Fresh Water]) performed by Louis Jouvet's company. He also tried unsuccessfully to have Gallimard bring out new inexpensive editions of his works and a separate edition of "Le Music-Hall" (the third part of *Le Jeune Européen*) with illustrations by German expressionist painter George Grosz. Now secure in his literary vocation, Drieu was nevertheless troubled by the poor sales of his books and worried fitfully about money. His first wife's wedding settlement was largely exhausted; his second wife's father went bankrupt in the crash. (Drieu and Alexandra Sienkiewicz separated in 1931 and divorced in 1933.) Drieu lived off advances against royalties on future books (never equaled by sales), disbursed loyally over the years by publisher Gaston Gallimard; when he needed extra money—for example in 1931 to secure the Ile Saint-Louis apartment with the extraordinary view described in Aragon's *Aurélien*—friends (frequently women such as Colette Jeramec and Victoria Ocampo) contributed. As Malraux's biographer Jean Lacouture has noted, many noted French writers of the 1920s and 1930s married wealthy women or lived off publishers and friends.

Le Feu follet (1931), inspired by the 1929 suicide of surrealist Jacques Rigaut, traces the final three days in the life of Alain, a drug addict. His ultimate efforts to reassemble a disintegrating existence are punctuated by failed human contacts: a few hours in bed with wealthy American Lydia, who leaves him money and escapes back across the ocean; a carnivalesque dinner at the sanitorium where Alain is failing at his last possible cure; a visit with a friend who has taken refuge in ethnology and a bestially placid marriage; a few hours with some depressingly bourgeois drug addicts; and dinner with friends in high society who refuse to recognize Alain's despair. The novel builds to its wrenching effect by assembling a heap of visual fragments that cubistically resume the contents of Alain's life. The fragments—represented by geometric shapes, carefully faceted planes, controlled primitive coloration, and snippets of dialogue—are gradually arranged into progressively smaller, more abstract compositions as Alain moves relentlessly toward the final obliteration of vision.

A failed writer, Alain greedily examines and mentally transforms the world around him; he sees other human beings as portraits, clowns, dummies, talking heads whose voices and words are less significant than the colors of their faces. Alain's Paris has the same gray, damp, metaphysical look as Eliot's London and some of its infernal structure. Women walk on ankles of clay like crumbling idols; taxis roll down streets like out-of-control billiard balls; the dining room of the sanitorium is "tapissée de littérature" (tapestried with literature). Alain is an instinctive lover of the primitive; he collects strange objects and arranges them into mysterious collages. Sickened by the imperfect structures that surround him, threatened by a profusion of images, Alain lives in an increasingly abstract world that approaches closure with the final chilling line of the novel. The remarkable prose style, skillful use of minimal dialogue, and relentless motion of this 192-page novel seem to have impressed Drieu's contemporary critics far less than its shocking subject matter. Intensely wounded by the novel's largely negative reception, Drieu bitterly insisted that the book was its own best defense. In recent decades, the novel has been widely translated and in 1963 made into a somewhat bowdlerized movie (Alain is an alcoholic; Lydia's money is part of a debt) by Louis Malle.

In 1932 Drieu visited Argentina, where he gave a series of well-attended public lectures on the current state of Europe to young South Americans. There Victoria Ocampo introduced him to Jorge Luis Borges, with whom he walked through the seemingly endless, darkened streets of Buenos Aires and from whom he heard the tale of a nineteenth-century Bolivian dictator that would become the basis of Drieu's 1943 novel, *L'Homme à cheval* (translated as *The Man on Horseback*, 1978). In his late political memoirs Drieu would date his "chute dans un destin politique" (descent into a political destiny) from the months in Argentina when–as the lionized "Français de Paris"–he began to conceive his role as historian-philosopher whose active involvement in politics would compensate for his too comfortable creative life. Soon the watershed of the 1930s would become pronounced, as French writers such as Gide, Aragon, Céline, and Malraux visited Russia and took stands on the choice between communism and fascism. Drieu would be one of those to drift to the extreme right. His memories of the South American continent and its reversed seasons, of "le vertige horizontal" (the horizontal vertigo) of Buenos Aires, fused in his mind with Spain, another "pays d'exil et de grandeur" (country of exile and of grandeur), and the delights of temporary expatriation would soon lead Drieu to visit other foreign countries as subjects for his journalistic writings, much in the manner of his character Blaquans. Drieu would then write on all fronts at once–as journalist, novelist, playwright, and critic. His relentless drive and ability to write, somewhat obscured over the years by the legends of "Drieu le paresseux" (the lazy Drieu) and Drieu the womanizer, fed by his own writings, resulted in the incredible production of the late 1920s and early 1930s; between 1927 and the end of 1934 Drieu published some thirteen books and wrote three plays and countless articles.

Drôle de voyage (1933), one of Drieu's finest novels, reintroduces Gille Gambier in a more complex incarnation. Now a few years older than in *L'Homme couvert de femmes* and occupant of a minor diplomatic post at the Quai d'Orsay, he visits La Béraude, the progressively modernized and degraded ancient Pyrenees chateau of wealthy Jewish friends Baptiste, Yves, and Gabriel Cahen-Ducasse, varied representatives of a dying bourgeois civilization, and their scrawny stepmother, who deludedly fancies herself aristocratic and passionate and lusts after Gille. The four young men engage in a strikingly cultured, musically brittle conversation on contemporary painting that is interrupted by the sudden arrival of English aristocrats Lord and Lady Owen and their daughter Béatrix en route to a winter home

in Granada. All present then participate in maneuvering Gille and Béatrix into a romantic situation; the two young people are almost immediately tempted by the idea of marriage. However, nothing is decided when the Owens leave for Granada after a few days. Twenty-four hours later Gille decides to visit them in Spain and travels to Granada, where he acts like a fiancé, but cannot bring himself to propose. On returning to Paris he initiates a passionate correspondence with Béatrix while becoming involved in a complicated affair with a married woman he meets at a movie house. Despairing of his fragmented and financially uncertain Parisian existence, he decides to marry Béatrix and give clear form to his life. The trip to Granada in December is a disaster. Gille is surprised to find Béatrix ugly and hopelessly virginal; the Owen "Spanish" home is typically chilly in the English style; and Granada looks like a dreary French provincial town. Feeling the marriage-and-money trap closing around him, Gille arranges to receive a telegram recalling him to Paris. While trying to explain his departure to Lady Owen, he finds himself beginning to seduce her. After a fruitless dialogue with Lord Owen in a room filled with antique weapons, Gille packs his bags and leaves.

The painterly, dramatic, and musical structure of *Drôle de voyage* is woven of vignettes and caricatures, plays within plays, and vocal arrangements. In his second appearance, Drieu's Gille is a skillful and always riveting *comédien* (actor), the traditional Pierrot (a clown, sometimes called *un gille*) darkly illumined by complex hindsight (he has fought in the war of 1914). As the clown-sage of a society he at once condemns and enjoys, Gille's presence transforms each of the novel's four parts into a full-scale play. Theatricality is carried to startling extremes. Rooms, houses, and natural scenery are all perceived as stage sets about to vanish when the curtain falls–contributing to the impression of a work of art about works of art, of pictures within pictures on every page. The sudden turns and pirouettes, verbal asides, and orchestrated character motions are doubled by Gille's mental impression of being surrounded by statues, drawings, silhouettes, and a few carefully selected paintings–a Cézanne Pyrenees landscape, several great "peintures de ruines" (paintings of ruins, that is, cubist paintings) by Picasso, and a few *fêtes galantes* (eighteenth-century costume entertainments) by Watteau. In reply to descriptions of his novel as the story of a young man who simply cannot make up his mind, Drieu wrote to critic Edmond Jaloux, "Je ne crois pas que Gille soit un indécis. Depuis le début, il sait que ça ne marchera pas, mais il feint.... J'ai voulu écrire une comédie comme celles de Watteau et de Marivaux et de Couperin ... où un Français sait comment le ballet finira" (Gille is not a man who cannot make up his mind. From the beginning, he knows it won't work, but he plays the game.... I wanted to write a comedy like those of Watteau, Marivaux, and Couperin ... where a French audience knows how the ballet will end).

Drôle de voyage was the best received of Drieu's novels to date, though it sold a bare six thousand copies, no more than *Le Feu follet*. Encouraged by comments referring to the emerging "real Drieu" and to "un roman concis et vigoureux de mœurs" (a concise and vigorous novel of manners), he began work on the stories that would comprise *La Comédie de Charleroi*. He also observed national and European politics and read of Hitler's election to the chancellorship of Germany in 1933 and installation as head of the German state in 1934 under the banner of national socialism as the rise of a popular hero capable of unifying his nation and initiating the pan-Europeanism Drieu had called for in *L'Europe contre les patries*. In February 1934 Drieu witnessed the Stavisky riots in Paris, in which leftists and rightists faced one another and the police in protest over a major government scandal. This clash appeared to him as a failed revolution that could have toppled the weak and corrupt Third Republic. On a trip to Berlin, he was impressed by the spectacle of young Nazi soldiers parading and by Otto Abetz, a cultured Francophile German who would become ambassador to France and director of cultural activities under the German occupation. In 1934 Drieu also cotranslated and wrote an extensive preface to *The Man Who Died*, a late allegorical novel by D. H. Lawrence, published the collection of stories *Journal d'un homme trompé* (Journal of a Deceived Man), and saw his play *Le Chef* (The Leader), a rather static exercise in "théâtre politique" (political theater) produced by Georges Pitoëff, run for only five performances. He began a series of newspaper articles based on trips to Rome, Czechoslovakia, and Hungary that elaborated an evolving semiotics of national salvation in troubled European capitals. In the midst of this intensely creative year, Drieu announced his conversion to "socialisme fasciste" (fascist socialism).

La Comédie de Charleroi, published in 1934 and awarded the Prix de la Renaissance, was Drieu's most successful book and sold eleven thousand copies. This carefully orchestrated volume of stories ranks with Céline's *Voyage au bout de la nuit* as one of the finest literary works to come out of the French experience of World War I. Intended in part as a corrective to the often positive view of war Drieu had expressed in *Interrogation*, *La Comédie de Charleroi* examines the war and its often contradictory revelations in a group of first-person narratives dealing at varying, sometimes multiple temporal distances with the battles of Charleroi and Verdun, with trench warfare in the Dardenelles, with an insignificant event in 1918, and with heroes and deserters after the war. Behind the stories of *La Comédie de Charleroi* stands a series of intertexts: illustrated children's books on the Napoleonic wars, Stendhal's *La Chartreuse de Parme* (The Charterhouse of Parma) with Fabrice del Dongo trying to find the battle of Waterloo, Tolstoy's *War and Peace* with Pierre observing Waterloo through Tolstoy's reading of Stendhal, Maupassant's acid tales of the Franco-Prussian war, Hemingway's *A Farewell to Arms*, and Céline's novel. Drieu assimilates these intertexts into a brilliantly theatricalized portrait of the major historical event of the early twentieth century.

Where Drieu's earlier fiction had dealt with the sexual, psychological, and artistic aftereffects of the war, *La Comédie de Charleroi* confronts the original events directly. Several narrators in several different voices attempt to give form to intensely lived experiences. The bare-bones style, at once poetic and unrhetorical, owes much to Hemingway and F. Scott Fitzgerald, but displays a quintessentially French—and highly modern—turn of phrase that is one of the hallmarks of Drieu's unique prose style. His use of colloquial language and slang is crisp, smooth, and utilitarian, radically different in effect from Céline's incantatory transformation of common speech. Shifts of tone and mood contribute to the effect of linguistic faceting, of mirroring, of multiple images superimposed. More vividly aural than Drieu's earlier fiction, *La Comédie de Charleroi* works through dialogues—between narrators and their own thoughts, between characters, and between individual stories. As Jonathan Dale has noted in an essay collected in Holger Klein's *The First World War in Fiction* (1976), critics who read *La Comédie de Charleroi* as simply another collection of Drieu's short stories missed its significance and misjudged its place in the context of 1930s war literature. Paul Fussell has shown, in *The Great War and Modern Memory* (1975), that much English literature dealing with World War II was shaped more by literary experience of World War I than by the actual events of 1939-1945. It can be demonstrated that Céline and Drieu had much the same effect in France.

In the title story the narrator is a veteran of the war who returns to Charleroi in 1919 in the company of his employer, Mme Pragen, whose son was killed in the 1914 battle there. The "comedy" is a complex interplay of pretense, recollection, image correction, social comedy, and splendid literary parody that focuses on the dual nature of the battle of Charleroi itself and on the use civilians make of experiences they can in no way understand. Unlike Mme Pragen, who insists on disinterring unidentified bodies in order to stage a funeral for the puny son she had so proudly sent off to die, the unnamed narrator must unwillingly relive the days in 1914 when he discovered—or so he thought—who he was in battle. His waves of recollection evoke the war, but fail to endow the experience with meaning. He can do little more than dramatize his discomfort at having to remember, but he is eloquent in describing the layers of mythology and personal pain that have become fused in his mind. The crushing irony of the tale's ending is Drieu at his most effective.

Drieu's artistic imagination strongly colored his 1935 trips to Germany and Russia. At the Nazi congress in Nuremberg (where he met Paris-based American journalist Janet Flanner) the staging of parades, speeches, and Wagnerian music struck him as a successful form of contemporary epic theater. Moscow, which he had expected to be as vital as Berlin, was disappointing; contemporary Soviet culture seemed to consist largely of bad movies and distressing *pompier* (tasteless bourgeois) art. Drieu's meeting in 1935 with Christiane Renault, wife of the French industrialist, initiated the most lasting liaison of his life. This strong, healthy woman appeared to Drieu a French *Victoire de Samothrace* (Winged Victory), an unliterary Victoria Ocampo with a complex life as mother, wife, and queen of Paris society that gave her a fascination which Drieu attempted to immortalize in *Beloukia*, a failed 1936 novel that transposed his passion for a married woman into an exotic tale set in ancient Baghdad. The secret liaison between the poet Hassib and the princess Beloukia, pitting political loyalty against passion,

reaches its apogee in a scene of sexual union narrated as a moment of mystical revelation. His tiresome exotic tale ignored by critics, Drieu deepened his involvement in journalism and politics. In 1936 he joined Jacques Doriot's new fascist group, the Parti Populaire Français, which Drieu saw as a vital form of communism without Moscow led by a strong, sweaty man with deep roots in the national psyche. Stirred by a desire to reach a broader audience, Drieu briefly took a more visible role in politics, publishing two very bad books on Doriot in 1936 and 1937 and delivering several stumbling, reedy-voiced speeches before political gatherings, where his personal charm and normally riveting presence totally evaporated. Journalistic expeditions in 1936 to North Africa and to Spain, where war was brewing, aroused a fleeting middle-aged nostalgia for the ambiguous glories of armed conflict.

Rêveuse Bourgeoisie (1937), Drieu's most traditional novel, is "une vaste machine" he hoped would be the real novel critics and readers seemed inclined to favor. The internal contradictions between three parts in the French realistic and naturalistic tradition and two parts closer to Drieu's modernist temperament create an impression of two separate books, one based on the lives of his grandparents and parents, the other a loosely mythologized account of a rather clichéd divided self. The Ligneul and Le Pesnel families belong to the world of Balzac and Zola reconceived through Maurice Barrès and Freud, while Yves and Geneviève Le Pesnel represent the action—art, male-female polarities that beset offspring of the "dreamy bourgeoisie." Polarities between Paris and the provinces, passion and money, sensuality and self-denial all come to bear on this story that has no real beginning, no real end, and almost no point. By the shift from an apparent third-person narrative to the revelation of a hidden tale-teller in part four Drieu accounts for the derivative cast of the first three parts: Geneviève can tell her family's story only by borrowing from outmoded fictional methodologies. If she frequently sounds like Balzac, the fault is with tradition and not with Drieu's novel. Geneviève herself has chosen a nonliterary form of "lying"—she is a professional actress. Striking descriptions of Norman beach holidays, of bourgeois Paris living rooms around 1910, of picturesquely attired secondary characters, of provincial views of the Babylon of Paris stand out in this long novel that seems to have tired Drieu after the first hundred pages. In depicting narrow-mindedness without recourse to satire, in espousing the viewpoint of a poorly defined, optimistic female character, Drieu worked totally against the grain. Despite a spirited send-off by Gallimard, *Rêveuse Bourgeoisie* failed to receive the critical acclaim shortly before accorded Aragon's *Les Beaux Quartiers* (*Residential Quarter,* 1936) and sold rather poorly (just over eight thousand copies).

As he began work on *Gilles* in 1937, Drieu also began to take stock of his artistic vocation. Clearly, he discovered, he preferred the solitude and personal freedom of art to the world of action. Drieu completed the first draft of his novel in August 1938, just before the Munich accords betrayed Czechoslovakia but seemed to avert war. He resigned from the Parti Populaire Français and worked at rewriting *Gilles,* observing with pleasure that some scenes had the power he admired in a few canvases by van Gogh, along with some of the "délicatesses choquantes" (shocking delicacies) of Manet. On completing *Gilles* in August 1939 Drieu wrote in a letter, "Cela m'a beaucoup détraqué.... C'est un jeu terriblement dangereux que la littérature..." (The writing has really unsettled me.... Literature is a terribly dangerous game...).

Drieu's major novel, *Gilles,* was published in a censored edition in December 1939, then reissued in complete form with an author's preface in July 1942. Painfully aware of the book's disastrous timing, Drieu continued to hope that its literary vision would ultimately prevail and find a comprehending audience. The reputation of this neohistorical, picaresque modernist work remained for many years obscured by reactions to Drieu's literary activities under the German occupation and to his fictional hero's political opinions. Republished in France in 1962, it has been translated into German, Spanish, Italian, and Japanese, but remains unavailable in English. A riveting and unforgettable novel, *Gilles* combines brilliant visual detail, striking satire, varied prose rhythms, and complex modulations of narrative tone in a sweeping dramatization of the interwar years in Paris. The novel's undulled verve continues to unhinge ideological critics, while its satirical portraits occupy source hunters reading it as a roman à clef. Traditionalist critics of fiction condemn the disjointed chronology and find in the admixture of varying rhetorical modes a symptom of the novelist's lack of skill. The objections resemble many of those first raised to novels by Joyce, Woolf, and Faulkner.

The ad for *Gilles* in the February 1940 *NRF* reads: "La Vie d'un homme de 1917 à 1937, n'est-ce pas la première fois qu'un romancier traite ce grand sujet?" (The life of a man from 1917 to 1937. This is the first time a novelist has dealt with this major subject). Gilles Gambier now has an *s* on his first name, since he is a multiple character–the Gille of two earlier novels and the several incarnations of this one. Like the clown of Watteau's major late painting, Drieu's Gilles stands at the center of the picture, playing successive roles as the soldier, the diplomat, the political journalist, and the exile about to die. The novel is not his history but a pictorial representation of his life, a series of "studies" showing him at various stages of his life. While time elapses between one major section and the next, its passage is imperceptible because the novel is fundamentally spatial rather than temporal. Gilles experiences the world primarily with his eyes; his generally fruitless efforts to understand others consist of trying to imagine what they see. His perceptions are largely composed of visual fragments, snatches of dialogue, speeches and harangues, and illustrated newspaper clippings and captioned cartoons. While the printed pages of *Gilles* do not include textual iconography, such as the key in *Ulysses* or the drawing of an eye replacing the word "eye" in *The Sound and the Fury,* all three novels share the techniques of literary cubism.

Gilles's adventures fuse the picaresque tradition, the cartoons of Goya and Daumier, the pictorial breakthroughs of Picasso and Braque, the discoveries in narrative checkmate of Flaubert's *Education sentimentale* (*Sentimental Education*), and the comic opera rhythms of Stendhal's *Le Rouge et le noir* (*The Red and the Black*). In the first part, "La Permission" (The Leave), Gilles returns to Paris on leave from the army in 1917. Immediately, he finds the world of civilians largely impenetrable. His marriage to Myriam, a wealthy, educated Jewish girl who represents the society to which he would like to belong, is unworkable and cruel from the first day. Gilles finds himself both a clown and a kind of criminal. In "L'Elysée" (The Elysee Palace, residence of the president of the Republic) Gilles, in a new position as a petty diplomat, becomes involved with Dora, a married American woman he loses largely because her image continues to elude him, and with some wild avant-garde literary figures. In "L'Apocalypse" (The Apocalypse, the name of a magazine he founds) Gilles leaves the ministry, becomes a journalist, and, after witnessing the 1934 Stavisky riots as his second wife Pauline lies dying of cancer, declares himself a fascist. His Parisian life is at an end. The "Epilogue" finds Gilles fighting in Spain in 1937 on the Franco side; the novel ends as he courts certain death on the steps of an abandoned bull ring. The vivid scenes of 1920 Paris music-hall audiences, of riots at avant-garde literary gatherings, of wealthy French Jews in their studiedly white-walled dining rooms all have the special bite that comes with being viewed by a man to whom everything is a picture. For almost twenty years Gilles plays the role of observer-clown in the small world of postwar Paris.

Gilles got a mixed reception. François Mauriac, in a January 1940 letter to Drieu, called it "un maître-livre" (a master-text), beautiful and grand, with an unusually healthy approach to eroticism. In the March 1940 *NRF* Marcel Arland reviewed it negatively. Few people actually read the novel, or read all of it, in those troubled months following the declaration of war, although it sold moderately well. While clinging to his dream of Hitler's unifying Europe under a supranational socialism, Drieu nevertheless became increasingly depressed as the Germans continued their march through Europe. After wondering in May if he should leave Paris, he set out for the Dordogne on 10 June. On 17 June Drieu wept upon hearing of the French surrender to the Germans. On 18 June de Gaulle spoke to the French from London, and on 19 June Himmler arrived in Paris. On 25 June Pétain announced the signing of an armistice with Germany dividing the country into two zones. Drieu returned in July to Paris, where the sight of the Nazi cross flying over French monuments shook him badly. However, after visiting Otto Abetz, now German ambassador to France, Drieu began to wonder how to make the best of the German presence. Ignoring Abetz's guarded warnings that German policy toward the occupied nation would soon become considerably harsher, Drieu began to think of reviving the *NRF* with himself as editor and discussed the idea with Jean Paulhan, the magazine's editor before the Occupation. With the Paris publishing houses and magazines now closed down and most French writers wondering how they would make a living, the resumption of literary activity seemed an excellent move.

Figaro carried a headline announcing the reappearance of the *NRF* and published an interview with Drieu. Mauriac offered to review books and Gide to contribute regularly from his residence in the south. In December 1940 the first issue of the revived *NRF* included among its contributors Gide, Aymé, and Giono. While many noted writers were announced for subsequent issues, Mauriac soon withdrew because he disliked the political slant of essays by Jacques Chardonne and Alphonse de Chateaubriant. Aragon refused to contribute, and Gide and the poet Paul Eluard dropped out in 1941. Drieu tried to keep the magazine balanced, but politics increasingly impinged on the world of literature. He soon wearied of day-to-day practical worries such as deadlines, securing paper, and dealing with the literary vanities of contributors, but stayed on as editor and a principal contributor, working quietly with Paulhan, whose office was on the same floor as his in the Gallimard enclave, until June 1943. When Drieu resigned, the magazine once again shut down, not to resume again until 1953.

Drieu's perceptions of his involvement with the Germans evolved as the Occupation deepened and changed character. In the winter of 1940-1941, with Paris colored by the blue-out designed to camouflage interior lights in cafés and apartments, Drieu began to put on paper the assessment of his life and work stirred up by the writing of *Gilles* and being brought to a head by the German presence in France. He fluctuated frequently between seeing German leadership as a drastic solution to France's problems and total detachment from historical and political matters. Still convinced that taking an active stand was part of his literary obligation, Drieu visited bureaucrats in Vichy, conferred with Abetz and other German officials in Paris, wrote for the collaborationist newspapers, and assessed contemporary literature. Now forty-eight years old, still dreaming of being a Stendhal who would find his audience posthumously, Drieu began to realize that the practical outcome of working with the Germans might be getting shot. He noted in his journal, "L'écrivain doit accepter la mort au bout de ses paroles" (A writer should accept death as a consequence of his written words). *Notes pour comprendre le siècle* (Notes for Understanding Our Century, 1941), a somewhat chaotic analysis of the French national character going back to the Middle Ages, reveals Drieu's increasing tendency to connect political with religious mysticism. The pages on Romanticism and realism, drawing connections between Baudelaire, Rimbaud, and Verlaine and the novelists of his own generation–Bernanos, Céline, Malraux–contain some of Drieu's best writing on the inherent limitations of the realist and naturalist fictional traditions and on the relationship between painting and literature.

When Jean Paulhan was imprisoned in May 1941 by the German authorities for involvement in a nascent resistance cell, Drieu secured his release. He also exacted a verbal agreement from Gerhard Heller, the official German censor of wartime literature in Paris, to guarantee the personal safety from arrest or harm of several key literary figures–Aragon, Malraux, Paulhan, Sartre, and Gallimard. In 1942 Drieu worked on a new novel set in Bolivia and arranged for the performance of his play, set during the French Revolution, by a traveling company touring fifteen provincial cities. *Charlotte Corday* (published in 1944) played to largely stony audiences and hostile journalists. Depressed by its failure and by the news of the Allied offensive in North Africa, in a dramatic gesture of despair and contempt Drieu rejoined the Parti Populaire Français in November. At times, he dreamed of ending his life on a battlefront somewhere.

By 1943 Drieu's mythologized image of Hitler had disintegrated; he felt certain of imminent German defeat and increasingly perceived the collaboration as a dangerous parade headed for violent consequences. His former wife Colette and her two children were arrested and imprisoned; Drieu secured their release. He noted in his journal that published anti-Semitic statements were not in conflict with his private actions on behalf of Jewish friends, because individual feelings had nothing to do with theories. He began to consider leaving France and made a trip to Switzerland that confirmed his inclination to remain in Paris. Malraux, visiting Paris early in 1943, urged Drieu to drop the *NRF* and get out of politics. Drieu began to dictate his memoirs, to arrange his papers, and to meditate on the historical role of the traitor.

The conflict between Drieu's political stance and his private doubts came into clearer focus with the publication of *L'Homme à cheval* in March 1943. His first novel since *Gilles* is a poeticized, mythologized tale of the confluences and differences between the man of action and the man of art and meditation. Set in Bolivia in the 1880s, it has the remote, simplified, and cinematically enlarged qualities of an American western movie. Felipe, the guitarist-theologian who narrates and whose ideas are put into action, and Jaime, the rising and then falling dictator whose

reality is communicated only through his actions and words, are costumed characters in a somewhat muddled morality play dealing with ambition, sensuality, class conflicts, the genius of indigenous peoples, the slippery role of women in political affairs, and the beauty of an imagined Bolivian landscape. Lacking the motion and plot interest of successful escapist fiction, *L'Homme à cheval* is exceedingly mannered, with prose rhythms that frequently lack Drieu's characteristic flexible modulations of tone. The postscript discrediting the manuscript's authenticity highlights Drieu's attempt at artificial distancing, but the literary game in no way masks the novel's obvious and painfully personal debate over the pitfalls of mixing dreams with politics. While a few critics praised what they read as Drieu's new detachment, the novel's general reception was cool. In the spring and summer of 1943 Drieu completed a new novel set in occupied France and began his last major journalistic venture, a series of articles in the *Révolution Nationale* that became increasingly critical of the Germans and formed what Grover has called "a resistance within the collaboration" noticed even by the German censors and a few of Drieu's enemies in the final months of the Occupation.

The journal entries of 1944 reflect Drieu's careful plotting of the progress of the Allied landing in Normandy, his ironic amusement at how pitiful a thing fascism had turned out to be, his disappointment at the crushing banality of Sartre's new play *Huis clos* (*No Exit*), his negative assessments of Paul Valéry and Jean Giraudoux, and a clear analysis of his fundamental error in assigning to history a rational order and plan. (Sartre's 1948 analysis of Drieu's active surrender to the fatality of history would be strikingly similar.) In this period Drieu also wrote a brief analysis of his late political career and an essay on the temptation of suicide.

The preface to *Les Chiens de paille* (Straw Dogs), published in April 1944, describes the novel as a short fable written in 1943 and intended to give artistic form to the most insidious current events. Constant Trubert, a fifty-year-old veteran of World War I recently escaped from a German prison camp, takes employment with a black-market network based in Paris. The operation's storage house in a marshy coastal zone of northwestern France turns out to be an arms cache. Individuals of all stripes of political persuasion–Gaullists, collaborators, Communists, nationalists–are involved in the action, which often has the qualities of a successful thriller novel or film. Constant is an interesting new figure in the Drieu gallery, middle-aged, still sensitive to the sensual beauty of women but no longer moved by sexual pleasure, passionate about painting and literature, and immersed in the study of religions. Despite his intellectual decision to become increasingly remote from life, Constant is an instinctive hedonist and man of action, fluctuating between violent deeds and uncommunicative silence; he plans to leave life in the plenitude of maturity but before the decrepitude of old age and chronic illness takes over. Constant admits to himself, in a cleverly handled critique of Nietzsche's internal contradictions, that he adopted Nietzsche as the guiding philosopher of his youth because he could not deal with abstract philosophy. Despite the somber historical frame, the narrative has remarkable wit and variety and several dazzling painterly sequences that predict the breakthroughs of *Mémoires de Dirk Raspe*. The lively evocations of occupied France in 1942 as a huge food-trading fair decorated with political banners rank with some of Céline's most Rabelaisian pages. Constant's skepticism, even about his own detachment and preoccupation with the myth of Judas, redeems his occasional tendency to lecture on Europe's drift toward chaos in the 1920s and 1930s. Indeed, the burst of fictional energy reflected by *Les Chiens de paille* casts an interesting light on Drieu's career after *Gilles*. From this novel and from numerous notebook entries and letters of the early 1940s, it appears that "le vice mortel" of fiction brought considerable brightness into the medieval tower Drieu often claimed to occupy in those difficult years.

In the last months of the Occupation, Drieu began his leave-taking. Journal entries of early August list the things and persons he had loved: wine, women, men, literature, painting, Aragon, Malraux, and his brother Jean. After organizing his papers, on 11 August 1944 Drieu made his first suicide attempt by taking a massive dose of luminal. His housekeeper, returning unexpectedly, found him unconscious but still alive on the twelfth. In the hospital he slashed his wrists and once again was rescued. After the liberation of Paris on 25-27 August Drieu hid out for several months at various friends' country homes near Paris. In October 1944 he began another novel, conceived as "une symphonie, une réponse à la peinture de Van Gogh" (a symphony, a reply to the painting of van Gogh); he completed the fourth of seven planned parts in the middle of Jan-

uary. At times, he thought of joining Malraux's Alsace-Lorraine brigade on the Eastern front (a whim to which Malraux had apparently agreed with the stipulation that Drieu conceal his identity from the other soldiers), then returned to his readings on Eastern religions. On 19 January 1945 writer Robert Brasillach was convicted of collaboration in Paris; he was executed on 6 February. In March, once again living in Paris, Drieu read in the newspaper that a warrant had been issued for his arrest. On 15 March, after leaving detailed instructions for the preservation and publication of his manuscripts with Malraux as literary executor, Drieu tore open the gas line in the apartment and took three tubes of gardenal. He was found the next morning; a note to his housekeeper asked her to make sure his papers were safe and to please let him sleep this time.

Although Drieu had some powerful literary defenders at the time of his death–Malraux, Gallimard, and Paulhan–his chances of avoiding arrest and probable execution were minimal. At the least he faced a long prison sentence, an alternative he found more unacceptable than dying. He could have gone to Switzerland or Spain; Heller had arranged the necessary passports a few days before Drieu's death. But he chose to live in Paris, or not at all.

Les Chiens de paille and *Le Français d'Europe* (A Frenchman of Europe, a 1944 collection of late political and literary essays), both published just before the Liberation, were seized and destroyed. The latter remains out of print, as does the volume containing the plays *Charlotte Corday* and *Le Chef*, also published in 1944. *Récit secret* (Secret Narrative), an essay on suicide written in 1944, appeared in a limited edition in 1951, then was republished in 1961 along with two other brief texts dealing with Drieu's political decisions. The riveting narrative voice Drieu adopted in these late pieces helped fuel the massive critical overemphasis on the political and confessional aspects of his work. *Histoires déplaisantes* (Disagreeable Tales), a collection of short stories written between 1935 and 1945, appeared in 1963, followed in 1964 by *Sur les écrivains* (On Writers), an arbitrarily organized anthology of critical pieces, excerpts on aesthetics and history, and snippets from the unpublished journals and letters. Drieu's unfinished last novel came out in 1966.

Loosely based on the life of van Gogh, *Mémoires de Dirk Raspe* is a first-person narrative tracing the discovery of Dirk's vocation as a painter. The first part narrates the difficult ten early years spent as a boarder with an English clergyman and his family, at the end of which Dirk tries a few tentative sketches. The second part jumps to his period in the employ of a London art dealer; he continues confusedly to paint and, surrounded by paintings both at the gallery and in the great museums of London, begins to distinguish canvases with an original vision from workmanlike exercises that simply repeat existing traditions. In a radical effort to understand the qualities that draw him to a few great painters of the past, Dirk mistakes their intensity of vision for detachment from reality. He decides to abandon art for a religious vocation. The third part finds him an evangelist in a poor mining town in Belgium, where he is overworked, misunderstood by the people he tries to help, and shriveling for lack of aesthetic and emotional nourishment; he falls into an intense despair. Then, in a vision that is piercing and clear, made visible and concrete during an electrical storm on an open plain, he understands that transcendence lies not in religious self-abnegation, but in light and in colors, "dans la lumière des peintres" (in the light of the painters). He returns to his sketches and to a few somber canvases. In the fourth part Dirk is living in The Hague, where his two attempts to end a crushing sense of isolation in relationships with women end in failure, and where he begins to meet resistance to his painting techniques from established artists. Drieu's ease of writing–highlighted in this unrevised manuscript–is breathtaking and profoundly saddening. Letters written during the novel's composition express a serene sense of artistic control and intense excitement at reaching for the link between fictional vision and painting his earlier novels had suggested. As Dirk tells his own story, noting that he is not a novelist and therefore not obliged to make linguistic compromises, the narrative at times achieves an intensity of painterly vision comparable to Proust's description of the patch of yellow wall in Vermeer's *View of Delft*, while retaining the concision and turn of phrase that mark Drieu's best writing.

Drieu's posthumous reputation has passed through several major phases. In the wake of his suicide, he became a literary character in the mythologies of other writers. For Sartre, who referred to *Gilles* as "un roman doré et crasseux" (a golden and dirty novel), Drieu was the figure of the collaborationist, the man so eager to predict history that he tries to go ahead of it. For Mau-

riac, Drieu was a frail and tragic ghost whose death represented the mortal wounds of an entire generation. Paulhan suggested that by committing suicide Drieu made it possible for lesser writers who had followed him into collaboration to survive. Apparently shaken by his death, Aragon refrained from even mentioning Drieu's name until 1959. By the 1950s, testimonies to Drieu's character and literary talent began to appear, spearheaded by Pierre Andreu's 1952 book *Drieu, témoin et visionnaire* (Drieu, Witness and Visionary) and continued by Frédéric Grover's *Drieu La Rochelle and the Fiction of Testimony* in 1958. In the 1960s Drieu's afterlife took several odd turns. As critical works dealing primarily with his "tentation politique" (political temptation) dominated, he also found a new audience among the disaffected youth of the Paris revolution of May 1968, who saw him as an apolitical brother in alienation, detested by the establishment. The structuralist wave of the 1970s failed to touch Drieu's critics, who devoted their energies to the psychosexual and historical roots of fascism; for them Drieu was a political writer with a warped personality who inadvertently wrote a few imperfect novels. Growing interest in World War I literature in the late 1970s resurrected "Drieu le témoin" (Drieu the witness), this time to an earlier war. Biographies in the late 1970s by Dominique Desanti and Pierre Andreu and Frédéric Grover have made available numerous fragments from the unpublished journals and letters; in the 1980s Robert Barry Leal did an introductory volume and Jean Lansard a massive study of the plays.

As a literary influence Drieu has been so deeply assimilated that he is almost invisible. Sartre's short stories owe much to *La Comédie de Charleroi*, while his *La Nausée* (*Nausea*) points clearly to *Le Feu follet*. Sartre's numerous studies of *le salaud* find their original model in *Blèche*. Camus's *L'Etranger* (*The Stranger*) silently acknowledges *Le Feu follet*, while *La Peste* (*The Plague*) resembles *L'Homme à cheval*. Numerous writers after the engaged generation were influenced by Drieu–François Nourissier, Félicien Marceau, Roger Nimier, Michel Déon, and Antoine Blondin, among others.

All these literary and critical images of Drieu, all these shadowy intertexts suggest a writer who is larger than the many explanations of his parts. In a letter satirizing the literary life of the Paris writer, Drieu suggested an explanation: "Chaque écrivain est ainsi retranché dans son for, comme un petit féodal, se trempant dans l'anarchie du royaume.... A chaque flèche reçue des autres, il gémit, se navre ... puis il remonte à son créneau et lance à son tour un carreau empoisonné" (Each writer is fortified in his castle, like a little feudal lord, enjoying the anarchy of the realm.... At every arrow that wings him, he groans, is cut to the quick ... then climbs back into his fortification and in his turn throws a poisoned tile). Only the substance and form of Drieu's best novels, those glowing poisoned tiles he left behind, can begin to explain what Dirk Raspe saw in a painting by Delacroix or in a storm on the Belgian plain, and what readers continue to see in *Le Feu follet, Drôle de voyage,* and *Gilles.*

Biographies:

Dominique Desanti, *Drieu La Rochelle ou le séducteur mystifié* (Paris: Flammarion, 1978);

Pierre Andreu and Frédéric Grover, *Drieu La Rochelle* (Paris: Hachette, 1979).

References:

Pierre Andreu, *Drieu, témoin et visionnaire* (Paris: Grasset, 1952);

Cahiers de l'Herne, special issue on Drieu La Rochelle, edited by Marc Hanrez (Paris: Editions de l'Herne, 1982);

Jonathan Dale, "Drieu La Rochelle: The War as 'Comedy,'" in *The First World War in Fiction,* edited by Holger Klein (London: Macmillan, 1976), pp. 63-72;

Défense de l'Occident, special issue on Drieu La Rochelle, 50 (February 1958);

Frank Field, *Three French Writers and the Great War: Studies in the Rise of Communism and Fascism* (Cambridge & New York: Cambridge University Press, 1975);

M. D. Gallagher, "Drieu et Constant: une parenté," *Revue d'Histoire Littéraire de la France,* 73 (July-August 1973): 666-675;

Frédéric Grover, *Drieu La Rochelle* (Paris: Gallimard, 1962);

Grover, *Drieu La Rochelle and the Fiction of Testimony* (Berkeley: University of California Press, 1958);

Marc Hanrez, "Le Dernier Drieu," *French Review,* 43 (Winter 1970): 144-157;

Julien Hervier, *Deux individus contre l'histoire: Drieu La Rochelle, Ernst Jünger* (Paris: Klincksieck, 1978);

Jean Lansard, *Drieu La Rochelle ou la passion tragique de l'unité. Essai sur son théâtre joué et inédit* (Paris: Aux Amateurs de Livres, 1985);

Robert Barry Leal, *Drieu La Rochelle* (Boston: Twayne, 1982);

Magazine Littéraire, special issue on Drieu La Rochelle, 143 (December 1978);

Parisienne, special issue on Drieu La Rochelle (October 1955);

Rima Drell Reck, "Drieu La Rochelle's *La Comédie de Charleroi:* A Long View on the Great War," *Romance Quarterly,* 34 (August 1987): 285-296;

Reck, "Drieu La Rochelle's *Etat civil* and the French Lost Generation," *French Review,* 58 (February 1985): 368-376;

Reck, "Drieu's Theater Criticism of the Twenties: Rituals, Spectators, and Subtext," *French Review,* 61 (October 1987): 50-59;

Paul Sérant, *Le Romantisme fasciste* (Paris: Fasquelle, 1959);

Allen Thiher, "*Le Feu follet:* The Drug Addict as Tragic Hero," *PMLA,* 88 (January 1973): 34-40;

Robert Wohl, *The Generation of 1914* (Cambridge: Harvard University Press, 1979).

Jean Genet
(19 December 1910-15 April 1986)

Joseph H. McMahon
Wesleyan University
and
Megan Conway
Tulane University

See also the Genet obituary in *DLB Yearbook, 1986.*

BOOKS: *Le Condamné à mort* (Fresnes, 1942); translated by Diane de Prima as *The Man Sentenced to Death* (N.p., 1950); translated by Steven Finch as *The Man Sentenced to Death* (San Francisco: Gay Sunshine Press, 1981);

Notre-Dame des Fleurs (Monte Carlo: Aux dépens d'un amateur, 1944); translated by Bernard Frechtman as *Our Lady of the Flowers* (Paris: Morihien, 1949; New York: Grove Press, 1963; London: Blond, 1964);

Chants secrets (Décines: L'Arbalète, 1945);

Miracle de la rose (Lyons: L'Arbalète, 1946); translated by Frechtman as *Miracle of the Rose* (London: Blond, 1965; New York: Grove Press, 1966);

Pompes funèbres (Bikini[?]: Aux dépens d'un amateur, 1947; revised edition, 1948); translated by Frechtman as *Funeral Rites* (London: Blond, 1969; New York: Grove Press, 1969);

Querelle de Brest (N.p., 1947); definitive version in *Œuvres complètes*, volume 3 (1953); translated by Gregory Streatham as *Querelle of Brest* (London: Blond, 1966); translated by Hollo Anselm as *Querelle* (New York: Grove Press, 1974);

La Galère (Paris: Y. Loyau, 1947);

Poèmes (Lyons: L'Arbalète, 1948); translated by Steven Finch as *Treasures of the Night: Collected Poems* (San Francisco: Gay Sunshine Press, 1981);

Haute Surveillance (Paris: Gallimard, 1949); translated as *Deathwatch* in *The Maids. Deathwatch: Two Plays* (1954); definitive French-language edition (Paris: Gallimard, 1965);

Journal du voleur (Paris: Gallimard, 1949); translated by Frechtman as *The Thief's Journal* (Paris: Olympia Press, 1954; New York: Grove Press, 1964; London: Blond, 1965);

L'Enfant criminel et 'Adame Miroir (Paris: Morihien, 1949);

Lettre à Leonor Fini (Paris: Y. Loyau, 1950);

The Maids. Deathwatch: Two Plays, translated by Frechtman (New York: Grove Press, 1954);

Les Bonnes, pièce en un acte. Les Deux Versions précédées d'une lettre de l'auteur (Sceaux: J. J. Pauvert, 1954); translated as *The Maids* in *The Maids. Deathwatch: Two Plays* (1954); definitive French-language version in *Œuvres complètes*, volume 4 (1968);

Le Balcon (Décines: L'Arbalète, 1956); revised by Genet and translated by Frechtman as *The Balcony* (London: Faber & Faber, 1957; New York: Grove Press, 1958); revised French-language version (Décines: L'Arbalète, 1960); definitive French-language version (Décines: L'Arbalète, 1962); translated by Frechtman (New York: Grove Press, 1960; London: Faber & Faber, 1966);

L'Atelier d'Alberto Giacometti. Les Bonnes, suivi d'une lettre. L'Enfant criminel. Le Funambule (Décines: L'Arbalète, 1958);

Les Nègres, clownerie (Décines: L'Arbalète, 1958); translated by Frechtman as *The Blacks: A Clown Show* (London: Faber & Faber, 1960; New York: Grove Press, 1960);

Les Paravents (Décines: L'Arbalète, 1961); translated by Frechtman as *The Screens* (New York: Grove Press, 1962; London: Faber & Faber, 1963);

Les Bonnes & Comment jouer Les Bonnes (Décines: L'Arbalète, 1963);

Lettres à Roger Blin (Paris: Gallimard, 1966); translated by Richard Seaver as *Letters to Roger Blin: Reflections on the Theater* (New York: Grove Press, 1969); republished in *Reflections on the Theatre, and Other Writings* (1972);

Jean Genet (photo Cartier-Bresson/Magnum)

Reflections on the Theatre, and Other Writings, translated by Seaver (London: Faber, 1972);

Un Captif amoureux (Paris: Gallimard, 1986).

Collections: *Œuvres complètes,* 5 volumes (Paris: Gallimard, 1951-1979);

The Complete Poems of Jean Genet (South San Francisco, Cal.: ManRoot, 1981).

PLAY PRODUCTIONS: *Les Bonnes,* Paris, Théâtre de l'Athénée, 19 April 1947;

Haute Surveillance, Théâtre des Mathurins, 26 February 1949;

Le Balcon, London, Arts Theatre, 22 April 1957; Paris, Théâtre du Gymnase, 18 May 1960;

Les Nègres, Paris, Théâtre de Lutèce, 28 October 1959;

Les Paravents, Berlin, Schlosspark State Theatre, June 1961; Paris, Théâtre de l'Odéon, 16 April 1966.

MOTION PICTURES: *Un Chant d'amour,* screenplay by Genet, 1950;

Mademoiselle, screenplay by Genet, 1965;

Genet, screenplay by Genet, 1981.

After Jean Genet's death in a modest Parisian hotel room, after a long bout with throat cancer, Jack Lang, the former minister of culture, said: "Jean Genet has left us, and with him, a black sun that enlightened the seamy side of things. Jean Genet was liberty itself, and those who hated and fought him were hypocrites." Earlier, when Genet was in prison, Lang's notion about the writer's being "liberty itself" probably would have astonished and enraged the convict; in his mature years, when his plays were being performed throughout the world by distinguished theatrical companies, he would have been angered by the observation that he had written to "enlighten the seamy side of things." At the beginning of his writing career, his purpose was somewhat different and vastly more audacious, for Genet's aim in his first prose works was to show that what to some was seamy in life was sublime to others and especially to him. In one early work, *L'Enfant criminel* (The Child Criminal, published with *'Adame Miroir,* 1949), he wrote brazenly: "Si mon chant était beau, . . . oserez-vous dire que celui qui l'inspira était vil" (If my song was beautiful, . . . who will dare to say that its inspiration was vile?). That question is a particularly rich one in the context of his works: it suggests that they were meant to be provocative; it indicates that Genet's writing was directed toward a public which was not going to understand him easily; and it conveys his conviction that careful aesthetic rendering, what he called his "lyrisme" (lyricism), can make any kind of material transcendent.

Though efforts have been made to associate Genet with other French writers–François Villon and Paul Verlaine, the Marquis de Sade and the Comte de Lautréamont–his work resists such attributions. He never retreated into the religious solace the first two found, and his intentions were quite different from those of the latter two. He is perhaps more readily comparable to Jean-Jacques Rousseau, the citizen of Geneva, who was to the eighteenth century what Genet became to the twentieth: a voice, articulate and powerful, insisting on making the literate public aware of levels of experience it had not previously considered worthy of its attention. As Rousseau was dedicated to speaking for the poor and raising disturbing questions about the legitimacy of those in authority, so Genet was devoted to speaking about outcasts and examining the meaning of their alienation from the establishment and its values. Both writers emerged slowly from obscurity to become highly controversial figures whose talent forced others to listen to them, sometimes with bafflement, but more frequently with fury. There were great differences between the two men: Rousseau came from a respectable artisanal background; Genet came from the gutter, and many believe that he should have stayed there. Another difference is that Rousseau's extension of the literary domain to include accounts of personal emotional experience was material in the birth of Romanticism and thus affected writers and readers for generations to come, whereas there is as yet no evidence that the topics Genet explored in his most controversial books will be central to a similar development.

From the time of his birth in Paris on 19 December 1910 Genet was an outcast because he was a bastard child; his father's name does not appear on his birth certificate, and his mother, Gabrielle Genet, abandoned him immediately after birth to the care of the state. Genet did not learn her name until he was twenty-one and examined his birth certificate. He remained a public charge until the age of eight when he was placed in the care of foster parents in the Morvan region of central France.

It is hard to find reliable data about the events of Genet's life and particularly of his youth, in part because of the absence of docu-

ments, in part because of conflicting reports about dates, but mostly because, in his semi-autobiographical novels, Genet mingled fantasies, wishful thinking, and facts in ways not easily sorted out. The novels include explanations of actions that conflict not only with each other but frequently with accounts in his journal as well.

One commentator has claimed that in his early youth Genet was the protégé of René de Buxheuil, a blind poet who saw to the boy's instruction in traditional cultural matters. In 1947 a writer for *La Presse* magazine claimed that Genet had received his education in a religious establishment, where he learned Latin and became familiar with the fine arts. It is possible that Genet was mute about such matters because they would not become consequential until later in his life, and in his youth they were greatly overshadowed by two events. One was the accusation that he was a thief, which he claims to have accepted by actually becoming a thief because it gave him a sense of identity; until then, he had considered himself an outcast of a society whose only coherence for him was its exclusion of him. In *Journal du voleur* (1949; translated as *The Thief's Journal*, 1954) he writes: "Cet ordre, redoutable, redouté, dont tous les détails étaient en connexion exacte avait un sens: mon exil" (This dreadful and dreaded order, all of whose details were exactly connected, had one meaning: my exile). Because of his thefts and other crimes he was remanded at the age of fifteen to the reformatory at Mettray, north of Tours, where he made the second significant discovery–the acknowledgment of his desire for other boys, which he had been experiencing since the age of eight or ten; this aspect of his identity also bore a defamatory label: homosexual.

In later years Genet insisted often that his sexual preference had made his years at Mettray happy; it led to passionate relationships with other boys in a setting where homosexual activity, though not approved, occurred routinely. He was not blind to the multiple forms of oppression, humiliation, and mystification which were the foundation of the institution; while the reformatory's practices hurt his feelings and offended his sensitivity, its look-the-other-way approach to his sexual orientation allowed him to satisfy his tastes. That preference brought him the scorn of some older boys and forced him to elaborate a rigorous personal discipline which he describes in the *Journal du voleur:* "Le mécanisme en était à peu près celui-ci: à chaque accusation

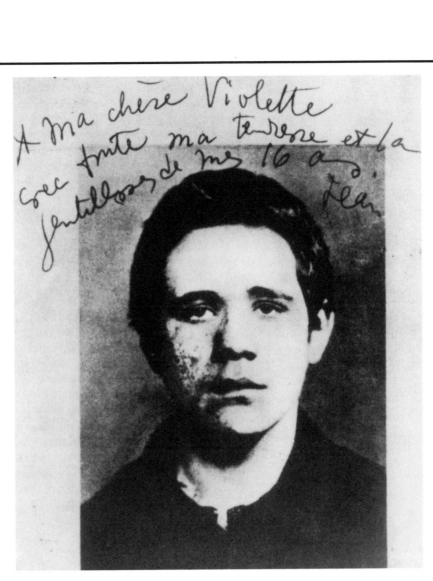

Photograph inscribed by Genet to Violette Leduc soon after his incarceration for theft at Mettray reformatory
(collection Violette Leduc)

portée contre moi, fût-elle injuste je répondrai oui. A peine avais-je prononcé ce mot . . . en moi-même je sentais le besoin de devenir ce qu'on m'avait accusé d'être. J'avais seize ans. . . . Je me reconnaissais le lâche, le traître, le voleur, le pédé qu'on voyait en moi" (Its mechanism was pretty much this one: to each accusation brought against me, however unjust it may be, I will answer yes. Hardly had I pronounced that word . . . than I felt within myself the need to become what I had been accused of being. I was sixteen. . . . I acknowledged being the coward, the traitor, the thief, the queer that they saw in me). He goes on to say that, after reflecting, he was always able to find within himself enough justification for being so named, and that the result was that he became abject. The label is one he placed on himself; he had to teach himself to live with it and find ways to derive a sense of triumph from

it. Abjection, in all its diverse forms, became a recurrent theme in both his novels and his plays, in which the consciousness of being abject does not automatically plunge those who experience it into paralysis or servitude.

Whether Genet's homosexual engagements were truly able to make him happy in the otherwise punishing conditions of the reformatory at Mettray is a question without an answer. Later in his life he asserted that his sexual proclivities had never posed any problem for him; he accepted them as he accepted the facts that his eyes were green and that he had two feet, and he believed that they helped to make him a writer by widening his range of personal experience. What is clear nonetheless is that the structures of homosexuality which Genet lived within during his years at Mettray were different from those which emerged from his novels. At Mettray his sexual role was that of the passive partner, a circumstance he then considered to be one of the signs of his abjection. His position was softened by the affection he had for his sexual partners and by what he believed was their nobility and glory within the hierarchy he perceived among the inmates.

How long Genet stayed at Mettray is not clear since he suggests several dates. In his novels the character based on himself claims that he escaped in 1929 or 1930. In an interview which he gave to Hubert Fichte in 1975 (published in *New Review*, April 1977), Genet said that he had been released in 1928, at the time when he was eligible for military service. Instead of being drafted, he claims to have joined the French Foreign Legion in order to benefit from the enlistment bonus and had been posted to Syria, where he claims to have had a happy love affair with a sixteen-year-old hairdresser. He told Fichte: "I felt really good with him, really good with his family, really good in Damascus."

In the early 1930s Genet apparently deserted the Legion and, wandering across Europe, became a vagabond, a thief, a drug runner, and a prostitute. These activities are described in detail in *Journal du voleur,* but as is always the case with Genet's works, the "I" who is the subject of the journal is not to be strictly interpreted as Genet himself. He was definitely in Czechoslovakia in 1937, where he was employed as a French-language instructor. There, he also established a connection with the League for Human Rights and met a journalist named Lily Pringsheim, who said, as paraphrased by Richard N. Coe in *The Theatre of Jean Genet* (1970), that Genet displayed a formidable knowledge of literature and spoke in strange poetic tones. According to Pringsheim, Genet had already accumulated a bundle of manuscripts. Pringsheim's claims about Genet's high level of literacy are supported by statements he later made to various interviewers.

While he was in custody at Mettray he often read popular novelists of the nineteenth century, but he also managed to obtain poems by the sixteenth-century poet Pierre Ronsard, and he was enchanted with what he read. During his time with the Foreign Legion, he read Dostoyevski's *Memoirs from the House of the Dead* and *Crime and Punishment.* He told Fichte: "For me, Raskolnikov was really alive, more alive than Léon Blum, for example." In the same interview he said that his favorite poets were Baudelaire,

Nerval, Rimbaud, and Mallarmé, some of whose verse he knew by heart.

Later in the 1930s he returned to France, drawn back by a desire to confront and undermine official institutions in his native country. There he continued to steal, and, although he remarked in an interview published in *Playboy* in April 1964 that he had not been unskillful as a burglar, he found himself jailed in 1939. In Fresnes prison he read with fascination novels by Proust, Dostoyevski, and Stendhal. He also started to write to ward off boredom and to demonstrate that he could create better poems than one of his cell mates. He may have succeeded—there is no way of knowing—but his poems are undistinguished, especially when their diction is compared to the verbal inventiveness found in his other works.

The first of his poems, *Le Condamné à mort* (1942; translated as *The Man Sentenced to Death,* 1950), was brought to the attention of the poet, novelist, and filmmaker Jean Cocteau by a friend of Genet's, who later showed Cocteau the manuscript of Genet's first novel. The poem and the manuscript were presumably smuggled out of prison by Olga Barbezat, whose husband ran a small press that occasionally published a literary review, *L'Arbalète.* Marc Barbezat took an active interest in Genet's work and became his first publisher. Through Cocteau and Barbezat, Genet's work and person became known to the established and not-yet-established: Marcel Jouhandeau, Jean-Paul Sartre, and Simone de Beauvoir.

In 1943, when Genet was again brought before the courts for theft and the sum total of his crimes in France—he allegedly already had nine convictions for burglary—mandated that he be given a sentence of life imprisonment, Cocteau intervened on the criminal's behalf, and Genet was released in 1944. Four years later Genet was again accused of theft and threatened with the same sentence. This time Cocteau and Sartre came to Genet's defense and addressed a petition to the president of the Republic, Vincent Auriol, asking that Genet be pardoned. That petition, published in the newspaper *Combat* and endorsed by its editors, urged Genet's pardon on the grounds that Genet was truly a great poet whose literary efforts had turned him away from a life of crime and because the theft of which he stood accused had been committed by another man,, Jean Decarnin, who had been Genet's lover and who had been killed while fighting for the Resistance. The petition was granted, and Genet be-

Genet with Jean-Louis Barrault at the Théâtre de France, 1960s (photo Bernand)

came a free man, honored by some and vilified by others.

All four of Genet's novels–*Notre-Dame des Fleurs* (1944; translated as *Our Lady of the Flowers,* 1949), *Miracle de la rose* (1946; translated as *Miracle of the Rose,* 1965), *Pompes funèbres* (1947; translated as *Funeral Rites,* 1969), and *Querelle de Brest* (1947; translated as *Querelle of Brest,* 1966)–were originally published either clandestinely or in expensive limited editions. The first appeared in an edition of 350 copies; the second in an edition of 475. It is difficult to assess what sort of public they reached. What is more certain is that they must have baffled most readers. Though Beauvoir, in her *La Force de l'âge* (The Prime of Life), remarked that she liked *Notre-Dame des Fleurs* and found that it renewed her faith in literature, she does not say what precisely in the novel, other than its style, produced those appreciations. Years later, a judge clearing *Notre-Dame des Fleurs* of charges of being a pornographic text made the observation that not many people would be willing to read the novel through to the end.

Notre-Dame des Fleurs, written while Genet was in Fresnes prison, is often considered his best work. The work, dedicated to the memory of a young murderer, Maurice Pilorge, whom Genet had known in prison, tells the story of a

young boy from the provinces, Louis Culafroy, who goes to Paris at the age of twenty and becomes a homosexual prostitute. To be more consistent with his new mode of living as a "queen," Culafroy changes his name to Divine. To underline this change, the author also shifts his use of pronouns and refers to Divine using the feminine while retaining the masculine when speaking of Culafroy. Although there are several flashbacks that deal with Culafroy's life in the country and particularly with his mother, Ernestine, who felt no love for him and had even tried to kill her son at one point, most of the book deals with Divine's love affairs and excursions into the Parisian underworld from where come most of "her" lovers. These men are not Divine's clients but individuals for whom "she" has strong emotional or sexual attachments. They include a variety of criminals and pederasts: Mignon-les-petits-pieds, a thief and pimp; Notre-Dame-des-Fleurs, a teen-aged murderer; Gabriel, a soldier later killed by the Nazis; and Seck Gorgui, a black. Mignon lives with Divine for six years before leaving to take another lover, named Mimosa II. Later, Mignon is arrested and jailed for shoplifting. After his desertion Divine lives with Gorgui and Notre-Dame. This lasts until Notre-Dame, whose real name is Adrien Baillou, confesses to a murder which he committed but of which he had not been accused. He is arrested, found guilty, and guillotined for having strangled a middle-aged homosexual named Ragon. As Divine grows older and less attractive–actually bald and toothless–"she" is reduced to paying her lovers and must endure the insults and insensitivity of those around her. Culafroy/Divine eventually dies of tuberculosis.

Although the story is easily summarized, the structure of the novel and Genet's treatment of his subject matter are quite complex. The action does not move along in a historical sequence but flips randomly backward and forward so that past and present events are presented concurrently. Rather than begin with Culafroy's arrival in Paris, the book opens with Divine's funeral; then the narration is broken by the intrusion of another character. This narrative voice represents Genet himself as he sits in prison awaiting trial, and it often interrupts the story to make observations about the other characters, to reminisce, or to express ideas about sexuality, crime, or Genet's personal situation. While largely an autobiographical novel, the autobiographical elements must be approached with caution for episodes in the life of Genet-as-author directly affect three characters in *Notre-Dame des Fleurs*–the young country boy who has already begun his career as a thief and experienced an attraction for other boys; Divine, who at first finds the life of a prostitute easy, then later is confronted with certain aspects of the homosexual's dilemma; and third, the narrator called Jean Genet. Having deliberately written himself into the book, Genet can take liberties with his own character, for, after all, *Notre-Dame des Fleurs* is a novel, and the narrator Genet does not necessarily represent the historical figure Genet.

This distinction between fact and fabrication–or rather the lack of it–is perhaps better understood when considered in terms of the whole book. *Notre-Dame des Fleurs* possesses a dreamlike quality, probably because it is presented as a conscious fictionalization with all the characters born out of Genet's imagination and not as a "real" story, which insulates it from the necessity of always conforming to an exterior reality. Genet supports this feeling with passages that read like poetry and others that are filled with almost religious exultation. His characters themselves indulge in fantasies and act out little rituals in their daily lives.

Juxtaposed to the often lush beauty of Genet's prose is the world of homosexuality, crime, and pimps that forms its subject. Never intending for the book to be read, Genet created a fantasy world to satisfy his own dreams, a circumstance which at least in part must have led Sartre to call the work "l'épopée de la masturbation" (an epic of masturbation). Genet's heroes in *Notre-Dame des Fleurs* represent his ideal men: young, virile, ruthless criminals. The sixteen-year-old Notre-Dame of the title is the "perfect" hero. He faces the consequences of his crime with unruffled composure; he is totally unafraid of death and because of his lack of fear is even stronger than death. Opposed to these heroes are the types of people Genet disliked intensely: the weak, the sentimental, the aging. It is only natural in Genet's world that these figures should become in one way or another, whether through betrayal, desertion, murder, violence, or ridicule, the victims of the strong.

This authorial attitude is part of what causes an uncomfortable reaction to the work on the part of the average reader. The world of Divine and "her" compatriots is far removed from normal experience and represents the inversion of a traditional outlook. In it, humiliation is a form of glory, abjection equals a form of sainthood, and evil is endowed with the mystic attributes of a religion. The most sacred images of the Catholic church–the Virgin Mary with her blue apron, the stigmata, and the Sacred Heart of Jesus–are evoked in the middle of scenes of crime, perversion, and infamy. Sacrilege is at the heart of the novel; Genet's characters are more shocking because they violate basic social taboos than because they contravene legal statutes. Even within the novel itself there is a consciousness of this hierarchy. Crime and violence in themselves are not very interesting except in that they place the offender outside the circle of acceptable society. Rather, it is the willful and complete descent into cruelty, degradation, and abjection that allows Genet's characters to experience a sort of spiritual ecstasy and makes Divine and Notre-Dame candidates for sainthood, at least within the fantasy world of the novel.

In Genet's presentation of the confrontation between the policed world and the criminal underworld, there is no readily discernible difference between the structures of these two worlds or between the functions of ambition and emotion which are found in each. Both are organized on hierarchical lines which, in theory, are to be rigidly

Scene from the first production of Les Paravents. *In a letter to director Roger Blin, Genet called the play a celebration of nothing (photo Bernand).*

regulated and respected: the motorist is supposed to heed the instructions of the traffic cop in order to avoid getting a ticket; the passive homosexuals obey their tough partners in order not to lose what little space they can claim in a relationship.

For Genet, the real differences between the operations of the two worlds spring from the claim to authority by the policed world and its power to defend that claim. Still, the policed society cannot persuade all who live within its precincts of the rectitude and preferability of all of its endeavors. All it can do is to police dissenters in an effort to thwart, coerce, or punish them. A Hegelian effect—the slave's realization that the master is more dependent upon him than he is on the master—comes into play once wilier criminals such as Notre-Dame and Mignon discover that the police, and the society whose values the police uphold, are dependent on their activities in order to affirm society's values. Criminals are essential to the performance of society's most important legal and symbolic rituals, as exemplified by Notre-Dame's trial and execution. That event is described as a sacrificial liturgy in which rules, robes, and rites are used impressively and

intimidatingly to reaffirm society's right to make judgments and punish transgressions.

Genet's second novel, *Miracle de la rose*, also written in prison, this time in La Santé and Tourelles in 1943, has much in common with his first book. It too portrays the outcast world of the criminal and the homosexual and is largely autobiographical in much the same fashion as *Notre-Dame des Fleurs*. There is a narrator who is identified as Jean Genet but who must be thought of as a character separate from the author Genet. Once again the other figures who people the novel are often projections of different sides of the author's personality—his ideal heroes and his alter egos—or are based on people he knew while in prison. As in *Notre-Dame des Fleurs* the distinction between past and present is blurred so that time is not subject to logical constraints.

The book is based largely on Genet's experiences in prison and at the reformatory of Mettray. Different from *Notre-Dame des Fleurs*, this second novel is not presented as the product of the narrator's fertile imagination in an effort to keep himself occupied and sexually gratified; *Miracle de la rose* is more realistic than Genet's first book in that it describes in detail the rigid structure of prison life and the hierarchical framework of the interrelationships of the inmates. Nevertheless, *Miracle de la rose* is still redolent with symbolism, mysticism, visions, and dreams. These elements are more important than the plot, which basically tells the story of the narrator's arrival and life at Fontevrault prison, his ecstatic and anguished emotional attachments to his fellow inmates Harcamone and Divers, both of whom he had previously known while incarcerated at Mettray, and to Bulkean, a young burglar who also spent time in Mettray, and the narrator's extensive actual and imagined sexual adventures with them and other inmates. These three characters, especially Harcamone, who is based on a young murderer named Maurice Pilorge whom Genet admired intensely, embody the type, full of strength and bravura, that Genet found so appealing. Bulkean, young, strong, and arrogant, is attractive primarily because of his savagery and ferocity. Divers was a former lover of the narrator at Mettray. Since they are of the same generation they share memories and experiences. Divers is another tough thug, a hardened bully. His status is not as high as Harcamone because Divers has not committed murder, but he is guilty of one of Genet's other favored crimes: Divers is the one who betrayed Harcamone to the police—he is both a traitor and a coward.

Before being converted into a prison Fontevrault was a Benedictine abbey with separate convents for men and women, and the narrator of *Miracle de la rose* constantly draws parallels between monastic and prison life. Like the monks of long ago all the inmates wear the same rough clothes, and they must obey a similar discipline of rising early, washing, dressing, eating, and working at prescribed times. Many of Genet's prisoners also spend part of their days in contemplation, lamentation, or silence as did the nuns and monks who once inhabited Fontevrault. Like the world within a medieval monastery, the prison community is isolated from the rest of the world and has its own hierarchy.

Harcamone, the "perfect" hero, the handsome, golden-haired, two-time murderer, is at the pinnacle of this prison hierarchy. Awaiting execution, he is kept in isolation from the rest of the prisoners. For the narrator this solitude is both mystical and sanctified—through Harcamone's transgression and unflinching acceptance of his condemnation, the murderer has transcended the judgments and morality of others. Har-

camone dominates the rest of the novel just as he dominates the other inmates by the glory of his acts, for he is never repentant of his strangling of a ten-year-old girl when he was sixteen nor of his murder years later of a prison guard who happened to be nice to him. His ascetic existence in solitude is like that of a saint shut away in his monastic cell and his absent presence has much the same inspirational effect on his fellow inmates, particularly the narrator, as a saintly figure would have had on his religious brothers.

Harcamone is the focal point of the miracle—actually there are two—referred to in the title. Both experiences involve the narrator, who is so dazzled by Harcamone's beauty and power when he sees the young criminal that he feels as if he is in the presence of some exceptional being, some deity. When the narrator sees Harcamone another time the murderer is bound hand and foot in heavy chains. Before the narrator's eyes the chains are transformed into garlands of white roses. In the second miracle, which takes place during Harcamone's final days in prison, the narrator is able to see into the murderer's cell and not only watch but feel the latter's experiences. During these visions Harcamone escapes the fetters of earthly constraints and walks through doors and walls; he also grows tremendously in size, and his heart is exposed as a monstrous and mystical rose. The rose, traditionally a symbol of innocent purity and beauty, becomes in Genet's novel the symbol of violence and debauchery epitomized in the character of the criminal Harcamone.

Genet's third novel, *Pompes funèbres*, written out of prison in 1947, differs substantially from the first two novels. Genet was at a turning point in his career and the emotional turmoil he was experiencing is reflected in his work. The criminal had discovered that writing was truly important to him, but he was being forced to decide just how important. In 1944 Genet had already faced the possibility of being imprisoned for the rest of his life for his criminal activities. He now had to make the decision whether to continue being a burglar or to give up that way of life to be a writer. Since Genet had specifically defined his existence in terms of the socially unacceptable outcast, giving up his propensity to steal meant potentially losing a good deal of his identity. Having struggled so intensely to arrive at a coherent view of himself, Genet could not settle down and become just another member of society. Crime had to be channeled in another way.

The answer was to make the act of writing become a surrogate for robbery: to make writing itself a form of criminal activity. By creating scenes of appalling violence and horror peopled by traitors, murderers, poisoners, and torturers, Genet attempted to make writing into an act of violence and thereby inflict pain and suffering on the reader, who represents society. In *Pompes funèbres* and many of his later works he seems to have succeeded in the endeavor. Indeed, Genet must have thought so himself for he did in fact forego his career as a burglar.

Much of the poetry and mysticism that colors the earlier works is gone; the narrative framework is more structured and Genet's style is consequently more rigid. While the characters are once again predominantly homosexuals, this book does not focus on the criminal world per se. In *Pompes funèbres* Genet has turned his interest to a new subject: the political forces of Nazism, communism, and socialism.

The story takes place in Paris during the last days of the Liberation. It is the glorification of the death of a young patriot, Jean Decarnin (a fictionalization of the historical man), a communist member of the French underground (the *maquis*) who has been shot by the Germans. The novel recounts what happens in the two days after the narrator (again, a fictional Genet) has spent an anguished day and a half in the morgue beside the body of his dead friend and lover. Agonizing over his loss, the narrator goes to the movies where he views a newsreel. At one point the action on the screen focuses on the combat between a young *maquisard,* a German soldier, and a collaborator. All three of these figures take on specific identities in the narrator's mind–the *maquisard* represents his murdered friend; the German becomes Erik Seiler, the lover of the dead hero's mother and possibly the one responsible for betraying Jean; and the collaborator becomes Riton, a French traitor whose defection, in the narrator's mind, is a result of Riton's love for Erik. At some point during the newsreel while the rest of the audience is reviling the actions of the German, the narrator finds himself, without any conscious decision on his part, cheering for the German soldier.

The narrator's cheering is not as contradictory as it might at first seem. In fact it is quite consistent with the author's notion that the only truly authentic existence is one outside that which is socially acceptable; if everyone in the theater was maligning the German, the narrator

could not do the same. For this very reason the narrator had felt himself compelled to leave Hitler's Germany, where he had been living. Hitler represented the triumph of evil, for he had made outcasts out of a whole nation. In this inversion of the normal social order, the narrator no longer stood alone and separate from the rest of society; to keep his identity he was forced to return to France where he would be reviled and hated–where he could be evil.

The question of evil is at the center of the novel. Jean Decarnin, the strong but kind, passionately devoted patriot, represents the good. With his death, good itself is destroyed. To cope with the terrible loss of his beloved, the narrator transfers the great love he has felt for his friend to the German soldier, possibly (probably) responsible for Decarnin's death. Love is therefore fused with hate as the narrator forces himself to love the most vicious of the enemy. The purity of this transference is at first disturbed by the fact of the powerful sexual attraction that the narrator experiences when he meets Erik, but he explains this by claiming that the attraction is another way of paying tribute to the dead hero. The narrator's goal is to align himself with evil, to become evil, in order to achieve its opposite. He pushes himself to the depths of degradation and betrayal to attain a sort of grace through the totality and completeness of his dedication. Self-martyrdom becomes a form of heroism. To love Erik is finally seen as being even better than having loved Decarnin, since the German represents the force that was stronger than the Frenchman.

Erik is not the only evil character in the book–Genet's pages are littered with less crucial but equally cruel and inhuman beings. Jean's vengeful mother, who takes her son's enemy for a lover, never acts as a real mother. Like Ernestine in *Notre-Dame des Fleurs,* she is a type rather than a real character. She is the "son-killer" that the author associated with his own motherless childhood; she even denies her own son. A more important character is the executioner from Berlin who appears in one of the flashbacks and who was Erik's first homosexual lover. During their two-year relationship they take on each other's personalities, until Erik becomes hard, brutal, and unfeeling and gratuitously murders a young boy, in an ultimate act of evil. Paulo, the dead hero's half brother, is also a murderer. A member of the *Milice,* a French procollaborationist organization, he is also a traitor and a torturer. Riton, another *milicien,* is equally ready to betray anyone standing in the way of the anti-order, of Hitler's regime.

The second most important theme of *Pompes funèbres* is, as the title would suggest, that of death. Genet himself was obsessed by the fear of death, and this novel was devoted to trying to face that fear and somehow understand it. Part of the pain and suffering that the narrator feels when meditating beside the body of his friend is caused not by grief but by fear of his own (and the author's) mortality. The narrator also mourns the passing of his own youth as he must face the fact of growing older. (This is a painful question that Genet had already raised with the unpleasant spectacle of the aging Divine in *Notre-Dame des Fleurs*.) The narrator cannot escape the problem for he sees death all around him: bodies, trees, the funeral service, the dead infant girl purported to be Decarnin's child by the family servant. In the end the narrator achieves a sort of victory over death, though whether or not the victory allays Genet's fears is questionable. He attends a church service and takes communion, but the bread and wine become the flesh and blood of Decarnin. As he feasts on his dead friend, he assimilates the dead lover through the act of cannibalism. By descending into the death of his friend, the narrator is able to give him new life within himself. By manipulating the creations of his imagination, the narrator puts himself on the level of God and is therefore beyond death; Decarnin bubbles up through the consciousness of his lover and lives again in the pages of *Pompes funèbres*.

The bulk of Genet's last novel, *Querelle de Brest*, was written the same year as *Pompes funèbres* but left unfinished until several years later. It was published by Gallimard in a revised form in 1953. (In 1983 it was made into a movie, written and directed by Rainer Werner Fassbinder.) For the first time Genet no longer figures as a character in his novel nor does the book make any claim to be even partially autobiographical. Genet avoids mentioning his own past experiences and tries his hand at being an omniscient narrator. As such, he breaks into the action with an occasional editorial comment or criticism. Like Genet's preceding works, *Querelle de Brest* involves homosexuality and crime, but in this book there is a new milieu, that of the seaman's world, a different structuring order. Here, sex is specifically related to power and, for the first time, there is a powerful female character, Madame Lysiane.

Querelle de Brest has a relatively coherent plot although the narrative itself is quite complicated. Genet plays even more complicated tricks with time than he does in his other novels, and the story is consequently very fragmented and chaotic. The characters are more autonomous than Genet's previous characters; they are born out of Genet's experience and creativity rather than based on specific persons that Genet knew or parts of his own personality. The title character is a sailor, thief, murderer, and opium smuggler. He murders his accomplice and friend Vic and lays the blame for his deed on Gil Turko, a young stonemason, whom Querelle incriminates by leaving Gil's cigarette lighter at the scene of the crime. Querelle sells the opium to Norbert, the husband of Madame Lysiane, who runs a stylish bordello named "La Féria," where much of the action of the book takes place. To expiate his crimes Querelle gives himself to Norbert, thereby symbolically sacrificing his manhood. Gil Turko is, in fact, guilty of a murder of his own for he stabbed another stonemason when the stonemason made homosexual advances toward him. Querelle discovers that Gil is hiding out in some old ruins and befriends him by bringing him food, clothing, and money. He arranges for Gil's "escape" to Nantes by train but informs the police so that Gil is caught and arrested. Querelle, free, ships out.

Querelle is another of Genet's strong and handsome heroes, but there are several significant differences between him and Genet's previous heroes. Querelle is the only one of Genet's criminals who benefits from his crimes or who actually gains from his act of betrayal. He manages to successfully hide the fruits of his robberies and to enjoy the profits from his opium smuggling. By foisting the responsibility for his killing onto Gil, Querelle keeps his desired freedom and manages, unlike most of Genet's characters, to stay out of jail. Perhaps even more significant is the fact that at the beginning of the story Querelle is not a homosexual. His discovery of his homosexual side is almost accidental and directly related to his crimes. He embarks upon his first homosexual relationship in order to expiate his acts of murder and betrayal. It is only as he lives out the affair on a day-to-day basis that homosexuality begins to infiltrate his whole being. What he had previously denied (the killing of the stonemason) now has risen to the surface where, once acknowledged, it can release Querelle from his feelings of guilt about his crimes.

*Genet (second from right) with Dolores V., Jacques-Laurent Bost, Jean Cau, and Jean-Paul Sartre at the café Pont-Royal
(photo Brinon-Gamma)*

This chain of events is almost paralleled by Gil's story. He, too, kills an aging homosexual in an attempt to deny that facet of his own personality. Yet he has unconsciously been in love with the fifteen-year-old brother of his girlfriend, a fact that he denies until after he has killed. Then Gil, who has expressed such an intense dislike for homosexuals and homosexuality, yields almost immediately to an attraction to Querelle.

Another character in the book criticizes homosexuality. He is Querelle's twin brother, Robert, who physically is almost an exact duplicate of Querelle. He is appalled by the affair between Norbert and his brother because he feels that it might somehow reflect on his own sexuality. Robert is also Madame Lysiane's lover and their love scenes show an unprecedented effort on the part of Genet to analyze a woman's sexuality.

Before *Querelle de Brest* Genet's female characters had been hags or harridans, prostitutes or drudges. Genet's misogyny is no secret; he never tried to hide the distaste he felt for women. In his portrayal of Madame Lysiane, Genet modifies her femininity, treating her more as a semi-magical object than as a woman. This modification of femininity is reflected in her precious

manner of speaking and the sumptuousness of her surroundings. His attitude combines humor and a sense of detachment as he describes the forty-five-year-old Madame Lysiane as a fat, haughty woman with cold feet, who is dedicated to providing her clients with the delights of love. Madame Lysiane is neither passive, humiliated, nor abject. If at the end of the book she is defeated because she has fallen in love with Querelle, who made her suffer, then abandoned her, her defeat is honest not degrading, for she has learned by it. This kind of feminine character will return again in a similar but more fully developed version, Madame Irma, in Genet's play *Le Balcon* (1956; translated as *The Balcony*, 1957).

Another major character in *Le Balcon* is also prefigured in *Querelle de Brest*. Mario, Brest's chief of police, has much in common with the later police chief. Both characters represent power and the established order but Genet shows the reader that such power depends on the actions and reactions of others. Mario, masculine and virile, is a homosexual, and he is strongly attracted to Querelle, with whom he has relations. Querelle soon discovers that even though Mario believes himself to be the dominant partner, the police chief is really dependent on Querelle for his pleasure.

Sex therefore is directly related to power. Madame Lysiane's husband, Norbert, asserts his dominance by having sexual relations with the young men that he fears will be taken as lovers by his wife. When Querelle discovers this he in turn forces himself to sleep with Madame Lysiane so that he can have his revenge on Norbert. Lieutenant Seblon, a latent homosexual who denies his tendencies because of timidity and social position, finds only debasement and degradation.

By the end of the book Genet's waning interest in writing novels is obvious. In the text the author comments several times that his characters are beginning to bore him. It seems as if once Genet had proven himself capable of writing about characters not related to himself, novels no longer seemed very important. For whatever reason Genet wrote no more fiction. Instead, he turned his energies to writing plays and composing his next book, *Journal du voleur*, published in 1949.

As in his earlier novels Genet intended his journal to be an explanation of his attitude toward life and society. The book recounts Genet's vagabond years in Spain and other European countries and describes the misery he endured, especially as a beggar and prostitute in Spain. Although the narrator of the journal is named Jean Genet, the reader must again be aware of the distinction between the character in the book and the author. While all the details of the *Journal* cannot be labeled false or misleading, neither can they be accepted as literally true simply because Genet has written them as if they were. The journal could be an accurate autobiography, but the reader cannot be certain because truth in Genet's world seems to depend largely on what point he is trying to make at the time. In his presentation of other characters Genet makes clear the difference, sometimes vast, between what they really were and the way he chooses to present them, admitting at one point that he is not writing about his past life so much as about his present way of interpreting it; he is imposing current meanings on earlier events in his life in order to give them a worth they really did not have. In this book there is none of the glamorization of Genet's heroes found in his earlier works. One criminal character, Armand, is depicted admiringly, but a large part of the narrator's respect for him stems from his recognition of the effort Armand has had to expend in order to live as he does.

The difference between past realities and present perceptions seems to be the result of Genet's realization that he was at a watershed in his career. He was making money from his writing and was in love with a young man who did not come from the criminal milieu in which Genet had spent his life. Having fairly well exhausted his examinations of that milieu, of which he himself was no longer truly a part, he looked to his future and found some direction for it. In the last, complex pages of the *Journal* Genet seems to be floundering between the notion that there is still more to be said to interpret his past and the sense that he is at a new beginning which forces him to place his past at some distance. The second volume, which the narrator promises in the last paragraph, never appeared.

By this time in his life Genet had become a celebrity and a cause of controversy in Paris because of the lack of traditional moral values in his works. At the end of the decade the publishing house Gallimard announced its intention to publish Genet's complete works and thereby provoked François Mauriac, in the 15 August 1950 issue of *Le Figaro Littéraire*, to protest such an endorsement and to describe Genet's "excremental" works as powerful evidence of the decline of the West. Public opinion, however, eventually began to waver in Genet's favor, largely because of favorable response to his early plays.

His first plays, *Haute Surveillance* (1949; translated as *Deathwatch*, 1954) and *Les Bonnes* (1954; translated as *The Maids*, 1954), were both literary successes. The former won the Prix de la Pléiade; the latter was commissioned and then presented in 1947 by Louis Jouvet, one of France's leading directors, at the Théâtre de l'Athénée. *Les Bonnes*, filmed in English in 1974 under the direction of Christopher Miles, deals with the rage and dissatisfaction of two domestic workers who deeply resent their inferior social condition and try to punish their mistress, who is blithely unaware of their bitterness, by betraying her lover to the police and murdering her. Their efforts are not successful, and they must resort to playacting in order to deal gesturally with what they have not been able to arrange in reality. In so doing each ultimately expresses a very different assessment of the meaning of the mistress's condition: one continues to want revenge, even if the form of vengeance is only symbolic; the other seems to believe that death is a worthy deliverance from her inescapable servitude. The play does represent a significant enlargement of Genet's preoccupations, for it is his first step into the analysis of the social structures of the bourgeois world he had hitherto been content to vilify. As he begins that analysis in his presentation of the mistress-servant relationship, he continues to use the categories of the Hegelian effect he had earlier described; here again it is present only in latent form.

Haute Surveillance, first performed in Paris in 1949 and brought to the American screen by Vic Morrow in 1966, is set in a prison cell where a convicted murderer is awaiting either his execution or his deportation to Devil's Island. It treats issues of perceived and real status within the criminal hierarchy by depicting the efforts of two other criminals to associate themselves with, or to make a hero out of, the right man–that is, out of the man who is truly at the top of the hierarchy. Neither succeeds, and their failure suggests that those who are not unfailingly clear-eyed in making such judgments can never hope for an improvement in their position.

Genet's increasing involvement in the productions of his first plays, the fact that he made a film, *Un Chant d'amour,* for which he was completely responsible for all elements, and the interest he developed in Chinese opera may help to explain the vast difference between the reach of the first two plays and that of the last three. What was original about *Les Bonnes* and *Haute Surveillance* was their subject matter; the one theatrical novelty that he proposed for one of them–to have the roles of the women in *Les Bonnes* played by male actors–was vetoed by Jouvet, who thought he had enough on his hands with the play itself. Nothing in those plays hints at the enormous theatrical originality that was to give such immense power to the later plays, each of which is a major work of twentieth-century theater and each of which enlarges and refines the analytical process begun in *Les Bonnes.*

For a time Genet's writing career seemed to be at an end, an occurrence he and others attributed to the supposedly devastating impact Sartre's penetrating study of his early works (*Saint Genet, comédien et martyr,* 1952) had had on him. But the fact is that his first period of literary aridity lasted from 1949 until the publication of *Le Balcon.* In the intervening years what he wrote was done in response to invitations; during that period he also turned his interest to the creation of a ballet, *'Adame Miroir* (Madame Mirror,

published with *L'Enfant criminel,* 1949), for which he wrote the scenario, and the making of a short, homoerotic film, *Un Chant d'amour* (1950). He remained in the public eye over those years because of the wider distribution given to his novels by the Gallimard edition and the presentation of his earlier plays in Parisian theaters.

Le Balcon did not reach a Parisian stage until 1960, when it was presented by Peter Brook at the Théâtre du Gymnase; a London production in 1957 was roundly condemned by Genet, who had to be forcefully ejected from the first-night performance because of his vociferous protests over the cheapening of his play by the director, Peter Zadek. In 1962 a film version was released under the title *The Balcony.* The title refers to the brothel which is the play's setting. It is not a commonplace bordello; rather it is Madame Irma's elaborate and versatile house of illusions where men can fulfill their fantasies and, in that process, reveal to the audience the brothel's meaning as a social institution.

It exists in order to satisfy the needs of its steady stream of clients; it is therefore an indication of the dissatisfactions its customers find in other social institutions, whose inadequacies are remedied by the bordello. Madame Irma's house is more than that; it is a place in which the realization of illusions demonstrates the illusory nature of some of the revered functions of bourgeois society; they are perceived by their supporters as bastions of order when in fact they are centers of power to which men are attracted, in part by their own sexual insecurities. The men who come to The Balcony in order to take on the roles of bishop, judge, and general know that, for they want only the illusion of the function, not its reality; they insist scrupulously that the rites they engage in must be gone through punctiliously, never losing sight of the sexual end being paid for and pursued. In the most striking of the tableaux which depict the unfolding of the illusions, Genet reiterates a major assertion from his preceding works; the client who repeats it does so as he is enacting the role of a judge in the presence of an accused woman and an executioner. He recognizes what, in Genet's view, most judges do not choose to understand: he is a doubly dependent man because he needs the criminal as the pretext of his work and the executioner as the agent of his judgment.

On this particular night the house is being disturbed by a revolution that is taking place outside it and that is capable of producing unknown consequences for the brothel and for the performances which take place within it. (It is quite possible that the rebellion is the most complex of the illusions staged by Irma.) The clients are not the only ones to be disturbed by the troubles in the street. The chief of police is also worried lest the revolutionaries attain a success that will strip him of his function, and so he decides to allow the other clients to pretend they really are the possessors of the functions they have been enacting. He uses them to mystify the people and put down the revolt. When victory is his, and when the clients decide that they want to go on exercising their roles in public, he rebukes them with contempt, reminding them that any apparent power they possess is dependent upon his; they continue to exist because he finds them useful, as dictators frequently do.

The chief, who is sexually impotent, has a worry even greater than the concern provoked within him by the revolution: he has not yet become part of the nomenclature of the brothel, for no client has yet appeared who wishes to find sexual gratification by taking on the role of a policeman; as a result, the chief has not yet been confirmed in his function by the authority of the brothel. At the end of the evening one of the defeated rebels comes to make that very request, to the chief's deep satisfaction; but to the chief's even deeper dismay, the client immediately castrates himself. His gesture is triply significant: it is the sign of his defeat; it replicates the chief's own sexual condition; and it suggests, in a world of rebellions, the end of the police's authority. In any case, it causes the chief to withdraw into the mausoleum he has had built for himself—confirmed by the brothel, he is also immobilized because the true nature of his function as a surrogate for sexual inadequacy has been unmasked at the very moment when his authority is being undermined by the rebellion.

As Madame Irma, the mistress of these elaborate and demystifying ceremonies, wearily closes her house down for the night, she turns to the audience and invites them to leave, telling them, "il faut rentrer chez nous, où tout n'en doutez pas, sera encore plus faux qu'ici" (you must now go home, where everything—you can be quite sure—will be even falser than here). The spectators are urged to see the acuity of her vision and to accept it as true: the policed world to which the audience belongs is itself a network of illusions, and Madame Irma invites the spectators to come back to the brothel to play out their own roles.

The presentation of such a message in Madame Irma's closing speech contains a suggestion that the public is still capable of taking it in and perhaps profiting from it in order to redesign its understanding of what forces are at play and in conflict throughout the world. Such implicit generosity is absent from Genet's next two plays, in which his theatrical ingenuity reaches new heights but where his contempt for his white, Western audiences is also manifest. *Les Nègres* (1958; translated as *The Blacks*, 1960)—the title is pejorative in French—received its first production in Paris, with an all-black cast, at the Théâtre de Lutèce in late 1959. Its major presupposition is that white audiences in Western societies are so locked into their racist myths that they are incapable of perceiving the new realities of their changed world. In a minstrel-show atmosphere they watch a group of blacks enact the fabricated story of a rape, which will reinforce the whites' image of them; the latter remain unaware of the revolutionary activities that other blacks are engaged in elsewhere. The whites have lost, or will soon lose, their control of the world. The play stands as the obituary of their mastery, which they will be allowed to hear but which many of them will not understand. Genet's last play, *Les Paravents* (1961; translated as *The Screens*, 1962), both extends that notion of Western paralysis and elaborates upon it. Though it uses situations related to the contemporary rebellion in Algeria against French colonial rule, the play has a much wider context. In it Genet is dealing with what he takes to be a new and capital reality: the accession of pariahs, of the class of outcasts throughout the world, to a sense of their historical exploitation by those against whom they are now rebelling. Unlike the whites in *Les Nègres*, most of the Westerners in this play become aware of the new menace to their longstanding privileges; some know that their colonial days are about to end, and that there is nothing they can do to forestall the decline. Still, the play is much less optimistic than its predecessor, whose ending had allowed for the belief that the blacks would attain their rights through revolutionary processes.

The principal character of *Les Paravents*, Saïd, offers no similar happy prospect. He is roundly unpleasant to everyone, including his mother and the woman he has married because of her ugliness. He operates on the basis of his belief, for which he has evidence, that unless pariahs are wary and noisy and always demanding they will risk being duped. Others, who feign to act in their interests, are actually looking to their own privilege, which is likely to entail the continued exploitation of the pariahs. The fact that Saïd's message is heard by more and more people during the play and that acts of rebellion and destruction are inspired by it does not change the content of the message. It is the message that Genet had been delivering in private and public for most of his life; what had changed was the fact that what was once considered a very individual way of reading the world had become a major issue of public policy in many countries of the world, with the result that Genet's voice was no longer a marginal one. On 1 May 1966 he told a reporter from *L'Algérien en Europe* that in writing the play he was writing a story of his own life. Three years later he told an acquaintance that with *Les Paravents* he had said all that he wanted to say.

Les Paravents, which was Genet's last play and the last major work published during his lifetime, was not performed in Paris until it was produced by Jean-Louis Barrault at the Théâtre de l'Odéon in 1966. The delay was the result of fears about the impact of the play on a public still suffering from the French retreat from Algeria and the high human cost of that defeat. The pandemonium that broke out on opening night justified the fears and forced André Malraux, France's minister of culture, to defend the presentation, in a nationally subsidized theater, of a play many thought was intended to subvert the state, which was underwriting the cost of the play's performances.

Controversy had become and was to remain a constant element of Genet's career. In 1956 he was condemned to a never-executed jail sentence and a heavy fine for pornographic works he had published in 1948; some believed that the harsh judgment against him was inspired by his published opposition to the French presence in North Africa. In the same year French editions of his novels were seized by British customs officers and impounded, an action which led to a debate in the House of Commons that was of no help in getting the books to their intended destination–the Birmingham City Library.

In the last two decades of his life Genet became increasingly dedicated to involvement with minority and Third World political causes–with the Zengakuren group in Japan during 1966, with the student unrest in Paris in 1968, with the people protesting against the Vietnam War at the Chicago Democratic National Convention in that

same year, with the Black Panthers in 1969 and 1970, and with the Baader-Meinhoff group in West Germany. Late in 1970 he was invited by the Palestinian Liberation Organization to visit its members in Jordan; he stayed with the Palestinians for fourteen years and became a vehement spokesman for that cause. All of his essays in these years were devoted to the explanation and defense of his political interests. In July 1974 he told a reporter from *Monde* that it was altogether natural that his attention should be turned to such groups, for they were not only disadvantaged but also crystallized dramatically his own hatred of the West. There was an irony in his dedication to radical revolutionary movements which he himself expressed in his interview with Fichte: "I'm not sure I really want a revolution. To be honest, I don't really want it . . . the revolution would probably not allow me a personal revolt."

Recognition and honors also came his way. In 1975 the French Ministry of Culture offered him a prize for the newly reissued film *Un Chant d'amour*, which he refused. The next year he was listed in Larousse's literary dictionary. In 1983 he received the Grand Prix National des Lettres. The year before his death his play *Le Balcon*, which had been rejected by five Parisian producers when it first became available, entered the repertory of the Comédie Française–the House of Molière, that partisan of moderation and a sane bourgeois order.

Upon Genet's death in 1986 Gallimard announced the forthcoming appearance of the writer's last work, *Un Captif amoureux*, published the same year. While Genet had been involved with the Palestinian revolutionaries, they had often urged that he write an account of exactly what he had seen and heard. After thinking about it at length Genet finally decided to follow the suggestion of his fellow rebels. *Un Captif amoureux* is a book of memoirs describing Genet's involvement in radical causes in the United States and particularly in the Middle East.

How future audiences and critics will judge Genet's work is difficult to say. Already his poetry has lost much of its appeal owing to its lack of originality. Because of its violence and cruelty, the homosexuality in his novels will continue to shock and disturb readers, despite society's increasing tolerance of homosexuals. Not even the accolades of Sartre, Cocteau, and Beauvoir can make the average reader feel comfortable with the cult of the criminal that Genet creates or truly understand the exultation embodied by the knowledge of being a complete outcast; yet Genet's affirmation of the underworld and its inhabitants reveals to the reader certain information about the structure and functions of the policed world. Perhaps these messages–that sex is power and self-affirmation, that the weak are made to be dominated by the strong, that illusion is often indistinguishable from reality–are clearer in Genet's plays; his fame seems assured as a result of his important contributions to modern theater.

Interviews:

Robert Poulet, *Aveux spontanés, conversation avec . . .* (Paris: Plon, 1963), pp. 109-114;

Playboy Interview with Jean Genet, *Playboy,* 11 (April 1964): 45-55;

Pierre Démeron, "Conversation with Jean Genet," *Oui,* 1 (November 1972): 62-102;

Hubert Fichte, "Jean Genet Talks to Hubert Fichte. Translated from the French by Patrick McCarthy," *New Review,* 4 (April 1977): 9-21; republished in *Gay Sunshine Interviews,* edited by Winston Leyland (San Francisco: Gay Sunshine Press, 1978).

Bibliography:

Richard C. Webb and Suzanne A. Webb, *Jean Genet and His Critics: An Annotated Bibliography* (Metuchen, N.J. & London: Scarecrow Press, 1982).

References:

Odette Aslan, *Jean Genet* (Paris: Seghers, 1973);

Georges Bataille, "Jean Genet," in his *La Littérature et le mal* (Paris: Gallimard, 1957), pp. 183-226; translated by Alastair Hamilton as *Literature and Evil* (London: Calder & Boyars, 1973);

Claude Bonnefoy, *Jean Genet* (Paris: Editions Universitaires, 1965);

Roger Borderie and Henri Ronse, eds., *Genet,* special issue of *Obliques,* no. 2 (1972);

Peter Brooks and Joseph Halpern, eds., *Genet, A Collection of Critical Essays* (Englewood Cliffs, N.J.: Prentice-Hall, 1979);

Robert Brustein, *The Theatre of Revolt: An Approach to Modern Drama* (Boston: Little, Brown, 1964), pp. 361-411;

Lewis T. Cetta, *Profane Play, Ritual and Jean Genet: A Study of His Drama* (University: University of Alabama Press, 1974);

Mohamed Choukri, *Jean Genet in Tangier,* translated by Paul Bowles (New York: Ecco Press, 1974);

Richard N. Coe, *The Theatre of Jean Genet: A Casebook* (New York: Grove Press, 1970);

Coe, *The Vision of Jean Genet* (New York: Grove Press, 1968);

Martin Esslin, "Jean Genet," in his *The Theatre of the Absurd* (Garden City: Doubleday, 1961), pp. 140-167;

David I. Grossvogel, "Jean Genet," in his *Four Playwrights and a Postscript* (Ithaca: Cornell University Press, 1962), pp. 133-174;

Jacques Guicharnaud, *Modern French Theatre: From Giraudoux to Genet,* revised edition (New Haven: Yale University Press, 1967), pp. 259-277;

Robert Hauptman, *The Pathological Vision. Jean Genet, Louis-Ferdinand Céline and Tennessee Williams* (New York: Peter Lang, 1983), pp. 1-50;

Josephine Jacobsen and William R. Mueller, *Ionesco and Genet: Playwrights of Silence* (New York: Hill & Wang, 1968);

Joseph H. McMahon, *The Imagination of Jean Genet* (New Haven: Yale University Press, 1963);

Jean-Paul Sartre, *Saint Genet, comédien et martyr* (Paris: Gallimard, 1952), translated by Bernard Frechtman as *Saint Genet, Actor and Martyr* (New York: George Braziller, 1963);

Jeanette L. Savona, *Jean Genet* (London: Macmillan, 1983);

Philip Thody, *Jean Genet: A Study of His Novels and Plays* (New York: Stein & Day, 1969).

Jean Giono

(30 March 1895-9 October 1970)

Walter Redfern
University of Reading

BOOKS: *Accompagnés de la flûte* (Manosque: Editions de l'Artisan, 1924);

Colline (Paris: Grasset, 1929); translated by Jacques Le Clerq as *Hill of Destiny* (New York: Brentano's, 1929);

Un de Baumugnes (Paris: Grasset, 1929); translated by Le Clerq as *Lovers Are Never Losers* (New York: Brentano's, 1931; London: Jarrolds, 1932);

Présentation de Pan (Paris: Grasset, 1930);

Naissance de l'Odyssée (Paris: Editions Kra, 1930);

Manosque-des-Plateaux (Paris: Emile-Paul, 1930);

Regain (Paris: Grasset, 1930); translated by Henri Fluchère and Geoffrey Myers as *Harvest* (New York: Viking, 1939; London: Heinemann, 1940);

Le Grand Troupeau (Paris: Gallimard, 1931); translated by Norman Glass as *To the Slaughterhouse* (London: Owen, 1969);

Solitude de la pitié (Paris: Gallimard, 1932);

Jean le bleu (Paris: Grasset, 1932); translated by Katherine A. Clarke as *Blue Boy* (New York: Viking, 1946; London: Routledge, 1948);

Le Serpent d'étoiles (Paris: Grasset, 1933);

Le Chant du monde (Paris: Gallimard, 1934); translated by Fluchère and Myers as *The Song of the World* (New York: Viking, 1937; London & Toronto: Heinemann, 1938);

Que ma joie demeure (Paris: Grasset, 1935); translated by Clarke as *Joy of Man's Desiring* (New York: Viking, 1940; London: Routledge & Kegan Paul, 1949);

Les Vraies Richesses (Paris: Grasset, 1936);

Refus d'obéissance (Paris: Gallimard, 1937);

Batailles dans la montagne (Paris: Gallimard, 1937);

Le Poids du ciel (Paris: Gallimard, 1938);

Lettre aux paysans sur la pauvreté et la paix (Paris: Grasset, 1938);

Précisions (Paris: Grasset, 1939);

Pour saluer Melville (Paris: Gallimard, 1941);

Triomphe de la vie (Neuchâtel: Ides et Calendes, 1941; Paris: Grasset, 1942);

L'Eau vive (Paris: Gallimard, 1943);

Jean Giono (photo Jacques Sassier, N.R.F.)

Théâtre de Jean Giono (Paris: Gallimard, 1943)—comprises *Le Bout de la route, Lanceurs de graines, La Femme du boulanger,* and *Esquisse d'une mort d'Hélène;*

Le Voyage en calèche (Monaco: Editions du Rocher, 1947);

Un Roi sans divertissement (Paris: Gallimard, 1947);

Noé (Paris: Table Ronde, 1947);

Fragments d'un déluge (Villeneuve-Saint-Georges: Fonteinas, 1948);

Fragments d'un paradis (Paris: Dechalotte, 1948);

Mort d'un personnage (Paris: Grasset, 1949);

Les Ames fortes (Paris: Gallimard, 1949);

Village (Paris: Prochaska, 1950);

Les Grands Chemins (Paris: Gallimard, 1951);

Le Hussard sur le toit (Paris: Gallimard, 1951); translated by Jonathan Griffin as *The Hussar on the Roof* (London: Museum Press, 1953); republished as *The Horseman on the Roof* (New York: Knopf, 1954);

Le Moulin de Pologne (Paris: Gallimard, 1952); translated by Peter de Mendelssohn as *The Malediction* (New York: Criterion, 1955; London: Museum Press, 1955);

Voyage en Italie (Paris: Gallimard, 1953);

Provence (Paris: Hachette, 1954);

L'Ecossais, ou La Fin des héros (Manosque: Aux dépens du Rotary-Club, 1955);

Notes sur l'Affaire Dominici, suivi d'un Essai sur le caractère des personnages (Paris: Gallimard, 1955); translated by de Mendelssohn as *The Dominici Affair* (London: Museum Press, 1956);

Le Bonheur fou (Paris: Gallimard, 1957); translated by Phyllis Johnson as *The Straw Man* (New York: Knopf, 1959; London: Redman, 1961);

Provence (Manosque: Imprimerie Rico et Auphan, 1957);

Provence (Paris: Belle Edition, 1957);

Angelo (Paris: Gallimard, 1958); translated by Alma E. Murch (London: Owen, 1960);

Hortense, ou L'Eau vive, by Giono and Alain Allioux (Paris: France-Empire, 1958);

Domitien, suivi de Joseph à Dothan (Paris: Gallimard, 1959);

Crésus: Livre de conduite du metteur en scène (Manosque: Rico et Auphan, 1961);

Le Désastre de Pavie, 24 février 1525 (Paris: Gallimard, 1963); translated and edited by Murch as *The Battle of Pavia, 24th February 1525* (London: Owen, 1965);

Deux Cavaliers de l'orage (Paris: Gallimard, 1965); translated by Alan Brown as *Two Riders of the Storm* (London: Owen, 1967);

Le Bal, L'Ecossais, Angelo, Le Hussard sur le toit (Paris: Gallimard, 1965);

Le Déserteur (Paudex/Lausanne, Switzerland: Fontainemore, 1966);

Provence perdue (Manosque: Edition du Rotary Club de Manosque, 1967);

Ennemonde et autres caractères (Paris: Gallimard, 1968); translated by David Le Vay as *Ennemonde* (London: Owen, 1970);

La Chute des anges, Un déluge, Le coeur cerf (Manosque: Printed by Rico, 1969);

L'Iris de Suse (Paris: Gallimard, 1970);

Les Récits de la demi-brigade (Paris: Gallimard, 1972);

Le Déserteur et autres récits (Paris: Gallimard, 1973);

Les Terrasses de l'Ile d'Elbe (Paris: Gallimard, 1976);

Faust au village (Paris: Gallimard, 1977);

Angélique (Paris: Gallimard, 1980);

Œuvres cinématographiques, edited by Jacques Mény (Paris: Gallimard, 1980);

Cœurs, passions, caractères (Paris: Gallimard, 1982);

Dragoon, suivi de Olympe (Paris: Gallimard, 1982);

Les Trois Arbres de Palzem (Paris: Gallimard, 1984);

Manosque-des-Plateaux, suivi de Poème de l'olive (Paris: Gallimard, 1986).

Collection: *Œuvres romanesques complètes,* 6 volumes, edited by Robert Ricatte (Paris: Gallimard, 1971-1983).

PLAY PRODUCTIONS: *Lanceurs de graines,* Geneva, Compagnie des Quinze, 30 September 1932; Paris, Théâtre de l'Atelier, October 1932;

Le Bout de la route, Paris, Théâtre des Noctambules, 30 May 1941;

Jofroi, by Jean-Pierre Grenier, based on Giono's *Jofroi de la Maussan,* Aix-en-Provence, Théâtre Municipal, 28 December 1941;

La Femme du boulanger, Paris, Théâtre des Ambassadeurs, May 1944;

Le Voyage en calèche, Paris, Théâtre du Vieux-Colombier, 21 December 1947;

Joseph à Dothan, by Joost Van den Vondel, adapted by Giono, Orange, 29 July 1952;

"J'ai connu Jean-Pierre Grenier," text for a stage presentation, Paris, Théâtre Marigny, 1959;

La Calèche, Paris, Théâtre Sarah-Bernhardt, 15 December 1965.

OTHER: Maria Borrély, *Le Dernier Feu,* preface by Giono (Paris: Gallimard, 1931);

Anton Coolen, *Le Bon Assassin,* preface by Giono (Paris: Grasset, 1936);

Marcel Pagnol, *Regain,* adapted from Giono's novel, preface by Giono (Paris & Marseilles: M. Pagnol, 1937);

Léon Isnardy, *Geógraphie du département des Basses-Alpes,* preface by Giono (Manosque: Mollet, 1939);

Dr. J. Poucel, *A la découverte des orchidées de France,* preface by Giono (Paris: Stock, 1942);

Herman Melville, *Moby Dick,* translated by Giono, Lucien Jacques, and Joan Smith (Paris: Gallimard, 1942);

Samivel, *L'Opéra des pics*, preface by Giono (Grenoble: Arthaud, 1944);

Anton Hansen Tammsaare, *La-Terre-du-voleur*, preface by Giono (Paris: Trémois, 1946);

Les Pages immortelles de Virgile, preface by Giono (Paris: Corrêa, 1947);

L'Iliade d'Homère, preface by Giono (Paris: Bordas, 1950);

Maurice Chauvet, *La Route du vin*, preface by Giono (Montpellier: Editions des Arceaux, 1950);

Charles Agniel, *Les Compagnons de la Bonne Auberge*, preface by Giono (Paris: Table Ronde, 1952);

Niccolò Machiavelli, *Œuvres complètes*, preface by Giono (Paris: Gallimard, 1952);

Albert Detaille, *La Provence merveilleuse*, preface by Giono (Marseilles: Detaille, 1953);

Félix Leclerc, *Moi, mes souliers*, preface by Giono (Paris: Amiot-Dumont, 1955);

Jacques Meuris, *Le Journal de Provence*, preface by Giono (Brussels & Paris: Dutilleul, 1955);

Maurice Pezet, *Les Alpilles*, preface by Giono (Paris: Horizons de France, 1955);

Bernard Buffet, preface by Giono (Paris: Hazan, 1956);

Romée de Villeneuve, *Dix Ans d'erreurs*, preface by Giono (Avignon: Presses Universelles, 1956);

Maurice Chevaly, *Fleurs artificielles*, preface by Giono (Aix: Editions de la Pensée Universitaire, 1958);

Rome que j'aime, preface by Giono (Paris: Sun, 1958);

Régina Wallet, *Le Sang de la vigne*, preface by Giono (Paris: Editions du Scorpion, 1958);

Georges Navel, *Chacun son royaume*, preface by Giono (Paris: Gallimard, 1960);

Tableau de la littérature française, volume 1, preface by Giono (Paris: Gallimard, 1962);

Tristan, preface by Giono (Paris: Livre de Poche, 1964);

Blaise de Monluc, *Commentaires*, preface by Giono (Paris: Gallimard, 1964);

Juan Ramón Jiménez, *Platero et moi*, preface by Giono (Paris: Rombaldi, 1964);

Merveilles des palais italiens, preface by Giono (Paris: Hachette, 1968).

Born 30 March 1895 to Jean-Antoine Giono, an anarchist shoemaker, and Pauline Pourcin Giono, Jean Giono spent his whole life, apart from holidays and abominated war service, in the small town of Manosque in Provence. In the late 1920s, released from work in a bank by his first writing successes, he began to devote his time to producing a cornucopian spread of fiction and teaching himself a wide culture. One of his texts, "Le Grand Théâtre," appeared in possibly the most exclusive book ever, encrusted with gems by Salvador Dalí, weighing 460 pounds, and valued at over a million dollars. In every way, Giono is a luxury writer.

He was fond of nature–a major theme throughout his work–and close to his parents, with whom his relationship seems to have been excellent. He particularly liked watching his father at work. In 1936, under the title "Les Vraies Richesses" (True Riches), he published in *Vendredi* a meditation on his father (later collected in *L'Eau vive*, 1943). The father liked to tell stories about his own father, an Italian carbonaro refugee who, Giono later suggested, became a model for one of the characters in his 1951 novel *Le Hussard sur le toit* (translated as *The Hussar on the Roof*, 1953). Giono attended school in Manosque. Very early he abandoned all religious faith, although he had gone to catechism classes; he found the Bible, which he read with his father, to be a marvelous book but said he could not believe in it, any more than he could believe in the *Odyssey*. He read the Greek and Latin classics–cheaper to buy than books by modern authors–and very early began writing.

At the end of 1914, after having been spared mobilization for two months, he was drafted into service in World War I. From 1916-1918 he participated as an infantry soldier in trench warfare and saw many friends fall near Soissons and at Chemin des Dames. During the battle in Flanders in 1918, he was gassed. After demobilization in 1919 he first worked at a bank in Marseilles and then returned to a bank in Manosque. He would work in various banks until 1929, when liquidation proceedings closed the office where he was employed, and he decided to try to make his living by writing. In 1920, shortly after the death of his father, he married Elise Maurin, a schoolteacher he had met before the war. From this marriage two daughters were born, Aline (1926) and Sylvie (1934).

Giono pursued his writing throughout the early 1920s and published his first work, a series of prose poems, in 1924 under the title *Accompagnés de la flûte* (Accompanied by the Flute). The early 1920s also saw the development of his close friendship with the painter Lucien Jacques. In 1928 the publisher Grasset turned

Le Paraïs, Giono's home in Manosque from 1929 until his death

down the manuscript of *Naissance de l'Odyssée* (Birth of the Odyssey), although he did publish it later, in 1930, after the success of Giono's novel *Colline* (translated as *Hill of Destiny*, 1929), which appeared under Grasset's imprint in 1929. Giono's literary career began to burgeon as he received the American Brentano Prize for *Colline* and won the critical attention and friendship of such writers as André Gide and Jean Paulhan. Later prizes would include the Northcliffe Prize for *Regain* (1930; translated as *Harvest*, 1939), the Prix Corrard in 1931, and the Grand Prix de Monaco in 1953 for the whole of his work. In 1954 he was elected to the Académie Goncourt. He practiced many genres, including literary criticism, historical narrative, and some of his own fabrication, halfway between poetry and prose, myth and novel. In 1932 his play *Lanceurs de graines*

(The Seed Throwers) was performed in Geneva and Paris; the next year it was staged in London. *Le Voyage en calèche* (The Carriage Trip), which opened in 1947, was a success, even more so in 1965-1966 in its revised version, *La Calèche*.

Giono was an avid reader (the classics, Henry David Thoreau, Walt Whitman, William Faulkner) as well as a prolific writer and also pursued his interest in painting and music, after he acquired a phonograph in the 1920s and was able to listen to favorite pieces by Bach, Handel, and Mozart. He cultivated family and friendship, frequently spending time with friends and family in other parts of France. His interest in filmmaking grew as his own works began to serve as points of departure for films, including some by Marcel Pagnol, and after World War II he began his own career as a scriptwriter, participating in some cases even in the directing of movies.

Giono's political ideas have been the topic of much commentary. His position, fortified by events of the 1930s, was resolutely pacifistic. The Contadour movement, an experiment in intermittent collective living and other group activities, was founded by him and associates in 1935 partly with the idea of promoting pacifism, as well as what would now be called ecological concerns. It lasted until the very eve of World War II. Giono made speeches and contributed to certain leftist journals as long as they were pacifist but broke with their editors when their views diverged. He also circulated petitions of his own and signed others in favor of nonintervention and disarmament, as late as 1939.

He did consent to be mobilized briefly when war broke out in September 1939; it was not, however, a gesture of cooperation, but rather the reluctance to cause trouble to the local authorities, people he knew well. After he refused to cooperate further, he was imprisoned for two months, including twenty days in solitary confinement, and then freed, partly on the intervention of admirers. Near the end of the war he was again imprisoned, this time for five months, as a collaborator, during the Communist-dominated purges, although he had done no active collaboration. His conclusion was that someone in his position was vulnerable to extremists of all persuasions. Although to some he remained persona non grata because of his refusal to participate in the French war effort, he was immensely popular as a writer after the war and remains an author of whom the French are proud, one of those eccentrics who stubbornly persists in holding his own values, and to whose quarters many readers have made pilgrimages.

Giono was an indefatigable storyteller with a rich and abundant imagination. He once foxed *Reader's Digest,* when it commissioned an ecological true story, by sending a totally made up but splendidly convincing tale of a shepherd, a kind of Johnny Appleseed, who year by year planted a forest of oaks over the whole of Upper Provence. The editor accused him of being a crook, but Raymond Queneau was surely nearer the mark when he granted Giono the accolade of "Homeric." Rooted but not regionalist, like Faulkner Giono created an imaginary South. His Provence is a product of his own vision expanded so as to embrace and transmute a geographical area into an entire mythology. With him cartography is less relevant than cartomancy. For him, the poet is a *dinamitero* who can alter the face of the exist-

ing world at will. As Giono wrote in *Cœurs, passions, caractères* (Hearts, Passions, Characters, 1982), "L'air est épais comme du sirop; à travers cette viscosité on voit double, ou triple, ou centuple, ou rien" (The air is as thick as syrup and through this viscousness you see double or triple or nothing).

Even, and especially, his autobiography of his childhood, *Jean le bleu* (1932; translated as *Blue Boy,* 1946), is heavily fictionalized. His complete works sing a hymn to the joys of lying.

The harsh, sunlit landscapes of Provence, with their gnarled olive trees, rugged rock formations, and desiccated river beds, fed his fond delusion that ancient Greece had magically been overlaid on southern France. Giono was a bookish "bard of nature," and, despite its undeniable corporeality, his fictional universe is intellectual as well. What he offers is landscapes with figures: individuals engendered by and molding in their turn a physical locale. Though there are exceptions, against the traditional depiction of country life as nasty, brutish, and short, Giono usually sets natural aristocrats, peasant thoroughbreds.

One of his first publications, and a key work, *Naissance de l'Odyssée* is an inverted epic, in which Ulysses is made a prey to his own imagination, which serves alternately to protect him from the world of others and of nature and to scarify himself. An inveterate liar, he encourages and becomes the subject of a fantastic legend of prowess which proliferates, by oral transmission, around his, in fact, rather seedy person. Hearing his own story embellished by a bard, he realizes the potentialities of verbal invention. Ulysses fears that his legend will get out of hand. He fears the day of reckoning with Antinous, Penelope's lover, when appropriately, as the legend has it, he will be saved from confrontation by a comically fatal accident which befalls his rival. Ulysses lives in some awe of the gods, hardly distinguished from the natural forces they embody, because he has usurped their monopoly of illusion-making. The lie—panicky, self-defensive, or self-assertive, but unmistakably passionate—is central to Giono's whole strategy. On reuniting, Penelope and Ulysses embark on a duet of falsehoods which whitewash their doings in the intervening years. A limp punch which Ulysses aims at another man lands with "le poids effroyable du mystère" (all the terrible weight of a mysterious reputation). As if to prove his point, Giono causes Telemachus' real adventures to bore listeners stiff: nobody wants to hear of

Giono in 1938

brute reality. *Naissance de l'Odyssée* is a marvelously inventive yarn, extremely bookish in inspiration, yet treating the revered Homer with loving mockery. Image-selling is seen already as a preoccupation of the earliest ages of mankind.

The first thing civilized man began doing was to lose his senses. In his "Pan trilogy," *Colline, Un de Baumugnes* (1929; translated as *Lovers Are Never Losers*, 1931), and *Regain*, Giono sets out to reinstate these underused faculties. One way is via mythology. By reintroducing the classical legends of Dionysus, Ceres, and Pan, Giono aims at enlarging and enhancing his native region. Ceres provides him with images of fruitful-

ness, Dionysus with those of violence and intoxicating participation, and Pan with metaphors of desire, transformation, and movement. Giono does not use these pagan deities as characters but endows his own creatures with these extra dimensions. It is his way of deeply involving his people with their habitat, creating myths to help people to make sense of their lives. The Pan trilogy transposes the mythological substratum of *Naissance de l'Odyssée* to peasant life in Provence. The catalyst was the *Leaves of Grass* of the American Pan, Walt Whitman.

Colline is composed in stanzalike paragraphs and is indeed an extended prose poem. Giono cunningly disarms criticism by talking in the preface of the "delectably false" sound of the French spoken in his area. And certainly this epithet suits the fanciful ravings of the paralyzed stand-in for Pan, Janet, as he curses the despoiling of the environment by his neighbors and pleads for a new gentleness in the relationship between man and beasts or soil. Janet is by turns described in terms of mineral, vegetable, and liquid: clearly he is offered as in tune with the natural cycle. Like *Naissance de l'Odyssée,* this novel is full of mystery and fears. Trees, as Jean-Paul Sartre's Roquentin would discover some years later, are more than just trees. Indeed the vision in Sartre's *La Nausée* (*Nausea,* 1938) of nature recapturing its lost domain by choking the erring city could have come straight from the recurrently apocalyptic strain in Giono's writing. Giono was prone to preach. *Colline* is a (pagan) sermon on the mountain. Its villagers are barely distinguishable from each other or from their milieu. The ending, when the villagers forget Janet's teaching and revert to unthinking greed, is ambivalent. Like a good anarchist, Giono knew in his heart that people resist being taught virtuous lessons. In the later collection of short stories, *Solitude de la pitié* (Solitude of Pity, 1932), he frequently laments the difficulty of communication between human beings, or between them and the beasts of the field. Barriers figure as much as openness in Giono's world.

Giono was a master of improvised oral narration. In *Un de Baumugnes,* varying his technique as he was to do periodically, he exploits the device of a softhearted but tough-spoken narrator to tell his tale of the triumph of goodness. The pure-hearted mountain dweller Albin rescues, with the help of his friend Amédée, an ill-used plains girl, whom he had loved previously but who has been sequestered by her ashamed parents after her misconduct. He courts her at a distance, playing "the song of the world" on his harmonica (a homely twist on Pan's pipes), thus evoking his uplands home in wordless music. He succeeds in delivering her and winning her love. *Un de Baumugnes* is a cordial book, not without belligerently sentimental dross. This is offset by the artful suspense of the elopers' return for a blessing from the dangerously crazed parents who might kill them with rage but with whom the young couple seek reconciliation. Though youth and goodness triumph, the undercurrent theme of bonds, stretched in conflicting directions, lends tension to the proceedings. When the final bond, linking the aging Amédée with his

protégé, is snapped, the tension resolves into a calm sadness. Amédée is the first of Giono's many "guérisseurs" (healers), or midhusbands, helpful to others but ultimately solitary.

Panturle in *Regain* is a lone wolf until he finds the missing half (the Platonic myth on the origin of the sexes is always crucial to Giono's vision) who will share his lonely, neglected plateau and aid him to rehabilitate it, and the couple in the process—the other side of the coin to *Colline,* in which human intervention is suspect. Nature is not ravished but nurtured. As in *Un de Baumugnes,* a much-used woman is saved and made anew by love, a love which is based on mutual physical charity and empathy. The world of this novel is a hardworking utopia. *Regain* is one of Giono's most erogenous books. The "wedding-wind" which drives the pair together inflames their desires. The lovers are bestial, which for Giono is a compliment. With none of D. H. Lawrence's residual complexes, or the cerebral eroticism of the French tradition, Giono celebrates frankly the body's needs. To those tempted to say of Giono what Voltaire said of Jean-Jacques Rousseau, that he was inviting humans to go back on all fours, it should be replied that the hunter Panturle is gradually and tenderly domesticated by his grateful wife into a resourceful farmer. Like all of Giono's work, however, *Regain* is also full of unabashed hyperbole: "Le ciel était collé si fort contre la terre qu'il fallait forcer de la tête pour passer entre les deux" (The sky on the plateau was so close to the earth that you had to push hard with your head to squeeze between the two). Nature presses humans hard. After the explosion of desire Panturle ends in epicurean contentment, able to contemplate his regenerated small universe with a calm mind. Even death is accepted serenely as part of the natural cycle. Here Giono captures, as Friedrich Wilhelm Nietzsche put it, "the skill to ruminate, which cows possess but modern man lacks."

The Pan trilogy is clearly utopian, while not uniformly joyous. A counterreality on each level (mountain, plains, and plateau, respectively) is constructed to gainsay the noxiousness of offered reality. The generous response would be to say, not that life is not like that, but rather: why cannot it be like that? Giono, however, never forgets the miseries of existence in his wishful thinking, though his tone is more often than not one of victory.

Giono's 1931 novel, *Le Grand Troupeau* (translated as *To the Slaughterhouse,* 1969), is his

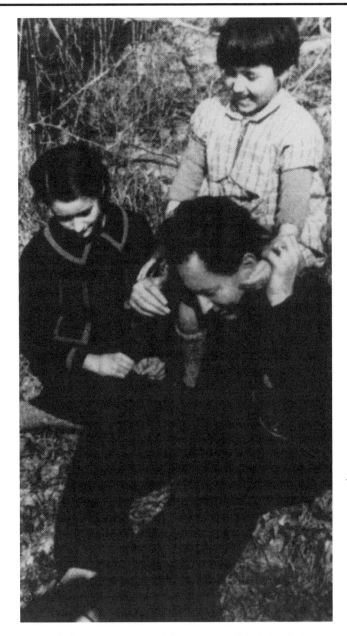

Giono with daughters Aline and Sylvie, 1939 (photo Gisèle Freund)

dystopia, the first work of his in which the modern age, in the amorphous and terrible shape of the 1914-1918 war, bursts into a private world that until then had seemed atemporal. This novel swings regularly between the country home of its heroes and the front line, and more than once Giono indulges in significant juxtapositions (for example, an abortion takes place to the accompaniment of the touching noises of a ewe tending her lamb). It has intermittent but real power, and there is one section of quite horrible beauty, describing the fastidious carnage of dead soldiers

by rats and crows—a feast beside which Ernest Hemingway's "A Natural History of the Dead" in *Death in the Afternoon* pales. The scene is a weird vision, which recurs with variations in later works, and in which it is hard to disentangle the protest at war's obscenity from a far from morose delectation. In Giono's hands the life force takes contrary forms. Similarly, his version of Pan—that most earthy of the pagan gods—can inspire in human beings either "poetry or madness."

    Le Grand Troupeau is the first novel by Giono to aim at being epic in scale; the biblical chapter headings reinforce its apocalyptic tone.

War is, in the fullest sense, against nature, both human and nonhuman, which are tightly bonded in Giono's view. The title links the two collectivities: the massive flock of sheep, forced by wartime manpower shortage to descend unseasonably to the plains in midsummer, in a brutal trek that kills many of them, and the mass departure of mobilized men to the slaughterhouse of the front. Giono's innate system of compensations ensures that this novel moves regularly between the death-dealing and the life-giving, despair and hope. Giono does not analyze the causes of war. He breaks down the matter of war, stressing the extraordinary malleability of the landscape under heavy bombardment. His impulse was always to reshape given material and to mold from it a hallucinatory hyperreality. The German enemy is seen throughout as "the other flock of men." In addition, Giono never limits himself to the man's-eye view and in the person of Julia evokes women's imperious sexuality. The constant switching between the country and the front keeps *Le Grand Troupeau* free from the monotony of many trench-confined war novels. *Le Grand Troupeau* was the first of Giono's novels to divide critics into sharply opposite camps, principally right-wing and pacifist. Giono was too radically utopian to say much usable about war itself, but he offers a more appealing picture of antiwar, of peace, than most other writers. He does not lie about war; he gives the lie to it, he gainsays it.

Le Chant du monde (1934; translated as *The Song of the World*, 1937) brings war home to his own favored region and gives it a justified place in human affairs. This is an epic tale with an adventurous plot (a quest for a lost son), grandiose passions (love, revenge, lust for freedom, devotion to healing and caring), numerous rituals, and a wild natural setting: it is a kind of European Western, set in a self-contained world from which the twentieth century is almost entirely excluded. It is a timeless and universal tale, a pure novel. A river is a leading character: blocking human progress in winter, releasing human enterprise in spring; its varying voices (part of the meaning of the title) accompany all the human action. Man and nature form a continuum, just as the water continues flowing beneath the frozen surface of the river.

Le Chant du monde is vital in all its parts. The hero Antonio is in harmony with his environment, the river, and respects its unpredictable ways. When with his companion Matelot he in-

vades the territory of the cattle baron Maudru to search for Matelot's lost son, the two sides play cat-and-mouse with each other. Besieged by Maudru's men during the winter in the sanctuary of Toussaint, a wise man and homeopathic healer of a strange malady infecting the area, the intruders eventually break out. Before they escape in spring downriver on a raft, Antonio and the refound son avenge Matelot's murder by burning down Maudru's ranch and stampeding his cattle. The violence is, however, measured—an exact eye for an eye. Tenderness softens the violence, too, when Antonio rescues and tends the blind Clara, a woman he finds in the forest. He protects her but learns to marvel at her extra sensitivity to the natural world, and in the finale they clearly need each other equally, as they head for their new home together.

Apart from one unfortunate section in which birds comment on the actions of humans, this novel fulfills its aim of rendering the diverse and captivating sounds of the physical world: river, trees, animals. As always in Giono, death and life intermingle, feed off each other. Giono's imagery is concrete, and it celebrates what it describes. Frequent comparisons serve to blend together the normally disparate segments of reality and thus to create a homogeneous fictional universe. Measure on the level of ethical codes gives way to *démesure* (inordinacy) in the descriptions. From the standpoint of some readers Giono's characters might appear underdeveloped, even primitive. Analysis for him meant breakdown, whereas he preferred to build up, to assert a totality, to concentrate on insistent presences. His people are living metaphors, all of a piece, *entiers* (like ungelded horses). They are not mutilated by the demands of modern society. Giono's standpoint, like that of his favorite Pan, is ubiquity. In turn he espouses every creature or phenomenon he depicts.

Despite the timeless perspective of *Le Chant du monde*, Giono in the 1930s could not permanently keep out the contemporary world. Given his pacifism, Giono found himself in the early 1930s drawn to the Left for a time, though he moved away when the official Communist line replaced hostility to war with a readiness for national defense and rearmament. Not that Giono's antiwar feelings were always orthodoxly pacifist. Against the spreading dictatorships of Left and Right, he dreamed of peasant *jacqueries* which would combine destruction of the machine-mad modern world with the rejuvenation of older societies. When asked, however, to write a book on a peasant Communist who tried to foment anti-Hitler uprisings, Giono refused. He could never be any kind of Socialist Realist. Increasingly, in the Popular Front era, he extolled the virtues of the Select Rear. Like the Norwegian writer Knut Hamsun, whom Giono championed as a "remedial writer" (and who later became a quisling), Giono at times hinted that nature was his private property and seemed to take refuge from personal accountability in the blind surrender to natural imperatives. Hitler, too, thought highly of fresh air on tanned bodies; Franco and Mussolini welcomed the willing acceptance of poverty by the majority. The back-to-nature call rings both clear and dubious.

Published in 1935, *Que ma joie demeure* (translated as *Joy of Man's Desiring*, 1940) retains its fascination, despite the flaw of excessive cracker-barrel preaching. It is this work that appealed and appeals most to hippies, anarchists, and subsistence farmers in minicommunes. It is a prophetic book in that it forecasts by its sorrowful ending–when the hero Bobi, who attempts to meld a dispersed community and to heal its existential maladies, is poleaxed by lightning for his presumption–the failure of Giono's practical experiment in refashioned collective life on the remote Contadour plateau.

Over five years, starting in 1935, Giono made annual hiking pilgrimages with friends to this spot, where they bought and refurbished a derelict farmhouse. The trip, which took place at Easter or in the summer, was basically a vacation for otherwise occupied people. Giono related stories, retold classical myths; they all listened to classical music. Numerous followers latched on. Those of the Contadour movement felt they were on an ark, watching Europe submerge under the rising tide of war. To outsiders, no doubt they seemed more a Ship of Fools, with their Quakerish bouts of "inspiration" and the fatal absence of voiced dissent. Some of the associates of the group, such as Lucien Jacques, lived for a while at or near the headquarters in the village of Le Contadour, and others spent varying lengths of time there; but the project did not have the cohesion of some other experiments in communal living, and, despite its publication, the *Cahiers du Contadour*, it did not have the literary importance of the group of the Abbaye de Créteil in the first decade of the century. The last gathering began at the end of August 1939, just before war was declared, and was immediately dispersed.

On his plateau in *Que ma joie demeure*, Bobi is a healer like Giono, but he lacks the ability to heal himself. The malady of the plateau-dwellers appears to be a luxury: not the result of a dearth of necessities but of a lack of appetite for life. This Bobi seeks to inject by his experiments: planting hawthorns in place of crops, setting farm animals free, feeding previously hoarded grain to birds, and entrancing the community with the impressive stag, Antoine, who represents the Dionysian spirit. Thus Bobi indulges and passes on his "passion pour l'inutile" (passion for the useless), against ancient peasant habits of cautious economy. Significantly, Bobi, a wandering acrobat, has come from fairgrounds; he knows the power of showmanship. The Dionysiac feast, built up by a drum-beat motif, makes the participants feel that they could truly live as one, eliminating selfish private ownership. They learn also to slow down the tempo of existence. Only collective activity, however, breeds unanimity. Pursuing more private concerns (love, for instance: Bobi magnetizes three women), the plateau-dwellers break the union. The narcissus is appropriately the favorite flower of these self-centered salvationists. All of Bobi's reforms are in essence rediscoveries, retrograde steps. The magical transformations do not last. His final inner debate with his skeptical alter ego questions the possibility of joy.

Giono's own innate doubts about the viability of any group dictate the course of this story. The paradox–organizing of anarchy–is not resolved. Before the cataclysmic end, however, Giono has provided his readers with a magnificent bestiary. The lovingly, lengthily described, untroubled mating of the horses as they roam the plateau points up Bobi's difficulties with love. Bobi tries to create a heaven below, an upland Fortunate Island, essentially static like all would-be idylls. What he eventually learns is that the attempt to translate a poetic idea into concrete practice is bound to fail, because of human frailty, including his own.

Whereas Giono intended *Que ma joie demeure* to embody an ideal of collective happiness, he wanted *Batailles dans la montagne* (Battles in the Mountains, 1937) to convey the physical combat for survival by men and women threatened by the elements, in this case a large-scale flood. Like *Le Grand Troupeau*, which critics have faulted for its propagandistic, episodic, and disconnected qualities, this second apocalyptic foray drowned in its own morass of excessive planning (Giono

First page of the first draft for Le Moulin de Pologne *(Pierre de Boisdeffre,* Giono, *Gallimard, 1965)* wanted its words to correspond to the moods and movements of Beethoven's Fourth Symphony). Though apparently close in this novel to the terrain of the Swiss novelist Charles Ramuz, Giono, in his stress on Prometheanism, is more akin to Victor Hugo. The hero is revealingly called Saint-Jean for, like his biblical predecessor, he is for Giono a "meditative athlete," climbing the heights weighed down with dynamite to blast the landslide clear and release the flood waters at the same time as he ponders human solitude. After saving his fellowmen, he slips away into the shadows; he is perilously reminiscent of the metaphysical boy-scout tradition of Antoine de Saint-Exupéry. The most powerful, though not necessarily the most readable, sections of this novel show Giono in his quintessential role of demiurge, amassing and mashing turgid chunks of fictional landscape, reworking the world, improving on God. A new Noah, Saint-Jean rescues people and animals on his raft. He wrestles with nature as Jacob wrestled with the angel.

In the late 1930s Giono took himself alternately for St. John the Baptist or a (pagan) Tolstoy. What he denounced in his several polemical essays was the twentieth century's song-and-dance about speed and linear progress, its fixation on packaging without content. He frequently mused on the conundrum, topical today in the threat of nuclear winter: how many would cope if suddenly stripped of the underpinnings of supposed civilization? The best hope, he concluded, lay with the peasants of the world, whom he saw as the true universal beings, capable of transcending national boundaries: "[Le paysan] a partout la même façon de se libérer de sa nation" (Peasants everywhere divorce themselves from their nation in the same way). He wanted smallholders to think small: localized interaid and bartering, but in general centripetal economic self-sufficiency. His arcadias are not melioristic but given over to the preservation of simplicity and hence largely static. The key myth-figures for Giono are Noah and Robinson Crusoe, and the crucial dictum is that of Voltaire: the world is a shipwreck, and it is every man for himself. To this end Giono advocated that farmers should withhold wheat from warmongering governments. No doubt few farmers read his messages or could, if they did, afford to comply. The logic of his unconditional pacifism made him a supporter of the Munich Pact in September 1938. Yet, despite his reiterated preaching in this period, it would be wrong to think of Giono as a true proselytizer.

Much of the extraordinary cosmic and global meditation in his 1938 work *Le Poids du ciel* (The Weight of the Sky) is given over to denouncing all who meekly or bellicosely follow the Fascist or Communist strong men of the age. The paradox, however, remains: the anarchist is temporarily tempted to act as leader, if only by example.

In the period 1939-1948 Giono took stock of his fictional domain and decided on extensions and refurbishing; his work underwent a considerable change of tone. Undoubtedly the war contributed, especially Giono's bitter experience of being jailed at the outset by men to his right and at the end by men to his left. During the war he sheltered refugees, entertained further Noah-like projects of escape, and contributed some nontopical and apolitical fiction to a collaborationist journal, *La Gerbe*. Cussed as always, his new bitterness begat a supreme love story, *Pour saluer Melville* (In Praise of Melville, 1941), instead of the work entitled "Eloge de la haine" (Praise of Hatred) that Giono thought at that time of composing. After translating *Moby-Dick* in 1941 with Lucien Jacques and Joan Smith, Giono invented in *Pour saluer Melville* a passionately chaste love affair for Melville during his stay in England. This invention embodies the instinctive system of compensation and displacement which Giono habitually imposed on reality. As with his later eulogy of Virgil in *Les Pages immortelles de Virgile* (Virgil's Immortal Pages, 1947), he annexes Herman Melville for purposes of self-definition and self-expansion. In the preface to *Les Pages immortelles de Virgile* he proclaims his need to be totally subjective, hostile to analysis which he always saw as a form of autopsy, and devoted solely to "l'admirable démesure" which he relished in classical antiquity, François Rabelais, William Shakespeare, Miguel de Cervantes, and Melville. The lesson of the microcosm had already been central to *Le Chant du monde* and *Que ma joie demeure*. The small contains the vast; if one opens one's eyes and other senses, riches are available. While a great projector, Giono was an impatient executor, though it could be argued that his defective structures chime in with his aim of suggesting but never clarifying mysteries. The autobiographical novel *Noé* (Noah), published in 1947, is a scrapbook crucial for this transition era. A mixture of seed bed and dustbin, it communicates the new tone of his vision: a mingling of cynicism and persistent idealism. His new heroes were Stendhal and Machiavelli. The rejuvenated prose offers a change of perspective: much less stress on analogies than on antitheses.

Fragments d'un paradis (Fragments of a Paradise, 1948) sums up this bridge period. In 1940 a crew takes flight on a sailing ship away from the loathsome spectacle of Europe and toward the unknown. They have many encounters with beauty and terror (meteors, a gigantic squid, bizarre birds–Giono's often medieval sensibility is at home with bestiaries) and are truly lifted out of themselves. A crew member experiences on the peak of the South Atlantic island Tristan da Cunha an entirely mineral universe of utmost stillness and isolation; he can hear the crackling of stars in infinite space. He feels a new life irrigate his whole being but remains serene during the whole episode, sensuously chewing his beloved quid of tobacco. By this small telling detail Giono captures the mysterious while sidestepping the mystical. Other parts of the tale irritate because of repetitious philosophizing about man's crucial need for spectacular monsters to enrich the "pauvreté d'âme" (soul-poverty) from which the so-called civilized world is dying. Some of the dialogue is roundabout and gnomic and thus doubly frustrating. Here, as so often, Giono is much more persuasive when he lets his fantastic animations of sea, sky, or land do his talking for him. Curiosity was for him always an aperitif to wonderment. The confrontation of man and the nonhuman is shown here as ambivalent, so that the human observer feels parallel uplifting and belittlement in the face of so much that is beyond him. Even so, it seems that the Promethean streak wins out, that Giono is only ever as terrified as he wants to be, and that such inviolable euphoria is a kind of mutilation.

Giono, who once spoke of contemporary man's fear of the past, was himself refreshed by it. In the 1940s he began plotting for his imaginary South a series of *Chroniques,* of which the first published was *Un Roi sans divertissement* (A King Left to His Own Devices, 1947). He used the term "chronicles" to indicate a linear development with a minimum of synthesis and explanation. His own reworked technique, as he described it, was "décrivant tout, sauf l'objet, et il apparaît dans ce qui manque" (describing everything but the object itself, which thus appears in the gap that remains). Thus, in *Un Roi sans divertissement* he presents, from several angles but always from the outside, Langlois, a lieutenant of the gendarmerie in the nineteenth century (the period when most of the *Chroniques* are set), who

Giono at work in his study, 1957 (photo F. Pervenchon)

discovers in himself an urge to ritual slaughter comparable to the one he detects in the murderer and the killer wolf he successively tracks down and executes on the spot. The reader can see easily enough that Langlois has an existential ennui, but Giono does not go into its causes. True to the author's description of his new technique, the center is missing, is conspicuous by its absence. Although Langlois magnetizes the curiosity and close attention of his neighbors, he has a profound but unspecified scorn for the age he lives in. The allusions to Pascal in the title (a king left to his own devices is a most wretched creature) and to the legend of Parsifal in the text (red blood dripping onto the white snow) serve alike to inflate this man who, when he finally commits suicide, does so in the grand style, by smoking a stick of dynamite.

There had been explosiveness and private misery in some of Giono's prewar texts but nothing so enigmatic as in this one. Yet the apparently new elements are more a matter of development than of a clean break. The description of the beech tree at the start of *Un Roi sans divertissement* is every bit as mythical, as Dionysiac, as superreal as any equivalent scene in the earlier work: "Il dansait comme seuls savent danser les êtres surnaturels, en multipliant son corps autour de son immobilité si inlassablement repétri par l'ivresse de son corps qu'on ne pouvait plus savoir s'il était enraciné par l'encramponnement de prodigieuses racines ou par la vitesse miraculeuse de la pointe de toupie sur laquelle reposent les dieux" (It danced as only supernatural creatures know how, by multiplying its body around its own central stillness . . . so tirelessly reshaped by the intoxication of its body that you could not tell whether it was moored by the grip of prodigious roots or by the miraculous spinning of the top on which the gods are poised).

What is relatively new is the sadistic dwelling on bloodletting, illicit or legal. (Sade was after all a "poet of nature.") Nature thus embraces from the start of Giono's postwar fiction far more cruel or ambivalent possibilities than previously. A second war had pulled Giono up with another jolt, and this time the response was to strike back. *Les Récits de la demi-brigade* (Stories of the Half-Brigade) contains stories centering on Langlois written by Giono earlier in his career but not published until 1972. Like the peasant heroes, Langlois is entirely self-reliant, and, though a servant of the established order, he prefers to settle his business with the brigands and dissidents he pursues man-to-man and without recourse to police apparatus. These *exercices de style* are concerned with styles of living. Clothes, facial expressions, ways of eating, fighting, or riding a horse–all these transmit messages to the receptive but uncommunicative Langlois. The trouble is that he is usually more perceptive than the reader and not overly eager to communicate: "Je suis comme les chasseurs de tempérament: je garde le gibier pour moi" (I'm like a true-blue huntsman; I keep the catch for myself). His political preferences are impossible to decipher. He sides with those who have brio or charm, without bothering much about their ideologies. Both author and hero cover their traces. Langlois is a mounted sleuth and an egoistic knight-errant.

Les Ames fortes (Sturdy Souls, 1949) further complicates Giono's picture of human nature. This novel grew out of a collection of stories, *Faust au village* (Faust in the Village, begun in the late 1940s but not published together until 1977). In these Giono experimented with various narrative techniques, especially antiphonal dialogue and the tendency to include cheeseparing information. Such willful perverseness as the latter chimes with the would-be satanic matter of the title story, "Faust au village." In the event this

lorry driver's tale of a courteous Devil who regularly hitches a ride in the middle of nowhere emerges as closer in spirit to diabolo than to diabolism. In these tales the mythomaniac Giono tells some real whoppers. "Le Cheval" is, as it were, a shaggy-horse story, about a noble beast so prescient about the weather that he programs his master's harvesting schedule for him. In "Monologue" the hyperbole is explosive. It swells from the proposition that some natural spots are so magnetically attractive that men are prepared to sell their souls for them, to the recycled mandrake myth of people hanging themselves for short periods to procure an inexplicit but guessable delectation in extremis: "Ce n'est pas respirer qu'on veut: c'est perdre le souffle" (They don't want to breathe, but to be breathless). Giono's people are mean with their money (and thus conform to the peasant stereotype of tightfistedness) but profligate with their passions. In "Silence" he draws up an awesome inventory of a man's property, which is his power; and it is the vertigo afforded by power that most excites the author and his creations.

The chief theme of Giono's later fiction figures heavily in these texts: the hunger for distraction from boredom. Violence had been an integral part of Giono's fictional society from the outset, but bloodletting, or the anticipation of it, becomes from this point on almost gratuitously endemic: a newfound land that Giono immediately overcolonizes. He does see also the comic side. In "Les Corbeaux" he offers a splendidly deadpan account of the difficulties inherent in dressing up for a wake a rapidly stiffening corpse. Violence, too, takes the form of obsessive surveillance of neighbors' every movement and of frenziedly wagging tongues. Giono always keeps one of his feet on the ground of recognizable behavior. He uses two tactics. One is to be so enigmatic (and structurally this entails starting hares with almost every new sentence) that eventually he courts the danger, like the proverbial firefly, of disappearing in incandescent bliss up his own fundament. The other is to be blatant, and this involves the endless hammering of one theme: for instance, blood, or the unstartling reminder that news-starved countryfolk take a lugubrious delight in dwelling on the deaths of neighbors. Either tactic is more akin to hectoring than to an art of persuasion. The author is as suicidal as his figments, for here, by the most perverse of paradoxes, Giono reverses the traditional constitution of genius and makes nothing (or at least a lessness) out of something. He gaily pulls the plug out of his fictional bathwater, evacuating where he had formerly pumped in and wallowed. Clearly he never thought of the undecidability of his latest crop of heroes as destructive of human contact, but rather as an endless source of permutations.

Giono adduces Thomas Hobbes to back up his own view that "L'homme est *naturellement* mauvais" (Man is *naturally* bad). From the late 1940s onward he tends to use the words *nature, naturel, naturellement* sardonically, though they still bear a magnetic charge. Giono projected a novel about a crook selling fake bonds, to be entitled in a perfect pun either "Les Mauvais Bons" (Fake Bonds/Evil Saints) or "Les Mauvaises Actions" (a twist on the "bonnes actions" of boy scouts: "dud deeds"). The title he once had in mind for a whole series of works was "La Chose naturelle, ou Rien dans les mains" (The Natural Thing, or Nothing up my Sleeve): archetypal conjuror's patter, and about as trustworthy. Like Alain-René Lesage (1668-1747), Giono equated the picaresque mode with diabolism, but his version of the devil is related to the seemingly banal, middle-aged gentleman of Dostoyevski's *The Brothers Karamazov.* The stress on the lust for newness, so as to ward off boredom, leads to the paradoxical upturning of norms: the banality of evil, the salaciousness of doves, the murder of loved ones. Such cynical eclogues are filled with vim, with a new kind of demotic lyricism. The emphasis falls on privileged moments of *jouissance* (enjoyment/orgasm) and risk-taking.

Les Ames fortes plays with plural truths. Giono provides several perspectives on the heroine Thérèse, who might be totally unscrupulous, or nobly self-abnegatory, or a pathological liar, as she conducts her not obviously sexual love affair with another married woman. In this text separate consciousnesses are engaged in internecine destruction. What Simone de Beauvoir theorized is here actualized and dramatized. It could be that the heroine's very lack of being, her inner void, leads her to rob others of theirs: she is the ogress of the couple she battens on. Giono had learned from his reading of *Moby-Dick* (1851) how the pursuit of a monster can breed monstrosity in the pursuer. In *Les Ames fortes* his adopted cynicism seems as hyperbolic as his earlier eudaemonism and is probably the same passion painted in different colors. Thérèse's dark avarice is made to seem the equally heroic pendant to the "générosité hémorragique" of earlier heroes (and later ones, such as Angelo Pardi of the

Hussar series). Both extremes, of giving and thieving, seek the same, lifelong goal: *démesure.* Flaubert spoke of "the gluttony of fasting." Giono's universe, also, is giddy, back-to-front. Panic exists, as before, yet Thérèse achieves a provocative serenity. At dawn, after her epic vigil during which she spins her intricate yarns, she is "fraîche comme la rose" (as fresh as a rose).

Similarly, in *Les Grands Chemins* (Highroads, 1951) the maneuvers of the characters are as much internal as open-air; even when sitting still, they are alive with action. A *voyageur immobile* himself, Giono reveled in both domains. The narrator (Giono was fond of the operatic term *le récitant*) maintains a unilateral passion for an unlovely object, a master cardsharper who successfully defies nemesis for a time. He is a confidence-man, but noticeably more laconic than the protagonist of Melville's *The Confidence-Man: His Masquerade,* and is significantly nicknamed L'Artiste. In order to flout retribution, he cheats in slow motion, a kind of tauromachy performed with pasteboard. Likewise, perhaps Giono himself was a Cretan liar not displeased at being caught in the act, for he wants readers to be aware of having been had. L'Artiste is finally executed by the narrator before the official forces of law and order can catch him. Giono had in mind Oscar Wilde's "All men kill the thing they love." Indeed, the current of homosexuality–reminiscences of Wilde, Walt Whitman, or John Steinbeck's *Of Mice and Men*–surfaces here as in *Les Ames fortes.* The narrator survives the catastrophe to anticipate new days on the road; his passion, protective even in the act of liquidating, has been his supreme divertissement.

Just as the character Thérèse in *Les Ames fortes* seems impervious, finally resistant to definitive interpretation, so the status of the narrator in *Le Moulin de Pologne* (1952; translated as *The Malediction,* 1955) baffles and frustrates. Is he a mediocrity or a perceptive genius? The partly grotesque fate of a family of latter-day Amalekites, which he recounts, was intended to be, like Mozart's *Don Giovanni,* "un dramma giocoso" (a ludic drama). It turned out something other. Whereas the earlier, lyrical Giono invented plenitudes, verbal equivalents to his own intuitive sense of "les vraies richesses" (the true riches) of life, the later plumps for gaps and absences. Giono liked quoting one of Gide's definitions of God: "Sac aux parois extensibles et qui ne contient que ce qu'on met soi-même dedans" (A sack with expanding sides which contains only what you yourself put into it), and linked it with the proverb of the Spanish inn, where one is served only what one himself supplies. Giono does not ask or help his readers to solve a mystery, but to undergo one. It is at least thinkable that he himself did not always know clearly what his postwar creations represented, apart from being proofs of his power to create with words a striking semblance of life. True art, besides, presumably dazes the originator as well as the receiver.

In *Le Moulin de Pologne* Giono reworks the fable of the stranger come to town; an exaggerated reputation collects around him, and this gives him sway over the townsfolk, who are presented as a series of aspirant, third-rank novelists. All men and women are for Giono inventors. The mysterious M. Joseph is another *guérisseur* figure, protector of the victimized, though the victimizer here is a joker-God. This novel reveals again Giono's epidemic imagination: a plague of catastrophes akin to the flood of lying in *Les Ames fortes* and the cholera in *Le Hussard sur le toit*, Giono's most highly acclaimed postwar novel.

Somewhat separate within the corpus of Giono's postwar fiction is the cycle of Hussar novels. In order of composition this comprises the trial run *Angelo* (published in 1958 and translated in 1960), *Mort d'un personnage* (Death of a Somebody, 1949), *Le Hussard sur le toit* (1951; translated as *The Hussar on the Roof*, 1953), and *Le Bonheur fou* (1957; translated as *The Straw Man*, 1959). The whole cycle was intended by Giono as romance, a set of chivalric adventures, but placed in a nineteenth-century context recognizably akin to the wars, natural disasters, and political machinations of the twentieth. The creation of the brave and often exquisitely sensitive Angelo Pardi enabled Giono for the first time to integrate his own wide and stylish culture into a fictional hero. Just as the prewar novels cannot be reductively labeled regionalist, so this cycle is not historical. As Alexandre Dumas the elder boasted of his "historical" romances: "J'ai violé l'histoire, mais je lui ai fait des enfants" (I've raped history, but she's borne me some children).

Le Hussard sur le toit parades what Giono described as "une hypertrophie des passions humaines" (a hypertrophy of human passions). The 1838 cholera epidemic is a marble surface on which he tests the authenticity of his gold coinage, the vivacious young colonel of hussars. Amid an epidemic, political intrigue, and chaos in everyday affairs, Angelo performs feats of arms and stamina and, most of all, preserves his integrity, remains pure, no matter what filth surrounds him. He lives at all times on an elevated level, as is suggested by his escapades in one section of the novel on the rooftops of Manosque. *Angelo* had shown him at the greenhorn stage, forever erring and rectifying himself or cursing his own naiveté. He is, from the beginning, made sympathetic by his compound of boyish charms and obvious, elegant manliness. He has an instant appeal for women of any age or social station.

In *Le Hussard sur le toit* he escapes contagion during the epidemic, not by avoiding the plague, for he nurses many of its victims, but by preserving his sense of balance. In this novel the comic counterbalances the cosmic. "La contagion me craint comme la peste" (Contagion avoids me like the plague), as he ironically notes. His spirit has antibodies. His egoistic happiness lifts him above the unhappy egoism of most of his fellowmen, though he teams up with some exceptional individuals who do not put self first in a mean-spirited way: the hardworking, ironic-eyed young doctor who reminds him of the preservative value of humor and the need to salvage every vestige of life; or the bustling, rough-tongued old nun, who cannot stall death yet washes the corpses of plague victims, striving to make them as clean as possible; and the entrancing, self-reliant Pauline de Théus, braver than most men but wholly feminine. They form a passionate partnership, united in their detestation of restraint (frontiers, barricades, quarantines) and their disgust for ignoble accidental death.

There is an extraordinary scene where Angelo massages the infected Pauline's body. She is shocked at such forced intimacy, but the exhausted hero falls asleep on her naked belly: extreme sensuality and decorum combined. The heroes of Camus's plague novel *La Peste* (1947) are hagridden by bureaucracy, in itself half in league with the pestilence. In Giono's work one sees a singular man face to face with the scourge. The two novels meet in their view of the plague as a revenge of nature on a stupid humanity.

As in Stendhal's fiction, which Giono confessed was a major inspiration for his own, heroic soliloquies abound. Angelo's most dramatic struggles take place within himself in his perpetual self-interrogations. Like Julien Sorel in *Le Rouge et le noir* (The Red and the Black, 1830), he knows he will be nothing if he loses his self-esteem. In *Le Bonheur fou* he kills in a duel his devoted half brother Giuseppe because Giuseppe is guilty of

Page from Giono's genealogy of his family (Claudine Chonez, Giono par lui-même, *Editions du Seuil, 1956)* treachery. It is no conventional code of morality that propels Angelo but an imperious urge to keep face before himself. Giono reworks Stendhal's periodic placing of his hero in ludicrous postures, the tongue-in-cheek footnotes, the nondemocratic liberalism of his outlook, the antisentimental taste for classification. Angelo, involved in the abortive 1848 revolution in Italy, grows as disillusioned over his fellow rebels in *Le Bonheur fou* as does Lucien Leuwen, the title character of Stendhal's posthumous 1894 novel, but kicks against being used as a straw man by the strategists in the wings.

It is likely that in *Le Bonheur fou* Giono was working off his deep resentment at the party-mindedness and the purges of the Liberation period. The novel centers on revolution, though Angelo learns that freedom is not a goal to be fought for by collective violence but an inner state to be defended against all incursions. However, if politics is mocked, war itself (and Giono later devoted a long study to the Renaissance battle of Pavia, *Le Désastre de Pavie, 24 février, 1525,* published in 1963) remained for Giono a divertissement on a grand scale. Just as Montaigne considered whether nature herself had implanted in human beings an impulse to be unnatural, so Giono accepted that to kill is also natural. Luckily, the need to love, the desire to protect are equally strong. For Giono, as for Stendhal, love is an ideal prison to which his characters commit themselves gladly. Angelo and Pauline at one stage take refuge from a storm with a hermit scholar, who propounds to them many theories about the plural meanings of the plague, in a long speech of startling verbal and intellectual pyrotechnics. No doubt he is, like Toussaint in *Le Chant du monde*, another idealized stand-in for the author. Again like *Le Chant du monde, Le Hussard sur le toit* is Giono's fiction at its very best: direct but with deep undercurrents, accessible but mysterious in an enriching, unfrustrating way.

Mort d'un personnage relates the harrowing death of an aged Pauline, tended devotedly by the grandson of her lover, Angelo. Giono's fondness for superimposition, connected with his system of compensations, provides an exquisite scene in which, in a feebly lit corner of a salon, Pauline stands behind a stooping girl and their two bodies fuse in one image: Pauline momentarily reacquires a youthful body and confers on this ordinary mortal's trunk the especial beauty of her own head. Two speeds of living for a mo-

ment run together: the old lady's precipitous and desperate urge toward death and the flirting round life of an adolescent. This novel powerfully embodies nothingness. Giono works in *Mort d'un personnage* to make nothingness, or ex-being, as enthralling as fullness; he has blown the egg, evacuated the substance. He calls this phenomenon "a natural monstrosity."

Deux Cavaliers de l'orage (1965; translated as *Two Riders of the Storm*, 1967) is a significant pivotal text, for its writing spanned nearly thirty years of Giono's career. In his apocalyptic spell of the late 1930s Giono caressed the idea of a novel on a peasant revolt against war. In *Deux Cavaliers de l'orage* this idea is transformed into a celebration of strength in a largely nonpolitical context. It is a family saga, with some pretensions to emulating the heroic world, full of brooding omens, of ancient Greece. It is told in the newer mode of external description of behavior, with little psychological speleology. It treats the themes of enemy brothers, of homicidal love, of homosexual incest and lustfully depicts epic bare-knuckle fights and several murders. Structurally, and given its protracted gestation, it is broken-backed, lurching from one section to another. Like all Giono's works, it has striking tableaux, such as the scene in which one brother rides his horse with a peacock perched on his shoulders, or another in which a runaway horse is killed stone dead with one Herculean punch. The refrain seems to be that men have an innate need to indulge in civil war, to test their strength, and women experience an equally magisterial need for verbal jousts. Even love and nursing (one section describes a violent cure for diphtheria) are brutal. Love means being in charge, to the point of deciding whether the loved one lives or dies.

Ennemonde et autres caractères (Ennemonde and Other Characters, 1968) celebrates the high country, the world of "maîtresses-femmes" (masterwomen, so to speak), in particular Ennemonde, monstrously obese, yet with exquisite ankles and, like the other denizens, absolutely set on independence and self-preservation. Here, too, actions speak louder than words. Giono stresses that these tough uplands are "une civilisation," by which he means a self-sufficient ethos, beyond good or evil. Being loved is not enough for Ennemonde; it is the power to dispose (in every sense) of others' lives that she adores. This ethos is totally pagan, and Ennemonde ends in the same Epicurean contentment as Panturle in *Regain:* "Conscience tranquille, elle regardait son monde" (With her mind at peace, she contemplated her universe).

L'Iris de Suse (The Iris of Suse, 1970) offers a hero, Tringlot, a robber on the run from criminal henchmen, hiding out with shepherds in the mountains. He indulges in flashbacks to his violent past, hears stories about local eccentrics, and involves himself in several destinies. At the end he cedes the loot to his pursuers and opts for looking after L'Absente, a mute woman whose husband has committed a spectacular double suicide with a baroness. This pair of weird lovers had conducted for years an affair of crisscrossing domination and subservience. Such is the central material of this robber's tale, in which the author defrauds the reader of clues to the motivation for the wayward passions of the characters. The various personages coincide only tangentially.

Giono operates here, as so often in the dispersive mode, throwing off his creations from the still center of himself. He can toss off scenes (a village fair, for instance) with the negligent ease of a Picasso. Hence there is a certain gratuitousness in this novel; or an arrogant form of self-affirmation. The fugitive Tringlot's deepest wish is to stop running, to become like a fish in water. This guerrilla tactic is comparable to Giono's own existential artifice of self-preservation, though some of his chosen people here select an opposite strategy: provocative salience. The general effect is of an in-game, of secret savoring, as if Giono were writing less to communicate than to withhold teasingly (possibly a sly way of suggesting that the old dog can outwit the New Novel puppies; that is, that he too can ignore the rules of the traditional well-made novel and change the center of interest in his text from plot and motivation to the free play of the imagination). As always, he proposes recipes (how to tame a mule, how to concoct scrumptious dishes), but they are expressed so gnomically that only the most expert could use them.

The title has several possible referents, a flower, a jewel, or, perhaps most important, an imaginary bone in a bird's skull which holds the framework together. The character who half-explains this fanciful anatomy seems something of a diabolical agent. There is something skeletal, indeed, about the people on display here: stripped to the bone of an overweening passion, aliens, inexplicable life forces. Bystanders, and possibly readers, are dismissed as mediocrities. Throughout, the word *modern* is used as a pejorative. Giono engenders the last fling of a dying

race. An alternative title he had in mind for the novel was "L'Invention du zéro." Zero, in Giono's fertile hands, is not a purely negating concept but rather a multiplier of possibilities. L'Absente, mute, barely evoked, is the ultimate self-container in this fictional universe, where autarky is the supreme value. It is strange to find something like Stéphane Mallarmé's Platonic flower ("la fleur absente de tout bouquet" [the flower which is missing from all bouquets]) in Giono's Provençal garden. Like that tiny bone, this figment holds together the disparate elements of this enigmatic text.

Giono's later heroes and heroines remain as self-reliant and reciprocally devoted as those he created in the pre-World War II years. Many of the abiding themes survive and prosper: death, for one. Every death begets joys. Giono could never resist being a profiteer, even from death, which is for him never the end but the beginning. (Remember that inverted picnic at which the beasts of nature grow sleekly fat on human flesh.) Karl Marx liked the French saying: "Le mort saisit le vif" (The dead one seizes the living). A great upturner, Giono says: "Le vif saisit le mort." It is by such twists or complications that he avoids freezing the concept of nature and making of it, as Roland Barthes would say, a mythology (that is, something man-made and unquestioned).

Giono's obsession with bloodletting or the opening of entrails suggests an erotic pull toward such spectacles. No doubt he would have abominated a real gladiatorial show, but his own imagined gore captivated him. Possibly it was an overspill from his zest for sensory experience, for gourmandise, open or covert, was dominant in his sensibility. The prewar pursuit of happiness, naked and unashamed, changed into a game reserve, often indeed a chilled preserve. Giono himself is so caught up in rendering the *volte-face* of his figures, or the voltage of charged situations, that he often neglects to tell his readers which game is entailing such high stakes. It resembles poker played in the dark. The stress falls on drawn out anticipation of pleasure, or foreplay. His later writings form a *Kama Sutra* of the art of right living. The chase, not the quarry, is the goal of this anti-Pascalian writer. To the pleasures of possession Giono adds those of willing loss.

In *Le Déserteur et autres récits* (The Deserter and Other Stories, 1973) Giono includes the strange tale of Charles-Frédéric Brun, who, about 1850, left France and his social class to settle in a remote Swiss valley, there to execute a series of naive ex-votive paintings. Giono both registers and maintains the mystery of this man's reasons for fleeing. Subsisting minimally, Brun is imagined as succeeding in his goal of devising a satisfactory soul for himself, indeed "un petit paradis terrestre" (a little earthly paradise).

Arbitrary and peremptory in tone, Giono's later fiction deals with fleecing or defrauding—financial, territorial, or authorial. This authorial short measure is offset to varying degrees by the endless generosity of his heroes to each other. Giono induces in his readers (luxury) hunger, a hunger for more (more explanation, especially): such hunger is an exhilarating, frustrating, and often nearly hallucinatory experience. Giono's imagination is essentially baroque, favoring the unformed, misformed or re-formed over the fixed form; matter in transformation or decomposition rather than in steady state; movement rather than immobility. He is heterogeneous. He offers a bizarre mixture of the ancient Greek (hyperbole), the Western film (poker faces, sibylline dialogue), and the Gothic (horrors narrated deadpan).

Recent critics have made out that there is metaphysical angst in Giono's later manner and material, though Giono plausibly claimed to be impermeable to religion: one is here to transform matter, and in due course to be transformed oneself. In *Ennemonde* he states unequivocally: "L'immortalité de l'âme est une grimace de clown pour amuser les enfants; ce qui éclate, ce qui s'étale au grand jour, c'est l'immortalité de la chair, l'immortalité de la matière, la chaîne des transformations" (The immortality of the soul is a clown's face to entertain the children; what leaps out and offers itself to full view is the immortality of the flesh, the immortality of matter, the great chain of transformations). Surely Giono belongs to the Platonist and Nietzschean traditions of the Original Oneness, and not to the Christian one of the Fall and the inner schism. Any tragic events in his work are offshoots and not premises. His creed is one of eudaemonism (and note the diabolical particle in that word). Joy can be attacked, like a citadel, but it antedates and most often survives its assailants. All told, it is an optimistic bloody-mindedness resolutely opposed to the twentieth century's preferred misery-mongering: the pursuit, enjoyment, and defense of private happiness, against all nay sayers. Woe unto him through whom joy comes: most people prefer bad news. Yet, if there is little fundamental tragedy, there remains that inevitable threat to all utopian ventures: boredom. Giono wrote to stave it off, in himself and in his readers. Attempts at psychology in depth slide over his broad and slippery back. Though his paganism was at times evangelical, he wrote principally to assert himself. When he did, rarely, use the word *metaphysics*, he gave it the sense of *rêverie*. "Qui rêve dîne": literally, he who dreams, dines, or, as the less gastronomically oriented English language has it, he who dreams forgets his dinner.

"Le pire loup c'est l'ennui" (The worst wolf is boredom), Giono wrote in *Le Déserteur*. Even here, he animalizes, and thereby energizes, the dreaded enemy. Giono does indeed ascribe intentions to all he touches: fire, wind, water, smells, flora, and fauna. Even negatives come alive: "On entendait le crépitement électrique du silence" (You could hear the electric crackle of silence). His sumptuous imagery, often comparing man to natural phenomena, is celebratory, non-pejorative: songs of praise, though they can veer into imagistic hiccuping, even convulsion. Often he crams so much in, that his creations are mixed metaphors, fit to bursting. Even in madness or depleted old age or when they are mutilated, Giono's people remain whole, so that the projected theme of "hemorrhage of the personality" in *Le Grand Troupeau* never really comes into play. In the postwar fictions Giono gradually substituted skeleton and muscle for his earlier tendency to opulent flabbiness. Despite the film adaptation of several of his books, his was not truly a visual imagination. His world exists in the mind, in the other senses, but seems betrayed when translated into moving or still images (a problem also not solved by any of his illustrators). He hoped to attain in film that simultaneity of action he deeply admired in the fugal music of Bach or the crowded canvases of Breughel. This was the only area in which he seemed to have doubts about the power of language to express vision.

This pacifist endured the irony of seeing both a nuclear establishment and army ranges set up near his cherished oasis of Manosque. He got his revenge in a text in which he has two old codgers throwing an entire nuclear research center into turmoil by their mere interrogative presence on its perimeter. Giono could write only of strength; weakness was not his forte. It is man's latent powers that Giono privileges, and not his only too obvious faults, which are the favorite hunting grounds of such Catholics as François Mauriac or Graham Greene, or such atheists as Jean-Paul Sartre. Giono's people are never types, social or professional. His stance toward them runs from one of intimate involvement, even impersonation (especially evident in his female characters), to an Olympian posture as impresario or demiurge. The early story "Prélude de Pan," published in the November 1929 issue of *L'Almanach des Champs*, is a self-advertisement, for, despite his distaste for other contemporary phenomena, image-selling (promising more than he actually delivers, often) characterizes his whole work and makes it a field day for would-be decoders and encoders. Like the Pan figure in that story who, to teach cruel villagers a harsh lesson for maltreating a bird, inebriates the whole gathering and sends them cavorting and coupling with a monstrous tide of animals, Giono is a spellbinder.

Often, as he admitted, his works have more words than clear sense. While many writers practice a stop-go economy, Giono favors galloping inflation. He urged Western society to think small technologically and individuals to think big imaginatively. The legless but stupendous Emperor Jules in *Noé* sprang from the mere glimpse of a tailor observed squatting to work. As Charles-Pierre Baudelaire said of Honoré de Balzac's concierges, all of Giono's people have genius; all live in the superlative mode. He worked always to belie the title of one of his stories, "La Fin des héros." The southern French call his brand of exaggeration "galéjade," the Irish would call it blarney, and the unromantic Anglo-Saxons bull. His imagination always ran best in circles. Unsurprisingly, the antique figure of Ouroboros, the serpent biting its own tail, was his favorite: a perfect image of self-containedness, self-sufficiency. Hence the largely closed circle of his imagery, mainly culled from the natural stock, with its attendant dangers of tedium and tautology. Magic circles can become vicious; a literature of joy a treadmill. (Perhaps Giono evicted the divisive Christian serpent too hastily.) Above all, Ouroboros is a loving symbol. Metaphors, like love, join together, throw bridges across the chasm of solitude.

Giono died of a heart attack in 1970. The armchair traveler came to final rest. How remedial was his life's effort? Giono set himself up early as a verbal faith healer. At his best he is a kind of horse doctor, bringing rough antidotes, or at least palliatives, charms against loneliness or vacuity. He has always enjoyed a wide readership and has been extensively translated. His readership must include those sickened by urban living or spoiled country life and those weary of the antinovelistic experimental novel. He has appeal for the lover of classic Westerns, for his work is a telling amalgam of pioneer landscapes, independence of spirit, ability to read the weather or to track man or beast and settle scores without recourse to officialdom, self-disciplined violence, comradeship, steadfast and cooperative love–all set in a timeless framework where the god in man can have its often ambiguous say. Giono's people are braver, tougher, more willful and yet more selfless, more sensitive than (except in fantasies) most human beings. One can look up to his elevated creatures, but prolonged looking up can be a pain in the neck. Balzac spoke of "un impossible presque croyable" (an almost believable impossibility), which well captures the writing of tall-tale-telling Giono, fan of mystery and mystification. His heart trouble in old age made his doctor forbid him salt, except for a few grains. He soon adapted and grew to see eternity in a few grains of salt. Likewise, his readers should keep the salt cellar within easy reach, as a reminder, though not as a spoiler. Giono indulges in the forbidden; he breaks taboos, mainly those imposed by common-sense reality. In *Ennemonde* he defines lying not as the opposite of truth but as the creation of another truth. In the same belligerent text he exalts "l'école buissonnière de la sensibilité" (the truancy of sensibility).

Ultimately, and this may be bad or good, one knows not where to place him. Yet one can clearly register what his life's work holds out: the intransigent pursuit of their heart's desires by rabid individualists. Written in a country more famous for its indoor, often hothouse, fiction, its psychological terrains, Giono's work embraces the great outdoors and the murky inside, in the most outward-turned kind of egocentricity imaginable. As Henry James said of Emile Zola, Giono enjoyed "a plentiful lack of doubt." He is an enormously affirmative writer, so much so that the doubting Thomas of a reader might occasionally feel that the plethora of words hovers above a central nothingness, just as Raymond Queneau observed that a full plate conceals the imminently empty one. Giono's euphoria can seem at times curiously evacuated.

Like Stendhal, Giono directed his latter-day enigmas to a "happy few" of like-minded souls, or like-souled minds. Yet any reader can enjoy his works, for he is a great creator (and, like

Siva, the Hindu god, a destroyer). He is much more than that quintessentially French product, the *moraliste,* except, that is, in the Nietzschean mode, beyond conventional categories of good and evil. He had a prodigious gift for physical detail, for surging imagery, for recycled proverbs, for the age-old art of telling a story. As for tempi, he could manage every one from plodding to hell-for-leather. Every sportsman knows that playing away calls for reserves of stamina, nerve, and imagination. One reads foreign literature in order to have foreign experiences. As Thoreau said, recommending "the tonic of wilderness," we need "to witness our own limits transgressed." Jean Giono can help us mightily in this direction. This luxury writer was a "wondrous necessary man."

Letters:

Correspondance Jean Giono-Lucien Jacques, 2 volumes, edited by Pierre Citron, *Cahiers Jean Giono* (Paris: Gallimard, 1981, 1983);

Correspondance André Gide-Jean Giono, edited by Roland Bourneuf and Jacques Cotnam (Lyons: Centre d'Etudes Gidiennes, 1983).

References:

Pierre de Boisdeffre, *Giono* (Paris: Gallimard, 1965);

Roland Bourneuf, ed., *Les Critiques de notre temps et Giono* (Paris: Garnier, 1977);

Bulletin de l'Association des Amis de Jean Giono (Marseilles: Association des Amis de Jean Giono, 1973-);

Jean Carrière, *Jean Giono* (Lyons: La Manufacture, 1985);

Jacques Chabot, *La Provence de Giono* (La Calade/Aix-en-Provence: Edisud, 1980);

Claudine Chonez, *Giono par lui-même* (Paris: Editions du Seuil, 1956);

Alan Clayton, *Pour une poétique de la parole chez Giono* (Paris: Minard, 1978);

Clayton, ed., *Jean Giono, imaginaire et écriture* (Aix-en-Provence: Edisud, 1985);

Henri Godard, *Album Giono* (Paris: Gallimard, 1980);

Jacques Mény, *Jean Giono et le cinéma* (Paris: Simoen, 1978);

Christian Michelfelder, *Jean Giono et les religions de la terre* (Paris: Gallimard, 1938);

Jacques Pugnet, *Jean Giono* (Paris: Editions Universitaires, 1955);

Walter Redfern, *The Private World of Jean Giono* (Oxford: Blackwell, 1967);

Pierre Robert, *Jean Giono et les techniques du roman* (Berkeley: University of California Press, 1961);

Maxwell A. Smith, *Jean Giono* (New York: Twayne, 1966);

Stephen Ullmann, *Style in the French Novel* (Cambridge: Cambridge University Press, 1957).

Julien Green

(6 September 1900-   )

John M. Dunaway
Mercer University

See also the Green entry in *DLB 4, American Writers in Paris, 1920-1939*.

BOOKS: *Mont-Cinère* (Paris: Plon-Nourrit, 1926); enlarged edition, translated by Marshall A. Best as *Avarice House* (New York & London: Harper, 1927; London: Benn, 1928); enlarged French-language edition (Paris: Plon, 1928);

Adrienne Mesurat (Paris: Plon, 1927); translated by Henry Longan Stuart as *The Closed Garden* (New York & London: Harper, 1928; London: Heinemann, 1928);

Christine (Abbeville: Printed by F. Paillart, 1927); translated in *Christine and Other Stories* (1930);

Les Clefs de la mort (Paris: J. Schiffrin, 1927); translated as *The Keys of Death*, in *Christine and Other Stories* (1930);

Suite anglaise (Paris: Cahiers de Paris, 1927);

Le Voyageur sur la terre (Paris: Gallimard, 1927); translated by Courtney Bruerton as *The Pilgrim on the Earth* (London: Blackmore/New York: Harper, 1929); republished in *Christine and Other Stories* (1930);

Christine, suivi de Léviathan (Paris: Cahiers Libres, 1928); translated in *Christine and Other Stories* (1930);

Léviathan [novel] (Paris: Plon, 1929); translated by Vyvyan Holland as *The Dark Journey* (New York & London: Harper, 1929; London: Heinemann, 1929);

Le Voyageur sur la terre–Les Clefs de la mort–Christine–Léviathan [story] (Paris: Plon, 1930); translated by Bruerton as *Christine and Other Stories* (New York & London: Harper, 1930; London: Heinemann, 1931);

L'Autre Sommeil (Paris: Gallimard, 1931);

Epaves (Paris: Plon, 1932); translated by Holland as *The Strange River* (New York & London: Harper, 1932; London: Heinemann, 1933);

Le Visionnaire (Paris: Plon, 1934); translated by Holland as *The Dreamer* (New York & Lon-

Julien Green

don: Harper, 1934; London: Heinemann, 1934);

Minuit (Paris: Plon, 1936); translated by Holland as *Midnight* (New York & London: Harper, 1936; London: Heinemann, 1936);

Journal, 12 volumes (Paris: Plon, 1938-1984); translated in part in *Personal Record, 1928-1939* (1939) and in *Diary, 1928-1957* (1964);

Personal Record, 1928-1939, translated by Jocelyn Godefroi (New York & London: Harper, 1939);

Varouna (Paris: Plon, 1940); translated by James Whitall as *Then Shall the Dust Return* (New York & London: Harper, 1941);

Memories of Happy Days (New York & London: Harper, 1942; London: Dent, 1944);

Les Œuvres nouvelles (New York: Editions de la Maison Française, 1943);

Si j'étais vous (Paris: Plon, 1947); translated by J. H. P. McEwen as *If I Were You* (New York: Harper, 1949; London: Eyre & Spottiswoode, 1950);

Moïra (Paris: Plon, 1950); translated by Denise Folliot (New York: MacMillan, 1951; London: Heinemann, 1951);

Sud (Paris: Plon, 1953);

L'Ennemi (Paris: Plon, 1954);

Le Malfaiteur (Paris: Plon, 1955); translated by Anne Green as *The Transgressor* (New York: Pantheon, 1957; London: Heinemann, 1958);

L'Ombre (Paris: Plon, 1956);

Chaque Homme dans sa nuit (Paris: Plon, 1960); translated by Anne Green as *Each in His Darkness* (New York: Pantheon, 1961; London: Heinemann, 1961);

Pamphlet contre les catholiques de France (Paris: Plon, 1963);

Partir avant le jour (Paris: Grasset, 1963); translated by Anne Green as *To Leave Before Dawn* (New York: Harcourt, Brace & World, 1967; London: Owen, 1969);

Diary, 1928-1957, selected by Kurt Wolff, translated by Anne Green (New York: Harcourt, Brace & World, 1964; London: Collins & Harvill, 1964);

Mille Chemins ouverts (Paris: Grasset, 1964);

Terre lointaine (Paris: Grasset, 1966);

L'Autre (Paris: Plon, 1971); translated by Bernard Wall as *The Other One* (New York: Harcourt Brace Jovanovich, 1973; London: Collins & Harvill, 1973);

Discours de réception de M. Julien Green à l'Académie Française. Réponse de Pierre Gaxotte (Paris: Plon, 1972);

Liberté (Paris: Julliard, 1974);

Jeunesse (Paris: Plon, 1974);

Memories of Evil Days, edited by Jean-Pierre J. Piriou (Charlottesville: University Press of Virginia, 1976);

La Nuit des fantômes (Paris: Gallimard, 1976);

Le Mauvais Lieu (Paris: Plon, 1977);

Ce qu'il faut d'amour à l'homme (Paris: Plon, 1978);

Dans la gueule du temps (Paris: Plon, 1978);

Pamphlet contre les catholiques de France, suivi de Ce qu'il faut d'amour à l'homme; L'Appel du désert; La Folie de Dieu (Paris: Gallimard, 1982);

Paris (Paris: Editions du Champ Vallon, 1983);

Frère François (Paris: Seuil, 1983); translated by Peter Heinegg as *God's Fool: The Life and Times of Francis of Assisi* (San Francisco: Harper & Row, 1985; London: Hodder & Stoughton, 1986);

Histoires de vertige (Paris: Seuil, 1984);

Demain n'existe pas; L'Automate (Paris: Seuil, 1985);

Villes (Paris: Différence/F. Birr, 1985);

Le Langage et son double/The Language and Its Shadow, bilingual edition, with translations by Green (Paris: Editions de la Différence, 1985);

Les Pays lointains (Paris: Editions du Seuil, 1987).

Collection: *Œuvres complètes*, 5 volumes, edited by Jacques Petit (Paris: Gallimard, 1972-1977).

PLAY PRODUCTIONS: *Sud*, Paris, Théâtre de l'Athénée-Louis Jouvet, 6 March 1953;

L'Ennemi, Paris, Théâtre des Bouffes-Parisiens, 1 March 1954;

L'Ombre, Paris, Théâtre Antoine, 19 September 1956.

OTHER: *Quand Nous Habitions tous ensemble*, in *Les Œuvres nouvelles*, volume 2 (New York: Editions de la Maison Française, 1943).

TRANSLATIONS: *Basic Verities: Prose and Poetry of Charles Péguy*, translated by Green and Anne Green (New York: Pantheon, 1943);

Men and Saints by Charles Péguy, translated by Green and Anne Green (New York: Pantheon, 1944);

God Speaks: Religious Poetry of Charles Péguy (New York: Pantheon, 1945);

The Mystery of the Charity of Joan of Arc, by Charles Péguy (New York: Pantheon, 1950).

Julien Green was the first American citizen to win membership in the prestigious Académie Française. When he was elected in 1971 to fill the vacancy created by the death of his longtime friend François Mauriac, it was the crowning of a long and productive career as a writer. He also won election to the Académie de Bavière, the Académie Royale de Belgique, the Academy of Arts and Letters, the Academie of Mainz, the Conseil Littéraire of Monaco, and the Légion d'Honneur. He has won the Prix Paul Flat (Académie Française) and the Prix Fémina, 1928, for *Adrienne Mesurat* (*The Closed Garden*); the Harper Prize, 1929-1930, for *Léviathan;* the Harper 125th Anniversary Prize, 1942, for *Memories of Happy Days;* the Grand Prix Littéraire de Monaco, 1951, for the whole of his work; the Grand Prix National des Lettres, 1966; the Prix Ibico

Reggino, 1968; the Grand Prix of the Académie Française, 1970; and the James Biddle Eustice Franco-American Award, 1972. The greater part of his popularity has grown out of his *Journal*, which has been published, volume by volume, from the late 1930s into the 1980s. But he is widely appreciated for his novels (some fourteen of them), several plays, a four-volume autobiography, and various other writings. In France he has enjoyed a large and faithful reading public. He is the last living major writer of what is known as the Catholic revival of letters (*le renouveau catholique*). Among those connected with the *renouveau catholique* in the 1920s, he was one of the three most important novelists, along with François Mauriac and Georges Bernanos.

Green's cultural identity is a curious blend. He was born 6 September 1900 in Paris, grew up there, and was educated in French schools, although he also attended the University of Virginia from 1919 to 1922. He has written only one book in English. However, his parents, Edward Moon and Mary Hartridge Green, had deep roots in the Old South (Georgia and Virginia), and their reverence for the genteel antebellum world has lived on, not only in Green's Paris apartment, where a large Confederate flag graces the wall, but also in his imaginative works, in which a kind of personal mythic version of the Old South is depicted in stories of tragic passion and violence. The most obviously dominant theme in his works is the conflict of spirit and flesh.

As a boy Green was bright and sensitive, very much taken with drawing and art. The Epicurean aspect of the rich French culture that played such an important role in his education provided a bold contrast to his stern puritanical family upbringing. Soon after the bitter trauma of losing his mother in 1914, he converted to the Roman Catholic faith and resolved while still a teenager to pursue a monastic vocation. However, the belated discovery of his long-repressed homosexuality was too great an impediment to his religious life, and there followed a period of nearly twenty years in which he remained outside the Church. Although he maintains that he never lost his faith, he says that during that time he became incapable of prayer. One of the most dramatic moments of his life was the day he literally turned his back on the crypt of the chapel in the rue Cortambert, where he was planning to take his monastic vows. In the description of the scene in his *Journal*, he describes the profound sadness

that he felt, pausing on the stairway to the crypt, as he thought of the world he would be giving up by entering a monastery. "Tout à coup je sentis se formuler en moi 'le grand refus' qui devait prêter à ma vie un aspect si particulier" (I felt suddenly that I had made "the great refusal" which was to give my life such a peculiar character). From that day on, Green's life and writings were branded by what Léon Bloy called the only sadness, that of not being a saint.

It was during Green's estrangement from the Church that his writing career began. Still struggling to reconcile the carnal side of his personality with his spiritual aspirations, he attempted to achieve what he called an "invisible style" during these early stages. By "invisible" he meant an unobtrusive style that would call as little attention as possible to the author. Unable to confront his own deepest personal dilemmas directly in his writings, he was hiding, as it were, behind characters who bore little apparent resemblance to himself and a consciously "invisible" style. The stories written during this period are violent ones that earned Green a label among critics as a practitioner of "magic realism." Appearing to present a faithful re-creation of exterior everyday reality, Green's early fiction reveals, at closer examination, a disquietingly otherworldly perspective.

His first published novel, *Mont-Cinère* (1926; translated as *Avarice House*, 1927), is a bleak portrayal of family life in a house afflicted with sterility brought on by human greed. The French title is the name of the house where the miserly Kate Fletcher and her daughter Emily live. The book opens with Emily brooding in her rocking chair while her mother sews. It is a picture of solipsistic alienation and deadly ennui that characterizes most of the action. The characters never truly communicate; the silence is broken only by trivial exchanges or hostile outbursts.

Mrs. Fletcher's obsession is economizing; Emily's is arriving at her majority and entering into full inheritance of the house. As a money-saving measure her mother allows fires to be lit in only two rooms, and one of the main tensions between the two is the struggle between comfort and economy. By plotting with her grandmother, Emily finally succeeds in driving her mother out of the house by marrying a young widower named Frank Stevens. But the marriage is a travesty. Emily and Frank, who was once gardener at Mont-Cinère, hardly ever see each other. They have a falling-out over his daughter, whom

Green with the ambulance he drove during World War I

Emily tries to strangle, and the novel ends with Mont-Cinère and Emily engulfed in flames. The fire that she so long coveted for comfort takes her life in a moment of madness and apocalyptic fury.

The theme of sexuality is notably absent from *Mont-Cinère*, especially in light of its importance in nearly all of Green's fiction. In this, his first novel, he concentrates instead on the motifs of boredom, greed, adolescent confinement, and conventional religious hypocrisy. The most powerful imagery has to do with the house itself, which constitutes perhaps the principal character. The near-personification of an imposing house at the thematic center of Green's novels was to become, in fact, a recurring pattern in his work. The Villa des Charmes in *Adrienne Mesurat* (1927; translated as *The Closed Garden*, 1928), Uncle Thomas Drayton's house in *Le Voyageur sur la terre* (1927; translated as *The Pilgrim on the Earth*, 1929), Ferrières in *Les Clefs de la mort* (1927; translated as *The Keys of Death*, in *Christine and Other Stories*, 1930), Nègreterre in *Le Visionnaire* (1934; translated as *The Dreamer*, 1934), Fontfroide in *Minuit* (1936; translated as *Midnight*, 1936), and Wormsloe in *Chaque Homme dans sa nuit* (1960, translated as *Each in His Darkness*, 1961) are edifices that have a living presence in the story and exert a powerful and mysterious influence on the action.

Mont-Cinère was given a warm reception by such distinguished reviewers as Edmond Jaloux and Georges Bernanos. Some confusion arose be-cause the author's name did not seem appropriate for a novel written in French, especially since the story was set in Virginia and the characters all had American names. One critic refused to read it, insisting that he preferred to read the original English text rather than a translation.

With the publication of *Adrienne Mesurat* in the Roseau d'Or series, directed by Jacques Maritain, Green's name began to be linked to the *renouveau catholique*. Other writers whose works appeared in the Roseau d'Or included Bernanos, Jacques Rivière, and Henri Ghéon. Maritain was to become one of Green's closest lifelong friends, and the chronicle of their relationship has been preserved in their correspondence, published as *Une Grande Amitié* (1979).

Adrienne Mesurat is, like *Mont-Cinère*, a tragic story of provincial bourgeois ennui, this time set in turn-of-the-century France. Once again the protagonist's struggle centers around the problem of adolescent confinement in a loveless family. And again the opening scene is a key to the interpretation: Adrienne is contemplating the gallery of family portraits depicting her ancestors. The group of twelve paintings of willful, aggressive physiognomies is referred to by the family as "le cimetière," or cemetery.

The action of the novel revolves around Adrienne's attempts to escape the drab monotony of life at the Villa des Charmes, where she is faced with the spectacle of a hypochondriac sister Germaine and a tyrannical father, incurably attached to his habits. André Maurois in his pref-

Green in 1935 (collection particulière)

ace to the English translation summarizes the story as that of "an hysterical girl, in love with a man to whom she has never spoken, and who will end in madness after having killed her father."

The progressive deterioration of Adrienne's strong character into obsession and insanity is a compelling tale of internalized horror. The psychologist Wilhelm Stekel reportedly said that *Adrienne Mesurat* was a truly psychoanalytical novel written by someone who knew nothing of psychoanalysis. The lines Green chose for the epigraph are from Marivaux: "Nous qui sommes bornés en tout, comment le sommes-nous si peu lorsqu'il s'agit de souffrir?" (How is it that we who are limited in everything are so unlimited when it comes to suffering?). He might have used the quotation from Racine of which Adrienne is reminded in the course of one of her solitary, sleepless nights of suffering: "C'était pendant l'horreur d'une profonde nuit" (It was during the horror of a deep, dark night).

Adrienne Mesurat was a significant success in Green's career. The English translation won the Bookman Prize and was a Book-of-the-Month Club selection, thus earning him a considerable American public. In France he was still viewed as something of an anomaly, and he was often placed under the convenient label of a sort of Franco-American version of Nathaniel Hawthorne or Emily Brontë. But amid the confusion

over this strange new writer who seemed quite out of step with the current fashion there was also considerable praise. Witness the Prix Paul Flat, which the Académie Française awarded him for *Adrienne Mesurat.*

The publication of two novellas and two stories during this period, however, gave clearer indications of the peculiarly Greenian fictional world. The titles themselves are richly evocative: *Le Voyageur sur la terre, Les Clefs de la mort, Christine* (separately published in 1927 and translated in *Christine and Other Stories,* 1930), and *Léviathan* (published in 1928 in a volume with *Christine* and translated in *Christine and Other Stories*). Here visionary reality overshadows everyday life and its terrible boredom. Daniel O'Donovan of *Le Voyageur sur la terre* is the first to embody a mythical quest motif that is intimately related to Green's experiences in the American South. It involves the struggle between saint and sensualist that is one of the keys to his fiction.

In *Les Clefs de la mort* Green offers the story of the young girl Odile's mysterious self-sacrifice, which prevents the main character, Jean, from committing murder. Both here and in *Christine,* we find an adolescent protagonist under the spell of a remote, beautiful girl who radiates a powerful spiritual appeal. *Léviathan* tells of the unexplained death of an unnamed passenger on a ship bound from France to America. It, too, incorporates the themes of guilt, crime, and boredom.

Having the same title as Green's 1928 story, his third novel, *Léviathan* (1929; translated as *The Dark Journey*, 1929), also appeared in the Roseau d'Or series. The protagonist, Paul Guéret, is a tormented young man who is driven to desperation by unrequited passion. The object of his desire, Angèle, is a beautiful prostitute imprisoned in a dreary routine at the café of the imperious Mme Londe. At the end Mme Londe denounces Guéret to the police for having attacked Angèle, leaving her disfigured for life. One of the most masterfully wrought passages of the book describes Guéret's flight from the scene of his crime to a coal yard. The evocation of the strange, somber forms bathed in moonlight is an example of magic realism at its best.

Léviathan is dominated by the theme of fate or destiny, and the title may represent, in some measure, the monster of a hostile, fatalistic force, which normally lies hidden beneath the surface but is capable of wreaking vast destruction. It also probably symbolizes the obsessions that lurk beneath the sea of the subconscious, personal demons which, unless exorcised or touched by some redemptive power, result in tragically empty lives like those of Guéret, Angèle, and Mme Londe.

Included among admirers of *Léviathan* was André Gide, who thought a movie should be made of it. Eventually, in 1962, Léonard Keigel did produce such a film, with Marie Laforêt in the role of Angèle. Gide was a close friend of Green, who was doubtless flattered by the highly regarded writer's interest and attentiveness. The author of *L'Immoraliste* (*The Immoralist*, 1902) was an avowed homosexual who preached a humanistic, individualistic doctrine of total sincerity. It is no accident that the two texts of Green's early fiction which most clearly foreshadow his eventual confession of his own homosexuality–*Le Voyageur sur la terre* and *L'Autre Sommeil* (The Other Sleep, 1931)–were published by Gallimard in the Editions de la Nouvelle Revue Française, where Gide exerted considerable influence.

The shortest of Green's novels, *L'Autre Sommeil* is also one of his most powerful. It combines the central themes of erotic and mystic desire in a struggle toward self-discovery that is at the heart of his fictional vision. The treatment of homosexuality is as delicate and discreet as it is intense. The first-person narrative of the hero, Denis, recounts the awakening of his consciousness to his true erotic nature without going into its actual development. Gide, in fact, was concerned at how platonic the narrative might seem.

Despite Denis's professed atheism, his story is far from a repudiation of religious faith. In fact, the mystical interpretation of Denis's drama is never overshadowed by the erotic. The masterful interweaving of themes makes *L'Autre Sommeil* reminiscent of Racine in his powerful yet restrained depictions of human passion.

Epaves (1932; translated as *The Strange River*, 1932) represents a change of direction for Green in several respects. It is one of only three of his novels that are set in Paris (along with *L'Autre Sommeil* and *Le Mauvais Lieu* [The Evil Place, 1977]). He is said to have attempted in *Epaves* to create characters unlike those in his previous fiction, in that they are not involved in the violent crimes of most of his heroes. Instead, they seem a kind of novelistic portrayal of T. S. Eliot's "hollow men," lukewarm antiheroes of boredom and mediocrity. The trio of main characters consists of Philippe, his wife Henriette, and her sister Eliane, who lives with them in their Paris apartment.

Epaves is a rather drab story of the rich, complacent bourgeoisie. Nothing remarkable happens. The themes of narcissism and impotence are portrayed against a backdrop of discreet Paris apartments and walks along the river Seine, which is the dominant image throughout. The novelist himself has said in his *Journal* that his characteristic capacity to "see" the action of the novel in a visionary way was at a low ebb during the composition of *Epaves,* and the emotional intensity that seems to accompany the visionary reality is noticeably absent.

The preoccupation with dreams and visions noted in *L'Autre Sommeil* was a foretaste of the next stage in the evolution of Green's fiction, a descent into the most mysterious regions of his subconscious, closely associated with a new interest in Oriental mysticism. Freudianism and surrealism must have had some influence on this period of Green's life, although this development can also be seen as a step in the direction that would lead to his "reconversion" to the Roman Catholic faith in 1939.

Green's new interest in Oriental mysticism was clearly reflected in the four novels of his midcareer: *Le Visionnaire, Minuit, Varouna* (1940; translated as *Then Shall the Dust Return,* 1941), and *Si j'étais vous* (1947; translated as *If I Were You,* 1949). They all mirror the author's struggle with the problem of death and suggest a kind of mystical escape from that obsession.

*Green at Hawthorne's grave, Concord, Massachusetts, 1939
(courtesy of Green)*

The seer of *Le Visionnaire*, Manuel, and Elisabeth, the protagonist of *Minuit*, are imprisoned, like so many other Greenian heroes, by the constraints placed on them in adolescence. They both desperately pursue deliverance, only to find death as the ultimate escape. Other forms of deliverance in their dramas include fantasy, dreams, and the "other" world of night, all of which are seen by both Manuel and Elisabeth in a strongly mystical perspective. And in each novel there is a mysterious castle where everyday reality is replaced by the visionary realm of fantasy.

In *Le Visionnaire* the author uses the two main characters as narrators (a technique he had already tried in *Epaves*). Marie-Thérèse's narrative is more conventional and realistic, whereas Manuel tells of events that may or may not have ever actually occurred in the mysterious château de Nègreterre. Escaping from the stifling influence of his aunt and guardian, Mme Plasse, the orphaned Manuel finds consolation in his own fantasy land, which has crystallized around the image of Nègreterre. He and Marie-Thérèse, who is Mme Plasse's daughter, often actually see the castle on their carriage rides in the country-

side, but he visits it only through the visionary medium.

The latter part of his account of his experiences at Nègreterre corresponds to the last days of Manuel's life, as he suffers from tuberculosis. Green has termed it Manuel's "apprentissage à la mort" (apprenticeship to death). This section culminates in an unprecedentedly erotic scene in which Manuel makes the viscountess his mistress, only to watch her swoon into death.

The itinerary of Elisabeth in *Minuit* constitutes a series of evasions of claustrophobic constraints in several households, some departures being occasioned by deaths of the inhabitants. She, like Manuel, is an orphaned adolescent who wanders in search of an elusive form of deliverance, haunted by death and fate. The most striking passages of this novel come after her arrival at the castle of Fontfroide, a former convent presided over by the eccentric M. Edme. Edme is the exponent of a mysticism of night, the realm that reminds one of everyday reality's transience and inconsequentiality.

Elisabeth is attracted not only by Edme's mystic appeal but also by the erotic appeal of a young, rebellious servant in the castle, Serge. Her fate is to die with the latter in an ambivalent scene that makes possible the interpretation that a kind of spiritual deliverance has taken place.

The visionary intensity of *Le Visionnaire* and *Minuit* is a high point in Green's fiction. The action is recounted with the authenticity of tone associated with things witnessed, and the interweaving of spiritual and erotic drives makes Manuel and Elisabeth two of Green's more memorable protagonists. They reveal much about the author's continuing struggle with the obsession of death and his study of Oriental mysticism.

For Green the year 1939 not only marked the beginning of a war that would drive him from his adopted country; it also brought the all-important religious reconversion that resulted in his definitive return to his adopted faith. The wartime exile that he spent in the United States and the insecurity of the period may have undermined his creativity. During these years (1940-1945) he lectured and taught at American colleges, wrote a memoir (*Memories of Happy Days*, 1942, the only book he ever wrote in English), and even wondered whether he would be forced to cease writing in French. In any case, his fictional works between *Minuit* and *Moïra* (1950) were on a lower level in terms of quality.

Green in 1954 (courtesy of Green)

Varouna and *Si j'étais vous* belong together both chronologically and thematically in Green's career. They take his meditations on the *Bhaghavad Gita*, the *Ramakrishna*, and other Eastern mystical writings to more extreme philosophical conclusions than *Minuit* and *Le Visionnaire*, exploring as they do the theme of metempsychosis.

Varouna offers the most exotic temporal escape of all Green's works. It is composed of three stories concerning three people at three distinct historical periods, linked in such a way as to suggest that they are three incarnations of the same soul. Hoël is a Welsh figure from pre-Christian times; Bertrand Lombard lives in sixteenth-century France; and Jeanne is a novelist whose story is set in the decade preceding World War I. The title is an allusion to the Vedic god of the night sky, who presides over the destinies of the guilty.

As Green has explained in his *Journal,* this novel illustrates the Buddhist belief that one generation is not sufficient for the working out of an individual destiny. The crime of a given individual may be expiated centuries later in a subsequent life. He also acknowledges in the *Journal*

that there are several details in *Varouna* that suggest implicitly his imminent return to the Catholic faith. One example is a metal chain that is passed down from Hoël to Bertrand to Jeanne. When the last one receives the chain, it has been exorcised, and from it hangs a cross.

The transmigration of souls finds a different twist in *Si j'étais vous,* a story whose broad outline Green had invented when he was a student at the University of Virginia. Fabien Especel makes a pact with the devil, acquiring the power to inhabit the bodies of other living beings of his choice simply by pronouncing the words of a magic formula. After having found several metamorphoses to be equally unsatisfactory, Fabien returns to his original identity and dies. Only once do the magic words fail to cast their spell: significantly, they are powerless to put Fabien into the body of a child in a state of grace. Again a comment from Green's *Journal* illumines the meaning of his story: "Il faudra indiquer que ce désir de transformations nécessaires correspond au désir de ne pas mourir" (I will need to show that this desire for transformations corresponds to the desire not to die). Green collaborated with Eric Jourdan in 1954 on a screen adaptation of *Si j'étais vous,*.

Green spent most of the period between the publication of *Varouna* in 1940 and *Si j'étais vous* in 1947 in the United States, where he wrote memoirs (*Memories of Happy Days*, 1942, and "Quand nous habitions tous ensemble" [When We All Lived Together], published in *Les Œuvres nouvelles,* 1943) and completed four translations (two in collaboration with his sister Anne) of the poetry of the French Catholic writer Charles Péguy. He also taught and lectured at various colleges and worked for the Office of War Information.

The publication of *Moïra* in 1950 inaugurated a new stage in Green's career, two decades that constitute his prime as a creative writer. *Moïra* is widely recognized as his masterpiece. Based on his experience as an undergraduate at the University of Virginia, it introduces one of the most implausible, unique characters in French literature. A red-haired fundamentalist from the mountainous backwoods, Joseph Day is the Greenian hero par excellence, torn between saintliness and sensuality. He is obsessed by the charms of Moïra, a mulatto temptress, and shocked by the loose morals on the campus, which he calls a city of the plain. He preaches hellfire and brimstone to the bemused students but privately worries about his own salvation. The violent crime he commits at the end of the novel is the result of omnipotent destiny; or is it the means God uses to humble and chasten his heart? (*Moïra* is Greek for fate, but it is also an Irish form of Mary, the blessed Virgin.)

Moïra was followed by three plays, all of which were performed successfully in Paris. *Sud* (South, published in 1953) is a powerful tragedy that takes place on a South Carolina plantation on the eve of the Civil War. *L'Ennemi* (The Enemy, 1954) is set in France just four years before the Revolution. *L'Ombre* (The Shadow, 1956) is the drama of an ill-fated protagonist named Philip Anderson and unfolds in Victorian England.

Green's return to fiction after his first three plays was the result of a rather complicated itinerary. *Le Malfaiteur*, Green's 1955 novel (translated in 1957 as *The Transgressor*) had a most curious development. He had begun the novel in 1936, abandoned it two years later, and did not resume it until 1955. It tells the story of a love triangle involving the lowly seamstress Félice, the shadowy, elusive Jean, and a young girl named Hedwige, all of whom live in the same house. The drama of unrequited love is played out here in the setting of bourgeois callousness that recalls *Epaves*, and the ending is characteristically violent and tragic.

Le Malfaiteur is one of the more direct treatments of the theme of homosexual desire, although it is again portrayed, as in *L'Autre Sommeil*, with great restraint and discretion. The puzzling fact that Green left the one-hundred-page manuscript in a drawer for nearly twenty years may best be explained by the difficulty of treating the subject of homosexuality in a character as distasteful as Jean. It is not, in the final analysis, one of Green's more effective novels, perhaps partly because of the unusual circumstances of its composition.

A more characteristic fruit of Green's fictional prime is the 1960 novel *Chaque Homme dans sa nuit*. The main character, Wilfred Ingram, is an excellent embodiment of the struggle between spirit and flesh as it is repeatedly portrayed in Green's work. He is a puritanical young American Catholic who is also an inveterate womanizer. His sexual activities, though rather extensive, are kept hidden from his acquaintances, who see on his face only the marks of the believer. Many look to him for spiritual support, and he sometimes finds himself used by God, almost in spite of himself. He is asked, for example, to minister comfort to his dying uncle Horace and to baptize his friend Freddie.

In addition to the tawdry liaisons that Wilfred pursues, he has two highly platonic relationships that are crucial to his search for identity. His cousin Angus also leads a rather dissolute sexual life, but he is an agnostic and makes no pretense of virtue. The semiconscious homosexual attraction that he feels for Wilfred is finally confessed openly but not acted upon. Another cousin's wife, Phoebe Knight, is Wilfred's Beatrice. He loves her from the first time he sees her but is attracted by her spiritual influence more than her physical beauty.

The most clearly satanic character in Wilfred's life is the cynical Max, who encourages debauchery and tries unabashedly to help Wilfred overcome his moral scruples. He leads him to a violent end in a sleazy part of the city, an ambivalent conclusion in which the ostensible tragedy is attenuated by the suggestion of Max's rehabilitation and of Wilfred's salvation. Wilfred's last words place him once more in the role of the chosen vessel of divine grace: "Chaque homme dans sa nuit s'en va vers la lumière" (Each man in his darkness proceeds toward the light), according to the poem by Victor Hugo from which Green took his title.

Following *Chaque Homme dans sa nuit*, Green turned his attention to autobiography, leaving a hiatus of eleven years during which he published no new fiction. *Partir avant le jour* (1963; translated as *To Leave Before Dawn*, 1967), *Mille Chemins ouverts* (A Thousand Open Paths, 1964), and *Terre lointaine* (Distant Land, 1966) are characterized by a new frankness with respect to his personal struggles, religious and carnal. For the first time Green speaks quite openly of his homosexuality, of the path that led him to it, and of the struggle to reconcile his sensual nature with his religious faith.

Already widely admired as a diarist, Green must have found that his new confessional mode was an important step in an ongoing personal quest. The desire to tell his own deepest truth ("dire sa vérité") moved him to exorcise the demons of his inner self, to deal therapeutically with his most difficult dilemmas, and thus to discover, along with the reader, his identity.

The year of Green's election to the Académie Française was also the year of the publication of his next novel, *L'Autre* (1971; translated as *The Other One*, 1973). The setting is unique for

Green, May 1970 (collection particulière, photo R. Laffont)

Green: Denmark immediately before and after World War II. The thematic focus, however, is familiar. Here the battle of spirit and flesh is waged at two different historical moments in two separate narratives in which the two protagonists exchange points of view. Karin in the first part of the book tells how Roger, a Frenchman, arrives in Copenhagen in 1939 and seduces her. She is a wild young girl at the time but also a believer, unlike Roger.

When Roger returns after the war, he is a chastened man whose newfound faith constrains him to make restitution to Karin. He feels responsible for the ruinous turn that her life has taken during the intervening war years. Having served the pleasure of the occupying Nazis, she is an outcast to the inhabitants of the city, who refer to her as "l'Allemande" (the German). She has not only lost her innocence and her dignity, but her faith as well.

Roger's narrative, the second half of the book, is largely a series of dialogues in which he strives to lead Karin back to salvation, almost as if the debate between spirit and flesh had taken dramatic shape in the two characters. Since the novel follows the unprecedentedly frank confes-

sion of the autobiography, one wonders if that long-awaited unburdening had not robbed Green's imagination of some of the emotional intensity evident in his earlier fiction. *L'Autre* is more, however, than an edifying story, as the rich setting of Copenhagen, its Tivoli gardens, its hotels and cafés, comes vibrantly alive.

After a fourth volume of autobiography, *Jeunesse* (Youth, 1974), Green published *Le Mauvais Lieu* in 1977. In this novel Green demonstrates once again that despite his advancing years, he is capable of producing a novel with the kind of burning authenticity that characterizes the fiction of his prime. Although he has lived almost all his life in Paris, it is the first time since 1932, oddly enough, that he has written a novel set in his beloved city, and *Epaves* and *L'Autre Sommeil* remain the only novels in which Paris has a significant imaginative presence.

The beautiful twelve-year-old Louise, a strangely aloof orphan who reminds one of Christine (in *Christine*) and Odile (in *Les Clefs de la mort*), is the inscrutable icon of *Le Mauvais Lieu*. She is the picture of innocence at the age of sexual awakening, and each of the main characters is fixated on her in some way. Her aunt and guardian, Gertrude, is a voluptuous widow who hides her frustrated sexuality in the attentions of a coterie of admirers she receives in her salon every Thursday. Gertrude imagines herself devoted to Louise but is secretly jealous of her. Gustave, Gertrude's brother, tries to play the role of the benevolent benefactor, while all the time planning to make his niece serve his own perverted pleasures. There are other shady characters surrounding the angelic Louise: Brochard, a sex-starved regular at the Thursday receptions; his pimp, Félix; Gertrude's palm reader, Zampa; and the misfit governess, Mlle Perrotte. Lina the cook is the only adult who represents a degree of solid maturity and wisdom. In the end Louise manages to escape boarding school in a heavy snowfall that hides her trail. The hideous adult world of bourgeois vanity and hypocrisy is left to collapse at the disappearance of the one creature who seems to symbolize the elusive and mysterious presence of purity.

Since 1977 several new titles have appeared under Green's name, some of which mark unprecedented directions for him. One notable example appeared in the same year as *Le Mauvais Lieu*. Bearing the intriguing title *Ce qu'il faut d'amour à l'homme* (What Love Man Needs, 1978), this book places Green very close to the *intégriste*, or traditionalist, movement in the Catholic Church, siding with rebel bishop Marcel Lefebvre against certain liberal reforms dating from the Second Vatican Council (1962-1965). Green's first attempt at biography, *Frère François* (1983; translated as *God's Fool: The Life and Times of Francis of Assisi*, 1985), is a solid piece of historical scholarship, as well as another incarnation of the typical Green protagonist torn between carnal and spiritual forces.

An interesting book of interviews with the critic Marcel Jullian was published in 1980 as *Julien Green en liberté* (Julien Green at Large). Another new departure for Green is *Paris* (1983), a lyrical essay dedicated to the city of his birth. Presented in the form of a kind of *poème-promenade* (or poetic walk around Paris), it is, perhaps, an overdue testimonial to the city of light, since so little of his fiction is set in the French capital.

Other titles by Green that have appeared since the mid 1970s include a children's mystery story entitled *La Nuit des fantômes* (The Night of the Ghosts, 1976) and two new plays, *Demain n'existe pas* (Tomorrow Does Not Exist) and *L'Automate* (The Automaton), published together in a single volume in 1985. *Histoires de vertige* (Stories of Vertigo, 1984) is a collection of stories from Green's long career, all previously unpublished in French. And *Le Langage et son double/The Language and Its Shadow* (1985) is an unusual bilingual volume of essays, unusual in that they were all written and translated by Green, some from French to English and the others from English to French. The French and English appear on facing pages.

In the spring of 1987 Green published his first novel in a decade, a 900-page chronicle of the Old South called *Les Pays lointains*. He told interviewers that it was a project he had begun in the 1930s, only to abandon it when he heard about Margaret Mitchell's *Gone With the Wind*. But he had found that it was a subject that just would not seem to remain unfinished in his mind. The sprawling narrative was an instant bestseller, and Green is now hard at work on a sequel at the age of eighty-eight.

Julien Green's popularity in France has been widespread. He is respected as a major writer, especially as a novelist and diarist. His fictional world is narrowly circumscribed, focused on the conflict of spirit and flesh. He might easily echo the self-commentary of the poet Alfred de Musset: "Mon verre n'est pas grand, mais je bois dans mon verre" (My cup may not be big, but I drink from it). One would not expect Green to treat grand historical, political, or philosophical themes. Nor would one find startling stylistic innovations. He remains completely detached from such movements as existentialism, the *nouveau roman*, and deconstructionism. His appeal rests, rather, on the authenticity of his imaginative vision and the classical purity of his style. His success proves that there is always room on the literary scene for a writer who can tell a good tale.

Letters:

Une Grande Amitié: Correspondance 1926-1972, by Green and Jacques Maritain, edited by Jean-Pierre Piriou (Paris: Plon, 1979).

Interview:

Marcel Jullian, *Julien Green en liberté* (Paris: Atelier Marcel Jullian, 1980).

References:

Pierre Brodin, *Julien Green* (Paris: Editions Universitaires, 1957);

Glenn S. Burne, *Julian Green* (New York: Twayne, 1972);

John M. Dunaway, *The Metamorphoses of the Self: The Mystic, the Sensualist, and the Artist in the Works of Julien Green* (Lexington: University Press of Kentucky, 1978);

Peter C. Hoy, "The Accessible Past," *Times Literary Supplement*, 12 September 1968, pp. 1026-1027;

Hoy, *Essai de bibliographie des études en langue française consacrées à Julien Green (1923-1967)* (Paris: Minard, 1970);

Nicholas Kostis, *The Exorcism of Sex and Death in Julien Green's Novels* (The Hague: Mouton, 1973);

Jacques Petit, *Julien Green: "L'homme qui venait d'ailleurs"* (Paris: Desclée de Brouwer, 1969);

Marilyn Gaddis Rose, *Julian Green: Gallic-American Novelist* (Berne: H. Lang, 1971);

Robert de Saint-Jean, *Julien Green par lui-même* (Paris: Seuil, 1967);

Samuel Stokes, *Julien Green and the Thorn of Puritanism* (New York: King's Crown Press, 1955).

Louis Guilloux

(15 January 1899-14 October 1980)

Walter Redfern
University of Reading

BOOKS: *La Maison du peuple* (Paris: Grasset, 1927);

Dossier confidentiel (Paris: Grasset, 1930);

Compagnons (Paris: Grasset, 1931);

Souvenirs sur Georges Palante (Saint-Brieuc: Aubert, 1931);

Hyménée (Paris: Grasset, 1932);

Angélina (Paris: Grasset, 1934);

Le Sang noir (Paris: Gallimard, 1935); translated by Samuel Putnam as *Bitter Victory* (New York: McBride, 1936; London: Heinemann, 1938);

Le Pain des rêves (Paris: Gallimard, 1942);

Le Jeu de patience (Paris: Gallimard, 1949);

Absent de Paris (Paris: Gallimard, 1952);

Parpagnacco; ou, La Conjuration (Paris: Gallimard, 1954);

Les Batailles perdues (Paris: Gallimard, 1960);

Cripure (Paris: Gallimard, 1962);

Le Sang noir, suivi de pages inédites du journal de l'auteur (Paris: Club Français du Livre, 1963);

La Confrontation (Paris: Gallimard, 1967);

Salido, Suivi de O.K. Joe! (Paris: Gallimard, 1976);

Coco perdu: Essai de voix (Paris: Gallimard, 1978);

Carnets 1921-1944 (Paris: Gallimard, 1978);

Carnets 1944-1974 (Paris: Gallimard, 1982);

L'Herbe d'oubli (Paris: Gallimard, 1984).

PLAY PRODUCTION: *Cripure,* adapted from Guilloux's *Le Sang noir,* Lyons, Théâtre du Cothurne, 12 February 1967.

OTHER: *Lettres de Pierre-Joseph Proudhon,* edited by Guilloux and Daniel Halévy (Paris: Grasset, 1929);

Margaret Kennedy, *L'Idiot de la famille,* translated by Guilloux (Paris: Plon, 1929);

Kennedy, *La Nymphe au coeur fidèle,* translated by Guilloux (Paris: Plon, 1929);

G. K. Chesterton, *La Vie de Robert Browning,* translated by Guilloux (Paris: Gallimard, 1930);

Claude MacKay, *Quartier noir,* translated by Guilloux (Paris: Rieder, 1932);

Le Lecteur écrit: Choix de lettres, edited by Guilloux (Paris: Gallimard, 1932);

Louis Guilloux (photo Danièle Pelletier)

Histoires de brigands, edited by Guilloux (Paris: Editions Sociales Internationales, 1936);

John Steinbeck, *Les Pâturages du ciel,* translated by Guilloux (Paris: Gallimard, 1948);

Jean Souvenance, *La Muflerie de la guerre,* preface by Guilloux (Vieux-Condé: Sol Clair, 1948);

C. S. Forester, *Capitaine Hornblower,* translated by Guilloux (Paris: Gallimard, 1950);

Pier-Antonio Quarantotti Gambini, *Nos Semblables,* translated by Guilloux (Paris: Gallimard, 1954);

Henri Weitzmann, *Itinéraires des légendes bretonnes,* preface by Guilloux (Paris: Hachette, 1954);

Alessandro Manzoni, *Les Fiancés,* translated by Guilloux (Geneva: Connaître, 1955);

Maksim Gorky, *Enfance,* preface by Guilloux (Paris: Livre de Poche, 1964);

Leo Tolstoy, *Nouvelles,* preface by Guilloux (Paris: Livre de Poche, 1967);

Gyula Illyes, *Ceux de Pusztas,* preface by Guilloux (Paris: Gallimard, 1969);

Claude Frégnac, *Merveilles des châteaux de Bretagne et de la Vendée,* preface by Guilloux (Paris: Hachette, 1970);

La Bretagne que j'aime, preface by Guilloux (Paris: Sun, 1973);

Souvenirs de Bretagne, preface by Guilloux (Paris: Chêne, 1977);

Jean Grenier, *Jacques,* preface by Guilloux (Quimper: Calligrammes, 1979).

At his best, Louis Guilloux was one of the finest French novelists of the twentieth century. Despite strong championing by such writers as André Malraux and Albert Camus, he has failed to receive widespread recognition and, because of his firm Breton base, has been regarded as a loner and a marginal. *Guilloux* in Breton means little devil. In his memoirs he speaks of himself as "ce petit dieu rieur, vigoureux, invulnérable, caché à tous" (this mocking, robust, invulnerable, invisible little deity), and so perhaps his peripheral status suits him. At the same time, few French writers have reviewed their navels less than Guilloux; he was unusually cosmopolitan in his receptivity.

Louis Guilloux was born the son of a militant shoemaker, Louis Guilloux, who helped to found the Socialist section in Saint-Brieuc. His mother was Philomène Marmier Guilloux. He grew up immersed in poverty and a loving, integrated family. He attended the *école communale* and the lycée of Saint-Brieuc, where he was a pupil of Georges Palante, a philosophy professor, columnist, and author of several tracts. After giving up his scholarship at the local lycée, he worked as a school monitor, held a series of diverse jobs in offices and commerce, and finally settled for three years (1921-1924) on the Paris newspaper the *Intransigeant,* as translator of English press cuttings. In 1924 he married Catherine Tricoire; their only child, Yvonne, was born in 1932.

In 1926-1927 he began to move in literary circles, and in 1927 *La Maison du peuple* (The People's House) appeared, his first and most autobiographical novel, and the winner of the Bourse Blumenthal that year. Its hero, Quéré, modeled on his father, is a man "all of a piece," a shoemaker who, in the period 1906-1914, acts as the natural but not self-seeking leader of the emerging Socialists in the still-feudal Saint-Brieuc. This group, a new class of industrious, respectable workers (mainly self-employed artisans and public-service employees) is relatively self-assured in their demands. The novel charts the growth of their sense of identity and rights, their setbacks when they are let down by opportunist politicians, and their gradual recovery from disunity to collaborate on building for themselves a "Maison du Peuple." This building is to be a concrete embodiment of their intentions, and combine educational, cultural, and syndical facilities. Education in particular is felt as crucial to social progress.

The politics of this novel are those of gradualism, "evolutionary socialism," seen on a mainly local level, for national, Paris-based parties are viewed with skepticism from this remote area. The stress falls on solidarity in the tradition of Pierre-Joseph Proudhon (1809-1865), the so-called father of anarchy. At the center of the novel is Quéré's family, an organic unit bonded by mutual support and fully integrated into its community and environs. The narration is from a child's viewpoint, consonant with the idealistic vision of the militants, whose hopes are suddenly suspended if not shattered by the outbreak of World War I. The stance is thus inward, compassionate, and governed by Guilloux's characteristic *pudeur* (discretion), saluted by Camus. The dialogue of these newly articulate militants is kept credible. In his portrayal of the workers, Guilloux achieves naivete but largely avoids sentimentality, condescension, exoticism, and inverted snobbery. He shows oases of joy amid much grimness: processions, the resurrected popular songs of the poor. One critic commented that the people of this story "make you wish you were poor." This was not what Guilloux intended, but is a tribute nonetheless to the persuasive understatement of one of his best fictions. He once complained that the French are gasbags. *La Maison du peuple* lacks hot air. Here people learn to take their social fate into their own calloused hands.

By reason of its communal theme, the emphasis of this novel does not fall on individual psychology. Guilloux enters this area sensitively in *Compagnons* (Companions, 1931), and unsuccessfully in *Dossier confidentiel* (1930). The latter is a short first-person narrative of an adolescent's impressions of World War I, from the coastal city where he lives. It is strangely abstract, icy, and dominated by an enigmatic guilt complex, more akin to Dostoyevski than to Guilloux. *Compagnons* centers on a post-1918 builder under sentence of death from heart disease; in his physical decline he is kept company by his supportive work-mate–a more intimate form of mutual aid than that depicted in *La Maison du peuple*. Despite his anger against the war and the damage it has done to whole peoples and to singular men, Kernevel dies in inexplicable peace and content-ment. The author's stance is that of a sympa-thetic witness trying to understand a terminal state. The tone is one of confidence: both a quiet imparting and a certainty of conviction which does not, of course, exclude doubts and myster-ies. Other early novels are *Hyménée* (Marriage, 1932) and *Angélina* (1934), a frankly poor at-tempt at a George Sand-like folk simplicity ex-pressed in a rarely convincing patois.

Guilloux always, however, resisted attempts to cram him into the "populist" pigeonhole. While politics pulls its weight in almost all of his novels, it never dominates them to the exclusion of private lives. Although his fidelity to his pau-per roots ensures his sympathy for the underprivi-leged, he makes room also for middle- and upper-class anguish. *Hyménée* focuses on the recip-rocal and tormented lying of a young bourgeois couple, caused by selfishness, self-doubt, and an obscure guilt which antedates any actual betrayal. With good intentions, they bend the truth, and the scenarios inside their heads anticipate, per-vert, and outdo their confrontations in person. Al-ternating viewpoints give the reader access to both sides of this noncoincidence of desire. The stoical ending ("Patience, patience"), after the hus-band's return from one of his periodic flights, is less than hopeful, as it seems unlikely that hon-esty will ever prevail in this relationship in which the partners are trapped.

From 1933 until 1939 Guilloux worked regu-larly for the Secours Populaire Français, a relief agency for the unemployed and for refugees from Hitler and Franco. In 1934-1935 Guilloux was secretary of the Congrès Mondial des Ecrivains Antifascistes; in 1936 he visited the U.S.S.R. with André Gide and Eugène Dabit. He was an anti-Fascist without becoming a fellow trav-eler of the French Communist party. He briefly edited the literary section of the Communist paper *Ce Soir*, but resigned in 1936 rather than criticize Gide's *Retour de l'U.R.S.S.* (*Return from the U.R.S.S.*).

He published in 1935 his finest novel, *Le Sang noir* (translated as *Bitter Victory*, 1936). Guilloux once called 1917 the last year of the nine-teenth century, the first of the age of murderers. *Le Sang noir* concerns one day in this pivotal year: the year of mutinies in the Allied armies, the carnage of battle, and the Russian Revolu-tion. The urge to rebel (or to cave in), the lethal ab-surdity of war, and the dimly hoped for new society all revolve around and intrude on the cen-tral character, Cripure, an agonized lycée profes-sor of philosophy. His very disturbed mind wanders and is affected by the local and national war psychosis. A mad world helps to finish off an already unhinged man.

Le Sang noir embraces the oppressed (sol-diers, young people, eccentrics) and the socially and psychologically depressed. The title, mislead-ingly rendered for the English translation, refers to the black bile of melancholy, often considered in the medieval doctrine of the humours as a fer-tile source of creativity, the negative of healthy red blood; it also refers to asphyxia, and the coagu-lating stain of Cripure's blood after his suicide. "Se faire du mauvais sang" means to fret and fume, which the hero does in abundance and to no avail. While seeing the impostures of estab-lished society, Cripure cannot bring himself to mu-tiny against them. His is the tragedy of a lucidity which does not lead to action, an intermittent cour-age mainly of the intellect. His crack-up illumi-nates the bankruptcy not only of his class but of its ineffectual dissidents as well. His energy goes as much toward self-laceration as toward social cri-tique. As his voluminous notes for his "Chrestoma-thy of Despair" suggest, his main tactic against the absurdity of existence is the absurdist one of accentuating its derisiveness (like the title charac-ter of Camus's play *Caligula*).

Cripure was also modeled partly on Georges Palante (subject of Guilloux's 1931 mem-oir), a "social atheist" who committed suicide when prevented from fighting a duel for honor. Mocked by his pupils and the townsfolk, scarred by the desertion of his wife, unable to complete his study of the philosopher Turnier (based on Jules Lequier, who was obsessed with the conflict between free will and predestination and who fi-nally swam out to sea until he drowned), Cripure clings to his pet dogs for consolation. With his goatskin coat, his monstrous feet, and his clumsi-ness, he is a freak himself, an albatross stranded on alien land. He is in the tradition of the absent-minded, otherworldly professor, derided by the common herd and regarded as subversive of public order, like Socrates. What keeps him resolutely of this world are those outsized feet (of clay), and his durable cohabitation with a humiliated slattern, Maïa. He is a Gulliver enmeshed by local paltriness and his own pettiness. This "bourgeoisophobe" enjoys unearned income from his investments. It is fittingly ironic that this man of some property should see his literary property, the aforesaid notes, chewed up by his beloved dogs.

His nickname, "Cripure de la raison tic," a schoolboy's twist on Immanuel Kant's title *Critique de la raison pure*, hints at both the honesty ("cri pur") of his anguish and his dottiness, his irrational tics. This split, and the ambivalence of his real name, Merlin (connoting both the magical and the sinister), give the novel its schizophrenic patterns. Cripure's often nightmarish vision conjures up a haunting grotesque that he calls le Cloporte (the Woodlouse), a demonic figure who performs a *danse macabre* in the streets. Cripure is similarly both creator and victim of the Ox, his image for the church of the town, which he thinks resembles an ox if he looks at it in a certain way. The church is an institution of warmongering bourgeois society and is thus a place of death ("Mortgorod") masquerading as life. With their mindless slogans of "Union Sacrée" and "Défense Nationale," the local notables support the official mystification of the common people and the ordinary soldiers. Cripure's fellow teachers, in particular, fail to be serious about the war, until it comes home to them personally via the death of sons. The town is ruled by *espionite* (spy mania), jingoistic speeches, hostility to all underminers and even faint hearts, and grotesque "bourrage de crâne" (brainwashing).

In the midst of this, Cripure, like Jean-Jacques Rousseau, suffers from persecution mania, and it is, as in Rousseau's case, partly justifiable, for there are indeed cabals, of the old and the young, against him. He has his admirers all the same–former students who thought he was on their side against cant but who live to be disillusioned by his failure to convert his bellyaching into positive action. His slap on the face of the unspeakable Nabucet, an old-world gesture, is his one true act, but even this act is spontaneous rather than willed. When the climactic duel is sidestepped, Cripure shoots himself. His funeral cortège is appropriately half-comic: Maïa, his dogs, and a mystical half-wit, Moka, follow the open cart, for Cripure inspires loyalty as well as disappointment and raillery. His chief error is to let his scorn for bourgeois society and his contempt for the intellect and its products dominate him instead of turning his *dérision* (contempt) into a means of struggle against false idealism. This Nietzschean *amor fati* (love of fate) veers close to defeatism. Guilloux shows how this affords a kind of resigned comfort, although he also stresses the anguishing possibilities of nihilism and misanthropy. Unforgettable in spite of his howling faults, Cripure is a dubious hero, however.

A rich cast of odd characters gravitates around Cripure: Moka, a Dostoyevskian saintly fool; Kaminsky, a Slav *vicieux* who terrorizes people and insists on seeing 1917 France in terms of czarist Russia, and who inspires a grand passion in the sixty-year-old Mme de Villaplane, who lives her life to the full. The young are in varying stages of revolt, some more determined than others. Cripure's ex-pupil, Lucien, strives to break out of provincial suffocation: he sails toward a new life in Russia at the end of the novel. He still retains faith in human potentiality. Unlike Cripure, he asks not "What are we here for?" but the Leninist question, "What is to be done?" The middle-aged generation is the main target of Guilloux's satire: cocksure of their rights, endlessly pontificating, heartless and mindless, until personal tragedy jolts them into humanity.

In *Le Sang noir* loaded satire, surrealist visions, grotesque hero, and other characters all give rise to a highly theatrical text. Cripure's pedantic-cum-slangy speech is ideal for his continual *rouspétance* (beefing) which, like hypochondria, is a French national sport. Jean Guéhenno, a fellow Breton who was from a similar background (his father was a shoemaker) and who was a Parisian journalist, associated notably with *Vendredi*, an important anti-Fascist journal of the 1930s, called Guilloux a *montreur* (displayer or showman). The phrase suggests both unobtrusive showing and histrionic showmanship, including some callousness. Indeed, Guilloux seems at times to go overboard willfully with the exuberant baroque of *Le Sang noir*, as if he wanted a change from the authorial self-denial of the earlier texts. Above all, the structure and language of *Le Sang noir* are fitted to its deepest purposes. Even if the world is absurd, Guilloux would later say, describing it as such is not. In tune with Malraux and Camus, he held that this unflinching description is perhaps the only way of striking back against absurdity.

Conflicting viewpoints and an unreliable hero make *Le Sang noir* richly ambiguous. It is a far livelier wasteland than T. S. Eliot's, though, like Eliot's poem and other modernist texts such as James Joyce's *Ulysses,* it is soaked in cultural allusion. It recycles: Flaubert's black comedy about the desperate antics of the human mind; Rousseau's antisocial grievances; Baudelaire's tactic of self-torment as described in "L'Héautontimorouménos" and his dreams of exotic escape; Alfred Jarry's Ubu—the grotesque bourgeois deflating the class he reflects; and numerous nineteenth-century Russian writers (Gogol, Chekhov, Dostoyevski). It foreshadows and, in many ways, overshadows Sartre's *La Nausée* (*Nausea,* 1938) in its concretizing of existential anguish and in the central phenomenon of the largely superfluous hero. It is an extremely self-aware novel but, unlike the elitist *La Nausée,* rooted in common humanity. A manic book, it is a virtuoso performance, in which fantasy is forced eventually to face the music. Its counterpoints—youth/age, peace/war, hope/despair—go beyond sterile allegory or mere patterns and support the making of a true and moving fiction.

During World War II, Guilloux gave help to underground workers, saw his home ransacked by the Vichy militia, and eventually had for a time to keep on the move, until the Liberation, when he acted as an interpreter for the U.S. Army (a period revived in the text *O.K. Joe!* of 1976). His sole publication of this period was *Le Pain des rêves* (Bread of Dreams, 1942), winner of the Prix Populiste and one of his most accomplished works. The title implies both that dreams can nourish and that they are fed by reality; that human beings do not live by bread alone. Despite the semblance of fatalism in his calm evocation of deprivation, Guilloux shows that much willpower clearly goes into making this state into a value, indeed almost paradisal. The virtue of necessity, the deep gratitude for small mercies, are the dominant criteria, as are the multiple forms that love can take: familial, matrimonial—the mother's unstinting love for her children and father, but equally for the husband who deserted them all. The stand-in head of the household, the grandfather, dominates the first half of the novel. An asthmatic, robotlike worker of fixed habits but seething with unspoken anger, he is a complex figure, a prisoner but a whole man, despite his inability to give vent to his love or his hatred. The tightly knit family leads a ghetto life, beyond the pale, inescapably subject to fleas and lice, evoked by Guilloux with a kind of poetic practicality.

Politics are absent in this novel except for the feudal dimension. This is conveyed by aristocratic charity offered to the crippled child, by the polarities of château and hovel, and by the child-like view of the grandfather as a dispossessed king. The apotheosis of this dream, at the end of the first half of the novel, shows the grandfather in his imagined glory yet still, characteristically, angry and brusque with his adoring grandchildren. It is not a deflation, but a complication. Appearances, then, are deceptive, and genuine love sees beyond them to the core of truth.

The second half of the novel, in contrast with the stasis, the imprisonment of the first, is more syncopated. The setting moves from a squalid cellar to a top-floor apartment, and the focus shifts to Aunt Zabelle, in her very different and extravagant way as much of a household deity as the grandfather. They are two contrasting, difficult to love yet loved, characters. The word *character* is particularly fitting here, since Guilloux makes considerable use, in the second half of the book, of the theater as a metaphor for life and a way of understanding it. Zabelle dramatizes her own life, consciously playing roles for her husband and other observers, reenacting choice scenes that always amaze the young narrator and provoke rage in her intimates. She even organizes an amateur company, which rents the town theater for its show. But such theatricality has its disappointments and cannot, despite Zabelle's flamboyance, be taken as a satisfactory substitute for life: the novelist shows how some traveling players have to beg onlookers who have stumbled onto a family scene to give them some privacy for their real drama.

This novel also dwells on growing up and the fear of losing or of being unfaithful to the past. As in Proust, memory is equated with conscience. This novel is a paean to childhood, to the dream-age: "Mes joies pleines d'espérances et depuis si mal désapprises" (My joys full of high hopes which I would never manage completely to abandon). The narrator's love for Gisèle, like that of Proust's narrator for Gilberte in *A la recherche du temps perdu,* is one-way, talismanic, chivalric, and total. Guilloux favors the image of mankind as sleepwalkers; people attempt to shut out the miseries of life by imagined existences. Such exclusion works both ways. If better-off folk marginalize the pauper family, the family is such a tight nucleus that it can shut out the rest.

Guilloux (left) with Louis Parrot and two unidentified women

While they hug themselves with the belief that they alone know what real love is, this does not lead to apartheid: "L'ennemi est aussi un homme, c'est la plus triste des choses" (The enemy is human, too, that's the saddest thing), a rueful admission of the difficulty of true hatred. One splendid scene shows how a bully shifts his shame on to his victim.

Le Pain des rêves is both open and secretive, vibrant. It is unembarrassed about moralizing or generalization, while recognizing the ultimate inadequacy of language ("A quoi bon vouloir interpréter les passions humaines, quand il est déjà si difficile de les nommer?" [What's the point of trying to analyze human passions, when it's already so hard even to put a name on them?]). This novel's final question, addressed to the reader, "Ai-je gagné ton amitié?" (Have I earned your friendship?), should be answered in the affirmative.

Le Jeu de patience (The Jigsaw Puzzle, 1949), winner of the Prix Théophraste Renaudot, embraces Guilloux's experiences and observations in World War II and earlier, as far back as 1912. Such a puzzle requires patient recomposition from the reader of this rich and complicated novel. Throughout there is an oscillation and mutual interpenetration between microhistory and macrohistory, ordinariness and high drama. Thus, the horrors and braveries of war—atrocities, deportation, the wretched partners in collaboration and the martyrs of resistance—as well as organized aid to the unemployed and to Spanish refugees, and politics (in its different strands—anarchism, socialism, Popular Front, right-wing coups), all mingle with and deeply influence the private dramas of love, betrayal, steadfast support, religion, and family life. In this melting pot recur figures from earlier novels, including Cripure, Zabelle, and the artisans of *La Maison du peuple*. *Le Jeu de patience* is often a roll call of the dead. Like Guilloux's best writing, it is a haunted book, sometimes to the point of having a hallucinatory quality. Despite its often tragic incidents, the recurring vision of "la Cité future," a crystalline symbol of harmony, keeps up a cyclical hopefulness amid the reiterated letdowns. *Durée*, here, implies both lived time, and endurance.

The narrator is unable to decide whether to organize his material, to bury it unpublished in a cupboard, or to burn the whole morass of papers. Partial memoirs, letters, records of oral reminiscences, and newspaper clippings form a misshapen ragbag. Like Flaubert, the narrator rages against the self-imposed curse of documentation that he cannot break. Time is of the essence: he marks time, he backtracks, he anticipates. He is plagued, like Cripure with his chrestomathy, by the multiple problems of ordering, classifying, and resolving chaos. The wider question of free will is raised: can the author *not* write his chronicle? This in turn brings in the issue of responsibility: the observer privileged to witness must bear witness. The chronicle must be comprehensive, in all senses of the word. While Guilloux would never subscribe to the limp truism "Tout comprendre c'est tout pardonner" (To understand everything is to forgive everything), his narrator feels both compassion and great discomfort in passing judgment even on proven or self-confessed traitors. The morality is clear but flexible. It is based on a firm sense of community and of common humanity which does not exclude the renegades.

Like Camus and like the Italian writer Ignazio Silone, Guilloux believed that human beings are all too sufficiently condemned by mortality ever to pose as automatically just judges. His sense of community depends on dialogue and sharing. The popular local verdict on Cripure, that he was a deserter, is queried as only part of the truth. He was, urges the narrator, "l'homme acculé," the man driven in on himself, desperately devoid of that consolation of solidarity which the narrator, though often in solitude like Cripure, sometimes experiences. Guilloux always marked his distance from organized religion, but retained an obsessive concern with guilt, judgment, and atonement. While priests are often dismissed as mere spokesmen, mouthing an alien script, Guilloux's works do feature many serious dialogues with priests, and in *Le Jeu de patience* several of these are the most outstanding of the Resistance heroes. Guilloux always avoids rigid categorization. He is much more taken with the prevalance of exceptionality and of overlap in human existence. Time, for instance, is seen not just as remorseless linearity, but as impinging, recurring: different periods are mutually allusive. Space, too, is ambivalent in this way. The narrator feels for his hometown, which saturates his consciousness, "des sentiments antinomiques et simultanés, dont me parlait notre vieux maître Palante, en se forçant à rire" (simultaneously opposite sentiments, such as our old master Palante used to talk about, with a forced laugh).

A very long work such as *Le Jeu de patience* relies on motifs. A dominating one is that of a poster depicting a military figure massacring women and children–the Apocalypse made more recognizable. Hints, trailed ideas or images, are presented, picked up later, and developed. There are many protracted flashbacks. This novel is a kaleidoscope or a crisscrossing and overlaying of strips of material. Great care is taken to situate every happening, for context is crucial to understanding. The narrator ranges back and forth in time, telling his myriad tales in a supple language, unaffectedly colloquial or highly literate, as the situation demands. Guilloux, and his spokespersons, command several registers. In a sense the novel has several narrators that together form a kind of collective voice, cumulative neighborly talk, as in Silone. Repetitions fulfill the task of keeping law and order amid the proliferating detail, just as habits, tics, and idiosyncrasies play a large part in typifying individuals. Guilloux alters reading rhythms; the narration is slow-motion, as befits the dominant value of patience. Just as in the game of patience, or solitaire, the player can succeed or fail, so patience as a virtue has to face both, and other, eventualities.

The periodic philosophizing in the novel is genuinely folk, not folksy or crackerbarrel: it is fully earned; it works its passage. Guilloux's dramatic gift for what Stendhal called "scènes probantes" (probing/proving scenes) emerges in several episodes where the witnessing, the inflicting, the enduring, or the salving of pain are enacted. The writer is a "remembrancer," finding salvation through saving others from oblivion, though the act of writing is shown to be analgesic or escapist as well as antiamnesiac. When the narrator speaks of "ma hantise du passé" (my obsession with the past), he means both that he tails the past and that it dogs him. Time past and time present are everywhere interleaved. Gradualism, whether in politics or in storytelling, is Guilloux's natural mode.

In the early 1950s Guilloux traveled widely in Europe, mainly to P.E.N. Club conferences, and was much involved in questions of popular culture on an international level. Yet, he wrote in *Absent de Paris* (Away from Paris, 1952), an extended letter to his lifelong friend Jean Grenier and a partial commentary on *Le Jeu de patience*, that populism, as a literary mode, had been killed off by the revelation of concentration camps, and that mere poverty was no longer enough to interest readers. Needing partly to renew his subject matter and partly to give himself a literary break, he published in 1954 *Parpagnacco; ou, La Conjuration* (Parpagnacco; or, The Conspiracy), a largely atemporal tale of magic set mainly in a mythologized Venice, and involving seafarers, an imprisoned girl, and a baleful cat. It is an ungripping mystery story, fey and close to pointless.

The publisher's blurb for Guilloux's next and very ambitious novel, *Les Batailles perdues* (Lost Battles, 1960), mentions "des hommes et des femmes, pris par l'histoire, [qui] veulent à la fois la faire et y échapper" (men and women, caught up in history, [who] want simultaneously to be involved and to escape from it). The novel also asks the question of whether or not it is prudent to embark on losing battles. This lengthy text starts off with bookish, disoriented young intellectuals, tempted to political activism but in effect marking time in a kind of limbo: inchoate misfits or parasites. Rather more serious but still marginal is Franz, a Jewish émigré from Austria, active in anti-Fascist politics, buoyed by the empowerment of the Popular Front government of Léon Blum, but disheartened by the Franco uprising in Spain and the arrest of his estranged wife by the Nazis. There are also fairy-tale elements (Breton folk yarns and superstitions); idealism and cynicism lock horns. The poor dream of being fabulously rich and the linked motifs of château and hovel, comfort and squalor, recur, as does the theme of buying and selling people (adoption, prostitution).

The overarching intention is to track the loss, maintenance, and reanimation of the revolutionary spirit (there are references to the French Revolution and the Paris Commune), culminating in the rise and vulnerability of the Popular Front, opposed by right-wing gangs. Soviet Russia, which Guilloux knew mainly through the trip made there by himself, Gide, and other sympathizers, represents a dubious pole of hope. Throughout, local history (the forced sale of farms in Brittany in the 1930s, and Breton separatist movements) is juxtaposed with world events. Some of the local history is narrated in the style of popular serialized fiction, making room for gossip and rumor as in oral narrative. The result is an often exclamatory style, as if some form of chorus were reacting to events, as in Knut Hamsun's *The Growth of the Soil* (1917). Yet it is a long and flawed novel, with much less of the pathos and the strength of *Le Jeu de patience*, *Le Pain des rêves*, *Le Sang noir*, or *La Maison du peuple*. One passage describes the art of storytelling as understood by a shoemaker-raconteur: "Il fallait prendre les choses de loin, amuser un peu, intriguer un peu, mener un peu les gens de-ci de-là, par le bout du nez, ... les tromper un peu, les détromper à moitié, les faire attendre, espérer, deviner, voir et croire qu'ils avaient déjà tout compris d'eux-mêmes quand justement le principal restait à dire, ... l'art étant de ne jamais insister" (The idea is to start way back, entertain, intrigue, lead people along by the nose, deceive them, undeceive them to some extent, make them wait, hope, guess and think they've got it all sorted out when the game is in fact just starting, the real trick being never to be blatant).

In *Les Batailles perdues*, a generosity of invention and of sympathy is combined with, and undermined by, one of squandering. The crowd scenes (religious processions and political demonstrations), so frequent in Guilloux's work, provide a means for the novelist to pursue multiple plot lines, as does the device of books-within-the-book. The theme of fighting lost causes puts more stress on the losing than the struggle; disengagement wins over engagement. Politics here is nearly always talk about action or desirable changes of state. There is not, as in the best political fiction (Silone, George Orwell), a strong resistance to ideology, a clear refusal of ready-made values and party lines, but something limper. It is as if Guilloux were implicitly confessing that neither he nor his fictional heroes had been properly cut out for the politicized life demanded by the age in which they live.

Guilloux's brand of politics had always been that of humanitarian socialism. In 1961 he made a long tour of West Germany, Greece, Austria, and Italy, on behalf of the United Nations High Commission for Refugees, visiting the residual camps. It was a period when, unsurprisingly, he felt a mixture of strangerliness, itchy feet, an urge to postpone settling down to write, yet a subterranean attachment to his roots. In 1967 *Compagnons* was adapted (as *Le Pain des rêves* would be in 1974) for television, and the play, *Cripure*, adapted from *Le Sang noir*, was staged in Lyons. Guilloux was awarded in 1967 the Grand Prix National des Lettres, and in 1973 the Grand Prix de Littérature de l'Académie Française, in recognition of his contribution to French literature. A decline set in.

La Confrontation (1967) had a working title of "Sans feu ni lieu" (No Fixed Abode), which at the time of writing reflected Guilloux's situation, occupying a succession of temporary rooms in Paris. It is a psychological detective story of a search for a missing person, which becomes a quest for the self, as the categories of journalist, policeman, biographer, and author–all of which entail the assembling of disparate material–overlap and coalesce. That ambiguous word *splice* (sunder/join) is suitable for this process of splintering and fusion. Despite formal coincidences with the New Novel of Alain Robbe-Grillet and company—the detective story used to overturn stock perceptions of reality, the confusion among characters—this novel in fact recoups many of Guilloux's lasting preoccupations, summed up in the Villonesque question: "Qu'as-tu fait de ta vie?" (What have you made of your life?)

Guilt, largely unspecified, lost love, disillusionment, imaginary dialogues, reconstructing a biography from documents and oral evidence, bread and dreams, the urge to sail away, the importance of the home as the center of life—all of these motifs are picked up from Guilloux's earlier fictions. The author plays hide-and-seek with the reader. As in Camus's *La Chute* (*The Fall*, 1956) the reader listens to a unilateral dialogue which is conducted by the split self; there is a largely symbolic use of place and a vision of innocence clouded with pervasive culpability. What distinguishes *La Confrontation* most from *La Chute* is its greater stress on forgiveness over accusation. In addition, the references are almost exclusively to private life, which encourages the Gidean motif of "mise en abyme," of mirror images and games. There is thus no check on what seems like self-indulgent proliferation of inquiry. The novel ends with an ambivalent image of mankind as prisoners waiting in condemned cells but with dawn about to break: the dawn of a second chance, or of execution?

In the 1960s Guilloux worked to promote provincial Maisons de la Culture—André Malraux's brainchild, intended to decentralize the arts in France—at Orléans, Bourges, and Saint-Brieuc. An effort along similar lines was his adaptation of works of literature for television: several tales of Joseph Conrad and Roger Martin du Gard's *Les Thibault*. In 1976 *Salido* and *O.K. Joe!* were published together, two short accounts developing incidents from Guilloux's memoirs, *Carnets*, which appeared in two volumes in 1978 and 1982.

Salido and *O.K. Joe!* are deadpan narratives. The first recounts the attempts of a refugee from Francoist Spain to escape German-occupied France to which he has fled. Determined to get to Moscow, he is helped by Guilloux and the local Communists, but gets lost in Paris. The author watches helplessly when he is arrested in Saint-Brieuc. *O.K. Joe!* relives Guilloux's spell as an interpreter for the U.S. Army. He officiates at the trials of several black GI's, all found guilty of rape, and one white officer, acquitted. Gentle but

telling irony is directed at his extremely hospitable and decent employers and their fervent but unreal democracy. The executions, not described in the novel, are yet another set of the atrocities of war. Guilloux's disquiet at his share in the judicial process is all the more patent for not being blatant.

His last work of fiction published in his lifetime was *Coco perdu* (The Lost Guy, 1978). Subtitled *Essai de voix* (Voice test), it is a monologue spoken by an aging man who eventually realizes that he has been deserted by his wife, ostensibly gone to Paris for a short visit. He is "en retraite," retired, indeed in retreat from life. Some odd snippets of overheard conversations resuscitate some of Guilloux's recurrent themes: the failure of revolution, the demoralizing spectacle of postwar Europe, and loneliness. It is a sad farewell to fiction. Were it not for the posthumously published *L'Herbe d'oubli* (The Herb of Oblivion, 1984), it might well seem there had been a gradual leaking away of creative energy after *Le Jeu de patience*.

L'Herbe d'oubli is less memoir than *récit*. Guilloux was always primarily a storyteller. The leitmotif of this text is "Rien n'est jamais fini" (Nothing is ever over once and for all). The title refers to a Breton tale of a magic plant, picked by ill-wishers to strew beneath the feet of those they want to curse, so that demons will seize them and dance them to death in an infernal round. For Guilloux, forgetfulness and oblivion (*oubli* covers both meanings) are as criminal and as pitiable as the *oubliettes* (secret dungeons) of the Ancien Régime. But memory is not infallible. Though Guilloux likens the stories he tells of people he has known, observed, or heard of to the leaves and branches of an old Breton oak tree with profound roots, he knows that one's memory houses as much dross as gold. Yet he remains convinced that without a devotion to remembering one commits moral crimes.

In *L'Herbe d'oubli*, Guilloux recounts his recurrent dream of sailing away from his home port, but also of returning to find everyone and everything the same exactly. This conjunction of escape and stasis, this sedentary nomadism, in fact produced largely the opposite: he mainly stayed where he was and imagined adventures. Within this framework he sought periodically to make himself anew. As he said in *Absent de Paris*, "Je voudrais en conter une . . . que je ne sache pas, dire une chose que je n'aurais pas vue" (I wish I could tell one [story] unknown to me, de-

Guilloux with Albert Camus

scribe something I had not seen). He criticized priests for parroting their divine scripts and, like Gide, wanted to, but doubted that he could, be truly inventive. His anarchist streak made him loathe commissioned tasks. The urge to be novel coexisted, as with Flaubert, with a limited but well-developed strain of veneration. Guilloux's habit of writing allusively, suggesting analogies of different sights, sounds, and faces, reveals a desire to widen out, to link up, to extend the apparently paltry. Soaked in culture and history himself, he saw the world in terms of resemblances. He freely admitted his debts to many writers: to Jules Vallès, the critique of schoolteachers as life-killers and the championing of society's marginals; Vallès was for Guilloux an initiator into a world "de santé, d'audace, de fierté, d'ironie, d'insolence, de liberté, vrai monde de la jeunesse" (of healthiness, audacity, pride, irony, insolence, freedom, the true world of youth). He was in debt to Rousseau especially for *Les Confessions;* also to Gogol, Dostoyevski, Tolstoy, Gorky, Dickens, and Thoreau. Guilloux is in some degree a French equivalent of Ignazio Silone: provincial roots, a durable humor, an allegiance to humanitarian socialism; the stress on the choice of companions, brotherli-

ness in a century fixated on strangerliness; an aversion to abstract dogma, and a deep love of the art of storytelling. What Guilloux learned above all from the nineteenth-century novel was the art of patience, the management of tempo, and the readiness to repeat and rework. His gift for mimicry helped him to impersonate a wide variety of characters, but his pastiching is controlled. He could manage understatement and knowingly go over the top.

While it is tempting when speaking of Guilloux to spend more time congratulating him on his sociable human qualities than on his creative powers, what in fact impresses most in his work is the breadth of his human interest and the depth of his sympathy, indeed empathy. For some, the tone of his narrative, filled with emotions of concern, pity, kindness, and fraternity, is probably more distinctive than his major theme: the condemnation of an unjust and corrupting society, where heroic failure is the best man can hope for. His friend Jean Grenier called Guilloux a novelist of imprisonment. Guilloux responded by suggesting that one should perhaps talk less of liberty and more of deliverance. It is strange that this most candid of writers should have said: "On n'écrit pas pour dire, mais pour cacher" (One writes not to reveal but to conceal). One of his favored expressions was "savoir à quoi s'en tenir" (to know what's what). This implies something that is clear to the person concerned but not to onlookers. Such reserve and discretion, while sometimes annoying to readers who wish to see more of the author in the work, or to have access to his private views, do not interfere with the proper understanding of his work and may even be considered a means to understanding.

Guilloux may not yet have received the recognition that is his due. Only one of his volumes has been translated into English. Yet he was admired by his contemporaries, including such major literary figures as Gide, Malraux, and Camus (a close friend). His work is important for both its content and its form. His varied use of narrative voices and different ways of handling time, including compressing the action of a full-length novel into twenty-four hours and expanding the main narrative time line by bringing in segments of the past, are noteworthy instances of the development of fictional technique in France during the first half of this century and even anticipate some of the technical departures of post-1950 novelists such as Claude Mauriac and Michel Butor. His constant concern for the modest classes, from which he came and which furnish the models for most of his fictional characters, makes him a major figure in the populist tradition of twentieth-century French fiction and an important spokesman for social concerns.

References:

François Bourgeat, ed., *Actualité de Louis Guilloux* (Marseilles: Laffitte, 1977);

Victor Brombert, *The Intellectual Hero* (London: Faber, 1964);

Eleanor Clark, "Death of a Thinker," *Kenyon Review*, 3 (Summer 1941): 322-334;

Mary Jean Matthews Green, *Louis Guilloux: An Artisan of Language* (York, S.C.: French Literature Publications, 1980);

Francis J. Greene, "Louis Guilloux's *Le Sang noir*: A Prefiguration of Sartre's *La Nausée*," *French Review*, 43, 2 (1969): 205-214;

Jean Grenier, *Les Grèves* (Paris: Gallimard, 1957);

Jean-Louis Jacob, *Louis Guilloux: Romancier du peuple* (Paris: Noroît, 1983);

Jacob, ed., *Louis Guilloux* (Quimper: Calligrammes, 1986);

Jonathan H. King, "Louis Guilloux's Ambiguous Epic: *Le Sang noir*," *Forum for Modern Language Studies*, 8 (January 1972): 1-14;

King, "Louis Guilloux's *Le Jeu de patience*: Time and the Novelist," *Trivium*, 1 (1972): 40-55;

King, "Louis Guilloux's Working Class Novels: Some Problems of Social Realism," *Modern Language Review*, 68 (January 1973): 69-76;

Yannick Pelletier, *Thèmes et symboles dans l'œuvre romanesque de Louis Guilloux* (Paris: Klincksieck, 1979);

Pelletier, ed., "Louis Guilloux," *Plein Chant*, 11-12 (1982);

Edouard Prigent, *Louis Guilloux* (Saint-Brieuc: Presses Universitaires de Bretagne, 1971);

Walter Redfern, "Political Novel and Art of Simplicity: Louis Guilloux's *La Maison du peuple*," *Journal of European Studies*, 1 (June 1971): 115-127;

Maurice Rieuneau, *Guerre et révolution dans le roman français, 1919-1939* (Paris: Klincksieck, 1974);

Geoffrey Strickland, "The Novels of Louis Guilloux: A Recommendation," *Cambridge Quarterly*, 5 (1970): 159-180.

Joseph Kessel

(31 January 1898-23 July 1979)

Alain D. Ranwez
Metropolitan State College

BOOKS: *La Steppe rouge* (Paris: Gallimard, 1922);

L'Equipage (Paris: Gallimard, 1923); translated as *Pilot and Observer* in *The Pure in Heart* (1928);

Au camp des vaincus, by Kessel and Georges Suarez (Paris: Gallimard, 1924);

Le onze mai, by Kessel and Suarez (Paris: Gallimard, 1924);

Mary de Cork (Paris: Gallimard, 1925);

Mémoires d'un commissaire du peuple (Paris: Champion, 1925);

Les Rois aveugles, by Kessel and Hélène Iswolsky (Paris: Editions de France, 1925); translated by G. and K. De Teissier as *Blinded Kings* (Garden City: Doubleday, Page, 1926; London: Heinemann, 1926);

Les Captifs (Paris: Gallimard, 1926);

Makhno et sa juive (Paris: Editions Eos, 1926);

Six Contes (Paris: Champion, 1926); republished as *Les Nuits cruelles* (Paris: Editions de France, 1932);

Le Journal d'une petite fille russe sous le bolchevisme (Abbeville: F. Paillart, 1926);

La Rage au ventre (Paris: Editions Eos, 1927);

Quatre Contes (Paris: Cahiers Libres, 1927);

Terre d'amour (Paris: Flammarion, 1927);

Les Cœurs purs (Paris: Gallimard, 1927); translated in *The Pure in Heart* (1928);

En Syrie (Paris: Editions Kra, 1927);

Nuits de princes (Paris: Editions de France, 1927); translated by Jack Kahane as *Princes of the Night* (New York: Macaulay, 1928; London: Richards, 1928);

The Pure in Heart (New York: Dodd, Mead, 1928; London: Gollancz, 1928)—comprises *L'Equipage* and *Les Cœurs purs;*

Belle de jour (Paris: Gallimard, 1928); translated by Geoffrey Wagner (New York: St. Martin's, 1962; London: Barker, 1962),

Nouveaux Contes (Paris: Cahiers Libres, 1928);

Dames de Californie (Paris: Hazan, 1928);

Les Nuits de Sibérie (Paris: Flammarion, 1928);

La Règle de l'homme (Paris: Gallimard, 1928);

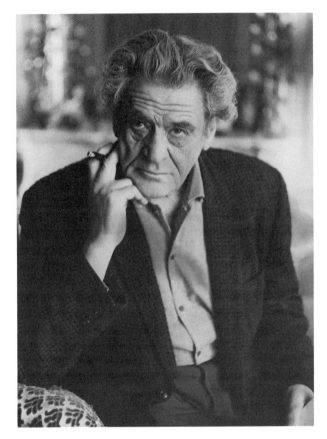

Joseph Kessel (photograph copyright © Jerry Bauer)

La Coupe fêlée. . . ; Un Drôle de Noël (Paris: Editions Lemarget, 1929);

Vent de sable (Paris: Editions de France, 1929);

Reine et Serre (Paris: Editions de France, 1929);

Secrets parisiens (Paris: Cahiers Libres, 1930);

Le Grand Sérail (Paris: Editions de France, 1930);

Le Coup de grâce (Paris: Editions de France, 1931); translated by Katherine Woods as *Sirocco* (New York: Random House, 1947);

Fortune carrée (Paris: Editions de France, 1932); translated by William Almon Wolff as *Crossroads* (New York & London: Putnam's, 1932; London: Grayson & Grayson, 1933);

Bas-fonds (Paris: Editions des Portiques, 1932);

Nuits de Montmartre (Paris: Editions de France, 1932);

Wagon-lit (Paris: Gallimard, 1932);

Marchés d'esclaves (Paris: Editions de France, 1933);

Les Enfants de la chance (Paris: Gallimard, 1934);

Stavisky, l'homme que j'ai connu (Paris: Gallimard, 1934);

Le Repos de l'équipage (Paris: Gallimard, 1935);

Une Balle perdue (Paris: Editions de France, 1935);

La Passante du Sans-Souci (Paris: Gallimard, 1936);

Hollywood, ville mirage (Paris: Gallimard, 1937);

La Rose de Java (Paris: Gallimard, 1937);

Mermoz (Paris: Gallimard, 1938);

L'Armée des ombres, chronique de la Résistance, edited by Jacques Schiffrin (Algiers: Charlot, 1943; New York: Pantheon, 1944); translated by Haakon Chevalier as *Army of Shadows* (London: Cresset, 1944; New York: Knopf, 1944); French version republished (Paris: Julliard, 1946);

Les Maudru (Paris: Julliard, 1945);

Le Bataillon du ciel (Paris: Julliard, 1947);

Terre de feu (Paris: Compagnie Parisienne du Livre, 1948);

Le Premier Amour de l'aspirant Dalleau (Paris: Fayard, 1949);

Le Tour du malheur, 4 volumes (Paris: Gallimard, 1950)—comprises *La Fontaine Médicis*, translated by Herma Briffault as *The Medici Fountain* (New York: St. Martin's, 1963; London: Barker, 1963); *L'Affaire Bernan*, translated by Charles Lam Markmann as *The Bernan Affair* (New York: St. Martin's, 1965); *Les Lauriers-roses;* and *L'Homme de plâtre;*

Le Procès des enfants perdus (Paris: Julliard, 1951);

La Nagaïka: Trois Récits (Paris: Julliard, 1951);

Au Grand Socco (Paris: Gallimard, 1952);

Les Amants du Tage (Geneva: Milieu du Monde, 1954);

La Piste fauve (Paris: Gallimard, 1954);

La Vallée des rubis (Paris: Gallimard, 1955); translated by Stella Rodway as *Mogok, The Valley of Rubies* (London: MacGibbon & Kee, 1960); republished as *The Valley of Rubies* (New York: McKay, 1961);

Témoin parmi les hommes, 6 volumes (volumes 1-3, Paris: Del Duca, 1956; volumes 4-6, Paris: Plon, 1968-1969)—comprises *Les Temps de l'espérance, Les Jours de l'aventure, L'Heure des châtiments, La Nouvelle Saison, Le Jeu du roi*, and *Les Instants de vérité;*

Hong Kong et Macao (Paris: Gallimard, 1957);

Le Lion (Paris: Gallimard, 1958); translated by Peter Green as *The Lion* (New York: Knopf, 1959; London: Hart-Davis, 1959);

Les Mains du miracle (Paris: Gallimard, 1960); translated by Denise Fulliot as *The Magic Touch* (London: Hart-Davis, 1961); translated by Helen Weaver and Leo Radites as *The Man With the Miraculous Hands* (New York: Farrar, Straus & Cudahy, 1961);

Inde, péninsule des dieux (Paris: Hachette, 1960);

Avec les alcooliques anonymes (Paris: Gallimard, 1960); translated by Frances Partridge as *The Enemy in the Mouth; An Account of Alcoholics Anonymous* (London: Hart-Davis, 1961); republished as *The Road Back: A Report on Alcoholics Anonymous* (New York: Knopf, 1962);

Tous n'étaient pas des anges (Paris: Plon, 1963); translated by Humphrey Hare as *They Weren't All Angels* (London: Hart-Davis, 1965; New York: McKay, 1965);

Discours de réception de M. Joseph Kessel à l'Académie Française et réponse de M. André Chamson (Paris: Gallimard, 1964);

Pour l'honneur (Paris: Plon, 1964);

Terre d'amour et de feu (Paris: Plon, 1966);

Les Cavaliers (Paris: Gallimard, 1967); translated by Patrick O'Brian as *The Horsemen* (London: Barker, 1968; New York: Farrar, Straus & Giroux, 1968);

Images, reportages, aventures (Paris: Plon, 1969);

Les Fils de l'impossible (Paris: Plon, 1970);

Des hommes (Paris: Gallimard, 1972);

Le Petit Âne blanc (Paris: Gallimard, 1973);

Les Temps sauvages (Paris: Gallimard, 1975).

Collection: *Œuvres complètes de Joseph Kessel*, 30 volumes (Paris: Rombaldi, 1975).

MOTION PICTURES: *Mayerling*, screenplay by Kessel and Irmgard von Cube, Pax, 1937;

Le Bataillon du ciel, screenplay by Kessel, Pathé-Cinéma, 1945;

Au Grand Balcon, screenplay by Kessel, CICC, and Raymond Borderie, 1949;

Le Grand Cirque, dialogues by Kessel, Imperator Films, 1949;

The Night of the Generals, screenplay by Kessel and Paul Dehn, Columbia, 1967;

Un Mur à Jérusalem, commentary by Kessel, Para-France, 1967; released in the United States as *A Wall in Jerusalem*, 1972.

OTHER: *Un Mur à Jérusalem, d'après le film de Frédéric Rossif, réalisé par Arthur Knobler*, commentary by Kessel (Paris: Denoël, 1968).

Joseph Kessel was a popular author of such adventure stories and best-sellers as *L'Equipage* (1923; translated as *Pilot and Observer*, 1928), *Belle de jour* (1928; translated, 1962), *Le Lion* (1958; translated as *The Lion*, 1959), and *Les Cavaliers* (1967; translated as *The Horsemen*, 1968). He was also a journalist and adventurer not unlike many of his fictional heroes. As both a personality and a writer Kessel might be considered a French counterpart to Ernest Hemingway. His characters, for the most part, are individuals seeking to fix existentially their rightful places in the world. He also has something in common with André Malraux, who was similarly driven to test himself through action, some of it dangerous, and in whose works adventure is a major theme. Kessel is, however, much less of a metaphysical novelist than Malraux and less concerned with the dynamics of history. Kessel is recognized along with Antoine de Saint-Exupéry as a pioneer of the literature of aviation. A powerful stylist, he combined a fierce social and historical realism with romantic themes. Emphasizing the individual, he avoided themes concerning the socioevolution of groups, and for this reason, he was for the most part ignored by French leftist critics of the late 1940s and early 1950s. His popularity with his readers, however, was great. In recognition of his literary merit he was awarded the Grand Prix du Roman de l'Académie Française in 1927 and elected to the Académie on 22 November 1962 as one of the few members not to have been born in France. He was also recipient of the Prix des Ambassadeurs (1958) and the Prix Rainier III de Monaco (1959). In 1965 he was honored with the Grande Médaille d'Or des Arts, Sciences et Lettres, and in 1977 he became Grand Officier de la Légion d'Honneur.

Kessel, the son of Samuel and Raissa Lesik Kessel, was born in 1898 in Clara, Argentina, where his father had volunteered his services as medical doctor in a Jewish agricultural community. The Kessels returned to the foothills of their native Ural mountains in Russia the following year and eventually settled in southern France (Lot-et-Garonne) in 1908. In order to enhance young Joseph's education upon his graduation from the lycée in Nice, the family moved to Paris, where Kessel attended the prestigious school Louis-le-Grand. After graduation he obtained a *licence* from the Sorbonne and took courses at the Conservatoire National d'Art Dramatique. In 1914 he initiated his journalistic career with the venerable Parisian daily *Journal des Débats*, abandoning his earlier dream of acting on stage. Too young to serve France at the outbreak of World War I, Kessel waited until 1916 to join the military and was immediately introduced to the world of aviation. As a young lieutenant pilot, he flew numerous combat missions for which he eventually received the Croix de Guerre and the Médaille Militaire. His military exploits make up the core of his second novel, *L'Equipage,* one of the earliest French aviation novels. It is a tale about the fervent sense of friendship and solidarity among pilots. It includes scenes of action–the sort that characterized World War I reconnaissance missions and aerial battles, in which planes flew very low and alone, and with only one or two crew members. But it is also concerned with the conflicts between duty and passion and the theme of sentimental treason. One of those who congratulated the author on it was Henry de Montherlant.

Immediately after the war Kessel volunteered to follow his squadron on an expedition to the Far East that enabled him to travel virtually around the world before he reached the age of twenty-one. It was during the course of this voyage that Kessel met Nadia-Alexandra Polizu-Michsunesti (better known as Sandi) in Shanghai. They married on 3 May 1921. She died of tuberculosis on 2 June 1928. The atmosphere of the Swiss sanatorium where she was treated for her illness became the major theme of *Les Captifs* (The Captives, 1926). It is a claustrophobic work in which the reader is confronted with acute existential solitude. It was this third novel which earned Kessel the Grand Prix du Roman.

Kessel's travels through China, Indochina, India, and Ceylon in 1919 inspired important articles for the daily press and nurtured his desire to write adventure stories. He was highly praised for his short work *Mary de Cork* (1925), set during the Sinn Fein uprising in Ireland. This moving tale traces the painful existence of two lovers torn apart by that national conflict. His first book, with a portrait of Kessel by his close friend, the writer and artist Jean Cocteau, had already received wide attention from the press. *La Steppe rouge* (The Red Steppes, 1922) centers on the Russian Revolution and reflects the author's consciousness of his ancestry. He returned to the revolution with his essay entitled *Les Rois aveugles* (1925; translated as *Blinded Kings*, 1926), a vivid historical panorama of Russia just prior to the fall of the Romanovs in 1916.

Catherine Deneuve and Jean Sorel in Luis Buñuel's 1968 film adaptation of Kessel's novel Belle de jour

In 1928 Kessel published *Belle de jour*. This novel's popularity was enhanced in 1968 when it was adapted for the screen under the direction of the Spanish director Luis Buñuel with Catherine Deneuve starring in the role of Séverine. This is a bitter tale about a married woman who can find refuge from daily life only by working in a brothel. In her desire to prostitute herself, Séverine reflects Kessel's characters, who prefer to live on the margins of insecurity and mystery in order to avoid the dreaded stagnation of life's routine. Like *L'Equipage*, this novel displays Kessel's skill at analyzing the nuances of sentimental and sexual attraction. It initially created a scandal, but the sales quickly surpassed 250,000 copies. Anticipating the novel's renewed popularity as a result of Buñuel's film, the Parisian publisher, Gallimard, brought out an edition of the novel with Deneuve's picture on the cover.

The confrontation between the individual and social norms is often taken up in Kessel's fictional work, as is the theme of battles between the spirit and the flesh. Kessel had lived these conflicts in his private life, and his feelings of guilt and remorse often appeared in his stories. For instance, he had angered and disappointed his parents by his first marriage and his choice to have no children; he had carried on love affairs while married, including the months when Sandi was dying in the sanatorium; he had squandered small fortunes and brought grief to Sandi and oth-

ers. Other behavior, such as taking opium and drinking heavily, inevitably caused problems. He had also witnessed family dramas, such as the liaison of his brother Lazare with a Gentile, Lazare's expulsion from home by Samuel Kessel, the birth of Lazare's illegitimate child, and finally his suicide. These conflicts are most explicit in his later novel *Le Tour du malheur* (1950). It consists of four volumes, entitled *La Fontaine Médicis* (translated as *The Medici Fountain*, 1963), *L'Affaire Bernan* (translated as *The Bernan Affair*, 1965), *Les Lauriers-roses* (Oleanders), and *L'Homme de plâtre* (The Plaster Man). This tetralogy portrays many characters and adventures involving war, ambition, love, glory, alcohol, drugs, and fervent moral torment. It is one of the most revealing portrayals in French of society between the two world wars. Kessel considered it his finest work and expected praise upon its publication. It was not well received by the critics, however, who at that time gave more attention to novelists such as Marguerite Duras, Boris Vian, Simone de Beauvoir, and Jean-Paul Sartre. Some columnists simply ignored it; others disdained the author's emphasis on adventure. Even François Mauriac, who had always admired Kessel, with whom he supported the Gaullist government, did not endorse the novel in the "Bloc-Notes" he wrote for the *Figaro*. Mauriac publicly apologized for this omission after the publication of Kessel's *Le Lion*.

In some ways, however, the 1930s were good years for Kessel. In 1934 he produced a portrait of Serge Alexandre Stavisky, *Stavisky, l'homme que j'ai connu* (Stavisky, the Man I Knew, 1934), concerning a swindler with government connections whose suicide or murder early in 1934 brought down the Radical Socialist government and was the occasion of riots. He spent much time during the decade observing the new aeropostal line, the Latécoère Company, which the young pilot-adventurer Jean Mermoz had helped establish between Europe and western Africa, and later in South America. The two men, who had much in common in their sense of daring, danger, unfailing devotion, and exuberance in life, became close friends. It was through that friendship that Kessel made the acquaintance of Antoine de Saint-Exupéry. Kessel's nonfiction work *Vent de sable* (Wind of Sand, 1929) is the result of personal experience with Mermoz and the flights Kessel made with him between Dakar and Casablanca. Along with Saint-Exupéry's *Courrier sud* (Southern Mail), it is one of the best documents in French on the early days of the French airmail routes and also affords much information on the situation of Europeans working in the 1920s in the dangerous zones of coastal northwest Africa, where dissident tribes still threatened life and property. Mermoz had fascinated Kessel with his perilous life, leaving no mission or task unfulfilled. Kessel admired the pilot's perpetual search for satisfaction and sense of individual accomplishment. On 7 December 1936, Mermoz's plane, the *Southern Cross,* disappeared off the African coast. Kessel was deeply affected by this loss and prepared his second biographical work in honor of his friend. *Mermoz* (1938) is an intimate portrayal of France's most important pilot of the period. This work, along with *L'Equipage* and *Vent de sable*, made Kessel the uncontested poet of early French aviation.

In 1934 Kessel traveled to Spain to cover the early rumblings of civil war. This experience offered him the plot for *Une Balle perdue* (Stray Bullet, 1935), which was admired by Hemingway; Kessel would later meet the American author in Spain in 1936. *Une Balle perdue* is a short novel depicting both the passion and the mediocrity visible in the Catalan uprisings. His accounts of the Spanish civil war for the French press represent well his journalistic style: Kessel emphasizes humanity over politics, portrayal over analysis, and stories of individuals over the collective sense of history. Kessel's vivid articles offered his readers an imperishable picture of an agonizing republican Spain. His commitment to journalism later led him to witness the British evacuation at Dunkirk, and he was the first reporter to write on the progress of the advancing German armies in June 1940 for the daily *Paris-Soir*. Kessel spent the first part of World War II in occupied France. He participated in the Resistance movement before he had to flee via Spain and Portugal in December 1942, when he was pursued by the Gestapo. Upon arrival in London he offered his services to General Charles de Gaulle; the general responded with a personal appeal that Kessel write an account of the French Resistance. *L'Armée des ombres* (1943; translated as *Army of Shadows*, 1944), based partly on Kessel's own experience and partly on what refugees told him in England, provides insight into the world of the French underground and a moving tribute to that movement. The account is true except in those instances when it was necessary to keep an individual's identity hidden to protect him or her. The documentary is made up of disconnected episodes, by which Kessel succeeds in conveying an awareness of the horror and violence of the Occupation.

During his stay in England Kessel and his nephew, Maurice Druon, who would himself become a prominent French novelist, composed "Le Chant des partisans" (Underground Song), which immediately became the anthem of the Resistance movement. The song was often broadcast over British radio and was played after de Gaulle's speech, at his personal request, on 6 June 1944. In 1962 the French government officially declared it to be a patriotic hymn. While in London Kessel also met Michèle Winifred O'Brien, who would become his third wife after his divorce from Catherine Gangardt, whom he had married 19 December 1939. In 1944 he joined the British Sussex Squadron, which helped prepare for the Allies' D day invasion through reconnaissance flights and secret missions, and, although age forty-six, he flew over occupied territory. Kessel was honored by the British government and also was awarded his second Croix de Guerre.

After the Liberation, Kessel began a long association with *France-Soir*. His assignments included covering the trial of Marshal Philippe Pétain for treason (this World War I hero and head of the collaborative Vichy government, 1940-1944, was sentenced to life imprisonment) and the Nuremberg trials. On 15 May 1948

Kessel was the first person to receive a visa for entry into the newly formed state of Israel. He became an ardent supporter of Israel in its struggle to exist, stressing his Judaism in his speech accepting entrance into the Académie Française and making known his commitment in *Terre d'amour et de feu* (Land of Love and Fire, 1966), a collection of articles which had originally appeared in *France-Soir*.

On other assignments and personal trips, Kessel traveled to India, Algeria, Burma, Hong Kong, Afghanistan, and East Africa. In Nairobi Kessel met the parents of a young girl who had befriended a lion cub to the point that they shared her baby bottle. In November 1957 he began composing a narrative based on her story. In December he told a journalist that it would not be an important book but would satisfy his contract with Gallimard, and that it could possibly be printed with illustrations as a children's book. Instead, he made of the story a full-fledged novel, *Le Lion*, which was a best-seller and which brought him international renown. Since the critical failure of *Le Tour du malheur*, Kessel had become better known as a newspaper reporter than a novelist. Consequently, he did not anticipate the success his new novel gave him. *Le Lion* received complimentary reviews even from the leftist press. With this charming tale Kessel became one of France's best-selling authors, along with Albert Camus, Saint-Exupéry, Malraux, and Françoise Sagan. As of 1980, *Le Lion* had sold over 1,771,600 copies. The English translation was warmly received in the United States, and almost all major publications reviewed it favorably.

Kessel again received critical acclaim for his last novel, *Les Cavaliers*, in 1967, although there was less unanimity among reviewers for the American press. It is an epic adventure which unfolds in Afghanistan: the young Uraz, star player of *buzkashi*, a game that resembles polo, breaks a leg just prior to the championship and then sets out on a journey back to his homeland during which he must triumph over nature.

Kessel wrote various travel books and published a book on Alcoholics Anonymous, an organization with which he kept close ties because of problems in his immediate family (his third wife, Michèle, was a lifelong alcoholic). He also coauthored, with Irmgard von Cube, a screenplay for the successful movie entitled *Mayerling* in 1937. Directed by Anatole Litvak, this cinematic adaptation of Claude Anet's *Mayerling* (Idyll's End, 1930) was well received by both the critics and the public. The film traces the true story of Rudolph of Austria and his tragic relationship with the young baroness Maria Vetsera. It starred Danielle Darieux and Charles Boyer, who had been a former schoolmate of Kessel's in Nice.

Although not widely translated into English, Kessel's work is important for its realistic portrayal of life during the two world wars, his sense of nostalgia for the heroic life, and the virtues of solidarity. His writings continue to celebrate the pursuit of higher rewards.

Kessel died in Paris suddenly, in 1979, after having had several warning bouts of heart and stomach trouble. He was surrounded by friends, even on the day of his death, but his relationship with his wife Michèle had deteriorated by then. Years earlier he had come to the conclusion that he would not be able to write anymore. *Les Temps sauvages* (Wild Times, 1975) had been his last best-seller, concluding his long series of semi-autobiographical fictional volumes. He was buried in Montparnasse Cemetery.

Interviews:

"Un Entretien avec Joseph Kessel," *Monde*, no. 9148, 14 June 1974, p. 1;

"Entretien avec Joseph Kessel: 'J'ai fait "le tour du malheur" parce que je n'ai jamais été d'accord avec moi,' " *Monde*, no. 9148, 14 June 1974, p. 20.

References:

Maryvonne Baurens, "Les Relations humaines dans le roman *L'Equipage* de Joseph Kessel," *Quaderni di Filologia e Lingue Romanze*, 4 (1982): 87-100;

Nicole Casanova, "L'Avion: l'ivresse du ciel," *Quotidien de Paris*, no. 1158, 16 August 1983, p. 27;

Richard Cobb, *Promenades: A Historian's Appreciation of Modern French Literature* (Oxford: Oxford University Press, 1980);

Yves Courrière, *Joseph Kessel; ou, Sur la piste du lion* (Paris: Plon, 1985);

Graham Daniels, "*L'Equipage*," *Le Français dans le Monde*, 79 (March 1971): 34-41;

Jean-Claude Perrier, "Wagons-lits: la poésie des grandes lignes," *Quotidien de Paris*, no. 1158, 16 August 1983, p. 28.

André Malraux

(3 November 1901-23 November 1976

Robert S. Thornberry
University of Alberta

BOOKS: *Lunes en papier* (Paris: Editions de la Galerie Simon, 1921);

La Tentation de l'Occident (Paris: Grasset, 1926); translated by Robert Hollander as *The Temptation of the West* (New York: Vintage Books, 1961);

Les Conquérants (Paris: Grasset, 1928); translated by Winifred Stephens Whale as *The Conquerors* (New York: Harcourt, Brace, 1929; London: Cape, 1929); enlarged edition of French version, with a postface by Malraux (Paris: Grasset, 1949); Whale's translation republished, with postface translated by Jacques Le Clercq (Boston: Beacon, 1956; London: Mayflower, 1956);

Royaume farfelu (Paris: Gallimard, 1928);

La Voie royale (Paris: Grasset, 1930); translated by Stuart Gilbert as *The Royal Way* (New York: Smith & Haas, 1935; London: Methuen, 1935);

Œuvres gothico-bouddhiques du Pamir (Paris: Gallimard, 1930);

La Condition humaine (Paris: Gallimard, 1933); translated by Haakon M. Chevalier as *Man's Fate* (New York: Smith & Haas, 1934); translated by Alastair MacDonald as *Storm in Shanghai* (London: Methuen, 1934); French version revised (Paris: Gallimard, 1946); *Storm in Shanghai* republished as *Man's Estate* (London: Methuen, 1948);

Le Temps du mépris (Paris: Gallimard, 1935); translated by Chevalier as *Days of Wrath* (New York: Random House, 1936); also published as *Days of Contempt* (London: Gollancz, 1936);

L'Espoir (Paris: Gallimard, 1937); translated by Gilbert and MacDonald as *Man's Hope* (New York: Random House, 1938); also published as *Days of Hope* (London: Routledge, 1938);

Les Noyers de l'Altenburg (Lausanne: Editions du Haut-Pays, 1943; Paris: Gallimard, 1948); translated by A. W. Fielding as *The Walnut Trees of Altenburg* (London: Lehmann, 1952);

Esquisse d'une psychologie du cinéma (Paris: Gallimard, 1946);

Scènes choisies (Paris: Gallimard, 1946);

N'était-ce donc que cela? (Paris: Editions du Pavois, 1946);

Dessins de Goya du musée du Prado (Geneva: Skira, 1947); translated by Edward Sackville-West as *Goya Drawings from the Prado* (London: Horizon, 1947);

Psychologie de l'art, 3 volumes (Geneva: Skira, 1947-1949)–comprises *Le Musée imaginaire, La Creation artistique*, and *La Monnaie de l'absolu;* translated by Gilbert as *The Psychology of Art*, 3 volumes (New York: Pantheon, 1949-1950) –comprises *Museum without Walls, The Creative Art*, and *The Twilight of the Absolute;* French version revised and enlarged as *Les Voix du silence* (Paris: Gallimard, 1951); translated by Gilbert as *The Voices of Silence* (Garden City: Doubleday, 1953; London: Secker & Warburg, 1954); part 1 of *Les Voix du silence* revised as *Le Musée imaginaire* (Paris: Gallimard, 1965); translated by Gilbert and Francis Price as *Museums without Walls* (Garden City: Doubleday, 1967; London: Secker & Warburg, 1967);

The Case for De Gaulle. A Dialogue between André Malraux and James Burnham, sections by Malraux translated by Spencer Byard (New York: Random House, 1948);

Saturne: Essai sur Goya (Paris: Gallimard, 1950); translated by C. W. Chilton as *Saturn; An Essay on Goya* (New York & London: Phaidon, 1957); French version revised as *Saturne, le destin, l'art et Goya* (Paris: Gallimard, 1978);

Le Musée imaginaire de la sculpture mondiale, 3 volumes (Paris: Gallimard, 1952-1954)–comprises *Le Musée imaginaire de la sculpture mondiale, Des bas-reliefs aux grottes sacrées*, and *Le Monde chrétien;*

Du musée (Paris: Editions Estienne, 1955);

La Métamorphose des dieux (Paris: Gallimard, 1957); translated by Gilbert as *The Metamor-*

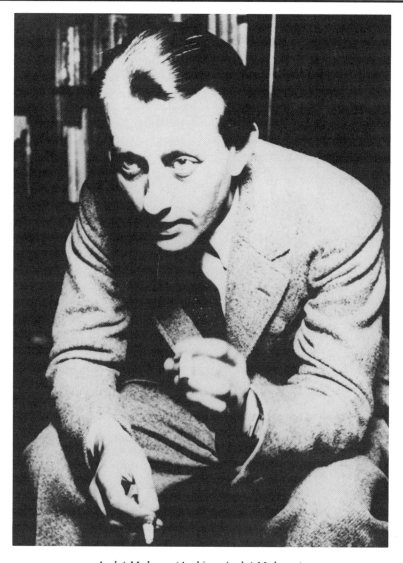

André Malraux (Archives André Malraux)

phosis of the Gods (Garden City: Doubleday, 1960; London: Secker & Warburg, 1960); French version revised and enlarged as *La Métamorphose des dieux*, 3 volumes (Paris: Gallimard, 1974-1977)–comprises *Le Surnaturel, L'Irréel,* and *L'Intemporel;*

Antimémoires (Paris: Gallimard, 1967); translated by Terence Kilmartin as *Antimemoirs* (London: Hamilton, 1968); translation republished as *Anti-Memoirs* (New York: Holt, Rinehart & Winston, 1968); French version revised and enlarged (Paris: Gallimard, 1972);

Le Triangle noir (Paris: Gallimard, 1970);

Les Chênes qu'on abat . . . (Paris: Gallimard, 1971); translated by Irene Clephane as *Fallen Oaks* (London: Hamilton, 1972); translation revised by Linda Asher as *Felled Oaks* (New York: Holt, Rinehart & Winston, 1972);

Oraisons funèbres (Paris: Gallimard, 1971);

Roi, je t'attends à Babylone . . . , illustrations by Salvador Dalí (Geneva: Skira, 1973);

Paroles et écrits politiques (1947-1972) (Paris: Plon, 1973);

Lazare (Paris: Gallimard, 1974); translated by Kilmartin as *Lazarus* (New York: Holt, Rinehart & Winston, 1977; London: Macdonald & Jane's, 1977);

La Tête d'obsidienne (Paris: Gallimard, 1974); translated and annotated by June Guicharnaud and Jacques Guicharnaud as *Picasso's Mask* (New York: Holt, Rinehart & Winston, 1976; London: Macdonald & Jane's, 1976);

Hôtes de passage (Paris: Gallimard, 1975);

La Corde et les souris (Paris: Gallimard, 1976);

Le Miroir des limbes, 2 volumes (Paris: Gallimard, 1976);

Et sur la terre . . . , illustrations by Marc Chagall (N.p.: Editions Maeght, 1977);

L'Homme précaire et la littérature (Paris: Gallimard, 1977);

De Gaulle par Malraux (Paris: Le Club du Livre, 1979).

Collection: *Œuvres,* 4 volumes, illustrated by André Masson, Chagall, and Alexandre Alexeieff (Paris: Gallimard, 1970).

MOTION PICTURE: *Sierra de Teruel,* screenplay by Malraux, Spain, 1938.

OTHER: Charles Maurras, *Mademoiselle Monk,* introduction by Malraux (Paris: Stock, 1923);

"D'une jeunesse européenne," in *Ecrits,* by Malraux, André Chamson, Jean Grenier, Henri Petit, and Pierre-Jean Jouve (Paris: Grasset, 1927), pp. 129-153;

Charles Clément, *Méditerranée,* preface by Malraux (Paris: Editions Jean Budry, 1931);

D. H. Lawrence, *L'Amant de Lady Chatterley,* translated by Roger Cornaz, preface by Malraux (Paris: Gallimard, 1932);

William Faulkner, *Sanctuaire,* translated by R. N. Raimbault and Henri Delgove, preface by Malraux (Paris: Gallimard, 1933);

Andrée Viollis, *Indochine S.O.S.,* preface by Malraux (Paris: Gallimard, 1935);

J. Bergeret and H. Grégoire, *Messages personnels,* "letter-preface" by Malraux (Bordeaux: Bière, 1945);

Michel Florisonne, *Van Gogh et les peintres d'Auvers chez le docteur Gachet,* includes "Fidélité," foreword by Malraux (Paris: Amour de l'Art, 1952);

Manès Sperber, *. . . qu'une larme dans l'océan,* translated by Blanche Gideon, preface by Malraux (Paris: Calmann-Lévy, 1952);

Tout l'œuvre peint de Léonard de Vinci, preface by Malraux (Paris: Gallimard, 1952);

Tout Vermeer de Delft, preface by Malraux (Paris: Gallimard, 1952);

Général Pierre Elie Jacquot, *Essai de stratégie occidentale,* prefatory "letter" by Malraux (Paris: Gallimard, 1953);

Albert Olliver, *Saint-Just ou la force des choses,* preface by Malraux (Paris: Gallimard, 1954);

Louis Guilloux, *Le Sang noir,* preface by Malraux (Paris: Club du Meilleur Livre, 1955);

Lazar and Isis, *Israël,* preface by Malraux (Lausanne: Editions Clairefontaine, 1955);

André Parrot, *Sumer* (Paris: Gallimard, 1960);

Pierre Lherminier, *L'Art du cinéma de Méliès à Chabrol,* includes "Ouverture," preface by Malraux (Paris: Seghers, 1960);

Louise Lévêque de Vilmorin, *Poèmes,* preface by Malraux (Paris: Gallimard, 1970);

Edmond Michelet, *La Querelle de la fidélité,* preface by Malraux (Paris: Plon, 1971);

José Bergamín, *Le Clou brûlant,* preface by Malraux (Paris: Plon, 1972);

Louis-Henri Boussel, ed., *Livre du souvenir* (on Charles de Gaulle), introduction by Malraux (Paris: Club Iris, 1973);

Maria van Rysselberghe, *Les Cahiers de la Petite Dame: 1918-1929,* Cahiers André Gide, Volume 4, preface by Malraux (Paris: Gallimard, 1973);

Pierre Bockel, *L'Enfant du rire,* preface by Malraux (Paris: Grasset, 1973);

Georges Bernanos, *Journal d'un curé de campagne,* preface by Malraux (Paris: Plon, 1974);

Jean Guéhenno and Romain Rolland, *L'Indépendance de l'esprit* (correspondence), preface by Malraux (Paris: Albin Michel, 1975);

Suzanne Chantal, *Le Cœur battant: Josette Clotis-André Malraux,* prefatory "letter" by Malraux (Paris: Grasset, 1976);

Martine de Courcel, *Malraux, être et dire,* includes "Néocritique," postface by Malraux (Paris: Plon, 1976).

André Malraux is one of the most misunderstood French writers of the twentieth century, both in his native land and in much of the English-speaking world. Despite numerous publications devoted to him, he remains, somewhat paradoxically, an unappreciated and often maligned author. Eulogized in the most extravagant terms by his admirers ("the last Renaissance man," "the intellectual as man of action"), denounced in a most vehement manner by his detractors ("a mythomaniac," "the only authentic French fascist"), he is an enigmatic, elusive, contradictory figure. There are many reasons for this.

First, as was the case with many of his contemporaries, particularly T. E. Lawrence, who intrigued Malraux to the utmost degree, his real significance, his originality, and his genius have been obscured by the legend surrounding his personal and political life: his adventures in Indochina, Yemen, Persia, and other parts of Asia, his polemic with the exiled Trotsky, his many anti-Fascist activities throughout the 1930s, his leadership of the Escadrille España and the Escadrille

Malraux with his father, 1917 (Archives André Malraux)

André Malraux during the first seven months of the Spanish civil war, his roles in the Resistance, his political *volte-face* in 1946, his special relationship with Gen. Charles de Gaulle, his career as minister of information and, later, minister for cultural affairs, his encounters with Nehru, Mao, Senghor and Picasso, and so forth.

Second, Malraux, who was an original and profound thinker, did not develop his ideas into a philosophical system. His writings defy conventional classifications, as the prefix in his title *Antimémoires* (1967; translated as *Antimemoirs*, 1968) clearly indicates, and, in addition to composing novels and essays, he contributed to a revival of such neglected genres as the preface, the epigram, the funeral oration, and the political speech. Most of the labels attached to him at differing stages in his career–cubist/surrealist, *écrivain engagé* (committed writer), art historian–are clearly inadequate and merely heighten the confusion. Like one of his mentors, the German philoso-

pher Friedrich Nietzsche, he preferred the aphorism, the epigram, and the essay to the logically coherent arguments of traditional Western philosophy, and his distrust of Cartesian reason was counterbalanced by an unrelenting appeal to lucidity, the cardinal Malraux virtue. An aversion to ideology, doctrine, and dogma, for closed systems in general, is a defining characteristic of Malraux's thought.

Third, Malraux's style is associative, evocative, and elliptical; its rhetoric has more affinities with the prose poem than with discursive logic, and, unfortunately, many of its subtle cadences virtually defy translation. Though Malraux has been well served by several translators, notably Haakon Chevalier and Terence Kilmartin, some of his most memorable sayings and pronouncements often seem sibylline when rendered into English. This barrier has undoubtedly made his incantatory prose somewhat inaccessible to those who read no French, and it probably accounts, at least in part, for his relative unpopularity in Great Britain, in particular.

Fourth, because he wrote about the "absurd" (a word he reintroduced into the French language), "the death of God," and the subsequent death of *given* values, Malraux is often presented as a forerunner of the atheist existentialism that flourished in France in the late 1940s and 1950s. While this identification is partly correct, it has not always been beneficial to his reputation, as it tends to blur the distinctions between his thought and, for example, that of Jean-Paul Sartre. In fact, the amalgam Malraux-Sartre-Camus tends to reduce Malraux to the status of a less gifted precursor of Sartrian philosophy whereas in fact his central preoccupations were not with freedom and bad faith, but with fraternity and metamorphosis. While the vogue for existentialism was at its height in France, Malraux was devising other responses to the absurd which, he often insisted, was not a philosophy or an answer to the human condition but, on the contrary, the starting point for a series of questions on the dichotomy between life and values, between being (*être*) and doing (*faire*).

Finally, Malraux's political evolution and his often contradictory allegiances–he has been described as anarchist, anticolonialist, Marxist, anti-Fascist, liberal, Communist (first a Trotskyist, then a Stalinist), Fascist, nationalist, Gaullist, reactionary, conservative–have generated much confusion and spawned many ephemeral but damaging pamphlets that have detracted from his stature as a writer of international repute. Though the man who defended Communist leaders imprisoned by Hitler may seem to have little in common with the minister who denounced communism just a decade later, the two positions are not necessarily incompatible.

It would hardly be an exaggeration to claim that Malraux's reputation as a writer, both in France and in the English-speaking world, rests almost exclusively upon the six novels he published from 1928 to 1943. Nevertheless, in terms of his total literary output (approximately thirty major works), this fifteen-year period, in which he wrote the two masterpieces most often associated with him, *La Condition humaine* (1933; translated as *Man's Fate*, 1934), and *L'Espoir* (1937; translated as *Man's Hope*, 1938), represents but a brief and brilliant hiatus in a career devoted as much to the essay form as to fiction. When his first novel, *Les Conquérants*, appeared in Paris in 1928 (and was translated as *The Conquerors* in 1929), Mal-

raux was primarily considered an obscure diagnostician of European decadence in the aftermath of World War I; and when fascism was finally defeated in the second conflagration to engulf Europe in a third of a century Malraux had abandoned the novel form and devoted himself to two ambitious projects on art and autobiography. On the other hand, from the early volumes of *Psychologie de l'art* (1947-1949; translated as *The Psychology of Art*, 1949-1950), a revised version of which appeared as *Les Voix du silence* in 1951 (translated as *The Voices of Silence*, 1953) down to the volumes of *La Métamorphose des dieux*, originally published in 1957, translated as *The Metamorphosis of the Gods* in 1960, and substantially rewritten in the 1970s, Malraux developed his concept of the "museum without walls" and sought to embrace the arts of mankind in a totalizing synthesis made possible by the perfection of photographic reproduction. On the other hand, with *Antimémoires*, which was to become, after substantial additions and amendments, part of the two-volume *Le Miroir des limbes* (1976), he defied conventional autobiography and re-created the genre by raising it to the level of philosophical discourse. Furthermore, Malraux's posthumously published works–*L'Homme précaire et la littérature* (Precarious Man and Literature, 1977), the only full-length study he ever wrote on literature, his reflections on numerous individual authors and painters; and the long opus on T. E. Lawrence, soon to be published in a Pléiade edition–are further proof of his predilection for the essay form.

Georges-André Malraux, the only child of Fernand Malraux and Berthe Lamy Malraux, was born on 3 November 1901 at 53, rue Damrémont in the Montmartre district of Paris. His parents, who had married in 1900, were separated in 1905 and divorced ten years later. His father remarried and by his second wife, Lilette Godard (d. 1946), had two sons, Roland, who died in 1945 during the deportation, and Claude, who was executed by the Germans in 1944. Malraux's relationship with his younger half brothers is shrouded by the same combination of privacy and discretion that was to characterize all his personal relationships with family and friends. Raised by his grandmother, his mother, and an aunt, the young Malraux grew up in relative comfort in the somewhat dreary Paris suburb of Bondy, where, in October 1906, he began to attend the Ecole de Bondy, a private school on the rue Saint-Denis. There he met Louis Chevasson, who was to accompany him to

Malraux at the time of his military service in Strasbourg (Archives André Malraux)

Indochina in the 1920s, and who remained a life-long friend. Malraux was an extremely precocious student whose omnivorous reading extended well beyond the orthodoxy of the school curriculum. At a very early age, he devoured the works of Hugo, Balzac, and Sir Walter Scott and years later he often acknowledged the impact that *Les Trois Mousquetaires* (by Alexandre Dumas père) and *Bouvard et Pécuchet* (by Flaubert) had upon his imagination. As of Oc- tober 1915 he went to the Ecole Primaire Secondaire (renamed Lycée Turgot after World War II) on the Rue de Turbigo and, when he was seventeen, found employment in the service of an entrepreneurial book dealer, publisher, and bibliophile, René-Louis Doyon. Impressed by Malraux's already vast knowledge of literature, which by that time embraced Baudelaire, Rimbaud, and Lautréamont as well as such older contemporaries as André Gide, Paul Claudel, and

André Suarès, Doyon employed him as a *chineur*, a sort of broker who combed the stalls along the banks of the Seine and secondhand bookshops in search of first editions, out-of-print titles, and other rare items. Malraux's "pay" was determined by the value of whatever treasures he managed to unearth. It is interesting to point out that Malraux's passion for the printed word, first as *chineur*, then as author and editor, was his primary means of livelihood for most of his life, and that he never "worked" (in the pedestrian sense of the word) at anything else.

In 1920-1921 he helped Doyon launch an ambitious but short-lived series of first editions called La Connaissance by editing two volumes of texts by Jules Laforgue (1860-1887). Their excellence brought him to the attention of another publisher, Lucien Kra, whose Editions du Sagittaire, a series of luxury books with woodcut illustrations, were intended to appeal to wealthy bibliophiles eager to find reliable means of combating the inflation and devaluations of the post-World War I period. From 1920 to 1922, Malraux edited various books by poets: Remy de Gourmont, Laurent Tailhade, Alfred Jarry, Pierre Reverdy, and Max Jacob; in 1926-1927, after the Indochina adventure, in partnership with Louis Chevasson and the Greek-born engraver Demetrios Galanis, he launched two series, A la Sphère, which published texts by François Mauriac and Paul Morand, and later, Aux Aldes, which printed luxury editions of works by Paul Valéry, Jean Giraudoux, André Gide, and Valery Larbaud. In 1928 Gallimard appointed him director for special Nouvelle Revue Française editions; he worked intermittently on numerous Gallimard projects–the most ambitious of which was an edition of the complete works of André Gide–until the outbreak of the Spanish civil war.

As editor of several successful series of luxury volumes of literature, Malraux had displayed an extreme sensitivity to all the technical components of book production, notably design, typography, and the importance of illustrations. His knowledge of the profession was perhaps equaled only by an all-consuming passion for art: "J'ai vécu dans l'art depuis mon adolescence" (I have lived in art since my adolescence), he reminded an interviewer in 1952. Though he had little or no formal training in art history, he would attend lectures at the Musée Guimet (which houses France's most extensive collection of Asian art) and the Ecole des Etudes Orientales

and assiduously visit the many museums and galleries of Paris. His contributions to the numerous avant-garde literary magazines that proliferated in the French capital brought the young Malraux into contact with such writers as Pierre Reverdy, Laurent Tailhade, Blaise Cendrars, and André Salmon, and soon afterward he sought out several of the artists he most admired: James Ensor, whom he went to visit in Ostend; the fauvist painter André Derain; and the poet-painter Max Jacob, to whom he dedicated his first book *Lunes en papier* (Paper Moons), which had appeared in 1921. This unusual tale, reviewed in the *Nouvelle Revue Française* and much appreciated by André Breton, leader of the burgeoning surrealist movement, had woodcuts by the cubist painter Fernand Léger and bore the following curious subtitle: "Petit livre où l'on trouve la relation de quelques luttes peu connues des hommes ainsi que celle d'un voyage parmi des objets familiers mais étrangers, le tout selon la vérité" (A little book in which are related some of man's lesser-known struggles and also a journey among familiar, but strange objects, all told in a truthful manner). *Lunes en papier* (which has never been translated into English) is a highly derivative piece of writing, which is understandable enough when one recalls that Malraux was nineteen when he wrote it. An indirect tribute to Max Jacob, the poet who had inspired it, it also bears the imprint of Hoffmann, Guillaume Apollinaire, and, more interestingly, Lautréamont, the subject of one of Malraux's earliest incursions into literary criticism. His article on Lautréamont's work, "La Genèse des *Chants de Maldoror*," appeared in the monthly review *Action*, and it was at a dinner celebrating the occasion that Malraux met the woman who was to become his first wife: Clara Goldschmidt, the daughter of a well-to-do Franco-German Jewish family. They were married on 21 October 1921.

"Si je ne vous avais pas rencontrée, j'aurais aussi bien pu être un rat de bibliothèque" (If I hadn't met you, I could have been just a bookworm), Malraux is alleged to have confessed to Clara, a highly intelligent, liberated woman who shared her companion's enthusiasm for art, literature, and the cinema. Together they discovered German and Flemish expressionism, Negro art, avant-garde films, and together they exulted in the simple pleasures of living in postwar Paris: frequenting cafés and restaurants, galleries, museums, and–the stock exchange. The couple indulged their love of travel by visiting Italy,

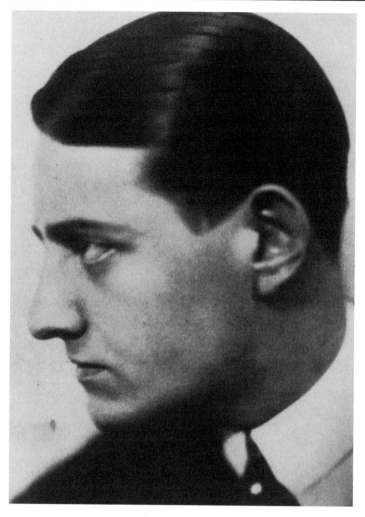

Malraux, circa 1920 (courtesy of Bernard Grasset)

Spain, Greece, Germany, and Czechoslovakia. However, their extravagant life-style quickly exhausted the funds, mostly Clara's. They had invested in stocks, and when the market suddenly collapsed, and with it their shares in Mexican mining stock, they were ruined. It was shortly after this financial disaster that Malraux decided to live out the dream he had been nourishing for some time: a journey to Asia, to explore the vestiges of the civilizations that fascinated him, specifically the Khmer monuments in Cambodia. He had already done much reading and research, and it was in fact his amazing knowledge of Khmer civilization that prompted the minister of colonies, Albert Sarraut, to recognize his proposed expedition.

In the late fall of 1923 André and Clara Malraux left Europe, that cemetery of "dead conquerors," in search of adventure, archaeological remains, and financial gain. In December of that same year, shortly after their arrival in French Indochina, where they joined their friend Louis Chevasson, they embarked upon an archaeological mission with some measure of official backing. Following the Ancient Royal Way that led through the jungle of Cambodia, from the Damreng mountains to Angkor, they eventually discovered, at Banteay Srei, a ruined Khmer temple from which they removed invaluable bas-reliefs. This act, by no means an uncommon occurrence, did not then have the same stigma attached to it as it has today, but, all the same, in Malraux's case, it had many unexpected repercussions. Caught in possession of stolen sculptures, he was arrested, tried, and sentenced to three years of imprisonment, a sentence that was appealed and ultimately dismissed after he had been subjected to several months of "house arrest." Clara Malraux had played an important part in bringing about this turn of events. As she recounts in her memoirs, she feigned suicide and was allowed to return to Paris, where she enlisted the moral support of writers as diverse as Gide, André Maurois, Mauriac, Jean Paulhan, Philippe Soupault, Louis Aragon, Doyon, Jacob, and André Breton, who signed a petition published in the *Nouvelles Littéraires* on 6 September 1924. A short article by Breton, "Pour André Malraux," had appeared in the same journal on 16 August.

The trial and the appeal had their share of farcical moments, with references to Rimbaud, poetic license, the immaturity and impetuousness of youth, Malraux's alleged Bolshevik connections and anarchist leanings, Clara Malraux's German origins, and so forth. At the same time it became increasingly obvious to Malraux that, irrespective of his deed, he was being tried and judged by representatives of a corrupt colonial administration bent upon punishing him for a crime perpetrated by many of its own high-ranking officials. In addition, the flagrant miscarriage of justice enabled Malraux to perceive a fundamental discrepancy between the so-called ideals of colonialism, Europe's "civilizing mission," and the cynical betrayal of the same ideals by the decadent French functionaries.

After a short visit to France in the winter of 1924-1925, mainly to raise funds and support for the struggle that lay ahead, Malraux returned to Saigon to found a newspaper, the *Indochine: Journal quotidien de rapprochement franco-annamite* (17 January-14 August 1925), later called the *Indochine Enchaînée* (4 November 1925-24 February 1926), which, in championing Annamite nationalism, was one of the first opposition papers to combat the oppressive realities of French colonial rule. With the help of a highly committed French lawyer named Paul Monin, and in agreement with Paris weeklies such as *Nouvelles Littéraires* and *Candide*, Malraux assembled an array of articles covering many subjects, from politics to art. Though only in his mid-twenties, Malraux wrote courageous, caustic editorials attacking and satirizing Maurice Cognacq, the unscrupulous governor of Indochina, and other influential officials. An important phase in the gradual awakening of his political consciousness had taken place.

When the *Indochine Enchaînée* finally folded in early 1926, Malraux vowed that he would never desert the Annamite cause, and, prior to his departure for Paris, he promised to continue the struggle in France. However, as most of his biographers have stressed, his promise was never

fulfilled, unless one interprets two articles–an indictment of military atrocities inflicted upon the population of Indochina ("S.O.S.–Les Procès d'Indochine" [S.O.S.–The Indochina Trial], *Marianne*, 11 October 1933) and his eloquent preface to the French journalist Andrée Viollis's book *Indochine S.O.S.* (1935)–as evidence of his continuing commitment. As was to be a pattern in his later life, Malraux was torn between two distinct, though not necessarily, incompatible, notions of *engagement*: that of the man of action, directly involved in a specific struggle, and that of the intellectual, more concerned with the origins and long-term implications of that same struggle. Prior to 1932, when Malraux's numerous anti-Fascist activities began to nurture (but never dominate) much of his writing, his political pronouncements were infrequent. During that same period, however, after his initial encounter with Asia, he wrote two essays, *La Tentation de l'Occident* (1926; translated as *The Temptation of the West*, 1961), and "D'une jeunesse européenne" (About European Youth, published in a 1927 volume entitled *Ecrits*), three novels, *Les Conquérants*, *La Voie royale* (1930; translated as *The Royal Way*, 1935), and *La Condition humaine*, many book reviews and articles that appeared in the *Nouvelle Revue Française*, and, just as important, parts of the much neglected *Royaume farfelu* (Whimsical Kingdom, 1928), dedicated to Louis Chevasson.

It would be ill-advised to dismiss Malraux's early attempts at writing short stories–*Lunes en papier*, *Royaume farfelu*, and fragments from unpublished works conceived in a similar vein that appeared in literary periodicals in the 1920s–as the frivolous failures of a precocious and ambitious yet inexperienced young author. After all, the two collections were republished with Malraux's consent in the handsome four-volume edition of his *Œuvres* (1970), with original engravings by Marc Chagall, André Masson, and Alexandre Alexeieff. This distinction was not conferred upon *Le Temps du mépris* (1935), a minor yet well-known novel translated into many languages (into English as *Days of Wrath*, 1936) and considered insignificant by both Malraux and his estate. The literary qualities of *Royaume farfelu* may be debatable, but, as Cecil Jenkins has emphasized in *André Malraux* (1972), virtually all the components of Malraux's vision are already present in this brief piece: "The cosmic ring, the pessimism, the exoticism, the violence, the insects, the image of blindness, the suffering, and the immanence of death . . . and the story itself–oddly foreshadowing Vincent Berger's Eastern adventure in *Les Noyers de l'Altenburg*–shows that Malraux's basic fable of arduous adventure and defeat is already in place." As much of *Royaume farfelu* was composed and parts of it already published in periodicals before Malraux's voyage to Indochina, one must beware of overstating the significance and relevance of that adventure to his basic fable. The voyage may be said to have crystallized, rather than determined, elements of his artistic vision.

In contrast, the intellectual content of both *La Tentation de l'Occident* and "D'une jeunesse européenne" bears the distinct imprint of Malraux's confrontation with the cultures of East Asia, China in particular, which provided the backdrop to his first three novels. *La Tentation de l'Occident*, his first major work, which was dedicated to his wife–"A vous, Clara, en souvenir du temple de Banteaï-Srey" (To you, Clara, in remembrance of the temple at Banteay Srei)–has been described by some critics as an epistolary novel. Essentially an exchange of letters between a young Chinese man, Ling, traveling in Europe, and a young Frenchman, A. D., traveling in China, the dialogue enables Malraux to compare and contrast the Western sensibility with its Eastern counterpart. The epistolary form provides him with flexibility in handling a wide variety of topics, and the two differing points of view obviate the subjective impressions of a diary or travelogue. Malraux is less interested, however, in events and places than in ideas, and, despite numerous passages of lyrical beauty, the book tends to be somewhat cerebral. A. D.'s contribution is much longer than Ling's, but the "dialogue" is less between an Easterner and a Westerner than between two disembodied voices that represent conflicting tendencies within Malraux's own mind.

Nevertheless, a fairly coherent line of reasoning may be distilled from the diversity of ideas expressed in *La Tentation de l'Occident*. Malraux's central concern is the moral and spiritual decadence of the West, whose values have been discredited, if not utterly shattered, by the debacle of World War I; and, in this respect, his general indictment of European civilization can be related to other intellectual, artistic, and social phenomena–Dadaism, surrealism, the resurgence of Catholicism, the forging of a new society in the U.S.S.R.–that marked the 1920s. Malraux's stance, however, was nonideological and nondoctrinal. He discerned in European man a fatal preoccupa-

tion with the individual, with selfhood, with a new demon, the subconscious, that he quickly associated with the absurd. In a characteristically memorable epigram–"After the death of the Sphinx, Oedipus attacks himself"–Malraux anticipates and deplores twentieth-century man's obsession with "interiority," the modern abyss. Both anti-Freudian and anti-Proustian–and explicitly so in his later pronouncements–he saw in his contemporaries' fascination with the self an inwardly spiraling, destructive force.

Malraux's own position was certainly not dualistic. *La Tentation de l'Occident* is not a simplistic valorization of the Orient at the expense of everything Western, even though the possibility of looking to Asia as a model for spiritual resurgence is one of the temptations suggested by the title. Malraux expresses the same idea more forcefully, in allegorical terms, when he prophesies the imminent reversal of colonial practices: Europe shall no longer impose herself and her values on an unwilling world, but shall in turn be transformed by an influx of aesthetic values from other cultures, not just from China. A. D. points out that the variety of paintings assembled in the Louvre by Napoleon had already profoundly disturbed a generation of artists "who were most sure of themselves," and he predicts that this malaise will spread to Europeans, who are weary of themselves, their crumbling individualism, and their "delicate framework of negation," and eventually generate new forms from the ferment. "Mais ce n'est plus l'Europe ni le passé qui envahit la France en ce début de siècle, c'est le monde qui envahit l'Europe, le monde avec tout son passé, ses offrandes amoncelées de formes vivantes ou mortes de méditations. . . . Ce grand spectacle troublé qui commence, mon cher Ami, c'est une des tentations de l'Occident" (But it is not Europe or the past which is invading France as this century begins, it is the world which is invading Europe with all its present and its past, its heap of offerings of living and dead forms, its meditations. . . . This great, troubled drama which is beginning, dear friend, is one of the temptations of the West).

Les Conquérants marks a turning point in the history of twentieth-century French literature: the exotic China of Claude Farrère, Pierre Loti, and Paul Morand gave way to the fermentation of prerevolutionary China, with its internecine struggles between nationalists and Communists, and the additional complications wrought by the machinations of terrorists, anarchists, and ideolog-

Clara and André Malraux in Indochina, 1923 (Archives Clara Malraux)

ically uncommitted adventurers. The novel was inspired by the aftermath of an event that occurred in Shanghai on 30 May 1925 (when Malraux was still in Saigon). A group of Chinese students, incensed by the existence of European-dominated "concessions," demonstrated against the foreign-controlled police of the International Settlement in Shanghai. After issuing warnings, the police opened fire, and the ensuing casualties–twelve dead, numerous wounded–had enormous repercussions: additional demonstrations, on a much vaster scale, against foreign usurpers, the boycotting of foreign goods, a total boycott of Hong Kong, and, in the long run the most damaging loss of all, the total discrediting of Western democratic institutions. A great revolutionary surge, which was mainly nationalist in inspira-

tion, swept through China, uniting every class behind it. *Les Conquérants* is set in the brief period from 25 June to 18 August 1925, when Malraux, as editor of the *Indochine*, was receiving dispatches and communiqués on the Chinese government's decree to paralyze Hong Kong, bastion of British imperialism and Western capitalism. It is little wonder then that many of his contemporaries, struck by the many vivid passages of description, should have viewed the novel as a kind of reportage. This was a significant factor in the growth of the myth of Malraux *témoin* (the witness), merely chronicling events he happened to have observed.

Serialized in the *Nouvelle Revue Française* from March to June 1928 before Grasset published the novel later that year, *Les Conquérants* provoked widespread commentary, ranging from outright condemnation to effusive praise. On 8 June 1929, at the Union pour la Vérité, it was the object of a memorable debate involving Jean Guéhenno, Julien Benda, Emmanuel Berl, Gabriel Marcel, and Malraux. Two years later the exiled Trotsky read the novel on the island of Prinkipo, just off the coast of Turkey. His reactions to it and Malraux's perceptive reply, in which he clarified his intentions and defended his aesthetics, appeared in the April 1931 issue of the *NRF*. The debate over *Les Conquérants* was revived in 1949 when Grasset reissued a "definitive" version of the novel, with the addition of an important "postface" by the author. Malraux, who had excised many political references, was singularly dismissive of "ce roman d'adolescent" (this young man's novel). He explained that its success was due less to his portrayal of episodes of the Chinese revolution than to his creation of a new hero "en qui s'unissent l'aptitude à l'action, la culture et la lucidité" (who combined a talent for action, culture and lucidity).

This new hero, or "new man," as both Pierre Drieu La Rochelle and Emmanuel Berl described him, is Pierre Garine, and much of the novel revolves around him. Garine, who was born in Switzerland, is "director of propaganda" and one of several Europeans who have sided with the Chinese in their efforts to oust their colonial masters. Neither a revolutionary nor a nationalist–he claims he is apolitical, in much the same way as other people are asocial–he can nevertheless sympathize with the oppressed masses in China, precisely because they are exploited and downtrodden. His success as a propaganda agent stems as much from his efforts to rekindle in the Chinese workers their sense of human dignity as from his appeals to liberty, equality, and justice. At odds with this strategy is the orthodox Russian Communist Mikhail Borodine, an actual historical figure, who strives to impose the successful Soviet model on Chinese society, but with scant regard for different structures. *Les Conquérants* is not a morality tale pitting wicked European imperialists against innocent Chinese victims, nor is it primarily an account of the Chinese people's struggle to eject their European conquerors. The main conflict is between Borodine, the doctrinaire party official who wishes to mass-produce revolutionaries the way Ford mass-produces automobiles, and Garine, for whom life, all life, is meaningless and absurd. The three-part structure of the novel–"Les

Approches," "Puissances," "L'Homme" (The Approaches, Powers, The Man)–establishes a progression away from the political events to the portrait rendered in "L'Homme" of the solitary individual whose illness, failure, and meaningless death are at the antipodes of revolutionary optimism, or even a liberal belief in the creation of a better future.

The forging of a more equitable society is not what motivates the two principal Chinese characters, Hong and Tcheng-Dai, either. The former (a forerunner of Tchen in *La Condition humaine*) is a terrorist propelled into committing gratuitous acts of violence by a burning hatred for the self-respect and complacency that, in his eyes, define the well-to-do. His political stance is basically Manichaean–"Il n'y a que deux races, les misérables et les autres" (there are only two races, the poor and the others)–and not predicated upon the attainment of specific political objectives. In the long term, his actions are ineffectual, as are those of Tcheng-Dai, a sort of Chinese Gandhi who embodies the ethical imperative in a self-aggrandizing way. Tcheng-Dai, a pacifist, prefers his actual role as *defender* of the oppressed to the virtual role of *liberator* of the oppressed, and his suicide, the supreme form of moral protest, valorizes the self over revolutionary praxis.

In his brilliant rejoinder to Trotsky's objections to his portrayal of the Chinese revolutionaries in *Les Conquérants*, Malraux made one of the earliest, as well as most succinct and cogently argued, statements about the functions of politics in his fictional world. In particular, he tried to dispel any uncertainty concerning the problematic relationship between politics and metaphysics. In response to Trotsky's notorious remark that a good inoculation of Marxism would have spared Garine many of the errors he had committed in Canton, Malraux issued the following clarification, which is crucial to any understanding of his aesthetics: "Ce livre est d'abord une accusation de la condition humaine. . . . Ce livre n'est pas une 'chronique romancée' de la révolution chinoise, parce que l'accent principal est mis sur le rapport entre des individus et une action collective, non sur l'action collective seule" (This book is first of all an accusation against the human condition. . . . This book is not a "fictionalized chronicle" of the Chinese revolution, because the main stress is placed on the relationship between individual and collective action, not on collective action alone). These words apply as much to *La*

Malraux and Louis Chevasson in Saigon, 1923 (Archives André Malraux)

Condition humaine as they do to *Les Conquérants,* but in between the two works set in China comes *La Voie royale,* where the stress is clearly on individual action.

When *La Voie royale* appeared in Paris in late 1930, after serialization in the August through October issues of the *Revue de Paris,* it was accompanied by an announcement of some promise: "*La Voie royale* consitue le tome premier des *Puissances du desert,* dont cette initiation tragique n'est que le prologue" (*The Royal Way* constitutes the first volume of *The Powers of the Desert,* to which this tragic initiation is merely the prologue). Less than a year later, Malraux used a similar expression in a letter dated 29 September 1931 to the editor of the review *Echanges,* in which he mentioned that he was working on "un roman très étendu dont *La Voie royale* constitue en quelque sorte la préface" (a very extensive novel to which *The Royal Way* constitutes a kind of preface). Most commentators have assumed that the projected novel, which never materialized, eventually became *La Condition humaine,* begun in September 1931, but Walter Langlois, the best informed of Malraux's biographers, doubts, in the 1978 publication *International Conference on the Life and Work of André Malraux,* that Malraux's masterpiece, published two years later, was the text in question. Similarly, in view of its classification as a tale of adventure—an apparent regression from the originality of subject matter, narrative coherence, and political acumen that had characterized *Les Conquérants*–many critics have concluded that the actual writing of *La Voie royale* must have preceded the composition of *Les Conquérants*. Recently this argument has been revived and given additional weight by Christiane Moatti in *"La Condition humaine" d'André Malraux* (1983), after attentive scrutiny of the pertinent manuscripts.

On the level of plot, *La Voie royale*, a fictionalized elaboration of the Indochina adventure, is a fairly straightforward novel. A young Frenchman, Claude Vannec, encounters a legendary Danish adventurer called Perken aboard a steamship destined for the Orient. Despite differences in age, education, background, and marital status, they soon discover that they have much in common, philosophically speaking, and decide to pool their resources. Claude, an amateur archaeologist with some semi-official backing from the French Institute, intends to explore a Buddhist temple on the Royal Way that leads from Angkor Wat to the lakes at Me Nam, but he has no experience in traveling in Indochina. Perken, who has some familiarity with the forests of Siam and the indigenous peoples (Xas, Stiengs) who live there, agrees to act as guide. Whereas Claude is motivated mainly by the desire to discover a small Khmer temple and remove its precious carvings, Perken wishes to seek out a masochistic ex-legionary by the name of Grabot, who had disappeared months before in mysterious circumstances in the same part of Indochina. After a harrowing trek through the jungle, Claude's archaeological expedition succeeds, and he is able to appropriate the sculptures he has so eagerly sought. Deserted shortly afterward by part of the native help they had requisitioned, Claude and Perken, in their quest for Grabot, are compelled to penetrate deeper and deeper into the jungle and further away from any semblance of civilization. Eventually, when they locate him, they are confronted by a chilling spectacle of degradation: Grabot, completely blinded and totally dehumanized, is tied to a millstone. Though they are by now encircled by hostile Stiengs, Perken manages to arrange a truce and negotiate Grabot's release. However, Perken falls upon a poisoned dart, and the novel ends with a description of his slow, painful demise. Gazing at the youthful features of the now hateful Claude, he learns that death, a metaphysical abstraction, does not exist: "Il n'y a pas . . . de mort. . . . Il y a seulement . . . moi. . . . moi . . . qui vais mourir . . . " (there is . . . no

death. . . . There's only . . . I. . . . I who . . . am dying).

Though it is obvious from this synopsis that Malraux has exploited many of the conventions of the traditional novel of adventure–the trek through tropical forests in search of hidden treasures, the pursuit of a legendary figure held captive by primitive tribes–it is less apparent how he molded this unoriginal raw material (there are echoes of Joseph Conrad and Rudyard Kipling) into a powerful statement of his own philosophical and metaphysical preoccupations. The suspenseful opening sentence of the novel–"Cette fois, l'obsession de Claude entrait en lutte" (Now Claude's obsession mastered him again)–sets the tone for what follows and suggests that one is dealing with more than just a simple tale. It soon becomes apparent that the obsession that has drawn Claude to Perken (and vice versa) is the obsession with death–"the irrefutable proof of the absurdity of life"–and the circular structure of the novel (death dominates the opening and closing scenes) reflects its inescapable finality.

In emphasizing Perken's tragic awareness of the inevitability and meaninglessness of death, Malraux has created a fictional world that is darkly pessimistic. However, the irremediable sense of solitude that pervades the work is never a pretext for acquiescence, resignation, or the passive acceptance of one's lot. On the contrary, it is the very consciousness of their own mortality that drives the main characters to act, although their actions never have any concrete political objectives, as was the case in *Les Conquérants*. It is possible to consider both Perken and Grabot as callous colonialists, cynically exploiting the vulnerabilities of indigenous peoples in order to satisfy their own inner cravings and desperate ambitions. Perken's oft quoted remark, "Je veux laisser une cicatrice sur la carte" (I want to leave my mark upon the map), can be interpreted as an expression of his imperialist dream, only partly fulfilled by the small kingdom he has already carved out in Siam. By the same token, the psychosexual leanings of at least two of the main characters–their desire to dominate, to imagine themselves as the "other" during erotic acts–suggest the sadomasochism that characterizes the colonial "master." Malraux's sympathy for the aspirations of the Chinese proletariat in *Les Conquérants* makes it difficult to ignore the political dimensions of *La Voie royale*, even if they are of secondary importance. Consequently, it must be acknowledged that it takes a novelist of considerable skill to shift the

Page from the manuscript of Les Conquérants, *Malraux's first novel (courtesy of the Langlois-Ford collection)* reader's attention away from these realities and on to the obsession with death that separates *La Voie royale* from the conventional tale of adventure. The novel won the 1930 Prix Interallié.

For both Claude and Perken death is not merely the antithesis of life, or the end of life; it is also a form of life based on acceptance and conformity, the craving for material comfort and success, the false security afforded by belief in established moral, intellectual, and spiritual values. In other words, the worst manifestation of death is the abject surrender to those forces that conspire to blunt man's apprehension of the "human condition." Perken and Claude persistently denounce this danger in their dialogues, and their decision to test their wills to the utmost limit in extreme situations is carried out in defiance of accepted bourgeois norms. The double alienation they endure–self-banishment from decadent Europe and estrangement from Indochinese customs and beliefs–is reflected in the jungle they choose to explore. Malraux describes the hostile background of the forests of Cambodia and Siam in terms of decay, disintegration, and decomposition; he emphasizes the proliferation of luxuriant vegetation, the prevalence of reptilian and insect life, the stifling atmosphere that envelops everything. In so doing, he has created an effective objective correlative to the adventurers' sense of alienation and isolation. The lyricism of these passages provides a sharp contrast with the ellipses and terse, telegrammatic prose he used in *Les Conquérants*. However, in his following novel, *La Condition humaine*, Malraux succeeded in fusing these two styles into a forceful demonstration of his artistic skills.

For this third novel, which was awarded the Prix Goncourt, Malraux returned to the raw material that had inspired *Les Conquérants. La Condition humaine* is set in Shanghai in the spring and summer of 1927, when General Chiang Kai-shek finally broke with his Communist allies, thereby plunging China into a protracted civil war. These crucial events are conveyed with such powerful immediacy, such concreteness of detail, and such immense sympathy for the crushed revolutionaries that it was again assumed, quite wrongly of course, that Malraux had actually witnessed them and simply transcribed his observations. This misunderstanding can be interpreted as an indirect tribute to Malraux's artistic genius; at the same time, it has detracted from a true appreciation of his creative powers. In 1927 Malraux was back in France, but, during the writing of *La Condition*

humaine (September 1931-May 1933), he embarked upon a second journey to Asia that took him to the cities Shanghai and Canton where revolutionary fervor had been most intense several years earlier.

La Condition humaine represents a major advance over the previous novels, mainly because none of its highly individualized characters is allowed to dominate the action as Garine had in *Les Conquérants* or Perken in *La Voie royale* and also because Malraux was more firmly in control of his subject matter. Abandoning the experimental approach adopted in *Les Conquérants*, he reverted to the omniscient third-person narrative, which allowed him greater latitude in handling the philosophical themes that are so important in the novel. As the title (dreadfully rendered as *Storm in Shanghai* in a 1934 English translation) clearly indicated, the metaphysical dimension, or what Malraux called "l'élément pascalien" (Pascalien element), outweighs the historical and the political. The reference to "la condition humaine" inevitably brings to mind both Pascal and Montaigne, and, in many respects, Malraux's best novel may be viewed as an illustration of the allegory outlined in a famous *pensée* of Pascal (which is quoted verbatim in Malraux's 1943 novel *Les Noyers de l'Altenburg* translated as *The Walnut Trees of Altenburg*, 1952): "Qu'on s'imagine un nombre d'hommes dans les chaînes, et tous condamnés à la mort, dont les uns étant chaque jour égorgés à la vue des autres, ceux qui restent voient leur propre condition dans celle de leurs semblables, et, se regardant les uns et les autres avec douleur et sans espérance, attendent à leur tout. C'est l'image de la condition des hommes" (Do but imagine a number of men in chains, all condemned to death, from whom some are taken each day to be butchered before the eyes of others. Those who remain see their own plight in that of their fellows and, looking at one another in hopelessness and grief, await their turn. In this image you see the human condition). In terms that evoke Dante and Goya as much as Pascal, this image is re-created and updated toward the end of part six, in which Malraux describes the fate of the defeated Communist revolutionary, burned alive in the cauldron of a locomotive.

More so than in *Les Conquérants*, in *La Condition humaine* the setting and recent history of China provide Malraux with an original backdrop to his portrayal of man's tragic solitude and search for some form of transcendence in a uni-

Malraux with Dutch poet Edgard du Perron, the friend to whom he dedicated La Condition humaine *(Archives André Malraux)*

verse without permanent values. All of the main characters and most of the secondary characters embody different responses to the burden of what one of them, old Gisors, calls "leur condition d'homme." A former professor of sociology at the University of Peking, Gisors finds in his addiction to opium an artificial paradise that offers him temporary release from the awareness of his own mortality and, at the same time, the wisdom with which to impart his insights to others. As the father of Kyo, mentor to Tchen, confidant of Ferral, and interlocutor to many others, Gisors has a pivotal role in enabling the reader to perceive and understand the various responses and

their inherent limitations. Had Malraux not wished to subordinate his political acumen and visionary sense to the elucidation of "man's fate," it is probable that his weltanschauung would have been less Europocentric. Virtually all the main characters are European: Ferral and Clappique are French, May is German, Katow is Russian; or Japanese, like Kama. Kyo is Eurasian, and of the central figures only Tchen is Chinese but, as the product of a Protestant upbringing, he too is steeped in European values.

Clappique, Ferral, and Tchen each embody an extreme response to the inherent absurdity of human existence. The bizarre baron de Clappique, whose antics recall the irony and whimsical humor of *Lunes en papier* and *Royaume farfelu*, is a mythomaniac, and undoubtedly Malraux's most unusual, as well as only recurring, character. (He returns in the *Antimémoires*.) His discordant voice is distinctly at odds with the tone of the rest of the novel. Fact and fiction, the real and the imagined, past and present, the pathetic and the grotesque, all are chaotically blended together in that peculiar vision which marks the mind of the mythomaniac. The psychic complexity of this pathetic individual, who seeks compensation in the creation of an imaginary world, cannot be dismissed as "relief" from the "seriousness" of the novel. He is after all one of the few main characters to survive. In addition, there are grounds for interpreting him as a prototype of the artist, but, in the last resort, he lacks both the skill and the willpower to shape the projections of his riotous imagination.

The imaginative excess of another extreme character, Ferral, epitome of the successful Western capitalist, serves a different obsession–the will to power. As president of the Franco-Asian consortium, Ferral is accustomed to exercising authority, to imposing his ideas and his desires upon his subordinates. Ultimately Ferral's power is shown to be illusory. Not only is he unable to exert any restraining influence over Chiang Kai-shek, but he is abandoned by the Paris banking community when the latter's repression leads to financial chaos. And, more important, Ferral's professional failures are echoed in the punishment he suffers at the hands of his strong-minded mistress, Valérie, who refuses to submit meekly to the sado-eroticism that marks their amorous encounters. Malraux here has concentrated in a single character both the limitations of economic power and the precariousness of power based on sexual constraint.

Whereas Ferral tends to externalize his neuroses and his complexes by victimizing others, Tchen's most anguished victim is himself. The murder he commits in the opening pages of the novel (one of Malraux's most brilliant scenes) should have bonded him to the revolutionary group he is helping. Instead, Tchen comes away with a feeling of extraordinary solitude, tortured by the realization that his irrevocable deed has severed him, irremediably, from the rest of mankind. From that moment on, he succumbs to the mystique of terrorism and seeks both self-fulfillment and self-destruction in murder. However, not only does he fail to kill Chiang

Kai-shek (whose car he had attempted to ambush), but he is deprived of the satisfaction of suicide as well. The shot that kills him is not self-inflicted but triggered by a blow dealt by one of Chiang Kai-shek's bodyguards. Tchen's failure is total: he dies in vain, because Chiang Kai-shek was not in his car that day, and, at the same time, he is unable to master the final moments of his life.

Clappique and Ferral (who survives the insurrection) and Tchen (who is destroyed by it) are not the only characters to resort to extremes in their struggle to thwart destiny. Both König, chief of Chiang Kai-shek's police, who derives perverse satisfaction from the acts of torture, and Vologuine, a Party hack who utterly subordinates himself to the Comintern, have also found ways of denying the self-consciousness that constitutes the "human condition." All of these tentative solutions–mythomania, the will to power, terrorism, torture, self-abasement–are essentially destructive and dehumanizing. However, the tragic contours of *La Condition humaine* envelop the protagonists, too, with equal intensity. Kama, a Japanese painter and Gisors's brother-in-law, assuages his sense of solitude through artistic creation: May, Kyo's wife and a doctor in one of the Chinese hospitals, embodies a love that is "a partnership consented, conquered, chosen," but her single act of infidelity reminds both her and Kyo of its fragility; and, in a novel that vividly dramatizes the spirit of revolution, even the most active militants, Kyo and Katow, cannot elude the grasp of solitude. Their failure, their suffering, their atrocious deaths confer upon the novel an aura of tragic finality.

Katow, one of the organizers of the insurrection, embodies the transcendental value of "fraternité virile." Condemned to be burned alive, along with several hundred captured comrades, in the boiler of a locomotive, he ennobles his dying moments by giving the cyanide he had carried with him in preparation for such an eventuality to two younger militants whose fear exceeds his own. Katow's final act of sacrifice is a summation of his life, but its tenuousness is understood by the unforeseen: one of the anonymous prisoners, terror-stricken, drops the precious capsules in the dark. For several suspenseful moments, it seems as if Katow's sacrifice has been in vain, destroyed by some cruel mocking destiny toying with human affairs. The cyanide is retrieved, and there are no further intrusions of fate. Nothing will alleviate the suffering of Katow.

In his 1938 review of *L'Espoir*, Graham Greene objected that Malraux had tried to make the events in *La Condition humaine* stand for too much, and that the horror actually drowned the scene: "It is not after all the human condition to be burnt alive in the boiler of a Chinese locomotive," he observed in the *Spectator*. Of course, this is much too literal an interpretation of a simple allegory. Earlier in the novel Malraux uses an equally powerful symbol of "man's fate" when Kyo, unable to recognize a recording of his own voice, which he hears for the first time, suffers a deep sense of alienation from himself. Almost twenty years later, in the concluding pages of *Les Voix du silence*, Malraux recalled that scene, which is crucial to an understanding of both his poetics and his metaphysics. "J'ai conté jadis l'aventure d'un homme qui ne reconnaît pas sa voix qu'on vient d'enregistrer, parce qu'il l'entend pour la première fois à travers ses oreilles et non plus à travers sa gorge; et, parce que notre gorge seule nous transmet notre voix intérieure, j'ai appelé ce livre *La Condition humaine*" (I have written elsewhere of the man who fails to recognize his own voice on the gramophone, because he is hearing it for the first time through his ears and not through his throat; and, because our throat alone transmits to us our own voice, I called the book *La Condition humaine*). Man's fate, man's estate, the human condition, the human situation: ultimately it remains one of muted anguish, fundamental incommunicability, the tragic awareness of one's solitude, and inevitable death. The somber chords of *La Condition humaine* did not lead Malraux to the brink of despair; on the contrary: they heralded a decade marked by a passionate involvement in the struggle against fascism, Nazism, racism, the decade in which he wrote *Le Temps du mépris* and *L'Espoir*.

It was not so much his sensitive portrayal of Kyo and Katow (or even his sympathy for real Chinese revolutionaries) that deepened Malraux's political commitment, but rather events much closer to home: the consolidation of fascism in Italy, the rise of Nazism in Germany, and additional threats to peace from belligerent autocratic movements in other parts of Europe. At the same time, as was the case with many of his contemporaries, notably André Gide, Malraux became increasingly supportive of the one force that then seemed most likely to stem the rising tide of right-wing totalitarianism–communism, as exemplified in the U.S.S.R. Contrary to what many have claimed, Malraux never joined the Communist

party, and if one bears in mind his treatment of Borodine and Vologuine, it is easy to understand why. To apply the crucial distinction made by Kyo in *La Condition humaine*, he saw in communism (Kyo had said Marxism) a sense of "fatalité" (destiny) and a sense of "volonté" (will); and, if Malraux was repulsed by the former, he was undoubtedly attracted by the latter. Though his relationship with the Communist party was always marked by mutual distrust, he nevertheless extolled the efforts of the Soviet Union to create a new humanism in which bourgeois *individualism* (which he had decried in *La Tentation de l'Occident*) would be supplanted by greater confidence in *mankind*. In addition, as a fellow traveler, he participated in numerous anti-Fascist organizations, most of which (though not all) were controlled or funded by the Soviet Union.

Malraux was an active member of the Amsterdam/Pleyel Peace Movement, as well as the Association of Revolutionary Writers and Artists, an influential organization that provided a forum for leftist intellectuals; with Gide, he copresided over a committee to defend the rights of German Communist leaders and writers, such as Ernst Thaelmann and Ludwig Renn, imprisoned under fascism. Like many other leftist writers, Malraux publicly denounced the fire that destroyed part of the German parliamentary chamber known as the Reichstag as the work of *agents provocateurs,* and, in a widely published visit to Berlin on 4 January 1934, he and Gide attempted to intercede, on behalf of the Bulgarian Communist Georgi Dimitrov, with Hitler, who refused to see them. Malraux was a regular speaker at rallies organized by the Communist party, and he contributed many articles to Communist publications such as *Commune, Regards, International Literature, Russie d'Aujourd'hui,* and *Avant-Poste;* he was a member of the International Writers' Association for the Defense of Culture; he participated in the League Against Anti-Semitism; and, in the summer of 1934, with Paul Nizan, Louis Aragon, Vladimir Pozner, and Jean-Richard Bloch (all members of the French Communist party), he visited the U.S.S.R. as a member of the official French delegation to the Congress of Soviet Writers.

The interviews Malraux granted during and after his stay in Russia, in addition to the speeches he delivered in Moscow, testify to his admiration for the achievements carried out under Stalin on socioeconomic questions. It would, however, be wrong to infer from this that he abdi-

Malraux at the time of his 1933 Prix Goncourt for La Condition humaine *(photo Gisèle Freund)*

cated his critical judgment and saw in Stalinist Russia a new "Utopia," a word later used by Gide. Two separate incidents indicate a reckless courage and a fierce independence of mind not usually associated with official guests of the U.S.S.R. During a banquet given in honor of the visiting writers, the author of *La Condition humaine* proposed a toast to the absent Trotsky, a brave but rash gesture that seems to have had no harmful consequences. And, more in keeping with his determination to champion the cause of artistic freedom, he launched a skillfully worded attack on the limitations of "socialist realism," the official literary doctrine sanctioned by Stalin. After outlining the deficiencies of realism, Malraux insisted that the artist, albeit "an engineer of the soul," was, like all engineers, above all a creator, and that artistic creation, which obeys its own logic, is predicated upon the notion of artistic freedom. Judgments such as these–and they were admittedly rare–were the price the Soviet leaders paid for their policy of a union of the

Left. Though Malraux's words undoubtedly shocked and offended, they should not have surprised, coming from an author whose first novel, *Les Conquérants,* had been banned in the Soviet Union.

Le Temps du mépris, Malraux's first novel set in Europe, was formed in the crucible of left-wing politics. (The title of the American translation, *Days of Wrath,* fails to communicate the Fascists' *contempt* for mankind expressed in the original.) It is a novel Malraux himself scathingly dismissed ten years later as "un navet" (rubbish, "third-rate"). In 1935 it was praised in the most lavish manner by virtually all orthodox Communist reviewers, mainly because its celebration of collective values and heroic idealism provided a useful corrective to the somber pessimism that had marked *La Condition humaine.* This judgment is not one likely to be repeated in contemporary criticism, and quite a few critics (Cecil Jenkins, Thomas Jefferson Kline) have questioned Malraux's own assessment. Though clearly inferior to *L'Espoir* and *Les Noyers de l'Altenburg, Le Temps du mépris* is an important novel, as much as for what it represents historically–it is one of the earliest works of fiction to reveal Nazi concentration camps–as for what Malraux was trying to accomplish aesthetically, a modern reworking of the myth of Prometheus. Furthermore, it has a preface which was adopted at that time as a manifesto of left-wing idealism and, somewhat paradoxically, as a succinct formulation of Malraux's philosophy, one he never repudiated, in spite of his later dislike for the novel. "Il est difficile d'être un homme. Mais pas plus de le devenir en approfondissant sa communion qu'en cultivant sa différence,–et la première nourrit avec autant de force que la seconde ce par quoi l'homme est homme, ce par quoi il se dépassé, crée, invente ou se conçoit" (It is difficult to be a man. But it is not more difficult to become one by enriching one's fellowship with other men than by cultivating one's individual peculiarities. The former nourishes with at least as much force as the latter, that which makes man human, which enables him to surpass himself, to create, invent or realize himself).

The value of "fellowship with other men" is illustrated and celebrated in a tale of compelling simplicity. A legendary Communist agent named Kassner is captured and interrogated by the Nazis, imprisoned in a stone cell and beaten until he loses consciousness. When consciousness returns, he is assailed by horrifying nightmares which he tries to ward off by remembering music. Failing in this and fearing the onset of madness, he contemplates suicide, but, in an adjacent cell, a fellow prisoner communicates with him by tapping out messages of hope and comradeship. After nine days of confinement, Kassner is suddenly released, because someone has surrendered in his place. (His interrogators had not succeeded in firmly establishing his real identity.) He is flown out of Germany to Prague, where he joins his wife and child and continues the fight against fascism. Malraux's dedication–"To the German comrades who were anxious for me to make known what they had suffered and what they had upheld, this book which is theirs"–dispels any doubt about the origins of the novel. The documentation had been provided by escapees from Nazi prisons and by such exiled German intellectuals and writers as Ludwig Renn and the Jewish author Manès Sperber. As always, Malraux incorporated into his work several personal experiences–the apparent reconciliation with family life after the birth of his daughter Florence, and a near brush with death when the airplane taking him back from his flight over the Yemen desert in search of the legendary capital of the Queen of Sheba ran into a storm–which he adapted to the requirements of plot and the psychological portrait of his main character. The simplicity of *Le Temps du mépris*, with its celebration of solidarity, forms a sharp contrast with the epic vision of *L'Espoir*, Malraux's novel on the Spanish civil war.

Malraux's dedication to the cause of Republican Spain in the immediate aftermath of the 17 July pronunciamiento is probably the most striking example of how the Spanish civil war moved an entire generation of writers as no other war had done before, or as none has done since. In May 1936, after the victory of the French Popular Front in the April elections, Malraux visited Spain, with Jean Cassou and Henri Lenormand, as a delegate of the International Association of Writers for the Defense of Culture. The purpose of their visit was to extend greetings to, and help establish fraternal relations with, the newly elected Spanish Popular Front government, and those intellectual and cultural organizations that had supported it. The three delegates were introduced to the president of the Republic, Manuel Azaña; they conferred with ministers (Francisco Barnés, Bernardo Giner de los Ríos), deputies (Vicente Uribe, Julio Alvarez del Vayo, Marcelino Domingo), and intellectuals (Américo Castro).

Up until this point Malraux's *engagement* was little different from that of many of his contemporaries–Louis Aragon, Paul Nizan, André Gide, Romain Rolland–who were equally active in the anti-Fascist struggle. The events of July 1936 changed all that. Faithful to the fighting and prophetic words he had uttered at the Ateneo in Madrid on 22 May 1936–"We know that our differences with the fascists will have to be resolved one day with machine guns"– Malraux arrived in Spain on 20 July some forty-eight hours after the military rebellion began. There are few traces of this first visit, but the second, which took place the same month, had a more official character. In his capacity as copresident of the Comité Mondial des Intellectuels contre la Guerre et le Fascisme, Malraux was asked to visit Spain and draw up a first-hand report on the situation. Conflicting interpretations of the pronunciamiento transmitted by radio stations in different parts of the peninsula had led to great confusion abroad as to its success or failure. On 25 July Malraux sent a telegram (published in *Humanité*) denying propaganda reports that Madrid had been encircled by the dissident armies. In all likelihood, it was during his second stay in Spain that Malraux first glimpsed the part he could play in stemming the rising tide of fascism. The novelist who had displayed an intuitive understanding of, and deep sympathy for, the aspirations of the Chinese revolutionaries had the opportunity not only to observe but also to participate in a revolutionary situation south of the Pyrenees.

Malraux quickly understood that the Republicans would require assistance from other democracies if the rebellion was to be checked. It was with this end in view that he undertook a series of actions that included: the purchase abroad of aircraft for the Spanish government; negotiations between the Popular Front governments of Spain and France, on whose behalf he acted as intermediary and spokesman; numerous appearances at pro-Republican gatherings in France; and, most striking of all, the leadership of an international air squadron of volunteers and mercenaries, the Escadrille España, which was renamed the Escadrille André Malraux when the mercenaries were dismissed in November 1936.

Malraux's leadership of the international volunteer air force was an unparalleled achievement, especially for a writer with no military experience, and he displayed a shrewd understanding of the crucial role aviation was to play

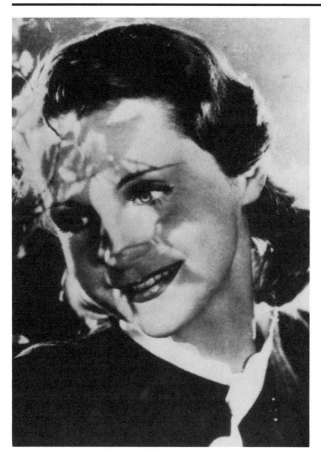

Josette Clotis, with whom Malraux lived from 1937 until her death in 1944 (photo © Harcourt)

during the civil war. Many Republican historians and indeed some Nationalist spokesmen have paid tribute to Malraux's prescience during the early stages of the war. However, as resistance to Franco was organized on more efficient lines, it became increasingly clear that his initiative was more or less obsolete. The squadron's last major mission involved protecting the civilian population fleeing Málaga after its capture on 8 February 1937; soon after it was disbanded and those who chose to remain in Spain were integrated into other units. The Republican government then decided that Malraux's status as a writer of international renown would be more profitably employed in other capacities, and they sent him on a mission to North America.

The Republican cause had fared rather poorly in United States newspapers, and President Franklin D. Roosevelt's determination to adhere strictly to a policy of neutrality in European affairs had deprived the Spanish government of a vital source of arms and equipment. Malraux could hardly be expected to help shift U.S. for-

eign policy, but he could help influence public opinion and counteract an effective pro-Franco propaganda machine wielded by the Catholic Church. As a Goncourt prizewinner and author of a recent Book-of-the-Month Club selection (*Days of Wrath*), he was assured extensive media coverage, particularly in liberal and leftist publications.

Malraux arrived in New York on 24 February 1937, and his six-week tour took him to Philadelphia, Washington, Cambridge, Boston, Los Angeles, San Francisco, Toronto, and Montreal. His visits were usually sponsored by local chapters of the American (or Canadian) League Against War and Fascism or the Committee to Aid Spanish Democracy. Everywhere he went, Malraux outlined the same ideas: he revealed Mussolini's expansionist policies with respect to the Mediterranean and the extent of the military aid Italy and Germany were giving Franco; he inveighed against American neutrality which, he argued, isolated Spain and bolstered fascism; he contrasted the values of the Fascists—"permanentes et particulières"—and their exaltation of differences such as race, nation, and class, that are "essentielles, irréducibles et constantes" with the Republican values, "humanistes parce qu'universalistes"; he attacked the treaty of nonintervention and criticized the International Red Cross for its apathy and ineffectiveness; he prophesied the outbreak of a worldwide civil war; and, by way of conclusion, he invited his audience to make donations for medical aid to help victims of the fighting. To illustrate his indictment of Fascist militarism ar^d his defense of the Republican cause, Malraux would recount incidents—the strafing of civilian refugees fleeing along the road from Málaga to Almería, the fraternal union of Spanish peasants and wounded foreign aviators during the descent from the mountain near Teruel—that he incorporated into *L'Espoir*, where they were invested with a poetical or mythical quality.

While fighting in Spain, or speaking on Spain's behalf in Europe and North America, Malraux continued to write. The experience of leadership and war he had acquired as commander of the International Air Force was transposed into *L'Espoir,* an epic novel that was published in Paris in late 1937 and appeared in the United States the following year under the title *Man's Hope.* Malraux's other artistic contribution to the anti-Fascist struggle was his only film, *Sierra de Teruel* (Teruel Mountains, 1938), made in well-nigh impossible conditions in and around Barcelona during the final stages of the civil war. This creation–an autonomous work and not a mere adaptation of *L'Espoir*–was awarded the Prix Louis Delluc in 1945. It has been described by some critics as one of the finest French films ever made. Thus, as squadron leader, propagandist, novelist, and director, Malraux, in less than three years of creative activity, provided an exemplum of *engagement* that remains unsurpassed.

A contributing factor in the defeat of the Republican armies at the hands of Franco was undoubtedly the disarray that prevailed among government troops, especially during the early stages of the war. Though it would be simplistic to portray the Nationalist forces as a homogeneous, highly disciplined unit, it is generally agreed that their army was better organized than the government's. The numerous pro-Republican groups–which included socialists, Communists, liberals, radicals, and anarchists–had to contend with fundamental ideological differences in their bid to create a united front. Even within the extreme Left, bitter hostility pitted orthodox Communists against Trotskyists and members of the POUM (Partido Obrero Unificacíon Marxista, or Marxist Workers' Unification Party). The highlight of *L'Espoir* is the victory in March 1937 at Guadalajara, a military success that ended the series of reversals suffered by the government side–or so it was expected. This is obviously one of the many hopes suggested by the title, and though they were undoubtedly shared by Malraux, he was not blinded by naive idealism or false optimism. The book is a rather unusual pro-Republican work in that it focuses frequently upon the weaknesses of the government army.

Insofar as it is possible to reduce the subtle political debates of *L'Espoir* to a single statement, Malraux's central argument may be summarized as follows: the spontaneous outpouring of enthusiasm that characterized the early weeks of the fighting, the "lyrical illusion," was by definition short-lived; and, unless this enthusiasm could be integrated into a military strategy, Republican chances of victory were slim, if they existed at all. As the Communists were the most disciplined group on the Republican side, and as the Soviet Union was both organizing the international brigades and forwarding arms and ammunition to the government, the Russians were seen as most capable of molding the numerous loyalist parties and groups into a force that could achieve victory. It would surely be false to infer from this portrayal that Malraux had cynically subordinated ethics to politics, or that he had completely jettisoned morality. Garcia, an intellectual who is one of his most eloquent spokesmen in *L'Espoir*, puts the matter into proper perspective when he declares: "On ne fait pas de politique avec la morale, mais on n'en fait pas davantage sans" (Though a moral code is not a concern of practical politics, it can't get on without one).

In fact, a distinguishing feature of *L'Espoir* is the number of intellectuals who appear there: Garcia, Alvear, Scali, Magnin, Manuel, Ximénès, to name the most significant. Their main function in the novel, aside from whatever responsibilities they may have as leaders, is to reflect upon many moral and intellectual issues at stake in the conflict, and to this effect they confront one another in a series of dialogues arranged contrapuntally. Questions raised at one moment by one character are later analyzed, explored, or indeed answered by another, usually after a new set of circumstances has entered into play. Many of these dialogues deal with concrete problems peculiar to the immediate historical situation–for example, the various factors undermining the Republican war effort. Others, without ever completely transcending the specific context of the war, examine questions of a more general nature and their application or relevance to the events in Spain. These highly original deliberations on such time-honored subjects as the end and the means, the antimony between politics and morality, the relation of the individual to a collectivity, the function of art, and man's attitude in the face of death have been praised unstintingly, even by right-wing critics who did not hesitate to write disparagingly about other aspects of the novel. There are, in the pages of these dialogues, an acuity of perception, a refinement of expression, and a depth of understanding that are worthy of Shakespeare or Tolstoy.

As is usually the case in Malraux's novels, scenes of dialogue alternate with scenes of action. Unlike *La Voie royale* or even *La Condition humaine* in which scenes of violence are described with a certain indulgence, *L'Espoir* is a moving indictment of the pain and suffering inevitably caused by war. Though Malraux briefly recounts atrocious death scenes as, for example, when Mercery, hit by bullets from a fighter plane, falls into the fire he was trying to extinguish, he also raises his voice in protest against the folly of war. Alvear, distraught over his son's blindness, remarks: "Rien n'est plus terrible que la dé-

Malraux with André Gide, Jean Guéhenno, and Paul Vaillant-Couturier at a public meeting, circa 1940 (photo A.F.P.)

formation d'un *corps* qu'on aime" (Nothing's more horrible than the mutilation of a *body* that one loves). In one of the most moving incidents in the novel, Manuel, wandering through a hospital room which resembles "un royaume éternel de la blessure" (the eternal kingdom of pain), hears the screams of a seriously wounded pilot and wonders: "Que valent les mots en face d'un corps déchiqueté?" (When the whole body is a quivering mass of pain, what use are words?) With its realistic accounts of the horrors taking place in Spain–the systematic bombing of open cities, the machine-gunning of refugees, the use of incendiary bombs, mass executions before open graves, acts of sabotage conducted by fifth columnists ready to welcome and collaborate with the enemy–*L'Espoir,* a novel about one particular war, is also a novel about and *against* war in general.

The defeat of Republican Spain, abandoned by the two democracies that had the most to lose from further Fascist advances, marked not only the final collapse of the "lyrical illusion" but the end of an era; and the nonaggression pact cosigned by Hitler and Stalin on 23 August 1939 had a demoralizing effect upon most anti-

Fascists, and many Communists. Shortly afterward, Malraux set out for Corrèze with the young writer Josette Clotis, who was to bear him two sons out of wedlock, Pierre-Gauthier (October 1940) and Vincent (November 1943), and, at Beaulieu-sur-Dordogne, in full view of a Romanesque church known for its exceptionally beautiful tympanum, he resumed work on *Psychologie de l'art,* begun as early as 1935. It was a brief respite. When World War II broke out, he returned to Paris to volunteer his services, but the air ministry, obviously unimpressed by his reputation as a squadron leader in Spain, rejected him out of hand. In November 1939, however, Malraux was accepted by the tank force. He was stationed at Provins, near Paris, where he endured the tedium and enjoyed the anonymity of being a private soldier, much as T. E. Lawrence had in 1922. On 15 June 1940 he was slightly wounded in a skirmish with a German patrol, taken prisoner, and interned in a camp halfway between Provins and Sens. Five months later he managed to escape to the free zone, the southern and central area of France presided over by Marshal Pétain after the signing of an armistice agreement on 22 June 1940. Four days earlier General de Gaulle had issued his famous appeal to the French to resist, and Malraux tried to establish contact with him. The message was intercepted, but, at the time, Malraux concluded that he had been ignored or rejected on account of his left-wing past. For the next three and a half years, until he joined the Resistance in Corrèze, he led a life of relative ease, given the circumstances, and devoted himself to his writings. Not only did he pursue his meditations on artistic creation, but he wrote a full-length study of T. E. Lawrence, "Le Démon de l'absolu" (The Demon of the Absolute, published only in excerpted form under the title *N'était-ce donc que cela?*, 1946), and his last novel, *Les Noyers de l'Altenburg*. This period of calm came to an end when the Germans invaded the free zone on 11 November 1942. Shortly afterward, Malraux and his family moved to the village of Saint-Chamant in the Dordogne, not far from Corrèze, where the maquis–supporters of the French underground–were hiding.

Though Malraux had been in touch with the maquis, mainly through his half-brother Roland, he remained on the fringes of the Resistance until late March 1944, at which time a small group of men, including Roland, were caught in the act of establishing radio communications with London and arrested by a detachment of the Gestapo. Malraux then joined the Resistance movement, and it is surely one of the numerous anomalies of his life that, in a matter of months, he was able to impose his authority on many of the small autonomous units operating in the Périgord and eventually unify them into a small force attached to the British networks of the Special Operations Executive. On 7 June, in conjunction with other commanders, Malraux and his men harassed the tanks and motorized infantry of the SS Panzer Division Das Reich and delayed its arrival in the north of France for the crucial battle of Normandy. In addition, he helped bring about what Gen. Colin McVean Gubbins, the head of the SOE, described as the most important parachute drop of the war, from Norway to Indochina. At the end of July the Citroën in which Malraux and four others were traveling was attacked by a German motorized column in the small town of Gramat. Because he was in uniform Malraux was pursued, captured, and imprisoned in the Saint Michel prison at Toulouse. He owed his life to an administrative error. His interrogators, having confused his file with that of his younger half-brother, never realized they had a famous French writer in their midst. Shortly afterward the German tanks were forced to evacuate Toulouse, and Malraux returned to lead the two thousand men under his command.

The last stage in Malraux's military career was to be marked by success. Because of the prestige he had acquired as a *résistant* in Corrèze, he was asked to lead the Brigade Alsace-Lorraine, which included a battalion led by another French writer, André Chamson. On 28 November 1944 the newly formed brigade captured the town of Dannemarie while the division of Gen. Philippe Leclerc took Strasbourg. From 20 December 1944 to 10 January 1945 the brigade helped defend Strasbourg against a mighty German offensive led by Field Marshal Karl Rudolf Gerd von Rundstedt. Malraux was decorated with the Légion d'Honneur by Gen. Jean de Lattre, and a fourth citation was added to his Croix de Guerre. The sense of triumph could not be shared by many of those closest to him. In addition to the friends and fellow combatants killed during the fighting, Claude Malraux died in a concentration camp in March 1944, Roland was killed five days before the end of the war, and, the cruelest blow of all, Josette Clotis was the victim of a ghastly accident. While attempting to alight from a moving train, she fell under the wheels and died, terribly mutilated, on 11 November 1944. It is perhaps because of these personal tragedies that the novelist who had conjured up vivid images of events in China and Nazi Germany, and who had written magnificently of his own experience in Spain was unable (or unwilling) to provide a fictionalized account of his twelve months in the Resistance. *Les Noyers de l'Altenburg*, his sixth and last novel, appeared in 1943, months before he personally encountered the "organisation de l'avilissement" (organized brutalization) of the Occupation.

Like *La Voie royale*, published thirteen years earlier, *Les Noyers de l'Altenburg* was originally conceived as the first part of a two-volume series; and, like the earlier work, which was announced as the prologue to *Puissances du désert*, it bore a resoundingly ambitious title, with biblical associations, *La Lutte avec l'ange* (Jacob Wrestling); and, to pursue the parallel, the reason for its incompletion has not been positively established, in spite of Malraux's explanation that the second part had been destroyed by the Gestapo. *Les Noyers de l'Altenburg* first appeared in Lausanne in 1943, because Malraux refused to "collaborate" with the Germans by having any of his books published in occupied Paris. However, during the war, ex-

Malraux in October 1944, when he was leading the Brigade Alsace-Lorraine under his nom de guerre, Colonel Berger (collection particulière)

cerpts were smuggled out of France and printed in Buenos Aires (*Lettres Françaises*), New York (*Twice A Year*), Geneva (*Semaine Littéraire*), Algiers (*Fontaine*), and eventually in liberated Paris (*Combat*), before Gallimard published the entire work, with an accompanying note by the author, in 1948. Stating that "on ne récrit guère un roman" (novels can hardly ever be rewritten), Malraux claimed that "lorsque celui-ci paraîtra sous sa forme définitive, la forme des *Noyers de l'Altenburg* sera sans doute fondamentalement modifiée" (when this one appears in its final form, the form of its first part, *The Walnut Trees of Altenburg,* will no doubt be radically changed). Malraux's intentions at that time are not known, but when *Les Noyers de l'Altenburg* did reappear in 1967 as part 1 of the *Antimémoires*, all that remained of the original volume was the central section, the magnificent colloquium on "permanence et métamorphose de l'homme," togeth-

er with the pages on Vincent Berger's suicide and Nietzsche's madness.

Unlike the previous five novels, *Les Noyers de l'Altenburg* is not based on current events, even though Malraux's own experience of imprisonment at Sens from June to November 1940 undoubtedly served as the inspiration for parts 1 and 5, which are set in Chartres. However, the question of transposing *le vécu* (the lived) is a less relevant and less fertile area of investigation in this transitional work. It begins on 21 June 1940 with an unidentified narrator recording his own observations and the remarks of his fellow prisoners as he gazes at the cathedral in Chartres, unrecognizable without its magnificent stained-glass windows. The soldiers around him, Senegalese and Arab as well as French, are not only the victims of a specific historical conjuncture or an implacable fate but, more significantly, they represent a universal, timeless situation, "la mémoire séculaire du fléau" (the age-old memory of the scourge). The idea of a continuum is introduced in the opening pages of the novel, in which the narrator evokes similar scenes of confinement through the ages. The prison is reminiscent of a prehistoric den, a Roman camp, and a Babylonian hovel, where captives with "faces gothiques" (gothic faces) are curled up like "les momies du Pérou" (Peruvian mummies). These associations suggest "la familiarité séculaire avec le malheur" (age-old familiarity with misfortune). As the Chartres setting is intended to convey, many of the images and cultural references (Breughel, the *fabliaux*) recall the medieval period, which is favorably contrasted with the modern age, precisely because it undertook to represent *mankind,* and not the *individual.* The narrator remembers a saying of his father, "Ce n'est pas à gratter sans cesse l'individu qu'on finit par rencontrer l'homme" (It's not by any amount of scratching at the individual that one finally comes down to mankind), and this position subsumes all of *Les Noyers de l'Altenburg.*

For example, in part 2, in which the narrator recalls his father Vincent Berger's involvement and eventual disillusionment with the Young Turk movement of Enver Pasha in 1913, and his rediscovery, upon returning to Europe, of "le fondamental," the emphasis is upon the common essence of humanity. Vincent Berger's firm belief, shared by the narrator, that a man's significance depends more on the values that shape his life than on whatever secrets he may harbor within him, is in no way undermined by the suicide of Dietrich Berger, the narrator's grandfather. In fact, this willful obliteration of "un passé de souvenirs et de secrets" (a past made up of memories and secrets) is not as much the pretext for introspection as for reflection upon the dead man's *vision du monde* (vision of the world) and mankind's millennial inability to accept the finality of death: "Les millénaires n'ont pas suffi à l'homme pour apprendre à voir mourir" (The millennia have not been long enough for man to learn how to look on death).

To insist too much on the finality of death is to run the risk of a metaphysical truism, and, in the central section of the novel, Malraux obviates this danger by shifting the discussion to the area of anthropology. The debate at Altenburg focuses upon the question: "Existe-t-il une donnée sur quoi fonder la notion d'homme?" (Is there any factor on which we can base the notion of man?), and the key speaker is an anthropologist named Möllberg, who is loosely modeled after Leo Frobenius (1873-1938). Möllberg is an Africanist who had attempted to produce a grandiose Hegelian synthesis of African cultures at a time when most of his colleagues opted for a pluralist approach to the same phenomenon. However, the results of his field work convinced him that every mental structure has its own absolute and that the premises governing his research were false. Möllberg concludes his intervention at the colloquium by conceding that if there are any universal values, or "permanence," it is "dans le néant" (in nothingness), at which point Vincent Berger interjects: "ou dans le fondamental" (in fundamental man). When Möllberg retorts that "L'homme fondamental est un mythe (Fundamental man is a myth), Berger can find no rejoinder. Möllberg's arguments are not refuted by another participant; they are undermined elsewhere in the novel by the choice of imagery, by numerous references to "timeless" occupations (that of the woodcutter, for example), and by the durability of the walnut trees, the principal symbols of "permanence."

Similarly, Vincent Berger's experience of fraternization between German volunteers and Russian soldiers during World War I (the main episode of part 4) is elevated to the value of a myth that illustrates man's capacity for triumphing over evil, in the face of overwhelming odds. The German volunteers, horrified by experiments with asphyxiating gases, forget the short-term goals of the fighting and, in an apotheosis of "fraternité maladroite et poignante" (pathetic, clumsy comradeship), rush to the aid of their former enemies. In the final short section of the novel, "Camp de Chartres," the narrator finds Pascal's allegory of the human condition a frighteningly apt description of modern warfare, but the prevalence of cosmic imagery points to some measure of reconciliation with the world around him.

Image: the word resounds like a clarion throughout Malraux's corpus of writing–fiction, criticism, essays on art, and autobiography. In *Les Noyers de l'Altenburg* a member of the narrator's family, in the course of a discussion on "le millénaire" (another key word in Malraux's vocabulary), expresses the following sense of wonderment at man's genius for transcending the temporal: "Le plus grand mystère n'est pas que nous soyons jetés au hasard entre la profusion de la matière et celle des astres; c'est que, dans cette prison, nous tirions de nous-mêmes des images assez puissantes pour nier notre néant" (The greatest mystery is not that we have been flung at random between the profusion of the earth and the galaxy of the stars, but that in this prison we can fashion images of ourselves sufficiently powerful to deny our nothingness). It is difficult to find a more adequate statement of the general principles governing Malraux's numerous books on art, from the earliest, *Psychologie de l'art* (three volumes, 1947, 1948, 1949) to the three revised volumes of *La Métamorphose des dieux: Le Surnaturel* (1977), *L'Irréel* (1974), *L'Intemporel* (1976). All of these works have lavish illustrations, and, consequently, they were rather expensive. In 1965 Gallimard published a revised and expanded version of *Le Musée imaginaire* (originally volume 1 of *Psychologie de l'art* and then part 1 of *Les Voix du silence*) in its inexpensive paperback collection Idées/Arts. As a result, Malraux's meditations upon artistic creation were made available to a much wider audience. Those readers already acquainted with his novels were not surprised to find in *Le Musée imaginaire* more sustained analyses of ideas–art as antidestiny, art as a humanization of the world–they had already encountered in *La Voie royale*, *L'Espoir*, and *Les Noyers de l'Altenburg*. Since *Le Musée imaginaire* is the most accessible of Malraux's books on aesthetics, it is a fitting source for a general account of his main concepts.

"Le Musée imaginaire," the imaginary museum or "museum without walls," is an extension of the real museum which, Malraux mentions, does not exist in lands where the civilization of

Malraux with Gen. Charles de Gaulle, 1946 (photo Dorka)

modern Europe is unknown. The real museum had already caused a metamorphosis in perceptions of art because it estranged works from their original functions, which were usually religious or sacred in nature, and made them into "images." The opening sentence of the essay—"Un crucifix roman n'était pas d'abord une sculpture, la *Madone* de Cimabué n'était pas d'abord un tableau, même l'*Athéna* de Phidias n'était pas d'abord une statue" (A Romanesque crucifix was not regarded by its contemporaries as a work of sculpture, nor Cimabue's *Madonna* as a picture. Even Phidias' *Pallas Athene* was not, primarily, a statue)—insists upon the museum's status as a "confrontation de métamorphoses." Just as the traditional museum had imposed a new hierarchy of values, by juxtaposing neglected or unknown masterpieces from other cultures beside those (primarily European works) which had been canonized by time, so too "le musée imaginaire" of photographic reproduction reveals new forms and revolutionizes the viewer's manner of seeing. In

addition, it resurrects other forms (mosaics, stained-glass windows, tapestries, frescos, much sculpture) excluded from the traditional museum and provides the "broadest artistic domain" man has never known. Unlike the real museum which is concrete, exclusive, restricted, the museum without walls is imaginary, all-inclusive, unrestricted; or, to use Malraux's terms, the mutilated possible conjures up the whole gamut of the possible.

In *Le Musée imaginaire*, Malraux interprets the history of European art as a gradual evolution away from a form of expression limited to two dimensions, toward the secrets of rendering volume and depth. However, the conquest of techniques of illusion and the creation of a semblance of reality that characterized both Flemish and Italian painting in the sixteenth century were as much a means for revealing the unreal as representing the real. During the next two centuries, art alternated between the maintenance of this "demiurgic power" (the creation of the real) and the representation of fiction. Malraux argues that the development and spread of photographic processes clearly demonstrate that, aside from a few centuries in which European artists aspired to capture the third dimension, two-dimensional painting is a universal phenomenon. In Europe, too, the model eventually became the basic material of an image, rather than the image being a reproduction of the model. In the twentieth century the representation of fiction has been appropriated by the cinema, and, consequently, the modern artist, indifferent to pictorial content and anthropomorphism, has reverted to a form of two-dimensional painting, which is both self-contained and autonomous. Malraux's striking synthesis, which owes something to Hegel and Nietzsche as well as to Walter Benjamin, combines religious terms (purification, idealization, resurrection, transfiguration, transcendence) with military terminology (conquest, imposition, dominance) to evoke and extol the artist's genius for transforming the world independently of verisimilitude.

In 1948 Malraux was officially divorced from his Clara and married Madeleine Lioux, the widow of his half-brother Roland. It was during the late 1940s and throughout the 1950s that Malraux finally found sufficient time to develop his aesthetics and complete the essays on art he had had to abandon at Beaulieu-sur-Dordogne in the summer of 1939. However, prior to publishing the three volumes of *Psychologie de l'Art* and *Les Voix du silence,* Malraux had met de Gaulle in 1945 and had been appointed "conseiller technique" (technical advisor), then "ministre de l'information" (minister of information) in the short-lived Gaullist government of November 1945-January 1946. A year later the Rassemblement du Peuple Français was founded, and until 1952 Malraux, as director of propaganda (following in the footsteps of Garine), was one of its most dedicated and eloquent spokesmen. The rest of the decade he devoted to writing (the three volumes of *Le Musée imaginaire de la sculpture mondiale* (1952-1954) and *La Métamorphose des dieux;* the essays on Goya, Leonardo da Vinci, and Vermeer de Delft; important prefaces to works by Louis Guilloux and Albert Ollivier, for example), and traveling: to Egypt and Persia; to New York, where he delivered a speech at the reopening of the Metropolitan Museum; to Stockholm, where he participated in the 350th anniversary of Rembrandt's birth. In 1958, with Sartre, Mauriac, and Roger Martin du Gard,

he addressed a letter to the French president, condemning torture in Algeria.

Shortly afterward, when de Gaulle was returned to power in 1959 as president of the Fifth Republic, Malraux was appointed "ministre d'Etat chargé des Affaires culturelles" (Minister of State for Cultural Affairs), and from April 1962 to April 1969 he was first in the hierarchy of ministers of State. The following excerpt from *Mémoires d'espoir* (*Memoirs of Hope,* 1970) by Charles de Gaulle describes the special relationship between the statesman-soldier and the writer-minister. "A ma droite j'ai et j'aurai toujours André Malraux. La présence à mes côtés de cet ami génial, fervent des hautes destinées, me donne l'impression que, par-là, je suis couvert du terre-à-terre. L'idée que se fait de moi cet incomparable témoin contribue à m'affermir. Je sais que, dans le débat, quand le sujet est grave, son fulgurant jugement m'aidera à dissiper les ombres" (On my right hand I have, and will always have, André Malraux. With this brilliant friend at my side, I somehow believed that I would be shielded from the commonplace. The image of me that this incomparable witness reflected continuously fortified me. In a debate, I always knew that his lightning judgment would help me to dispel the shadow).

During his ten years in the Ministry of Cultural Affairs Malraux found himself in a somewhat ambiguous position, an ambiguity that is reflected in the wording of the mandate entrusted to him: "to make accessible the major works of mankind in general and of France in particular to the greatest number of Frenchmen, to ensure the largest audience for the cultural heritage and to encourage the creation of the works of art and of the minds that enrich it." On the one hand, as minister, he was responsible for a series of short-term policy decisions that had to be implemented more or less immediately, and on the other, as writer and thinker, he continued to elaborate and refine concepts of culture whose complexities he had already outlined as early as 1926, in *La Tentation de l'Occident.* The minister often talked in terms of somewhat outmoded nineteenth-century approaches to culture that had found favor again in the 1930s, but these were often tainted by appeals to conservative nationalism (along the lines of "enhancing the glory of France," "restoring France to its position as the world's foremost cultural nation," and so forth). The philosopher, however, had to contend with a more recent phenomenon (which he

Malraux and Marc Chagall viewing the painter's fresco for the ceiling of l'Opéra de Paris, 1963. Malraux commissioned the work while he was Minister of State for Cultural Affairs (photo Izis © A.D.A.G.P., 1986).

had foretold in *La Tentation de l'Occident*) and its many implications: the growing awareness of the plurality of *cultures* in a world increasingly impervious to imperialist, Europocentric, and anachronistic notions of the word. To pose Malraux's dilemma in this fashion is neither to privilege the philosopher at the expense of the minister, nor to belittle his accomplishments, which were substantial. In spite of severe budgetary limitations—less than half a percent of the national budget—Malraux's ministry will be remembered for the following innovations and achievements: the creation of Maisons de Culture, multipurpose arts centers at Amiens, Bourges, Caen, Firminy, Grenoble, Le Havre, Ménilmontant, Reims, Rennes, St. Etienne, Thonon, and other French towns; an inventory, to be completed by the end of the century, of French national monuments and artistic riches; the restoration, above all in Paris, of famous historical buildings (the Louvre, the Grand Palais); numerous initiatives in favor of contemporary art, particularly the commissioning of major works from Masson and Chagall; the organization of important exhibitions on treasures of India (1960), Persian art (1961), Mexican art (1962), Picasso (1966), Tutankhamen (1967), and the Spanish *siglo de oro,* or Golden Age; the establishment of the Paris orchestra; cultural exchanges between France and other countries, for example, Mexico (1960). In addition, Malraux frequently served as de Gaulle's special envoy to distinguished leaders such as Mao Tse-tung and Nehru, and he was called upon to proclaim the independence of Tchad, Gabon, Congo, the Central African Republic, and other former French colonies.

On the negative side, the dismissal of France's most prestigious director, Jean-Louis Barrault, for having supported the students who had occupied the Odéon, a leading State theater, during the riots of May 1968; a regrettable altercation with Henri Langlois, founding father and director of the Cinémathèque, France's film archives; and his failure to help improve the quality of French television were highly publicized blemishes that detracted from an otherwise enviable record. When Malraux resigned in June 1969, several months after de Gaulle, the tension between his two involvements with culture was resolved, and for the remaining seven years of his life he was free to meditate upon one of his key concepts: "metamorphosis."

In the concluding pages of *Les Voix du silence* Malraux had insisted upon the transforming power of the artist and his capacity for immortalizing some "supreme moment," not by reproducing it, but by subjecting it to a metamorphosis ("S'il advient que l'artiste fixe un instant privilégié, il ne le fixe pas parce qu'il le reproduit mais parce qu'il le métamorphose" [If an artist happens to arrest a privileged instant, he does not fix it because he reproduces it but because he metamorphosizes it]). Many of the most illuminating passages of his writings illustrate this insight into how one culture selects and transforms the images of another in terms of its own values. In this respect, it is surely significant that the work Malraux revised most extensively in the 1970s was *La Métamorphose des dieux,* expanding it into three volumes, *Le Surnaturel, L'Irréel,* and *L'Intemporel.* Revised versions of other previously published writings on art (for instance, *Saturne, le destin, l'art et Goya* [1978; published in 1950 as *Saturne: Essai sur Goya* and translated as *Saturn: An Essay on Goya,* 1957]); the luxurious limited editions of volumes produced in collaboration with

Dalí (*Roi, je t'attends à Babylone . . .* [1977]) and Chagall (*Et sur la terre . . .* [1977]): and the moving filmed interview conducted by Pierre Dumayer and Walter G. Langlois and entitled *La Métamorphose du regard* (1973) provide further proof of Malraux's elevation of art to a form of secular religion.

During the same fertile last seven years of his life that followed his retirement from politics, Malraux completed an additional venture, which had begun with the publication of the *Antimémoires* in 1967. This book was greeted with near-unanimous praise from critics of all persuasions and became an immediate best-seller in France. Scenes from previously published fiction (*Le Temps du mépris* and *Les Noyers de l'Altenburg*) are interspersed with reminiscences upon lived experiences, recollections of dialogues with illustrious historical figures, and numerous reflections upon art, history, philosophy, and death. Malraux subordinates the self, the principal subject of traditional, narcissistic autobiography, to an atemporal, somewhat discontinuous meditation on "la condition humaine." In subsequent volumes, despite the variety of subject matters, he pursued his interrogation in much the same vein: *Les Chênes qu'on abat . . .* (1971; translated as *Fallen Oaks,* 1972) is a reconstruction of his last conversations with de Gaulle, on 11 December 1969, in the latter's library at Colombey; *Lazare* (1974; translated as *Lazarus,* 1977), based on his own near-fatal encounter with death in 1973, evokes the transience of all human activity; *La Tête d'obsidienne* (1974; translated as *Picasso's Mask,* 1976), a tribute to Picasso, both celebrates and questions the ability of art to ward off "le néant"; and *Hôtes de passage* (Passing Guests, 1975), which discusses the events of May 1968 and de Gaulle's fall from power, reveals among other things a fascination with the field of parapsychology. These four works were later reconstituted into *La Corde et les souris* (The Cord and the Mice, 1976), which, with a substantially revised version of the *Antimémoires,* became parts 1 and 2 of *Le Miroir des limbes,* published in 1976, shortly before Malraux's death from a pulmonary embolism on 23 November. As was the case with his key writings on art, *Le Surnaturel* (his most systematic book on literature) and the essay on Goya were published posthumously.

L'Homme précaire et la littérature (Precarious Man and Literature, 1977) is Malraux's only major full-length study on literature. "L'homme précaire" referred to in the title is twentieth-

Malraux at work (photo © Roland Dourdin/Rapho)

century man, who enjoys the dubious distinction of living in a civilization, on a planet, capable of self-annihilation. Though at the time of writing, Malraux's health was precarious, *L'Homme précaire et la littérature* is a vigorously youthful work. It is characterized by a lucidity and a verve which utterly belie the author's struggle with death. It weaves together strands both old and new and reveals a mind that is often perplexing, to say the least. On the one hand, Malraux is sensitive to many contemporary phenomena, particularly the intrusion of the audiovisual into our world of perceptions; yet, at the same time, benignly indifferent to many recent developments, such as structuralism or semiotics, that challenge acquired norms for reading literature. The enigma is all the more bewildering when one realizes that the most modern authors to figure briefly in the book are James Joyce and Marcel Proust.

Malraux's own contemporaries do not exist. But *L'Homme précaire et la littérature* is not literary criticism in the usual senses of the word: it is, rather, a long philosophical essay, which refers to history and the plastic arts as well as to literature, and which asks as many questions as it answers. Arguments are buttressed by aphorisms and analogies more than by logical development, and provocative comparisons challenge many received ideas on specific authors, works, and literary movements. Like so many of Malraux's works, it resists efforts to classify it in terms of a specific genre.

The cornerstone of *L'Homme précaire et la littérature* is Malraux's notion of *metamorphosis*, which had already provided a conceptual framework for his writings on art, from *Les Voix du silence* to *L'Intemporel,* and which is applied *mutatis mutandis* to the world of literature. Just as Giotto had discovered painting through the canvases of another artist, and not through the contemplation of a pastoral scene in Italy, so too the poet or novelist discovers literature not through sentiment or a *fait divers* (little incident) but as a result of reading poetry or novels. In both instances the painter and the writer react to, and will eventually react against, other forms. Malraux dispels romantic misinterpretations of the creative mind by making a crucial distinction between *l'imagination* (le domaine du rêve, the world of dreams) and *l'imaginaire* (le domaine des formes, the world of forms).

L'Homme précaire et la littérature is also a general indictment of certain critical approaches which were more prevalent when Malraux was writing than they have been in subsequent years and which, in Malraux's judgment, are mistaken precisely because they are content-oriented. His hostility to Freudo-Marxism and his distrust of realism, be it socialist or bourgeois realism, had been expressed as early as the 1930s. He maintains that even novels such as Emile Zola's *Germinal* (1885), which have workers as heroes and deal with the class struggle, have ultimately to contend with "l'irréalité fondamentale de la fiction"; and, in one of those perplexing equations that are peculiar to his thinking, Malraux adds that "les classes sont égales devant l'imaginaire comme les âmes devant Dieu" (classes are as equal before the imaginary as souls are before God). He rejects the myth of perfection in art, denounces subjective, impressionist criticism, and, in a more modernist vein, he stresses the shortcomings of criticism as interpretation.

In the first chapter Malraux identifies himself with those who attached "plus d'importance à l'art de La Fontaine qu'à sa biographie, sa morale, son temps" (more importance to the art of [seventeenth-century poet and fabulist Jean de] La Fontaine than to his biography, his ethics, his times). The context makes it abundantly clear that he was protesting against the limitations of positivism–the prevailing credo, during the interwar years, of the literary establishment, identified with the Sorbonne, the Académie Française, and the *Revue des Deux Mondes*–on the grounds that positivism reduced the creative impulse to "une combinaison de réels" (a combination of realities). This "combinaison de réels," the tendency to quantify the different components of a literary text, is not only reductive, but it also fails to acknowledge that autonomy to which the nineteenth-century novel, in particular, increasingly aspired. Throughout *L'Homme précaire et la*

littérature, Malraux compares and contrasts two different ways of reading a novel or of viewing film. For example, to read Flaubert's *Madame Bovary* or Stendhal's *Le Rouge et le noir* (*The Red and the Black*) in terms of "moyens d'information" (means of information) as opposed to "moyens de suggestion" is to ignore, or fail to see, not only "l'imaginaire de l'écriture" (the imaginary in writing) but that sense of the *irrémédiable* which great art seeks to express.

It is precisely this concern with the irremediable that prevents one from interpreting Malraux's concept of literature as an annexation of formalism, despite his undoubted interest in forms and their transformations. What is enigmatic, unknowable, unfathomable in the human condition cannot be communicated by rational means–what Malraux calls *l'argumentation*–but rather by *la contagion*. And the same holds true of literary criticism. Ultimately, the uniqueness of great literature, of Flaubert and Dostoyevski, for example, cannot be accounted for, even though the critic's analysis may illuminate such specific factors as the author's narrative techniques, use of plot, character, tropes, and so forth. Furthermore, in accordance with his abiding interest in metamorphosis, Malraux considered the creative process as fruitful an area of research as the final product. For example, in claiming that the study of Balzac's proofs and corrections to his manuscripts is more revealing than a scholarly article, he is projecting his own fascination with the transmutation undergone by *le vécu* when it is subjected to the alchemy of artistic creation. That this very process should escape the writer is borne out by Malraux's contention that theories advanced by the novelist are less revealing of his genius than those other works: the *Correspondance* in the case of Flaubert, the *Notebooks* in the case of Dostoyevski, in which "le mécanisme createur–qui se dérobe" (the creative mechanism, which escapes conscious control), is made manifest in its pristine purity.

L'Homme précaire et la littérature also raises, in its own peculiar and pertinent way, the question of the value of literature in a world whose precariousness is more apparent with each passing day. For Malraux, despite the emphasis he places upon form and metamorphosis, precariousness is indissolubly linked to the ethical imperative, and, in this respect, he is curiously consistent with the precocious youth who had written *La Tentation de l'Occident* some fifty years earlier. While conceding that literature both instructs and pleases, that it often edifies and uplifts, Malraux sees in the greatest works of art an expression of man's Promethean spirit. The precariousness of individual life is a metaphysical commonplace, but the precariousness of civilization is less so, and Malraux has illuminated contemporary man's predicament by adapting Paul Valéry's warning of 1919, "Nous autres civilisations, nous savons maintenant que nous sommes mortelles" (We civilizations, we know now that we are mortal), as "Nous autres chrysalides, nous savons maintenant que nous sommes provisoires" (We chrysalises, we know now that we are provisional).

Literature too is provisional, like the literature and library of Alexandria, and precarious too if by that we mean of doubtful or uncertain duration. But the term precarious, *precarius* in Latin, also designates that which is obtained by entreaty or by prayer, and it is difficult not to relate Malraux's choice of title to his conviction that a profound spiritual metamorphosis is quite conceivable as a response to the aleatory and the absurd. In the final pages of the last work he wrote, he does not relinquish his choice of agnosticism, as far as religion is concerned, but *L'Homme précaire et la littérature* concludes with an unanswered question, "Nous souviendrons-nous que les événements spirituels capitaux ont récusé toute prévision?" (Will we remember that spiritual events have challenged all foresight?). It is this very question, more than anything else, that separates Malraux's reflections on literature from those of the majority of his contemporaries.

In the last fifteen years of his life he received numerous honorary degrees–from the University of São Paulo (1959), the University of Benares (1965), Oxford University (1967), Jyväskylän University in Finland (1969), and Rajshahi University in Bangladesh (1973). He was also awarded the Nehru Prize for Peace (1973) and the Mexican government's Alfonso Reyes Prize (1976).

Interviews:
Roger Stéphane, *Chaque Homme est lié au monde,* volume 2, *Fin d'une jeunesse* (Paris: Table Ronde, 1954), pp. 40-69;
Guy Suarès, *Malraux, celui qui vient (Entretiens)* (Paris: Stock, 1974); translated by Derek Coltman as *Malraux: Past, Present, Future. Conversations with Guy Suarès* (London: Thames & Hudson, 1974; Boston: Little, Brown, 1974);

Frédéric J. Grover, *Six Entretiens avec André Malraux sur des écrivains de son temps (1959-1975)* (Paris: Gallimard, 1978);
Stéphane, *André Malraux: Entretiens et précisions* (Paris: Gallimard, 1984).

Bibliographies:
Walter G. Langlois, *André Malraux, 2. Première livraison. Malraux Criticism in English (1924-1970)* (Paris: Lettres Modernes, 1972);
Joseph D. Gauthier and John J. Michalczyk, "André Malraux: 1901-1976 (A Bibliography of Commemorative Items)" *Mélanges Malraux Miscellany,* 9-10 (Autumn-Spring 1977-1978): 5-54;
Robert S. Thornberry, "Mise à jour bibliographique. Ouvrages consacrés à André Malraux (1945-1984)," *Mélanges Malraux Miscellany,* 17 (Spring/Fall 1985): 122-139;
Thornberry, "Mise à jour bibliographique. Ouvrages consacrés à André Malraux (1984-1986)," *Revue André Malraux Review,* 18 (Fall 1986): 158-160.

Biographies:
Clara Malraux, *Le bruit de nos pas,* 6 volumes (Paris: Grasset, 1963-1979); translated in part by Patrick O'Brien as *Memoirs* (New York: Farrar, Straus & Giroux, 1967);
Walter G. Langlois, *André Malraux: The Indochina Adventure* (New York: Praeger, 1966);
Robert Payne, *A Portrait of André Malraux* (Englewood Cliffs, N.J.: Prentice-Hall, 1970);
Pierre Galante, *Malraux. Quel roman que sa vie* (Paris: Plon, Paris-Match & Presses de la Cité, 1971); translated by Haakon Chevalier as *Malraux* (New York: Cowles, 1971);
Jean Lacouture, *André Malraux: Une Vie dans le siècle* (Paris: Seuil, 1973); translated by Alan Sheridan as *André Malraux* (London: Deutsch, 1975; New York: Pantheon, 1975); French version revised and enlarged (Paris: Seuil, 1976);
Axel Madsen, *Malraux: A Biography* (New York: Morrow, 1976; London: Allen, 1977);
Suzanne Chantal, *Le Cœur battant: Josette Clotis-André Malraux* (Paris: Grasset, 1976);
Martine de Courcel, *Malraux, être et dire* (Paris: Plon, 1976);
Brigitte Friang, *Un Autre Malraux* (Paris: Plon, 1977);
Alain Malraux, *Les Marronniers de Boulogne* (Paris: Plon, 1978).

References:

Charles D. Blend, *André Malraux: Tragic Humanist* (Columbus: Ohio State University Press, 1963);

Gerda Blumenthal, *André Malraux: The Conquest of Dread* (Baltimore: Johns Hopkins Press, 1960);

Denis Boak, *André Malraux* (Oxford: Oxford University Press, 1968);

Robert Bréchon, *"La Condition humaine" d'André Malraux* (Paris: Hachette, 1972);

Barrie Cadwallader, *Crisis of the European Mind: A Study of André Malraux and Drieu la Rochelle* (Cardiff: University of Wales Press, 1981);

Jean Carduner, *La Création romanesque chez Malraux* (Paris: Nizet, 1968);

Philippe Carrard, *Malraux ou le récit hybride: Essai sur les techniques narratives dans "L'Espoir"* (Paris: Lettres Modernes, 1976);

Paul Raymond Côté, *Les Techniques picturales chez Malraux: Interrogation et métamorphose* (Sherbrooke, Quebec: Editions Naaman, 1984);

Jeanne Delhomme, *Temps et destin: Essai sur André Malraux* (Paris: Gallimard, 1955);

Jean-Marie Domenach and others, *Malraux* (Paris: Hachette, 1979);

Françoise E. Dorenlot, *Malraux ou l'unité de pensée* (Paris: Gallimard, 1970);

Dorenlot and Walter G. Langlois, "Les *Antimémoires* devant la critique française (1967)," *Mélanges Malraux Miscellany,* 2 (Autumn 1971): 3-15;

Henri Dumazeau, *"La Condition humaine": Malraux, Analyse critique* (Paris: Hatier, 1970);

Georges Duthuit, *Le Musée inimaginable,* 3 volumes (Paris: José Corti, 1956);

Elizabeth A. Ellis, *André Malraux et le monde de la nature* (Paris: Lettres Modernes, 1975);

Elizabeth Fallaize, *Malraux: La Voie royale* (London: Grant & Cutler, 1982);

Brian T. Fitch, *Les Deux Univers romanesques d'André Malraux* (Paris: Lettres Modernes, 1964);

Wilbur Merrill Frohock, *André Malraux* (New York & London: Columbia University Press, 1974);

Frohock, *André Malraux and the Tragic Imagination* (Stanford: Stanford University Press, 1952);

Pol Gaillard, *André Malraux* (Paris: Bordas, 1970);

Gaillard, *Les Critiques de notre temps et Malraux* (Paris: Garnier, 1970);

Gaillard, *"L'Espoir": Malraux, Analyse critique* (Paris: Hatier, 1970);

Edward Gannon, S.J., *The Honor of Being A Man: The World of André Malraux* (Chicago: Loyola University Press, 1957);

Serge Gaulupeau, *André Malraux et la mort* (Paris: Lettres Modernes, 1969);

James W. Greenlee, *Malraux's Heroes and History* (De Kalb: Northern Illinois University Press, 1975);

Bernard Halda, *Berenson et André Malraux* (Paris: Lettres Modernes, 1964);

Geoffrey T. Harris, *André Malraux: L'Ethique comme fonction de l'esthétique* (Paris: Lettres Modernes, 1972);

Geoffrey H. Hartman, *André Malraux* (London: Bowes & Bowes, 1960; New York: Hilary House, 1960);

François Hébert, *Triptyque de la mort: Une Lecture des romans de Malraux* (Montreal: Presses de l'Université de Montréal, 1978);

James Robert Hewitt, *André Malraux* (New York: Frederick Ungar, 1978);

J. A. Hiddleston, *André Malraux: "La Condition humaine"* (London: Arnold, 1973);

Joseph Hoffmann, *L'Humanisme de Malraux* (Paris: Klincksieck, 1963);

Violet M. Horvath, *André Malraux: The Human Adventure* (New York: New York University Press, 1969; London: University of London Press, 1969);

Cecil Jenkins, *André Malraux* (New York: Twayne, 1972);

Ileana Juilland, *Dictionnaire des idées dans d'œuvre d'André Malraux* (The Hague & Paris: Mouton, 1968);

Thomas Jefferson Kline, *André Malraux and the Metamorphosis of Death* (New York & London: Columbia University Press, 1973);

Rodolphe Lacasse, *Hemingway et Malraux: Destins de l'homme* (Montreal: Editions Cosmos, 1972);

Walter G. Langlois, *Via Malraux,* edited by David Bevan (Wolfville, Nova Scotia: Malraux Society, Acadia University, 1986);

Emile Lecerf, *André Malraux* (Paris: Richard-Masse, 1971);

R. W. B. Lewis, ed., *Malraux: A Collection of Critical Essays* (Englewood Cliffs, N. J.: Prentice-Hall, 1964);

André Lorant, *Orientations étrangères chez André Malraux: Dostoïevski et Trotsky* (Paris: Lettres Modernes, 1971);

Denis Marion, *André Malraux* (Paris: Seghers, 1970);

André Marissel, *La Pensée créatrice d'André Malraux* (Toulouse: Edouard Privat, 1979);

Claude Mauriac, *Malraux, ou le mal du héros* (Paris: Grasset, 1946);

Mélanges Malraux Miscellany (Laramie, Wyo., 1969-1983; Edmonton, Alberta, 1983-1986);

John J. Michalczyk, *André Malraux's "L'Espoir": The Propaganda/Art Film and the Spanish Civil War* (University, Miss.: Romance Monographs, 1977);

Christiane Moatti, *"La Condition humaine" d' André Malraux: Poétique du roman d'après l'étude du manuscrit* (Paris: Lettres Modernes, 1983);

Moatti, *Le Prédicateur et ses masques: Les Personnages d'André Malraux* (Paris: Publications de la Sorbonne, 1987);

Stefan Morawski, *L'Absolu et la forme: L'Esthétique d'André Malraux* (Paris: Klincksieck, 1972);

Will Morrisey, *Reflections on Malraux: Cultural Founding in Modernity* (Lanham, Md., New York & London: University Press of America, 1984);

Janine Mossuz, *André Malraux et le gaullisme* (Paris: Armand Colin, 1970);

New York Literary Forum, special issue on Malraux, edited by Françoise E. Dorenlot and Micheline Tison-Braun, 3 (1979);

Nouvelle Revue Française, special issue on Malraux, no. 295 (July 1977);

Gaëtan Picon, *André Malraux* (Paris: Gallimard, 1945);

Picon, *André Malraux par lui-même* (Paris: Seuil, 1953);

Revue André Malraux Review (Edmonton, Alberta, 1986-);

Revue d'Histoire littéraire de la France, special issue on Malraux, 81 (March-April 1981);

William Righter, *The Rhetorical Hero: An Essay on the Aesthetics of André Malraux* (London: Routledge, 1964);

John Beals Romeiser, *Critical Reception of André Malraux's "L'Espoir" in the French Press: December 1937-June 1940* (University, Miss.: Romance Monographs, 1980);

Pascal Sabourin, *La Réflexion sur l'art d' André Malraux: Origines et évolution* (Paris: Klincksieck, 1972);

Roch Smith, *Le Meurtrier et la vision tragique: Essai sur les romans d' André Malraux* (Paris: Didier, 1975);

Sud, special issue on Malraux, no. 21 (1977);

Claude Tannery, *Malraux, l'agnostique absolu ou la métamorphose comme loi du monde* (Paris: Gallimard, 1985);

Ralph Tarica, *Imagery in the Novels of André Malraux* (Rutherford, Madison & Teaneck: Fairleigh Dickinson University Press/London & Toronto: Associated University Press, 1980);

Brian Thompson and Carl A. Viggiani, eds., *Witnessing André Malraux: Visions and Re-visions* (Middletown, Conn.: Wesleyan University Press, 1984);

Robert S. Thornberry, *André Malraux et l'Espagne* (Geneva: Droz, 1977);

Micheline Tison-Braun, *Ce Monstre incomparable . . . : Malraux ou l'énigme du moi* (Paris: Armand Colin, 1983);

Twentieth Century Literature, special issue on Malraux, 24 (Fall 1978);

André Vandegans, *La Jeunesse littéraire d' André Malraux: Essai sur l'inspiration farfelue* (Paris: Pauvert, 1964);

Wascana Review, special issue on Malraux, 14 (Spring 1979);

David Wilkinson, *Malraux: An Essay in Political Criticism* (Cambridge: Harvard University Press, 1967);

Yale French Studies, special issue on Malraux, no. 18 (Winter 1957).

Papers:

Malraux's papers are at the Bibliothèque Nationale and the Fonds Jacques Doucet, both in Paris, and at the Harry Ransom Humanities Research Center, University of Texas at Austin.

Henry de Montherlant

(21 April 1896-21 September 1972)

John Fletcher
University of East Anglia

BOOKS: *La Relève du matin* (Paris: Société Littéraire de France, 1920; definitive edition, Paris: Grasset, 1933);

Le Songe (Paris: Grasset, 1922); translated by Terrence Kilmartin as *The Dream* (London: Weidenfeld & Nicolson, 1962; New York: Macmillan, 1963);

Les Olympiques, 2 volumes (Paris: Grasset, 1924)– comprises *Première Olympique: Le Paradis à l'ombre des épées* and *Deuxième Olympique: Les Onze devant la porte dorée*;

Chant funèbre pour les morts de Verdun (Paris: Grasset, 1925);

Les Bestiaires (Paris: Grasset, 1926); translated by Edwin Gile Rich as *The Bullfighters* (New York: Dial, 1927; London: Cape, 1928);

Aux fontaines du désir (Paris: Grasset, 1927);

Sans remède (Paris: Trémois, 1927);

Un Désir frustré mime l'amour (Paris: Lapina, 1928);

Pages de tendresse (Paris: Grasset, 1928);

Pour le délassement de l'auteur (Paris: Hazan, 1928);

Earinus: Troisième Olympique (Paris: Hazan, 1929);

L'Exil (Paris: Editions du Capitole, 1929);

Le Génie et les fumisteries du divin (Paris: Nouvelle Société, 1929);

Hispano-moresque (Paris: Emile-Paul, 1929);

La Petite Infante de Castille (Paris: Grasset, 1929);

Sous les drapeaux morts (Paris: Editions du Capitole, 1929);

Au petit mutilé (Paris: Editions des Portiques, 1930);

Pour une vierge noire (Paris: Editions du Cadran, 1930);

Mors et vita (Paris: Grasset, 1932);

Les Célibataires (Paris: Grasset, 1934); translated by Thomas McGreevy as *Lament for the Death of an Upper Class* (London: Miles, 1935); republished as *Perish in Their Pride* (New York: Knopf, 1936); translated by Kilmartin as *The Bachelors* (London: Weidenfeld & Nicolson, 1960; New York: Macmillan, 1960);

Henry de Montherlant (photograph copyright © Jerry Bauer)

Encore un instant de bonheur (Paris: Grasset, 1934; enlarged edition, Paris: Editions Rombaldi, 1951);

Il y a encore des paradis: Images d'Alger (Algiers: Soubiron, 1935);

Service inutile (Paris: Grasset, 1935; revised edition, Paris: Gallimard, 1952);

Les Jeunes Filles (Paris: Grasset, 1936); translated as *Young Girls* in *Pity for Women* (1937);

Pasiphaé (Tunis: Editions de Mirages, 1936; Paris: Grasset, 1938);

Pitié pour les femmes (Paris: Grasset, 1936); translated in *Pity for Women* (1937);

Le Démon du bien (Paris: Grasset, 1937); translated as *The Demon of Good* in *Costals and the Hippogriff* (1940);

Flèche du sud (Paris: Maurice d'Hartoy, 1937);

Pity for Women (London: Routledge, 1937; New York: Knopf, 1938)–comprises *Les Jeunes Filles*, translated by McGreevy as *Young Girls*, and *Pitié pour les femmes*, translated by John Rodker as *Pity for Women;*

L'Equinoxe de septembre (Paris: Grasset, 1938);

Les Lépreuses (Paris: Grasset, 1939); translated as *The Lepers* in *Costals and the Hippogriff* (1940);

Costals and the Hippogriff, translated by Rodker (New York: Knopf, 1940); republished as *The Lepers* (London: Routledge, 1940)–comprises *Le Démon du bien* and *Les Lépreuses;*

La Paix dans la guerre (Neuchâtel: Ides et Calendes, 1941);

Le Solstice de juin (Paris: Grasset, 1941);

La Reine morte; ou, Comment on tue les femmes (Paris: Grasset, 1942; revised edition, Paris: Gallimard, 1947); translated as *Queen After Death* in *The Master of Santiago, and Four Other Plays* (1951);

La Vie en forme de proue (Paris: Grasset, 1942);

Fils de personne (Paris: Gallimard, 1944); translated as *No Man's Son* in *The Master of Santiago, and Four Other Plays* (1951);

Un Incompris (Paris: Gallimard, 1944);

Un Voyageur solitaire est un diable (Paris: Lefebvre, 1945);

Malatesta (Lausanne: Marguerat, 1946; Paris: Gallimard, 1948); translated in *The Master of Santiago, and Four Other Plays* (1951);

Carnets XXIX à XXXV, du 19 février 1935 au 11 janvier 1939 (Paris: Table Ronde, 1947);

Le Maître de Santiago (Paris: Gallimard, 1947); translated in *The Master of Santiago, and Four Other Plays* (1951);

Pages catholiques (Paris: Plon, 1947);

Carnets XLII et XLIII, du 1 janvier 1942 au 31 décembre 1943 (Paris: Table Ronde, 1948);

Demain il fera jour (Paris: Gallimard, 1949); translated as *Tomorrow the Dawn* in *The Master of Santiago, and Four Other Plays* (1951);

L'Etoile du soir (Paris: Lefebvre, 1949);

Celles qu'on prend dans ses bras (Paris: Gallimard, 1950);

Coups de soleil, Afrique-Andalousie (Paris: Palatine, 1950);

Notes sur mon théâtre (Paris: Arche, 1950);

Le Théâtre complet, 6 volumes (Neuchâtel: Ides et Calendes, 1950);

La Cueilleuse de branches (Paris: Horay, 1951);

España sagrada (Paris: Wapler, 1951);

L'Infini est du côté de Malatesta (Paris: Gallimard, 1951);

The Master of Santiago, and Four Other Plays, translated by Jonathan Griffin (New York: Knopf, 1951; London: Routledge & Kegan Paul, 1951)–comprises *La Reine morte; ou, Comment on tue les femmes*, *Fils de personne*, *Malatesta*, *Le Maître de Santiago*, and *Demain il fera jour;*

La Ville dont le prince est un enfant (Paris: Gallimard, 1951); translated by Vivian Cox and Bernard Miles as *The Fire That Consumes* (San Francisco: Ritchie, 1980);

Le Fichier parisien (Paris: Palatine, 1952; enlarged, 1955; definitive edition, Paris: Gallimard, 1974);

Textes sous une occupation, 1940-1944 (Paris: Gallimard, 1953);

L'Histoire d'amour de "La Rose de sable" (Paris: Plon, 1954); translated by Alec Brown as *Desert Love* (London: Elek, 1957; New York: Noonday Press, 1957);

Port-Royal (Paris: Gallimard, 1954);

Carnets XXII à XXVIII, du 23 avril 1932 au 22 novembre 1934 (Paris: Table Ronde, 1955);

Brocéliande (Paris: Gallimard, 1956);

Carnets XIX à XXI, du 19 septembre 1930 au 26 avril 1932 (Paris: Table Ronde, 1956);

Carnets, années 1930 à 1944 (Paris: Gallimard, 1957);

Don Juan (Paris: Gallimard, 1958); revised and republished as *La Mort qui fait le trottoir* (Paris: Gallimard, 1972);

Romans et œuvres de fiction non théâtrales (Paris: Gallimard, 1959);

Le Cardinal d'Espagne (Paris: Gallimard, 1960);

Selected Essays, translated and edited by John Weightman (London: Weidenfeld & Nicolson, 1960; New York: Macmillan, 1961);

Le Chaos et la nuit (Paris: Gallimard, 1963); translated by Kilmartin as *Chaos and Night* (London: Weidenfeld & Nicolson, 1964; New York: Macmillan, 1964);

Discours de réception à l'Académie Française (Paris: Gallimard, 1963);

La Guerre civile (Paris: Gallimard, 1965); translated by Griffin as *The Civil War* in *Theatre of War*, edited by Robert Baldick (Harmondsworth, U.K.: Penguin, 1967);

Va jouer avec cette poussière: Carnets 1958-1964 (Paris: Gallimard, 1966);

La Rose de sable (Paris: Gallimard, 1968);

Montherlant in his infantry uniform, 1916

Les Garçons (Paris: Gallimard, 1969); translated by Kilmartin as *The Boys* (London: Weidenfeld & Nicolson, 1974);

Le Treizième César (Paris: Gallimard, 1970);

Un Assassin est mon maître (Paris: Gallimard, 1971);

La Tragédie sans masque: Notes de théâtre (Paris: Gallimard, 1972);

Mais aimons-nous ceux que nous aimons? (Paris: Gallimard, 1973);

Tous feux éteints: Carnets 1965, 1966, 1967, carnets sans dates, carnets 1972 (Paris: Gallimard, 1975);

Romans II (Paris: Gallimard, 1982);

Moustique (Paris: Table Ronde, 1986).

Collections: *Théâtre* (Paris: Gallimard, 1955); enlarged as *Théâtre de Montherlant* (Paris: Gallimard, 1968);

Essais (Paris: Gallimard, 1963);

Œuvre romanesque, 8 volumes (Paris: Editions Lidis, 1963-1964).

PLAY PRODUCTIONS: *Pasiphaé*, Paris, Théâtre Pigalle, 6 December 1938;

La Reine morte, Paris, Comédie-Française, 8 December 1942;

Fils de personne, Paris, Théâtre Saint-Georges, 18 December 1943;

Le Maître de Santiago, Paris, Théâtre-Hébertot, 26 January 1948;

Montherlant in 1920 (photo Martini-Viollet)

Demain il fera jour, Paris, Théâtre-Hébertot, 9 May 1949;

Celles qu'on prend dans ses bras, Paris, Théâtre de la Madeleine, 20 October 1950;

Malatesta, Paris, Théâtre Marigny, 19 December 1950;

Port-Royal, Paris, Comédie-Française, 8 December 1954;

Brocéliande, Paris, Comédie-Française, 1956;

Don Juan, Paris, Théâtre de l'Athénée, 1959;

Le Cardinal d'Espagne, Paris, Comédie-Française, 1960;

La Guerre civile, Paris, Théâtre de l'Œuvre, 27 January 1965;

La Ville dont le prince est un enfant, Paris, Théâtre Michel, 8 December 1967.

Considered by some to be one of the most impressive French writers of the twentieth century, Montherlant made his reputation with a series of outrageously antifeminist novels in the 1930s. Then, at the height of his powers, he wrote sev-

eral plays which are considered to be among the finest in the French language. Finally, toward the end of his life, he returned to the novel. Throughout his career he had been a prolific and influential essayist. His collected writings fill several substantial volumes of some fifteen hundred pages each. And yet his work remains in large measure outside the mainstream of contemporary French literature. Lucille Becker, one of his most perceptive English-language critics, makes clear why in her *Henry de Montherlant* (1970): "His glorification of the exceptional exploits and moral superiority of the hero is aristocratic, in a day when literature of that class has died out. While the majority of modern authors are preoccupied with the problems of the time, Montherlant, in conformity with the great classical tradition, is concerned with the eternal problems of the human soul. His emphasis on stylistic perfection is in contrast to the indifference of so many contemporary authors, for whom language is only a means used to transmit their ideas."

And yet Montherlant is fully of the twentieth century. His pessimism, his unsentimental attitude toward relations between the sexes, and his robust and vigorous writing style all situate him in a contemporary context. Frequently compared with the great French classical dramatists Corneille and Racine, he lacked their confident belief in transcendent values: for him, as for Jean-Paul Sartre, man was "une passion inutile" (a useless passion), and a pretty ridiculous one at that. He said that his true spiritual home was the ancient world, whose stoical beliefs were close to his own. But his neoclassicism was a studied affair, almost a self-conscious pose, a way of being different, the reverse of misty nostalgia of the kind indulged in by Anatole France.

The key to Montherlant's personality lies in his sexual orientation. He was, technically speaking, bisexual, in that he had relations with both male and female partners, but this "flamboyant creator of several Don Juan figures was at least three-quarters paedophiliac, so that *la chasse* or *la drague* [prowling the streets in search of a pickup] which he refers to so often in his novels and diaries was the pursuit of adolescent boys, rather than of girls or women," writes another perceptive critic, John Weightman, in a 1986 review of *Moustique* (1986) in the *Times Literary Supplement*. As a fellow writer, cited by Weightman, remarked, "Il n'est pas difficile de détester les femmes, quand on ne les aime pas" (It's not difficult to loathe women when you're none too keen on them).

Montherlant's biographer, Pierre Sipriot, believes that the notorious misogyny arose from the invert's compulsion to "murder the woman within himself." At the same time, Montherlant, who despised "crusading" homosexuals and, in fact, positively reveled in the deceits which persecution of gay men necessitated at that time, kept his personal life hidden from view and adopted the pose of a compulsive womanizer in his works. Believing that "un homme est ce qu'il cache" (a man is what he conceals), Montherlant created a whole series of fictions (in both novel and play form) which simultaneously divulge and deny the homosexual adventures that he both craved and feared in daily life.

Montherlant, the son of Joseph Millon and Marguerite Camusat de Riancey de Montherlant, was born in Paris on 21 April 1896. His personal situation was complicated by intense relationships with his mother (who nearly died in giving birth to him) and his adored grandmother, whose

Montherlant, circa 1930 (photo Harlingue-Viollet)

house he shared for many years. Not surprisingly, Montherlant never married. However, the cult of virility and of open contempt for women (viewed with few exceptions as weak, sentimental, dishonest, and mercenary) was not merely an individual invert's method of self-concealment, but also part of the spirit of the age. Other writers— André Malraux and Pierre Drieu La Rochelle in particular—glorified maleness at the expense of femininity (albeit from an exclusively, even aggressively heterosexual viewpoint), to say nothing of the obsession with "masculine" qualities by national leaders on the Fascist edge of contemporary politics. The Nazis were notorious for their propaganda in favor of warrior menfolk and homemaking womenfolk, and it is not without significance that Montherlant glorified both war and competitive sports, just as the Nazis did.

Nevertheless, it would be to caricature this writer to present him as a Fascist. Apart from the fact that Fascism, officially at least, is totally opposed to homosexuality and particularly pederasty, Fascists would have found Montherlant's irony and skepticism very little to their liking. As Robert B. Johnson puts it in *Henry de Montherlant* (1968), "Montherlant is French literature's twentieth century maverick," and mavericks do not, on the whole, endear themselves to political bigots. Although his failure to throw in his lot demonstratively with the Resistance led to his being mildly punished during the period immediately after the liberation of France in 1944, there was never any suggestion that Montherlant had seriously compromised himself by his alleged acts of collaboration with the Germans. Whereas other writers were executed for active support of the losing side, he was merely condemned to have nothing published for twelve months. Characteristically, he used the enforced leisure to write a masterpiece, *Le Maître de Santiago* (1947; translated as *The Master of Santiago,* 1951).

Now that the political passions aroused by the World War II period have cooled, it is clear that Montherlant's fastidious disdain for, even cynicism about, all enthusiasms not connected with the seduction of attractive boys was mistaken for active treachery. Clearly there are moments in human history when it is dangerous to be agnostic and positively foolhardy to make a virtue of agnosticism, as Montherlant did all through his life. It says more for the hysteria of 1944 that he had to go into hiding for a while, just as it says something for his basic integrity as a writer that, when the case was looked into, it was quite clear that he had done nothing more reprehensible than publish in journals that were not banned by the Germans.

Such an attitude of disdainful detachment smacks of the aristocrat, and indeed Montherlant had noble ancestry on both his father's and his mother's side. He was baptized in the Ancien Régime manner, held in the arms of a pauper over the font, and given the names Henry Marie Joseph Frédéric Expedite Millon de Montherlant. His early education took place at home, but at the age of about ten he was enrolled at the lycée Janson-de-Sailly, a leading Paris high school, where he discovered the language and culture of ancient Rome (particularly through Henryk Sienkiewicz's 1896 novel *Quo Vadis?*), which were to influence him for the rest of his life. After a year at the lycée he was taught briefly at home again and then went to the Ecole Saint-Pierre de Neuilly, a private Catholic high school near his home in the Paris suburb of Neuilly. It was here that he experienced passionate love for the first time, and it is clear that after this revelation he would never be able to envisage love other than with partners of his own sex. In doing so, he was following the precepts and example of the ancients whom he idolized.

In 1909, on a trip to visit the shrine at Lourdes with his grandmother, he discovered the ecstasy of the bullfight at a corrida in Bayonne. From then onward, to be involved in the bullring was for him to experience pleasures as intense as any, including sexual ones. In particular, this passion gave rise to his second novel, *Les Bestiaires* (1926; translated as *The Bullfighters,* 1927). There is an obvious comparison here with Ernest Hemingway, who also discovered bullfighting at an impressionable age, but unlike the American writer, Montherlant emphasized the pagan blood-cult aspects of the sport as much as its power to affirm macho principles of virility in the struggle for supremacy between (male) toreador and (male) bull.

In 1911 Montherlant moved to the Ecole Sainte-Croix-de-Neuilly, another private Catholic high school, to prepare for the *baccalauréat,* but before he could take the examination he was expelled for homosexual conduct. Although he passed the *baccalauréat* easily enough as an independent candidate, he never forgot the shame of this public scandal. The experience was, however, like everything else in Montherlant's life, put to good literary use: the circumstances surrounding his expulsion are the subject of the play *La Ville dont le prince est un enfant* and the novel *Les Garçons,* works which he began in 1914 but did not publish until much later, in 1951 and 1969, respectively. (The English translations, *The Fire That Consumes* and *The Boys,* appeared in 1980 and 1974.)

Montherlant at the time he wrote Le Maître de Santiago

In 1912, like many upper-class high-school graduates of the time, Montherlant began law studies. Although he soon dropped out of school, his vague status as a student enabled him to lead an active social and amorous life. The outbreak of World War I in 1914 would have brought this "student-prince" existence to an abrupt end had his mother, who felt death approaching, not implored him to postpone his intention to enlist. She died in 1915, to Montherlant's great grief, but it freed him to submit to an army medical examination, which he failed because of suspected cardiac problems. He was probably not unduly upset over this, since his enthusiasm for the virile experience of action on the front line, the subject of his first novel, *Le Songe* (1922; translated as *The Dream*, 1962), was more literary and theoretical than strictly practical; once again, the comparison with Hemingway, who based *A Farewell to Arms* (1929) on his experiences in the Italian campaign, is instructive.

When Montherlant was finally declared fit for military service in September 1917, it was for auxiliary work only, and so he found himself for a time working on a farm substituting for men who had gone to the front. No one reading the somewhat inflated rhetoric of Montherlant's rather tasteless panegyric of war in *Le Songe*

Mony Dalmès and Jean Yonnel in the 1942 Comédie-Française production of La Reine morte *(photo Bernand)*

would guess that its author, far from braving enemy fire, was hosing turnips in the rear. In early 1918 he completed his first major work, the volume of essays *La Relève du matin* (The Morning Relief); failing to find a publisher, Montherlant had the work printed two years later at his own expense.

Soon after completing these essays, he moved from auxiliary to active service and in June 1918 was wounded. He was transferred to duties as an interpreter with the U.S. Army and finally discharged in August 1919. At a loss for something to do, he became involved in the public campaign to build an ossuary for the Verdun dead at Douaumont and served as its general secretary until 1924. In 1925 he published *Chant funèbre pour les morts de Verdun*, dedicated to his "chers camarades" (dear comrades), a text (mostly in prose) that began as a sort of homage to the Verdun dead and developed into a long and perceptive meditation on war in twentieth-century Europe. While not extolling war, and recognizing that the conflict of 1914-1918 had been worse than most other wars, he argued that one should "ramener dans la paix les vertus de la guerre" (bring to peace the virtues of war), for

peace is in some ways an inferior status and certainly not to be taken for granted in a nation that has neglected civic virtue. He played soccer often during this period, and his experiences in the stadium led to the two-volume semi-fictional collection of prose, poetry, and drama, *Les Olympiques* (The Olympics, 1924), which appeared when his work for the ossuary scheme came to an end.

The year 1925 proved a turning point in Montherlant's life. His grandmother having died, nothing kept him in the family home at Neuilly. He moved to an apartment in Paris, and for the next thirteen years treated it only as storage space: he did not even unpack his trunks. He traveled widely instead, in search of exotic experiences. Montherlant, predictably, went to Spain (where he fought bulls and was more than once gored by them), and from Spain to North Africa where, as André Gide and other homosexual writers knew, the boys were both willing and inexpensive. Montherlant, like other affluent amateurs, took an occasional youth under his protection, apparently never fully aware (as Weightman puts it) that he was thereby "buying himself a sort of human pet." During these years he had affairs with women, too, particularly with a certain

Jeannine, whom he nearly married: a situation fictionalized in *Les Lépreuses* (1939; translated as *The Lepers* in *Costals and the Hippogriff*, 1940) in the broken engagement between Costals and Solange Dandillot, a character closely modeled on Jeannine.

During the late 1920s and the 1930s Montherlant established a solid notoriety as a particularly caustic and even iconoclastic novelist. He was much feted during his occasional sojourns in Paris. The books which made him famous were the Costals quartet–Costals, Montherlant's alter ego, being their amoral hero–published from 1936 to 1939 and known by the general title *Les Jeunes Filles*. But before writing this tetralogy–which comprises *Les Jeunes Filles* (1936; translated as *Young Girls* in *Pity for Women*, 1937), *Pitié pour les femmes* (1936; translated as the title work in *Pity for Women*, 1937), *Le Démon du bien* (1937; translated as *The Demon of Good* in *Costals and the Hippogriff*, 1940), and *Les Lépreuses*–he had already produced a substantial corpus of fiction, all of it stylish, sophisticated, and more or less shocking to conventional readers.

His first novel, *Le Songe*, set the tone. Like much of Montherlant's writing, it is semiautobiographical, being based on his war experiences (somewhat flatteringly fictionalized, it is true). Published in 1922, it introduces an upper-class young man, Alban de Bricoule, who was to figure again in *Les Bestiaires* some four years later. Alban, like his creator, is excused from active service for health reasons, but he rebels at the idea of being left out. He wants to join what he calls the "saint ordre mâle" (holy virile order) and stand side by side with his school friend Prinet under fire. Before leaving for the front he says goodbye to the two young women in his life. Between them these girls are the prototypes of nearly all the female characters in Montherlant's fiction.

Dominique Soubrier is an athlete and represents the virile, intellectual type, with whom genuine friendship is possible for a man. By the same token, the hero's relationship with her must remain purely platonic; when Dominique, moved by the proximity of death on meeting Alban behind the lines, becomes amorous, Alban is disgusted. The other female character, Douce, who is only briefly mentioned in the novel, is, as her appropriately chosen name meaning soft or gentle implies, the kind of woman a man "takes in his arms"–Montherlant's title for his 1950 play is *Celles qu'on prend dans ses bras* (Those That One

Takes in His Arms)–the passive mistress, the sensual primitive, the sex object, in contemporary parlance. Montherlant believed in the absolute division of relations between people: there were those one used for sensual gratification and those with whom one shared conversation, aesthetic experience, ideas. The two elements, spirituality and physicality, could not be found in the same relationship; to hope otherwise was, Montherlant maintained, to be guilty of sentimentality; and sentimentality in his eyes was the cardinal weakness of human beings. It is not difficult to see that it was Montherlant's inversion which led him to this rather desperate view of human love: as a pederast he sought out boys for gratification–and boys from deprived backgrounds, or from different cultures, for the most part–and reserved his "virile friendship" for such close homosexual friends as Roger Peyrefitte, with whom he corresponded intimately for several years but with whom he always used *vous*, the formal mode of address.

Having taken his departure, Alban plunges into the intoxication of military life, and has no fear of death: on the contrary, the idea of falling in action is exhilarating, even sensual in its intensity. On killing his first enemy soldier he feels fully initiated into manhood, his virility confirmed. He is, however, no sadist, and does not hate the Germans, so that he can give heed to the agonized plea of a dying prisoner for an instant of companionship to help his passing. Alban's conduct is perhaps explained by the fact that he is quite agnostic about the rights and wrongs of the conflict; he does not consider that he is fighting for his country, but engaged merely in "useless service" (a 1935 Montherlant title is *Service inutile*) which is undertaken for its own sake, without illusions and above all without sentimentality, in a pact of pure friendship and of self-sacrifice solemnized with one's comrades in arms.

The cruelty which Alban does inflict is not on France's invaders but on Dominique, whose craving for love he cynically belittles and destroys. He is the first of a long line of Montherlant heroes who abandon lovers who become dependent on them precisely because of the women's pathetic dependence. Ultimately, therefore, such men are not happy; but then, happiness is not something by which one would expect the unsentimental Montherlant to set great store. This stoical attitude is expressed in *Le Songe* in language of remarkable toughness and of graphic vividness which evokes, often bril-

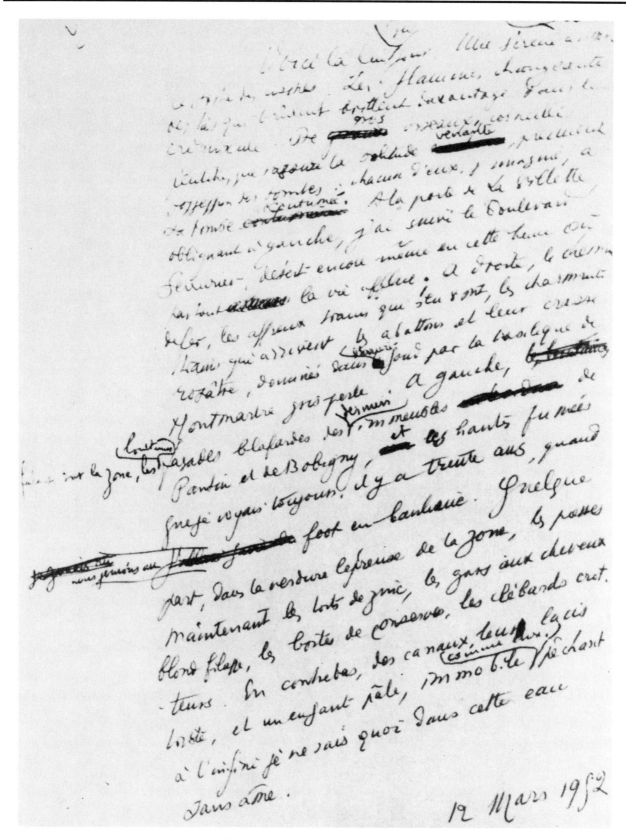

Last page of the manuscript for the story "Pantin parisien," which was published in Le Fichier parisien *(Pierre Sipriot,* Montherlant par lui-même, *Editions du Seuil, 1963)*

liantly, the sharp reality of physical things. Although flawed as first novels often are–in this case, the war scenes detract from the real focus of the book, which is Alban's lonely quest for identity–*Le· Songe* announced unmistakably that an important French stylist had arrived on the literary scene, one who, however perverse the sentiments expressed in his writings, was a force to be reckoned with. For Montherlant, election to the Académie Française was only a matter of time.

In his next work of fiction, *Les Olympiques*, published in 1924 to coincide with the holding of the Olympic Games in Paris after the war, Montherlant turned to sports in an attempt to rekindle enthusiasm for the physical self-transcendence and virile emulation which characterized life at the front. In competitive games, he declared, war was carried on with less murderous weapons, and he sought in them the calm and ordered violence, the courage, simplicity, and salubrity which he loved in war. Like military service, sports contribute to the development of character and to the building of physical fitness and inculcate that faith which for Montherlant was more important than any other, faith in oneself. They create order in a chaotic world; they glorify the isolation of the individual repudiating an effete society. The hero of this meditation on the austere beauty of sport is Jacques Peyrony, the real name of an athlete whom Montherlant befriended at this time.

With the 1926 novel *Les Bestiaires* Montherlant returned to his semi-fictional protagonist Alban de Bricoule. Alban has become a bullfighter facing not a national enemy–in any case, the story is set in the prewar period–but an equally worthy opponent, the black *toro* of the Spanish bullring. As the novel opens, Alban is restless to leave Paris, where he finds society and caste oppressive; once across the frontier into Spain he sheds the trappings of his bourgeois world with relief. He travels not only in space, however; in a sense he also travels in time, because in undergoing initiation into the mysteries of bullfighting he is also partaking in the cult of Mithra, the sun god of ancient Rome. Mithra's symbol is the sacrificed bull whose blood, marrow, and sperm provide mankind with everything–wine, corn, and meat–that supports life.

This mystical dimension to the novel is underpinned by realistic descriptions of the rearing and combating of the *toro;* there is also an erotic interest in the proposal by the woman Soledad to grant her favors to Alban if he will fight a particularly fearsome bull. True to type, he conquers the bull but disdains the girl's offer afterward; the corrida serves not to impress foolish women but to assert the power, virility, and supremacy of the hero in the world's eyes: "Il apparut à tous qu'au centre de l'arène une puissance souveraine agissait, qui seule était capable de ce détachement presque nuancé de dédain: la souveraineté de l'homme apparut à tous. Ce n'était plus un combat, c'était une incantation religieuse qu'élevaient ces gestes purs, plus beaux que ceux de l'amour, voisins de ceux qui domptent avec le taureau de grossiers spectateurs, et leur font venir les larmes aux yeux. Et celui qui les dessinait, soulevé de terre comme les mystiques par un extraordinaire bonheur corporel et spirituel, se sentait vivre une de ces hautes minutes délivrées où nous apparaît quelque chose d'accompli, que nous tirons de nous-même et que nous baptisons Dieu" (It appeared to everyone that in the center of the arena a sovereign power was active, one alone capable of this detachment tinged with disdain: the sovereignty of man was evident to all. It was no longer a combat, it was a religious incantation raised by those pure gestures which are more beautiful than those of love, and are similar to those which subdue not only the bull but also coarse spectators, bringing tears to their eyes. And he who performed them, raised above the earth as mystics are by an extraordinary physical and spiritual happiness, felt that he was living one of those moments of great gift in which we are vouchsafed a vision of something accomplished, which we derive from within ourselves and which we name God). In mastering the bull, Alban affirms his control over his own destiny, untrammeled by sentimental distractions. He also exemplifies the glorification of the body and the single-minded pursuit of physical pleasure which Montherlant propounds in his early novels. Although this theme was very much in the air at the time, he gave eloquent expression to it and thus stood out from other writers who held similar views but lacked the vivid descriptive style to create the same impact.

A slight piece of fiction, *La Petite Infante de Castille* (The Little Infanta of Castille), based on the traditional tale of a knight who encounters the Castilian infanta in a tree only to lose her because he hesitates, was published in 1929 and closed the short cycle of works with a Spanish setting. In the same year Montherlant wrote a book which opened a new series, but he immediately suppressed it because of its controversial subject matter; it finally appeared, long after his death, in 1986. *Moustique* (Mosquito) is the story of a shoe-shine boy who gives his name to the title and is hired in Marseilles by the author (who writes in his own name) as a manservant and companion. The couple travels widely and the relationship lasts eight years. The narrative, which peters out into disjointed notes, appears to end with Moustique's falling ill and dying in a hospital. The work is coy about the precise nature of the relationship between Montherlant and the boy, no doubt through loss of nerve on the author's part. Dealing with such a sensitive topic in his own name was clearly too much for Montherlant, who abandoned this work and returned to the subject later, in a less personal form, in *Les Garçons*.

La Rose de sable (The Sand Rose), written in 1930, was immediately suppressed because Montherlant feared that its attack on the abuses of French colonialism in North Africa would harm France's international interests at a time of increasing political tension in the world. In 1954 he published part of it–a love story able to stand on its own–under the title *L'Histoire d'amour de "La Rose de sable"* (translated as *Desert Love*, 1957), and the whole novel finally appeared in 1968 in a definitive edition, some years after the last French soldier had departed from France's former North African possessions. The hero, Lucien Auligny, is an ambitious young officer who gets himself transferred to a military fort in Morocco, where he hopes that promotion will come his way more rapidly than is likely to be the case if he remains in mainland France. He suffers, however, from isolation and boredom, which he seeks to relieve by taking up with a fifteen-year-old Arab girl, the prototype of Costals's mistress Rhadidja in *Les Lépreuses*. In *La Rose de sable* she is called Ram, and she is compared to a sand rose, that is, a small petrified formation in the sand of the desert surface which is beautiful to look at but only cold, inertly mineral, in reality. Thus, when Auligny falls in love with her she cannot reciprocate. When he puts his love before duty and declines to lead his men into battle in order to stay with her, she sees his action merely as weakness. Fully aware, however, of the futility of the sacrifice of his honor, Auligny earns the author's admiration–and election to the select club of Montherlant heroes–when he is killed, by the very natives whom he refused to fight, in a death as absurd as it is useless.

La Rose de sable has inevitably not exerted the impact it might have, had it been published in 1932 when it was completed; it was, to say the least, quixotic of the author to withhold a work of social and political relevance when he was prepared to offend his readers' susceptibilities in other ways. One cannot help feeling that some types of outrage were more to his taste than others: he was delighted to offend such women readers as Simone de Beauvoir with the *Jeunes Filles* tetralogy, but he held back works that revealed his pederasty too openly, or which might have upset the political establishment. It would have been more courageous, perhaps, to have published this solid work of realist fiction, which violently criticizes French society and vehemently repudiates the values of the modern world, at a time when it could have had an influence on the course of events.

Montherlant's next novel is also a work of literary realism. *Les Célibataires* (1934; translated as *Lament for the Death of an Upper Class* in 1935 and, more literally, as *The Bachelors* in 1960) was his first big commercial success, and it deploys all the traditional devices of the nineteenth-century novel, in particular a firm, linear time scheme with flashbacks clearly signaled. Two eccentric bachelors (based on Montherlant's uncles), ruined members of the aristocracy, fail to come to terms with the modern world, so imprisoned are they by their notions of caste and birth. The novel begins with the revelation of their dire financial straits; things soon go from bad to worse in a gloomy atmosphere of fatalism which reminds one of the novels of classic Russian writers. The end follows inevitably with the squalid, lonely death of one of the bachelors. "Léon est la victime désignée," writes Michel Raimond in *Les Romans de Montherlant* (1982), "*Les Célibataires*, c'est, aussi, l'histoire d'une mise à mort" (Leon is the scapegoat; *The Bachelors* is, too, the story of an execution). As the hero dies, he hears the wild geese flying south and, in spite of everything, "il confondait sa propre espérance avec cette autre espérance qui volait au haut des cieux" (his own hope merged with this other hope which was flying high up in the sky). There then follows a characteristically fine set-piece description of the migrating birds, hurrying as if they knew only too well "qu'on peut mourir pour une minute de trop qui n'est pas du bonheur" (that one can die for having wasted one moment of happiness).

Montherlant's best-known work of fiction, the four-volume *Les Jeunes Filles*, appeared at inter-

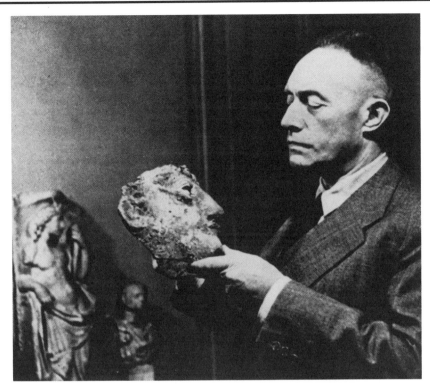

Montherlant at his home, 1954 (photo Match-*Jean Mangeot)*

vals during the late 1930s. With this major work Montherlant returned to the semi-autobiographical mode at which he excelled. The tetralogy is basically the chronicle of Pierre Costals's chequered relationships with various women, principally the provincial bluestocking Andrée Hacquebaut, from whom he receives many letters which he never even opens (although they are included in full for the reader), and the beautiful and rather stupid Solange Dandillot, whom he enjoys making love to and almost marries. When she (or rather her bourgeois mother) becomes too pressing about tying the knot, he escapes to North Africa where he has an incandescent–but entirely physical–affair with a young Arab girl who turns out to be suffering from leprosy. As if to mortify the flesh while at the same time proclaiming his sublime indifference to death, Costals does not stop sleeping with her after this discovery, but on the contrary revels in the danger. But as he has been exposed to syphilis and tuberculosis in the past and not caught anything from the women he associated with, he hopes to escape the consequences again this time. Somewhat bathetically, he is assured, after he returns to Paris and is examined by a specialist, that he has not contracted the sickness. At the same time he finally breaks with both Andrée

and Solange: Andrée when with characteristic incompetence in practical matters she fails to keep a rendezvous and thus involuntarily stands Costals up, and Solange when she marries a man (whom Costals dismisses as an "imbécile") simply because she wishes to avoid being an old maid like Andrée. In line with Montherlant's dualism, the stupid, sensual woman has given priority to her appetite, and the intellectual has muffed the one opportunity she might have had to share the life of the man she hero-worships.

This provocative work is often unfair to women, but it can be hard on men, too. Costals's vanity and heartlessness are laid bare just as harshly as the girls' sentimentality; their self-delusion, Andrée's pretentiousness, and Solange's vulgarity are all exposed for what they are. So it is not a complacent male view; rather, it offers an unflattering picture of human beings of both sexes: sexes whom nature has paired but who, Montherlant believes, simply do not suit each other. It is decidedly not a book for the romantically inclined, but also not a book to be taken very seriously. It is an amusingly cynical work but not one that merits a detailed feminist critique. Despite its qualities, it suffers from being at once sententious and anecdotal, weak on narrative and prolix on aphoristic moralizing; highly characteristic of its age but not strong on potential to endure.

In 1939 Montherlant moved to another flat in Paris. This was to remain his home for the rest of his life: indeed, it was there that he committed suicide in 1972. The move ushered in the second phase of his writing career, that of the dramatist. His first major play, *La Reine morte* (published in 1942; translated as *Queen After Death* in 1951), was written on an Iberian theme at the suggestion of the head of the Comédie-Française, Jean-Louis Vaudoyer. Once the idea had been discussed Montherlant wrote this play about the legendary Inés de Castro quickly, and it was put on at the Comédie-Française in Paris in December 1942, with the celebrated actress Madeleine Renaud in the title role. In the closing years of the war Montherlant wrote two other plays, *Fils de personne* (1944; translated as *No Man's Son*, 1951) and *Malatesta* (1946; translated, 1951); *Le Maître de Santiago* (1947; translated as *The Master of Santiago*, 1951) followed soon after. For the next two decades Montherlant was to devote most of his creative energies to the theater. Two other important events occurred during these busy years: in 1959 he suffered severe sunstroke, as a result of which his health (never robust) started to deteriorate; and in 1960 he was elected to the Académie Française even though he had refused, characteristically, to be a candidate or to canvas votes.

In the last phase of his life—during the late 1960s and the early 1970s—he returned to his first love, the novel, while still enjoying success in the theater with plays already written. In 1968 he lost the sight of his left eye. In 1970 he destroyed the only four extant typescript copies of a novel on an ancient Roman theme, "Le Préfet Spendius" (The Prefect Spendius), which he felt was too virulently anti-Christian to be published; he did not believe he should add to the Church's difficulties in an increasingly secular society. Then, on 21 September 1972, he took the step which he had been preparing to take all his life: fearing that he was going blind in his right eye as well, he stoically put an end to his sufferings by killing himself. His body was, as he had requested, cremated, a relatively unusual procedure in France, and his ashes were scattered appropriately in Rome, the ancient imperial city which he had admired since his school days.

The novels of Montherlant's last period reflect the darkening situation in his private life. *Le Chaos et la nuit* (1963; translated as *Chaos and Night*, 1964) deals with the chaos of life and the night of death. The hero is an anarchist veteran of the Spanish civil war who has lived ever since in exile in France. Over the years he has lost touch with the reality of Spain, and so it comes as a shock, when he finally returns in connection with a legacy, to discover that he is as much an exile in his own country, which has come to terms with Franco, as he was in France. His daughter in particular disappoints him because she soon feels completely at home in the postwar situation. Then, to crown it all, he tries to fulfill a longing he has cherished for twenty years, to see a bullfight, but that leaves him with a taste of ashes, too. There is nothing left for him to do but die himself, like the baited bull. Even death is not the final humiliation: his daughter flouts his wishes and gives him a church funeral followed by burial in consecrated ground. Everything he has stood for and believed in has come to nothing; his whole life and struggle are shown to have been totally futile; the only enemy he now confronts is the bland indifference of his fellow Spaniards for whom the late civil war, so potent a symbol still to the hero, is now merely an embarrassment.

Les Garçons appeared in 1969 after a long period of gestation and offers further variations on the theme of death. It centers on the character who figures prominently also in the play *La Ville dont le prince est un enfant,* the atheist priest de Pradts, for whom everything is meaningless except his much-loved work as an educator of boys, but who comes in the end to an intellectual belief in God. This novel also features the death of Alban's mother, Madame de Bricoule, a former beauty whose decline is described in painful detail as she learns to accept her approaching end with indifference. These two deaths, together with those of the boys of the school where de Pradts teaches who have been killed on active service in World War I, sound the knell of a whole era. There is something distinctly poignant about Montherlant's meditation on such a theme so many years after the end of that war and so few years before his own suicide.

His last novel, *Un Assassin est mon maître* (A Murderer Is My Master), was published in 1971. Again, the subject was one he had been meditating upon for many years: since 1928, in fact, when he met in Algiers the government official who was the model for the protagonist of this book. Once again Montherlant "nous raconte les derniers mois d'un malheureux abandonné à lui-même, victime de sa névrose, incapable de regarder les choses en face, de voir ce qui est et d'agir en conséquence" (recounts the last months of an unfortunate left to his own devices, a victim of neurosis, unable to face up to things, to see them as they are and to act accordingly), writes Michel Raimond, who describes the novel as a critique of an improper use of Freud's work, in that the hero attempts to treat himself on the basis of his reading of Freud and sinks ever more deeply into insanity.

It is not easy to determine how posterity will judge Montherlant's contribution to the novel. Like other French writers of his time he tended to use the art of fiction to express his own opinions and air his own prejudices, as if novel-writing were merely a more fanciful manner of drafting an essay. "De beaux livres, avec des pages d'anthologie" (fine books, with several pages worthy of being anthologized) is Raimond's considered verdict, and it seems an eminently fair one. Montherlant could certainly write memorable passages; whether he ever wrote a whole novel which will stand the test of time is, however, another question.

Letters:

Henry de Montherlant/Roger Peyrefitte: Correspondance (Paris: Laffont, 1983).

Biography:

Pierre Sipriot, *Montherlant sans masque: l'enfant prodigue 1895-1932* (Paris: Laffont, 1982).

References:

Lucille Becker, *Henry de Montherlant* (Carbondale: Southern Illinois University Press/London: Feffer & Simons, 1970);

John Cruikshank, *Montherlant* (Edinburgh: Oliver & Boyd, 1964);

Robert B. Johnson, *Henry de Montherlant* (New York: Twayne, 1968);

Michel Raimond, *Les Romans de Montherlant* (Paris: S.E.D.E.S., 1982);

John Weightman, "Incomplete Attachments," *Times Literary Supplement*, 5 September 1986, p. 979.

Paul Nizan

(7 February 1905-23 May 1940)

Walter Redfern
University of Reading

BOOKS: *Aden, Arabie* (Paris: Rieder, 1931); translated by Joan Pinkham (New York & London: Monthly Review Press, 1968);

Les Chiens de garde (Paris: Rieder, 1932); translated by Paul Fittingoff as *The Watchdogs: Philosophers of the Established Order* (New York & London: Monthly Review Press, 1971);

Antoine Bloyé (Paris: Grasset, 1933); translated by Edmund Stevens (New York & London: Monthly Review Press, 1973);

Le Cheval de Troie (Paris: Gallimard, 1935); translated by Charles Ashleigh as *The Trojan Horse* (London: Lawrence & Wishart, 1937; New York: Fertig, 1975);

Les Acharniens, adapted from Aristophanes' *The Acharnians* (Paris: Editions Sociales Internationales, 1937);

La Conspiration (Paris: Gallimard, 1938);

Chronique de septembre (Paris: Gallimard, 1939);

Paul Nizan, intellectuel communiste, 1926-1940: Articles et correspondance inédite, edited by Jean-Jacques Brochier (Paris: Maspero, 1967; enlarged, 2 volumes, 1970);

Pour une nouvelle culture, edited by Susan Suleiman (Paris: Grasset, 1971);

Complainte du carabin qui disséqua sa petite amie en fumant deux paquets de Maryland; Hécate ou la méprise sentimentale (Le Revest-les-Eaux: Spectres Familiers, 1982).

OTHER: Theodore Dreiser, *L'Amérique tragique,* translated by Nizan (Paris: Rieder, 1933);

Louis Fischer, *Les Soviets dans les affaires mondiales,* translated by Nizan (Paris: Gallimard, 1933);

"Marx philosophe," in Karl Marx, *Morceaux choisis,* edited by Henri Lefebvre and Norbert Guterman (Paris: Gallimard, 1933);

Henri Lefebvre, *Le Nationalisme contre les nations,* preface by Nizan (Paris: Editions Sociales Internationales, 1935);

Les Matérialistes de l'antiquité: Démocrite–Epicure–Lucrèce, edited, with a preface, by Nizan

Paul Nizan

(Paris: Editions Sociales Internationales, 1936).

Born to Pierre Nizan, a fairly prosperous railway engineer of illiterate Breton peasant stock, and Clémentine Nizan née Métour, a conventional, pious mother, Paul-Yves Nizan in his tragically curtailed life proved himself the best writer the French Communist party has so far had in its ranks and a classic twentieth-century novelist in his own right. His friend Jean-Paul Sartre was instrumental in rescuing his work from the oblivion imposed largely by the efforts of his former colleagues who wished to silence Nizan for leaving the party because of the Hitler-Stalin pact of mutual nonaggression in 1939. In the previous decade Nizan had worked hard, as a lycée teacher, a party militant, a journalist, a parliamentary candidate, and as a writer of fiction and essays, in order to serve the joint but often warring causes of communism and truthfulness.

A second child (his sister died at the age of seven), Nizan attended primary school first at Tours, then at Périgueux and the lycées Henri IV and Louis-le-Grand in Paris. He satisfied his teachers with his keen studying but also gave early notice of his budding independence of mind. He met and made friends with Sartre at school in Paris and renewed the friendship later at the Ecole Normale Supérieure. There were many intellectual and even personal resemblances between the two, both in their backgrounds and in their physical appearances. They were very close throughout their university years, despite growing differences in their views on politics, literature, and women. Sartre later realized that his friend had bidden farewell much sooner than he did to the idols of Western culture, especially literature and philosophy, and that Nizan had reached a remarkably mature political consciousness while still young. Generally their early passions were much more literary than political, though Nizan briefly joined Faisceau, the right-wing group of Georges Valois. In 1927 he joined the Communist party, and on 24 December of that year married, in a ceremony witnessed by Raymond Aron and Sartre, Henriette Alphen, the daughter of a genteel, prosperous, somewhat artistic middle-class family. The marriage produced two children, Anne-Marie (born in 1928) and Patrick (born in 1930). In 1926-1927, before his marriage, he held a post as tutor to a rich Anglo-French family in Aden, on the southwestern coast of the Arabian peninsula.

Despite being tempted by offers of a lucrative position by his employer, Antonin Besse, Nizan turned his back on capitalism, and in his first book, *Aden, Arabie* (1931; translated, 1968), began his caustic polemical analysis of the contemporary West. He later wrote in his novel *La Conspiration* (The Conspiracy, 1938): "Un jeune homme est le seul être qui ait le cœur de tout exiger et de se croire volé s'il n'a pas tout" (A young man is the only one with guts enough to demand all or nothing and to feel robbed if he does not get it). In *Aden, Arabie* he had expressed, dialectically, the counterproposition: "J'avais vingt ans. Je ne laisserai personne dire

que c'est le plus bel âge de la vie" (I was twenty. I will not allow anyone to tell me that youth is the best time of life). It is this alternation between passion and cold-eyed judgment that gives Nizan's writing its characteristic charge.

As a student Nizan had experienced the "Ecole dite Normale et prétendue Supérieure" (the so-called Normal and would-be Superior School) as a hothouse insulated against external reality; he lived there in a largely verbal universe. Like many well-educated young Frenchmen, Nizan was a bookish youth. Like Albert Camus's Clamence in *La Chute* (The Fall, 1956), he could well have asked "Ai-je lu cela, ou l'ai-je pensé?" (Did I read that somewhere, or did I think it up for myself?) It was in reaction to such enervating contamination that Nizan chose for his twin targets in *Aden, Arabie* the French *Université* (that is, the whole of the higher educational system) and capitalist imperialism: the parochial and the universal. The connection is that the spurious values inculcated by the first agency (the cult of impersonal reason, which leads to an ahistorical stance and political abstentionism) encourage the practice of the second enterprise. In Aden familiarity with the colonialist regime quickly bred contempt, just as distance from France led to disenchantment with the home country. Aden, for Nizan, was a microcosm, a compressed version of Europe, where foreign exploitation produced the extremes of powerful but mostly abstract wealth (that is, vast sums exchanged by bank drafts and checks) and real, extensive poverty.

Aden lies at the center of an extinct volcano, like a huge shell-crater, and it is mainly sterile. Nizan's description of this apocalyptic landscape as the "mouth of hell" is hardly an exaggeration. Fishbones exposed on the beach led him to see Aden as a skeletal image of Europe.

In the East Nizan found his true orientation: the decision to wage war, by the means at his disposal–writing and militancy–on those who live off the awe they unjustifiably inspire. *Aden, Arabie* is a bitter, violent, often pompous, but essentially tonic essay. Seeking to deal a blow to his class of origin as a small gesture of solidarity with exploited workers, and in line with Lenin's injunction to steal back from and use against the bourgeoisie what it had stolen from the people, Nizan exploits capitalist imagery (for example, from accountancy). His critique is nonetheless also self-criticism, a response to what he felt was a baleful warning of his own imminent collapse into death-in-life. *Aden, Arabie* is the charged account of a near miss, in which Nizan treats sardonically his own foolish need to travel abroad in order to discover home truths. He narrowly escaped death in a car accident, having been overcome by sunstroke. He was always vulnerable. His work is built on the tensions of the narrow escape, last-ditch salvage, precarious survival. The movement of *Aden, Arabie* goes less from dilemma to solution (Nizan mocked, a long time before Sartre's *Les Mots* [*The Words*, 1964], the concept of the writer-as-savior), than from nameless panic, which provoked the flight, to identifiable opponents to be confronted on their home ground, France. Pascal Ory, in *Nizan, destin d'un révolté* (1980), describes *Aden, Arabie* as the work of a young man more "enragé" than "engagé"; the book received only slight critical attention. Yet the writing of this first publication cleared the way for Nizan to join the Communist party, possibly at the outset more for ethical or provocative reasons than truly political ones.

In July 1929 Nizan passed the examination for the *agrégation*, the highest degree leading to a teaching career, with a specialization in philosophy. He then had to spend a year doing his military service. The young couple lived with his wife's parents. After his military service, he briefly worked in journalism and resumed his writing. He also maintained ties with former classmates at the Ecole Normale Supérieure and the Sorbonne, including Sartre, Simone de Beauvoir, and others, some of whom were militant Marxists.

His first journalistic efforts went to writing for university Marxist periodicals, where he often disconcerted his more anarchistic colleagues by his orthodox plugging of the party line on class war. He started in the area he knew best: education, the French intellectual elite. In his second book, *Les Chiens de garde* (1932; translated as *The Watchdogs*, 1971), published while he was teaching philosophy at the lycée in Bourg-en-Bresse, he locates the twin mystiques of the French governing classes in the cult of impersonal, atemporal reason and the belief in the superiority of the "inner man": two pretexts for social inaction. While this essay is part of the unending internecine war between French intellectuals of antagonistic camps and suffers from the taking of lycée or university for the whole of France, the text still strikes home. Nizan's "watchdogs" (teachers, state inspectors, ministers of education, and those bourgeois who seek to justify their self-appointed mission to be bosses by reference to some

intellectual hierarchy), unfortunately, exercise real influence. They are a sort of ersatz clergy. Because Nizan sees abstract philosophy as the ultimate form of equivocation and intelligence as merely a tool available to all sides in any conflict, he can offer no guaranteed truth. All he can do is pinpoint the social consequences of particular philosophical stances. For him, professional philosophers talk shop, their inky emissions insulating them like squids. It is into this vicious circle that Nizan intrudes, deflating the Cartesian idol of reason.

In *Les Chiens de garde* Nizan shows off less than he does in *Aden, Arabie*; even the extensive footnotes are strictly functional. Nizan asks here the awkward questions: Why do human beings let themselves live so badly? Who does their thinking for them, and why? Marx is quoted on the revolutionary impulse that springs from shame. To this Nizan adds a horror of the void. The tone is one of arrogantly phrased humility, Tacitean pungency: "Et ils nomment cette hygiène Philosophie" (And they call this sterility Philosophy). Amid the delectable iconoclastic rudeness, Nizan makes a rueful admission that he himself had all but been taken in by the soothing conformist teachings of Alain, Henri-Louis Bergson, and Emile Durkheim.

After *Aden, Arabie* and *Les Chiens de garde* (which, like *Aden, Arabie*, sold only few copies), Nizan needed to anchor his critique of contemporary French society in concrete particulars and to give it a historical basis. In *Antoine Bloyé* (1933; translated, 1973), he rewrote the life story of his father (who had died in 1930), in order to brood more comprehensively on the question of the unlived life. The novel, which received one vote for the Prix Goncourt, starts and ends with the death of its unextraordinary hero. In between, his life is delineated as a journey on a treadmill. He is a brighter-than-average lad of peasant stock, directed by his social betters to a technical education designed to provide middle management for the railway boom of the late nineteenth century. He moves steadily through the stages of apprentice, driver, engineer, and depot manager, in the course of a life which is outwardly successful but inwardly unfulfilled and frustrated. At intervals this inarticulate good worker senses that much of his being lies fallow, that he has sold himself or been sold short, but he does nothing to get himself off the rails of his seemingly preordered existence. Apart from one traumatic and fruitless attempt to whip up collective protest when he

Nizan (standing at right) with Jean-Paul Sartre (seated on chimney) and other students on the rooftop of the Ecole Normale Supérieure, 1927 (Collection particulière, photo Editions Gallimard)

was a student, he never integrates his spasmodic anger into political action.

Though written by a Communist, this novel describes a pre-Communist man. The kind of Marxism informing Nizan's approach and language places a strong emphasis on personal responsibility as well as on economic determinism. When Bloyé has to collaborate, as a manager, in strike-breaking, his creator makes no bones about calling him a traitor to his class of origin, betrayal being an unforgivable act when the group in question is the working class. As this novel castigates its hero's treachery, it piles the agony on thick; there is nothing skeletal here. Antoine Bloyé is trapped not only in the spider's web of capitalist industrialism, but also in the saccharine slavery of a respectable middle-class marriage. More willing to acknowledge the theories of Freud than was common among Marxists in the 1930s, especially in France, where there was resistance to Freud generally, Nizan makes full room for psychology—the role of dreams, the private idiosyncratic self—in the total picture. Indeed, the most impressive section of this powerful novel deals with the aging of Bloyé: his impotent sexual furies, his naked terror of dying before he has truly lived, his desperate and belated attempts to make living contact with other human beings. He has been living what Louis-Ferdinand Céline would later call "la mort à crédit"—death on the installment plan.

This novel accommodates not only Marx, Freud, and Zola (the last in Nizan's densely textured, naturalistic, documentary account of an age, 1860-1920) but also Pascal. Bloyé's life is one long *divertissement*, or distraction. In a rare moment of awareness, he telescopes a lifespan of seventy years into one day. The idea of dying at midnight instead of in some vague future, "thirty years hence," carries a real Pascalian punch. Shortly before his actual death, Bloyé sees "cette image vaine de lui-même, cet être décapité qui marchait dans le cendre du temps à pas précipités, sans repères" (this defeated image of himself, that headless being who walked in the ashes of time with hurrying steps, aimlessly). The undeniable morbidity is not gratuitous but stems rather from a concern for what men sadly fail to do in order to counteract their imposed fates. There is an underlying compassion and sustained effort of comprehension, especially in the section on the tragically brief life of Bloyé's first child, ill with a terminal disease from her birth. Nizan's first novel accentuates the negative, but as a preparation for the positive. Its protagonist, or rather agonist, submits to the call of the tame, but his son's growing anger foretells different options for members of the next generation, who will reject more forcefully the offer to repeat their fathers' lives. *Antoine Bloyé* says in effect: here are the facts of life. Now what is one to do with what is done to him? "Quel homme sait triompher de sa division? Il n'en triomphera point tout seul, car les causes de sa division ne sont pas en lui" (Can a man surmount his inner divisions? He cannot do it alone, for the causes of these divisions are outside him). Throughout this work Nizan shows himself to be an acute reader of signs. His critical intelligence slices through the camouflaging rhetoric not only of official mystifications but also of the day-to-day fallacies and lies with which man cushions his existence. The virtues of this novel are not dramatic but cumulative. It deals a measured, heavy jolt to complacency. Its bleak but not dispiriting lesson is that everything has to be paid for. But equally: no one is a nobody.

In the 1930s Nizan wrote several articles on proletarian literature. While no doubt inhabited by guilt at his own privileged position, he betrayed no urge to become, or even to envy from a distance, a manual worker. He had therefore serious doubts about some of the premises that would lead to the official Soviet doctrine of Socialist Realism. For Nizan, converts (laudable traitors) from the bourgeoisie must work by constant practice to associate their efforts, by emotional, intellectual, and political training, with the aims and values of the proletariat, whose spokesmen they are.

In *Antoine Bloyé* Nizan speaks through and for his hero. The danger is obviously that the author might appropriate too far, and the dearth of dialogue certainly makes this an authorially commanding narrative. One must recognize that Nizan is exploiting an exploited man as a means of protesting against exploitation. The Marxist standpoint is used as a means of correcting vision and not, as with Louis Aragon, as a substitute for sight. The Communists' reaction to *Antoine Bloyé* was grudging; no doubt they were annoyed at Nizan's portrait of an amorphous, unguided proletariat, though in the period he covers this version was unarguably truer than the party line of a consciously revolutionary working class. Sartre's later neo-Freudian diagnosis of the text in *Situations IV* (1964) places too reductive a stress on family civil war and underplays the more universal kinds of alienation examined in *Antoine Bloyé*. In short, Sartre offers too exclusively pathological and melodramatic a reading of this novel to do it proper justice, though his efforts at refamiliarizing the public of the 1960s with Nizan's writings were invaluable.

As a teacher of philosophy at Bourg in 1931-1932, Nizan opposed the Marxist as well as the establishment varieties of brainwashing; teach-

ing was not a machine dispensing ready-made opinions. He kept his pedagogical and his militant functions quite separate but soon upset local sensibilities by his out-of-school agitation, his efforts to persuade the unemployed of Bourg to affiliate with the central workers' syndicate after forming their own union. Despite being denounced in the local press as a "Red Messiah," Nizan persevered and ran in the 1932 legislative elections, where his minimal score of votes mirrored the national electoral disaster of the Communist party. He had simply wanted to involve himself in the concrete processes of politics at the grass-roots level, to see for himself what were the obstacles to radical renewal. As well as his journalism in Communist or antifascist papers and journals (book reviews, articles on politics and on education), Nizan taught courses at the Université Ouvrière (Workers' University in Paris) on Soviet literature and the history of materialist philosophy. In 1936 he produced a useful anthology, *Les Matérialistes de l'antiquité* (The Materialists of Antiquity). At the party's Ecole Centrale, Nizan ran courses on Marx, Lenin, and the histories of Ireland and of Russia. He was for a time, with his wife, in charge of the bookshop run by the Communist paper *Humanité*. He was continuously busy. In 1933 he was appointed editorial secretary of *Commune*, soon to become the leading Communist cultural periodical and the organ of the Association des Ecrivains et Artistes Révolutionnaires. Its aim was to widen the antifascist front.

Nizan spent the year 1934 in Russia, partly to edit some issues of *La Littérature Internationale* and partly to study the Soviet experiment firsthand and to attend the 1934 Soviet Writers' Congress, which attracted Communist intellectuals and fellow-traveling or sympathizing writers from many countries. While he was there Nizan worked on an adaptation of Aristophanes' play *The Acharnians* for the Jewish State Theatre in Moscow, preserving the essentials of its witty antiwar message. He traveled extensively in Soviet Central Asia, which he evoked with considerable force in several long articles. He insisted on the rich diversity of Russian peoples and the need to tame nature in this pioneer area of virgin soil, but was equally aware that the land marks man as well as being marked by him. Perhaps from his Breton roots, Nizan always retained a strong feeling for the countryside while rejecting the antiindustrial visions of Jean Giono or Charles-Ferdinand Ramuz. Nature could both be harnessed to human needs and transformations and admired as a source of awesome beauty. This attitude saved him from existing, like so many French intellectuals, in a cerebral hothouse insulated against the weather outside.

His report on Soviet Russia was no panegyric but a measured account of a nascent society, still messy and unjust, but containing the seeds of hope. He was clinging to the tactic of giving the benefit of the doubt. He kept largely silent on the purges of dissidents, no doubt aware of his own precarious status as a never completely trusted intellectual member of the party. On one issue he was fully himself: his obsession with death. Everywhere he went, he asked Russians whether the new disposition gave any more solid sense to their lives and thereby reduced the awfulness of death but received only ambiguous responses or answers that were not reassuring. Amid urgent public and collective duties and sacrifices, the private self remained precious yet violable.

Nizan applied to the novel what Marx said of philosophy: that it must force people (inside or outside its covers) to be conscious of themselves and their world. He was always saying in the 1930s in briefer terms what Sartre would say in 1947 in "Qu'est-ce que la littérature?" Writers must renounce their traditional narcissism; the problems they choose to embody in literature should enlarge the nineteenth-century idea of "character"; and the new literature must be one opening on the future and based on will, not one harking back to the past and centered on description. Seeking a concrete image for the contemporary situation (a compound of hope and ignorance, the area of the provisional), Nizan chose the common place of street-level political confrontation for his 1935 novel *Le Cheval de Troie* (translated as *The Trojan Horse*, 1937), part of which he wrote in Russia.

The early 1930s had already seen violent street clashes in Paris between right-wing and antifascist groups. This novel switches from the solitary man, Antoine Bloyé, to the militant group: Communist workers and intellectuals cooperating in a provincial town. *Le Cheval de Troie* opens with a breathing space, Nizan's description of a Sunday outing to the country; but later events of the narrative are present embryonically in the peaceful opening. The bodies lying in the grass are a prelude to those prostrate on the bloody pavements at the finale. Nizan's economy as a writer, his balance of optimism and doubts, and

his critical intelligence help to keep this text from lapsing into the excesses of propaganda. His group of characters has no idealized corporate soul; within it, pairs quarrel. The theme of secretion recurs here, as it does in all of Nizan's work. The property owners create their own protective shells; a married couple harbors mutual bitterness; all humans hug the skeletons in their own cupboards; and all secrete death. The title provides an image of concealment, but also a potential breakout from constriction.

Through his spokesman Pierre Bloyé (son of Antoine), a teacher, Nizan recognizes that to see such utterly bereft and dejected people as the Armenian textile workers as human beings demands an act of faith and will. Bloyé serves to link the differing social levels in this novel. His colleague at the lycée, Lange, is an opposite and cerebral pole to the militant Bloyé: an amalgam of Pierre Drieu La Rochelle and the Sartre of the 1930s. Lange has a mind that is ceaselessly ticking over and building up lustful visions of cataclysms; he is excited by reports of brutality in Hitler's Reich. Thus this novel houses the middle, bottom, and top of the social pyramid: metaphysics (the luxury but real despair of Lange) as well as economics; sexual problems alongside and intermingled with politics, for one of the militant couples seeks an abortion of the child they cannot afford. The Communists are learning to work in concert with Socialists and Radicals, just as the bullies of the Fascist street gangs win guarded sympathy from local bigwigs (industrialists, an army commander, the prefect). Bloyé has undergone the same education at the Ecole Normale Supérieure as Lange but has recovered from the lack of gravity in abstract speculation. Though still preoccupied by mortality, he uses it more as a reminder of the urgent need to act: "On ne change rien qu'au risque de la mort. On ne transforme rien qu'en pensant à la mort" (Nothing is changed except by risking death. Nothing is changed except by thinking of death).

The climax of the novel is the street battle. Perhaps recalling his own brief adhesion in the 1920s to the Faisceau, or Chemises Bleues (Blue Shirts), of Georges Valois, Nizan takes care to motivate the enemy, to avoid making them cardboard dummies. The Fascist thugs are drawn by sporting desires, by opportunism, by confused longings for change and emancipation, "un effort maladroit pour respirer" (a clumsy attempt to breathe properly). While the confrontation builds up, Catherine, who has had the abortion she

Nizan and André Gide at the International Writers' Congress for the Defense of Culture, Paris, 1935 (photo Gisèle Freund)

sought, is suffering a hemorrhage alone in a room. She agonizingly loses her life, as does Antoine Bloyé, by asphyxiation–social as much as medical. These episodes are not counterpointed but concurrent. Political commitment does little to abolish private grief. In Nizan's nonmiraculous world, everything has to be paid for in full. The would-be separatist Lange gets caught up in the crowd among the Fascists. Hit by a stone, he fires the tiny revolver he has picked up on the street. Unattached thought, for Nizan, can veer into such lethal options. The book-bound intellectual has erupted with a gesture of terrorism. The normal Sunday life of the town goes on around the fighting. After the Fascists have been routed, the riot police charge the antifascists but are forced to withdraw from combat in the narrow backstreets. The total event is as yet of mainly local significance, but a new tradition has been born, of resistance, solidarity, and self-assertion. On a few occasions, Nizan allows rhetoric to inflate the scale of events. At such times the propagandist tone is unabashed. But Nizan's artistic instinct made him offset, or at least complicate, this single-mindedness with doubt, defeats, wasted energy, and death.

Le Cheval de Troie can no more be dismissed as edifying than *Antoine Bloyé* as purely negative. This novel ends with a dawn, but a chill one; hopefulness, but not untainted. Lange and Catherine are as important in this book's natural balance as

are the political issues. For all its dogmatism, it is an open-ended work. The battle is a dubious one. What matters most is that after centuries of cowed acquiescence a partly prepared but largely spontaneous upsurge (and not the glamorous exploits of elite individuals in the fashion of André Malraux's novels) unites formerly atomized people in a collective struggle. It is a show of strength, possibly a courageous lie, such as those saluted by Nizan in the works of Dickens and Tolstoy.

While writing his novels, Nizan was also functioning as a party hack or at least journeyman (he joined *Humanité* in 1935), with some privileged high spots, such as the Congrès International des Ecrivains pour la Défense de la Culture in Paris, which he attended in 1935; the Communist party dialogues with liberal Catholics, which helped to clear the way for the Popular Front; and lecture tours around France. Nizan widened his political education by going to Spain in 1936 to write reports on the first stages of the Spanish civil war for *Regards*. In these he displayed Stendhalian powers of swift, evocative notation and judgment of what he observed on the spot. He was never an armchair journalist any more than he was a *communiste de salon*. His accounts were well informed and balanced, though he witnessed only the more hopeful overture of the war. In 1937 he joined the new upmarket Communist evening paper *Ce Soir* (the editors were

Louis Aragon and Jean-Richard Bloch; contributors included Jean Renoir and Robert Desnos) and took charge of foreign-affairs coverage, as well as contributing many book reviews of a more freewheeling nature than was possible when he was writing for *Humanité* in the early 1930s. He also covered the Tour de France cycle race, which enabled him to visit most of France. Though no sports buff himself, he had always valued physical expenditure and enjoyment as a counterbalance to the cerebral French tradition. This tradition in the intelligentsia receives full analysis and caustic evaluation in Nizan's best novel, *La Conspiration*, which won the Prix Interallié. In his study of this work, Sartre wondered whether it was possible for a Communist to write a good novel, since he had no right to be the accomplice of his almost inevitably bourgeois characters. Sartre's question is more loaded than Nizan's novel.

The group of young men at the center of *La Conspiration* are at the awkward age of French middle-class studenthood, in their early twenties. It includes Rosenthal, who sees himself as the leader; Simon, who is later arrested and imprisoned for stealing documents; Pluvinage, a Communist who betrays another party member being sought by the police; and Laforgue. Nizan's own experiences as a young man provide some of the details of the plot. Typically, the group members operate mainly from a comfortable home base, are supported financially by their families, and pursue their studies in very eclectic fashion. Their posture, or imposture, comes under the author's keen scrutiny: their preference for believing that a thought is an action, that the mere fact of verbalization alters situations. Nizan's young rebels indict their society, which they persist in envisaging as a macrocosm of their family situations, and conspire against what they see as the plot of their families to neutralize them by providing safe careers. As well as reading Spinoza, Hegel, Marx, and Lenin, they are influenced by the surrealist movement of the 1920s. Despite their articulateness and cultural know-how, they are ignorant of the real world of the mass of men. The periodical that they launch (subsidized by capitalist philanthropy), the *Guerre Civile*, is aimed much more against the idealist official philosophy of the Sorbonne than toward militant action. From the start Nizan both understands and mocks these youths' ambitions. "Ils ne savaient pas encore comme c'est lourd et mou le monde, comme il ressemble . . . à un amas sans queue ni tête de gélatine" (They were unaware as yet just how heavy and flabby the world is, how close it is to a shapeless mass of gelatine). This statement sets the tone for the whole novel: an intelligent disgust with misapplied intellect, combined with a profound sense of a world ruled by multiple and enigmatic conspiracies.

The first issues of the group's would-be radical review elicit that phenomenon intolerable to rebels: impunity, or repressive tolerance. Rosenthal begins to hanker for some definitive commitment but ignores the obvious step of joining the Communist party, preferring mystique to politics. He sounds like an existentialist when he demands not good intentions but proof in action. To aid the cause of revolution, he sets up a small network of industrial and military espionage, but in the time-honored bourgeois mode, he does not do the work himself; instead, he sends Simon, who is to procure military contingency plans in the event of civil insurgence. Although Laforgue frequently criticizes Rosenthal's cloak-and-dagger exploits, and knows that his friend seeks above all a boost to his own ego, Laforgue acquiesces in another project of industrial espionage. Besides, he likes the idea of stealing secrets from his own father's engineering works, because his father had used him in a time-and-motion study on the workers: "ce mouchardage à chronomètre" (spying with a stopwatch). Rosenthal's attitude toward his family is even more hostile. He frets over "les poisons de famille que son foie et ses reins n'élimineraient pas toujours" (the family poisons which his liver and kidneys would not always succeed in evacuating). Essentially rootless and faithless, he feels only scorn for his fellow Jews, rich and poor alike. He has a love affair with his sister-in-law, Catherine, which, he feels, is a slap in the face of class and family values. The affair is another of Rosenthal's conspiracies; his efforts to make Catherine commit herself to him founder on her passive resistance. She is part of that gelatinous reality against which these young men make so little headway.

Nizan analyzes Catherine in terms of her social class: both are characterized by a fragmented consciousness, allied with a conveniently short memory that clings to the status quo. Futile as the affair turns out, it does force Rosenthal into direct confrontation with his family, which separates the lovers, although it does not punish him. He takes poison as an act of protest against the society that has duped him, partly because he has not resisted forcefully enough.

It is a measure of Nizan's imaginative strength that he can persuade readers both that Rosenthal is a *poseur* and that his suicide is a sad waste. In contrast, Laforgue (named after one of Nizan's favorite writers, the premodernist dandy poet Jules Laforgue) is much concerned with the dynamics of transition from youth to manhood. He values the definitive nature of the initiation rites he has read about in his anthropological studies, whereas European youths are left to wallow in their psychic malaise. When he falls seriously ill, for the first time in his life he is obliged to involve himself totally in an experience. When he begins to recover, he is bowled over by the sheer joy of survival and feels himself as never before a living entity. His second go at life begins, but the price he pays is the knowledge that, after twenty years of marking time, he is now living toward death.

The lucid but not paralyzing consciousness of death is crucial to Nizan's concept of how to live authentically. Laforgue embodies the unavoidability of painful transitions. Some of the elements of Nietzsche's recipe for rebels in an unrebellious age are already active within him: "Objection, joyous distrust, and love of irony are signs of health: everything absolute belongs to pathology."

La Conspiration includes among its characters two men from an older generation, the liberal writer Régnier and the party member Carré. Régnier hovers on the brink of conversion to communism, whereas Carré has made the leap. For him, communism is a total faith in which politics and ethics are wedded in a unified life-style, although one never sees this life-style in action, but always on the run, its leaders harassed by the police. When Régnier asks the inevitable liberal question of how an intellectual can reconcile himself to the discipline imposed by the party, Carré's scornful reply is that Régnier's view of freedom is essentially negative. Yet, Carré's own blanket acceptance of ideology may conceal compromises. Similarly, although party membership gave Nizan a sense of purpose and of companionship, an authentication of his private revolt, one might conclude, given his final break with the party and his favored image of the Trojan horse, that he too *secreted*, kept something in reserve, not letting hackwork stultify his mind.

In line with Nizan's sense of values and countervalues, he makes Pluvinage the antithesis of Carré: not a man of equilibrium and maturity, but a pathological misfit. From the outset, he is

the odd man out. Carré is arrested in a police swoop, and, suspecting Pluvinage's part in the operation, Laforgue and Rosenthal subject him to an embarrassing inquisition and denounce him to the party. In a scene that resembles episodes in Sartre's *La Nausée* (Nausea), published the same year as *La Conspiration*, the suspect feels himself turned to stone by judging gazes, however furtive. Nizan adds that it was the judging gaze of his family which had in the first instance induced in the as yet guiltless adolescent a sense of guilt. Just as Rosenthal took his own life, Pluvinage hands over his in a gesture of moral suicide; together they represent two forms of betrayal after two abortive existences. Pluvinage's diary had already revealed the conditioning and the motivation which led him to denounce Carré, while posing the question of how inevitable it was. So perspicacious is Nizan's presentation of Pluvinage that, after Nizan left the party in 1939, his erstwhile comrades clamored that he was an arrant traitor and that his understanding of Pluvinage proved it. Instead, all it proves is that he knew his duty as a novelist: know your enemy, think his thoughts.

Through Pluvinage, Nizan warns that communism may be the salvation only of those who devote themselves generously to its ends; it is not a foster home for the misused children of the bourgeoisie who refuse to grow up. But *La Conspiration* does not finish with Pluvinage's deadend; it ends on Laforgue's return from illness, his symbolic death and rebirth, an as yet directionless but incipient transformation. It not only presents individual case histories but also inserts these consistently into the wider context of social processes. One of the few collectively invigorating moments experienced by the group is the day in 1924 when the ashes of the assassinated Socialist leader Jean Jaurès are triumphantly transferred to the Pantheon. Despite attempts by government officials to appropriate the memory of the great man, the anonymous and volatile crowd turns the occasion into one of joyous solidarity (it was in fact the first mass demonstration organized by the Communist party). For once in their lives, the young members of the group feel elated to be part of a collective show of strength. Later in the novel, a contrasting scene, the funeral of Marshal Foch, shows the upper classes in the ascendancy.

The physical world, too, counts, intrudes, influences behavior. When Rosenthal visits Naxos to see his sister, after being initially blinkered by

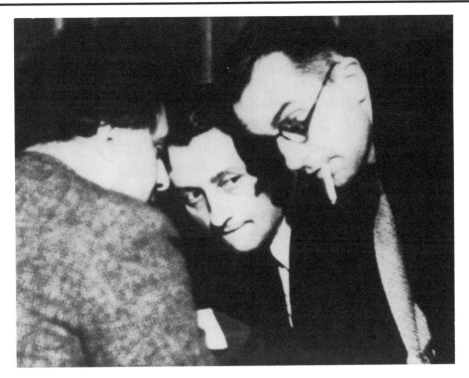

Nizan with André Malraux and Ilya Ehrenburg (back to camera) at the International Writers' Congress in Paris, 1935 (photo Gisèle Freund)

cultural reflexes, he gradually learns to value the self-contained, self-explanatory Greek landscape. These pages reveal in Nizan a capacity for measured lyricism; irony was not his only mode. Similarly, family life is treated with nuance. Just as in *Les Chiens de garde* where Nizan castigates the bourgeois view of Marxism as an alien malady introduced into the body politic, here the family blames Rosenthal's suicide on a foreign agency: the undesirable company he kept. But Nizan's bourgeois are never entirely predictable, nor does he ever maintain that they can be laughed, or argued, away. Part of the educational process, too, of this novel is sentimental and sexual education. Love proper, like political choice, is like aspiration—a counteraspiration to that of death. Just as Nizan speaks up for communism, so he affirms unashamedly his own belief in the value of shared love. Honest and generous love would be one of the indispensable bases of that more authentic life of which his young men dream.

Probably the dominant feature of Nizan's outlook was a refusal of establishment, an unending vigilance, as if he were forever operating on enemy territory. In *La Conspiration,* families, police, Communists, and the young and dubious heroes are all conspiratorial. Here conspiracy theory is given a realistic foundation. It is also

given true style. Nizan's tone is distinctive: a constant amused irony, a mixture of connivance with, and mockery of, youth's melodramatic imaginings. He works midway between Stendhalian fiction, with its fluctuating emphasis on politics, and the type portrayed by George Orwell or Arthur Koestler, almost totally dominated by politics. If not open-minded, the novel is open-ended in a limply ecumenical way. It was meant to be continued by "La Soirée à Somosierra" (of which the manuscript was buried and never found after Nizan's death). It was to show Laforgue finding his feet during the Spanish civil war as well as coping in Geneva with a love affair. Nizan always stressed his aversion to "dead-end" literature, convinced as he was that the novel was an instrument of knowledge, a means of understanding both oneself and others. The ending of *La Conspiration* is neither tragic nor sanguine, but problematic. Nizan proves Sartre wrong: complicity and judgment can be combined.

It should be noted that *La Conspiration* includes various techniques of narration. Nizan models some of the formal structures on André Gide's *Les Faux-Monnayeurs* (*The Counterfeiters,* 1925), and very suitably, given the ambivalence of Nizan's principal characters. First, there is a chapter of letters, an appropriate means for these bookish young men to air their theories and prejudices; second, Régnier's notebook, which ensures a distancing from the group; third, Pluvinage's diary, his melancholy *apologia pro vita sua,* addressed to Laforgue. This too offers a different slant on Pluvinage's peer group, who are by turns hero-worshipped and condemned.

La Conspiration is a densely packed novel, intelligent, taut, by turns harsh and generous. The chief movement goes from the provisional, the stalling, to the definitive; from *disponibilité* (virtuality) to death or to a second chance. Nizan shows the plurality of paths by which human beings can certainly damn, and possibly save, themselves. The novel's complexities offset the dogmatism that Nizan often slipped into in his more polemical writings. As Sartre said, "Ce révolutionnaire manquait d'aveuglement" (This revolutionary was singularly lacking in blindness).

Nizan brought the subtleties of his fiction to his later journalism, which gave it added perception. In the 1936-1939 period he traveled often in Europe, accompanying governmental missions and increasing his grasp of foreign affairs. In *Chronique de septembre* (September Chronicle, 1939), Nizan exemplified historian Jacques Fauvet's comment that in the late 1930s the Communist party in France was behind the times in home affairs and ahead of them in international affairs. This postmortem examination of the Munich crisis also contains Nizan's journalistic credo: a combination of psychological and forensic field work, a full awareness of when one is simplifying. Nizan's capacity for free thought was put to its severest test in August 1939, when Hitler and Stalin signed their pact of mutual nonaggression. When Nizan was mobilized for active military service, he submitted his resignation from the Communist party. Yet he never ceased to think of himself as a Communist after leaving the party and remained caustic toward line-toeing Stalinists. He was principally concerned about the future for French communism, and the need to restructure a ruined organization. He was very alive to the whole deadly farce of the Phoney War period, and his observations on military life remained clear-eyed. Transferred from a Pioneer regiment to a British one as an interpreter and liaison agent, he was hit in the head by a German bullet during the retreat from Dunkerque in May 1940.

His instinct that his name would be defamed proved justified. Denounced during the war by the party leader Maurice Thorez as a traitor and police informer, Nizan was similarly described after the war as an expert in treachery—witness his fictional characters: Lange, Antoine Bloyé, Pluvinage. The same false accusations are suggested again in Aragon's novel *Les Communistes* (1949-1951). Sartre took charge of his defense, aided by Nizan's widow, Henriette. In an article published in *Temps Modernes* and other periodicals, he challenged the Communists, especially the historian Henri Lefebvre, to prove their allegations that Nizan had given to the minister of the interior information about the Communist party. A petition by leading intellectuals (Raymond Aron, Julien Benda, Roger Caillois, Albert Camus, Maurice Merleau-Ponty, Jean Paulhan) protesting the attacks on Nizan's reputation was sent to the party, which refused to comment. Sartre also used Nizan as a basis for the character Schneider in *Les Chemins de la liberté* (*The Roads to Freedom,* 1945-1949). Schneider is a complex and troubling figure who represents a tormented but recognizably human brand of communism. In his 1960 preface to the republication of *Aden, Arabie,* Sartre betrays strong envy of his friend and appears to live vicariously through this "vigorous corpse," whom he proposes as a living example to the restless but shiftless youth of 1960. Sartre undoubtedly romanticizes Nizan and makes his anguish far less socially oriented than it was.

Nizan had a definite individual style of being and of acting, recognized even by his detractors. It was one of elegant self-containment, and a troubling kind of detachment that often secreted anger and scorn. Many were discomfited by his habit of gazing at his fingernails in the middle of discussions. More perceptive witnesses speak equally of his reliable sense of fun, *la fête.* He gave the impression of having reserves—of energy and of doubt. He could work in the middle of a noisy room, no doubt inured to distractions by his journalistic experience of having to meet deadlines. He made very few notes, and his manuscripts exhibit hardly any deletions. Gide often claimed that the "gait" (*allure*) of a writer reveals more about him than any other stylistic feature. Nizan's gait adjusts itself to his subject: plodding, or swirling around a central vacancy, in *Antoine Bloyé*; nervous, often exalted and proud, in *Le Cheval de Troie*; alternately expansive and stabbing in *La Conspiration.*

He was fond of repeating Dostoyevski's advice to writers: guess, and make mistakes. He was a risk-taker, and hence the leitmotif of the near miss in his work. It is tempting to speculate on what stand he would have taken if he had escaped death at Dunkerque. What seems likely is that he would not have become a dedicated anti-communist of the Koestler type, for communism had informed him through and through. He was finally a heretic but not a renegade; his break represented a schism and not a desertion. He once wrote that the revolutionary is the man who has triumphed over solitude. He would not have had the strength to leave the party if he had lacked the strength to support it. Since his death his work has been alternately scorned and salvaged for recycling—the latter in 1968, when young rebels replaced him, without reading him closely or at all, in the ranks of the ultra-Left, outflanking the party.

Nizan was one of the most intelligent of the French Communist novelists, expressing a genuine sensibility. In his book reviews, he went straight to the core of the book under discussion, asking: what is behind all this? What is the premise, the working hypothesis (Sartre would later say, more airily, the metaphysics)? His own premise was a fusion of the best in the Marxist and existentialist traditions: a human being is not doomed to one unchanging nature; he can will himself to be other, not merely in mental attitude but also in social practice. His photos make him look disconcertingly like Harold Lloyd, one of his culture-heroes. He was an existential funambulist. He was as obsessed with the death-defying (what Malraux would more pompously call *l'anti-destin*) as he was with death itself. In Dylan

Thomas's words, Nizan's life and his works urge: "Do not go gentle into that good night."

Biography:

Pascal Ory, *Nizan, destin d'un révolté* (Paris: Ramsay, 1980).

References:

Annie Cohen-Solal and Henriette Nizan, *Paul Nizan, communiste impossible* (Paris: Grasset, 1980);

Etiemble, *Hygiène des lettres*, volume 1 (Paris: Gallimard, 1952);

Franco Fe, *Paul Nizan, un intellettuale comunista* (Rome: Nuova Sinistra, 1973);

Ariel Ginsbourg, *Paul Nizan* (Paris: Editions Universitaires, 1966);

Youssef Ishaghpour, *Paul Nizan, une figure mythique et son temps* (Paris: Le Sycomore, 1980);

Adèle King, *Paul Nizan, écrivain* (Paris: Didier, 1976);

Jacqueline Leiner, *Le Destin littéraire de Paul Nizan* (Paris: Klincksieck, 1970);

Magazine Littéraire, no. 59, "Dossier," special section on Nizan (December 1971): 8-23;

Walter Redfern, *Paul Nizan: Committed Literature in a Conspiratorial World* (Princeton: Princeton University Press, 1972);

Jean-Paul Sartre, "*La Conspiration* par Paul Nizan," in his *Situations I* (Paris: Gallimard, 1947), pp. 26-30;

Sartre, "Paul Nizan," in his *Situations IV* (Paris: Gallimard, 1964), pp. 130-188;

Susan Suleiman, *Authoritarian Fictions* (New York: Columbia University Press, 1983).

Raymond Queneau

(21 February 1903-25 October 1976)

Vivian Kogan
Dartmouth College

BOOKS: *Le Chiendent* (Paris: Gallimard, 1933); translated by Barbara Wright as *The Bark Tree* (London: Calder & Boyars, 1968; New York: New Directions, 1971);

Gueule de Pierre (Paris: Gallimard, 1934); revised with *Les Temps mêlés* (1941) as *Saint Glinglin* (1948);

Les Derniers Jours (Paris: Gallimard, 1936);

Chêne et chien (Paris: Denoël, 1937);

Odile (Paris: Gallimard, 1937);

Les Enfants du limon (Paris: Gallimard, 1938);

Un Rude hiver (Paris: Gallimard, 1939); translated by Betty Askwith as *A Hard Winter* (London: Lehmann, 1948);

Les Temps mêlés (Paris: Gallimard, 1941); revised with *Gueule de Pierre* as *Saint Glinglin* (1948);

Pierrot mon ami (Paris: Gallimard, 1943); translated by J. McLaren Ross as *Pierrot* (London: Lehmann, 1950);

Les Ziaux (Paris: Gallimard, 1943);

Loin de Rueil (Paris: Gallimard, 1944); translated by H. J. Kaplan as *The Skin of Dreams* (Norfolk, Conn.: New Directions, 1948);

Bucoliques (Paris: Gallimard, 1947);

Exercices de style (Paris: Gallimard, 1947; revised, 1947; revised and enlarged, 1963); translated by Wright as *Exercises in Style* (London: Gabberbocchus, 1958; New York: New Directions, 1981);

On est toujours trop bon avec les femmes, as Sally Mara (Paris: Editions du Scorpion, 1947); republished in *Les Œuvres complètes de Sally Mara* (1962); translated by Wright as *We Always Treat Women Too Well* (London: Calder, 1981; New York: New Directions, 1981);

L'Instant fatal (Paris: Gallimard, 1948);

Saint Glinglin (Paris: Gallimard, 1948);

Bâtons, chiffres et lettres (Paris: Gallimard, 1950; revised and enlarged, 1965);

Journal intime, as Sally Mara (Paris: Editions du Scorpion, 1950); republished in *Les Œuvres complètes de Sally Mara* (1962);

Petite cosmogonie portative (Paris: Gallimard, 1950);

Le Dimanche de la vie (Paris: Gallimard, 1951); translated by Wright as *The Sunday of Life* (London: Calder, 1976; New York: New Directions, 1977);

Si tu t'imagines, 1920-1951 (Paris: Gallimard, 1952); revised as *Si tu t'imagines, 1920-1948* (Paris: Gallimard, 1968);

Zazie dans le métro (Paris: Gallimard, 1959); translated by Wright as *Zazie* (London: Bodley Head, 1960; New York: Harper, 1960);

Entretiens avec Georges Charbonnier (Paris: Gallimard, 1962);

Les Œuvres complètes de Sally Mara (Paris: Gallimard, 1962);

Bords: Mathématiciens, précurseurs, encyclopédistes (Paris: Hermann, 1963);

Le Chien à la mandoline (Paris: Gallimard, 1965);

Les Fleurs bleues (Paris: Gallimard, 1965); translated by Wright as *Between Blue and Blue* (London: Bodley Head, 1967); also published as *The Blue Flowers* (New York: Atheneum, 1967);

Une Histoire modèle (Paris: Gallimard, 1966);

Courir les rues (Paris: Gallimard, 1967);

Battre la campagne (Paris: Gallimard, 1968);

Le Vol d'Icare (Paris: Gallimard, 1968); translated by Wright as *The Flight of Icarus* (London: Calder & Boyars, 1973; New York: New Directions, 1973);

Chêne et chien, suivi de Petite cosmogonie portative (éd. rev. et corr.) et de Le Chant de Styrène (Paris: Gallimard, 1968);

Fendre les flots (Paris: Gallimard, 1969);

Raymond Queneau en verve, edited by Jacques Bens (Paris: Horay, 1970);

Raymond Queneau: Poems, translated by Teo Savory (Santa Barbara, Cal.: Unicorn, 1971);

Le Voyage en Grèce (Paris: Gallimard, 1973);

Morale élémentaire (Paris: Gallimard, 1975);

Contes et propos (Paris: Gallimard, 1981);

Pounding the Pavements; Beating the Bushes; and Other Pataphysical Poems, translated by Savory (Greensboro, N.C.: Unicorn, 1985);

Raymond Queneau (photo Gisèle Freund)

Journal 1939-1940, suivi de Philosophes et voyous (Paris: Gallimard, 1986).

MOTION PICTURES: *Monsieur Ripois,* screenplay by Queneau, 1953);
La Mort en ce jardin, screenplay by Queneau, 1956;
Le Dimanche de la vie, screenplay by Queneau, 1967.

PERIODICAL PUBLICATIONS: "Récit de rêve," *Révolution Surréaliste,* no. 3 (15 April 1925): 5;
"Texte surréaliste," *Révolution Surréaliste,* no. 5 (15 October 1925): 3-4;
"Sur quelques aspects relativement peu connus du verbe en français," *Surréalisme Révolutionnaire,* no. 1 (1948): 36;
"Philosophes et voyous," *Temps Modernes,* no. 63 (January 1951): 1193-1205;
"Zazie dans son plus jeune âge," *Lettres Nouvelles,* new series 2 (1959): 5-7;
"Premières Confrontations avec Hegel," *Critique,* nos. 195-196 (August-September 1963): 694-700;
"L'Analyse matricielle du langage," *Etudes de Linguistique Appliquée,* no. 3 (1964): 37-50.

Raymond Queneau has been celebrated as one of the most amusing and versatile French writers of the twentieth century. He was a poet, novelist, critic, editor, playwright, filmmaker, philosopher, mathematician, and even a painter. He is best known as a novelist whose production spans the period from surrealism to the New Novel. Except for his early participation in surrealism, Queneau kept his distance from literary movements. And, because Queneau was not in the mainstream of literary fashion, he was, until recently, given marginal attention by critics. During most of his career his work was both greeted enthusiastically and underestimated. Author of a best-seller, *Zazie dans le métro* (1959; translated as *Zazie,* 1960), for which he was awarded the Prix de l'Humour Noir, and a hit song, "Si tu t'imagines" (If You Think), Queneau delighted his public with his idiomatic expressions, his fictional game-playing and his "jocoserious" tone, though his readers often ignored the implications. Yet, neither the playing nor the expression nor the tone is inconsequential, for they liberate readers from the servitude of certain narrow perspectives from which they still tend to view art— as a serious communication in which the enlightened writer dispenses his superior wisdom to a passive receptor according to sacrosanct conventions. Queneau undermines those conventions while revealing what they are. The explosive nature of his literary production was visible to few. Only the philosopher Gaston Bachelard was able to anticipate future critics when he exclaimed: "Queneau, c'est de la dynamite, déguisée en barbe à papa" (Queneau is dynamite disguised as cotton candy).

Born in Le Havre at the turn of the century of haberdasher parents, Auguste and Josephine Mignot Queneau, Queneau came to Paris to study philosophy in 1920 and remained there. He received his *licence ès lettres* in 1926. That same year he was called to military duty in Algeria and Morocco as a Zouave during the Rif wars. He returned to Paris in 1927. A year later he married Janine Kahn, sister-in-law of André Breton, leader of the surrealist movement. In 1934 they had a son, Jean-Marie, who became a painter. During the 1920s and 1930s Queneau took odd jobs that allowed him to scrape together a living: he gave private lessons; he sold paper tablecloths to cheap restaurants; he translated books from English into French; he did some journalism, writing a column called "Connaissez-vous Paris?" (Do You Know Paris?) for the daily, *Intransigeant*, from 1936 to 1938. In 1938 he became a reader of manuscripts at the prestigious firm Gallimard, which had already published four of his first five books, all novels, and would produce almost all his subsequent works.

Queneau's editorial career was briefly interrupted by World War II. Drafted in August 1939, he spent his time during the war in provincial towns. He was promoted to corporal just before being demobilized in July 1940. He returned to Paris. Despite the hardships of the war, the period was one of intense literary production. Queneau collaborated on clandestine publications and wrote a weekly column for *Front National* until 1945, receiving his card as a professional journalist in the same year. These activities were conducted in addition to his editorial responsibilities at Gallimard, where he was now general secretary and where he remained for the rest of his life.

Queneau did not like to move. He did travel, including trips to England in 1922, to Greece in 1932, to Scandinavian countries in 1945, and to the United States in 1950, the last in the company of the choreographer Roland Petit. But Queneau was not fond of the picturesque or the exotic; he preferred intellectual voyages. The first significant influence on Queneau's writing was surrealism. He participated in surrealist activities in 1924-1925 and again from 1927 to 1929. He published a poem and two samples of automatic writing in the *Révolution Surréaliste*, André Breton's journal for disseminating the group's ideas. Queneau's interest in surrealism was centered above all on the way of life it represented, one of total revolt against societal values. Queneau eventually quarreled with Breton for personal, not ideological, reasons, he said, and left the group in 1929.

His break with surrealism left Queneau somewhat adrift. Although he never severed his relations with most of his friends and even renewed his acquaintance with Breton, the crisis led him to reexamine his life through psychoanalytic therapy and to reevaluate his literary views and aspirations. Queneau abandoned surrealistic experimentation and began writing his own fiction. His first novel, *Le Chiendent* (the word, meaning both *crabgrass* and *problems*, was rendered as *The Bark Tree* in the 1968 English translation), was published in 1933. It was not a commercial success and brought Queneau little public attention. His literary reputation began to be established after the war.

He participated in several groups interested in literary invention and games, though most are not as well known as the surrealists. One such organization was the Collège de 'Pataphysique, which he joined in 1950. The term 'Pataphysique is an invention of the early-twentieth-century writer Alfred Jarry. 'Pataphysics is defined as the science of the realm beyond metaphysics; it is the science of the particular, of the laws governing exceptions, and of imaginary solutions. To construct a system of values and invent an idea of truth is the most imaginary of solutions. 'Pataphysics is an inner attitude; there is nothing beyond 'Pataphysics.

In 1960 Queneau and a mathematician friend, François Le Lionnais, founded a subgroup of the Collège de 'Pataphysique called the Ouvroir de Littérature Potentielle, or Oulipo. The participants partook of a series of festive games. They set themselves explicit constraints, game rules of a mathematical or linguistic nature, and illustrated the rules established in texts. An example of the application of a mathematical rule was Queneau's transposition of David Hilbert's mathematical theses to literature: "Les Fondements de la littérature d'après David Hil-

Queneau in 1928

bert" (The Foundations of Literature According to David Hilbert). Queneau eventually wrote an essay on the German mathematician, and the "Théorie des nombres sur les suites s-additives" (The Theory of Numbers on the S-additive Series) was presented to the French Academy of Sciences in 1968. As for linguistic games, they included such activities as playing with anagrams or the writing of texts in which a vowel, such as the letter *e*, was missing, the most notable example of which is Georges Perec's *La Disparition* (The Disappearance, 1969). The function of the group was not necessarily to produce new texts but to create new literary forms and to renew the use of old ones. The Oulipo project generated a lucid reconstruction of poetic language.

Queneau was elected to the Académie Goncourt in 1951; he was named to the Académie de l'Humour the following year. Queneau was also a member of the mathematical society in France from 1948 and of the American Mathematical Society from 1963. Queneau's participation in such a variety of literary and mathematical societies begins to suggest his enormous curiosity and appetite for knowledge. He investigated many subjects, from oriental philosophy to the writings of literary madmen. He compiled an anthology of the latter, for which he could never find a publisher. His investigation of, and expertise in, a variety of disciplines ultimately led to his reputation for impressive erudition.

Queneau's fiction seeks to revitalize the genre. His innovations concern the subjects considered proper to literature, modes of expression, and form. His first novel, *Le Chiendent,* describes the awakening of the principal character, Etienne Marcel, from the status of a two-dimensional shadow whose gestures are mechanical because his life has been unexamined. Under the transformational gaze of an observer, Pierre Le Grand, Etienne develops into a character concerned about Cartesian reality beyond appearances. He seeks absolute knowledge, rather than inquiring about his wife who makes off with another man. Queneau is clearly not interested, here, in the psychological coherence of the characters or in a traditional plot. As Etienne develops his intellectual capacities, the temporal framework of the novel seems to regress; other characters regress morally. Thus the morbid Mme Cloche, who derived joy from bloody accidents and intrigue, becomes Miss Aulini (Mussolini), military leader of the Etruscans, who are decimating the Gauls. Finally, the only actors left are Etienne, Mme Cloche, and her brother, a janitor-writer. At the close of the novel these characters meet by accident and comment on their status as fictional creations. Mme Cloche is particularly unhappy with the credulousness that characterizes her in earlier episodes. Etienne and her brother advise her to erase the book. But what about time? she exclaims. No one answers, as the novel returns to its very first sentence.

This circular form of the novel provides a kind of closure in the absence of other types of resolution. The work is self-conscious and deliberate in form. Queneau stressed technical composition in his early texts in particular. Nothing is left to chance. In addition to its circular form, there is a numerical pattern of formal divisions in *Le Chiendent,* governing the number of chapters, the reappearance of the characters, and so on. Queneau explained how he composed his novel in the enlarged edition of *Bâtons, chiffres et lettres* (Sticks, Numbers and Letters, 1965). He recognized his debt to James Joyce in the formulation of his technique, for the author of *Ulysses* organized every detail of his text according to a specific strategy. In Queneau's early work the organization is arithmetical in nature, no doubt a result of his mathematical penchant. *Le Chiendent* consists of 91 (7 X 13) sections. The author indicated that he perceived the number 13 as benefi-

cent because it negated happiness. As for the number 7, he took it to be the numerical image of himself, since his first name and surname are each composed of seven letters, and he was born on February 21 (3 X 7). Thus, although it is not autobiographical in appearance, the form of the novel expresses what the content sought to disguise. There is also a doubling and a pairing of characters and situations, which gives a sense of rhyme to the novel just as words do in a poem. Indeed, Queneau has claimed that he never saw a difference between the novel, as he wished to write it, and a poem. There are two principal observers who are acquainted but observe independently of each other. There are also two characters observed: Etienne and, by coincidence, his wife Alberte. Such parallels and the introduction of several kinds of discourse–dream, journalistic writing, letters, telegrams, conversations, interior monologue–draw attention to the composition of the novel rather than to its plot.

In 1936 Queneau produced *Les Derniers Jours* (The Last Days). This novel juxtaposes the lives of two principal groups of characters. One is formed about Vincent Tuquedenne, a student, who (like Queneau) has come to Paris from Le Havre. He spends his days studying, seeking sexual initiation, and participating in literary and philosophical movements. As he roams the streets of Paris, he alternately ponders Western culture and "nothing," mainly the latter. In so doing he is representative of a type of protagonist found frequently in Queneau's fiction. They are likable young men on the fringes of society who often appear vacuous, yet whose very emptiness is valued as a sign of intellectual activity or at least integrity. Vincent's interest in Dada, his reading of Proust and Gide, his discovery of Apollinaire and cubism do not alter the fact that his dominant experience is boredom or that he recognizes that he has everything to learn.

The initiation of Vincent and his friends into the intellectual life of Paris in the 1920s is somewhat satirical, as is the treatment of the contrasting series of events, the final stages in the lives of two older men. One, Brabbant, is a petty swindler who makes it fairly big; the other, Tolut, is a retired geography teacher who has never traveled. He therefore feels that he swindled his students. When he finally has the opportunity to make a journey, it is to London to pay his respects to his dying brother, and the trip is a catastrophe. The unifying center of the novel is Alfred, a philosopher-waiter in a Parisian café. Al-

Queneau with André Blavier on the day Queneau was awarded the Prix de l'Humour Noir for Zazie dans le métro
(photo Anatole Jakovsky)

fred can read the stars and figure out unerringly which horses will win the races. He recuperates in this way the fortune his father once lost gambling. Alfred also makes occasional commentaries on the various characters. He observes the cyclical nature of their appearances as well as the repetitions in their behavior. As Queneau explains in *Bâtons, chiffres et lettres,* every sixth chapter in *Les Derniers Jours* constitutes a pause. Alfred plays the role of Greek chorus. He is also the one who has the final word. The form of the novel consists of narrative zones which give it a sense of simultaneity and imbalance.

In *Chêne et chien* (Oak and Dog, 1937), described by Queneau as a "novel in verse," the author chooses to describe his own psychoanalytical treatment in the second part of the book. In the first part he focuses on his childhood from birth to his sexual initiation. The final sequence, entitled "La Fête au village" (The Village Festival), is the account of a celebration. It indicates the victory of collectivity over the morbid, solitary introspection characteristic of the psychoanalytic cure. *Chêne et chien* suggests the impossibility of recovering the past and of establishing with certainty the identity of the subject. But this is not cause for despondency; the book ends with a celebration.

The title refers to two etymologies that Queneau offers for his own name: *quêne*, meaning *oak* in Norman dialect, and *quenêt*, meaning *dog*. The author uses this linguistic pair to refer to opposing impulses in him: one toward nobility, the other toward baseness. The creation of his personal myth culminates in a break in the tension between the opposing poles of his character, the lofty, as symbolized by the oak, winning over the decadent impulses. In this book Queneau mocks virulently the reductive aspect of psychoanalytic symbolism in which everything represents either the phallus or the family. His innovation is to make psychoanalysis a theme of his novel in verse and to exploit the comic aspects of his own contradictions.

In the novel *Odile*, published in the same year as *Chêne et chien*, the autobiographical elements are so thinly disguised that the author, ever reticent, hesitated to have the book republished. Writing it undoubtedly served as a kind of exorcism of the traumas associated with his tearing away from surrealism, which he clearly attacks. The book is a roman à clef. In Anglarès, Queneau clearly satirizes the tics and megalomania that identify André Breton. The main character, however, is Roland Travy, a young Queneau, from whose perspective the novel is written.

Philippe Noiret and Catherine Demongeot in Louis Malle's 1960 film adaptation of Zazie dans le métro *(photo* les Nouvelles Editions de film)

Travy's narrative begins with a vision, the sight of an Arab on a road in Morocco during the 1920s. Travy projects onto this figure the qualities of nobility, poetic invention, and philosophical mastery he wishes to make his own. Travy takes this image as a directive for the future and breaks with the past, with his own childhood. This break is duplicated in Travy's rejection of Anglarès and his followers, who, like the surrealists, view childhood as a privileged state. In the novel they are shown to play childish games. Travy's evolution suggests the difficulties and benefits of growing up. It is also a love story. Travy, who had initially refused love and life in order to find refuge in the world of mathematical ideals, ends by accepting the love of a woman, Odile, and following the path of ordinary men. Queneau does not necessarily give value to the banal in this novel, but rather reveals Travy's initial refusal of happiness in search of an absolute as both immature and misguided.

Whereas the form of *Odile* is that of a traditional narrative, the following novel, *Les Enfants du limon* (The Children of the Earth, 1938), is fragmented. The reader learns gradually that the various characters are linked because they share a common patriarch, Jules Limon, an industrialist who committed suicide during the Depression.

His grandchildren–Agnès, Noémie, Daniel–lead generally idle lives at the beginning of the novel, though their fortune is less than secure. They are envied by others less privileged than they, people to whom they are related in obscure ways. There is an Italian grocer, Gramigni (meaning *crabgrass* or *weeds*, in Italian the equivalent of the French *le chiendent*), who marries a maid of the Limon family. She is an illegitimate daughter of Limon. Another member of the proletariat is named Bossu (which means *hunchback*). He is the illegitimate son of Chambernac, who is the brother-in-law of Sophie, Limon's daughter. She and her second husband, Baron Hachamoth, try to keep the family from sinking into poverty.

Politics plays a key role in the novel. Agnès and her husband, for example, start a Fascist organization called the Nation without Classes. Agnès becomes imbued with political zeal and ambition only to die in the streets during an attempted coup. Daniel does not die, but he suffocates periodically in extreme asthma attacks. His condition leads him to discover evil as unredeemable suffering. His sister Noémie marries her uncle Astolphe, Sophie's brother, who becomes a paper manufacturer. The novel ends with the birth of their child and on the word *délivrance*. The term means *birth* and marks the beginning as well as

The 1961 Prix Goncourt jury. Standing left to right: Gérard Bauer, Queneau, Philippe Hériat, Alexandre Arnoux, Pierre Mac Orlan. Seated: Roland Dorgelès, André Billy (photo A.F.P.).

the continuation of life, of the Limon family, and also of a liberation by joy from suffering and fanaticism.

In addition to plotting the lives of the Limon grandchildren, the novel includes the story of Chambernac's project to compile an encyclopedia of inexact sciences. One of the most curious aspects of Chambernac's project is the way in which he acquires his assistant, Purpulan. The latter is a small-time devil just learning the art of becoming a parasite. He tries to frighten Chambernac into hiring him as a teacher in the school where Chambernac is director. But Chambernac turns the tables on him. He makes him sign a pact in blood and indentures him as his assistant. Purpulan finally dissolves in the Seine. At the end of the novel, and just prior to the birth, Chambernac encounters a character named Raymond Queneau who wants to use Chambernac's anthology of literary madmen in a novel he is writing, in which, coincidentally, a character is writing an encyclopedia of inexact sciences. The circularity of presenting himself, the author, as a character in his novel indirectly

poses a number of Borgesian questions about the nature of fiction.

Un Rude Hiver (1939; translated as *A Hard Winter*, 1948) continues in the direction of less emphasis on mathematical constraints. Published prior to the outbreak of World War II, the novel anticipates the forthcoming conflict as it looks back on World War I. Queneau's protagonist, Bernard Lehameau (his surname means *the hamlet*), is a widower in his thirties, recuperating in Le Havre from injuries sustained at the front. He expresses pro-German sympathies, but all his other emotions seem to have been paralyzed as a result of the death of his wife in a fire thirteen years before. He appears charmed by a Miss Weeds, a WAC, yet he gives a German spy information that allows the enemy to torpedo the ship on which she is returning to England. He then denounces the spy. He eventually finds happiness in his engagement to a fourteen-year-old girl named Annette Rousseau. Queneau's novel is full of uncertainties. Does Bernard espouse the Fascist sentiments he expounds, or is his posture a cover to dupe authentic German spies? Does he care about Miss Weeds even though he allows her to die? Does he prefer her death to her departure? He ultimately finds happiness with a girl almost half his age. Is he an average male, or Nabokov's Humbert Humbert? The uncertainties of motivation and hence of the reader's ability to evaluate the characters and events are a function of the elliptical form of the novel and the techniques of distancing. The first chapter is revelatory. The novel opens with a celebration of the Chinese New Year. The description is disorienting. It is only later that the reader discovers that the parade takes place in Le Havre, not in the Orient.

In *Pierrot mon ami* (1943; translated as *Pierrot*, 1950) the questions posed and the mystery posited are more literary in nature. The main character, Pierrot, having been deprived of his job at an amusement park known as the Luna-parc and of the affections of Yvonne, the daughter of the park's owner, is displaced by her from the very house that had been willed to him. The person from whom he would have inherited the house, had he not lost the codicil to the will, was the guardian of a chapel where a Poldavian prince is said to have died. There are indications in the novel that there was really no prince, that the person in question was really a French animal trainer who is alive and well and living in Palinsac. When the Luna-parc burns down, there are several hypotheses as to who did it. The owner himself is not above suspicion since his fondest wish is to expand and modernize the park. In the epilogue to the work Pierrot reflects upon the actions that constitute the novel and thinks about the detective story it might have made (but did not), with its crime (which one?), a guilty party, and a detective. Certainly the potential for constructing a detective novel is there, but it is not exploited. It is only designated. Making the act of reading into a theme in this way is a recognition of the reader's demand for meaning. Queneau nevertheless refuses to suggest that meaning. It is his way of playing the literary game and unmasking it at the same time.

Loin de Rueil (1944; translated as *The Skin of Dreams*, 1948) is another comic work in which it is frequently impossible to distinguish between dreams and films, fantasies and events, desires and "reality." The main character, Jacques L'Aumône, becomes the American actor James Charity as a result of the most farfetched metamorphoses. Film provides the novel not only with a theme but also with several techniques. The most frequently used is the jump cut, which separates episodes of Jacques's improbable transformations into chemical engineer, dancer, boxer, breeder of giant lice, and researcher trying to cure "ontalgia," an existential disease that afflicts the poet Des Cigales. Jacques even tries to become a saint. He finally appears transcendent in all the mythified glory of celluloid fame as the star of a movie. Opposed to Jacques's various manifestations is the unifying motif of the novel, lice, which appear as a topic of discussion in each chapter of the book. This motif serves as a counterpoint of inescapable banality and as a universal connection that is opposed to the exceptional adventures of Jacques. *Loin de Rueil* has been viewed as a parody of the existential themes of anguish, freedom, and the absurd. Is it also an exploration of the mythmaking function of film and its relation to wish fulfillment? Certainly Queneau celebrates film as a new popular artistic medium, of which he was very fond, one which would one day compete with literature.

The nature of literature is the underlying subject of Queneau's *Exercices de style* (1947; translated as *Exercises in Style*, 1958). In this text the author presents an insignificant incident: someone gets on a bus, has his feet trampled by another passenger, and sits down. He is later seen in the company of an acquaintance who gives him advice regarding a button on his coat. This incident is recounted in ninety-nine different ways or styles, each one varying the arrangement of events and the choice of diction, tone, and emphasis. One such style is termed metaphoric, another tactile, still others exclamatory and vulgar. These variations can be seen as mathematical permutations. There are even two variations called permutations, the first consisting of increasingly larger groups of letters and the other of increasingly larger groups of words. What this humorous text shows is that there is clearly no privileged subject for art; a writer can and does create significant forms from the most banal, trivial pretexts. In making his point Queneau deflates the myth of literature. He also draws the reader's attention to the manner of expression, rather than to content, although the characters are modified by the style adopted. By contrasting the similarity of events and the different modes of their expression, Queneau invites the reader to view all of literature as a series of permutations that have no ultimate or "authentic" text as their origin. Queneau claims that his intentions are therapeutic rather than destructive of literature; his purpose is to rid literature of its rusty, crusty conventions. In fact, Queneau's *Exercices de style* so pleased his public that some of the "exercises" were set to music and performed by the Frères Jacques.

Saint Glinglin (1948) is a reworking of two previously published novels, *Gueule de Pierre* (Stoneface, 1934) and *Les Temps mêlés* (1941), into one. It concerns an imaginary society that combines features of Western societies and those of primitive ones. In several chapters the approach is anthropological in perspective, as if a foreign observer were attempting to inform the reader of the society's principal characteristics. A good illustration is the amusing description of a potlatch, which has the effect of provoking questions regarding nature and culture in general. After the potlatch–or as part of it–Queneau's characters destroy part of what it was made of: the pots and other crockery. Other chapters of the novel's seven sections are narrated by individuals from the Nabonide ruling family and present extremely subjective, even mad, visions of the world. The first is written from the point of view of Pierre Nabonide. He has been sent to Foreign City to learn its language. Finding it incomprehensible, the narrator ponders the mysteries of existence ("eggzistence" and "eksistence" are among the spellings of the word) at the aquarium.

Pierre feels exiled from Native City, his hometown, where his father is mayor. The father has sent Pierre's sister, Hélène, to another city and imprisoned her. Jean Nabonide, Pierre's brother, writes that there may be changes in the city's yearly festival, Saint Glinglin, the celebration of a fictitious saint whose name in popular French means *never*. Pierre, Jean, and their brother, Paul, whose names evoke the New Testament, follow, in Freudian terms, an Old Testament pattern of behavior: they rebel against their authoritarian and castrating father, who falls to his death in the Petrifying Spring. Pierre replaces his father as mayor of the city. He makes radical changes, abolishing the festival and the device known as the *chasse-nuages* (cloud-chaser) responsible for the perpetual splendid weather. He thereby inaugurates the reign of wetness. The last chapter shows the preparations for revolt by unhappy citizens. The advent of a new mayor, Paul, and the sacrifice of Jean as scapegoat for the troubled times, returns Native City to its previous order and to its role as a never-never land. The feast of Saint Glinglin and the sunny weather are restored.

In this novel there are echoes of multiple sources and disciplines, including psychoanalysis, anthropology, sociology, literature, and philosophy. There are allusions to Swift's *Gulliver's Travels* and to Montesquieu's *Les Lettres persanes* (*The Persian Letters*), as well as several themes and expressions that recall the Bible, but in a fragmented and often ironic way.

The title of Queneau's 1951 novel, *Le Dimanche de la vie* (translated as *The Sunday of Life*, 1976), as Alexandre Kojève pointed out in his 1952 essay for *Critique*, "Les Romans de la sagesse," refers to the glorious period after "the end of history" as announced by Hegel. But if the protagonist Valentin Brû represents that posthistorical sage, as Kojève claims, most readers are surprised, at least at first, for he seems rather mindless, the antithesis of a sage. As the novel begins, Julie, also called Julia, has decided to marry Brû, the attractive young soldier she has seen but not yet met. She is a middle-aged notions dealer who, with the help of her attractive sister, realizes her desire. But she is unable to leave her business for a honeymoon, which is nevertheless deemed indispensable by the spouses. They decide that Valentin must take the trip alone. His naiveté and inexperience cause him to get lost in Paris; he falls prey to an unscrupulous taxi driver, manages to get his money back, and goes off to visit the site of Napoleon's famous victory, Jena. But the pro-German tour guide leads his tour group to the site of French defeats.

When Julie's mother dies, she and Valentin inherit a shop in the twelfth arrondissement in Paris. Valentin sells picture frames and spends much time watching the hands of the clock move, while Julie becomes a medium, Madame Sophie, without informing Valentin. When she falls ill, she asks Valentin to take on the medium's role. When war is declared, everyone but Valentin is surprised. He fulfills his military service in the provinces, where he decides to become a saint. His name, after that of Valentinus, a gnostic heretic, does not seem to predispose him to such a vocation, and he fails. When he is last seen by Julie and the reader after the French defeat, he is helping girls climb into a train by the window–in order to be able to put his hand on their backsides–to Julie's intense amusement.

In this comic and often bewildering novel, events normally considered important, such as marriage, war, and career decisions, are not described. The actions narrated are the banal, daily events that both reveal and conceal much about the characters and their actions. Furthermore, the novel does not indicate the significance of the episodes presented. How is one to evaluate Valentin as he watches the hands of the clock move, trying to capture time in its pure state? Is he a sage or simply vacuous? It is ironic that the novel, written after World War II, deprives every character except Valentin of the knowledge of forthcoming events; he is the only one to predict the conflict. For this reason he may be seen as on the other side of history.

In the 1959 novel *Zazie dans le métro* World War II is still fresh in the memory of adults and provides them with a common point of reference. Zazie comes to Paris to spend forty-eight hours with her uncle, Gabriel, and his wife, Marceline, while Zazie's mother remains with her lover. Zazie is a prepubescent adolescent. Her age is significant, because it places her in a transitional phase between childhood and maturity, sharing the qualities of each state. The language she uses is often inappropriate. She either speaks in imitation of adults, often without understanding the meaning of what she says, or she refuses the rhetoric of adults by brutally interjecting vulgarity. Her fondest wish is not to visit the great monuments, as the adults presume, but rather to ride the metro. In this most surrealistic of Queneau's fiction, she both realizes her desires and does not. She does get to ride the subway, but she is asleep at the time.

In this novel the familiar Parisian setting becomes as strange and as unsettling as it does in Louis Aragon's *Le Paysan de Paris* (*Nightwalker*, 1926). The reader of *Zazie dans le métro* is repeatedly surprised by unpredictable turns of phrase and events, often disoriented by the characters. Gabriel is also known as Gabriella; he dances, dressed in a tutu, in a gay night club. Marceline is really Marcel. Other characters lose their identities only to adopt new ones derived from *The Arabian Nights* and cartoons. Pédro-surplus, a "satyr," becomes Trouscaillon, a policeman, and ultimately Aroun Arachide, master of this world and adjoining territories. At the end of the novel, anarchy seems to prevail. After fighting a quasi-epic though inconclusive battle with the elusive and protean forces of evil, the protagonists disperse; one of them even exchanges places with his parrot as he leaves. The story and characters are undone, unraveled as the novel reaches its formal, circular closure. In *Zazie dans le métro*, more clearly than in his other fiction, Queneau questions certain ordering factors in civilization and

undermines outworn conventions of language and literature.

Les Œuvres complètes de Sally Mara (The Complete Works of Sally Mara), published in 1962, comprises two earlier novels, *On est toujours trop bon avec les femmes* (1947; translated as *We Always Treat Women Too Well*, 1981) and *Journal intime* (Private Diary, 1950), plus a shorter piece entitled "Sally plus intime" (More Intimate Sally). It is a volume that also plays with the elements and limits of fiction. In this case it is not only the character that is exploited as imaginary but the author as well. The two novels "written" by Ms. Mara are "edited" by Queneau. The preface is by Mara. One explanation for Queneau's use of the pseudonym is that he was asked to write some erotic fiction for the new series Editions du Scorpion, but he did not want the work attributed to him, even though these books are parodies of the titillating and violent thrillers in the French Série Noire, a cheap detective book series. Certainly there is a focus on sex and violence that distinguishes the texts attributed to Sally Mara from most of Queneau's fiction.

Journal intime is an engaging work. Although it was published after *On est toujours trop bon avec les femmes*, it appears before it in *Les Œuvres complètes de Sally Mara*. Written as a diary that begins in 1934 and ends eighteen months later, it traces the apprenticeship of a young Irish woman, Sally Mara, to the nuances of the French language and to the world of sexuality. Totally ignorant of sex and of sexual innuendo in French, she has to look up the word *virgin*, and she wonders how her brother could be the father of the cook's child, because they are not married. She progresses so well that she ends up married. This, the novel suggests ironically, is the termination of sexual curiosity. Another aspect of her activities is learning Gaelic, for reasons of patriotism. Her only novel, *On est toujours trop bon avec les femmes*, will be written in that language. In *Journal intime* Queneau satirizes not only fictional conventions but also national and sexual stereotypes.

On est toujours trop bon avec les femmes is said to have been written in Gaelic by Sally and translated by Michel Presle. The events take place in Dublin during the Easter rebellion of 1916. Seven Irish revolutionaries take over a post office while Gertie Girdle, an employee, is in the ladies' room. She becomes their prisoner while the post office is besieged. Fearful for her life, she offers herself, losing her virginity to one rebel, embrac-

Queneau in later life (photograph copyright © Jerry Bauer)

ing a second in the same way, and fellating a third. She is also sodomized by two others. While she is thus engaged, the other rebels fight and go about their business. She is finally rescued by her fiancé, Commodore Cartwright. The parody is amusing, with its allusions to Joyce in the choice of the rebels' names and their password, "Finnegans Wake," and very discreetly erotic, Queneau's descriptions being rarely straightforward.

In 1965 Queneau produced what is perhaps his most complex and profound text, *Les Fleurs bleues* (translated in England as *Between Blue and Blue* and in the United States as *The Blue Flowers*, 1967). In Bettina Knapp's *French Novelists Speak Out* (1976) Queneau summarizes the plot of his novel: "In *The Blue Flowers*, I focus on a person who goes back in time—and one who emerges from some past era. In other words, modern and ancient. My historical character lived in the thirteenth century and reappears every one hundred and seventy-five years until he meets the other protagonist and becomes his contemporary. There is an old Chinese saying in this connection: 'I dream that I am a butterfly and pray

there is a butterfly dreaming he is me.' The same can be said of the characters in my novel–those who live in the past dream of those who live in the modern era–and those who live in the modern era dream of those who live in the past."

Because each protagonist dreams the actions of the other, the reader wonders whether they are one character or two, alter egos or two aspects of the same psyche. One critic, Anne Clancier, proposes a Freudian model in a 1966 review for *Arc*: she identifies the Duke of Auge, the historical character, with the ego, while associating Cidrolin, the modern one, with the id. But the stories of Auge and Cidrolin can also be interpreted according to other systems of oppositions: the conscious and the unconscious, metaphor and metonymy, or time and space, for example. Auge, although a fictional character, appears in the context of Queneau's "historical" moments. From the past, Auge dreams of the future even as he reappears every 175 years. Auge does not evolve during his odyssey, which has so far covered a span of 700 years, but his historical situation and his language do. In that sense, Auge can be seen to represent time. The narrative of Cidrolin, in contrast, emphasizes his place of residence, a stationary barge called L'Arche. Indications of distance and direction, and points of departure and destination evoke spatial associations, reinforced by the absence of temporal progression. Time is even reversed as Cidrolin's situation stagnates. At the beginning of the novel Cidrolin explains that it is a fine autumn day; toward the end of the novel autumn is said to be approaching. Just as in dreams, the events in this narrative are temporally indeterminate.

Queneau also situates dreams in the context of the philosophical tradition of illusion and reality. The epigraph he chose for the novel, "He heard a dream for a dream," is taken from Plato's *Theaetetus*. In it the two main sources of human error are defined: the relativity of knowledge, which depends on the background and point of view of the knower, and dream or illusion, which may be experienced as real. But what is reality in a novel? In Queneau's narrative that question is even more striking since each character is the dream of the other. Perhaps one is to understand that dreams are the true reality.

Queneau's reference to the Chinese adage in connection with *Les Fleurs bleues* suggests that the dreamer captures an essential part of his own identity in his dream. The butterfly represents the dreamer to himself. It reveals his being and his desires with a freedom that is not possible in waking life, where repressions and others' expectations hold one in their web.

The variety of interpretations the text makes possible is not only a function of the identity of the protagonists and the themes of the novel; it is also a function of its form. Composed of two narrative lines, it is the relationship between the lines that captivates readers. Initially distant, the historical line eventually meets the spatial or modern one as Auge enters the twentieth century. The novel concludes with a timeless myth. Auge and his entourage arrive, board Cidrolin's ark, and depart through the flooding rains to a new Mt. Ararat, a shore abloom with blue flowers.

The phrase "les fleurs bleues," which gives the novel its title, has several meanings. When attributed to a person, it can suggest outdated notions regarding love, manners, or ideals, whether they be ideals of purity or of decorum. Or the noun can refer to a specific moment, when knighthood was in flower, when the ideals of chivalry were in effect. In the novel Auge gives vent to his nostalgia for less degraded times. His desire for purity is ultimately fulfilled by a transformation of the Noah myth. At the end of the novel the blue flowers reemerge from beneath the deluge; they are now a symbol of hope and regeneration. The title also evokes the use of flowers as the ancient figure for rhetoric, suggesting the bouquet of tropes, even the decorative use of "flowery" prose–to which Auge is occasionally given. As for the adjective "blue," it is used in connection with literature to indicate tall tales or popular literature, elements of which are found in *Les Fleurs bleues*. Finally, the title calls to mind specific texts, such as Novalis's *Heinrich von Ofterdingen*. The hero of Novalis's fiction seeks the blue flower of poetry. Reading Queneau's work in the light of the German romantic text allows one to grasp the evolution of the novel as a genre.

It should be added that while Queneau's title has several connotations, the expression "les fleurs bleues" is still a ready-made one in French. It is not original with Queneau, and this may be seen as revealing his attitude toward literary language: that literature is not composed of a special language but is merely one of the "uses" to which ordinary language can be put. The title engages the reader to examine the linguistic codes that each adapts to his own unique purpose. Queneau's puns, his play with different registers

of language from the most noble to slang, and his surprising associations engage the reader to play as well and to enjoy the novel at different levels.

In a similar way, the readers of Queneau's last novel, *Le Vol d'Icare* (1968; translated as *The Flight of Icarus*, 1973), cannot escape involvement with the literary process. This work is both a quest and an inquest of fiction, as the detective story pretext amply illustrates. The fictional turn-of-the-century character, novelist Hubert Lubert, searches in vain for his hero, Icarus, a character escaped from his book: Icarus was blown away into the "real" world and out of his "creator's" novel by a sudden gust of wind. Hubert calls upon the detective Morcol to retrieve him. The novelists that number among Hubert's friends lose their characters in turn. But whereas most of the other characters go back, Icarus, enthralled by all manner of machinery, takes off in an airplane and crashes before the eyes of Hubert. The text, written almost entirely in dialogue form, points to the fact that there are no levels of reality in fiction; no word is closer to the world than any other. There are only narrative conventions generally accepted as models of how events are recounted. Queneau dismisses the traditional causality of plot in favor of a linguistic motivation: each episode is based on one of the various meanings of the verb *voler*: to fly, to steal, and of its composite *s'envoler*, to take off. The novel points to itself as a verbal artifact and explores the way in which literature re-creates existing fictions and myths that are already endowed with structure and meaning. *Le Vol d'Icare* recuperates and modifies the myth of Icarus. Queneau thereby attracts the reader's attention to the codes of language and literature, to the interplay of referential and contextual signification. He does not communicate a "vision" or a philosophy; he engages the reader in active experimentation with the tools and techniques of the literary process. Readers can thus attain a heightened awareness of linguistic potentialities and a greater understanding and acceptance of new forms of literary expression that can more adequately give symbolic expression to their living situation.

Letters:
Correspondance Raymond Queneau-Elie Lascaux (Verviers: Temps Mêlés, 1979);
Une Correspondance: Raymond Queneau-Boris Vian (Levallios-Perret: Association des Amis de Valentin Brû, 1982).

Bibliographies:

Wolfgang Hillen, *Bibliographie des études sur l'homme et son œuvre* (Cologne: Gemini, 1981);

Claude Rameil, Bibliography of Queneau's writings, *Les Amis de Valentin Brû*, no. 23 (1983).

References:

Arc, special issue on Queneau, no. 28 (February 1966);

Renée Baligand, *Les Poèmes de Raymond Queneau* (Montreal, Paris & Brussels: Didier, 1972);

Jacques Bens, *Queneau* (Paris: Gallimard, 1962);

Andrée Bergens, *Raymond Queneau* (Geneva: Droz, 1963);

Cahiers Raymond Queneau (Levallois-Perret: Association des Amis de Valentin Brû, 1986-);

Jean-Pierre Dauphin, ed., *Raymond Queneau plus intime* (Paris: Gallimard, 1978);

Europe, special issue on Queneau, no. 650-651 (June-July 1983);

Paul Gayot, *Raymond Queneau* (Paris: Editions Universitaires, 1967);

Jacques Guicharnaud, *Raymond Queneau* (New York: Columbia University Press, 1965);

L'Herne, special issue on Queneau, no. 29 (December 1975);

Vivian Kogan, *The Flowers of Fiction: Time and Space in Raymond Queneau's "Les Fleurs bleues"* (Lexington, Ky.: French Forum, 1982);

Magazine Littéraire, special issue on Queneau, no. 94 (November 1974);

Jean Queval, *Essai sur Raymond Queneau* (Paris: Seghers, 1960);

W. D. Redfern, *Queneau: "Zazie dans le métro"* (London: Grant & Cutler, 1980);

Christopher Shorley, *Queneau's Fiction: An Introductory Study* (Cambridge, London, New York, New Rochelle, Melbourne & Sydney: Cambridge University Press, 1985);

Claude Simonnet, *Queneau déchiffré (Notes sur "Le Chiendent")* (Paris: Julliard, 1962);

Temps Mêlés: Documents Raymond Queneau (Paris: Argon, 1978);

Allen Thiher, *Raymond Queneau* (Boston: Twayne, 1985).

Papers:

Queneau's publications and criticism of Queneau's work are in a special collection supervised by André Blavier at the Bibliothèque Municipale, Verviers, Belgium.

Antoine de Saint-Exupéry

(29 June 1900-31 July 1944)

Catharine Savage Brosman
Tulane University

BOOKS: *Courrier sud* (Paris: Gallimard, 1929); translated by Stuart Gilbert as *Southern Mail* (New York: Smith & Haas, 1933);

Vol de nuit (Paris: Gallimard, 1931; New York & London: Harper, 1939); translated by Gilbert as *Night Flight* (New York & London: Century, 1932; London: Harmsworth, 1932);

Terre des hommes (Paris: Gallimard, 1939); translated by Lewis Galantière as *Wind, Sand and Stars* (New York: Reynal & Hitchcock, 1939; London: Heinemann, 1939; revised edition, London: Heinemann, 1970);

Pilote de guerre (New York: Editions de la Maison Française, 1942); translated by Galantière as *Flight to Arras* (New York: Reynal & Hitchcock, 1942; London: Heinemann, 1942); French version republished (Paris: Gallimard, 1942);

Lettre à un otage (New York: Brentano's, 1943; Paris: Gallimard, 1944); translated by Jacqueline Gerst as *Letter to a Hostage* (London: Heinemann, 1950);

Le Petit Prince (New York: Reynal & Hitchcock, 1943; Paris: Gallimard, 1945); translated by Katherine Woods as *The Little Prince* (New York: Reynal & Hitchcock, 1943; London: Heinemann, 1944);

Citadelle (Paris: Gallimard, 1948); translated by Gilbert as *The Wisdom of the Sands* (New York: Harcourt, Brace, 1950; London: Hollis & Carter, 1952);

Carnets (Paris: Gallimard, 1953; revised edition, 1975);

Un Sens à la vie (Paris: Gallimard, 1956); translated by Adrienne Foulke as *A Sense of Life* (New York: Funk & Wagnalls, 1965);

Ecrits de guerre, 1939-1944 (Paris: Gallimard, 1982); translated as *Wartime Writings, 1939-1944* (New York: Harcourt Brace Jovanovich, 1986).

Collection: *Œuvres* (Paris: Gallimard, 1953).

Antoine de Saint-Exupéry (photo Viollet)

MOTION PICTURE: *Courrier sud*, screenplay by Saint-Exupéry, France, 1937.

To readers throughout the world, Saint-Exupéry is known chiefly as the author of *Le Petit Prince* (1943; translated as *The Little Prince*, 1943)—that is, as the charming, imaginative writer and illustrator of a fable appreciated by both children and adults—and also for *Vol de nuit* (1931; translated as *Night Flight*, 1932), a novel on flying, and his poetic volumes *Terre des hommes* (1939; translated as *Wind, Sand and Stars*, 1939) and *Pilote de guerre* (1942; translated as *Flight to Arras*, 1942), all of which have been published in many languages. In France, he is viewed not only as the greatest writer on aviation, but also as a master of French prose and a moral spokesman of his generation, whose works have a significance that goes well beyond their immediate topics. Changing literary tastes in the decades since his death and the birth of a new criticism that has ignored him almost completely have not affected his stature among those who appreciate a classic French style, sober and controlled even when poetic, and those who find in his searching comments on man and his planet tools for their own understanding of human activity and its meaning. In his biography, Curtis Cate quotes publication figures for Saint-Exupéry's books as listed in the 1970 *Quid?* almanac: almost two and a quarter million copies of *Vol de nuit* had been sold, and well over a million and a half of *Terre des hommes* and *Le Petit Prince* each. He is the only author of the century to have three books among the top ten bestsellers of the period. (There are two by Albert Camus.)

He is not a great novelist in the manner of Balzac or Proust, not a powerful creator of characters and their own fictional society, but his books all reflect a vision which is immediately recognizable as his and which transforms ordinary perception. Both his two fictional works—based considerably on personal experiences—and the more numerous volumes in which he speaks directly of his own and his companions' activities and meditates on their meaning provide to the reader not only a thrilling vicarious experience of flight but also an invitation to see the world and its dilemmas from perspectives that are at once characteristic of the author and nearly universally recognizable. His work thus fulfills the condition that André Gide, who admired him, identified as the hallmark of a classic: rendering the general through the particular. It is unfortunate that much writing on his work is marred by adulation and an excessive occupation with his person, approaches which obscure some of the qualities of the writing and set the artisan above the object he produced, the thinker above his thought; there has also been an unfortunate tendency to give questionable religious interpretations to his work.

Antoine de Saint-Exupéry was born on 29 June 1900 in Lyons, the third child of Count Jean de Saint-Exupéry and his wife, née Marie de Fonscolombe. Both parents came from aristocratic families—from Provence on the maternal side and Limousin on the paternal side. Two other children were born before the father died

in 1904. Saint-Exupéry's writings and letters depict what was apparently a very happy childhood: he was devoted to his mother and, at the two châteaux where the family stayed alternately (Saint-Maurice in the department of the Ain, and La Mole in the Var), he romped cheerfully with his brother and sisters. What is perhaps the most striking in his reminiscences is his account of the games—not just playing them, but inventing them. Although it would be erroneous to consider aviation a game for him, a strong ludic impulse is visible in his work. Many of his pages are concerned with childhood, but his evocation of the past, or what Baudelaire called the "vert paradis des amours enfantines" (green paradise of childhood loves), is a happy one, not tinged with the morbid regret that characterizes the theme in the writings of Proust.

Saint-Exupéry's first education took place at home. From 1909 through 1914 he was a day student at a Jesuit school in Le Mans; this schooling was followed by brief studies at Villefranche-sur-Saône (autumn 1914), then two years at the Marianists' school in Fribourg, Switzerland. In 1917-1918, after the death of his brother François, he attended two Parisian institutions, the Ecole Bossuet and the Lycée Saint-Louis, in preparation for the entrance examinations for the Ecole Navale. He liked mathematics and showed aptitude for it, but, after passing the written examinations, despite a low score in French composition, he did not pass the orals. After studying architecture briefly, he began his military service. He was soon writing to his mother that he wanted to obtain his pilot's license.

Flying was not new to him; he had been a passenger briefly in 1912. In Strasbourg, where he was assigned to an aviation regiment, he was not a pilot trainee but was able to take flying lessons in his spare time and received his civilian license. Later he was transferred to Rabat, in Morocco, where he was certified as a military pilot. In 1922 he returned to France and studied at the school for air cadets at Avord, then, holding the rank of second lieutenant, finished his military obligation in the 33rd aviation group, assigned to Le Bourget, near Paris. There, in 1922, he had a serious accident (after a minor scrape at Strasbourg), the first in what would be a series of crashes.

Meanwhile Saint-Exupéry had met and become affianced to Louise de Vilmorin, who would later be recognized as a minor writer and would be the last companion of André Malraux.

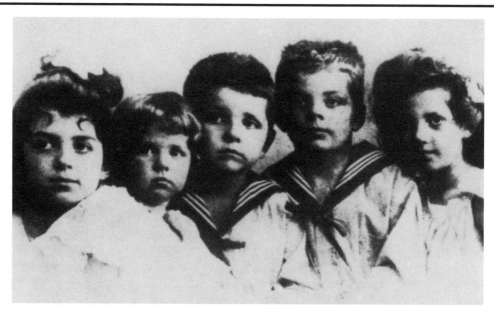

Marie-Madeleine, Gabrielle, François, Antoine, and Simone de Saint-Exupéry, 1907

The career in the air force, which Saint-Exupéry wanted after his obligatory service, was a prospect the Vilmorin family could not accept; the young man therefore took instead a position with a tile manufacturer–arranged by his fiancée's family. Little of this life is reflected in his work; but when the reader comes upon passages in *Courrier sud* (1929; translated as *Southern Mail*, 1933), *Terre des hommes*, and *Un Sens à la vie* (1956; translated as *A Sense of Life*, 1965; more aptly, A Meaning to Life) that deal with the *termitière* or *fourmilière* (termite or ant hill), with busloads of weary office workers, he glimpses the author's dissatisfaction with a bureaucrat's life and his judgments on the society that produces it. At the time, his chief recourse was to continue flying as much as possible.

When Louise de Vilmorin broke the engagement in 1923–perhaps under family pressure, perhaps because she was much more interested in such matters as social visits and furniture than in the intellectual concerns of Saint-Exupéry–he attempted to find other work, including a position in journalism, and in letters to his mother he began to speak of "mon roman" (my novel). He did some flying in 1926 as an instructor, then accepted a job with a truck-manufacturing firm, as a traveling salesman–a job he rather liked for a while but at which he was singularly unsuccessful. Meanwhile, his first work (excluding a manuscript entitled "Manon," never published) appeared in a little magazine, the *Navire d'Argent*, in 1926. Entitled "L'Aviateur" (and later collected

in *Un Sens à la vie*), it had been planned as a longer story, to be called "L'Evasion de Jacques Bernis" (The Escape of Jacques Bernis). It is to some degree a first version of parts of *Courrier sud*. Some of the author's favorite themes are already present: the experience of takeoff, the relationship between the pilot and his plane, the importance of camaraderie with other pilots, and even the contrast between the pilot's life and the Parisian society to which he returns.

That same year, thanks to a former professor who introduced him to the director of the Latécoère aviation company, Saint-Exupéry was hired and assigned to Toulouse, where he met Didier Daurat, the local head, who was to exercise over him a strong influence, through his own devotion to his work and his way of making the highest demands on his pilots and thereby gaining their respect. After working at the Toulouse base for some months, Saint-Ex (as his colleagues called him) became a pilot in 1927 on the southern postal route, which transported mail from Toulouse to Dakar via several stops on the west coast of Africa. It was as if the job had been designed for him. He was doing what he had wished to for years; he had an admirable supervisor; he was happy with his fellow pilots, of whom some later became famous on their own, such as Jean Mermoz, and others were immortalized by him. And he was back in the desert, which he had discovered in Morocco and which was to play a role in his work no less considerable than the part it plays in the writings of Camus.

Saint-Exupéry with his sister Marie-Madeleine (at left) at Saint-Maurice de Rémens, the family's house in Ain, 1918

Before long Saint-Exupéry was made head of the tiny post at Cape Juby in the Spanish Sahara, surrounded by dissident tribes. His time there–close to a year–is reflected in several works written later, for it was crucial to his intellectual development, but it is especially visible in letters of the period and in *Courrier sud*. He lived an ascetic life and had long periods of near-solitude. In addition to supervising the landings and take-offs of mail planes, he was successful in fostering good relations with the Spanish authorities there and obtaining extensions of air-space rights for the French line. He also took it upon himself to engage in rescue missions that were dangerous and, in one case, against regulations. As a result of his negotiations and strategy–a combination of persistence and daring–he was able to effect the rescue of several downed pilots, the recovery of a plane, and the exchange of pilots being held for ransom. He learned a little Arabic and came to know some of the local chieftains, who respected him, and to appreciate their way of life. And he learned to know the desert itself, as well as the sea, which at high tide lapped at his hut.

The novel *Courrier sud*, his first full-length work, is a development of material from "L'Aviateur," some of which appears verbatim. Bernis, an alter ego of the author, is the central character, but the author also appears as an unnamed voice who says "I," the head of the Cape Juby airfield who relates Bernis's experiences, quite autobiographical in content. The two men

were friends as boys and are now fellow flyers; moreover, they both loved as youths a charming girl named Geneviève, now married and living in Paris, with whom Bernis is still in love. The novel is divided into three parts, one and three concerned with the southern mail route, the central one with Bernis on leave in Paris, trying among the Parisians to retain his identity as a pilot–that is, with a different vantage point from that of others–and seeing Geneviève again.

The sections on flying, written at the latest when the author was twenty-seven, are remarkable for both style and content. Like similar passages in *Terre des hommes* and other later texts, instead of attempting to describe at length the experience of piloting over Spain and Africa, they indicate it by equivalents: psychological notations (suggesting the effect on the pilot of what he is doing and seeing) and metaphoric correspondences. The author proceeds by light touches and telling details. The style is often sparse and at times literally telegraphic, composed of wireless reports. How things appear is one of the principal interests. In 1923 Saint-Exupéry had written to a friend, "Il ne faut pas apprendre à écrire mais à voir" (One must not learn to write but to see). The plane is an instrument, an extension of the self, which reveals everything differently–earth, sky, sea, and the body that is temporally and spatially a part of them. Sartre wrote in "Qu'est-ce que la littérature?" (*What is Literature?*, 1948) that he admired Saint-Exupéry because he showed how the plane was an instrument of perception. Spain is no longer a peninsula on the globe or an abstract entity, but some orange trees, a field, a stream, a few fishermen on the beach–that is, an example of the microgeography which is the world of small planes flying at low altitudes.

Bernis and the narrator live for the route, for the regular flights of a network which seems to have its own being. To speak of duty in this connection would be to suggest that the text is colored by moralizing. It is not a question so much of doing one's duty as of living *through* the act. This is what makes Saint-Exupéry seem congenial to those well-read in the existential writers of the same generation: Malraux, Sartre, and to some degree Camus. There is absolutely no heroism, however: this is flying experienced from the inside, where one does not feel himself to be a hero but rather an enabler of an act, a doer.

In part 1 Bernis appears principally in his function as a pilot; although the focus is on his experience, his flight from Toulouse to Alicante, which is recounted by the narrator using a mix of grammatical persons, reveals an agent more than a particularized human being. In part 2 the narrator relates what Bernis, upon returning from Paris, tells him about his stay there. The account is marked by a sense of alienation, both geographic and moral, and by the failure of his love affair with Geneviève. The latter, based probably on Louise de Vilmorin as well as on other female acquaintances of the author, had so charmed Bernis as a girl that she remains connected in his mind with the delights of childhood–imagination and spontaneity. Now, married to a dull, authoritarian husband, she turns to Bernis for some of the warm and witty conversation she has missed. Her only child dies while Bernis is in Paris. The event is treated with stylistic control, but a sense of anguish pierces through, which reflects perhaps the author's own upon the death of his brother. Disappointed in her husband, and in grief over the death, Geneviève goes away briefly with Bernis.

This rather ordinary plot is transformed by Saint-Exupéry's understanding of feminine psychology and his way of expressing it. Avoiding the vocabulary of psychological analysis that has been the stock-in-trade of the French novel for generations, he uses instead exterior referents–the chill, a crowded hotel, trees along the road–to stand for mental events, revealed thereby to both character and reader. Geneviève's inability

to forget Paris, for instance, is conveyed by her forgetting her fur coat. The author's treatment of his heroine has something in common with Jean Giraudoux's portraits of young women, particularly in the depiction of her rather ethereal qualities. The failure of Bernis and Geneviève's escape together is not plumbed psychologically but seems inevitable. Bernis's attempts to find meaning in religion at Notre Dame and in Parisian night life are even greater failures.

In part 3 the narrator recounts Bernis's return to Cape Juby after a dangerous flight in bad weather, and relates what his friend tells him of the dying Geneviève, whom Bernis visited just before she lost consciousness. Her death is conveyed as a loosening of ties of recognition and belonging. Although for some tastes the passage may be too fanciful, essentially it suits the character–not an oneiric figure, but somehow less of the world than of the mind. Bernis's own death on his next flight, which can be considered an "escape" (just as his visit to Paris and departure again are echoes of the escape mentioned in the abandoned short-story title), is told entirely from the point of view of his task: a mail plane does not arrive; there is a break in the chain. Only when the narrator discovers Bernis's crashed plane in the desert and telegraphs a short description of the wreck, ending with the notation that the mail is intact, does the reader have a visual image of a downed aircraft, a dead man, and what that means.

Courrier sud is sometimes considered weak. Reviewing it for the *Nouvelles Littéraires*, Edmond Jaloux acknowledged that it was well written, in terms of style, but found it unimpressive in content, since it consisted of rather ordinary romantic adventures, transposed into a modern setting, and since the psychology was superficial, or at least ill explained. Yet it was recognized by many as expressing an original voice, and Gallimard gave the author a contract for other books. Although the author had not yet acquired a total mastery of his craft, even if he had written nothing else, this novel would probably have kept a place on the literary bookshelf.

By March 1928 Saint-Exupéry was back in France after a brief leave the previous fall and further service in Africa. The Latécoère company sent him to Brest to study aerial navigation, as preparation for the new post he was to occupy in South America, which he assumed in October 1929. He found there several close friends, including Henri Guillaumet, and his former chief,

Saint-Exupéry at age twenty-one in Rabat, Morocco, where he received his certification as a military pilot

Daurat, and soon Mermoz. Named head of the Argentinian subsidiary of the Compagnie Générale Aéropostale, he was to extend the company's routes throughout the southern tip of the continent. The airfields he set up became famous through *Vol de nuit;* his descriptions of Tierra del Fuego and other stops occupy a place in *Terre des hommes.* By April 1930 he had established the weekly mail service from Patagonia to Buenos Aires, and, the next month, the entire France-Patagonia route was opened. In June 1930 his friend Guillaumet crashed in the Andes on a crossing from Santiago. The fruitless efforts of Saint-Ex and other pilots to spot the wreckage from the air, the man's determination to survive

and his amazing resistance to extreme cold and starvation, the joy of his return a week later– these create, in the section of *Terre des hommes* devoted to the author's comrades, a superb narrative.

Saint-Exupéry spent eighteen months in South America. When he returned to France on leave in 1931 he brought with him the manuscript of *Vol de nuit* and a fiancée, Consuelo Suncin, widow of an Argentinian journalist. Gide, who would soon write the preface for the new novel, observed in his diary that he hoped the bride would be as good as the literary work. From the relatively scant evidence available, it is clear that the marriage was not a satisfactory one.

The wife apparently did not understand her husband's need for creative solitude, although she herself had some artistic ambitions. They lived apart for several periods in addition to those occasioned by the war. Saint-Exupéry's works do not reflect this marriage directly; only two women besides Geneviève–pilots' wives in *Vol de nuit*–play a role in his work. Some critics, however, have seen in the vain, demanding rose of *Le Petit Prince* a reflection of Consuelo.

Vol de nuit was published in 1931 and was awarded the Prix Fémina. Part of the critical interest it aroused may have been due to the prize; some may have arisen also from Gide's preface, which attracted the attention of the reviewer Jaloux in the *Nouvelles Littéraires* because it showed a severe, moralizing side to the great immoralist. The preface to the first edition emphasizes the paradoxical truth of the novel: that happiness is found not in freedom but in the acceptance of a duty. Some readers have found the role of duty excessive and have even seen the text as proto-Fascist–a reading which has seemed justified by certain statements in the author's posthumously published works, but which is inaccurate. The book is a poem as well as a *récit*–a poem to the heroism (although they do not see it as such) of those who inaugurated night flying on the South American routes. While it includes several plots, its coherence is provided by the nocturnal setting and a vision which portrays the night sky in marine terms–waves of clouds and winds, stars like shore lights–and humanizes the earth below–villages like a scattered flock.

Coherence is provided also by the central character, Rivière, based principally on Didier Daurat but also on the author himself (reflecting his responsibilities as director of the Argentinian line). As director of Aéropostale, Rivière does not fly, but commands the network of routes and planes, indicated on a map in his office, as though it were his own nervous system. Mail is collected at Buenos Aires from three South American points–Patagonia, Chile, and Paraguay–then sent on to Rio de Janeiro and Africa. At night, Rivière waits anxiously for the three planes to arrive, and prepares the departure of the fourth. The existence of the line demands high standards, and he exercises severe discipline, dismissing, for instance, an old and devoted mechanic who has made a careless mistake and demanding that an inspector–the most ineffectual of Saint-Exupéry's characters–write a reprimand against a pilot, not because the latter has erred, but to off-

set the effects of the friendship he had tried, against policy, to establish with him. Rivière, who sees his task as the creation of character as well as of an enterprise, tells a pilot that what he had called a cyclone, which had made him turn back, was really his own fear. "Aimez ceux que vous commandez. Mais sans le leur dire" (Love those you command, but without telling them) is his formula for a superior's role, one aspect of the theme of responsibility crucial to Saint-Exupéry's work.

The pilots experience this same sense of duty, although they also know the exhilaration of flight, the discovery of villages nestled at twilight on the plain, and the grandeur of the stars and moon above the clouds. The questions arise implicitly from the text: why devote one's life to an air route; why risk dying so that mail can reach Europe faster? Saint-Exupéry's answers grow out of Rivière's meditation on man. It is not known, he concludes, *what* surpasses man–for neither the character nor the author indicates belief in God– but men always act *as if*–as if they must reach beyond themselves, to build something greater which will endure, and for which they see themselves as tools. The author thus answers in advance Henry de Montherlant's statement in *Le Solstice de juin* (Summer Solstice, 1941) that it is idiotic to risk one's life for trivial love letters or petty commercial correspondence. Again, it is not a question of sheer heroism. Saint-Exupéry wrote more than once on the topic of courage, agreeing with Plato that it occupied the lowest rank among virtues, being composed of vanity, anger, stubbornness, and sporting pleasure. Rather, it is a question of building something, first the self and its spirit, and then something that goes beyond the self and can be called man.

Saint-Exupéry's method of presentation is noteworthy. The novel is written in the third person, but includes numerous passages in which the reader is placed at the center of consciousness of the pilots as they fly and experiences with them by means of metaphors and impressions their progress at night toward Buenos Aires. These passages alternate with others centered on the office, where Rivière monitors the route. He is seen sometimes from the outside, but glimpses are afforded also of the inner man, particularly of his solitude and his concern for creating, with his life, something of lasting value. The author devotes small scenes to several pilots, including pages that describe the transatlantic pilot as he is awakened by his wife, who helps him, as in a rit-

Saint-Exupéry, Beppo de Massimi, director general of the Société Aéropostale, and Jean Mermoz, Saint-Exupéry's fellow pilot and best friend, 1930

ual, into his heavy aviator's suit. Only one pilot, Fabien, is followed the length of his route, and it is to him that the inevitable accident occurs, which is prefigured by a sense of dread concerning night flying. Based perhaps on Mermoz, he represents total dedication to his route. Yet he is married, and his wife, after learning that her husband is lost, appears at the office. Her voice as she telephones for reports, and her confrontation with Rivière represent the legitimate claims of one type of happiness; Rivière's counterclaims— the route, the conquest of fear—are just as legitimate. Their confrontation can only be tragic. Fabien flies through a cyclone, as Saint-Exupéry himself had, which blows him out to sea, far off course. Although during the storm he is tense, clutching the controls, his last minutes, when he is nearly out of fuel, are expressed poetically: he has been lured by a star which he mistook for a light.

The severity of these themes and of Rivière's character and the account of Fabien's death must not be allowed to obscure warmer aspects of the book. Saint-Exupéry's characters are not interested in the plane as machine—that is, mechanical power for its own sake—but in what it allows them to do. Like Jacques Bernis they feel it as an extension of themselves, allowing them to transform distance into human ties, and to see the earth below as alive with the cares and concerns of the heart that make the planet truly the "earth of men."

Saint-Exupéry at the time he was awarded the Prix Fémina for Vol de Nuit

While *Vol de nuit* is characterized by lyricism as well as pithy observations on character and values, its construction is balanced and its style carefully chiseled, the result of the author's laborious trimming of a long manuscript. It is the least autobiographical of his books and, of his two novels, the one with wider appeal. In its insistence on action as a creative force and on the importance of creating something enduring, its ethical viewpoint parallels and anticipates the writings of Malraux and Camus. Its severe morality of discipline and sacrifice make it distasteful to those who fear authoritarianism, but it fits well into the author's work as a whole, which, as he matured, became increasingly concerned with values and standards for action.

While Saint-Exupéry was in France on leave in 1931, the Compagnie Aéropostale broke up in South America, a result of complicated political and commercial dealings. He lost his post there, as did Daurat, to whom he remained loyal in the ensuing series of accusations. For a time, he returned to piloting in Africa, where he realized that the heroic days of the line were over, and did some piloting of hydroplanes for the Latécoère firm. In a serious accident in the Mediterranean, he nearly drowned; a consequence was that he lost his position. In 1934, however, he obtained employment as a publicity agent with Air France, recently formed from other companies, and wrote articles for its magazine. He also participated in the filming of a publicity movie and, later, in the filming of *Courrier sud*. In 1935 he traveled to Moscow for *Paris-Soir*, a daily. Thus began a short but distinguished career as a journalist. His reports from Moscow and later from Spain, for the *Intransigeant* as well as for *Paris-Soir*, do not resemble in the least the common fare of newspaper journalism. They usually focus on revealing details and incidents rather than on sensational news; the one exception, the crash of the airship *Maksim Gorky,* is treated from a very personal point of view. Local political issues are present, but are seen in the larger context of human issues. What makes each place unique—the quality of human experience, the justification of political points of view, and the question of values—is conveyed through carefully chosen vignettes and authorial comment. The Spanish reports in particular, done in the midst of the civil war, are searching; they deserve a place with other well-known chronicles of the conflict, such as Malraux's *L'Espoir* (*Man's Hope,* 1937) and Hemingway's *For Whom the Bell Tolls* (1940). Saint-Exupéry later included parts of them in *Terre des hommes,* and the whole series can be found in *Un Sens à la vie.*

Toward the end of 1935, after his return from Moscow, Saint-Exupéry learned of a contest, sponsored by the Air Ministry, in which a prize would be awarded to the pilot who could break the time record between Paris and Saigon. On 29 December he set off with his mechanic, Prévot. After an initial delay because of a fuel leak, they set out again. On the lap from Benghazi to Cairo they were disoriented and, with their progress slowed by a head wind, they crashed on a rocky dune in the Libyan desert. One of the best-known sections of *Terre des hommes* recounts their struggle to survive (they had almost no provisions). When, after vain marches of many kilometers in other directions, they were found on the fifth day as they walked east, by Bedouins, they were very close to death from dehydration. The author's homage to the nomad who first spotted him, whom he calls simply *man,* is as noble a page as can be found in contemporary French letters.

Back in France, Saint-Exupéry returned to journalism, and after the war broke out in Spain was sent there in 1936 and again in 1938. He also did some flying for Air France to reconnoiter a new route in Africa and visited Nazi Germany. Early in 1938 he traveled to New York with plans to undertake another long flight, this time from New York to Punta Arenas at Cape Horn. On 16 February, at Guatemala City, he and Prévot were seriously injured in a crash after a refueling stop. They were hospitalized there for weeks, and then Saint-Exupéry returned to New York City for the rest of his convalescence. He had with him a manuscript which he had promised Gallimard he would complete, and which would become *Terre des hommes.* It was finished over a period of some months, in New York and then France. Before returning to Europe the author left a copy of the manuscript with his American publisher, with instructions for it to be translated; meanwhile, he reworked, pared, and developed the French text; when both versions appeared early in 1939, the French version was noticeably different.

Although *Terre des hommes* received the Grand Prix du Roman, given by the Académie Française, for 1939, it is by no means a novel, nor even a personal narrative with a developed story line. Rather it groups together anecdotes, reminiscences, and meditations on flying, the planet, especially the desert, the war in Spain and other political topics, and what the author calls simply "men." Perhaps the award reflects the jury's admiration for previous works by Saint-Exupéry also or a penury of meritorious novels for 1939. Well crafted and stylistically beautiful, it is, like his other volumes, an invitation to see the world in the light of the author's experiences. The author's view, however, is not self-centered, but rather one which underscores general and lasting human values.

For instance, in the last episode, the often-anthologized passage "Mozart assassiné," taken from his Moscow reports, Saint-Exupéry evokes his train ride from France east toward Russia, and especially a group of Polish workers returning home after having lost their work in French mines. The highly graphic picture of the families with their tired children and small bundles of possessions has as a counterpart the writer's meditation on their individual lives and their destiny. Avoiding facile pity and patronizing, he recognizes that they too have known happiness—courtship and the first years of marriage, for instance—but that life has worn them down. In the child sleeping on the hard seat he sees not an individual victim but a loss for the human race, because his potentialities will never be realized. Like roses (one of his favorite images), human beings need cultivation, but "il n'est point de jardinier pour les hommes" (there is no gardener for men). When riches are lost for the human race, it is as if Mozart were assassinated.

Similarly, he recounts Guillaumet's struggle to survive the cold of the Andean winter. The flyer, after spending two nights near his wrecked plane, decided to try to traverse the rugged terrain when he thought of his wife and friends: "Ma femme, si elle croit que je vis, croit que je marche" (If my wife believes I'm alive, she be-

Saint-Exupéry and his wife, Consuelo, in 1936 (photo Keystone)

lieves I am walking). His purpose was to get far enough down so that his frozen body would be spotted from the air when the snow melted and his wife could collect the insurance; otherwise she would have to wait four years for the legal declaration of death. Ignoring his desire to sleep, he continued his painful descent for days. His statement to Saint-Exupéry, "Ce que j'ai fait jamais aucune bête ne l'aurait fait" (No animal would have done what I did), becomes a key phrase for the author. It is not a question of endurance or the instinct to survive but of considering one's responsibility to the community—wife and friends—and thereby forging human spirit.

Another episode from South America is called "L'Oasis." This is not a geographic oasis but a human one, the house of some country people who took in Saint-Exupéry after an emergency landing. The warm spirit of the family is visible everywhere; the household gods are *laisser-aller* and ease. The two daughters, who observe him carefully at dinnertime, are versions of the young Geneviève, spontaneous and pure. When he successfully passes the test to which they subtly put him (whether or not he will be frightened of the snakes in a hole under the table), he remembers his own childhood and knows that he is still one of the elect; but he wistfully foresees the day when a stranger—that is, a suitor—will fraudulently pass with a high score and take the girls away forever from the oasis of their youth, toward inevitable disappointment.

Other particularly reflective passages of *Terre des hommes* recount Saint-Exupéry's first experiences in the desert, his and Prévot's ordeal in Libya and his reflections when he thought he would die, unable to reach the "shipwrecked" (that is, his wife and friends, desperately calling out to him from France), and his visits to the front and to Madrid during the Spanish civil war. He stresses the human values for which both sides were fighting in that war, recognizing that they differed in their understanding of honor, loyalty, and Spain itself, but that in both cases the soldiers, so many of whom were volunteers, were fighting for values which surpassed their immediate circumstances. The corporal who is trying to teach botany to some unlettered recruits, the sergeant who is awakened early so that he may lead a few men in their inevitably futile attack against well-fortified positions, the volunteer who has left a comfortable trade to join the troops— all are reaching beyond themselves, trying to make something of the potentiality of their lives. A similar concern is visible in passages taken from his 1938 *reportage* on the Munich crisis and in many other pages.

Terre des hommes was a critical success on both sides of the Atlantic. The translation, by Lewis Galantière, won several prizes, including a National Book Award. In 1939, on 14 July, the author also had the satisfaction of breaking the transatlantic speed record with his friend Guillaumet, who died the next year. When war broke out in September, he was mobilized and, at his own urging, was assigned to Reconnaissance Group 2/33 at Orconte, in the north. In this instance, as later, he insisted on participating fully in operations, repeatedly refusing attempts by well-meaning friends to have him kept out of action. This attitude is consistent with his sense of responsibility and his understanding of community, the ties and relations which bind men together–as he had observed during the Spanish civil war–and create the values for which they are fighting.

The action which he saw, after several transfers, was both dangerous and futile. His several missions in 1940 included the flight of 23 May that became the basis for *Pilote de guerre*. The purpose was photographic reconnaissance over German-occupied territory. But it hardly made sense in the utter military chaos that prevailed in northern France; the information would be use-

less even if successfully gathered. Yet he and his crew flew to Arras and back, through heavy flak, carrying out orders as if they could have some meaning. He was decorated afterward with the Croix de Guerre. In June, with the fall of France, he flew to Algeria, like most other air officers, then was demobilized and returned to France in August. At the end of 1940, he arrived, via Portugal, in New York, for an exile of over two years that was both a productive and an unhappy period in his career, marked by his distress over the internecine quarrels of French exiles in New York and the suffering in his country itself. During this period he composed *Pilote de guerre, Lettre à un otage* (1943; translated as *Letter to a Hostage*, 1950), and *Le Petit Prince*, and worked on his manuscript for *Citadelle* (1948; translated as *The Wisdom of the Sands*, 1950). All four texts reveal his concern for moral values that, he was persuaded, were essential for the rebuilding of Europe.

Pilote de guerre was published first in New York, in French and English, then later the same year in Paris. It is not fiction, but, unlike *Terre des hommes,* it has a sustained narrative structure, to which are added anecdotes, short retrospective passages, and reflections. The memorable flight to Arras, which is the central event, is recounted against a background that includes portraits of Commander Henri Alias and other members of Group 2/33, brief evocations of the village where they are billeted, accounts of the French exodus across northern France after the German invasion, and considerations on the futility of the mission. The author seems to be at pains to avoid making himself and his comrades appear heroic, that is, exceptional. This attitude is consistent with his concern for identifying values that can be held by all and for motivating others to recognize these values. The France for which the group was sacrificing itself (about three-quarters had already been taken by Germany by the time he flew to Arras) was the patrimony of all. He is concerned to show that others also felt and acted through a patriotic devotion which was at once generous and natural, and which would have been unvoiced and almost unnoticed, had he not been there to record it.

His narrative begins with an account of preparations for the flight and of his understandable resentment at having to make it; it continues with indications about mechanical and navigational problems and his reflections while in flight. He repeatedly calls upon memories, particularly of his

Saint-Exupéry giving a radio talk during his visit to New York, 1938

childhood, to shed light on the experience. Remembering, as he crosses antiaircraft fire, his Tyrolian governess Paula, who put arnica compresses on his bumps, he muses, "Je vais avoir fameusement besoin d'arnica" (I am going to need arnica very badly). He recalls a game in which he and his brother and sisters tried to avoid being touched by raindrops, comparing it to his flight through flak, and elsewhere imagines that he and his crew are simply going for an evening walk. The flight is an experience of transformation. Literary transformations–that is, metaphors–by which he depicts the sky and earth in poetic terms disguise the treachery of the experience, in which a blue evening sky and peaceful countryside below conceal mortal danger. The

sense of time is likewise transformed, when at any moment there can be an explosion and a crash.

Most of all, his body is transformed. Unlike many other moralists, who have written out the body, Saint-Exupéry writes it into his vision of the world and indeed writes from it. The body, he discovers, is a means and not an end. Daily preoccupations with its care mask the necessity of going beyond it; but it is itself a going beyond, and its meaning comes only from its acts. It is the way for a father to save his son from a fire, the way to make discoveries, care for the sick, and save one's nation. The essential part of man is a "nœud de relations" (knot of relationships) with others, and the body is a currency to be exchanged for this community. Just as the refugees below live the defeat–that is, the assault upon their sense of nation–in their bodies, the pilot lives in his hands gripping the controls because it is an action of and for France, not of himself.

As the crippled plane returns miraculously from low passes over Arras and other areas infested with German defenses, the author finds himself changed, and this is the moral drama, paralleling the tension of the mission itself. "Chaque obligation fait devenir" (Every obligation leads to becoming). His resentment at carrying out the mission is replaced, in the context provided by a literal passage through fire, by the affirmation of his oneness with the suffering French people and of the moral values of French civilization, which are reaffirmed by each action carried out in their defense. These values, he recognizes, spring from Christianity; he even uses the sacramental image of bread. But they are not in themselves Christian. A misreading of the conclusion to *Pilote de guerre* has made several critics insist on the Christian content of Saint-Exupéry's ethics. Rather, he identifies principles such as responsibility, freedom, duty, and fraternity–all taking their meaning from the collectivity–as the cornerstones of a humanism which knows, or should know, no confessional or national boundaries. The closing of the book is a personal credo that those who prefer unstated moral conclusions or none at all can only find preachy. It marks the existential current in Saint-Exupéry's thought and reveals much about his understanding of the needs of France.

The short *Lettre à un otage*, dedicated to the author's friend Leon Werth, deals not only with the latter's precarious situation as a Jew in occupied France but also with all the French held hostage by the Germans and, by extension, with the values of French civilization. The letter is a paean to friendship, to the quality of man which French civilization had cultivated, and to the whole nation, with which Saint-Exupéry affirms his solidarity from abroad. He insists in particular on the principle of respect for man as essential in all political organizations, and contrasts it to Nazism. The letter is also a cry of distress at the divisions among Frenchmen and a call for moral and political unity. He disclaims, however, any right to *found* France: her truth is not represented in his words but in the lives of forty million hostages and her soldiers, whose existence, even in the darkness of wartime Europe, magnetizes and gives meaning to his.

The same appeal for values is found, in a different mode, at the heart of *Le Petit Prince*, dedicated to Werth. This fanciful tale of a little traveler from a distant asteroid is both a critique of a certain false civilization, that of a termite hill–businessmen, merchants, geometers, all who live by figures–and an affirmation of what the writer had discovered earlier about bonds and responsibility, the interdependency of human beings in a community which gives meaning to their lives and leads them to surpass themselves. In the desert setting made familiar by *Courrier sud* and *Terre des hommes*, the little prince, who has left a tyrannical rose that he has cultivated, and searched in vain for meaning on other planets, recounts to the narrator his adventures. The desert fox, whom he tamed and thus formed bonds with, tells him a secret: that one sees well only with the heart. "L'essentiel est invisible pour les yeux" (Essential things are invisible to the eyes). He realizes that protecting and loving his rose had given meaning to his life, and recognizes his responsibility to her. His death, which reflects in its tenderness the scene of the brother's death in *Pilote de guerre*, marks not just his return to his distant planet but also the narrator's transformation: henceforth the skies will have a different meaning for him. The theme of responsibility, as well as the fact that the narrator's plane has crashed in the desert where he encounters the little prince, ties the fable to Saint-Exupéry's earlier works on aviation and to his concerns of the 1940s.

In addition to composing *Pilote de guerre, Lettre à un otage*, and *Le Petit Prince* during the years in the United States, where Consuelo had come to join him, Saint-Exupéry wrote articles for American publications such as the *New York Times Magazine, Senior Scholastic*, and *Harper's* and gave lectures. Virtually all his writing and speaking had as its purpose the defense of France and her values, and the reconciliation of various French political factions. In 1942 he made a radio broadcast in which he appealed to the French in exile to go beyond the defeat and the Vichy regime and prepare the future together, whether under General Henri Giraud or Charles de Gaulle. These texts and others of the period, some not published previously, have been collected in *Écrits de guerre, 1939-1944* (1982; translated as *Wartime Writings, 1939-1944*, 1986). His conciliatory spirit was not appreciated by all. He was never popular with the Gaullists, who eyed him with suspicion, since he had never accepted de Gaulle's right to sole and entire leadership of the anti-Vichy French. But his appeal in 1942 may have had some effect.

In the spring of 1943 Saint-Exupéry sailed for North Africa, and immediately visited his old 2/33 group, stationed at Laghouat. The remaining fifteen months of his life were spent in efforts to rejoin the group–difficult because of his age–followed by short-lived success and then grounding–and ultimately a series of reconnaissance missions from bases in Algeria and Sardinia, for which permission was obtained from the Americans. He insisted on participating, even though rules and common sense forbade it. Some commentators have assumed that he no longer cared about living; and it is true that texts such as his "Lettre au Général X" in *Un Sens à la vie* reveal, in a disabused tone, his pessimism, inspired by doubts about the quality of life that would follow the war's end. He sensed that material values alone would dominate and that they would leave little place for what concerned him. But those who knew him well in Africa have argued that he wished to serve, not throw away his life. His presence in North Africa was a tonic to others; those who had been waiting for a chance to fight were delighted to see someone they considered a spokesman for their country as well as an important writer and aviator. Moreover, he was still working on *Citadelle*, begun in 1936 and expanded in New York, which had reached nearly a thousand pages of manuscript when he died. On his final mission, 29 July 1944, he was apparently shot down, although there is no confirmation of the circumstances of his death. Ironically, the mission was to be his last; permission to extend the allowed maximum would be granted no longer.

Citadelle was published four years later in its entirety with no editorial changes except mechanical ones. The work, as lengthy as all his previously published writing put together, was far from complete; the author had intended to work on it for years. However, even in its rough form, it is a masterpiece.

The setting of *Citadelle* is the desert, which takes on more clearly than ever a moral dimension. The voice is that of a Berber chieftain who recounts his youth, the assassination of his father, his assumption of leadership, and his deeds. But this is by no means a novel. It is more like a series of variations on themes or an extended prose poem, with elements of the Oriental tale. The highly wrought style bears resemblance to the Bible (narrative books, Ecclesiastes, the Psalms, and the parables), the prose of Gide (early works such as *El Hadj*, 1899), and especially the poetic prose of Saint-John Perse, with whose epic *Anabase* (*Anabasis*, 1929) Saint-Exupéry's text has striking stylistic and narrative resemblances.

The reference of the title is triple: the desert city which is the geographical center and, by extension, its traditions and values; the city of God–for the prince is building for Him as well as his people; and the fortress within each man: "Citadelle, je te construirai dans le cœur de l'homme" (Citadel, I shall build you in the hearts of men). The morality which underlines such edification is not a facile one, and some readers detected there germs of Nietzschean philosophy or fascism. It is conservative insofar as it insists upon personal virtue as the foundation for any genuinely just and virtuous society. The themes of responsibility and interdependency, seen in earlier works, reappear here as the chief's responsibility to his people and the people's responsibility to what he asks of them, something greater than themselves that they can become. What Rivière called in *Vol de nuit* the perishable body (an echo perhaps of St. Paul), to be exchanged for what surpasses it, is the fundamental concern. Ultimately, the goal toward which man strives would be God, and the text abounds in references to the search for God and what He means–without, however, any statement by which Saint-Exupéry assumes this belief as his own. The metaphor of the cathedral as a dynamic creation, used in *Pilote de guerre*, is present again. A cathedral is not merely an assemblage of stones; but in it stones find their meaning. Other images–sand, fountain or well, tree, and ship–tie the vision of *Citadelle* to some of the author's previous works but bear more weight here than in the novels and *récits*. Indeed, the whole text is highly lyrical, not in a personal manner but a general one, where the beauty and vastness of desert and sky stand for a vision of history and what man could become.

The unity of Saint-Exupéry's work derives from his style, his poetic vision of the world, and his moral concern, which begins in *Courrier sud* by focusing on the quality of the individual, seen in relation to his tasks, and ends in *Citadelle* by posing the principles for the city of man. While the political and historical circumstances which gave rise to many of his reflections no longer prevail, it would be hard to argue that no contemporary parallels can be found, and in any case his treat-

Saint-Exupéry in 1944, shortly before his death

ment of particular problems always moves toward the universal. Adventure in aviation and heroic confrontation with adversity in his works will doubtless continue to appeal to readers for whom action is a value, but above the plane of action is the ethical plane, to which action points. Saint-Exupéry will have a permanent place in French literature among those who have drawn on both the lyrical and the sententious strains of the language to give enduring form to their reflections on man.

Letters:
Lettres de jeunesse, 1923-1931 (Paris: Gallimard, 1953);

Antoine de Saint-Exupéry: Lettres à sa mère (Paris: Gallimard, 1955).

Biographies:
Maxwell Smith, *Knight of the Air* (New York: Pageant Press, 1956);
Marcel Migeo, *Saint-Exupéry* (Paris: Flammarion, 1958); translated by Herma Briffault (New York: McGraw-Hill, 1960; London: MacDonald, 1960);
Pierre Chevrier, *Antoine de Saint-Exupéry* (Paris: Gallimard, 1958); revised as *Saint-Exupéry* by Chevrier and Michel Quesnel (1971);
Curtis Cate, *Antoine de Saint-Exupéry* (New York: Putnam's, 1970).

References:

R.-M. Albérès, *Saint-Exupéry* (Paris: Albin Michel, 1961);

Clément Borgal, *Saint Exupéry, mystique sans la foi* (Paris: Centurion, 1964);

Cahiers Saint-Exupéry (Paris: Gallimard, 1980-);

André-A. Devaux, *Saint-Exupéry* (Brussels: Desclée De Brouwer, 1965);

Luc Estang, *Saint-Exupéry par lui-même* (Paris: Seuil, 1956);

Carlo François, *L'Esthétique d'Antoine de Saint-Exupéry* (Neuchâtel & Paris: Delachaux & Niestlé, 1957);

Yves Le Hir, *Fantaisie et mystique dans "Le Petit Prince" de Saint-Exupéry* (Paris: Nizet, 1954);

Serge Losic, *L'Idéal humain de Saint-Exupéry* (Paris: Nizet, 1965);

Jean-Louis Major, *Saint-Exupéry, l'écriture et la pensée* (Ottawa: Editions de l'Université d'Ottawa, 1968);

Brian Masters, *A Student's Guide to Saint-Exupéry* (London: Heinemann, 1972);

Yves Monin, *L'Esotérisme du Petit Prince* (Paris: Nizet, 1975);

Réal Ouellet, *Les Relations humaines dans l'œuvre de Saint-Exupéry* (Paris: Minard, 1971);

Joy D. Marie Robinson, *Antoine de Saint-Exupéry* (Boston: Twayne, 1984);

Jules Roy, *Passion de Saint-Exupéry* (Paris: Gallimard, 1951); republished as *Passion et mort de Saint-Exupéry* (Paris: Gallimard, 1964);

Bruno Vercier, ed., *Les Critiques de notre temps et Saint-Exupéry* (Paris: Garnier, 1971).

Jean-Paul Sartre

(21 June 1905-15 April 1980)

Catharine Savage Brosman
Tulane University

SELECTED BOOKS: *L'Imagination* (Paris: Alcan, 1936); translated by Forrest Williams as *Imagination: A Psychological Critique* (Ann Arbor: University of Michigan Press, 1962);

La Nausée (Paris: Gallimard, 1938); translated by Lloyd Alexander as *Nausea* (Norfolk, Conn.: New Directions, 1949); republished as *The Diary of Antoine Roquentin* (London: Lehmann, 1949);

Le Mur (Paris: Gallimard, 1939); translated by Alexander as *The Wall, and Other Stories* (New York: New Directions, 1948); republished as *Intimacy and Other Stories* (New York: New Directions, 1948; London: Nevill Spearman, 1949);

Esquisse d'une théorie des émotions (Paris: Hermann, 1939); translated by Bernard Frechtman as *The Emotions: Outline of a Theory* (New York: Philosophical Library, 1948);

L'Imaginaire: Psychologie phénoménologique de l'imagination (Paris: Gallimard, 1940); translated by Frechtman as *The Psychology of Imagination* (New York: Philosophical Library, 1948);

L'Etre et le néant: Essai d'ontologie phénoménologique (Paris: Gallimard, 1943); translated in part by Hazel E. Barnes as *Existential Psychoanalysis* (New York: Philosophical Library, 1953); complete translation by Barnes as *Being and Nothingness: An Essay on Phenomenological Ontology* (New York: Philosophical Library, 1956; London: Methuen, 1957);

Les Mouches (Paris: Gallimard, 1943); translated in *The Flies and In Camera (Huis clos)* (1946), and in *No Exit (Huis clos) and The Flies (Les Mouches)* (1947);

Huis clos (Paris: Gallimard, 1945); translated in *The Flies (Les Mouches) and In Camera (Huis clos)* (1946), and in *No Exit (Huis clos) and The Flies (Les Mouches)* (1947);

L'Age de raison, volume 1 of *Les Chemins de la liberté* (Paris: Gallimard, 1945; revised, 1960); translated by Eric Sutton as *The Age of Rea-*

Jean-Paul Sartre (photo Bernand)

son (New York: Knopf, 1947; London: Hamilton, 1947);

Le Sursis, volume 2 of *Les Chemins de la liberté* (Paris: Gallimard, 1945); translated by Sutton as *The Reprieve* (New York: Knopf, 1947; London: Hamilton, 1947);

L'Existentialisme est un humanisme (Paris: Nagel, 1946); translated by Frechtman as *Existentialism* (New York: Philosophical Library, 1947); translated by Philip Mairet as *Existentialism and Humanism* (London: Methuen, 1948);

Morts sans sépulture (Lausanne: Marguerat, 1946); revised in *Théâtre* (1947); translated as *The Victors* in *Three Plays* (New York, 1949), and

331

as *Men without Shadows* in *Three Plays* (London, 1949);

La Putain respectueuse (Paris: Nagel, 1946); translated as *The Respectful Prostitute* in *Three Plays* (New York, 1949), and in *Three Plays* (London, 1949);

Réflexions sur la question juive (Paris: Morihen, 1946); translated by George J. Becker as *Anti-Semite and Jew* (New York: Schocken Books, 1948); translated by Erik de Mauny as *Portrait of the Anti-Semite* (London: Secker & Warburg, 1948);

The Flies (Les Mouches) and In Camera (Huis clos), translated by Stuart Gilbert (London: Hamilton, 1946); republished as *No Exit (Huis clos), a Play in One Act, and The Flies (Les Mouches), a Play in Three Acts* (New York: Knopf, 1947);

Baudelaire (Paris: Gallimard, 1947); translated by Martin Turnell (London: Horizon, 1949; Norfolk, Conn.: New Directions, 1950);

Situations, I (Paris: Gallimard, 1947); translated in part in *Literary and Philosophical Essays* (1955);

Les Jeux sont faits (Paris: Nagel, 1947); translated by Louise Varèse as *The Chips Are Down* (New York: Lear, 1948; London & New York: Rider, 1951);

L'Homme et les choses (Paris: Seghers, 1947);

Les Mains sales (Paris: Gallimard, 1948); translated as *Dirty Hands* in *Three Plays* (New York, 1949), and as *Crime passionnel* in *Three Plays* (London, 1949);

Situations, II (Paris: Gallimard, 1948); translated in part by Frechtman as *What Is Literature?* (New York: Philosophical Library, 1949; London: Methuen, 1950); republished as *Literature and Existentialism* (New York: Citadel, 1962);

L'Engrenage (Paris: Nagel, 1948); translated by Mervyn Savill as *In the Mesh* (London: Dakers, 1954);

Visages, précédé de Portraits officiels (Paris: Seghers, 1948);

La Mort dans l'âme (Paris: Gallimard, 1949); translated by Gerard Hopkins as *Iron in the Soul* (London: Hamilton, 1950); republished as *Troubled Sleep* (New York: Knopf, 1951);

Situations, III (Paris: Gallimard, 1949); translated in part in *Literary and Philosophical Essays* (1955);

Nourritures, suivi d'extraits de La Nausée (Paris: Damasé, 1949);

Three Plays, translated by Lionel Abel (New York: Knopf, 1949)—comprises *Les Mains sales, La Putain respectueuse*, and *Morts sans sépulture;*

Three Plays, translated by Kitty Black (London: Hamilton, 1949)—comprises *Les Mains sales, La Putain respectueuse*, and *Morts sans sépulture;*

Le Diable et le Bon Dieu (Paris: Gallimard, 1951); translated by Black as *Lucifer and the Lord* (London: Hamilton, 1953); and as *The Devil and the Good Lord* in *The Devil and the Good Lord, and Two Other Plays* (1960);

Saint Genet, comédien et martyr (Paris: Gallimard, 1952); translated by Frechtman as *Saint Genet, Actor and Martyr* (New York: Braziller, 1963; London: Allen, 1964);

Kean, adapted from *Kean ou Désordre et génie*, by Alexandre Dumas père (Paris: Gallimard, 1954); translated by Black as *Kean; or Disorder and Genius* (London: Hamilton, 1954), and in *The Devil and the Good Lord, and Two Other Plays* (1960);

Literary and Philosophical Essays, translated by Annette Michelson (New York: Criterion, 1955; London: Rider, 1955)—comprises parts of *Situations, I* and *Situations, III*; republished as *Literary Essays* (New York: Philosophical Library, 1957);

Nekrassov (Paris: Gallimard, 1956); translated by Sylvia Leeson and George Leeson (London: Hamilton, 1956), and in *The Devil and the Good Lord, and Two Other Plays* (1960);

The Transcendence of the Ego, edited and translated by Forrest Williams and Robert Kirkpatrick (New York: Noonday Press, 1957); published in French as *La Transcendance de l'ego* (Paris: Vrin, 1965);

Les Séquestrés d'Altona (Paris: Gallimard, 1960); translated by Sylvia Leeson and George Leeson as *Loser Wins* (London: Hamilton, 1960); republished as *The Condemned of Altona* (New York: Knopf, 1961);

Critique de la raison dialectique, Volume I: Théorie des ensembles pratiques (Paris: Gallimard, 1960); translated in part by Black as *Search for a Method* (New York: Knopf, 1963); translated by Alan Sheridan-Smith as *Critique of Dialectical Reason: Theory of Practical Ensembles*, edited by Jonathan Rée (London: NLB/Atlantic Highlands, N.J.: Humanities Press, 1976);

The Devil and the Good Lord, and Two Other Plays, translated by Black, Sylvia Leeson, and George Leeson (New York: Knopf, 1960)—

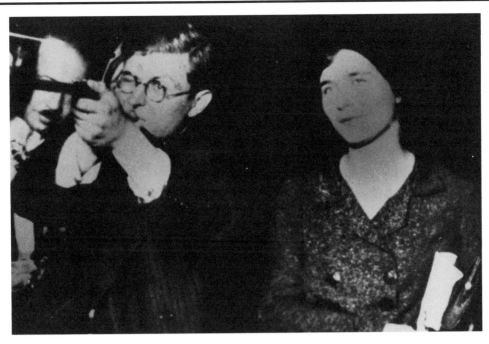

Sartre with Hélène de Beauvoir, Simone de Beauvoir's younger sister, summer 1929 (collection particulière, photo
Editions Gallimard)

comprises *Le Diable et le Bon Dieu, Kean,* and
Nekrassov;

Sartre on Cuba (New York: Ballantine, 1961);

Théâtre (Paris: Gallimard, 1962)–comprises *Les
Mouches, Huis clos, Morts sans sépulture, La Putain respectueuse, Les Mains sales, Le Diable et
le Bon Dieu, Kean, Nekrassov,* and *Les Séquestrés d'Altona;*

Bariona, ou Le Fils du tonnerre (Paris: Atelier Anjou-
copies, 1962);

Les Mots (Paris: Gallimard, 1964); translated by
Frechtman as *The Words* (New York: Brazil-
ler, 1964); translated by Irene Clephane as
Words (London: Hamilton, 1964);

Situations, IV (Paris: Gallimard, 1964); translated
by Benita Eisler as *Situations* (New York: Braziller, 1965; London: Hamilton, 1965);

Situations, V: Colonialisme et néo-colonialisme (Paris:
Gallimard, 1964);

Situations, VI: Problèmes du marxisme, 1 (Paris: Gallimard, 1964); translated in part in *The Communists and Peace* (New York, 1968), and in *The
Communists and Peace* (London, 1969);

Qu'est-ce que la littérature? (Paris: Gallimard,
1964);

Il Filosofo et la politica, translated by Luciana Tren-
tin and Romano Ledda (Rome: Riuniti,
1964);

Situations, VII: Problèmes du marxisme, 2 (Paris: Galli-

mard, 1965; translated in part in *The Communists and Peace* (New York, 1968), and in *The
Communists and Peace* (London, 1969); translated in part by Martha H. Fletcher as *The
Ghost of Stalin* (New York: Braziller, 1968);

Les Troyennes, adapted from Euripides' play
(Paris: Gallimard, 1966); translated by Ronald Duncan as *The Trojan Women* (New
York: Knopf, 1967; London: Hamilton,
1967);

On Genocide (Boston: Beacon, 1968);

The Communists and Peace, translated by Fletcher
(New York: Braziller, 1968)–comprises parts
of *Situations, VI* and *Situations, VII;*

Les Communistes ont peur de la révolution (Paris: Didier, 1969); translated by Elaine P. Halperin
as "Communists Are Afraid of Revolution:
Two Interviews," *Midway,* 10 (Summer
1969): 41-61;

The Communists and Peace, translated by Clephane
(London: Hamilton, 1969)–comprises parts
of *Situations, VI* and *Situations, VII;*

L'Idiot de la famille: Gustave Flaubert de 1821-1857,
3 volumes (Paris: Gallimard, 1971-1972);
translated by Carol Cosman as *The Family
Idiot: Gustave Flaubert, 1821-1857* (Chicago:
University of Chicago Press, 1981);

Situations, VIII: Autour de 68 (Paris: Gallimard,
1971); translated in part in *Between Existentialism and Marxism* (1974);

Situations, IX: Mélanges (Paris: Gallimard, 1972); translated in part in *Between Existentialism and Marxism* (1974);

Plaidoyer pour les intellectuels (Paris: Gallimard, 1972);

Un Théâtre de situations, edited by Michel Contat and Michel Rybalka (Paris: Gallimard, 1973); translated by Frank Jellinek as *Sartre on Theatre* (New York: Pantheon, 1976);

Politics and Literature, translated by J. A. Underwood and John Calder (London: Calder & Boyars, 1973);

Between Existentialism and Marxism, translated by John Matthews (London: NLB, 1974; New York: Pantheon, 1975)–comprises parts of *Situations, VIII* and *Situations, IX;*

Situations, X: Politique et autobiographie (Paris: Gallimard, 1976); translated by Paul Auster and Lydia Davis as *Life/Situations: Essays Written and Spoken* (New York: Pantheon, 1977);

Sartre (Paris: Gallimard, 1977); translated by Richard Seaver as *Sartre by Himself* (New York: Urizen, 1978);

Sartre: Images d'une vie (Paris: Gallimard, 1978);

Œuvres romanesques, edited by Contat and Rybalka (Paris: Gallimard, 1981);

Cahiers pour une morale (Paris: Gallimard, 1983);

Les Carnets de la drôle de guerre (Paris: Gallimard, 1983); translated by Quintin Hoare as *War Diaries of Jean-Paul Sartre: November 1939-March 1940* (New York: Pantheon, 1984); republished as *War Diaries: Notebooks from a Phoney War* (London: Verso, 1984);

Le Scénario Freud (Paris: Gallimard, 1984); translated by Hoare as *The Freud Scenario* (New York: Pantheon, 1984; London: Verso, 1985);

La Mauvaise Foi, edited by Marc Wetzel (Paris: Hatier, 1985);

Mallarmé, la lucidité et sa face d'ombre (Paris: Gallimard, 1986).

PLAY PRODUCTIONS: *Les Mouches,* Paris, Théâtre de la Cité, 3 June 1943;

Huis clos, Paris, Théâtre du Vieux-Colombier, 27 May 1944;

Morts sans sépulture, Paris, Théâtre Antoine, 8 November 1946;

La Putain respectueuse, Paris, Théâtre Antoine, 8 November 1946;

Les Mains sales, Paris, Théâtre Antoine, 2 April 1948;

Le Diable et le Bon Dieu, Paris, Théâtre Antoine, 7 June 1951;

Kean, Paris, Théâtre Sarah-Bernhardt, 14 November 1953;

Nekrassov, Paris, Théâtre Antoine, 8 June 1955;

Les Séquestrés d'Altona, Paris, Théâtre de la Renaissance, 23 September 1959;

Les Troyennes, Paris, Théâtre National Populaire, 10 March 1965.

MOTION PICTURES: *Les Jeux sont faits,* script by Sartre, dialogues by Sartre and Jacques-Laurent Bost, Gibé-Pathé, 1947;

Les Mains sales, dialogues by Sartre, Rivers, 1951;

La P. . . . respectueuse, dialogues by Sartre and Jacques-Laurent Bost, Marceau, 1952;

Huis Clos, dialogues by Sartre, Marceau, 1954;

Les Sorcières de Salem, script and dialogues by Sartre, based on Arthur Miller's play, Borderie, C.I.C.C., S.N. Pathé (France), Defa (Germany), 1957;

Le Mur, dialogues by Sartre, Procinex-Niepce, 1967.

OTHER: Francis Jeanson, *Le Problème moral et la pensée de Sartre,* preface by Sartre (Paris: Editions du Myrte, 1947); translated by Robert V. Stone as *Sartre and the Problem of Morality* (Bloomington: Indiana University Press, 1980);

"Orphée noir," in *Anthologie de la nouvelle poésie nègre et malgache de langue française,* edited by Léopold Sédar Senghor (Paris: PUF, 1948); translated by S. W. Allen as *Black Orpheus* (Paris: Gallimard, 1963);

Hervé Bazin and others, *L'Affaire Henri Martin,* commentary by Sartre (Paris: Gallimard, 1953);

Henri Cartier-Bresson, *D'une Chine à l'autre,* preface by Sartre (Paris: Delpire, 1954); translated by Edward Hyams as *China in Transition: A Moment in History* (London: Thames & Hudson, 1956);

"Une Victoire," in *La Question,* by Henri Alleg (Lausanne: La Cité, 1958; Paris: Pauvert, 1966); translated by John Calder as *The Question* (London: Calder, 1958);

Roger Garaudy, *Perspectives de l'homme: Existentialisme, pensée catholique, marxisme,* letter by Sartre (Paris: Presses Universitaires de France, 1959);

Marxisme et existentialisme: Controverse sur la dialectique (Paris: Plon, 1962; revised, 1983)–comprises contributions by Sartre, Roger Garaudy, Jean Hyppolite, and others;

Sartre, a second-class private in the meteorological corps, and his superior, Corporal Pierre, 1939 (collection particulière, photo Editions Gallimard)

"Doigts et non-doigts," in *Wols en personne,* by Wols (Paris: Delpire, 1963); translated by Norbert Guterman as "Fingers and Non-Fingers" in *Watercolors, Drawings, Writings* (New York: Abrams, 1965);

Ronald D. Laing and David G. Cooper, *Reason and Violence: A Decade of Sartre's Philosophy, 1950-1960,* foreword by Sartre (London: Tavistock, 1964);

Que peut la littérature? (Paris: Union Générale d'Editions, 1965)–comprises contributions by Sartre, Simone de Beauvoir, Jean-Pierre Faye, and others;

Georges Michel, *La Promenade du dimanche,* preface by Sartre (Paris: Gallimard, 1967);

Matta, *Un Soleil, un Viêt-nam,* text by Sartre (Paris: Cassé, 1967);

Jean-Paul Sartre, Opening speech at the International Tribunal Against War Crimes in Vietnam, and other texts, in *Tribunal Russell: Le Jugement de Stockholm* (Paris: Gallimard, 1967); translated as *Against the Crime of Si-*

lence (New York & London: Bertrand Russell Peace Foundation, 1967);

Roger Pic, *Au cœur du Vietnam,* preface by Sartre (Paris: Maspero, 1968);

Le Procès Régis Debray, text by Sartre (Paris: Maspero, 1968);

Michel Contat and Michel Rybalka, *Les Ecrits de Sartre,* includes previously unpublished material by Sartre (Paris: Gallimard, 1970); translated by Richard C. McCleary as *The Writings of Sartre* (Evanston: Northwestern University Press, 1974);

"Le Socialisme qui venait du froid," in *Trois Générations: Entretiens sur le phénomène culturel tchécoslovaque,* edited by Antonin J. Liehm (Paris: Gallimard, 1970); translated by Helen R. Lane as "The Socialism That Came In from the Cold," *Evergreen Review,* 14 (November 1970): 27-32, 65-73;

Gisèle Halimi, *Le Procès de Burgos,* preface by Sartre (Paris: Gallimard, 1971);

Michèle Manceaux, *Les Maos en France,* foreword by Sartre (Paris: Gallimard, 1972);

On a raison de se révolter (Paris: Gallimard, 1974)–comprises contributions by Sartre, Philippe Gavi, and Pierre Victor.

The name Jean-Paul Sartre is recognized by millions around the world. By the time of his death in 1980 he was a public figure throughout Europe and something of a French and even worldwide intellectual property. His volumes have been translated into dozens of languages; he gave interviews to journalists from numerous countries; during his later years he supported the political causes of many groups and nations. While Albert Camus was perhaps more widely admired, especially during his lifetime, no mid-twentieth-century French writer was more notorious. If it is true of anyone, it can be said of him that he dominated his age.

He was par excellence the spokesman for *la littérature engagée* (committed literature); for him, writing was action. In literary history his work falls roughly between, on the one hand, surrealism and the great modernists such as André Gide and Marcel Proust, and, on the other, the New Novelists, between which he is in more than one way a transitional figure. In philosophy he occupies a pivotal place between Cartesianism and phenomenology, on the one hand, and neo-Marxism on the other. His legacy is such that it is possible to speak of a post-Sartrean period as well as a Sartrean one. To different readers, or

Sartre and Simone de Beauvoir with Boris and Michèle Vian (photo Yves Manciet)

simply the man in the street, he represents different things. Some know him as the author of stories and novels, although perhaps only half of these have been widely read; others think of him principally as the author of plays, successful on the French stage and elsewhere and popular with the reading public. To still other readers he is chiefly a philosopher, known either as the author of the difficult *L'Etre et le néant* (1943; translated as *Being and Nothingness*, 1956) or the proponent of a popular existentialism, whose texts are often included in anthologies despite some coolness toward his work among professional philosophers, and to whom the so-called New Philosophers are indebted. He is, and should be, recognized also as a major critic of literature and art and an important biographer. The most common image of him doubtless includes some of all these aspects. Above all, especially in France, the image of Sartre is that of the political essayist and activist, the would-be renewer of Marx and the supporter of Maoists and other radicals. Memories remain vivid of newspaper photos showing Sartre (often with Simone de Beauvoir) distributing radical

tracts in the streets; nor have older French readers forgotten his signing of controversial petitions during the Algerian War and of other political statements. The result is that his name still evokes strong reactions; he is anathema to some, a model or an idol to others. When such polarized opinion subsides with time, readers will be faced with reevaluating the enormous body of work he left, in order to identify its enduring value. Probably, however, the figure of the man also will remain fascinating for his brilliance, energy, and contradictions.

Sartre was born on 21 June 1905 in Paris, the son of a naval engineer, Jean-Baptiste Sartre, and his wife Anne-Marie, née Schweitzer, first cousin of Albert Schweitzer. Both families, as Sartre stresses at the outset of his autobiographical volume *Les Mots* (1964; translated as *The Words*), were marked by eccentric behavior and difficult relationships, a fact which is perhaps less surprising than one might think for his period and class, which had an enormous underground current of deviation. Much like a naturalistic novelist, he suggests a connection between the type of people who surrounded him and the man he became. It would, however, be improper to interpret simplistically his understanding of the relationship between the man and the milieu, for his assumption goes well beyond naturalism's cause-and-effect mechanism to become an elaborate method of biographic reading called progressive-regressive. His own reading of himself is not, of course, to be accepted without examination; but critics so far have used it as a foundation for both biographic and psychoanalytic studies.

When the child was just over a year old, Jean-Baptiste Sartre died of fever he had contracted in Indochina. The absence of a father led, Sartre wrote, to his lack of a superego–a lack which he interpreted later as very advantageous, since he did not have to live up to the paternal image. One should observe, however, that some of his works are marked by fascination with father figures. Anne-Marie Sartre returned to live with her parents at Meudon and then Paris. Charles and Louise Schweitzer were the ones who raised the boy; he and his mother were called "the children." The commanding figure of Charles Schweitzer, a professor of German, was something of a relic from the nineteenth century; he took himself, Sartre wrote, for Victor Hugo. With others he was stern; with the boy, indulgent. They shared a world of delight and make-believe–or so Sartre recalls. But the grandfather's playacting, which Sartre identifies as a reflection of the mendaciousness of middle-class French society at the time, led the boy to make the false assumption that life was a comedy. When he discovered that there were also "serious" things, to which children were not admitted, and "indispensable" people, next to whom his make-believe self counted for nothing, he was devastated. Throughout the rest of his life he had a keen eye for sham, which is a theme in several of his works. He was also so struck by the contingency–groundlessness–of his existence that it became a major philosophical topic for him.

Charles Schweitzer shared the nineteenth-century humanistic sense of the sacred. Among the "holy" objects were words and books; the latter lined his study, and the boy supposed that wisdom was contained in them like healing in medicine. His precocious reading experiences soon led to a childish desire to write–which the grown-ups indulged with pride. He sensed (or so he indicated later) that writing was a way of overcoming contingency, assuring his being, his place; that is, literature was justification. Some-

what later, however, he discovered that while scholarly books and scholars themselves were acceptable to Schweitzer, anyone who proposed to be a professional man of letters was thought to be a fool, heading for certain ruin, like the drunkard Paul Verlaine. Sartre's very ambiguous literary career, which illustrates both his adoration and his disdain for the written word, would seem to derive from the ambivalent attitude of Schweitzer; Sartre said later, as he considered his career, that he had covered so many thousands of pages with ink in a futile effort to please the shade of his grandfather–who surely would have disapproved of nearly every line.

The boy's education was begun at home and continued irregularly at various schools. Having played alone, he had trouble playing with other children. His life changed radically at age eleven when his mother remarried; at age twelve he joined her at La Rochelle, where his stepfather, Joseph Mancy, directed a shipyard. There Sartre attended the lycée and learned what adolescent cruelty, even violence, was like. Despite his denials it is probable that he also felt antipathy toward his stepfather, whose interests in science and mathematics and emphasis on discipline contrasted with the cultivation of letters and music and atmosphere of indulgence at the Schweitzers'. Sartre also realized, as an adolescent, that he had none of the religious faith that the catechism lessons given him (by a Catholic priest, since his grandmother was nominally of that church) were intended to promote. After some months at La Rochelle, he returned to Paris and finished his lycée work in 1922 at Henri IV.

Whereas Sartre wanted to write, Schweitzer had insisted that he take up teaching. At the Ecole Normale Supérieure he prepared for this career, studying philosophy, which had attracted him at Henri IV when he read works of Henri Bergson. He wrote a thesis on images and passed the *agrégation* exams at the head of his class in 1929, after a failure the previous year (perhaps because his essay had been quite removed from the usual treatment of the topic). Taking the exam with him, and passing in second place, was Simone de Beauvoir, whom he had met at the Ecole and with whom he and several fellow students had formed a close-knit group. The lifelong friendship between the two was both intellectual and sexual. She wrote that they considered marriage only once–when there was a possibility that Sartre would go to Japan to teach.

Sartre addressing the Congress for World Peace in Vienna, November 1952 (photo Lessing-Magnum)

Their relationship may have been morally monogamous much of the time, but throughout, each had what she called "contingent" (chance or nonessential) loves, with whom on occasions they made up a trio or quartet. Some of these affairs played a considerable role in Sartre's life, almost from the start of his liaison with Beauvoir, and sexuality was enormously important to him, as readers long suspected and publications of the 1980s made clear. In the mid 1930s he became emotionally and sexually involved with Olga Kosakiewicz, a pupil of Beauvoir's whom she and he decided to take responsibility for and tutor; the three were to form a "trio." (The story is reflected in Beauvoir's novel *L'Invitée* [*She Came to Stay*, 1943].) At the end of the decade he became involved with her sister. During the period 1946-1950, he and a woman he met in New York, Dolorès V., carried on a liaison made difficult by long geographic separations and other factors. After the separation between the writer Boris Vian and his wife Michelle, Sartre and Michelle became close and were frequently traveling companions. Nevertheless, on the intellectual plane, Beauvoir and Sartre remained entirely faithful: merciless critics, sometimes, of each other's writing but vigorously supportive and united by nearly identical views and assumptions. Sartre

was the dominant figure of the pair for decades—it was he who elaborated the philosophy which she helped illustrate—but he acknowledged that she had contributed greatly to his intellectual life.

Sartre's career may conveniently be divided into several periods. The first covers the 1930s, from the time he finished his military service in 1931 to the beginning of World War II in 1939. It was a time of considerable activity, although little compared to what he would undertake subsequently. He taught at provincial lycées, including that in Le Havre, before being assigned to the Lycée Pasteur on the outskirts of Paris in 1937. As a teacher of philosophy he was popular with his students, eschewing an authoritarian, paternal role for a nearly fraternal one. Class discipline displeased him, although intellectual discipline was one of his strengths, and it is uncertain how well he fulfilled his pedagogical role. He pursued his philosophical investigations, begun at the Ecole Normale, stressing the psychology of the imagination. In 1933-1934 he spent a year at the Institut Français in Berlin, reading contemporary German philosophy, notably the phenomenology of Edmund Husserl, whose contribution to epistemology and ontology had great appeal for the student heretofore nurtured in Cartesianism and the earlier German idealism. At the same time he began writing fiction, some of which is closely connected to his reading in philosophy.

His first publications—excluding short student pieces in the 1920s—are an outgrowth of his study of the contemporary Germans; they all stress the operations and structure of consciousness. In 1936 he published *L'Imagination* (translated into English in 1962), a treatise based partly on his university work, in which he took issue with several classic and recent theories of the imagination and proposed his own, which reflected his interest in hallucinations and other aspects of abnormal psychology. "La Transcendance de l'ego" (published in 1937 in *Recherches Philosophiques* and in 1965 in book form) similarly aimed at showing the flaws in the concept of the self in the works of several philosophers, including Kant and Husserl. Sartre argued for a self that was essentially posterior rather than prior to experience, that is, reflexive. A third essay of the period is his *Esquisse d'une théorie des émotions* (1939; translated as *The Emotions: Outline of a Theory*, 1948), which sets forth his phenomenological method as well as his thesis that emotion is chosen behavior. He also published critical articles on such recognized or emerging literary figures as François Mauriac, Jean Giraudoux, Camus, and the Americans John Dos Passos and William Faulkner, whose narrative technique and approach to time influenced his fiction as well as that of other French writers. He did not, however, write political essays. While he was already antiestablishment to the core, probably by reaction to the class in which he had been raised, and was convinced that European capitalism and bourgeois democracy were doomed to failure, he was inactive politically, unlike his close friend Paul Nizan. In his work a certain malaise is visible when he mentions the Spanish civil war, reflecting perhaps the feeling that he should have protested actively against French nonintervention. It would, however, be ungracious to reproach for political passivity someone who would become so active after World War II.

His first fiction also dates from the 1930s and, like his philosophical treatises, was an outgrowth of his studies as well as his personal experience. *La Nausée* (1938; translated as *Nausea*, 1949), originally entitled "Melancholia" (after Albrecht Dürer's engraving), seems to have developed from drafts of a treatise on contingency dating from the first part of the decade. It also reflects his literary reading, particularly of the surrealists, Proust, and Louis-Ferdinand Céline. The common assumption that it expresses his existentialism and the core of *L'Etre et le néant* is only partly correct. To the degree that it is a philosophical novel, it was, rather, more of an occasion for working out, in literary form, certain insights which later contributed to parts of his philosophic system; and in some respects, the hero is still the dupe of beliefs which will later be dismantled. Chiefly it is not an exemplum but a work of art–precisely the sort which the young Sartre had dreamed of creating, which would impose itself (and, by extension, its author) as an autonomous object.

The work was both self-castigation and self-justification, though not so radical as *Les Mots* would be. In the form of an erratically kept journal with "editor's notes" (the old "found manuscript" device), it concerns Roquentin, a scholar who formerly worked abroad and now has settled in Bouville (Mudville, that is, Le Havre) to do research on a minor eighteenth-century figure. Of independent means, he has only minimal contact with others: a few words, a superficial sexual encounter; Sartre has set him up as a loner, the better to show what man really is when the social

layers are peeled off. Realizing, part way through the diary, that he will not write his proposed book because it is a meaningless as well as false project to resuscitate the dead and live by them (that is, justify oneself by writing on them), he goes through a profound crisis that has been building since the inception of the story. It is both emotional and intellectual. He experiences loss of function and ground. He discovers that the past is dead and the future does not exist; he cannot live through others (as in love) or through beliefs (he has none, and even if he had they would have no grounding); everything is contingent, or by chance, and no explanation for existence can be found. "Tout existant naît sans raison, se prolonge par faiblesse et meurt par rencontre" (Every existing thing is born without reason, prolongs itself out of weakness and dies by chance). There are no values, and those who persuade themselves that such values exist and who live in function of them (usually to their own social advantage) are "salauds," or bastards. The apparent instrumentality of things is only a human invention; the world, a random assemblage of disquieting objects, has no purpose. This is the Sartrean form of the absurd. Roquentin's reaction is a profound disgust or nausea, which bears resemblances to existential *angoisse* or angst. His sometime companion, an *Autodidacte* (Self-Taught Man) who haunts libraries and is both a closet socialist and a pederast, is a mirror figure: maladjusted, trying to kill time and fill the void in his life, looking for meaning in books. His ultimate disclosure as a pervert and his disgrace reflect, in the mode of pathos, the meaninglessness of his project and the solitude of the individual. Roquentin ultimately despises him as much as he does those who condemn him and seems to identify more with an exhibitionist who may have raped and murdered a child.

When Roquentin has lunch, as he had agreed, with the Self-Taught Man, he experiences his most acute attack of nausea as he confronts the pathetic but irritating self-deception of the bookworm. Activity no longer means anything at all to him; he could just as well stab the Self-Taught Man with his knife as eat his cheese with it, and the food disgusts him. In a state of panic he leaves the restaurant, runs through the streets, gets on a streetcar for no reason, and ends up in the public garden, where, in a trance-like state, he has a revelation of existence and the world, emptied of meaning when the observer no longer "intends" or projects his meaning onto

Sartre, in his only film role, with Jean-Pierre Aumont in Nicole Védrès's 1952 film La Vie commence demain
(photo Radio-Cinéma)

them. He decides to leave Bouville for Paris, where he will live meagerly on his income and do nothing. He hopes that his former mistress will rescue him from utter futility, but she denounces their past and goes away with another man. However, Sartre, in entire seriousness (although in hindsight it seems ironic), does not leave him with this failure, for he discovers the aesthetic solution. It comes to him by way of a jazz song, which seems to have its own raison d'être and to surpass in the mode of the ideal the record on which it has been preserved. He resolves to try to do something similar in the form of a book, not history, since "jamais un existant ne peut justifier l'existence d'un autre existant" (no existing thing can ever justify the existence of another), but a fiction that will refer to nothing outside itself, be hard like steel, and, as he says, make people ashamed of their existence, while redeeming his.

In several ways *La Nausée* fits the traditional pattern of the quest novel but entirely on the intellectual plane. Roquentin begins his diary because something seems changed in his life, and he wants to find out what and why. Even though the search is a mental, indeed a metaphysical, one, there are parallels to the traps and monsters of old quest novels. The development is basically linear, though there are detours and false starts. The text almost ends after he has the Sartrean equivalent of an epiphany, when he finds out what he was seeking–the utter meaninglessness of things. But then there is the added dimension of redemption through a project which surpasses the individual. Although to some readers it might seem that nothing happens, the mental events and rare external ones are important moments in the disclosure of reality which, in true phenomenological fashion, is the book's plot.

Nor is the text lacking in vividness, drama, even humor. The element of social criticism, introduced each time the hero depicts the hypocritical, right-thinking bourgeoisie who built Bouville and dominate its industry and institutions, includes superb characterizations (by speech and gesture) reminiscent of Proust's character sketches, as well as acid dismissals. Scenes such as that when Roquentin, in a crisis of paranoia, runs through the middle of the street and when he has lunch with the Self-Taught Man are very funny. The first-person narration allows the reader to experience these episodes as Roquentin does, and yet the book constantly provides ironic qualification of the hero's (or antihero's) insights, save the final one. The most dramatic moments may be those when, studying a chestnut tree in the garden, he realizes that the world is occupied by *existants*–things: meaningless, nameless phenomena that are utterly absurd. Like several other episodes, this meditation is highly poetic, for the world is transformed before Roquentin's eyes, each thing being a metaphor for another, with no ultimate referent. A tramway seat, for instance, could just as well be a dead, bloated donkey, with thousands of tiny feet sticking up; a root is a giant serpent or a seal.

Sartre wrote in *Les Mots* that he had achieved in his first novel the tour de force of making others ashamed of their existence while vindicating his own. Only later did he denounce the aesthetic project, which *La Nausée*, somewhat like Proust's great novel, both announces and illustrates. Even then, it remained one of his favorites among his own books–although he did write that it (like all literature) did not count when weighed against the suffering of one child. It was favorably received by discerning readers and was a considerable success; it remains his best piece of fiction, still striking fifty years after its composition. Both the character of the hero and the phenomenological approach had some influence on the development of the New Novel. The style, a mixture of pithy Cartesian deductions and sometimes surrealistic impressionism, is one of Sartre's best achievements.

The five stories of *Le Mur*, collected in 1939 (and translated into English as *The Wall* in 1948), display a considerable range of the author's talent, while reflecting his various preoccupations of the 1930s. Like parts of *La Nausée*, the stories were morally offensive to many because of crude language and topics which at that date were still not generally broached in print. Their subjects range from the Spanish civil war, in the title story, to sexual impotence and insanity. Like the novel, but more so, they deal with varieties of what Sartre was later to call inauthenticity, which includes the mode of the *salaud* and any kind of self-deception. The tension created in the volume by the unquestionable authorial mastery of plot, scene, and dialogue, on the one hand, and the loss of control over themselves which most of the characters experience, on the other, is one of the collection's strengths.

The title story seems to reflect Sartre's reading of Hemingway, not only in its crisp sentences but also in the hero's sense of himself as he tries to remain "dur" (hard) as he approaches the mo-

ment of death before a firing squad. Yet the desire to remain hard is not just derivative; it is also very much a part of Sartre's view of the self, which was founded in part on a sense of malaise with his own body (perhaps a reflection of his oft-noted homeliness) and his general ambivalence concerning embodiment, that is, the physical aspect of reality. The repugnance Pablo feels when confronting butterlike flesh and faces turned ashen with fright, a reaction which mirrors his own fear of resembling them, is one of many passages in Sartre in which the flesh is felt as obscene. Another major Sartrean current of the story is the theme of absurdity, visible in this instance when the hero, unintentionally in jest, reveals to the Fascists his leader's hiding place–thereby condemning him to death and producing his own release. The O. Henry-like ending does not seem out of place in Sartre's absurd, ironic world, which is seen by Pablo as a colossal joke.

"La Chambre" ("The Room") and "Intimité" ("Intimacy") have as their topic human relationships, which they explore in characteristic Sartrean ways. In the first a wife is emotionally tied to her insane husband Pierre, whose hallucinations she attempts to espouse by denying that they are delusions; yet she cannot really convince herself, and the project is a failure. In "Intimité" a wife considers leaving her impotent husband for her lover, but–as she sensed all along without admitting it–will not do so because she prefers, ultimately, a man who is dependent. In both stories, as in *La Nausée*, fantasy plays an enormous role: characters dream of accomplishing things but do not carry out their desires and thus, in Sartre's terms, are inauthentic. The stories also focus on embodiment. The same is the case in "Erostrate," which takes its title from Erostratus, the Greek who gained lasting fame by burning down the temple at Ephesus. Paul Hilbert, a loner and a sexual pervert, dreams of a similar act, one that will impose him on others and destroy, in the process, a few of the consciousnesses that have been judging him. But he fails in his plan to shoot six people because the act appears to him as empty, absurd, and in the end he is cornered in a public toilet.

The final story in *Le Mur*, by far the longest, might appear on the surface to recount a successful education. Lucien, the hero of "L'Enfance d'un chef" ("The Childhood of a Leader"), overcomes the difficulties of childhood and obstacles of adolescence to become a proper young man, the worthy heir to his father's business. Those

Sartre circa 1957

who know *Les Mots* immediately recognize the considerable autobiographic element in the story, less in the facts than in the character's mentality. The boy Lucien feels that he has no being, no justification. Efforts to gain a sense of self end up in an experience of nothingness or shame. His solution, unlike Sartre's own, is to adopt a political position—anti-Semitism—which guarantees him by allowing him to define himself as what he is not. This choice gives him such confidence that he can claim his place in society, becoming the "leader" he was born to be, a member of an oppressive class, a prig and a true *salaud*. The story must be read in the light of other Sartrean texts, especially Roquentin's judgment on the "leaders" he sees in the famous museum scene of *La Nausée:* Sartre is castigating not only a social class and its political positions but also any choice by which one lives an external imperative.

As the 1930s drew to a close Sartre was known chiefly in intellectual circles—to the readers who bought his two volumes of fiction, published by Gallimard, and the smaller number who knew his philosophical essays. Such novelists as Céline and André Malraux were considerably more widely known, not to mention the giants from previous decades such as Proust and Gide, Mauriac and Roger Martin du Gard. Had World War II not swept Europe, his career would have developed in ways that cannot be known. It is certain that the outbreak of the conflict in September 1939, when he was immediately mobilized, changed his art as well as his circumstances. For a while he was assigned to a post at the Eastern border, where Beauvoir visited him several times. Their letters from this period reflect his vast reading and intellectual activity; *Les Carnets de la drôle de guerre* (1983; translated as *The War Diaries of Jean-Paul Sartre: November 1939-March 1940*, 1984) is an even better record of his intellectual development at the time.

In June 1940 he was involved in troop actions, though he did no real fighting, and was captured on the twenty-first. Until late winter of the next year he was a prisoner of war, first in a French camp, then at a German stalag. Although its effect was not immediately visible in his work, the experience changed him deeply. For the first time he was a member of a unit that was neither a family-based nor an intellectual one, and he discovered his solidarity with his fellow prisoners. At Christmastime he wrote and produced a play for them, *Bariona* (unpublished until 1962, when it appeared in a limited edition); this was his first attempt at theater since his university days. He formed a close friendship with a priest, with whom he discussed Heidegger as he reread that German philosopher. After he was repatriated in March 1941, he told Beauvoir that he no longer saw his work as separate from the social and political circumstances in which he lived; he was convinced that it must be rooted in the present situation and directed toward the cause of socialist revolution. This marks the beginning of a new period in his career, characterized by his awareness of historicity. For ten years or so his literary activity increased; the 1940s are par excellence the decade of Sartrean existentialism. And for the rest of his life he was to write, and often demonstrate, on behalf of groups that sought to replace bourgeois capitalism in France with some sort of socialist state; but his position with respect to the French Communist party (which he never joined), the Soviets, and other European socialist parties varied widely, from explicit support for the U.S.S.R. to condemnation of its policies at the time of the Hungarian uprising of 1956 and the revolt in Czechoslovakia in 1968.

Back in Paris, he resumed his teaching, first at the lycée Pasteur, then at the lycée Condorcet until 1944. He wrote film scripts, became friends with Jean Genet and, later, Camus (until the rift of 1952), briefly was connected with a Resistance network, worked on his philosophical summa *L'Etre et le néant*, wrote plays, and labored on a lengthy fictional project that became *Les Chemins de la liberté* (*The Roads to Freedom*), a trilogy plus fragments. By 1945 he had published the philosophical study, seen two plays produced and two of the novels published, and had become lionized, especially on the Left Bank. Although many had not read his works, he was widely known as the apostle of a new philosophy that gave to nihilism its definitive form and yet was, paradoxically, also a vigorous call to action; he was seen also as the spokesman for a new society, rejecting inherited values and prewar politics, whose bankruptcy seemed even more striking than it had after World War I because the old attitudes had led to, among other things, the defeat of France. That year he also helped found what was to become the very influential journal of commentary, *Temps Modernes,* and gave a public lecture on existentialism which was then published as *L'Existentialisme est un humanisme* (1946; translated as *Existentialism,* 1947), a text which gave widespread currency to the term (not of his coining) and to several basic concepts of Sartrean philosophy, especially the idea that man is the sum of his acts, although his use of the term *humanism* collides somewhat with his rejection in previous works of traditional human values. Other plays and important essays followed; the final volume of the trilogy appeared in 1949.

L'Etre et le néant is a systematic presentation, in difficult, sometimes technical, philosophical language, of what the author calls his phenomenological ontology, that is, the examination of being (the world and mankind, or what he calls *en soi* and *pour-soi*) via the phenomenological method. It owes a great deal to his reading of Husserl, which suggested especially Sartre's method of reduction, or *epochè.* It also has Cartesian elements and echoes of Martin Heidegger. It develops systematically insights and concepts which had appeared in Sartre's three short philosophical essays of the 1930s, plus his longer volume

Sartre on the balcony of his apartment at 42 Rue Bonaparte, Paris (photo Gisèle Freund)

L'Imaginaire: Psychologie phénoménologique de l'imagination (1940; translated as *The Psychology of Imagination,* 1948), and even his early fiction. There are similarly close ties between it and some works of the mid 1940s, especially *Huis clos.* It is itself a very literary work in the sense that, after pages of abstract argumentation, the reader comes upon sections that are highly concrete and factual and others in which concepts are illustrated by fictional situations. It reveals Sartre's conviction that philosophy must be rooted in experience, thus close to literature. Indeed, many of its concerns are familiar literary themes: for instance, the fundamental problems of how people perceive reality, of how they view themselves (including their bodies) and others, and especially how they relate to others.

Such classic problems of philosophy and psychology as time, reality, knowledge, free will, and the nature of sexuality receive very particular treatment at Sartre's hands. He stresses especially the utter, radical freedom of what he calls human reality and the consequent total responsibility of each person. Some of his statements on being and especially human beings have been so frequently quoted that they are almost clichés: "L'homme est condamné à être libre" (Man is condemned to be free), "L'homme est une passion inutile" (Man is a useless passion). The volume does not purport to furnish an ethics, only an ontological investigation; Sartre suggests that any valid ethics would have to be founded on human freedom and the absence of God. In the following years he wrote parts of what was to become a treatise on morality, but the project was not completed; fragments appeared and after the author's death the finished portion was published as *Cahiers pour une morale* (Notebooks for an Ethics, 1983).

Five of Sartre's plays were written and produced during the 1940s. In them he revealed himself to be a superb creator of scene and character. In *Les Mouches* (translated as *The Flies*, 1946), a version of the legend of Electra and Orestes, produced in 1943 during the Occupation, he has his characters discover freedom; even Jupiter is powerless before human choice. The intention was probably chiefly philosophical, in accord with the ontology of *L'Etre et le néant*, but many viewers interpreted it in political terms. Its success was mixed, reviewers being rather harsh on the play's formal qualities. *Huis clos* (produced in 1944, published in 1945, and translated as *In Camera*, 1946, and as *No Exit*, 1947) grew from Sartre's desire to write a play with three main roles, each of which would have equal importance; it became a tense, incisive dramatization of key philosophical concepts concerning human relationships. All of its dynamics come from competition among different images of self and others in perpetual conflict. The discovery made by the three characters, ostensibly dead and in hell together, that "l'enfer c'est les autres" (hell is other people) arises from the desire and failure of each consciousness to impose itself on others and thereby achieve ratification. Each consciousness tries then to "kill" the others, that is, to eliminate their freedom. The pattern of the trio is not the classic love triangle but rather embodies the complication of subject-object relationships whereby each pair, itself in continuous sadomasochistic conflict, is always an object to an observer, or voyeur. Sartre later said that he had not meant to indicate that all human relationships were doomed to failure but rather that they would continue to be so as long as relationships with others were fundamentally twisted.

La Putain respectueuse (produced and published, 1946; translated as *The Respectful Prostitute*, 1949), which gave rise to the euphemism "la respectueuse," is much less accomplished than the first two plays because of its reliance on stereotypes and its melodramatic plot; but even using such stock characters as the generous prostitute and the hypocritical senator (the action takes place in an unnamed southern state of the United States), the playwright is able to illustrate how a person's being is a function of his or her role, his or her presence for others, and is thus inauthentic. A fourth play, *Morts sans sépulture* (produced and published, 1946; translated as *The Victors*, and as *Men without Shadows*, 1949), was not successful when it premiered, doubtless because it dealt with the sensitive subject of torture practiced by the Vichy militia under the Occupation. Like *Le Mur* and *Huis clos*, it presents characters who are sequestered, and their awful drama arises from the necessity of making choices under duress for which they are nevertheless utterly responsible. The play illustrates well the dread and anguish analyzed in *L'Etre et le néant*, which come from one's discovery of both responsibility and inadequacy and the ironic absurdity of action.

The last play of the 1940s is also the longest and most complex. *Les Mains sales* (produced and published, 1948; translated as *Dirty Hands*, 1949, and as *Crime passionnel*, 1949), favorably received on the stage, is Sartre's version of the Hamlet dilemma in a modern political setting. Modeled considerably on the dramatist himself, at least as a child, Hugo, the young bourgeois hero, an idealist and a political absolutist, wants to prove to his comrades in the Communist party that he is truly one of them, responsible and capable. Yet when faced with the difficult task he has been assigned—the assassination of Hoederer, an opportunist leader too ready for compromises and *Realpolitik*—he hesitates, not through cowardice but because Hoederer, something of a substitute father, has converted him to his own views. However, the assassination is ultimately carried out when Hugo shoots Hoederer as a result of sexual jealousy. The political conflict between idealism and pragmatism is left unresolved, though the audience's sympathies usually go toward Hoederer. The philosophical dilemma is even more difficult: when the political winds blow in favor of expediency and the dead Hoederer becomes a hero, should Hugo assume his act and thereby identify what he is with what he has done, or denounce it as an error? His final refusal to denounce it–to let the Party call it a mistake and thus explain it away–marks one of the few moments in Sartre's theater when an existentialist choice resembles what is usually understood by heroism.

In composing these plays Sartre was concerned with the social function of drama. Following his politicization after wartime captivity, he wished to change the place and function of theater in France from one of entertainment for the middle and upper classes, revolving usually around love triangles and other sentimental topics, to one of provoking social change, with plays addressed to the proletariat and petty bourgeoisie. He wanted a drama of praxis, or action. This was not to be accomplished through didacticism but what he called a theater of situations, which would deal with crucial issues in a way that would have meaning for the audience and in which it would be clear that, instead of deriving from absolutes, ethical choice was a function of situation, always characterized by conflict. Ironically, although Sartre's drama had a wide general appeal, mostly to middle-class audiences, it seems to have played no political role; nor did it change French theater, which remained much the same after the war until the advent of the theater of the absurd and, later, a new political theater under the influence of Bertolt Brecht.

Sartre's fiction of the 1940s was also his last. Before the war began, he had already been planning another novel. Upon returning from prison he knew what direction he wished to give the work, a direction indicated by the general title, *Les Chemins de la liberté*. In 1945 the first two volumes appeared: *L'Age de raison* (translated as *The Age of Reason*, 1947) and *Le Sursis* (translated as *The Reprieve*, 1947). Volume three, *La Mort dans l'âme* (translated as *Iron in the Soul*, 1950, and as *Troubled Sleep*, 1951), appeared in 1949, followed by "Drôle d'amitié" (Strange Friendship) in *Temps Modernes* (1949). Posthumously published fragments included in the Pléiade edition of Sartre's fiction (*Œuvres romanesques*, 1981) show the proposed development of characters from earlier volumes but omit any precise resolution to the dialectical problem of the conflict between personal freedom and social responsibility; the series thus remains problematical both aesthetically and ideologically.

Like other fiction of the 1930s and 1940s by writers such as Malraux and Camus, *Les Chemins de la liberté* marks the confrontation of the traditional enlightenment view of human rights with

Sartre at the time of his refusal of the Nobel Prize
(photo Berretty-Rapho)

the contemporary concern for the rights of groups and political bodies. This dialectic between individual and collective freedom is paralleled by the theme of ontological liberty and the resulting moral dread. Sartre begins with a hero, Mathieu Delarue, who resembles him–a philosophy professor, with a few friends and a mistress but no real ties–and who is obsessed with remaining free. This is negative freedom, or freedom misunderstood; whereas true freedom, as *L'Etre et le néant* shows, means total responsibility for oneself in a valueless world, Mathieu's understanding of it is simply to remain unmarried and, thanks to his teaching job, enjoy an assured income. According to the logic of the series he is gradually led along the roads to genuine freedom. His progress–recalling again the basic pattern of the quest or journey novel–is paralleled by the sentimental and political adventures of a wide range of other characters, mainly from the middle classes but displaying varying behavior and preoccupations. *L'Age de raison* turns on Mathieu's efforts to arrange for an abortion for his mistress so that he will not have to accept the responsibility of paternity. Subplots of the volume deal with the same theme: Boris tries to avoid the commitment required when one accepts being loved; Ivich fails in her university work so that she will not have to accept the self-definition and duties associated with a degree and a profession–even though she loathes the idea of returning to her hometown in the provinces. A related theme is bad faith, in which all the characters live, notably Mathieu's homosexual friend Daniel, who tries to hide his penchant from himself; Mathieu himself attempts to avoid making decisions in existential dread by denying the need for such decisions.

Despite these themes, which closely tie *L'Age de raison* to Sartre's philosophic works of the 1940s, the novel is very lively. Even when exasperating, the characters are also convincing and vividly drawn, especially through their conversations and the long passages of interior monologue in the first or third person. The multiple plots, developed in parallel chapters but connected via Mathieu at the center, convey well something of life on the Left Bank before the war. The sense of lived experience is very strong. Certain scenes, such as Daniel's masochistic efforts to drown his cats and mutilate himself, and Ivich's and Mathieu's stabbing of their hands in a nightclub, are powerful dramatizations of moral and existential sickness.

In volume two, *Le Sursis,* Sartre adopted a radical technique of simultaneity, for which he was indebted somewhat to Dos Passos. Whereas in the first volume the multiple characters and plots are kept distinct by being grouped in separate chapters, in the sequel a much greater number of simultaneous plots are woven together, often on the same page and in the same sentence, with no explicit transitions between them. The effect is what the novelist wanted: *Le Sursis,* extremely difficult on first reading, provides the experience of simultaneity and ubiquity, or what he called multidimensionality. As he argued in "Qu'est-ce que la littérature?," first published in 1947 (later collected in *Situations, II,* 1948, and translated as *What Is Literature?,* 1949), this is consistent not only with modern physics but also with his atheistic philosophy, which denies a single godlike point of view, and with contemporary political realities, according to which isolation is impossible and the political destiny of Europe must be seen as a whole. In other words, the novel corresponds to what Sartre would later call a detotalized totality: a Hegelian synthesis in the making, in which dialectical forces are operating on all levels, but which cannot be completed.

The title of the second volume refers to the few days in September 1938 when the Nazi armies invaded Czechoslovakia to annex the territory where the Sudeten Germans were a majority and, in one of the century's most notorious acts of appeasement, Great Britain and France signed with Hitler the Munich Pact, which Sartre rightly takes as the end of the interwar period. For a few days his characters live on the brink of war and then, when it is averted, believe that the return to normal conditions of living will be permanent. As a political novel its aim is to show the folly of such appeasement and the necessity of commitment, and to attack the wealthy bourgeois who were more apprehensive about communism than fascism and, above all, sought to protect their investments. As the continuation of Mathieu's story the volume draws him into situations in which his awareness of responsibility is increased to the point that he feels uneasy, although not yet ready to commit himself, unlike his Communist friend Brunet. He has a revelation of his entire freedom and gratuitousness. Mathieu's other acquaintances from *L'Age de raison* reappear here, all in circumstances which situate them with respect to themselves and also the collectivity. A wide range of new characters, including the historical figures Hitler, Daladier, and Chamberlain, some appearing only briefly, illustrate reactions to their circumstances and to the approaching war and the pact that vary between appropriate, responsible action and utter bad faith. Jacques Delarue, Mathieu's brother, demonstrates the middle-class apprehension of communism. Daniel, who wishes for war, has punished himself at last by marrying Mathieu's pregnant mistress, who disgusts him; Boris hopes to escape through military service the unacceptable demands of being loved by Lola; Philippe, the coward, prepares to flee to Switzerland; Gomez, who fought as a volunteer in Spain on the Republican side, argues against giving in to Hitler's blackmail.

The third volume is probably the least satisfactory and the least reread, although Michel Contat and Michel Rybalka, in *Les Ecrits de Sartre* (1970), consider it the best in the series. It matches neither the technical achievement of *Le Sursis* nor the range of human and social interest in *L'Age de raison* and at this remove seems dated. Yet Sartre's effort to carry further on the fictional plane the theme of freedom is not without historical and political interest. The title, *La Mort dans l'âme,* refers to the discouragement of those who fought, briefly and futilely, against the Ger-

Sartre and Robert Gallimard in Sartre's study at 222 Boulevard Raspail, circa 1978 (photo Jacques Robert–Editions Gallimard)

mans in May and June 1940 and then were defeated and of those who wished to build a socialist France. The volume is divided into two parts, the first dealing with several characters from previous volumes, principally Mathieu, during the retreat in June, the second with French captives in an internment camp and as they are transferred to a German stalag. But the interest is less military than political and moral.

The first part of the volume is structured like *L'Age de raison,* with different characters grouped in separate chapters. One chapter, for instance, concerns Gomez in New York, suffering so from the defeat that what has meant the most to him previously–painting–loses all significance. Another depicts refugees streaming along provincial roads, and still others, the final days of the war after the rout of Mathieu's squad. Another deals with Daniel, rejoicing in the German occupation of Paris, and with Philippe, who did not cross the border after all and whom Daniel proposes to "reeducate" after saving him from a suicide attempt. In the only well-known scene Mathieu participates in a heroic defense of a village, despite its obvious futility, and, at last apparently freed from his near-paralysis of action, shoots at the invading Germans from the church belfry, each shot identified with an act he had not had the courage to perform before. This ac-

tion has often been taken as the perfect expression of Mathieu's freedom, but Sartre specified elsewhere that it was still negative.

The second part of the novel depicts Brunet as a prisoner of war. The emphasis is not, however, on physical hardship but on the reaction of prisoners to their condition, with contrasts drawn particularly between Communists, such as Brunet, and the others, who have neither discipline nor a political faith and think only of their comfort. The main questions are how to deal with the defeat and what attitude to adopt toward the U.S.S.R. after the 1939 Nazi-Soviet pact (a problem that Sartre's friend Paul Nizan had to face), which put in an ideological strait French patriots who were also Communists. Brunet's conclusion that internment is better than liberation for the French soldiers is based on his conviction that only deprivation and hardship can bring about the radical change in their attitude necessary if France is ever to be rebuilt on a socialist foundation.

Like much that Sartre published in the 1940s and subsequently, *Les Chemins de la liberté* created a sensation; the author was attacked for his immorality, though a few perceptive critics saw the novels' value. As he realized himself, the series referred to a period that, while only a few years distant, seemed almost foreign in the *après-*

guerre period of 1945-1950. His aim, as he stated it, was to write for his own time, but psychologically and morally the tone had changed at the war's end and especially by 1950; he felt that the subject was distant from him and that he could not express the ambiguities of the present moment in terms of even the recent past. Readers also may have felt distant from it: the series as a whole did not carry in most readers' eyes the moral weight of Camus's 1947 novel *La Peste* (*The Plague*), although the setting of the latter is even farther removed from postwar France.

Sartre seems also to have had difficulty in going beyond the critical aspect of the theme of liberty to develop fictionally what he understood by true existential freedom and the way it could be realized in contemporary society. Instead of completing the fourth volume, which was to have shown through the characters who had appeared previously what genuine free action entails, he published separately the long fragment "Drôle d'amitié." Though connected to the series, it can stand on its own, since there is a unified, coherent action, supported by excellent character portraits. At its center are Brunet and a fellow prisoner, Schneider, both in a German camp; Mathieu, as posthumously published fragments show, was not killed in the village but is elsewhere. The complexities of human relationships are paralleled by those of political questions. The episode ends in anguish and violence when an escape attempt fails. Some of Sartre's best scenes of action and human dynamics are included in this fragment, despite its heavy ideological element.

By 1950 Sartre was widely known in France and to a certain degree in the rest of Europe and North America. His reputation in the United States was in part the result of his first trip there in 1945, which, like many of his subsequent travels throughout Europe and the two Americas, produced provocative essays. His brand of existentialism, for which Beauvoir offered further illustrations in her work, was publicized in many different organs as the philosophy of the hour. It informed *Temps Modernes* and his many journalistic articles and critical essays, including those that were collected in the important ten-volume series *Situations* (1947-1976). Christian commentators on the one hand and Communist critics on the other felt themselves obliged to answer in writing many of his assertions, giving rise to important polemics; and some of those who were in his circle, such as Raymond Aron, Maurice Merleau-Ponty, and Camus, began disagreeing with him publicly,

especially after the Korean War began. While he had aligned himself with no single political movement or party except for a brief association in 1948 with the Rassemblement Démocratique Révolutionnaire (RDR), he had spoken out on crucial issues such as the conflict in Indochina and what seemed to him to be the warmongering of the United States and right-wing elements in France, criticizing all vigorously. Successful as a playwright, novelist, essayist, and philosopher, he was nevertheless on the verge of a personal and intellectual crisis, which was to have ramifications so great that no portrait of him would be complete without taking it into consideration. Moreover, although his last fiction was published in 1949, he remained so important as a literary figure that it is appropriate to trace the remainder of his career in some detail.

The crisis was due to a number of factors, it would seem. One was the near failure of his political efforts, especially during his connection with the RDR. In a France increasingly divided, after the brief euphoria of post-Liberation accord among many Resistance groups, he had been unable to succeed either directly or by writing in creating a nonaligned Leftist movement; caught in the Cold War, the country was being polarized between Communists, with their allegiance to the Soviet Union, and the parties whose allegiance was to the West. Fearing war, Sartre had to hope for a Soviet victory, though it would mean the end of France as he knew it. Another cause of the crisis, probably, was his radical questioning of the status of the literary work as privileged–something that one would not have foreseen in the 1930s but to which his politicization had led him. A third cause was, paradoxically, his success. Whether because he was the descendant of strict Protestants and could not help looking upon fame as suspect, even diabolical, or because his vanity was so great that success–that is, popular ratification–represented to him an appropriation and a denigration, or whether it was simply a question of always going beyond himself in a nihilation of the past and re-creation of the present self, according to his existentialist understanding of man as project, Sartre attempted to reject the image of himself which was that of the successful creative writer. This was tantamount to a radical reexamination of himself and his positions, or what he called self-contestation, which he attempted to practice throughout the rest of his career.

Sartre (back to camera) at a meeting with the Temps Modernes *editorial board (from left): Jacques-Laurent Bost, Beauvoir, and Claude Lanzmann (photo* Paris-Match/de Potier)

The decade of the 1950s, marking a third period in his development as a writer, was characterized by the prolongation of this crisis and remarkable literary and political consequences. In literature the crisis led to the permanent abandonment of fiction and a near withdrawal from other genres, though two great plays and two others were composed during the decade. In politics and philosophy the crisis and reevaluation were a function of, and led to, continued rereading of Marx and Marxist historians, which culminated in the 755-page study of 1960, *Critique de la raison dialectique* (translated as *Critique of Dialectical Reason*, 1976). In criticism it produced several essays, including his study of Tintoretto, entitled "Le Séquestré de Venise," in 1957 published in *Temps Modernes* and later collected in *Situations, IV,* and earlier an article on Mallarmé, published in *Les Ecrivains célèbres* in 1953 and collected in *Situations, IX.* Most notably the crisis resulted in his lengthy existentialist psychoanalytic study of Jean Genet. Entitled *Saint Genet, comédien et martyr* (1952; translated as *Saint Genet, Actor and Martyr*, 1963), the study is a creative application of principles from *L'Etre et le néant* to the criminal who became a famous and admired author. It insists upon Genet's self-creation as *comédien* or actor, beginning with his so-called original choice to *be* a

thief in accordance with society's labeling of him, through his homosexuality and his assumption of social evil as a good. The argumentation relies highly on the sort of dialectical reasoning which Sartre had learned from Marx, transferred to the area of existentialist psychoanalysis and ethics. The volume illustrates how, for Sartre, genius is a response to a situation; Genet's genius lay in his creative forming of himself, which then gave rise to literary expressions.

Critique de la raison dialectique is an attempt to review classical Marxism, considered by Sartre ossified, in the light of existentialism. It proposes to furnish a new method for historical analysis, based on Hegel and Marx but departing from them in several respects, especially the insistence on the freedom of subjects. Neither entirely a study of politics, nor history, anthropology, sociology, nor philosophy, it draws on all these disciplines in its aim of providing the means for social revolution. Verbose and obscure, it was written partly under the influence of amphetamines, as well as with the conviction that Europe and civilization were on the edge of disaster. It denounces, in addition to bourgeois capitalism and Western democratic structures, almost all the social relationships and institutions of the modern world (including those in socialist societies such as the

U.S.S.R.), which he calls series and which are inauthentic and tyrannical; it calls for new relationships based on structures Sartre identifies at certain dynamic moments in history, notably the French Revolution. Analytic reason—the type of Cartesian logic that gave rise to modern science and mathematics and is found every day in the common notion of cause and effect—is denounced in favor of Marxist dialectical reason, which proceeds by triads and which Sartre illustrates at length. Departing from his earlier position, he acknowledges freedom as conditionable and conditioned by circumstance, but it remains as both a given and an end.

The critical reception given *Critique de la raison dialectique* by philosophers and political scientists varied. Some found it derivative, others obscure, others brilliantly creative. It is such a complex and difficult work that early appraisals were very incomplete and biased, and even now it can by no means be considered well understood, but an abundant corpus of criticism on it in the 1970s and 1980s indicates its richness and vitality; Marxist social critics in English-speaking countries have been particularly attentive readers.

Sartre's two principal plays of the 1950s, though antedating *Critique de la raison dialectique* (since they were produced in 1951 and 1959 respectively), are closely connected to the dialectical reasoning for which he argued in the 1960 volume. Indeed, he was working on the later play as he composed the *Critique*. The earlier one, *Le Diable et le Bon Dieu* (published, 1951, and translated as *Lucifer and the Lord*, 1953, and as *The Devil and the Good Lord*, 1960), is a long, complex drama with multiple characters and scenes, violence of language and action, and strong contrasts; these characteristics, which are the signs of the baroque, make it conform well to its setting and subject matter—the religious and political conflicts in pre-Reformation Germany, especially the violence among temporal powers and princes of the church. The play introduces one of Sartre's favorite figures, the bastard (also visible in *Saint Genet*, which is closely connected to the drama). The theme of the bastard is related to that of treason, one of the most important currents in *Le Diable et le Bon Dieu* and other texts and something which attracted Sartre.

The main topics, however, are good and evil as absolutes—and hence the existence of God—and the foundation for human action. The hero, Goetz, the natural son of a peasant and a noblewoman, has systematically practiced evil, like Genet.

On a bet he vows henceforth to pursue only good, including the emancipation of serfs and the seizing of lands belonging to the nobility. The impossibility of doing only good—not through human frailty but because of the nature of action in and on the world—is illustrated in a rich and complex plot development. In particular it becomes clear to Goetz that all action, being rooted in a historical moment, must fit that moment to be effective: a revolt that is premature is worse than no revolt, because of its negative consequences. Sartre illustrates thereby the limits of action or praxis, set by what he calls the practico-inert, that is, the counteraction of "objects" (matter, series, individuals) in response to action. Goetz's failure is both personal and practical (he has not been able to free the peasants). His response is to denounce both evil and good as absolutes and to choose pragmatic action in a situation, directed toward a specific end. On the philosophical plane this means the denial of God's existence, and *Le Diable et le Bon Dieu* is Sartre's most dramatic and, in a sense, positive expression of atheism. Successfully produced in Paris with an impressive cast, it was vociferously criticized, notably by François Mauriac, who found its contents morally offensive, and Elsa Triolet, who attacked it for political reasons.

For production in 1953 Sartre wrote a very free adaptation of Alexandre Dumas père's play *Kean ou Désordre et génie*, concerning the great English actor who was also a bastard. Witty, although melodramatic in plot, Sartre's *Kean* (published, 1954; translated as *Kean; or Disorder and Genius*, 1954) presents several favorite Sartrean themes: identity, role playing, the relationship between self and others, authenticity, and social oppression. This brilliant adaptation was followed by a political farce, *Nekrassov* (1956; translated, 1956; republished in *The Devil and the Good Lord, and Two Other Plays*, 1960), which, in a Cold War context, attacked the press and public paranoia about the Soviet Union; it closed after a few performances and now seems very dated.

Les Séquestrés d'Altona, Sartre's last play (produced, 1959; published, 1960; and translated as *Loser Wins*, 1960, and as *The Condemned of Altona*, 1961), excluding his 1965 adaptation of Euripides' *The Trojan Women*, is, like *Le Diable et le Bon Dieu*, lengthy, difficult to produce, and somewhat unwieldy in plot. Despite its shocking subject matter, it was very successful on the stage. The dramatist had a hard time finishing it, partly because of poor health, and production was post-

Procession for Sartre's funeral, 19 April 1980 (photo X.–D.R.)

poned. Although such is not immediately obvious, it reflects the time at which it was written, that is, the Algerian war, which had been expanding since 1954. By 1957 it had become clear that torture had been practiced systematically by French units in Algeria against civilians and rebel soldiers alike. The consequent debate on the means of conducting the war and on the war itself was tearing France asunder. Knowing that censorship under the Gaullist Fifth Republic would not allow him to depict episodes from the conflict directly, Sartre chose instead to deal in a World War II context with the questions of torture and a commercially inspired war. The concerns of the play go well beyond these moral questions, however, important as they are, to embrace topics that range from madness to a dialecti-

cal view of history. The drama deals with a German family after the defeat of 1945 and especially the son Frantz (a name that commentators generally interpret as standing for France), who has sequestered himself in an attempt to maintain the illusion of German victory and prosperity. His madness, which represents a free choice, is in part a function of his having seen a Jew handed over to the SS and beaten to death and having tortured partisans in Russia. Tense family relationships involving the father, the other son, the sister Leni, and the sister-in-law recall those in *Huis clos;* hostility alternates with dependence and need for the other, which in the case of Leni and Frantz is full-blown incest. Frantz's hallucinations are not only a fully conscious choice; they are also prophetic as he envisages–what accord-

351

ing to Sartre's view of militaristic capitalism is inevitable–the destruction of the human race. Many of the author's concerns and obsessions are woven into the text: fascination with the sister and the father, the oppressiveness of the bourgeois family, problems of authenticity and self-identity, crab motifs (frequent throughout his work), food images, the functioning of capitalism, the theme of treachery, and an apocalyptic view of history that incorporates concepts from *Critique de la raison dialectique*.

If one compares Sartre's intellectual posture in 1960 to that of the late 1930s, it is clear that a radical change had taken place, although not a complete break. Gone was the novelist he had wanted to be and had been successfully; gone also was the philosopher preoccupied chiefly with phenomenological questions. Even the playwright would compose no more original dramas. The idealistic conviction–which he called his imposture–that art represented personal redemption because the status of the art object was superior to that of lived experience had been destroyed. Yet the man of letters remained, as the rest of his career shows. There are at least two explanations for this. One is that he retained his belief in a literature of action, whether essay, play, or other form, which could have meaning for his contemporaries and be instrumental in achieving change; but this literature would be only one, and not the principal, means of action on the world, a complement to political involvement such as that he practiced in 1960 by signing the "Manifeste des 121" (Letter of 121) urging French military recruits to refuse obedience and by saying that he would, if necessary, "porter des valises" (carry suitcases, that is, transport incendiary material) in the cause of the Algerian rebels. Another reason for his continued activity as a writer was his inability–visible in *Les Mots* (begun in 1953, finished in the early 1960s and published in book form in 1964)–to renounce wholly the words by which he had so long lived. While he insisted that he had lost his belief in literature, Sartre's self was so bound up with words, and he was so interested in his own thought, that he could not give up writing; *Les Mots*, a renunciation of literature, is a superb literary production. When he refused the Nobel Prize for Literature awarded him in 1964, it was not an antiliterature gesture but rather a political statement. His concern was to remain radical; thus he felt obliged to reject the "appropriation" by the middle

classes and Western humanism which accepting the prize would signify.

From 1960 on until the mid 1970s, when he lost much of his eyesight and could neither read nor write, Sartre continued producing texts–in addition to *Les Mots*, many political essays, articles, and interviews, the most important of which were reprinted in *Situations*. He was very active politically, supporting many different causes. He spoke against the American involvement in Vietnam and participated in the Russell Tribunals, formed to judge American war crimes. He generally supported Israel but made attempts to act as an intermediary between Arab nations and the Israeli state. He found himself involved with radical political movements in France and ended by acting as editor of the *Cause du Peuple* and other extreme left-wing publications. He also composed his last major critical text, *L'Idiot de la famille* (1971-1972; translated as *The Family Idiot*, 1981), a three-volume work of almost three thousand pages. The idiot is Gustave Flaubert, who had long interested Sartre, just as Mallarmé had; certain resemblances between the author of *Madame Bovary* and his twentieth-century critic may be at the source of this interest, although the differences are enormous. Sartre had written biography before: his 1947 study *Baudelaire* (translated into English in 1949), the book on Genet, *Les Mots*. Like the previous studies, *L'Idiot de la famille* emphasizes childhood, for even though he rejected much of Freud, Sartre saw the crucial relationship between a writer's first years and his development. *L'Idiot de la famille* studies at length, in a difficult style reminiscent of *Critique de la raison dialectique* and using its concepts, the milieu into which Flaubert was born–not just his family and the professional upper class but the entire French industrial society of the early nineteenth century, which Sartre condemns vigorously as neurotic and whose neuroses were mirrored in the profoundly maladjusted Gustave. The biography is thus social criticism more than literary criticism, and although Flaubert's achievement in fiction did interest Sartre–he wanted to pursue the investigation by concentrating on *Madame Bovary* but was unable to do so–what he was mainly concerned with was castigating French structures in both the nineteenth and the twentieth centuries, and the analytic reason and capitalism on which they were based.

After Sartre became unable to pursue his reading and writing, he turned to other lines of activity: music (of which he was very fond); conversations with Beauvoir and other friends, especially the Algerian Jewish girl Arlette El Kaïm, at one point his mistress, whom he had adopted legally in 1965; giving additional interviews; and political activities such as marching and signing petitions. He remained enthusiastic about the Maoists in France, with whom he had earlier collaborated. In his last years he was cared for by friends, especially Beauvoir; despite his repeated affairs with other women and her displeasure especially over the seriousness of his liaison with El Kaïm, their relationship at the last was like that of devoted spouses who have held the same values and pursued identical undertakings for fifty years. He died in April 1980 after suffering for some time from circulatory and other difficulties.

His legacy is still being reviewed by critics. Books on him proliferated shortly before and after his death, ranging from psychoanalytic studies to political analysis to highly specialized examinations of currents in his work. He is still quoted frequently in journals of commentary. But in certain reassessments, skepticism is visible; the present generation of intellectuals is old enough to have known his influence, young enough to have gone beyond it. Already in May 1968, at the time of the Parisian student riots, few of the leaders cited his work as inspiration for the uprising, mentioning instead other philosophers and revolutionaries such as Marx, Trotsky, Mao, Castro, and Guevara. And several Marxist philosophers in France and elsewhere have surpassed his efforts to modernize Marxist thought, especially by the use of structuralism, and are now considered more influential. By 1985 critics writing in *Débat* dismissed him—perhaps in reaction against his previous intellectual sway. He was not, moreover, the only novelist of his generation to condemn in a lucid, biting prose the selfishness of the bourgeoisie and the corruption of French society; Céline certainly insisted even more clearly on the cruelty of the upper classes and misery of the lower. Nor was he the first to emphasize authenticity: Gide, whose example he acknowledged, had sounded that note earlier in the century. Malraux and Camus, to name only two, had written of silent heavens and the absurd. But Sartre did so much, of so many different kinds. He renewed old literary themes such as the love triangle and ennui, introduced new ones, used dialogue brilliantly, created striking characters and situations in his plays and novels, and gave a name to experiences of dread, shame, hostility, solitude, embodiment, emptiness, and others which

readers recognized as their own. He combined irony, crisp analysis, and pithy formulas with passages of impressionistic prose which render the very feel and taste of experience. He was indefatigable in supporting causes in which he believed, illustrating what it meant truly to be a committed writer. Of all twentieth-century French writers he succeeded best at rationalizing his own positions on art, politics, ethics, and the human situation, and his career illustrates better than that of any French figure since the eighteenth century the union of fiction and drama with philosophy.

Letters:

Lettres au Castor et à quelques autres, 2 volumes (Paris: Gallimard, 1983); translated in part by Matthew Ward, Irene Ilton, and Marilyn Myatt as *Thoughtful Passions: Jean-Paul Sartre's Intimate Letters to Simone de Beauvoir, 1926-1939* (New York: Macmillan, 1987).

Interviews:

"Existentialist," *New Yorker*, 22 (16 March 1946): 24-25;

Paul Carrière, "*Les Jeux sont faits?* Tout le contraire d'une pièce existentialiste," *Figaro*, 29 April 1947, p. 4;

Roderick McArthur, "Author! Author?," *Theatre Arts*, 33 (March 1949): 11-13;

Joseph A. Barry, "Sartre Enters 'a New Phase,'" *New York Times Magazine*, 30 January 1949, pp. 12, 18-19;

Gabriel d'Aubarède, "Rencontre avec Jean-Paul Sartre," *Nouvelles Littéraires*, 1 February 1951, p. 6;

"Avant la création de *Nekrassov* au Théâtre Antoine, Sartre nous dit . . . ," *Monde*, 1 June 1955, p. 9; translated by Rima Drell Reck as "Said Jean-Paul Sartre," *Yale French Studies*, 16 (Winter 1955-1956): 3, 7;

"Jean-Paul Sartre nous parle du théâtre," *Théâtre Populaire*, 15 (September-October 1955): 1-9;

"Sartre Views the New China," *New Statesman and Nation*, 50 (3 December 1955): 737-739;

"Après Budapest, Sartre parle," *Express*, 281 (9 December 1956, supplement); translated as "After Budapest," *Evergreen Review*, 1 (1957): 5-23;

Olivier Todd, "Jean-Paul Sartre on His Autobiography," *Listener*, 57 (6 June 1957): 915-916;

"Deux Heures avec Sartre," *Express* (17 September 1959); translated by Richard Seaver as

"The Theater," *Evergreen Review*, 4 (January-February 1960): 143-152;

Madeleine Chapsal, "Jean-Paul Sartre," in her *Les Ecrivains en personne* (Paris: Julliard, 1960);

Oreste F. Pucciani, "An Interview with Jean-Paul Sartre," *Tulane Drama Review*, 5 (March 1961): 12-18;

Kenneth Tynan, "Sartre Talks to Tynan," *Observer*, 18 (June 1961);

Jacqueline Piatier, "Jean-Paul Sartre s'explique sur *Les Mots*," *Monde*, 18 April 1964, p. 13; translated by Anthony Hartley as "A Long, Bitter, Sweet Madness," *Encounter*, 22 (June 1964): 61-63;

"L'Ecrivain doit refuser de se laisser transformer en institution," *Monde*, 24 October 1964, p. 13; translated by Richard Howard as "Sartre on the Nobel Prize," *New York Review of Books*, 17 December 1964, pp. 5-6;

"Pourquoi je refuse d'aller aux Etats-Unis: Il n'y a plus de dialogue possible," *Nouvel Observateur*, 1 April 1965; translated in part by Lionel Abel as "Why I Will Not Go to the United States," *Nation*, 200 (19 April 1965): 407-411;

"Jean-Paul Sartre," *Playboy*, 12 (May 1965): 69-72, 74-76;

Madeleine Gobeil, "Sartre Talks of Beauvoir," translated by Bernard Frechtman, *Vogue*, 146 (July 1965): 72-73;

Léonce Peillard, "Entretien avec Jean-Paul Sartre," *Biblio-Livres de France*, 17 (January 1966): 14-18; translated by Elaine P. Halperin as "Communists Are Afraid of Revolution," *Midway*, 10 (Summer 1969): 53-61;

"L'Intellectuel face à la révolution," *Point* (Brussels), 13 (January 1968); translated by Bruce Rice as "Intellectuals and Revolution," *Ramparts*, 9 (December 1970): 52-55;

Arturo Schwarz, "Sartre: Israël, la Gauche et les Arabes," *Arche*, 152 (26 October 1969): 32-40, 73, 75; translated as "Sartre Looks at the Middle East Again," *Midstream*, 15 (August-September 1969): 37-38;

"Itinerary of a Thought," *New Left Review*, 58 (November-December 1969): 43-66;

John Gerassi, "Sartre Accuses the Intellectuals of Bad Faith," *New York Times Magazine*, 17 October 1971.

Bibliographies:

Allen J. Belkind, *Jean-Paul Sartre and Existentialism in English: A Bibliographical Guide* (Kent, Ohio: Kent State University Press, 1970);

Michel Contat and Michel Rybalka, *Les Ecrits de Sartre* (Paris: Gallimard, 1970); translated by Richard C. McCleary as *The Writings of Jean-Paul Sartre*, 2 volumes (Evanston: Northwestern University Press, 1974);

François H. Lapointe and Claire Lapointe, "A Bibliography of Jean-Paul Sartre, 1970-1975: The Anglo-American Response to Jean-Paul Sartre," *Philosophy Today*, 19 (Winter 1975): 341-357;

Robert Wilcocks, *Jean-Paul Sartre: A Bibliography of International Criticism* (Edmonton: University of Alberta Press, 1975);

François H. Lapointe and Claire Lapointe, "A Selective Bibliography with Notations on Sartre's *Nausea* (1938-1980)," *Philosophy Today*, 24 (Fall 1980): 285-296;

François H. Lapointe, *Jean-Paul Sartre and His Critics: An International Bibliography (1938-1980)*, revised and enlarged edition (Bowling Green, Ohio: Philosophy Documentation Center, 1981).

Biographies:

Francis Jeanson, *Sartre par lui-même* (Paris: Seuil, 1959);

Philip Thody, *Sartre: A Biographical Introduction* (New York: Scribners, 1971);

Francis Jeanson, *Sartre dans sa vie* (Paris: Seuil, 1974);

Axel Madsen, *Hearts and Minds: The Common Journey of Jean-Paul Sartre and Simone de Beauvoir* (New York: Morrow, 1977);

Kenneth Thompson and Margaret Thompson, *Sartre, Life and Works* (New York: Facts on File, 1984);

Annie Cohen-Solal, *Sartre: 1905-1980* (Paris: Gallimard, 1985); translated by Anna Cancogni as *Sartre: A Life* (New York: Pantheon, 1987).

References:

Thomas Anderson, *The Foundations and Structure of Sartrean Ethics* (Lawrence: Regents Press of Kansas, 1979);

Ronald Aronson, *Jean-Paul Sartre–Philosophy in the World* (London: NLB, 1980);

Aronson, *Sartre's Second Critique* (Chicago & London: University of Chicago Press, 1981);

Hazel E. Barnes, *The Literature of Possibility: A Study in Humanistic Existentialism* (Lincoln: University of Nebraska Press, 1959); republished as *Humanistic Existentialism: The Literature of Possibility* (Lincoln: Bison Books, 1962);

Barnes, *Sartre* (Philadelphia: Lippincott, 1973);

Barnes, *Sartre and Flaubert* (Chicago: University of Chicago Press, 1981);

George H. Bauer, *Sartre and the Artist* (Chicago: University of Chicago Press, 1969);

Simone de Beauvoir, *La Cérémonie des adieux, suivi de Entretiens avec Jean-Paul Sartre* (Paris: Gallimard, 1981); translated by Patrick O'Brien as *Adieux: A Farewell to Sartre* (New York: Pantheon, 1984);

Catharine Savage Brosman, *Jean-Paul Sartre* (Boston: Twayne, 1983);

Catharine Savage [Brosman], *Malraux, Sartre, and Aragon as Political Novelists* (Gainesville: University of Florida Press, 1964);

Michel-Antoine Burnier, *Les Existentialistes et la politique* (Paris: Gallimard, 1966); translated as *Choice of Action: The French Existentialists on the Political Front Line* (New York: Random House, 1968);

Ronald A. Carson, *Jean-Paul Sartre* (Valley Forge, Pa.: Judson Press, 1974);

Joseph S. Catalano, *A Commentary on Jean-Paul Sartre's "Being and Nothingness"* (New York: Harper & Row, 1974);

Catalano, *A Commentary on Jean-Paul Sartre's Critique of Dialectical Reason, Volume 1, Theory of Practical Ensembles* (Chicago & London: University of Chicago Press, 1986);

Peter Caws, *Sartre* (London: Routledge & Kegan Paul, 1979);

Robert Champigny, *Sartre and Drama* (Columbia, S.C.: French Literature Publications, 1982);

Champigny, *Stages on Sartre's Way* (Bloomington: Indiana University Press, 1959);

Max Charlesworth, *The Existentialists and Jean-Paul Sartre* (New York: St. Martin's, 1976);

Stuart L. Charmé, *Meaning and Myth in the Study of Lives: A Sartrean Perspective* (Philadelphia: University of Pennsylvania Press, 1984);

Pietro Chiodi, *Sartre and Marxism*, translated by Kate Soper (London: Harvester, 1976);

Douglas Collins, *Sartre as Biographer* (Cambridge: Harvard University Press, 1980);

Ian Craib, *Existentialism and Sociology: A Study of Jean-Paul Sartre* (Cambridge: Cambridge University Press, 1976);

Arthur Danto, *Jean-Paul Sartre* (New York: Viking, 1975);

Débat, special issue on Sartre, 35 (May 1985);

Wilfrid Desan, *The Marxism of Jean-Paul Sartre* (Garden City: Doubleday, 1965);

Desan, *The Tragic Finale: An Essay on the Philosophy of Jean-Paul Sartre* (Oxford: Oxford University Press/Cambridge: Harvard University Press, 1954; revised edition, New York: Harper, 1960);

Paul John Eakin, *Fictions in Autobiography: Studies in the Art of Self-Invention* (Princeton: Princeton University Press, 1985);

Esprit Créateur, 17, special issue on Sartre (Spring 1977);

Joseph P. Fell, *Heidegger and Sartre* (New York: Columbia University Press, 1979);

Thomas R. Flynn, *Sartre and Marxist Existentialism: The Test Case of Collective Responsibility* (Chicago: Chicago University Press, 1984);

French Review, special issue on Sartre, 55 (Summer 1982);

Marc Froment-Meurice, *Sartre et l'existentialisme* (Paris: Nathan, 1984);

Gila J. Hayim, *The Existential Sociology of Jean-Paul Sartre* (Amherst: University of Massachusetts Press, 1980);

Christina Howells, *Sartre's Theory of Literature* (London: Modern Humanities Research Association, 1979);

Francis Jeanson, *Sartre et le problème moral* (Paris: Gallimard, 1947; revised, 1965); translated by Robert V. Stone as *Sartre and the Problem of Morality* (Bloomington: Indiana University Press, 1980);

Edith Kern, ed., *Sartre: A Collection of Critical Essays* (Englewood Cliffs, N.J.: Prentice-Hall, 1962);

Douglas Kirsner, *The Schizoid World of Jean-Paul Sartre and R. D. Laing* (St. Lucia: University of Queensland Press, 1976);

Dominick LaCapra, *A Preface to Sartre* (Ithaca: Cornell University Press, 1978);

James Lawler, *The Existential Marxism of Jean-Paul Sartre* (Amsterdam: Grüner, 1976);

Benny Lévy, *Le Nom de l'homme: Dialogue avec Sartre* (Lagrasse: Verdier, 1984);

Dorothy McCall, *The Theater of Jean-Paul Sartre* (New York: Columbia University Press, 1969);

Joseph H. McMahon, *Humans Being: The World of Jean-Paul Sartre* (Chicago: University of Chicago Press, 1971);

István Mészáros, *The Work of Sartre, Volume 1: Search for Freedom* (Atlantic Highlands, N.J.: Humanities Press, 1979; Brighton, U.K.: Harvester, 1979);

Phyllis Sutton Morris, *Sartre's Concept of a Person: An Analytic Approach* (Amherst: University of Massachusetts Press, 1976);

Obliques, special issue on Sartre, nos. 18-19 (1979);

Papers in Romance, special issue on Sartre, 3 (Spring 1981);

Philosophy Today, special issues on Sartre, 19 (Winter 1975), 24 (Fall 1980);

William Plank, *Sartre and Surrealism* (Ann Arbor: UMI Research Press, 1981);

Gerald Prince, *Métaphysique et technique dans l'œuvre romanesque de Sartre* (Geneva: Droz, 1968);

Alain D. Ranwez, *Jean-Paul Sartre's "Les Temps Modernes": A Literary History, 1945-1952* (Troy, N.Y.: Whitston, 1981);

Peter Royle, *The Sartre-Camus Controversy: A Literary and Philosophical Critique* (Ottawa: University of Ottawa Press, 1982);

Paul A. Schilpp, ed., *The Philosophy of Jean-Paul Sartre* (La Salle, Ill.: Open Court, 1981);

William Ralph Schroeder, *Sartre and His Predecessors: The Self and the Other* (London & Boston: Routledge & Kegan Paul, 1984);

Michael Scrivin, *Sartre's Existential Biographies* (London: Macmillan, 1984);

Hugh Silverman and Frederick Elliston, eds., *Jean-Paul Sartre: Contemporary Approaches to His Philosophy* (Pittsburgh: Duquesne University Press, 1980);

George Stack, *Sartre's Philosophy of Social Existence* (St. Louis: Green, 1977);

Michael Theunissen, *The Other: Studies in the Social Ontology of Husserl, Heidegger, Sartre, and Buber,* translated by Christopher Macann (Cambridge: Massachusetts Institute of Technology Press, 1984);

Mary Warnock, *Sartre: A Collection of Critical Essays* (Garden City: Doubleday, 1971);

Margaret Whitford, *Merleau-Ponty's Critique of Sartre's Philosophy* (Lexington, Ky.: French Forum Monographs, 1982);

Colin Wilson, *Anti-Sartre* (San Bernadino, Cal.: Borgo, 1981).

Papers:

The Bibliothèque Nationale in Paris has manuscripts of several of Sartre's works. The bulk of his papers remain in private hands.

Georges Simenon
(13 February 1903-   )

Catharine Savage Brosman
Tulane University

BOOKS: *Au rendez-vous des terre-neuvas* (Paris: Fayard, 1931); translated as *The Sailor's Rendezvous* in *Maigret Keeps a Rendezvous* (1940);

Le Charretier de la "Providence" (Paris: Fayard, 1931); translated as *The Crime at Lock 14* in *The Triumph of Inspector Maigret* (1934); published with *The Shadow in the Courtyard* (New York: Covici, Friede, 1934);

Le Chien jaune (Paris: Fayard, 1931); translated as *A Face for a Clue* in *Patience of Maigret* (1939);

Un Crime en Hollande (Paris: Fayard, 1931); translated as *A Crime in Holland* in *Maigret Abroad* (1940);

La Danseuse du Gai-Moulin (Paris: Fayard, 1931); translated as *At the "Gai-Moulin"* in *Maigret Abroad* (1940);

M. Gallet décédé (Paris: Fayard, 1931); translated as *The Death of Monsieur Gallet* (New York: Covici, Friede, 1932); translated as *The Death of M. Gallet* in *Introducing Inspector Maigret* (1933);

La Nuit du carrefour (Paris: Fayard, 1931); translated as *The Crossroad Murders* in *Inspector Maigret Investigates* (1933); translation published separately (New York: Covici, Friede, 1933);

Le Pendu de Saint-Pholien (Paris: Fayard, 1931); translated as *The Crime of Inspector Maigret* in *Introducing Inspector Maigret* (1933); translation published separately (New York: Covici, Friede, 1933);

Pietr-le-Letton (Paris: Fayard, 1931); translated as *The Case of Peter the Lett* in *Inspector Maigret Investigates* (1933); translated as *The Strange Case of Peter the Lett* (New York: Covici, Friede, 1933);

Le Relais d'Alsace (Paris: Fayard, 1931); translated as *The Man from Everywhere* in *Maigret and M. l'Abbé* (1941);

La Tête d'un homme (Paris: Fayard, 1931); translated as *A Battle of Nerves* in *Patience of Maigret* (1939);

Georges Simenon, 1943

L'Affaire Saint-Fiacre (Paris: Fayard, 1932); translated as *The Saint-Fiacre Affair* in *Maigret Keeps a Rendezvous* (1940);

Chez les Flamands (Paris: Fayard, 1932); translated as *The Flemish Shop* in *Maigret to the Rescue* (1940);

Le Fou de Bergerac (Paris: Fayard, 1932); translated as *The Madman of Bergerac* in *Maigret Travels South* (1940);

La Guinguette à deux sous (Paris: Fayard, 1932); translated as *Guinguette by the Seine* in *Maigret to the Rescue* (1940);

"Liberty Bar" (Paris: Fayard, 1932); translated in *Maigret Travels South* (1940);

L'Ombre chinoise (Paris: Fayard, 1932); translated as *The Shadow on the Courtyard* in *The Triumph of Inspector Maigret* (1934); published as *The Shadow in the Courtyard* with *The Crime at Lock 14* (1934);

Le Passager du "Polarlys" (Paris: Fayard, 1932); translated as *The Mystery of the "Polarlys"* in *Two Latitudes* (1942); translated as *Danger at Sea* in *On Land and Sea* (1954);

Le Port des brumes (Paris: Fayard, 1932); translated as *Death of a Harbour Master* in *Maigret and M. l'Abbé* (1941);

Les Treize Coupables (Paris: Fayard, 1932);

Les Treize Enigmes (Paris: Fayard, 1932);

Les Treize Mystéres (Paris: Fayard, 1932);

L'Ane rouge (Paris: Fayard, 1933); translated by Jean Stewart as *The Nightclub* (New York: Harcourt Brace Jovanovich, 1979);

Le Coup de lune (Paris: Fayard, 1933); translated as *Tropic Moon* in *Two Latitudes* (1942); translation published separately (New York: Harcourt, Brace, 1943);

L'Ecluse no. 1 (Paris: Fayard, 1933); translated as *The Lock at Charenton* in *Maigret Sits It Out* (1941);

Les Fiançailles de Mr. Hire (Paris: Fayard, 1933); translated as *Mr. Hire's Engagement* in *The Sacrifice* (1956);

Les Gens d'en face (Paris: Fayard, 1933); translated as *The Window Over the Way* in *The Window Over the Way* (1951);

Le Haut-mal (Paris: Fayard, 1933); translated as *The Woman in the Grey House* in *Affairs of Destiny* (1942);

Inspector Maigret Investigates, translated by Anthony Abbott (London: Hurst & Blackett, 1933)–comprises *La Nuit du carrefour* and *Pietr-le-Letton;*

Introducing Inspector Maigret, translated by Abbott (London: Hurst & Blackett, 1933)–comprises *M. Gallet décédé* and *Le Pendu de Saint-Pholien;*

La Maison du canal (Paris: Fayard, 1933); translated as *The House by the Canal* in *The House by the Canal* (1952);

L'Homme de Londres (Paris: Fayard, 1934); translated as *Newhaven-Dieppe* in *Affairs of Destiny* (1942);

Le Locataire (Paris: Gallimard, 1934); translated as *The Lodger* in *Escape in Vain* (1943);

Maigret (Paris: Fayard, 1934); translated as *Maigret Returns* in *Maigret Sits It Out* (1941);

Les Suicidés (Paris: Gallimard, 1934); translated as *One Way Out* in *Escape in Vain* (1943);

The Triumph of Inspector Maigret (London: Hurst & Blackett, 1934)–comprises *Le Charretier de la "Providence"* and *L'Ombre chinoise;* republished as *The Shadow in the Courtyard [and] The Crime at Lock 14* (New York: Covici, Friede, 1934);

Les Clients d'Avrenos (Paris: Gallimard, 1935);

Les Pitard (Paris: Gallimard, 1935); translated as *A Wife at Sea* in *A Wife at Sea* (1949);

Quartier négre (Paris: Gallimard, 1935);

Les Demoiselles de Concarneau (Paris: Gallimard, 1936); translated as *The Breton Sisters* in *Havoc by Accident* (1943);

L'Evadé (Paris: Gallimard, 1936); translated by Geoffrey Sainsbury as *The Disintegration of J. P. G.* (London: Routledge, 1937);

Long cours (Paris: Gallimard, 1936); translated by Eileen Ellenbogen as *The Long Exile* (San Diego: Harcourt Brace Jovanovich, 1983);

45 à l'ombre (Paris: Gallimard, 1936);

L'Assassin (Paris: Gallimard, 1937); translated as *The Murderer* in *A Wife at Sea* (1949);

Le Blanc à lunettes (Paris: Gallimard, 1937); translated as *Talata* in *Havoc by Accident* (1943);

Faubourg (Paris: Gallimard, 1937); translated as *Home Town* in *On the Danger Line* (1944);

Le Testament Donadieu (Paris: Gallimard, 1937); translated by Stuart Gilbert as *The Shadow Falls* (London: Routledge/Toronto: Musson, 1945; New York: Harcourt, Brace, 1945);

Ceux de la soif (Paris: Gallimard, 1938);

Chemin sans issue (Paris: Gallimard, 1938); translated as *Blind Path* in *Lost Moorings* (1946); translation republished separately as *Blind Alley* (New York: Reynal & Hitchcock, 1946);

Le Cheval blanc (Paris: Gallimard, 1938); translated by Norman Denny as *The White Horse Inn* (New York: Harcourt Brace Jovanovich, 1980);

L'Homme qui regardait passer les trains (Paris: Gallimard, 1938); translated by Gilbert as *The Man Who Watched the Trains Go By* (London: Pan, 1945; New York: Reynal & Hitchcock, 1946);

La Marie du port (Paris: Gallimard, 1938); translated as *A Chit of a Girl* in *Chit of a Girl* (1949);

La Mauvaise Etoile (Paris: Gallimard, 1938);

Monsieur La Souris (Paris: Gallimard, 1938); translated in *Poisoned Relations* (1950);

Les Rescapés du "Télémaque" (Paris: Gallimard, 1938); translated as *The Survivors* in *Black*

Simenon (standing at left) with Russian students and anarchists, 1918 (courtesy of Centre d'Etudes Georges Simenon, University of Liège)

Rain (1949); published separately (San Diego: Harcourt Brace Jovanovich, 1985);

Les Sept Minutes (Paris: Gallimard, 1938)—comprises *Le Grand Langoustier, La Nuit des sept minutes,* and *L'Enigme de la "Marie Gallante";*

Les Sœurs Lacroix (Paris: Gallimard, 1938); translated as *Poisoned Relations* in *Poisoned Relations* (1950);

Le Suspect (Paris: Gallimard, 1938); translated as *The Green Thermos* in *On the Danger Line* (1944);

Touriste de bananes (Paris: Gallimard, 1938); translated as *Banana Tourist* in *Lost Moorings* (1946);

Les Trois Crimes de mes amis (Paris: Gallimard, 1938);

Le Bourgmestre de Furnes (Paris: Gallimard, 1939); translated by Sainsbury as *The Bourgomaster of Furnes* (London: Routledge & Kegan Paul, 1952);

Chez Krull (Paris: Gallimard, 1939); translated in *A Sense of Guilt* (1955);

Le Coup de vague (Paris: Gallimard, 1939);

Patience of Maigret, translated by Sainsbury (London: Routledge/Toronto: Musson, 1939; New York: Harcourt, Brace, 1940)—comprises *Le Chien jaune* and *La Tête d'un homme;*

Les Inconnus dans la maison (Paris: Gallimard, 1940); translated by Sainsbury as *Strangers*

in the House (London: Routledge & Kegan Paul, 1951; New York: Doubleday, 1954);

Malempin (Paris: Gallimard, 1940); translated by Isabel Quigly as *The Family Lie* (London: Hamilton, 1978);

Maigret Abroad, translated by Sainsbury (London: Routledge/Toronto: Musson, 1940; New York: Harcourt, Brace, 1940)—comprises *Un Crime en Hollande* and *La Danseuse du Gai-Moulin;*

Maigret Keeps a Rendezvous, translated by Margret Ludwig (London: Routledge, 1940; New York: Harcourt, Brace & World, 1941)—comprises *Au rendez-vous des terre-neuvas* and *L'Affaire Saint-Fiacre;*

Maigret to the Rescue, translated by Sainsbury (London: Routledge/Toronto: Musson, 1940; New York: Harcourt, Brace, 1941)—comprises *Chez les Flamands* and *La Guinguette à deux sous;*

Maigret Travels South, translated by Sainsbury (London: Routledge, 1940; New York: Harcourt, Brace, 1940)—comprises *Le Fou de Bergerac* and *"Liberty Bar";*

Bergelon (Paris: Gallimard, 1941); translated by Ellenbogen as *The Delivery* (New York: Harcourt Brace Jovanovich, 1981);

Cour d'assises (Paris: Gallimard, 1941); translated as *Justice* in *Chit of a Girl* (1949);

Il pleut bergère (Paris: Gallimard, 1941); translated as *Black Rain* in *Black Rain* (1949);

Maigret and M. l'Abbé, translated by Gilbert (London: Routledge, 1941; New York: Harcourt, Brace, 1942)—comprises *Le Relais d'Alsace* and *Le Port des brumes;*

Maigret Sits It Out, translated by Ludwig (London: Routledge/Toronto: Musson, 1941; New York: Harcourt, Brace, 1941)—comprises *L'Ecluse no. 1* and *Maigret;*

La Maison des sept jeunes filles (Paris: Gallimard, 1941);

L'Outlaw (Paris: Gallimard, 1941); translated by Howard Curtis as *The Outlaw* (San Diego: Harcourt Brace Jovanovich, 1986);

Le Voyageur de la Toussaint (Paris: Gallimard, 1941); translated by Sainsbury as *Strange Inheritance* (London: Routledge & Kegan Paul, 1950);

Affairs of Destiny, translated by Gilbert (London: Routledge/Toronto: Musson, 1942; New York: Harcourt, Brace, 1944)—comprises *Le Haut-mal* and *L'Homme de Londres;*

Le Fils Cardinaud (Paris: Gallimard, 1942); translated as *Young Cardinaud* in *The Sacrifice* (1956);

Maigret revient (Paris: Gallimard, 1942)—comprises *Cécile est morte*, translated by Ellenbogen as *Maigret and the Spinster* (London: Hamilton, 1977; New York: Harcourt Brace Jovanovich, 1977), *Les Caves du Majestic*, translated by Carolyn Hillier as *Maigret and the Hotel Majestic* (London: Hamilton, 1977; New York: Harcourt Brace Jovanovich, 1978), and *La Maison du juge*, translated by Ellenbogen as *Maigret in Exile* (London: Hamilton, 1978; New York: Harcourt Brace Jovanovich, 1979);

Oncle Charles s'est enfermé (Paris: Gallimard, 1942); translated as *Uncle Charles Has Locked Himself In* (San Diego: Harcourt Brace Jovanovich, 1987);

Two Latitudes, translated by Gilbert (London: Routledge/Toronto: Musson, 1942)—comprises *Le Passager du "Polarlys"* and *Le Coup de lune;*

La Vérité sur Bébé Donge (Paris: Gallimard, 1942); translated by Sainsbury as *The Trial of Bebe Donge* (London: Routledge & Kegan Paul, 1952); translated as *I Take this Woman* in *Satan's Children* (1953);

La Veuve Couderc (Paris: Gallimard, 1942); translated by John Petrie as *Ticket of Leave* (London:

Simenon with his first wife, Régine, 1936 (courtesy of Centre d'Etudes Georges Simenon, University of Liège)

Routledge & Kegan Paul/New York: British Book Service, 1954);

Les Dossiers de l'agence O. (Paris: Gallimard, 1943);

Escape in Vain, translated by Gilbert (London: Routledge/Toronto: Musson, 1943; New York: Harcourt, Brace, 1943)—comprises *Le Locataire* and *Les Suicidés;*

Havoc by Accident, translated by Gilbert (London: Routledge, 1943; New York: Harcourt, Brace, 1943)—comprises *Les Demoiselles de Concarneau* and *Le Blanc à lunettes;*

Le Petit Docteur (Paris: Gallimard, 1943); translated by Stewart as *The Little Doctor* (London: Hamilton, 1978; New York: Harcourt Brace Jovanovich, 1978);

Les Nouvelles Enquêtes de Maigret (Paris: Gallimard, 1944);

On the Danger Line, translated by Gilbert (London: Routledge, 1944; New York: Harcourt,

Brace, 1944)–comprises *Faubourg* and *Le Suspect;*

Le Rapport du gendarme (Paris: Gallimard, 1944); translated as *The Gendarme's Report* in *The Window over the Way* (1951);

Signé Picpus (Paris: Gallimard, 1944)–comprises *Signé Picpus*, translated by Sainsbury as *To Any Lengths* in *Maigret on Holiday* (1950), *L'Inspecteur Cadavre*, translated by Helen Thomson as *Maigret's Rival* (London: Hamilton, 1978; New York: Harcourt Brace Jovanovich, 1980), *Félicie est là*, translated by Ellenbogen as *Maigret and the Toy Village* (London: Hamilton, 1978; New York: Harcourt Brace Jovanovich, 1979), and *Nouvelles exotiques;*

L'Aîné des Ferchaux (Paris: Gallimard, 1945); translated by Sainsbury as *Magnet of Doom* (London: Routledge/Toronto: Musson, 1948); translated as *The First Born* (New York: Reynal & Hitchcock, 1949);

La Fenêtre des Rouet (Paris: Editions de la Jeune Parque, 1945); translated by Petrie as *Across the Street* (London: Routledge & Kegan Paul, 1954);

La Fuite de Monsieur Monde (Paris: Editions de la Jeune Parque, 1945); translated by Stewart as *Monsieur Monde Vanishes* (London: Hamilton, 1967; New York: Harcourt Brace Jovanovich, 1977);

Je me souviens (Paris: Presses de la Cité, 1945);

Le Cercle des Mahé (Paris: Gallimard, 1946);

Lost Moorings, translated by Gilbert (London: Routledge, 1946)–comprises *Chemin sans issue* and *Touriste de bananes;*

Les Noces de Poitiers (Paris: Gallimard, 1946); translated by Ellenbogen as *The Couple from Poitiers* (San Diego: Harcourt Brace Jovanovich, 1985);

Trois Chambres à Manhattan (Paris: Presses de la Cité, 1946); translated by Lawrence G. Blochman as *Three Beds in Manhattan* (Garden City: Doubleday, 1964; London: Hamilton, 1976);

Au bout du Rouleau (Paris: Presses de la Cité, 1947);

Le Clan des Ostendais (Paris: Gallimard, 1947);

Maigret et l'inspecteur malchanceux (Paris: Presses de la Cité, 1947)–comprises *Le Client le plus obstiné du monde*, translated as *The Most Obstinate Man in Paris* in *The Short Cases of Inspector Maigret* (1959), *Maigret et l'inspecteur malchanceux*, *On ne tue pas les pauvres types*, and *Le Témoignage de l'enfant de chœur;*

Lettre à mon juge (Paris: Presses de la Cité, 1947); translated by Louise Varèse as *Act of Passion* (New York: Prentice-Hall, 1952; London: Routledge & Kegan Paul, 1953);

Maigret à New York (Paris: Presses de la Cité, 1947); translated by Adrienne Foulke as *Maigret in New York's Underworld* (Garden City: Doubleday, 1955);

Maigret se fâche (Paris: Presses de la Cité, 1947);

Le Passager clandestin (Paris: Editions de la Jeune Parque, 1947); translated by Nigel Ryan as *The Stowaway* (London: Hamilton, 1957);

La Pipe de Maigret (Paris: Presses de la Cité, 1947);

Le Bilan Maletras (Paris: Gallimard, 1948); translated by Emily Read as *The Reckoning* (London: Hamilton, 1984; San Diego: Harcourt Brace Jovanovich, 1984);

Le Destin des Malou (Paris: Presses de la Cité, 1948); translated by Denis George as *The Fate of the Malous* (London: Hamilton, 1962);

La Jument perdue (Paris: Presses de la Cité, 1948);

Maigret et son mort (Paris: Presses de la Cité, 1948); translated by Stewart as *Maigret's Special Murder* (London: Hamilton, 1964); republished as *Maigret's Dead Man* (Garden City: Doubleday, 1954);

La Neige était sale (Paris: Presses de la Cité, 1948); translated by Varèse as *The Snow Was Black* (New York: Prentice-Hall, 1950); translated by Petrie as *The Stain on the Snow* (London: Routledge & Kegan Paul, 1953);

Pedigree (Paris: Presses de la Cité, 1948); translated by Robert Baldick (London: Hamilton, 1962);

Les Vacances de Maigret (Paris: Presses de la Cité, 1948); translated as *Maigret on Holiday* in *Maigret on Holiday* (1950); republished separately as *No Vacation for Maigret* (Garden City: Doubleday, 1953);

Black Rain, translated by Sainsbury (London: Routledge & Kegan Paul, 1949)–comprises *Les Rescapés du "Télémaque"* and *Il pleut bergère;*

Chit of a Girl, translated by Sainsbury (London: Routledge & Kegan Paul, 1949)–comprises *La Marie du port* and *Cour d'assises;*

Les Fantômes du chapelier (Paris: Presses de la Cité, 1949); translated as *The Hatter's Ghost* in *The Judge and the Hatter* (1956); translated by Willard R. Trask as *The Hatter's Phantom* (New York: Harcourt Brace Jovanovich, 1976);

Le Fond de la bouteille (Paris: Presses de la Cité, 1949); translated as *The Bottom of the Bottle* in *Tidal Waves* (1954);

Maigret chez le coroner (Paris: Presses de la Cité, 1949); translated by Francis Keene as *Maigret and the Coroner* (London: Hamilton, 1980); republished as *Maigret at the Coroner's* (New York: Harcourt Brace Jovanovich, 1980);

Maigret et la vieille dame (Paris: Presses de la Cité, 1949); translated by Robert Brain as *Maigret and the Old Lady* (London: Hamilton, 1958); published in *Maigret Cinq* (1965);

Mon Ami Maigret (Paris: Presses de la Cité, 1949); translated by Ryan as *My Friend Maigret* (London: Hamilton, 1956); republished as *The Methods of Maigret* (Garden City: Doubleday, 1957);

La Première Enquêtte de Maigret, 1913 (Paris: Presses de la Cité, 1949); translated by Brain as *Maigret's First Case* (London: Hamilton, 1958); published in *Maigret Cinq* (1965);

Les Quatre Jours du pauvre homme (Paris: Presses de la Cité, 1949); translated as *Four Days in a Lifetime* in *Satan's Children* (1953);

A Wife at Sea, translated by Sainsbury (London: Routledge & Kegan Paul, 1949)—comprises *Les Pitard* and *L'Assassin;*

L'Amie de Madame Maigret (Paris: Presses de la Cité, 1950); translated by Helen Sebba as *Madame Maigret's Own Case* (New York: Doubleday, 1959); republished as *Madame Maigret's Friend* (London: Hamilton, 1960);

L'Enterrement de Monsieur Bouvet (Paris: Presses de la Cité, 1950); translated by Eugene Mac-Cown as *The Burial of Monsieur Bouvet* (Garden City: Doubleday, 1955); republished as *Inquest on Bouvet* (London: Hamilton, 1958);

Maigret on Holiday, translated by Sainsbury (London: Routledge & Kegan Paul, 1950)—comprises *Signé Picpus* and *Les Vacances de Maigret;*

Un Nouveau dans la ville (Paris: Presses de la Cité, 1950);

Les Petits Cochons sans queue (Paris: Presses de la Cité, 1950);

Poisoned Relations, translated by Sainsbury (London: Routledge & Kegan Paul, 1950)—comprises *Monsieur La Souris* and *Les Sœurs Lacroix;*

Tante Jeanne (Paris: Presses de la Cité, 1950); translated by Sainsbury as *Aunt Jeanne* (London: Routledge & Kegan Paul, 1953);

Les Volets verts (Paris: Presses de la Cité, 1950); translated by Varèse as *The Heart of a Man* (New York: Prentice-Hall/Toronto: McLeod, 1951); published in *A Sense of Guilt* (1955);

Maigret au "Picratt's" (Paris: Presses de la Cité, 1951); translated as *Maigret in Montmartre* in *Maigret Right and Wrong* (1954); translated by Cornelia Schaeffer as *Inspector Maigret and the Strangled Stripper* (Garden City: Doubleday, 1954);

Maigret en meublé (Paris: Presses de la Cité, 1951); translated by Brain as *Maigret Takes a Room* (London: Hamilton, 1960); republished as *Maigret Rents a Room* (Garden City: Doubleday, 1961);

Maigret et la grande perche (Paris: Presses de la Cité, 1951); translated by J. Maclaren-Ross as *Maigret and the Burglar's Wife* (London: Hamilton, 1955); republished as *Inspector Maigret and the Burglar's Wife* (Garden City: Doubleday, 1956);

Marie qui louche (Paris: Presses de la Cité, 1951); translated by Thomson as *The Girl with a Squint* (New York: Harcourt Brace Jovanovich, 1978);

Les Mémoires de Maigret (Paris: Presses de la Cité, 1951); translated by Stewart as *Maigret's Memoirs* (London: Hamilton, 1963);

Un Noël de Maigret (Paris: Presses de la Cité, 1951)—comprises *Un Noël de Maigret*, translated as *Maigret's Christmas* in *The Short Cases of Inspector Maigret* (1959), *Sept petites croix dans un carnet*, and *Le Petit Restaurant des Ternes;*

Le Temps d'Anaïs (Paris: Presses de la Cité, 1951); translated by Varèse as *The Girl in His Past* (New York: Prentice-Hall, 1952; London: Hamilton, 1976);

Une Vie Comme neuve (Paris: Presses de la Cité, 1951); translated by Joanna Richardson as *A New Lease on Life* (London: Hamilton, 1963; New York: Doubleday, 1963);

The Window over the Way, translated by Sainsbury (London: Routledge & Kegan Paul/New York: British Book Service, 1951)—comprises *Les Gens d'en face* and *Le Rapport du gendarme;*

Les Frères Rico (Paris: Presses de la Cité, 1952); translated as *The Brothers Rico* in *Violent Ends* (1954); published in *Tidal Waves* (1954);

The House by the Canal, translated by Sainsbury (London: Routledge & Kegan Paul, 1952)—comprises *La Maison du canal* and *Le Clan des Ostendais;*

Maigret, Lognon et les gangsters (Paris: Presses de la Cité, 1952); translated by Varèse as *Inspector Maigret and the Killers* (Garden City: Doubleday, 1954); republished as *Maigret and the Gangsters* (London: Hamilton, 1974);

La Mort de Belle (Paris: Presses de la Cité, 1952); translated as *Belle* in *Violent Ends* (1954); published in *Tidal Waves* (1954);

Le Revolver de Maigret (Paris: Presses de la Cité, 1952); translated by Ryan as *Maigret's Revolver* (London: Hamilton, 1956);

Antoine et Julie (Paris: Presses de la Cité, 1953); translated as *The Magician* in *The Magician [and] The Widow* (1955); published separately (London: Hamilton, 1974);

L'Escalier de feu (Paris: Presses de la Cité, 1953); translated by Ellenbogen as *The Iron Staircase* (London: Hamilton, 1963; New York: Harcourt Brace Jovanovich, 1977);

Feux rouges (Paris: Presses de la Cité, 1953); translated as *Red Lights* in *Danger Ahead* (1955); republished as *The Hitchhiker* in *Destinations* (1955);

Maigret a peur (Paris: Presses de la Cité, 1953); translated by Margaret Duff as *Maigret Afraid* (London: Hamilton, 1961; San Diego: Harcourt Brace Jovanovich, 1983);

Maigret et l'homme du banc (Paris: Presses de la Cité, 1953); translated by Ellenbogen as *Maigret and the Man on the Boulevard* (London: Hamilton, 1975); republished as *Maigret and the Man on the Bench* (New York: Harcourt Brace Jovanovich, 1975);

Maigret se trompe (Paris: Presses de la Cité, 1953); translated as *Maigret's Mistake* in *Maigret Right and Wrong* (1954); published in *Five Times Maigret* (1964);

Satan's Children, translated by Varèse (New York: Prentice-Hall, 1953)—comprises *La Vérité sur Bébé Donge* and *Les Quatre Jours du pauvre homme;*

Le Bateau d'Emile (Paris: Gallimard, 1954);

Crime impuni (Paris: Presses de la Cité, 1954); translated by Varèse as *Fugitive* (Garden City: Doubleday, 1954); translated by Tony White as *Account Unsettled* (London: Hamilton, 1962);

Le Grand Bob (Paris: Presses de la Cité, 1954); translated by Eileen Howe as *Big Bob* (London: Hamilton, 1954);

L'Horloger d'Everton (Paris: Presses de la Cité, 1954); translated as *The Watchmaker of Everton* in *Danger Ahead* (1955); published with *The Witnesses* (1956);

Maigret à l'école (Paris: Presses de la Cité, 1954); translated by Daphne Woodward as *Maigret Goes to School* (London: Hamilton, 1957); published in *Five Times Maigret* (1964);

Maigret chez le ministre (Lakeville, Conn., 1954; Paris: Presses de la Cité, 1955); translated by Moura Budberg as *Maigret and the Minister* (London: Hamilton, 1969); republished as *Maigret and the Calame Report* (New York: Harcourt, Brace & World, 1969);

Maigret et la jeune morte (Paris: Presses de la Cité, 1954); translated by Woodward as *Maigret and the Young Girl* (London: Hamilton, 1955); republished as *Inspector Maigret and the Dead Girl* (Garden City: Doubleday, 1955);

Maigret Right and Wrong (London: Hamilton, 1954)—comprises *Maigret au "Picratt's,"* translated by Woodward as *Maigret in Montmartre*, and *Maigret se trompe*, translated by Alan Hodge as *Maigret's Mistake;*

On Land and Sea, translated by Victor Kosta (Garden City: Hanover House, 1954)—comprises *Le Passager du "Polarlys"* and *Les Gens d'en face;*

Les Témoins (Lakeville, Conn., 1954; Paris: Presses de la Cité, 1955); translated as *The Witnesses* in *The Judge and the Hatter* (1956); published with *The Watchmaker of Everton* (1956);

Tidal Waves (Garden City: Doubleday, 1954)—comprises *Le Fond de la bouteille*, translated by Schaeffer as *The Bottom of the Bottle, Les Frères Rico*, translated by Ernst Pawel as *The Brothers Rico*, and *La Mort de Belle*, translated by Varèse as *Belle;*

Violent Ends (London: Hamilton, 1954)—comprises *Les Frères Rico*, translated by Pawel as *The Brothers Rico*, and *La Mort de Belle*, translated by Varèse as *Belle;*

La Boule noire (Paris: Presses de la Cité, 1955);

Les Complices (Paris: Presses de la Cité, 1955); translated as *The Accomplices* in *The Blue Room [and] The Accomplices* (1964); published separately (London: Hamilton, 1966);

Danger Ahead, translated by Denny (London: Hamilton, 1955)—comprises *Feux rouges* and *L'Horloger d'Everton;*

Destinations (Garden City: Doubleday, 1955)—comprises *Feux rouges*, translated by Denny as *The Hitchhiker*, and *L'Enterrement de Monsieur Bouvet*, translated by MacCown as *The Burial of Monsieur Bouvet;*

The Magician [and] The Widow (Garden City: Doubleday, 1955)—comprises *Antoine et Julie,* translated by Sebba as *The Magician,* and *La Veuve Couderc,* translated by Petrie as *The Widow;*

Maigret et le corps sans tête (Lakeville, Conn., 1955; Paris: Presses de la Cité, 1955); translated by Ellenbogen as *Maigret and the Headless Corpse* (London: Hamilton, 1967; New York: Harcourt, Brace & World, 1968);

Maigret tend un piège (Paris: Presses de la Cité, 1955); translated by Woodward as *Maigret Sets a Trap* (London: Hamilton, 1965; New York: Harcourt, Brace & World, 1972);

A Sense of Guilt, translated by Woodward (London: Hamilton, 1955)–comprises *Chez Krull* and *Les Volets verts;*

Un Echec de Maigret (Paris: Presses de la Cité, 1956); translated by Woodward as *Maigret's Failure* (London: Hamilton, 1962); published in *A Maigret Trio* (1973);

En cas de malheur (Paris: Presses de la Cité, 1956); translated by Sebba as *In Case of Emergency* (Garden City: Doubleday, 1958; London: Hamilton, 1960);

The Judge and the Hatter (London: Hamilton, 1956)–comprises *Les Fantômes du chapelier,* translated by Ryan as *The Hatter's Ghost,* and *Les Témoins,* translated by Budberg as *The Witnesses;*

The Sacrifice (London: Hamilton, 1956)–comprises *Les Fiançailles de Mr. Hire,* translated by Woodward as *Mr. Hire's Engagement,* and *Le Fils Cardinaud,* translated by Brain as *Young Cardinaud;*

The Witnesses [and] The Watchmaker (Garden City: Doubleday, 1956)–comprises *L'Horloger d'Everton,* translated by Denny as *The Watchmaker of Everton,* and *Les Témoins,* translated by Budberg as *The Witnesses;*

Le Fils (Paris: Presses de la Cité, 1957); translated by Woodward as *The Son* (London: Hamilton, 1958);

Maigret s'amuse (Paris: Presses de la Cité, 1957); translated by Brain as *Maigret's Little Joke* (London: Hamilton, 1957); republished as *None of Maigret's Business* (Garden City: Doubleday, 1958);

Le Nègre (Paris: Presses de la Cité, 1957); translated by Sebba as *The Negro* (London: Hamilton, 1959);

Le Petit Homme d'Arkhangelsk (Paris: Presses de la Cité, 1957); translated by Ryan as *The Little Man from Archangel* (London: Hamilton, 1957); published with *Sunday* (1966);

Maigret voyage (Paris: Presses de la Cité, 1958); translated by Stewart as *Maigret and the Millionaires* (London: Hamilton, 1974; New York: Harcourt Brace Jovanovich, 1974);

Le Passage de la ligne (Paris: Presses de la Cité, 1958);

Le Président (Paris: Presses de la Cité, 1958); translated by Woodward as *The Premier* (London: Hamilton, 1961);

Les Scrupules de Maigret (Paris: Presses de la Cité, 1958); translated by Robert Eglesfield as *Maigret Has Scruples* (London: Hamilton, 1959); published in *Versus Inspector Maigret* (1960);

Une Confidence de Maigret (Paris: Presses de la Cité, 1959); translated by Lyn Moir as *Maigret Has Doubts* (London: Hamilton, 1968; New York: Harcourt Brace Jovanovich, 1982);

Dimanche (Paris: Presses de la Cité, 1959); translated by Ryan as *Sunday* (London: Hamilton, 1960); published with *The Little Man from Archangel* (1966);

The Short Cases of Inspector Maigret, translated by Blochman (Garden City: Doubleday, 1959);

La Vieille (Paris: Presses de la Cité, 1959); translated by Stewart as *The Grandmother* (New York: Harcourt Brace Jovanovich, 1978);

Maigret aux assises (Paris: Presses de la Cité, 1960); translated by Brain as *Maigret in Court* (London: Hamilton, 1961);

Maigret et les vieillards (Paris: Presses de la Cité, 1960); translated by Eglesfield as *Maigret in Society* (London: Hamilton, 1962); published in *A Maigret Trio* (1973);

L'Ours en peluche (Paris: Presses de la Cité, 1960); translated by John Clay as *Teddy Bear* (London: Hamilton, 1971; New York: Harcourt Brace Jovanovich, 1972);

Le Roman de l'homme (Paris: Presses de la Cité, 1960); translated by Bernard Frechtman as *The Novel of a Man* (New York: Harcourt, Brace & World, 1964);

Versus Inspector Maigret (Garden City: Doubleday, 1960)–comprises *Les Scrupules de Maigret,* translated by Eglesfield as *Maigret Has Scruples,* and *Maigret et les témoins récalcitrants,* translated by Woodward as *Maigret and the Reluctant Witnesses;*

Le Veuf (Paris: Presses de la Cité, 1960); translated by Baldick as *The Widower* (London: Hamilton, 1961);

Betty (Paris: Presses de la Cité, 1961); translated by Alastair Hamilton (London: Hamilton, 1975; New York: Harcourt Brace Jovanovich, 1975);

Denyse and Georges Simenon at the Venice Film Festival, August 1958 (courtesy of Keystone Press Agency)

Maigret et le voleur paresseux (Paris: Presses de la Cité, 1961); translated by Woodward as *Maigret and the Lazy Burglar* (London: Hamilton, 1963); published in *A Maigret Trio* (1973);

Le Train (Paris: Presses de la Cité, 1961); translated by Baldick as *The Train* (London: Hamilton, 1964);

Les Autres (Paris: Presses de la Cité, 1962); translated by Hamilton as *The Others* (London: Hamilton, 1975); republished as *The House on Quai Notre Dame* (New York: Harcourt Brace Jovanovich, 1975);

Maigret et le client du samedi (Paris: Presses de la Cité, 1962); translated by Tony White as *Maigret and the Saturday Caller* (London: Hamilton, 1964);

Maigret et les braves gens (Paris: Presses de la Cité, 1962); translated by Thomson as *Maigret and the Black Sheep* (London: Hamilton, 1976; New York: Harcourt Brace Jovanovich, 1976);

La Porte (Paris: Presses de la Cité, 1962); translated by Woodward as *The Door* (London: Hamilton, 1964);

Les Anneaux de Bicêtre (Paris: Presses de la Cité, 1963); translated by Stewart as *The Patient* (London: Hamilton, 1963; New York: Harcourt, Brace & World, 1964);

La Colère de Maigret (Paris: Presses de la Cité, 1963); translated by Eglesfield as *Maigret Loses His Temper* (London: Hamilton, 1964; New York: Harcourt Brace Jovanovich, 1974);

Ma Conviction profonde (Geneva: Cailler, 1963);

Maigret et le clochard (Paris: Presses de la Cité, 1963); translated by Stewart as *Maigret and the Dossier* (London: Hamilton, 1973); republished as *Maigret and the Bum* (New York: Harcourt Brace Jovanovich, 1973);

La Rue aux trois poussins (Paris: Presses de la Cité, 1963);

La Chambre bleue (Paris: Presses de la Cité, 1964); translated as *The Blue Room* in *The Blue Room [and] The Accomplices* (1964); published separately (London: Hamilton, 1965);

The Blue Room [and] The Accomplices (New York: Harcourt, Brace & World, 1964)—comprises *Les Complices*, translated by Frechtman as *The Accomplices*, and *La Chambre bleue*, translated by Ellenbogen as *The Blue Room;*

Five Times Maigret, translated by Woodward (New York: Harcourt, Brace, 1964)—comprises *Maigret au "Picratt's," Maigret se trompe, Maigret à l'école, Les Scrupules de Maigret,* and *Maigret et les témoins récalcitrants;*

L'Homme au petit chien (Paris: Presses de la Cité, 1964); translated by Stewart (London: Hamilton, 1965);

Maigret et le fantôme (Paris: Presses de la Cité, 1964); translated by Ellenbogen as *Maigret and the Ghost* (London: Hamilton, 1976); republished as *Maigret and the Apparition* (New York: Harcourt Brace Jovanovich, 1976);

Maigret se défend (Paris: Presses de la Cité, 1964); translated by Hamilton as *Maigret on the Defensive* (London: Hamilton, 1966); republished as *Maigret on the Defensive* (New York: Harcourt Brace Jovanovich, 1981);

Maigret Cinq, translated by Brain (New York: Harcourt, Brace, 1965)–comprises *Maigret et la vieille dame, La Première Enquête de Maigret, Maigret en meublé, Maigret et la jeune morte,* and *Maigret s'amuse;*

La Patience de Maigret (Paris: Presses de la Cité, 1965); translated by Hamilton as *The Patience of Maigret* (London: Hamilton, 1966); republished as *Maigret Bides His Time* (San Diego: Harcourt Brace Jovanovich, 1985);

Le Petit Saint (Paris: Presses de la Cité, 1965); translated by Frechtman as *The Little Saint* (New York: Harcourt, Brace & World, 1965; London: Hamilton, 1966);

Le Train de Venise (Paris: Presses de la Cité, 1965); translated by Hamilton as *The Venice Train* (London: Hamilton, 1974; New York: Harcourt Brace Jovanovich, 1974);

Le Confessional (Paris: Presses de la Cité, 1966); translated by Stewart as *The Confessional* (London: Hamilton, 1967; New York: Harcourt Brace Jovanovich, 1968);

La Mort d'Auguste (Paris: Presses de la Cité, 1966); translated by Frechtman as *The Old Man Dies* (New York: Harcourt, Brace & World, 1967; London: Hamilton, 1968);

Maigret et l'affaire Nahour (Paris: Presses de la Cité, 1966); translated by Hamilton as *Maigret and the Nahour Case* (London: Hamilton, 1967);

Sunday [and] The Little Man from Archangel, translated by Ryan (New York: Harcourt, Brace & World, 1966)–comprises *Dimanche* and *Le Petit Homme d'Arkhangelsk;*

Le Chat (Paris: Presses de la Cité, 1967); translated by Frechtman as *The Cat* (New York: Harcourt, Brace & World, 1967; London: Hamilton, 1972);

Le Démenagement (Paris: Presses de la Cité, 1967); translated by Christopher Sinclair-Stevenson as *The Neighbors* (London: Hamilton, 1968);

republished as *The Move* (New York: Harcourt, Brace & World, 1968);

Le Voleur de Maigret (Paris: Presses de la Cité, 1967); translated by Ryan as *Maigret's Pickpocket* (London: Hamilton, 1968; New York: Harcourt Brace Jovanovich, 1968);

L'Ami d'enfance de Maigret (Paris: Presses de la Cité, 1968); translated by Ellenbogen as *Maigret's Boyhood Friend* (London: Hamilton, 1970; New York: Harcourt Brace Jovanovich, 1970);

Maigret à Vichy (Paris: Presses de la Cité, 1968); translated by Ellenbogen as *Maigret Takes the Waters* (London: Hamilton, 1969); republished as *Maigret in Vichy* (New York: Harcourt Brace Jovanovich, 1969);

Maigret hésite (Paris: Presses de la Cité, 1968); translated by Moir as *Maigret Hesitates* (London: Hamilton, 1970; New York: Harcourt Brace Jovanovich, 1970);

La Main (Paris: Presses de la Cité, 1968); translated by Budberg as *The Man on the Bench in the Barn* (London: Hamilton, 1970; New York: Harcourt Brace Jovanovich, 1970);

La Prison (Paris: Presses de la Cité, 1968); translated by Moir as *The Prison* (London: Hamilton, 1969; New York: Harcourt Brace Jovanovich, 1969);

Il y a encore des noisetiers (Paris: Presses de la Cité, 1969);

Maigret et le tueur (Paris: Presses de la Cité, 1969); translated by Moir as *Maigret and the Killer* (London: Hamilton, 1971; New York: Harcourt Brace Jovanovich, 1971);

Novembre (Paris: Presses de la Cité, 1969); translated by Stewart as *November* (London: Hamilton, 1970; New York: Harcourt Brace Jovanovich, 1970);

La Folle de Maigret (Paris: Presses de la Cité, 1970); translated by Ellenbogen as *Maigret and the Madwoman* (London: Hamilton, 1972; New York: Harcourt Brace Jovanovich, 1972);

Maigret et le marchand de vin (Paris: Presses de la Cité, 1970); translated by Ellenbogen as *Maigret and the Wine Merchant* (London: Hamilton, 1971; New York: Harcourt Brace Jovanovich, 1971);

Quand j'étais vieux (Paris: Presses de la Cité, 1970); translated by Helen Eustis as *When I Was Old* (New York: Harcourt Brace Jovanovich, 1971; London: Hamilton, 1972);

Le Riche Homme (Paris: Presses de la Cité, 1970); translated by Stewart as *The Rich Man* (London: Hamilton, 1971; New York: Harcourt Brace Jovanovich, 1971);

La Cage de verre (Paris: Presses de la Cité, 1971); translated by Antonia White as *The Glass Cage* (London: Hamilton, 1973; New York: Harcourt Brace Jovanovich, 1973);

La Disparition d'Odile (Paris: Club Français du Livre, 1971); translated by Moir as *The Disappearance of Odile* (London: Hamilton, 1972; New York: Harcourt Brace Jovanovich, 1972);

Maigret et l'homme tout seul (Paris: Presses de la Cité, 1971); translated by Ellenbogen as *Maigret and the Loner* (London: Hamilton, 1975; New York: Harcourt Brace Jovanovich, 1975);

Maigret et l'indicateur (Paris: Presses de la Cité, 1971); translated by Moir as *Maigret and the Flea* (London: Hamilton, 1972); republished as *Maigret and the Informer* (New York: Harcourt Brace Jovanovich, 1972);

Choix de Simenon, edited by Frank W. Lindsay and Anthony M. Nazzaro (New York: Appleton-Century-Crofts, 1972);

Les Innocents (Paris: Presses de la Cité, 1972); translated by Ellenbogen as *The Innocents* (London: Hamilton, 1973; New York: Harcourt Brace Jovanovich, 1973);

Maigret et Monsieur Charles (Paris: Presses de la Cité, 1972); translated by Marianne A. Sinclair as *Maigret and Monsieur Charles* (London: Hamilton, 1973);

A Maigret Trio, translated by Woodward (New York: Harcourt, Brace & World, 1973)—comprises *Un Echec de Maigret*, *Maigret et les vieillards*, and *Maigret et le voleur paresseux;*

La Piste du Hollandais (Paris: Presses de la Cité, 1973);

Lettre à ma mère (Paris: Presses de la Cité, 1974); translated by Ralph Manheim as *Letter to My Mother* (London: Hamilton, 1976; New York: Harcourt Brace Jovanovich, 1976);

Un Homme comme un autre (Paris: Presses de la Cité, 1975);

Des Traces de pas (Paris: Presses de la Cité, 1975);

A la découverte de la France, edited by Francis Lacassin and Gilbert Sigaux (Paris: Union Générale d'Editions, 1976);

A la recherche de l'homme nu, edited by Lacassin and Sigaux (Paris: Union Générale d'Editions, 1976);

Maigret's Christmas, translated by Stewart (London: Hamilton, 1976; New York: Harcourt Brace Jovanovich, 1977);

Les Petits Hommes (Paris: Presses de la Cité, 1976);

Vent du nord, vent du sud (Paris: Presses de la Cité, 1976);

A l'abri de notre arbre (Paris: Presses de la Cité, 1977);

L'Aîné des Ferchaux (Paris: Gallimard, 1977);

Un Banc au soleil (Paris: Presses de la Cité, 1977);

De la cave au grenier (Paris: Presses de la Cité, 1977);

Maigret's Pipe, translated by Stewart (London: Hamilton, 1977; New York: Harcourt Brace Jovanovich, 1978);

La Main dans la main (Paris: Presses de la Cité, 1978);

Tant que je suis vivant (Paris: Presses de la Cité, 1978);

Vacances obligatoires (Paris: Presses de la Cité, 1978);

A quoi bon jurer? (Paris: Presses de la Cité, 1979);

Au-delà de ma porte-fenêtre (Paris: Presses de la Cité, 1979);

Je suis resté un enfant de chœur (Paris: Presses de la Cité, 1979);

Point-virgule (Paris: Presses de la Cité, 1979);

Les Libertés qu'il nous reste (Paris: Presses de la Cité, 1980);

Maigret and the Mad Killers (Garden City: Doubleday, 1980);

On dit que j'ai soixante-quinze ans (Paris: Presses de la Cité, 1980);

Le Prix d'un homme (Paris: Presses de la Cité, 1980);

Quand vient le froid (Paris: Presses de la Cité, 1980);

La Femme endormie (Paris: Presses de la Cité, 1981);

Jour et nuit (Paris: Presses de la Cité, 1981);

Mémoires intimes (Paris: Presses de la Cité, 1981); translated by Harold J. Salemson as *Intimate Memoirs* (San Diego, New York & London: Harcourt Brace Jovanovich, 1984).

Collection: *Œuvres complètes*, 72 volumes, edited by Gilbert Sigaux (Lausanne: Rencontre, 1967-1973).

André Gide considered Georges Simenon to be one of the finest novelists of the century. He even went so far in 1939 as to state (as quoted in *Cahiers de la Petite Dame*, volume 4, 1977, p. 263) that he was "le plus grand peut-être et le plus vraiment romancier" (the greatest, the one who is most truly a novelist). This judgment is shared and even surpassed by those admirers who consider him the best novelist of all time. Yet to innumerable readers in France and throughout the world he is little more than a prolific author of detective novels. Although apparently contradictory, these two views–one coming from a demanding critic–can be reconciled if one realizes that in detective fiction plot is supreme, making it appeal to those who read for the story alone, and yet, since a measure of craftsmanship and considerable invention, sometimes great ingenuity, are required, the detective novel also appeals to connoisseurs of fiction, especially those who see it as a construct of the mind, an intellectual game. The genre also favors the development of fictional psychology and allows a writer to attach to the plot a wide range of observations on human society and behavior. This has been the case to some extent since the Gothic novels of Ann Radcliffe, which are among the ancestors of the modern detective novel, the tales of Edgar Allan Poe, and the classic works of the so-called Golden Age of the genre in England, best illustrated by Agatha Christie.

In fact, the mystery novel and detective novel are not so far apart as may be supposed from other types of fiction, despite the unfavorable reputation of the genre among those who disdain such famous French examples as the cheap thrillers of the *Fantomas* series of Marcel Allain and the charming but unpretentious Arsène Lupin books by Maurice Leblanc, featuring a gentleman *cambrioleur* (burglar) who sometimes turns detective himself. As Michel Butor has pointed out, fiction often develops around a process of discovery or disclosing of truths, whether to hero or reader or both. There are elements of detection in many novels not normally associated with the genre, including, in the twentieth century, Gide's works, such as *L'Immoraliste* (*The Immoralist*, 1902)–a psychological mystery–*Isabelle* (1911)–a literal mystery in which the narrator tries to act as detective–and *Les Faux-Monnayeurs* (*The Counterfeiters*, 1925), which includes both adult and juvenile criminals. To these can be added Marcel Proust's *A la recherche du temps perdu* (*Remembrance of Things Past*, 1913-1927)–again, a psychological mystery, complete with clues; François Mauriac's *Thérèse Desqueyroux* (1927); and most of Georges Bernanos's novels, to name only some. The adoption by French New Novelists such as Butor, Alain Robbe-Grillet, and Claude Ollier of certain formulas of the detective novel shows how it can be adapted to the serious purpose of revealing aspects of reality; indeed, one of the oldest detective plots known, the Oedipus story, is also the

material of great classical drama. Simenon's own career shows the connection, for he wrote, in addition to his detective stories, countless other works–which sometimes he called *romans durs* (hard novels) or *romans sérieux* (serious novels), sometimes *romans-romans*, and in which his earlier experience at recounting crimes and detection served him well in developing plot and character and establishing atmosphere.

Georges Joseph Chrétien Simenon was born in Liège, Belgium, on 13 February 1903, the son of Désiré Simenon, an accountant, and Henriette Brüll Simenon. His younger brother was born three years later. His antecedents were mostly from the petite bourgeoisie and seem to have been of Breton, Dutch, and German blood as well as Belgian. One of his biographers, Stanley G. Eskin, has noted the importance of the boy's childhood experiences in the development of his character. He seems to have felt considerable disappointment with respect to his mother, a somewhat mean-spirited, class-conscious, and neurotic woman who instinctively emphasized the unimportant. (She was superstitious enough to have his birthdate registered as 12 February, fearing the inauspicious number thirteen, and she was constantly warning him about what he should avoid doing so that he would not be like the riffraff.) He admired his father, who worked for an insurance agency and was the image of orderliness in habits and mind. His death in 1921 deprived the boy of an admired model. There were countless aunts, uncles, and cousins on both sides, some more successful than others; a number of them, particularly the down-and-out Uncle Léopold, seem to have furnished models for characters or types in Simenon's novels. To the wide range of family members that the boy could observe were added a number of roomers, once his mother decided to take in lodgers to augment her husband's too-modest salary. A number of these had come from Eastern Europe to study in Liège; they were, as a rule, strange, or at least appeared so to the boy.

Simenon attended a number of local schools, including the Collège Saint-Louis and the Collège Saint-Servais, which he left at age fifteen, when his father's heart trouble was discovered, in order to start earning a living. He did a variety of odd jobs, read a good deal, and wrote for his own amusement, perhaps with the vague idea of becoming a professional writer. In 1919 he got a job on the *Gazette de Liège*, where he remained until 1922, and was very successful, espe-

Simenon with his daughter, Marie-Georges (photo François Gonet)

cially for a beginner, reporting on many different topics and even writing his own column. He associated with the arty and bohemian crowd of Liège, centered around the Académie des Beaux-Arts, but he did not envisage himself as a garret poet, despite some literary aspirations, and his tastes, it would become clear, were too expensive for him to adopt such an existence.

In December 1922, after having fulfilled his military service, partly in occupied Germany, Simenon left Liège and went to Paris to pursue his journalistic and literary career. He was provided with letters of introduction to a few minor

writers and others. Thanks to one of these contacts he obtained a job as a factotum for a literary hack and right-wing political organizer; this led to a position as secretary to an aristocrat whom he followed from residence to residence. Thanks to the time spent with these employers he was able to observe a variety of human specimens that he had not seen in Liège, including members of the upper nobility. He eventually met some better-known writers, including the poet Paul Fort, the nationalist novelist Maurice Barrès, and Colette, who was literary editor of the newspaper *Matin* and who accepted some of

Simenon's short stories for its pages. Paris, and especially the colorful sections such as Montmartre and Montparnasse, held immense charm for him and is the locale of many of his stories and novels. It is, however, often not the Paris of bohemians and artists or that of tourist guides and postcards, but rather the city of its residents, seen as working people see it, from the sidewalk or a shop or the open windows of a nondescript apartment.

Simenon's first novel, the pseudonymous *Au pont des Arches* (On the Bridge of Arches), written when he was sixteen, appeared in 1921. (For a bibliography of Simenon's pseudonymous publications see Stanley G. Eskin, *Simenon: A Critical Biography* [1987], pp. 275-279.) Under some seventeen or eighteen different pseudonyms, he composed before the end of the decade literally hundreds of stories, many of them somewhat titillating treatments of sexual themes, and nearly two hundred potboiler novels of adventure (including westerns), romance, eroticism, and detection. This frenetic writing pace allowed him to live from 1924 on by his pen, which had already been sharpened by journalism; it also permitted him to develop his considerable gifts for characterization and taught him the value of a good plot. Perhaps it was also responsible for his distaste for rewriting (he later claimed that he never revised; other indications are that he did sometimes re-read to pare down his already spare narrative): how could a hack writer find time to do so, and to what purpose? It was, in any case, the sort of literary apprenticeship that will lead to nothing in the indifferent writer but, in a man of talent, affords an unrivaled chance to sharpen his skills. It was not only practical considerations, however, that dictated such a pace, at least in the following decades, when his popularity would have allowed him to live comfortably without selling so many books. There was in him a compulsive streak that usually took the form of obsessive writing and sexual adventures but also was displayed in other ways, such as the acquisition of furniture and properties (including houses he hardly lived in) and extensive travel, almost unrelentingly for a while.

After 1929 he began using his own name. Starting in the next year, he published more than eighty novels featuring the detective Maigret and well over a hundred *romans durs*, which he wished to have taken seriously, as literature. If one adds to these his pseudonymous works and his volumes of memoirs and autobiography—more than a score—one arrives, accord-

Simenon, circa 1968 (photograph copyright © Jerry Bauer)

ing to Eskin's count, at some 418 separate volumes, not counting short stories. Increasingly, after World War II, Simenon favored the social and psychological novel over the mystery novel. His works have been translated into fifty-five languages and have reached immense worldwide sales figures; a UNESCO survey of 1972, quoted by Fenton Bresler, indicates that he is the most translated writer in the world after Lenin. More than fifty of his books have been made into films and some have been adapted for television.

Simenon was, from adolescence, strongly attracted to, even obsessed with, women and boasted in print of his conquests (which his good looks and charm, and later his fame, facilitated). It appears that he sought sensual pleasure with women of all classes, including ordinary prostitutes. During both his marriages there were many periods when in essence he was living with two women (or more) in a ménage à trois. His novels furnish many reflections of these relationships and of a few women in particular, including his wives and the American dancer Josephine Baker, one of the most talked-about attractions in Paris in the 1920s, with whom he was apparently in love. Something of his attitude toward relationships between the sexes—an attitude both of casualness and a highly developed amateur's appreciation—can be seen in Maigret's matter-of-fact approach toward sexuality. In certain of the nondetective novels, such as *Le Temps d'Anaïs* (1951; translated as *The Girl in His Past*, 1952), sexuality is a principal topic.

On 24 March 1923 Simenon married Régine Renchon, a student from the Académie des Beaux-Arts in Liège, to whom he gave the nickname Tigy. The sister of a friend, she came from a proper family but was set on a career as a painter. They had become engaged before Simenon left Liège; she followed him to Paris to pursue her painting, but they returned briefly to Liège for the wedding. It does not seem to have been a marriage of love; he considered her jealous and continued to seek out relationships with a wide variety of women. The marriage produced one son, Marc, born in 1939.

As Simenon had increasing success with his popular novels of the 1920s, paid for by line count, and his wife also sold some paintings, they were able to move from their cramped quarters to an apartment on the Place des Vosges, known for its beautiful seventeenth-century townhouses, and then to leave Paris for extended periods. They began by taking vacations first on the Channel coast, then on a Mediterranean island not far from Toulon, and later, by boat, on the canals of central and northern France and eventually as far as the North Sea, Norway, and Lapland. In 1928 he bought a fifteen-foot boat, the *Ginette*, where he did a great deal of writing as well as touring. The following year he replaced it with a thirty-foot vessel, the *Ostrogoth*, in which he and his wife lived for over two years. He continued his writing pace, some eighty pages a day, even in dry dock. In addition to his novels, he turned out stories for a publication called *Détective*, edited by Joseph Kessel and his brother Georges. He also contributed to several other magazines and newspapers. There are numerous reflections in Simenon's fiction of life on board, his fishing expeditions, the ports they visited, and sights along the canals. For instance, the novella "Sous peine de mort" (Under Death Sentence) is set in a small Mediterranean fishing port; Simenon evokes graphically its docks and ferry, the houses

rising from the shore, and the daily routine, which serve as the backdrop for an outstanding study of the confrontation of enemies who had never met before.

After their return to Paris the couple lived in a fashionable section of the city, and Simenon associated with some of the most famous people of the day, both in the arts and in society. Later in the decade he moved to a country place at Nieul-sur-Mer, near La Rochelle, on the Atlantic coast. In the interval he and Tigy lived on the Riviera and elsewhere on the Mediterranean coast, among other locations. They had made a trip around the world (at the expense of several newspapers), by way of New York, Central and South America, several island groups in the Pacific, Australia, the Indian Ocean, and the Suez canal. They also had visited Africa, where Simenon was disgusted with the colonial representatives (including his own brother, in the Belgian Congo) but rather taken with the primitive tribes. These travels left many traces in his fiction, although even before seeing such distant spots he had used them as the settings for many stories and novels, relying upon atlases and encyclopedias for background information and details of local color. *Le Coup de lune* (1933; translated as *Tropic Moon* in *Two Latitudes*, 1942), for instance, is set in Libreville in the Congo and is based on some gossip he picked up there as well as his observations; it was the object of an unsuccessful lawsuit by a hotel keeper who thought she had been used as a model for an unsavory character.

Although the appeal of Simenon's novels is more varied than those who know only his detective stories may realize, he was long known chiefly as the creator of Commissioner Maigret, a likable, rather ordinary investigator of the *police judiciaire* (criminal investigation unit) in Paris. It is difficult to establish with certainty the date of conception of this figure, known by all connoisseurs of the genre. The name was used in *Train de nuit* (Night Train), a novel composed in 1930 and published under the pen name Christian Brulls; the figure to whom it shortly corresponded—a middle-aged, somewhat portly police inspector—appeared in other texts at the end of the 1920s. In *Pietr-le-Letton* (1931; translated as *The Case of Peter the Lett* in *Inspector Maigret Investigates*, 1933) the name and the figure have come together. The novel also introduces other recurring characters, including the inspector's wife and his associate Torrence. The

Teresa, Simenon's companion since 1970, circa 1980 (courtesy of Centre d'Etudes Georges Simenon, University of Liège)

first starting in 1936, the second in the early 1940s with the publication of *Maigret revient* (*Maigret Returns*, 1942), a one-volume collection of three novels, including the outstanding *Les Caves du Majestic* (translated as *Maigret and the Hotel Majestic*, 1977), *Cécile est morte* (translated as *Maigret and the Spinster*, 1977), and *La Maison du juge* (translated as *Maigret in Exile*, 1978).

Maigret is married, wears a bowler hat, smokes a pipe, is often seen warming himself near a stove, and is at home with ordinary people–"les petites gens"–who can be found in modest cafés and shops. He not only brings a kind of unity to the multiplicity of Simenon's detective fiction; he seems to be an alter ego of the author, who also smokes a pipe. (In his habits, he also resembles the author's father.) Unlike his counterpart in detective novels of the Golden Age, he does not proceed by systematic, rigorous induction, based on an accumulation of often odd pieces of evidence that, together, produce the only possible conclusion; his method, if it can be called that, is closer to intuition, or a sort of intellectual sympathy. Intuition is based on observation and involvement; he is not an aristocrat in slippers and only rarely plays the role of the armchair detective. He studies the locale and atmosphere of the crime, the streets, cafés, and other spots frequented by suspects. Simenon writes of him in *La Pipe de Maigret* (*Maigret's Pipe*, 1947): "Il était là, comme une éponge, à s'imprégner lentement de tout ce qui suintait autour de lui" (He was there, like a sponge, letting everything that oozed around him penetrate him).

Maigret has been compared to the tough detectives of the American "hard-boiled" school of detective fiction (Raymond Chandler and Dashiell Hammett both admired him). Although there is less gore and crude violence in many of the Maigret stories than in the typical story by the Americans, the commissioner is capable, if the circumstances require it, of wrestling with a burly man younger than himself, throwing him down, and securing his revolver; he prefers also to do much of the spade work himself, questioning witnesses, pursuing leads, following a suspect in the streets. To some degree he disdains the judicial process that should normally follow the discovery and arrest of a suspect; in *Pietr-le-Letton* he lets the criminal kill himself, rather than take him into custody forcibly.

His success is based on a generous measure of psychology, not only the insight and induction that Simenon must grant to him, but also, in the

plot involves international intrigue, fraud, and the murder of Maigret's own brother.

Maigret appears in a score of novels from the early 1930s, of which one of the best examples is *Le Chien jaune* (1931; translated as *A Face for a Clue* in *Patience of Maigret*, 1939). They were a great commercial success and, with exceptions, were well received by the press. Among well-known critics who from the earliest volumes praised the Maigret books, or at least some aspects of them, were the poet and critic Jean Cassou and the novelist Robert Brasillach; Janet Flanner (Genêt), writing in the *New Yorker*, predicted great future success for Simenon. There were two other sequences of Maigret novels, the portraits of other characters, plausible motivation. Maigret relies on his understanding of others, which allows him to put himself in their positions. His thesis is that a criminal is not usually a deviant being, marked from the start by the essence of criminality, but rather an ordinary person, like millions of others, who finds himself one day in a situation from which he can extricate himself only by an illegal, sometimes violent act. There is a peculiar sympathy in Maigret for those on the margin of society, the *malchanceux* (unlucky ones) and *ratés* (failures); this sympathy is seen likewise in Simenon's other fiction. While far from a failure himself, Simenon had seen failure at close range, partly in his own family at Liège and also among the boarders and others he had known as a boy. This tendency must not, however, be taken as full-fledged social criticism, which is not developed systematically in his fiction. (Even his unfavorable observations on colonial administrators during his travels in central Africa did not lead to a topical essay, but only to scattered comments.)

The gift of understanding character, together with interest in it, seems to have been Simenon's from the start. He wanted to know how everyone else lived, what it was like for others to go home to their families in the evenings, to do their work, to follow their routines. This pursuit of the human being, from the inside as well as the outside, which may have been one of the things that appealed to Gide, produced convincing portraits. Simenon's characters are not just eccentrics with one or two striking features that mark them for the reader's memory and indicate the use to which they will be put in the plot; they are portrayed as they would be in a social novel, for what they are and what they reveal about their milieus and humankind. The plot exists as much to reveal them as it does for itself. As R.-M. Albérès writes in *Histoire du roman moderne*, "Un roman de Simenon est, en effet, toujours construit *autour* d'un fait divers–généralement un crime–mais il le dépasse, dans la mesure où il ne fait que l'utiliser pour révéler le fond un peu terne de la conscience humaine et ses mensonges" (A Simenon novel is, to be sure, always built *around* a small incident–generally a crime–but it goes beyond it, to the degree that it uses it only to reveal the somewhat dull heart of human conscience and its lies). In Simenon's hands the detective novel thus approaches the realistic novel in the Balzacian mode; indeed, he has been compared to Balzac for his evocation of places and characters–in both his detective and nondetective fiction–as well as his inventiveness and prolific output.

Simenon's style illustrates what the romantic-realistic writer Prosper Mérimée called the best style: the one that goes unnoticed. It is lean, quick, sometimes almost telegraphic. It is the style both of an observer, who depicts things and people through rapid characterizing touches, and a thinker, with flashes of insight but without laborious reproduction of the thought process. Colette, said Simenon, told him that he must cease writing "literature"–that is, abandon pretentiousness and stop looking for refined stylistic effects. His use of language is almost always entirely pragmatic: every sentence is to serve a purpose of either setting the scene, advancing the plot, developing character, or suggesting something about human behavior. He is a master at quick characterization. A fat woman in a negligee who is seen washing the sidewalk in front of her doorstep; a woman retired from a creamery, her complexion still fair but her eyes red around the edges, who spends her time exchanging unfinished sentences with a neighbor about the shortcomings of their menfolk; a middle-aged widow, in shock over her husband's death the day before but dressed and made up with consummate taste–these characters and countless others are quickly sketched in such a way that the reader senses immediately their essential characteristics, the things that make them different from others.

Characterization and exposition are often accomplished in dialogue. This is eminently practical and allows the novelist to display his keen ear for a variety of speech patterns. It contributes to the fast pace of much of his fiction and suggests that for him speech reveals the person; it also is a factor in the working out of the solution, as Maigret asks questions, listens to the answers, perhaps takes a different tack, and lets his interlocutors indicate, by what they both reveal and conceal, how he should next proceed. Simenon also develops, in the Balzacian manner, the relationship between the milieu and the characters. He is deft at evoking an ambience, such as a Paris café, a run-down inn on the outskirts of the city, or a drab suburban apartment and its occupants, on the borderline between respectability and poverty. This does not mean, however, that he agrees with the nineteenth-century naturalists that the environment dictates character; rather, objects and places reveal character.

Simenon at his home in Lausanne, April 1979 (photograph by Ben Lee)

In the last years of the 1930s Simenon and his wife, and then their young son, Marc, continued their peregrinations in Europe, some prompted by political events, others by his whims. They spent the early months of World War II at Nieul and most of the rest of the war period in Vendée, living alternately in town and on a vast farm, well provided with livestock and produce. When the war ended and travel was again possible, at least for those who could persuade the authorities to grant them visas, Simenon decided to go to North America. He and his family arrived in New York in October 1945. He was very much pleased with the city—one of his love affairs with places, he later wrote. They soon moved to Canada, however, settling near Montreal.

Simenon's marriage to Tigy was remarkably enduring, if one considers his habit of pursuing other women and the demands made on her strength and patience by the frequent changes of residence and lengthy travels. In the 1930s there was a crisis, provoked by his behavior on shipboard in the Pacific Ocean, but it was weathered, and the birth of Marc helped cement their relationship, which was, as he wrote later, a marriage of friendship. It was greatly strained, however, in the postwar years and then ended when Simenon became involved in a liaison that proved more serious than others. In 1945, in New York, while Tigy and Marc were in Canada, Simenon met Denyse (or Denise, as he spells it) Ouimet, a French Canadian, then twenty-five years old. The best-seller *Trois Chambres à Manhattan* (1946; translated as *Three Beds in Manhattan*, 1964), an excellent example of his nondetective fiction, recounts, in barely veiled terms, their meeting and the beginning of the passionate liaison that ensued. Like many other Simenon novels, it is full of local color, describing their prowling about in New York, in rather drab settings (a departure from fact); it is also marked by scenes of heavy drinking, quarrels, and fits of jealousy. It was admired by the novelist Pierre Benoit and the filmmaker Jean Renoir, but it was Marcel Carné who made a movie of it in 1965.

For some years Denyse served as Simenon's secretary and mistress, accompanying him, Tigy, Marc, and other household members from Montreal to New York to Florida to Arizona. She became his second wife on 22 June 1950, after Tigy obtained a divorce in Reno, Nevada. They had three children, Jean (born in September 1949), Marie-Georges (born in February 1953), and Pierre (born in May 1959).

After living for a while in California, Simenon and Denyse returned to the East, taking up residence on a huge estate in Connecticut, where they remained until 1955. During this period he composed some twenty-six volumes. He remained fond of the United States, where fifteen of his novels are set, many in Florida and Arizona. The family subsequently lived near Cannes, in France, and then in Switzerland, near Lausanne.

This marriage also was ultimately a failure, and in 1970 or 1971 (the accounts vary), after several temporary separations, the two finally parted, on very bad terms, without divorcing because of the financial complications that would have ensued. Both husband and wife drank excessively, and in Simenon's novels of the period alcohol plays a significant role–a point he has in common with Raymond Chandler. Denyse was intermittently under psychiatric care. She wrote a roman à clef, *Un Oiseau pour le chat* (A Bird for the Cat), to portray herself and her husband (she saw herself as a bird with whom the cat played). The subsequent suicide in 1978 of Marie-Georges, known as Marie-Jo, whom Simenon adored, brought him great grief. Like her mother, she had been under the care of a psychiatrist. She had been driven to despair, he claimed, by her mother's book. Under the pseudonym Odile Dessane, Denyse published another roman à clef, *Le Phallus d'or* (The Golden Phallus), stronger this time, portraying a sexually obsessed egomaniac.

Simenon recounted events leading up to his daughter's death, and much of his earlier life, in *Mémoires intimes* (1981; translated as *Intimate Memoirs*, 1984), one of the principal sources of information on Simenon's life. It is a massive work, somewhat self-serving even though self-accusatory. While the style is not remarkable, the characters visible on its pages often are, not excluding the author himself. In an appendix he included scraps of Marie-Jo's own writing (letters, transcriptions of lengthy cassette recordings she made, and songs she composed and sang, accompanying herself on the guitar). This autobiographical work was preceded by others, including a memoir, *Je me souviens* (I Remember, 1945), and a fictionalized account of his life, *Pedigree* (1948; translated, 1962). The former was written with Simenon's first son in mind, at a time when the novelist had been told (because of a misdiagnosis) that he had only two years to live; it was to acquaint the boy with his father and his paternal ancestors. The second, much lengthier, grew out of the first after Gide suggested to Simenon that he should tell his past in the form of a novel rather than by employing the customary, less interesting, first person. He also published some of his diary under the title *Quand j'étais vieux* (1970; translated as *When I Was Old*, 1971) to mixed reviews. He published no fiction after 1972, with *Maigret et Monsieur Charles* (translated in 1973).

Simenon's next companion was an Italian woman named Teresa, who entered his household as a maid while he was still living with Denyse and for a time acted as both servant and mistress. He is extremely reticent about her, and little biographic information has been gleaned by biographers and other interviewers, although Simenon revealed some intimate details of their relationship.

Simenon professed to disdain honors and once said he would refuse election to the Académie Française, if it took place, or the Nobel Prize, for which he had been rumored to be a candidate. But in 1952 he accepted election to the Académie Royale Belge de Langue et Littérature Françaises, sailing to Belgium from the United States so that he could be inducted. He was also a member of the American Academy of Arts and Letters and was president of the Mystery Writers of America. His reputation as a writer of outstanding detective fiction is worldwide, but critical opinion on him varies considerably. He was admired as an author and was personally liked by a large number of other writers, including François Mauriac, Jean Cocteau, Anaïs Nin, Henry Miller, and Thornton Wilder. Although he attempted to persuade critics and publishers that he should be taken seriously as an author of *romans sérieux*, sales figures suggest that the Maigret series and a few other books in the same vein have the most appeal, and his fame continues to rest principally on them. This is probably appropriate. What he wrote about in other novels–family, love, conflict, failure, the desire to escape from untenable situations or oneself–is the stuff of much fiction in France and elsewhere; some of it is excellent, some ordinary. Despite his ambitions to surpass himself, and the convictions of friends that he possessed the genius to do it, he was not able to give to these topics a treatment that would make them stand out, not through lack of craft but lack of the unusual insight, the thoughtfulness, the probing style that mark the great realists. As Gide wrote in his *Journal 1939-1949*, "Les *sujets* de Simenon sont souvent d'un intérêt psychologique et éthique profond; mais insuffisamment indiqués, comme s'il ne se rendait pas compte lui-même de leur importance" (Simenon's subjects often have deep psychological and ethical interest; but they are insufficiently indicated, as though he himself did not realize their importance). His serious novels do not offer wisdom or illumination, and, despite the strong characterization, the reader does not enter into their world, as is the case with Mauriac and Roger Martin du Gard. In the detective mode, however, his work sets the standard, rather than following it; there, his gifts for character portrayal and plot development (including the creation of suspense and the ironic twist) and his sense of the dynamics of human action work together to produce a fictional mechanism that works on all levels.

Bibliography:

Trudee Young, *Georges Simenon* (Metuchen, N.J.: Scarecrow Press, 1976).

Biographies:

Fenton Bresler, *The Mystery of Georges Simenon* (New York: Beaufort Books, 1983);

Stanley G. Eskin, *Simenon: A Critical Biography* (Jefferson, N.C. & London: McFarland, 1987)– includes bibliography of Simenon's pseudonymous publications.

References:

R. -M. Albérès, *Histoire du roman moderne* (Paris: Albin Michel, 1962), p. 296;

Lucille F. Becker, *Georges Simenon* (Boston: Twayne, 1977);

Michel Butor, *Repertoire, Etudes et conférences 1948-1959* (Paris: Editions de Minuit, 1960);

Carvel Collins, "The Art of Fiction IX: Georges Simenon," *Paris Review*, 9 (Summer 1955): 71-90;

Brendan Gill, "Profiles: Out of the Dark," *New Yorker* (24 January 1953): 35-45;

Francis Lacassin and Gilbert Sigaux, *Simenon* (Paris: Plon, 1973);

Michel Lemoine, *Index des personnages de Georges Simenon* (Brussels: Editions Labor, 1986);

Thomas Narcejac, *The Art of Simenon* (London: Routledge, 1952);

Maurice Piron, *L'Univers de Simenon* (Paris: Presses de la Cité, 1983);

John Raymond, *Simenon in Court* (New York: Harcourt, Brace & World, 1968);

Charles J. Rolo, "Simenon and Spillane: The Metaphysics of Murder for the Millions," in *New World Writing* (New York: New American Library of World Literature, 1952), pp. 235-245.

Papers:

Simenon's papers are at the Centre d'Etudes Georges Simenon in Liège, Belgium, and at the Simenon Center, Drew University, Madison, New Jersey.

Elsa Triolet
(25 September 1896-16 June 1970)

Konrad Bieber
State University of New York at Stony Brook

BOOKS: *Na Taiti* (Leningrad: Ateney, 1925); translated as *A Tahiti* in *Œuvres romanesques croisées d'Elsa Triolet et Aragon*, volume 1 (1964);

Zemlyanichka (Moscow: Coopérative des Ecrivains "Le Cercle," 1926); translated by Léon Robel as *Fraise-des-bois* (Paris: Gallimard, 1974);

Zashchitny tsvet (Moscow: Fédération, 1928); translated by Robel as *Camouflage* (Paris: Gallimard, 1976);

Bonsoir Thérèse (Paris: Denoël, 1938);

Maïakovski, poète russe (Paris: Editions Sociales Internationales, 1939); translated by John Rodker as *Mayakovsky, Poet of Russia: Reminiscences from a Longer Work* (London: Hogarth, 1939);

Mille Regrets (Paris: Denoël, 1942);

Le Cheval blanc (Paris: Denöel, 1943); translated by Gerrie Thielens as *The White Charger* (New York & Toronto: Rinehart, 1946); translated by Mervyn Savill as *The White Horse* (London & New York: Hutchinson, 1951);

Les Amants d'Avignon, as Laurent Daniel (Paris: Editions de Minuit, 1943); collected in *Le Premier Accroc coûte deux cents francs* (1945) and translated as "The Lovers of Avignon" in *A Fine of 200 Francs* (1947);

Yvette, as Laurent Daniel (N.p.: Bibliothèque Française, 1943);

Qui est cet étranger qui n'est pas d'ici? ou Le Mythe de la Baronne Mélanie (Paris: Seghers, 1944); republished as *Le Mythe de la Baronne Mélanie* (Neuchâtel & Paris: Ides et Calendes, 1945);

Ce n'était qu'un passage de ligne (Paris: Seghers, 1945);

Le Premier Accroc coûte deux cents francs (Brussels: Denoël, 1945; Paris: Egloff, 1945); translated by Francis Golffing as *A Fine of 200 Francs* (New York: Reynal & Hitchcock, 1947; London: Hutchinson, 1949);

Personne ne m'aime (Paris: Editeurs Français Réunis, 1946); republished with *Les Fantômes armés* (1947) as *Anne-Marie* (1952);

Elsa Triolet

Dessins animés, by Triolet and Raymond Peynet (Paris: Bordas, 1947);

Les Fantômes armés (Paris: Bibliothèque Française, 1947); republished with *Personne ne m'aime* as *Anne-Marie* (Paris: Bibliothèque Française, 1952);

L'Inspecteur des ruines (Paris: Bibliothèque Française, 1948); translated by Norman Cameron as *The Inspector of Ruins* (London: Weidenfeld & Nicolson, 1952; New York: Roy, 1953);

L'Ecrivain et le livre; ou, La Suite dans les idées (Paris: Editions Sociales, 1948);

Le Cheval roux; ou, Les Intentions humaines (Paris: Editeurs Français Réunis, 1953);

L'Histoire d'Anton Tchekhov, sa vie, son œuvre (Paris: Editeurs Français Réunis, 1954);

Pour que Paris soit, by Triolet and Robert Doisneau (Paris: Editions Cercle d'Art, 1956);

Le Rendez-vous des étrangers (Paris: Gallimard, 1956);

Le Monument (Paris: Gallimard, 1957);

Roses à crédit, volume 1 of *L'Age de nylon* (Paris: Gallimard, 1959);

Luna-Park, volume 2 of *L'Age de nylon* (Paris: Gallimard, 1959);

Les Manigances: Journal d'une égoïste (Paris: Gallimard, 1962);

L'Ame, volume 3 of *L'Age de nylon* (Paris: Gallimard, 1963);

Le Grand Jamais (Paris: Gallimard, 1965);

Ecoutez-voir (Paris: Gallimard, 1968);

La Mise en mots (Geneva: Skira, 1969);

Le Rossignol se tait à l'aube (Paris: Gallimard, 1970);

Chroniques théâtrales, edited by M. Lebre-Peytard (Paris: Gallimard, 1981).

Collections: *Elsa Triolet choisie par Aragon*, edited by Louis Aragon (Paris: Gallimard, 1960);

Œuvres romanesques croisées d'Elsa Triolet et Aragon, 42 volumes (Paris: Laffont, 1964-1974).

OTHER: M. Iline, *Les Montagnes et les hommes*, translated by Triolet (Paris: Editions Hier et Aujourd'hui, 1946);

Ina Konstantinova, *La Jeune Fille de Kachine: Journal intime et lettres*, translated by Triolet (Paris: Editeurs Français Réunis, 1951);

Nikolay Gogol, *Le Portrait*, translated by Triolet (Paris: Editeurs Français Réunis, 1952);

Vladimir Mayakovski, *Maïakovski: Vers et proses de 1913 à 1930*, edited and translated, with an introduction, by Triolet (Paris: Editeurs Français Réunis, 1952);

Anton Chekhov, *Théâtre*, 2 volumes, translated by Triolet (Paris: Editeurs Français Réunis, 1954, 1962);

La Poésie russe, bilingual edition, edited by Triolet (Paris: Seghers, 1965).

The works of Elsa Triolet, a Russian-born French novelist and essayist, vary from critical essays on the theater and translations of Russian poetry, plays, and novels into French to novels of fanciful soul searching; of love and death; of loneliness in the middle of the crowd; of high-flying ideals and coldly calculating political and finan-

The Kagan family (left to right): Lili, Helena Youlievna Berman, Yuri Kagan, and Elsa (L'Humanité)

cial scheming. Her books first found acceptance in France, then in translation throughout the world.

Born Elsa Kagan, the daughter of Yuri Kagan, a lawyer specializing in contracts for artists and writers, and Helena Youlievna Berman, a pianist, Triolet studied architecture at the Lycée Valitzki in her native Moscow and earned her diploma in that field. An older sister, Lili, was married in 1912 to Ossip Brik, a lawyer and literary critic. The poet Vladimir Mayakovski courted both sisters; he became Lili's lover and a lifelong friend and inspiration to Elsa. Her friends, above all Roman Jakobson, the linguist, and Viktor Shklovski, the literary critic, urged her to write. Her earliest publications, three novels, were in Russian and appeared during the 1920s. All of them are to some degree autobiographical and all have been translated into French.

In Moscow, during the revolution, she met a French military attaché, Capt. André Triolet, and married him in 1918 in Paris. The couple went to live in Tahiti in 1919, but in 1920 Elsa alone returned to Europe. Although she was separated and later divorced from Triolet, he agreed to let her keep his name. A stay in London was marred by financial difficulties, and Elsa went back to Paris. A longer stay in postwar Berlin led to an affair ·with the painter Ivan Pougny. During these various sojourns Triolet kept careful notes to use in her writing. Maksim Gorky, who had encouraged Triolet to write, helped her gain readmittance to Russia, where she returned for the first time in 1925 for a short period. From there, via Berlin, she went on to Paris where she was to live more or less permanently in small hotels, a fact often reflected in her prose.

In 1928, after several liaisons, Triolet met Louis Aragon, then at the height of his surrealist phase. Though initially not attracted to her (he was still smarting from the break-up of his long-time affair with Nancy Cunard and an attempted suicide), once Aragon began to know Elsa, he became increasingly certain that he had found the woman meant for him. They began living together in late 1928, and on 28 February 1939 they married. Aragon was to dedicate to Triolet five of his best-known volumes of poetry, every one of them bearing the name Elsa in its title.

During World War II both Triolet and Aragon were active in the Resistance. They were members of the Comité National des Ecrivains, of which she later became the honorary president, and contributed to *Les Lettres Françaises*, a Resistance publication; both of these included noncommunists and Communists. She and Aragon continued their writing, in the southern zone (unoccupied until November 1942), publishing a number of clandestine texts, what they called "prose de contrebande." For a while they lived in Nice, then moved to an isolated spot, then to Lyons, and finally, as associates feared more and more for their safety, to a secret location. They were both active in passing documents and other dangerous work, for which they were nearly apprehended once. She later received the Médaille de la Résistance for her service in this period.

In the early days of the German occupation both had been able to publish legally, Triolet through her French publisher, Denoël, the first to bet on her writing talent, in 1938, when her first novel in French, *Bonsoir Thérèse* (Good Evening, Theresa), appeared. This work, more a collection of short stories with tenuous links between them than a novel of organic unity, already demonstrated Triolet's talent for observation and for subtle, wistful character depiction. Subsequent short stories—those collected in *Mille*

Triolet's sister, Lili, with the poet Vladimir Mayakovski, a lifelong friend and source of inspiration to Triolet (photo Roger-Viollet)

Regrets (A Thousand Regrets, 1942), for example—are more colorful and dramatic. Her first true novel, *Le Cheval blanc* (1943; translated as *The White Charger*, 1946), is a bold attempt at creating a saga. Michel Vigaud is a gifted, confused, impetuous artist, apt at impressing people with his talents as an entertainer. His many flights from reality are balanced by his strong sense of justice, of fairness. The book, set in France during the interwar years and World War II, was well received by critics and popular among members of the Resistance and with those confined in the prisons of occupied France. It tended to be read as an allegory–Vigaud's mission, as a kind of Knight of the Grail, is to rid the earth of monsters while maintaining his virtue. His heroic end in battle while saving a comrade keeps him from becoming a "raté," a social outcast through failure. Some characters in this graceful novel are to be found again in other fictional contexts.

When publication "above ground" became impossible for both Aragon and Triolet, she resorted to writing under the pen name Laurent Daniel, which became known overnight with the clandestine publication later in 1943 of *Les Amants d'Avignon* (The Lovers of Avignon). This *récit*, which was collected in the 1945 volume *Le Premier Accroc coûte deux cents francs* and translated in *A Fine of 200 Francs* (1947), did much to earn the author the Prix Goncourt in 1945, the first awarded since 1939. It also won for Triolet the admiration of Joë Bousquet, who praised its style—more sober than that of previous works such as *Le Cheval blanc*—and its authentic sense of humanity. Juliette, the heroine of *Les Amants d'Avignon*, travels through southern France in search of hiding places for young Frenchmen at odds with the collaborationist government. The writing depicts the oppressive atmosphere of the German occupation in simple, direct touches. The courage it takes to oppose the invaders is described as something so natural, so matter-of-fact, as to minimize the heroism of the resisters. One minor theme noticeable throughout Triolet's fiction—the rat race—is here a sort of background music, as the rats rush to and fro in the attic of the unoccupied farm where Juliette finds shelter. Juliette's escape from the arresting Nazi police through the "traboules" or tunnels under the houses of Lyons is an especially memorable passage, and *Les Amants d'Avignon* is a widely anthologized work by Triolet.

Personne ne m'aime (Nobody Loves Me) and its sequel, *Les Fantômes armés* (Armed Ghosts), were published in 1946 and 1947. As a narrative in the first person, *Personne ne m'aime* succeeds in focusing on one woman—who eventually dies under mysterious circumstances—and then switching to the narrator herself without losing momentum. The theme of the book is the solitude of the artist, whom others envy but who finds the isolation brought about by fame to be unbearable. The beautiful film star Jenny Borghese kills herself when she realizes that she cannot find an enduring love.

In *Les Fantômes armés*, one of Triolet's most bitter works, one finds, prophetically, what Jacques Madaule, in the June 1971 issue of *Europe*, calls "la grande rupture des années 1947-1950, la rupture entre les vainqueurs, entre l'Union Soviétique et les Occidentaux" (the great rupture of 1947-1950, the break between the victors, between the Soviet Union and the Western powers). It evokes the rubble of defeated Germany and the postwar corruption that replaced the patriotism of the Resistance. *Les Fantômes armés* sustains the suspense begun in the first book and develops at the same time a psychologi-

Triolet in Berlin, 1923 (photo AFP)

cally satisfying portrait of a thinker able to act in extraordinary situations and a truthful description of the intricate military and political circumstances of the Resistance movements.

Although Triolet was married to the foremost poet and novelist within the Communist orbit, one who remained a Stalinist longer than any of the other leading artists or writers, she maintained a critical attitude toward party politics and never joined the Communist party. In fact, her novel *Le Monument* (1957) affords the reader an insight into the workings of Eastern European political culture. Her allegiance was firmly with the Left, but her relative political independence made her a better artist, freed from the shackles of Socialist Realism that marked Aragon's writing for a while. Often attacked by Communist critics because of this very political independence, she also was the target of those who abandoned the party: witness Dominique Desanti's 1983 book on Triolet, *Les Clés d'Elsa*. Desanti never forgave her for avoiding the "betrayal" that leaving the party meant for so many French intellectuals.

Again, in *L'Inspecteur des ruines* (1948; translated as *The Inspector of Ruins*, 1952), perhaps her finest novel, Triolet showed an uncanny mastery in rendering the conditions in postwar Western Europe, in sharp contrast to the confusion reigning in the mind of her protagonist. Antonin Blond is to some extent the spiritual brother of Alfred Döblin's Franz Biberkopf, the tragic hero of *Berlin Alexanderplatz* (1929), though he lacks Biberkopf's criminality. The book is narrated by the hero, Blond, who was first a prisoner of war and then was imprisoned in a concentration camp, from which he successfully escaped. He returns home to find his wife dead beneath their bombed-out house. Having lost his past, and having no sense that there is a future, he drifts through a series of fantastic adventures, including some in Germany, where he meets a dreamlike Italian actress, Bianca, in a partially destroyed theater. He recounts his experiences with good humor, but the overall tone remains somber. Many scenes are also highly dramatic, with a superb sense of the commonplace and of the exceptional. Most secondary characters in this novel are well developed, some of them memorably. Though Antonin's life is viewed with more than a touch of irony, of cynically sober evaluation of his potential, the overall impression the reader derives from this book is one of the author's empathy with her protagonist, whose destiny is typical of the turmoil caused by the historical events of the twentieth century. The "ruins" inspected here are not just material; they are in people's hearts and minds.

Triolet's subsequent fiction does not always equal this high point. *Le Cheval roux; ou, Les Intentions humaines* (The Red Horse; or, Human Intentions, 1953) is an ambitious and often gripping projection of the danger of atomic energy. An uneven work, it is an attempt at continuing the Voltairean tradition of warning mankind of the dangers of endless "progress." The world seen after an atomic war is described in strong, brutal colors as the few survivors go through harrowing experiences that cannot be shrugged off.

Le Rendez-vous des étrangers (Meeting Point for Foreigners, 1956) suffers even more from excessive creative ambition as Triolet attempts to combine her usual sharp observation of reality with personal experience and at the same time to display sensitivity to the condition of being a foreigner—something she had known herself and

which was one of her concerns in postwar Europe, with its many displaced persons.

L'Age de nylon (The Age of Nylon, 1959-1963) is a trilogy with little, if any, unity. Volume 1, *Roses à crédit* (Roses on the Installment Plan, 1959), is a well-devised study in contrasts. Its heroine, Martine, growing up in squalor and poverty, appears to be cut out for a leading role as a social activist. Instead, she concentrates her considerable gifts of intelligence and adaptability on the acquisition of gadgets, all of them on the installment plan, to the point that, despite her abilities, she loses first some of her gadgets and then her husband as her marriage disintegrates. She perishes, tragically, in the same hovel where she had grown up. The title of the trilogy points to Triolet's satire: the author considers the twentieth century the time of synthetics, and the ridicule here attached to material goods as an end in themselves is applied mercilessly and with good effect.

The second volume, *Luna-Park* (1959), appearing only months after the first one, is a narrative made murky by overlong quotations from a supposed treasure trove of letters a movie director has found in the villa he has just bought. The title is meant to be a pun: the never seen and slightly crazy letter writer had wished to participate in the first flight to the moon. Although Triolet does make some sound psychological observations in this novel, the work suffers from repetition, an almost complete lack of suspense, and a tendency toward melodrama intensified by Triolet's unwitting caricatures of a few secondary characters.

L'Ame (The Soul, 1963), the third volume of the series, is the best. Like some of Triolet's earlier works, it is a delicate, imaginative, and stimulating story. At its center is another victim of a Nazi concentration camp, this time a woman of powerful magnetism, although physically ruined by the Nazi doctors' experiments. She is the focal point that dominates every one of the highly diversified people who rotate about her. Intellectually, politically, and morally this book is perhaps one of the finest French novels of the twentieth century.

Les Manigances (Wangling, 1962) is not as satisfying artistically. Subtitled *Journal d'une égoïste* (Journal of an Egoist), it is an uneven work. The heroine, as so often in Triolet's work, is a performing artist. Although some of the dialogue is lively, several episodes seem unnecessary, and the whole novel is a bit contrived. The author noted that because the writing of this book represented

Triolet with Louis Aragon at their home, circa 1945 (photo Izis)

an interruption of the series *L'Age de nylon,* she felt she could afford, instead of undertaking new investigations and more research, to "eat the grass right underfoot, not running to distant quarters."

Le Grand Jamais (It Will Never Happen, 1965) is another vast enterprise. Triolet uses the flashback technique to revive interest in a historian after his death. His young wife, Madeleine, is shown in her ambivalence. She admired her late husband, Régis, who also turns out to be an author of fiction. But when some of his disciples want to magnify his importance, she becomes suspicious. When a religious bias is claimed for the deceased Régis, who had always been a skeptic, she decides to counter the cult-building. The novel deals with the impossibility of knowing another,

even through love, even through the cult of another's memory. The widow's image of her husband must compete with, and ultimately yields to, the public image, the man appropriated by others. Unfortunately, the novel is stilted, often contrived. The plot rambles on pretentiously; the characters, too, are rather lifeless.

In contrast, *Ecoutez-voir* (Look and Listen, 1968), the equally ambitious sequel to *Le Grand Jamais,* is a challenge to the reader. Triolet attempts to bolster the effect of her written words by including hundreds of photographs, meant to be viewed contextually, in the book, a technique that has its flaws–most prominently, the reader's effort to agree with the author on the force sought in pictorial emphasis. However, the novel progresses at a rapid pace, and its three main narrators forcefully synthesize the anguish felt by Régis's widow, Madeleine. Not without *coquetterie*, the author, following a long-established tradition of authorial intervention, shows her own face now and then. This feature lends the novel an additional note of irony. However, the various pursuits of the three main characters are not always convincingly portrayed. In particular, Madeleine's frenzy, her obsession with noise, and her need for fresh air do not seem to be enough to motivate her erratic behavior.

Le Rossignol se tait à l'aube (The Nightingale Falls Silent at Dawn, 1970) is the novelist's swan song, with more than a small measure of autobiographical allusions. A slim volume, it has a modest framework, relating a reunion of elderly people near death. The dialogue sounds right, direct, true; the characters, fragile and sometimes silly, are movingly portrayed in their discrete fears and hopes.

Also known as a biographer of Russian poets, a translator and interpreter of Russian dramatists, a drama critic, and an editor of literary periodicals (*Europe, Les Lettres Françaises*), Elsa Triolet stands as an imaginative and powerful creator of fiction and a subtle critic. Her novels mirror the sense of people's isolation in the crowd as Samuel Beckett came to express it slightly later. Her empathy for refugees and other uprooted foreigners living in France before, during, and after World War II is constant.

The death of Triolet in June 1970 was mourned by friends in many countries. The French actor and director Jean-Louis Barrault and the Chilean writer Pablo Neruda were among those who read tributes to her at a memorial ceremony, and a number of Russian writers composed memorial essays. Her popularity in France and other countries of Europe sprang in part from her activity in the Resistance and in part from her role in the Aragon-Triolet couple, a model, to many, of the shared intellectual life. She also represented, to those friendly to the Soviet Union, ties with the early revolutionary era and some of its most creative thinkers. Since the publication of the *Œuvres romanesques croisées d'Elsa Triolet et Aragon* (1964-1974), her writing has taken on more and more the appearance of a joint product, something that belongs not only to her but to Aragon and ultimately to the age in which they were both deeply involved. She should be remembered for novels and stories such as *Le Cheval blanc* and *Le Premier Accroc coûte deux cents francs* that show how she was committed both to the art of fiction and the truth of her time as she knew it.

References:

Konrad Bieber, "Ups and Downs in Elsa Triolet's Prose," *Yale French Studies*, no. 27 (1961): 81-85;

Dominique Desanti, *Les Clés d'Elsa* (Paris: Ramsay, 1983);

Elsa Triolet [exhibition catalog] (Paris: Bibliothèque Nationale, 1972);

Europe, special issue on Triolet and Louis Aragon, no. 454-455 (February-March 1967); special issue on Triolet, no. 506 (June 1971);

Jacques Madaule, *Ce que dit Elsa* (Paris: Denoël, 1961);

Marie-Monique Pflaum-Vallin, "Elsa Triolet and Aragon: Back to Lilith," *Yale French Studies*, no. 27 (1961): 86-89;

Monica Stirling, "Elsa Triolet," *Atlantic Monthly*, 184 (September 1949): 76-78.

Boris Vian

(10 March 1920-23 June 1959)

Zvjezdana Rudelic
Duke University

BOOKS: *J'irai cracher sur vos tombes,* as Vernon Sullivan (Paris: Editions du Scorpion, 1946); translated by Vian and Milton Rosenthal as *I Shall Spit on Your Graves* (Paris: Vendôme Press, 1948);

Vercoquin et le plancton (Paris: Gallimard, 1946);

L'Ecume des jours (Paris: Gallimard, 1947); translated by Stanley Chapman as *Froth on the Daydream* (London: Rapp & Carroll, 1967); translated by John Sturrock as *Mood Indigo* (New York: Grove Press, 1968);

L'Automne à Pékin (Paris: Editions du Scorpion, 1947; revised edition, Paris: Editions de Minuit, 1956);

Barnum's Digest (Paris: Deux Menteurs, 1948);

Et on tuera tous les affreux, as Vernon Sullivan (Paris: Editions du Scorpion, 1948);

Cantilènes en gelée (Limoges: Editions Rougerie, 1949);

Les Fourmis (Paris: Editions du Scorpion, 1949);

Elles se rendent pas compte, as Vernon Sullivan (Paris: Editions du Scorpion, 1950);

L'Equarrissage pour tous; Le Dernier des métiers (Paris: Editions Toutain, 1950); *L'Equarrissage pour tous* translated by Marc Estrin as *Knackery for All* in *Plays for a New Theater, Playbook 2* (New York: New Directions, 1966);

L'Herbe rouge (N.p.: Editions Toutain, 1950);

L'Arrache-cœur (Paris: Vrille, 1953); translated by Chapman as *Heartsnatcher* (London: Rapp & Whiting, 1968);

En avant la zizique . . . et par ici les gros sous (Paris: Livre Contemporain, 1958);

Fiesta (Paris: Editions Heugel, 1958);

Les Bâtisseurs d'empire; ou, Le Schmürz (Paris: Collège de 'Pataphysique, 1959); translated by Simon Watson Taylor as *The Empire Builders* (New York: Grove Press, 1967; London: Methuen, 1971);

Le Goûter des généraux (Paris: Collège de 'Pataphysique, 1962); translated by Taylor as *The General's Tea Party* (New York: Grove Press, 1967);

Je voudrais pas crever (Paris: Pauvert, 1962);

Boris Vian

L'Herbe rouge; Les Lurettes fourrées (Paris: Pauvert, 1962);

Théâtre, 2 volumes (Paris: Union Générale d'Editions, 1965, 1971);

Textes et chansons (Paris: Union Générale d'Editions, 1966);

Trouble dans les Andains (Paris: Editions de la Jeune Parque, 1966);

Chroniques de jazz, edited by Lucien Malson (Paris: Editions de la Jeune Parque, 1967);

Le Chevalier de neige (Paris: Christian Bourgois, 1974);

Petits Spectacles (Paris: Christian Bourgois, 1977).

PLAY PRODUCTIONS: *J'irai cracher sur vos tombes,* Paris, Théâtre Verlaine, 22 April 1948;

L'Equarrissage pour tous, Paris, Théâtre des Noctambules, April 1950;

Les Bâtisseurs d'empire, Paris, Théâtre Récamier, 22 December 1959;

Le Dernier des métiers, Paris, Café-Théâtre de la Grande-Sévérine, 1964;

Le Goûter dés généraux, Paris, Théâtre de Gaîté-Montparnasse, 18 September 1965.

OTHER: August Strindberg, *Mademoiselle Julie,* translated by Vian (Paris: Arche, 1952);

A. E. van Vogt, *Le Monde des A,* translated by Vian (Paris: Gallimard, 1953);

Nelson Algren, *L'Homme au bras d'or* (Paris: Gallimard, 1956).

PERIODICAL PUBLICATION: "Approche indirecte de l'objet," *Dossiers Acénonètes du Collège de 'Pataphysique,* 12 (1960).

Above all a novelist and a playwright, Boris Vian is also remembered for his versatility: an engineer, poet, and songwriter, as well as an actor, scriptwriter, and translator, Vian was also a composer, a painter, a member of the Collège de 'Pataphysique, and from 1947 to 1950, a jazz trumpeter at the clubs of Saint-Germain-des-Prés. Despite his many interests the fifteen years of Vian's literary career were extremely productive. He left some twenty volumes of published work and pages of notes with ideas for projects never completed owing to his premature death. Vian died suddenly from a heart attack on 23 June 1959 during a private showing of the film version of his controversial novel *J'irai cracher sur vos tombes* (1946; translated as *I Shall Spit on Your Graves,* 1948).

"Etre connu, c'est être méconnu" (To be famous is to be misjudged) Vian used to say. Indeed, his reputation has been just as ambivalent as his artistic career was: idealized and adored by a generation of French youth, studied by critics and academics, inspiration for such diverse contemporary figures as Alain Robbe-Grillet and Serge Gainsbourg, Vian and his work suffered as much as they profited from their fame. Stigmatized sometimes as "scandalous" or "superficial," or purely "humoristic," the work has been on occasion easily dismissed. Yet to classify it thus is to ignore one of the main characteristics of Vian's writing: through his literary creations, Vian attempted to force the reader out of habitual patterns of approaching text and reality, to make him question traditional barriers between the comic and the serious, between simple "being" and intellectual "existing," and, finally, between light amusement and pure art.

The ambiguity of the myth of Vian partly results from the scandal surrounding the publication of his first book, *J'irai cracher sur vos tombes.* The novel was written as a result of a bet. Jean d'Haullin, an editor and a friend of Vian, was searching for ways to improve business at his publishing house, Editions du Scorpion. He asked Vian to advise him as to which American author to publish, American literature being much in fashion. Vian responded that he would write a best-selling American-type potboiler himself. During a vacation, within two weeks, he wrote *J'irai cracher sur vos tombes.* Published under a pseudonym, supposedly a translation by Boris Vian of a work by an American novelist named Vernon Sullivan, *J'irai cracher sur vos tombes* is one of Vian's four Vernon Sullivan novels and his only important success during his lifetime.

The novel focuses on racial problems in America, an issue Vian learned about from his friends, black jazz musicians. The narrator is a mulatto who can easily pass for a white person. In order to avenge his brother, lynched for having kept company with a white woman, he sleeps with two sisters, both beautiful, rich, and white. He then reveals his true identity and brutally kills both. After a long pursuit by the police he is caught.

The success of the novel was enhanced by the scandalous affair of Edmond Rougé, a sales agent who in April 1947 strangled his female friend in a hotel room at Montparnasse, leaving next to the corpse a copy of *J'irai cracher sur vos tombes,* opened to the page describing the death of one of the women. The press immediately accused the novelist of having inspired the murder. Vian, who was brought to trial for offending public morals, denied authorship until late 1948. On 3 July 1949 the government forbade the sale of the book, and in 1951 Vian was sentenced and fined one hundred thousand francs. Vian himself, with the assistance of an American, Milton Rosenthal, did an English translation of the work, which was published in Paris in spring 1948. This may have been in order to capitalize on the book's success; it was also intended to vindicate him, perhaps, by presenting the "American" version as the original, according to the claim on

Vian and Yehudi Menuhin, circa 1933, the year Vian's father rented his villa to the Menuhin family (collection Alain Vian)

the title page of the French that it had been translated from English. (However, *Bibliographie de France* for 9 July 1948 identifies the newer book as a translation from the original French.)

Vian later remarked, not without some regret, that while *J'irai cracher sur vos tombes* broke all records, "his own" novels hardly sold at all. Thus, although the novel, which sold five hundred thousand copies, provided Vian with economic security, it deprived him of the kind of literary career to which he aspired. Partly because of the affair of *J'irai cracher sur vos tombes*, Vian became a legend in his lifetime; only after his death did critics begin to appreciate the specifically literary qualities of his work. Consequently, the main difficulties faced by Vian critics are distinguishing the Vian myth from Vian the man and above all separating both from his literary creations.

Born on 10 March 1920 in Ville-d'Avray, Vian was the second child of Paul and Yvonne Ravenez Vian. He had a sister and two brothers, his brother Lélio being the oldest. His childhood resembled a fairy tale: isolated and protected by his parents, he was brought up in a peaceful suburb of Paris. First he was taught by a private tutor, who provided him with a sound education: at the age of five he was able to read and write,

and by the age of eight he had read many of the classics of French literature.

Beginning in the early 1930s, Vian studied at the Lycée Hoche in Versailles. His health was precarious after a bout of rheumatic fever which affected his heart in 1932 and a case of typhoid fever that interrupted his studies in mid decade. In 1936 he entered the Lycée Condorcet in Paris to study mathematics in preparation for admission to the Ecole Centrale des Arts et Manufactures. In 1933, after having experienced financial difficulties, Paul Vian began selling homeopathic pharmaceutical products, only to move into the real estate business in 1938. The Vian family began living more modestly: they rented their villa to the biologist Jean Rostand and later to the family of the future violinist Yehudi Menuhin and moved themselves into the adjoining, more modest residence. Later Paul Vian built in the back of the garden a pavillion with a small dance hall, designed especially for the amusement of his carefully guarded children. At this pavillion the famous "surprise parties" described by Vian in his 1946 novel *Vercoquin et le plancton* (Vinegrub and the Plankton) took place.

One of the crucial periods in Vian's life began in 1938: through Duke Ellington's Paris concerts he discovered jazz and learned to play

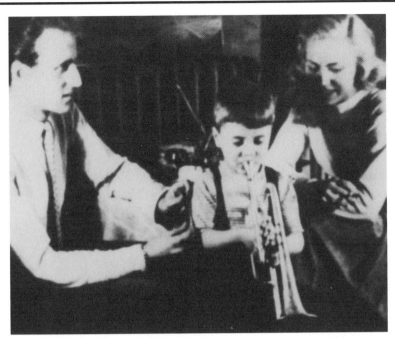

Boris, Patrick, and Michèle Vian in 1946 (collection Alain Vian)

the trumpet. Music, jazz in particular, continued to fascinate Vian until the end of his life and remained one of his favorite activities. In 1939 Vian entered the Ecole Centrale to study engineering, a profession in which he actively engaged in for several years. In 1940 he met Jacques Loustalot (known as Le Major), whose personality animates several of Vian's fictional characters. He represented for Vian the essence of youthful joie de vivre and rebellion, with no inhibitions and utter disregard for social usages and institutions. The same year Vian also met Michèle Léglise, whom he married in 1941. In 1942, their son Patrick was born, and Vian received his degree from the Ecole Centrale. He started work as an engineer with the Association Française de Normalisation (AFNOR), while also writing his first poems and filmscripts.

During the winter of 1942-1943 he began his *Trouble dans les Andains* (Trouble in the Swaths). The novel was published posthumously in 1966. As is often the case with Vian's novels, the title bears no apparent relation to the work itself. The hero, Adolphin de Beaumashin, searches for a stolen "barbarin fourchu." This mysterious forked object (the word *barbarin* does not exist in French) gains its identity from the associations of the reader as the search progresses. Eventually, the "barbarin" is found, but a character named Le Major throws it into the sea. The novel is rather bizarre, but Vian's language is al-

ready as playful, inventive, and humorous as in his more mature works.

In 1943-1944 Vian also wrote *Vercoquin et le plancton*, dedicated to Jean Rostand. When he wrote *Vercoquin et le plancton*, Vian was twenty-three. In a nostalgic mood, in this novel set at a surprise party given for Le Major's twenty-first birthday, Vian attempts to revive his teens, or the "bon vieux temps" (good old times), as he calls them. The characters are all young, living only for the present moment. Enchanted by freedom and opposed to all conformity and conventionality, the young men explore not only the world around them but also their own sexual as well as social identities. The world of work, such as Vian encountered it in AFNOR, is described as excessively boring, and it contrasts with the other world, built solely around amusement. Vian's humorous approach obviously aims at ridiculing both, but as critics have noted, each to a different extent. Violence seems inherent in the apparently carefree world of amusement: at the end of the surprise party at Le Major's house, in order to take revenge for all the damage caused by the guests, Antioche kills one out of every four guests with a machine gun, and in the final explosion, survived only by Le Major and Antioche, the entire block is ravaged.

As in other Vian novels the real and the imaginary are mixed. In *Vercoquin et le plancton*, the characters are real in their attitudes, unreal in the

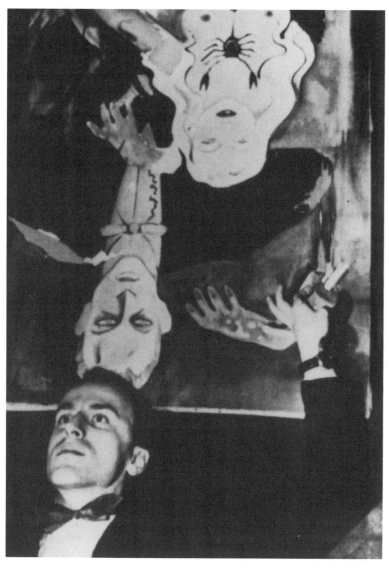

Vian with Jean Boullet's portrait of him and Michèle (collection Michèle Léglise-Vian)

world they inhabit. While the characters are based on Vian's friends and acquaintances–Le Major and the Rostand family, for example–the charm of the novel resides mainly in what can be called its humorous and yet forceful "wor(l)d play." Thus, what appears at first as only a humorous attitude toward language grows into a philosophy and way of life.

Starting in 1942, Vian played in Claude Abadie's amateur jazz orchestra, and in 1944 they performed numerous concerts, many for the American army. That same year he also wrote several short stories later collected in *Les Fourmis* (Ants, 1949). On 22 November 1944 Vian's father was killed accidentally when, in the middle of the night, he interrupted a robbery in progress in his house. The killers were never identified.

Vian was one of many of his generation who threw themselves frenetically into the exciting intellectual life and popular culture of the immediate post-World War II period in Paris. Already knowledgeable about jazz, he frequented the Left Bank jazz clubs that, through a loose association (or none at all) with well-known existentialist writers and their friends, became known as existentialist night spots. He was enthusiastic about Jean-Paul Sartre's writings and attended in October 1945 the crowded meeting at the Club Maintenant, at which Sartre delivered the lecture published in 1946 as *L'Existentialisme est un humanisme* (*Existentialism and Humanism*). In the spring of 1946 he made the acquaintance of Sar-

Vian in the back room of his brother Alain's music store (collection Michèle Léglise-Vian)

tre and Simone de Beauvoir. The former's gospel of personal and social freedom, his theme of metaphysical absurdity, and his staunchly anti-establishment posture appealed strongly to Vian, doubtless more than the concomitant element of responsibility in his philosophy. Thanks to the connection with Sartre, Vian was able to begin contributing to *Temps Modernes.* He was not, however, above mocking the existentialist fashion, the fanaticism of its adherents, and even the writer himself, who was soon to be transformed into Jean-Sol Partre in one of his novels and whose works and themes are parodied there.

The year 1946 was an extremely fruitful one for Vian. In February he left AFNOR to become an engineer in a paper and carton factory. In March of the same year he began *L'Ecume des jours* (1947; translated as *Froth on the Daydream,* 1967, and as *Mood Indigo,* 1968) and completed it in May. A number of chapters were first published in *Temps Modernes.* That same spring his first publication appeared in the magazine *Jazz-*

Hot, under the pseudonym of Bison Ravi. But it was with the publication of *L'Ecume des jours* that Vian began to consider himself a serious writer. Hoping to dedicate himself to writing and composing music, soon after the publication of *L'Ecume des jours,* he left his job at the factory.

L'Ecume des jours is probably Vian's most popular novel. Although Raymond Queneau called it "le plus poignant des romans d'amour contemporains" (the most poignant of contemporary love stories), critics generally agree that the novel can hardly be reduced to its surface structure of a simple love story. Nevertheless, this playful, unrealistic narrative is structured around the relationship of two young couples, Colin and Chloé and Chick and Alise. The protagonists at first share a carefree world of love and well-being, but, beginning with Colin and Chloé's honeymoon, unhappiness invades the story to the point of eventually destroying everything and everyone. The main characters succumb to the magic of the world furnished with things, "les choses," which, although they exist at first to pamper and reassure the protagonists of their self-sufficiency, eventually force the human beings from their world. (For instance, a necktie that someone is knotting suddenly closes shut and crushes a finger; the corners of a room become rounded.)

The most striking example of the way things dominate and crush human beings is Chloé and Colin's apartment, which literally shrinks out of existence. Chloé is eventually completely absorbed by her sickness–a water lily that grows in her lungs, eventually causing her to suffocate. Colin is not very likely to survive her, and Chick and Alise are destroyed by Chick's passion for Jean-Sol Partre. In the last scene, as if the violent endings of the protagonists were transposed, a mouse, Colin and Chloé's companion, convinces a cat that he wishes to commit suicide. The cat prepares to bite off the mouse's head. But he will wait until someone steps on his tail. Just then eleven little blind girls from an orphanage come by. Thus the novel concludes.

When it was published, the novel had very little success. Yet it has since become Vian's most widely read work. Even though Jean-Sol Partre is killed by Alise, by means of an "arrache-cœur" (heart extractor), Beauvoir wrote in *La Force des choses* (*The Force of Circumstance*) that she and Sartre liked the novel, and Sartre supported it, unsuccessfully, for the Prix de la Pléiade. (It was awarded to Jean Grosjean.)

Vian's next novel, *L'Automne à Pékin* (Fall in Peking), was completed in November 1946 and published in 1947. It is the only novel that Vian reworked. The revised edition, with important changes such as chapter reorganization and textual alterations, appeared in 1956. *L'Automne à Pékin* was the third novel to appear under Vian's own name. It is undoubtedly the most difficult one, mainly because of the multiplicity of characters often only loosely related to the main story line. Four apparently independent episodes open the novel in a cinematographic way. They describe events leading to an apparently gratuitous reunion of the main characters in the desert of Exopotamie.

An exotic desert, Exopotamie is nevertheless easily accessible. Amadis Dudu arrives at Exopotamie by simply taking bus number 975. He appears to ignore his surroundings, and, his desk firmly planted in the sand, he continues to work. Finally he persuades the Administrative Council to build a railroad in Exopotamie. The railroad serves no practical purpose, only a narrative one: it brings the other characters into the desert, among them the two young men, Anne and Angel, and a secretary, Rochelle.

Anne, Rochelle, and Angel form a strange love triangle. Angel loves Rochelle, who in turn loves Anne. The two men seem to be parts of the same character. They come from the same school, both are engineers, one is hardworking, the other lazy. They complement each other so well that taken together their love for Rochelle is complete: Anne's is sensual and Angel's idealistic.

As in *L'Ecume des jours*, love eventually destroys its object: Chloé and Rochelle both perish from *usure* (wearing out). Abandoned by the cynical Anne, used up by love, Rochelle passes into the hands of Angel, who cannot help loving her, although she is obviously very ordinary. While *L'Ecume des jours* is marked by joy and tenderness as well as cruelty, the protagonists of *L'Automne à Pékin* no longer seem able to conceive of love and happiness. Angel ends by killing Anne, his erstwhile rival, and then Rochelle, through hostility to her and her inferiority.

L'Automne à Pékin is Vian's least accessible novel. This is partly because of the large number of characters, partly because of the loose structure of the book and the casual way in which the characters are attached to the plot. The novel is divided into three main "mouvements" (sections), preceded, separated, and followed by four "passages," in Vian's term, which are commentaries by the author. These transitional passages, in which the voice of the author addresses his readers directly, include indications of how the plot will develop and comments on the characters. The passages do not, however, simplify much a story that is marked by unexplained connections and an illogical plot development. Secondary characters have been identified as illustrations of Vian's traditional themes of anticlericalism, contempt for medicine, and hatred of bureaucracy, but critics agree on the need for more elaborate, refined techniques of interpretation.

The play *L'Equarrissage pour tous*, completed in 1947, was produced and published in 1950, then translated into English (as *Knackery for All*) in 1966. The action of this "paramilitary vaudeville" takes place on a farm in Arromanches, on D-Day, 6 June 1944. The knacker and his family see an entire military squad land at their house. They, however, are interested only in the wedding of their daughter Marie (one of the two daughters who have the same name) to Heinz Schittermach, with whom she has been sleeping

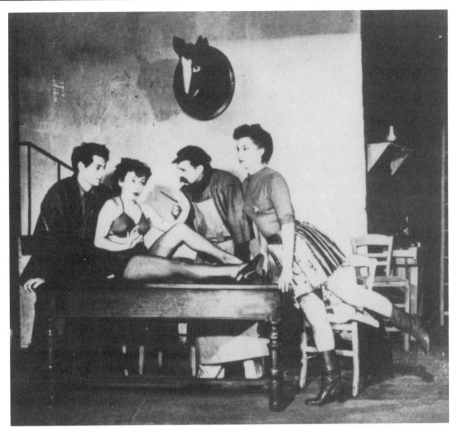

Scene from the Théâtre des Noctambules production of Vian's controversial play L'Equarrissage pour tous, *Paris, 1950 (photo Roger-Viollet)*

for four years. Two other children, both paratroopers, Jacques under the American flag and Catherine for the Russians, "land" to attend the wedding. In the end a French lieutenant and a captain arrive at the knacker's home to announce on behalf of the Ministry of Reconstruction that the house–the only one not entirely destroyed–is not "in line." A boy scout brings a box of dynamite, and the lieutenant, the only survivor after the explosion, cries out: "Et vive la France!" while a terribly off-key "Marseillaise" resounds hollowly.

It was still considered in 1950 not only bad taste but unpatriotic to make fun of the armies that had liberated France in 1944-1945, especially to make light of the Resistance and France Libre (the Free French, or Gaullist movement); only after the Algerian rebellion was well underway did antimilitarism become fashionable. When the play was produced, by André Reybaz and the company of Myrmidon at the Théâtre des Noctambules in Paris, it provoked considerable ire. Elsa Triolet, writing in *Lettres Françaises*, was one of several who criticized Vian for attacking, even spitting on, the Liberation. The play was a failure,

acclaimed only by those who considered themselves " 'pataphysicins." The play did earn Vian membership in the Collège de 'Pataphysique–a group of writers who cultivated the unusual and the parapsychological.

In 1947 Vian began working on several translations. English translations remained his main means of support until the end of his life. Although many are commercial, several remain authoritative: his 1952 version of August Strindberg's play *Miss Julie,* for instance, or his translation of *The World of A* by A. E. van Vogt, the first American science-fiction writer popular in France.

In 1948, the year Vian's daughter, Carole, was born, a new Sullivan title was published. *Et on tuera tous les affreux* (And We'll Kill All the Ugly Ones) is considered the most original of the Vernon Sullivan books. Vian modeled a number of the characters on acquaintances of his, using transparent pseudonyms. This, as well as the tone of the novel, caused considerable uproar. In fact, *France-Dimanche*, which had published part of it in serialized form, interrupted publication be-

Ursula and Boris Vian, Cité Véron, 1955 (collection Ursula Vian-Kubler)

cause of protests from readers. It is set in California, where Rock Bailey, just elected Mr. Los Angeles, decides to remain a virgin until the age of twenty in order to preserve his handsome muscular body, a choice which aggravates the pressing assaults of his female acquaintances. He finally gives in when the attractive Sunday Love comes along. Rock also becomes involved in a search for several beautiful young women, all mysteriously missing. During his quest, unexpectedly, he encounters a certain doctor Schutz, a Hitlerian who engages in strange experiments aiming at perfecting the human species by eliminating all those he deems ugly. Fortunately, not all of Dr. Schutz's operations are successful, and the "betterment" of the human species is doomed to failure. In fact, Vian suggests that it would not be betterment. Perfect beauty is dull; in an experiment women who are themselves beautiful prefer ugly men to uniformly handsome ones because they are more interesting. The novel criticizes eugenics as a method and uniformity as an aim for the human race.

On 4 June 1948 Vian gave an important lecture, "Approche discrète de l'objet" (Discreetly Approaching the Object), at the Musée des Arts Décoratifs in Paris. Among other topics, it dealt with war, treated in a half-serious, half-comic

vein but fundamentally critically. War, he said, was the best way to "s'objectifier" (be objectified), by being killed. It is better than suicide, which requires too much reflection. Unfortunately, there is a certain risk: one is not always killed. Conscientious objectors who oppose this are "détracteurs de l'objet" (detractors of objects). Vian also presented the paradoxical thesis that objects are superior to human beings, even quoting from the philosopher Gaston Bachelard to support his position, since Bachelard was interested in the objectification of psychological phenomena. Vian suggested that objects were a much more flexible field of investigation than people. There were also explicit allusions to the German philosopher Karl Jaspers and many implicit ones to Sartre and his theories on subjectivity and objectivity. Vian also explicitly denied the presence of logic and reasoning–that is, the Cartesian method–in his remarks. These anti-Cartesian and apparently antihumanistic positions are characteristic of his mind, which rejected boundaries, classifications, and traditions in favor of spontaneous and apparently illogical thought. Although the speech preceded Vian's official association with the Collège de 'Pataphysique, it clearly announced his orientation away from Aristotelian and Cartesian thought.

Three years after the publication of *L'Automne à Pékin*, *L'Herbe rouge* (Red Grass) appeared. It was unnoticed by the general public, and only one thousand copies were sold. Like other Vian novels, *L'Herbe rouge* resists paraphrase, and critics have often preferred to search in the novel for intimate personal confessions of the author, an approach that lends little to an understanding of the narrative. The main characters of *L'Herbe rouge* are two couples: Wolf and Lil, and Saphir Lazuli and Folavril. Wolf, who is an engineer, constructs a machine for time travel with the help of his mechanic, Lazuli. He undertakes four trips, each of which corresponds to one or two sessions of psychoanalysis. He reviews his relationships to family, religion, love, and sex. Hoping to escape from the exigencies of his present, Wolf is eventually caught up in his own past. Finally, his trips into the past ruin his relationship with Lil. Lazuli's relationship with Folavril is never fully realized either. Although very attracted to her, he is unable to make love, because at the crucial moment a shadow of a man appears and disturbs him. He eventually kills the shadow man, only to realize that to make him disappear he must die himself.

Characteristic of Vian's work, the unreal space in which the action takes place, with complete absence of recognizable décor, receives considerable emphasis in *L'Herbe rouge*. Characters appear to be living in a vacuum. Like the desert background of *L'Automne à Pékin*, the narrative space of *L'Herbe rouge* seems forced into being by the existence of the characters.

In 1949 Vian's collection of nineteen poems, under the title *Cantilènes en gelée*, was published. Fascinated by linguistics and semantics, Vian explores in his poetry the ways in which words escape the command of the author. Aware of the creative power of words themselves and their ability to generate unusual associations, Vian disassociates his language from traditional meanings. As he writes in the poem "Un de plus" (One More), from the 1962 collection entitled *Je voudrais pas crever* (I Don't Want to Die), the only alternative to the creative process is silence: "Comment voulez-vous que je fasse/Un poème avec ces mots-là?/Et bien tant pis j'en ferai pas" (How do you expect me to create/A poem with those words? /Well, too bad, I won't write any).

In the summer of 1949, at a cocktail party organized by the publisher Gaston Gallimard, Vian met Ursula Kubler. Vian's marriage had already become stagnant despite Carole's birth in 1948. He and Ursula first lived together in an apartment in the Cité Véron, facing the terrace of the Moulin Rouge, and following Vian's divorce in 1952, were married on 8 February 1954.

In July 1949 Vian's collection of short stories, *Les Fourmis*, which was originally to be entitled "Les Lurettes fourrées" (Furry Long-agos), appeared. The first story gives the title to the collection and is generally considered the most important. A soldier tells in fifteen episodes, most of which do not exceed a paragraph in length, what happens around him during a disembarkation. The story introduces the theme of the absurdity of war, particularly characteristic of Vian's theater.

Thus the play *Le Goûter des généraux* (1962; translated as *The General's Tea Party*, 1967), originally written in 1951 but produced and published in revised form in the 1960s, opens with a scene in which an infantile general, James Audubon Wilson, is alerted by President Léon Plantin that France, suffering from overproduction, can cure its ills only through war. During a tea party Audubon persuades generals Dupont-d'Isigny, Lavaste, and Juillet that the country should declare a war, but he suddenly realizes that he does

not know on whom. In the second act Plantin meets with generals Jackson (American), Korkiloff (Russian), and Ching-Ping-Ting (Chinese). Unfortunately, none of them is willing to enter the war with France. Finally, they decide that the only solution for France is to declare war on Morocco and Algeria. In the third act, two years later, Plantin, a clergyman named Tapecul, and all the generals except Jackson are in a shelter in Sweden. They start playing Russian roulette. Each protagonist sings a verse, shoots from a revolver and falls dead, accompanied by the joyous laughter of the survivors. In the end there is only one general left. Suddenly, the "Marseillaise" is heard and the general crosses the scene dressed in a festive uniform, grotesquely pulling behind him a miniature canon.

When it was first completed in 1951, *Le Goûter des généraux* was considered an interesting but extremely dangerous play and no producer was willing to take the risk. As critics have pointed out, Vian's obvious allusions to the Vichy government leader Marshal Henri Philippe Pétain, in the terms such as those the author uses, seemed inconceivable in the decade following World War II; ten years later, though, the public greatly appreciated the play, staged at the Théâtre de Gaîté-Montparnasse, and *Le Goûter des généraux* was the big success of the 1965 season: from September 1965 to August 1966, it was performed 309 times, for eighty-six thousand spectators. The play earned Vian the reputation of being a genius of satire, burlesque, and surrealism.

In 1952 Vian officially joined the Collège de 'Pataphysique as an "équarrisseur de première classe" (knacker of the first class). Although Alfred Jarry, whose 1896 play *Ubu Roi* had inspired the Collège, and Vian shared the same eccentricity and taste for farce, Vian was primarily interested in pataphysical nondogmatic, non-Aristotelian logic of equivalence, which gives equal importance to the serious and the comic.

During the early 1950s Vian also wrote most of the poems published posthumously under the title *Je voudrais pas crever* (1962). They are marked by a spontaneous, free lyricism that is the opposite of strict French versification and places Vian in the modern poetic tradition of Guillaume Apollinaire, Paul Eluard, and Jacques Prévert. Vian uses rhyme and lines with the same number of syllables but dispenses with punctuation and substitutes popular language and odd spellings for elevated poetic speech. The poems

Burial of Vian, 30 June 1959 (photo France-Soir)

are direct, unpretentious, and often musical; they deal with love, poetry, and especially death. (Vian long predicted that he would not live past forty.)

In January 1953 Editions Vrille published *L'Arrache-cœur* (translated as *Heartsnatcher*, 1968), the last novel that appeared during Vian's lifetime. Like the preceding ones, it passed unnoticed. One of the main characters, the psychiatrist Jacquemort, arrives at the pregnant Clémentine's house just in time to deliver her three little boys, called Joël, Noël, and Citroën. Throughout her pregnancy, and especially after a painful delivery, Clémentine has abhorred her husband, Angel. She ends by completely excluding him from both her life and the life of their children. A grotesque caricature of an overly protective mother, Clémentine is ready to sacrifice herself completely for her children. Her husband leaves her, and her protective love for the three "salopiots" (dirty brats) increases: hysterically afraid that they might hurt themselves when they are out of her sight, she at first isolates the garden from the outside world and eventually puts the three little boys into a specially made cage; only then can she rest. David Noakes has observed that Vian's mother was a model for Clémentine, although the possible excesses of her love for her children were not at all monstrous; in fact, Clémentine can be considered as the opposite extreme from the mother in Hervé Bazin's

Vipère au poing (*Viper in the Fist*, 1948), who ruins her children's lives through hostility to them.

The other main plot of *L'Arrache-coeur* concerns the efforts of the psychiatrist Jacquemort to find some meaning in his life; that is, to cure himself. His failures point to Vian's skepticism about certain practitioners of Freudian psychoanalysis, if not Freud himself. Having failed to establish identification with the pasts of his patients and thus to find himself, Jacquemont tries identifying himself with a cat through incorporating into himself its "substance mentale." But this does not satisfy him. He then gets an old man, La Gloïre, from a village not far from Clémentine's house, to tell him about his past. When the old man dies, Jacquemort assumes his role in the village, but it does not represent success as a transfer of personalities so much as capitulation: he will be an ordinary, indeed a mean, person, and the psychological truths he sought have value for him no longer. The glory suggested by the old man's name (despite the strange spelling), which is antiphrastic to start with since his job was to use his teeth to fish garbage and other debris from the river—that is, to assume others' shame—could be taken symbolically as an indication of his role as a scapegoat; but more likely it is Vian's way of criticizing those who keep their consciences clean by paying others to do their dirty work.

Vian thought that a "shock effect" should accompany a work of art. *L'Arrache-cœur*, probably more than any of his other novels, fulfills that design. Clémentine makes love on a table with an invisible power, whereas Jacquemort, while longing for a meaningful relationship, indulges in relations with women who seem to draw no pleasure from the sexual act. Whether because of its erotic scenes or the scenes of violence, such as the fair that Jacquemort attends where old people are sold as children's toys, the novel has not ceased to surprise and disconcert its readers.

The title of the novel seems to have little in common with the work. It reminds readers of the heartsnatcher with which, in *L'Ecume des jours*, Alise kills Jean-Sol Partre; there is, it is important to note, no heartsnatcher in the later novel. The apparent inappropriateness of the title is a common phenomenon in Vian's work, and like the story which evades paraphrase, Vian's titles lend themselves ambiguously to interpretation. They defy any automatic associations and the only philosophical message they seem to have is precisely their lack of message.

The years 1954-1955 inaugurated a period of Vian's life marked by intense activity in the field of music. In five years he wrote over four hundred songs. The most famous ones, "Le Politique" and "Le Déserteur," are strongly antimilitaristic; the second was, in essence, an invitation to conscripts to refuse military service. As a result Vian had difficulties with government censors and veterans' organizations, since the Algerian war was in progress. In 1955, in addition to several lesser-known works, he wrote the first French rock-and-roll songs. Because his health had worsened, Vian was advised not to play the trumpet any longer and instead contributed regularly to the magazine *Jazz-Hot* and devoted himself to composing.

In only a few days, in July 1957, Vian wrote *Les Bâtisseurs d'empire; ou, Le Schmürz* (1959; translated as *The Empire Builders*, 1967). It is mostly to this play that Vian owes today his reputation as a playwright, although the play was produced for the first time several months after his death. The Dupont family of *Les Bâtisseurs d'empire*, chased by a menacing and inexplicable noise, moves from one apartment to another, each time climbing one floor. As they move up, they lose a few things, and the apartment diminishes in size and comfort. In one of their lodgings the family finds a strange creature covered with bandages, the *schmürz*. The Dupont parents constantly brutalize the *schmürz* while simultaneously pretending not to see it. Zénobie, the daughter, not only notices the existence of the *schmürz* but is also the

only one to note openly the constant deterioration in the family's circumstances and remember the life before the changes began. Disgusted, the maid leaves and the father eventually sacrifices the daughter and the wife to save his own skin. When faced with the *schmürz*, Dupont, still incapable of confronting his own egoism and hypocrisy, dies, crying out "Je ne savais pas" (I did not know).

Critics tried to attribute meaning to both the strange noise and the *schmürz*. Commonly, the strange noise was associated with Vian's heart disease, whereas most interpretations of the *schmürz* followed Ursula Vian's explanation of the coinage of the word. Derived from the German word *Schmerz*, meaning pain, in the circles of Vian's friends *schmürz* represented an object, a thing that opposes itself to human beings: anything that happens to be in one's way. A materialized essence, *schmürz* was thus also meant to represent the mute hostility of "anti-being."

Critics have suggested that if Vian's three other plays seemed less successful in comparison with *Les Bâtisseurs d'empire*, this is partly because they conformed less to the rules of the theatre of the absurd. As Eugène Ionesco does in his absurdist plays, Vian constantly calls language into question. Several characters often bear the same name, although the usual function of a name is to identify by making distinctions. He uses different nouns to indicate the same things, with the result that statements lose meaning. Indeed, the main function of the language in *Les Bâtisseurs d'empire* seems not to represent or communicate; rather, as in Vian's novels, the language itself becomes the "wor(l)d."

From approximately 1960 on, beginning with the staging of *Les Bâtisseurs d'empire*, which premiered in December 1959, and the publication of number 12 of the *Dossiers Acénonètes du Collège de 'Pataphysique*, with its important bibliography of Vian's writings, his fame as an author, not just as a jazz trumpeter, songwriter, and *mystificateur* (joker), began to spread. Since the early 1960s, there have been numerous republications of his works, and unpublished ones have appeared; he has been the subject of a number of critical studies. At first considered scandalous and controversial, his work continues to challenge traditional literary definitions. Rich linguistic invention, unexpected, vertiginous associations, audacity of thought and word are but a few rewards awaiting the reader of Vian. Demanding, challenging, and provoking, Vian's work questions even textual foundation and aims at Arthur Rimbaud's systematic "déréglement" (disordering) and reinvention. As Vian himself puts it in verses from *Je voudrais pas crever:*

> Ils cassent le monde
> En petits morceaux
> Ils cassent le monde
> Mais ça m'est égal
> Il en reste assez pour moi
> Il en reste assez
> Il suffit que j'aime
> Une plume bleue

> (They break the world
> in little pieces
> They break the world
> But I don't care
> There is still enough left for me
> Still enough
> It's enough for me to love
> a blue pen).

Bibliography:
François Caradec, "Pour une bibliographie de Boris Vian," *Dossiers Acénonètes du Collège de 'Pataphysique,* 12 (1960): 111-138; supplemented in *Dossiers Acénonètes du Collège de 'Pataphysique,* 18-19 (1962): 123-127.

Biographies:
Noël Arnaud, *Les Vies parallèles de Boris Vian* (Paris: Union Générale d'Editions, 1970);
Michel Fauré, *Les Vies posthumes de Boris Vian* (Paris: Union Générale d'Editions, 1975).

References:
Noël Arnaud, *Les Dossiers de l'affaire "J'irai cracher sur vos trombes"* (Paris: Christian Bourgois, 1974);
Jacques Bens, "Un Langage-univers," in Vian's *L'Ecume des jours* (Paris: Union Générale d'Editions, 1963), pp. 175-184;
Bizarre, nos. 39-40, combined issue on Vian (February 1966);
Boris Vian: Colloque du Centre Culturel International de Cerisy-la-Salle, 23 juillet au 2 août 1976, edited by Arnaud and Henri Baudin (Paris: Union Générale d'Editions, 1977);
Pierre Christin, "Gloire posthume et consommation de masse: Boris Vian dans la société française," *Esprit Créateur,* 7 (Summer 1967): 135-143;
Alfred Cismaru, *Boris Vian* (New York: Twayne, 1974);
Jean Clouzet, *Boris Vian* (Paris: Seghers, 1966);
Alain Costes, *Lecture plurielle de "L'Ecume des jours"* (Paris: Union Générale d'Editions, 1979);
Dossiers Acénonètes du Collège de 'Pataphysique, 12 (1960); 18-19 (1962);
Michel Gauthier, *"L'Ecume des jours," analyse critique* (Paris: Hatier, 1973);
Daniel Grojnowski, "L'Univers de Boris Vian," *Critique,* no. 212 (January 1965): 17-28;
David Noakes, *Boris Vian* (Paris: Editions Universitaires, 1964);
Obliques, 8-9, combined Vian issue (1976);
Michel Rybalka, *Boris Vian: Essai d'interprétation et de documentation* (Paris: Lettres Modernes/Minard, 1969).

Marguerite Yourcenar

(8 June 1903-17 December 1987)

C. Frederick Farrell, Jr., and Edith R. Farrell

University of Minnesota at Morris

BOOKS: *Le Jardin des chimères* (Paris: Perrin, 1921);

Les Dieux ne sont pas morts (Paris: Sansot, 1922);

Alexis; ou, Le Traité du vain combat (Paris: Sans Pareil, 1929; revised edition, Paris: Plon, 1965); translated by Walter Kaiser, in collaboration with the author, as *Alexis* (New York: Farrar, Straus & Giroux, 1984; Henley-on-Thames: Ellis, 1984);

La Nouvelle Eurydice (Paris: Grasset, 1931);

Pindare (Paris: Grasset, 1932);

La Mort conduit l'attelage (Paris: Grasset, 1934);

Denier du rêve (Paris: Grasset, 1934; revised edition, Paris: Plon, 1959; definitive edition, Paris: Gallimard, 1971); translated by Dori Katz, in collaboration with the author, as *A Coin in Nine Hands* (New York: Farrar, Straus & Giroux, 1982; Henley-on-Thames: Ellis, 1984);

Feux (Paris: Grasset, 1936; revised edition, Paris: Gallimard, 1974); translated by Katz, in collaboration with the author, as *Fires* (New York: Farrar, Straus & Giroux, 1981; Henley-on-Thames: Ellis, 1982);

Les Songes et les sorts (Paris: Grasset, 1938);

Nouvelles orientales (Paris: Gallimard, 1938; revised, 1963, 1975); translated by Alberto Manguel, in collaboration with the author, as *Oriental Tales* (New York: Farrar, Straus & Giroux, 1985; Henley-on-Thames: Ellis, 1985);

Le Coup de grâce (Paris: Gallimard, 1939); translated by Grace Frick, in collaboration with the author, as *Coup de Grâce* (New York: Farrar, Straus & Cudahy, 1957; London: Secker & Warburg, 1957); French version revised (Paris: Gallimard, 1978); translation revised (New York: Farrar, Straus & Giroux, 1981; Henley-on-Thames: Ellis, 1983);

Mémoires d'Hadrien (Paris: Plon, 1951); enlarged as *Mémoires d'Hadrien, suivis des Carnets de notes des "Mémoires d'Hadrien"* (Paris: Club du Meilleur Livre, 1953); first edition translated by Frick, in collaboration with the au-

Marguerite Yourcenar (courtesy of Mme Yourcenar)

thor, as *Memoirs of Hadrian* (New York: Farrar, Straus & Young, 1954; London: Secker & Warburg, 1955); enlarged as *Memoirs of Hadrian and Reflections on the Composition of "Memoirs of Hadrian"* (New York: Farrar, Straus, 1963; London: Secker & Warburg, 1974); French version enlarged again as *Mémoires d'Hadrien. Suivi des Carnets de notes des "Mémoires d'Hadrien" et d'une note de l'auteur* (Paris: Gallimard, 1971);

L'Ecrivain devant l'histoire (Paris: Centre National de Documentation Pédagogique, 1954);

397

Electre; ou, La Chute des masques (Paris: Plon, 1954); translated as *Electra* in *Plays* (1984);

Les Charités d'Alcippe & autres poèmes (Liége: Flûte Enchantée, 1956); translated by Edith R. Farrell as *The Alms of Alcippe* (New York: Targ Editions, 1982); French version revised and enlarged (Paris: Gallimard, 1984);

Présentation critique de Constantin Cavafy, 1863-1933 (Paris: Gallimard, 1958; revised, 1978);

Sous bénéfice d'inventaire (Paris: Gallimard, 1962); translated by Richard Howard and Frick, in collaboration with the author, as *The Dark Brain of Piranesi and Other Essays* (New York: Farrar, Straus & Giroux, 1984; Henley-on-Thames: Ellis, 1985);

Le Mystère d'Alceste, suivi de Qui n'a pas son Minotaure? (Paris: Plon, 1963); *Qui n'a pas son Minotaure?* translated as *To Each His Minotaur* in *Plays* (1984);

L'Œuvre au noir (Paris: Gallimard, 1968); translated by Frick, in collaboration with the author, as *The Abyss* (New York: Farrar, Straus & Giroux, 1976; London: Weidenfeld & Nicolson, 1976);

Présentation critique d'Hortense Flexner (Paris: Gallimard, 1968);

Théâtre, 2 volumes (Paris: Gallimard, 1971); volume 1 comprises *Rendre à César*, translated as *Render unto Caesar* in *Plays* (1984); *La Petite Sirène*, translated as *The Little Mermaid* in *Plays;* and *Le Dialogue dans le marécage;* volume 2 comprises *Electre; ou La Chute des masques*, translated as *Electra* in *Plays; Le Mystère d'Alceste;* and *Qui n'a pas son Minotaure?,* translated as *To Each His Minotaur* in *Plays;*

Discours de réception à l'Académie royale belge de langue et de littérature françaises, 19 mars 1971 (Paris: Gallimard, 1971);

Souvenirs pieux, suivi de L'Album de Fernande (Monaco: Editions Alphée, 1973);

Archives du Nord (Paris: Gallimard, 1977);

Suite d'estampes pour Kou-Kou-Hai, woodcuts by Nancy McCormick (Seal Harbor, Maine: High Loft, 1980);

Mishima, ou la vision du vide (Paris: Gallimard, 1980); translated by Manguel as *Mishima: A Vision of the Void* (Henley-on-Thames: Ellis, 1986);

Discours de réception de Mme Marguerite Yourcenar à l'Académie française et réponse de M. Jean D'Ormesson (Paris: Gallimard, 1981);

Anna, Soror . . . (Paris: Gallimard, 1981);

Comme l'eau qui coule (Paris: Gallimard, 1982); translated by Kaiser, in collaboration with the author, as *Two Lives and a Dream* (New York: Farrar, Straus & Giroux, 1987; Henley-on-Thames: Ellis, 1987);

Le Temps, ce grand sculpteur (Paris: Gallimard, 1983); translated by Kaiser, in collaboration with the author, as *That Mighty Sculptor, Time* (Henley-on-Thames: Ellis, 1987);

Plays, translated by Yourcenar and Katz (New York: Performing Arts Journal Publications, 1984).

Collection: *Œuvres romanesques* (Paris: Gallimard, 1982).

OTHER: Virginia Woolf, *Les Vagues,* translated by Yourcenar (Paris: Stock, 1937);

Henry James, *Ce que savait Maisie,* translated by Yourcenar (Paris: Laffont, 1947);

Oppian of Syria, *Cynégétique,* translated by Florent Chrestien, preface by Yourcenar (Paris: Société des Cent Une, 1955);

Jayadeva, *Gita Govinda,* translated by François Di Dio and others, preface by Yourcenar (Paris: Emile-Paul, 1957);

Giovanni Battista Piranesi, *Les Prisons imaginaires,* preface by Yourcenar (Paris: Kieffer, 1964);

Fleuve profonde, sombre rivière: Les Negro Spirituals, translated, with commentaries, by Yourcenar (Paris: Gallimard, 1964);

La Couronne et la lyre: Poèmes traduits du grec, translated by Yourcenar (Paris: Gallimard, 1979);

James Baldwin, *Le Coin des "Amen,"* translated by Yourcenar (Paris: Gallimard, 1982);

Blues et gospels, translated by Yourcenar (Paris: Gallimard, 1984);

Cinq Nô modernes, translated by Yourcenar and Jun Shiragi (Paris: Gallimard, 1984);

Le Cheval noir à tête blanche, edited by Yourcenar (Paris: Gallimard, 1985);

La Voix des choses, edited, with translations, by Yourcenar (Paris: Gallimard, 1987).

PERIODICAL PUBLICATIONS: "L'Ile des Morts," *Revue Mondiale,* 1 (1928): 394-399;

"Diagnostic de l'Europe," *Revue de Genève,* 68 (June 1929): 745-752;

"Caprée," *Revue Bleue,* 67 (1929): 371;

"Le Premier Soir," *Revue de France,* 9, no. 6 (1929): 435-449;

"Oscar Wilde," *Revue Bleue,* 67 (1929): 621-627;

"Le Changeur d'or," *Europe,* 29 (1932): 566-577;

"Maléfice," *Mercure de France,* 241 (January 1933): 113-132;

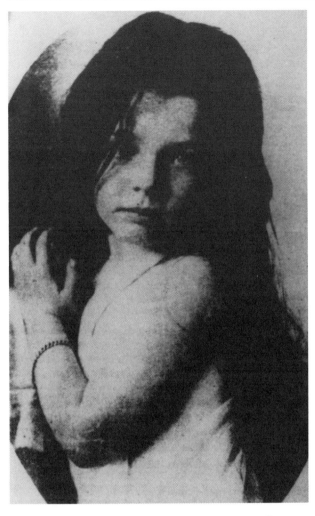

Marguerite Cleenewerck de Crayencour at age five

"Essai de généalogie du Saint," *Revue Bleue,* 72 (June 1934): 460-466;

"Mozart à Salzburg," *Revue Bleue,* 75 (1937): 88-89;

"Mythologies I, II and III," *Lettres Françaises,* 11 (April 1944): 41-46; 14 (October 1944): 33-40; 15 (June 1945): 35-45;

"Carnets de notes d'*Electre*," *Théâtre de France* (1954): n.pag.;

"Carnet de notes 1942-1948," *Table Ronde* (1955): 83-90;

"Lettre à Charles du Bos," *Cahiers Charles du Bos* (9 November 1964): 53-54;

"Animaux vus par un poète grec," *Revue de Paris* (February 1970): 7-11;

"André Gide Revisited," *Cahiers André Gide,* no. 3 (1972): 21-44;

"Le Japon de la mort choisie," *Express* (10 March 1980): 96-98;

"Lettres à Mademoiselle S.," *Nouvelle Revue Française,* no. 327 (April 1980): 180-189;

"Les Charmes de l'innocence: Une Relecture d'Henry James," *Nouvelle Revue Française,* no. 359 (December 1982): 666-673;

"Amrita Pritam: Poèmes," by Yourcenar, Rajesh Sharma, and Charles Brasch, *Nouvelle Revue Française,* no. 365 (June 1983): 166-178;

"Les Trente-trois Noms de Dieu," *Nouvelle Revue Française,* no. 401 (June 1986): 101-117.

Marguerite Yourcenar was the first woman elected to the prestigious Académie Française. A self-taught scholar, novelist, poet, dramatist, essayist, and translator, widely traveled and well read, Yourcenar brought a broadly based sensibility to her literary work. Her writings treat the dawn of time and the future; the physical and the spiritual worlds; characters ranging from peasants to emperors, from courtesans to Hindu gods; nature and civilizations; the arts and religion. Although she frequently ignored or defied literary styles, the advice of critics, and the conventions of Parisian literary life, Yourcenar managed to reach and appeal to a wide audience in France and throughout the world.

Despite her prediction that *Mémoires d'Hadrien* (1951; translated as *Memoirs of Hadrian,* 1954) would find an audience of "a few students of human destiny," it is her best-known work, in part because of its portrayal of the ideal prince, a type that no doubt appealed to readers in the immediate post-World War II period. But for several reasons recognition as one of the leading figures of modern French literature was a long time coming for Yourcenar. She refused to be lionized; she lived from 1939 until her death in 1987 in the United States; she ignored popular trends in order to write about what seemed important to her (ancient Greek verse, alchemy, the Roman Empire, Asia, political allegory), reworking earlier manuscripts or published writings with which she was dissatisfied rather than composing new ones, writing historical novels and refusing alliances with such literary groups as the New Novelists.

Some of the attention that Yourcenar has received has been based on an unseemly interest in her personal affairs rather than on her works. Especially because her books include several bisexual protagonists and because her 1936 book, *Feux* (translated as *Fires,* 1981), is based on her relationship with an unidentified lover, some critics turned to speculation on her private life. Among the qualities in Yourcenar's work in a country that values its language is her style, which is considered exemplary. She has helped to revive forms, such as the *récit*, that anchor her solidly in French literary tradition. With her use of classical myths and standard forms, and more attention to plot and characterization than is common to many of her contemporaries, she has acquired readers who believe in her values and have confidence in her good example. Conservative from a literary point of view, although liberal and universalist in her thinking, she has appealed to a wide enough audience to make her acceptance as the first woman in the Académie Française a national issue and her election to it a major event. A woman who worked for conservationist and ecological causes, consumer protection, and civil rights on the one hand, and on the other a writer whose scholarship, command of her craft, and far-ranging knowledge in many fields were very striking, she occupies a privileged place in twentieth-century letters.

Marguerite Antoinette Jeanne Marie Ghislaine Cleenewerck de Crayencour was born on 8 June 1903 to a French father, Michel, and a Belgian mother, Fernande de Cartier de Marchienne, both of whom came from old and influential families, from Flanders and the Walloon section of Belgium respectively. Because of her mother's wish to be near her relatives, Yourcenar was born in Brussels, although she was immediately registered as a French citizen.

Following Yourcenar's mother's death (ten days after she was born), Yourcenar was brought to Mont-Noir, the ancestral home of the Crayencour family, where she spent the summers during her childhood; winters were spent in Lille for the first two years and afterward in the south of France. At Mont-Noir Yourcenar made contact with the land, with country people, and with animals–all of which had an influence on her life. When she was nine, Yourcenar and her father moved to Paris, where the world of books, museums, and art expanded her environment.

Her first contact with war and exile came in 1914 when, while visiting Ostende, Belgium, she and her father had to flee from the advancing German armies across the channel to England, where they lived for a year before making their way to southern France. It was while at Aix-en-Provence that Yourcenar completed her early education, with her father and with tutors, and received her *baccalauréat* at the age of sixteen. She had already begun to write. The first poems

she wrote, *Les Dieux ne sont pas morts* (The Gods Are Not Dead), which she later referred to as the equivalent of a music student's scales, were privately published in 1922 as her second book. They show her to have been an admirer of the classics, a person sensitive to art, myth, and religions–especially the Roman Catholicism of her own upbringing, as well as other ways of experiencing the divine.

Her first publication, also privately printed, came in 1921, and for it she and her father invented the pen name Yourcenar, a near anagram of Crayencour and the name under which all of her works were published. *Le Jardin des chimères* (The Garden of Chimeras) proved her able to write in the standard French alexandrine, sometimes with Hugoesque twists, and to interpret and expand myths in order to express her own views. This work shows the aspirations of a young person, as Icarus is drawn to Helios, in contrast to the archetype of the wise old man, Daedalus. It is written in the heavily "literary" style not uncommon at the time and introduces such themes as purity, renunciation, spirituality, going beyond the self, and the oneness of the world that remained an integral part of the works of her maturity. Although the work did not receive much notice from critics–one called it "très ambitieux, très long et très ennuyeux" (very ambitious, very long and very boring)–it attracted the attention of the Nobel laureate Rabindranath Tagore, who wrote to the young poet, inviting her to visit him in India.

She chose instead to remain with her father, with whom she traveled during the 1920s. Her preoccupations at this stage show many of the lines which she followed later. Her ambition at twenty, she said, was to be the anonymous author of a few sonnets appreciated by fewer and fewer readers in each generation. This romantic notion was quickly abandoned, and she began to imagine a novel, "Remous" (Eddies), that would weave together characters and plots which crossed geographic and temporal boundaries to form a vast panorama of Renaissance Europe. The emperor Hadrian, too, had already claimed a share of her attention. Later in the 1920s she wrote her first play, *Dialogue dans le marécage* (Dialogue in the Swamp), modeled on a Japanese Nô, and additional poetry, including *Les Charités d'Alcippe* (The Alms of Alcippe), which would not be published in book form for almost thirty years.

In 1929 three events occurred that altered the course of Yourcenar's life. The first, in Janu-

Yourcenar with her father at Mont-Noir, circa 1910

ary, was the death of her father/friend/mentor after a long illness. The second was the Wall Street crash, which caused Yourcenar to lose three-quarters of her fortune, inherited from her mother, signaling the approaching end of the privileged existence she had enjoyed. The third, and most important, was the publication of her first novel, *Alexis; ou, Le Traité du vain combat* (translated, after revisions, as *Alexis* in 1984).

The novel, which is based on the lives of two men of Yourcenar's acquaintance, is written as a letter in the sober prose of the traditional *examen de conscience* (examination of conscience). The story is about the development of an artist faced with opposition from his family and from society. Alexis's letter to his young wife, written after he has left her, attempts to explain his actions. He traces an unhappy childhood, the growth of his love for music, his discovery and "vain struggle" against his homosexual leanings,

the relationship between love and pleasure, his attempts at conforming to the expectations of his family (of which his marriage and child are the most notable), and finally his departure to seek the freedom to express himself through his art. He concludes, "Je vous demande pardon, le plus humblement possible, non pas de vous quitter, mais d'être resté si longtemps" (With the utmost humility, I ask you now to forgive me, not for leaving you, but for having stayed so long).

This book, because of its subtitle echoing André Gide's *La Tentative amoureuse, ou Le Traité du vain désir* (*The Lover's Attempt*, 1893), its bisexual theme, and its form—the *récit*—has frequently been compared to Gide's work, although Yourcenar denied direct influence from him, citing Rainer Maria Rilke instead. Images of Alexis's ancestral home, mirrors (including pools of water and portraits), music, and silence carry forward the theme of the alienation of a young man who perceives himself as different but refuses to accept guilt as a result. *Alexis* was an important step for Yourcenar. It was the first work accepted by a commercial publisher; she even received a small advance for it, which she invested immediately in a blue Lalique vase. It was also the only one of her important works read and appreciated by her father.

The 1930s were the period in which Yourcenar's life and talents took on new dimensions and found new means of expression. During this decade Yourcenar, although in the orbit of Paris as much as any young French writer, spent much of her time living and traveling in Italy, Germany, and, especially, Greece. This was a time of challenge, a time to try new methods, to publish what she had already written, to discover herself as she discovered the world she had loved in books, and to experience the only love of which she speaks—even if indirectly—in her works.

Her books from this period include nine works in various genres. *La Nouvelle Eurydice* (The New Eurydice, 1931) is, like *Alexis*, a first-person novel, but one whose theme of the possibility of understanding another is not well realized. Yourcenar considered it "infiniment raté" (a total failure) and never allowed its republication. *Pindare*, published in 1932 but written ten years earlier, is an imaginative biography and critique on the Greek poet; it has been superseded by her commentary on the poet in the 1979 anthology of Greek poetry in translation, *La Couronne et la lyre* (The Crown and the Lyre), in which she makes "honorable amends" for her youthful at-

Yourcenar in June 1923 at her Paris apartment, where she lived with her father following the publication of her first two books (courtesy of Mme Yourcenar)

tempt, which lacked the scholarship of the later work. *La Mort conduit l'attelage* (Death Drives the Team, 1934), well received at the time of its publication, is a collection of three novelettes, taken from the unfinished novel "Remous": "D'après Greco," "D'après Rembrandt," and "D'après Dürer" ("D'après" meaning "after," "in the manner of " each). *Denier du rêve* (1934; translated, after revisions, as *A Coin in Nine Hands* in 1982) is a major novel, although it received little critical attention. It explores the boundaries of dream and reality, the points of intersection between myth and life. Written in and about the Italy of 1933, this remains Yourcenar's only novel with a contemporary setting. The characters constitute a modern commedia del l'arte, and each has a mythological counterpart. Although clearly a condemnation of fascism, with a plot that concerns attempts to assassinate Mussolini, the novel focuses primarily on the lives of individuals, on their beliefs, values, and ways of coping with political reality and with each other. The contrast between appearance and reality is constantly stressed. Of Dida it is noted, "On la disait mauvaise: elle était dure comme la terre, avide comme la racine . . ." (She had the reputation of being mean: she was hard as the earth, eager like a root . . .). Rome, as home to the characters, art center, political reality, and historic archetype of the City, also plays an active role in the novel.

Feux is an unclassifiable work. It is a collection of prose poems, short stories, and sketches on many kinds of love (for a lover, God, justice, and so forth) interspersed with *pensées*, or reflections, taken primarily from the author's diary, in which the progress of an "amour fou" (mad love affair) is not so much recounted as alluded to. The *pensées* also comment on the poems and are, in turn, elucidated by them. Excellent examples of Yourcenar's more elaborate style, both *Feux* and *Denier du rêve* repay close stylistic study. In these volumes the theme of religion, already present in Yourcenar's earlier works, is highlighted in several important scenes, while dreams assume a major role for the first time. Themes relating to the family, the mother and child, the artist, purity, the soul and the body, the outlaw, and death, especially suicide, are important.

A volume of short stories, *Nouvelles orientales*, reveals a wide range of Eastern and Near Eastern interests fostered by travel and reading. The collection has been twice revised since its first publication in 1938, once in 1963 by dropping one story, rewriting the ending of one, and retitling two others, and again in 1975 by adding a new tale. The English version, *Oriental Tales*, appeared in 1985. Sources range from Taoist and Hindu stories to Japanese literature to Balkan legends to an item in a Greek newspaper. The themes include love, again in very diverse forms; the relationship of man and God; art; heroism; and several possible reactions to the human condition. "Comment Wang-Fô fut sauvé" and "La

Yourcenar with American poet Hortense Flexner, whose work Yourcenar translated (courtesy of Mme Yourcenar)

Veuve Aphrodissia" are especially worthy of mention.

During the same period Yourcenar produced *Les Vagues* (1937), a translation of Virginia Woolf's 1931 novel *The Waves,* and the essay *Les Songes et les sorts* (Dreams and Destinies, 1938). The latter recounts Yourcenar's important recurring dreams, which contain images and symbols basic in her life. The book is prefaced by a refutation of Freudian dream theory.

Other translation projects of these years include works not published until later: *Ce que savait Maisie* (What Maisie Knew) by Henry James (1947), the beginning of her work on Negro spirituals, which was to become *Fleuve profonde, sombre rivière* (Deep River, Dark River, 1964), and poems later included in *Présentation critique de Constantin Cavafy* (1958), her critical volume on the Greek poet.

Yourcenar's final pre-World War II novel is

Le Coup de grâce (1939; translated as *Coup de Grâce,* 1957), considered by many to be among her finest. Constructed like a classical tragedy, with, as one commentator put it, unities of "time, place and danger" and in a very restrained style, the novel, set in Kurland during the Russian Revolution, treats a love triangle. Another first-person narrative, the story is remembered by Eric von Lhommond, a mercenary, half-German, half-French, recently wounded in Spain during the 1930s civil war. From his early days as an anti-Bolshevik resistance fighter, he recalls Conrad, the young man whom he loved, or, at least, whom he cast as Patrocles to his Achilles, and Conrad's sister, Sophie, who loved Eric, but who was rejected by him. In despair she joined the Bolsheviks and was eventually captured and executed—by Eric's hand in accordance with her last request. Eric reflects: "J'ai pensé d'abord qu'en

Yourcenar with her spaniel, Valentine, at Petite Plaisance, 1967 (courtesy of Mme Yourcenar)

me demandant de remplir cet office, elle avait cru me donner une dernière preuve d'amour et la plus définitive de toutes. J'ai compris depuis qu'elle n'avait voulu que se venger, et me léguer des remords. Elle avait calculé juste . . ." (At first I thought that in asking me to perform this duty she had intended to give me a final proof of her love, the most conclusive proof of all. But I understood afterward that she only wished to take revenge, leaving me prey to remorse. She was right in that . . .).

When World War II began Yourcenar once again found herself trapped. Low on funds, unable to find a position, and prevented from returning to Greece as she had planned, she accepted the invitation of her American friend and translator Grace Frick to make her second visit to the United States (where she had stayed briefly in 1937, taking notes on Hadrian at Yale) for a six-month lecture tour. Although Yourcenar traveled abroad for periods of as much as two years, she established her permanent home in the United States at that time.

The break in her life around 1940 was profound. Not only did she suffer, as did many exiles, from a forced separation from the places and people that had been part of her life, but she was also obliged for the first time to earn a living, taking jobs in journalism and commercial translation before accepting a position as parttime instructor at Sarah Lawrence College in 1942. She found teaching–particularly to American students with a background very different from her own–extremely trying.

"Le désespoir d'un écrivain qui n'écrit pas" (The despair of a writer who does not write) enveloped Yourcenar during much of this decade. She spent much of the time required for commuting to work in New York from Hartford reading the Loeb series classics. She was a frequent visitor at the Hartford museum, and she became involved with that city's Wadsworth Athenaeum Theater, led by Everett (Chic) Austin, for which she wrote the play *La Petite Sirène* (1971; translated as *The Little Mermaid* in *Plays,* 1984). She wrote articles on Greek myth, published in *Lettres Françaises* in Buenos Aires; and first versions of the plays *Le Mystère d'Alceste* (The Mystery of Alcestes) and *Electre; ou, La Chute des masques* (*Electra*), also published in journals. In poetry, she wrote imitations and produced translations of Negro spirituals as well as of Constantin Cavafy and ancient Greek poets.

404

The break with her past life was formalized in 1947 when she became an American citizen and, at the same time, took Marguerite Yourcenar as her legal name. It was further reinforced in 1950 when she, with Grace Frick, acquired Petite Plaisance, the modest white house on Mount Desert Island in Maine, where she lived until her death.

The arrival in 1948 of trunks Yourcenar had deposited in Lausanne before the war provided the spark needed to reactivate her literary career. Among other old letters, one beginning "Mon cher Marc" (My dear Mark) was, she realized with shock, what remained of her former attempt to write the life of the Emperor Hadrian. From that moment on, she knew she had to finish the project. The three years of intense work that followed, described in "Carnets de notes des *Mémoires d'Hadrien*" (published in the 1953 revised edition of the novel and translated in *Memoirs of Hadrian and Reflections on the Composition of "Memoirs of Hadrian,"* 1963), involved scholarship and "sympathetic magic," as she attempted to look at the second century with the soul of a second-century observer in order to attain a closer communion over time with the emperor.

The novel is an imagined first-person narrative in letter form, written by Hadrian shortly before his death, when action has had to yield to contemplation and analysis of his accomplishments. Published in 1951, Yourcenar's attempt to "refaire [l'histoire] du dedans" (redo [history] from within) shows Hadrian primarily as the Good Prince; his meditations on classical art, dreams, destiny, religions, women, freedom, and so forth make him an extremely well-rounded character. Similarly, the events of his life in politics, love, and war are documented, chronicling the self-improvement that allows him to realize his own potential and his plans for the Roman Empire. The book was almost universally admired, critics and the public alike being particularly attracted to the episode of Hadrian's love for the handsome Bithynian, Antinoüs.

Mémoires d'Hadrien changed Yourcenar's life. The fulfillment of her youthful plans, ones that she had renounced as impossible several times, the unexpected international success of the book, which received the Fémina-Vacaresco prize and an award from the Académie Française, among other honors, served to establish Yourcenar firmly in the line which she would continue to follow over the next decades.

Yourcenar at work in her study (courtesy of Mme Yourcenar)

In the 1950s she spent much of her time in travel, visiting such spots as Spain, England, northern France, Belgium, and Germany that would serve as bases for future works. In this decade, too, the essay assumed greater importance in Yourcenar's work, with the appearance of several interesting examples of the genre and reflections on the writing of *Mémoires d'Hadrien* and of *Electre* ("Carnets de notes d'*Electre*," published in *Théâtre de France* in 1954), precursors of the substantial prefaces she characteristically included in later works. Having reached middle age, she also began the task of completing, refining, and consolidating the corpus of her literary production. Other kinds of work appeared in book form for the first time: the final version of her play *Electre; ou, La Chute des masques* was published in 1954; *Les Charités d'Alcippe* (1956; translated as *The Alms of Alcippe,* 1982) is a collection of her poetry, including a few poems revised from her first volume; Yourcenar wrote prefaces for French translations of the Hindu *Gita Govinda* (1957) and for Oppian's *Cynegetica* (*Cynégétique*, 1955); and, most important, she began the task of reconsidering and rewriting her early works. *Denier du rêve* was the first to be revised, in 1959. Almost half of it was changed, giving both the events and the characters greater definition and therefore greater impact. She planned to revise the collection of three novelettes entitled *La Mort conduit l'attelage* but instead decided to transform one story only, that of the philosopher-alchemist Zeno, into a major novel, *L'Œuvre au noir* (1968; translated as *The Abyss*, 1976), which took ten years to complete. During this decade also, Yourcenar became ever more concerned about social evils and involved in groups and programs aimed at combatting them. She joined both American and European societies fighting for civil rights, world peace, protection of the environment, endangered or mistreated animals, and consumer protection, as well as groups against nuclear proliferation and overpopulation.

The 1960s saw the continuation or completion of several projects, fiction and nonfiction, all reflecting Yourcenar's deepening concern with the need to speak out unambiguously against evil and with the parallel concern of preserving and appreciating the good and the beautiful that human beings have produced. Two more plays were published during the decade, both based on Greek myth, of which *Qui n'a pas son Minotaure?* (1963; translated as *To Each His Minotaur* in *Plays*, 1984) most clearly bears the stamp of this activist period of her life. A new version of the Theseus legend, it shows characters moving blindly toward the Minotaur as Yourcenar had seen people moving toward the horrors of the concentration camps or the front lines. Their leader, Theseus, the antithesis of Hadrian, is shallow, vain, insensitive, fickle, and egocentric. Ariadne's closing scene is particularly noteworthy as a capsulized vision of the progress of a soul toward the divine and a striking contrast to the youthful picture of Icarus in Yourcenar's first work. This play, like others by Yourcenar that have been staged, was not well received. Although her novels have much of the dramatic, her dramas have too much of the novelistic to play well. They are better read, when one has time to stop, savor, and interpret for himself.

Her first collection of essays, *Sous bénéfice d'inventaire*, written over the preceding ten years, was published in 1962 and won the Prix Combat;

in 1984 it appeared in English translation as *The Dark Brain of Piranesi and Other Essays*. *Fleuve profonde, sombre rivière*, her collection of Negro spirituals and freedom songs, appeared two years later, with an introductory essay on the songs' artistic value and on the historical and current condition of blacks in America. As in her novels, Yourcenar finds no easy solution to the problem of inequality, nor does she attribute blame; all of humanity is implicated.

Her master work of the 1960s is *L'Œuvre au noir* (1968), a historical panorama of sixteenth-century Europe that rivals that of second-century Rome in *Mémoires d'Hadrien*. Although critics responded very favorably to this novel, which won the Prix Fémina, some readers find it difficult. The story centers around the lives of two young men, Henry-Maximilian Ligre and Zeno, his bastard cousin. While both were born into the wealthy Ligre family, whose textile and banking interests make it a power in Europe, Henry sets out at sixteen to find love and glory as a soldier. For Henry, "Il s'agit d'être homme" (One wants to be a man), while Zeno, at twenty, sees fifty years of study before him, which will include theology, medicine, and alchemy: "il s'agit d'être plus qu'un homme" (for me it is a matter of being more than a man). Neither has great respect for the path chosen by the other, but each believes that it would be ridiculous to die without at least attempting to travel the path one sees before him.

The first section, entitled "La Vie errante" (The Wanderings), tells the story of Zeno's early life and travels that are portrayed in "D'après Dürer" of *La Mort conduit l'attelage*. While working on what was to be the last part of the novel, however, Yourcenar, in a monastery in Salzburg on one of her many trips abroad, met the man who served as the model for the character of the Prior, which changed the direction of her almost completed novel. Already Yourcenar had depicted the political unrest, the misery of Renaissance workers in contrast to the ostentatious life-style of the rich, the conditions prevalent in seminaries and at the Sorbonne, the Reformation and the Counter-Reformation; the story now turns to philosophy, alchemy, and mysticism, and broadens into an interplay of conflicting powers: the church, the state, the wealthy, the right-thinkers. Two long chapters, "La Conversation à Innsbruck" (A Conversation in Innsbruck) and "L'Abîme" (The Abyss), provide a philosophic counterpart to Zeno's life of study, work, and travel, just as Hadrian's meditations counterbalanced his life as ruler and soldier.

Zeno's development is frequently conveyed in alchemical symbolism and parallels the successive stages of the alchemists' great task: "l'Œuvre au noir" or the Black Work (of separation and dissolution), the White Work (of purification and serving one's fellowman), and the Red Work (a fusion of the soul and the body with the absolute in a blinding vision). All of life overflows this canvas, which sometimes teems like Bosch's *Garden of Earthly Delights* and sometimes focuses on one figure like Dürer's *Melancholia,* which inspired the original tale's title. About one quarter of the minor characters in this work were taken by Yourcenar from local chronicles and some of the others are historical figures, but the central characters are fictional. Their souls are the battlegrounds of conflict, and many of them are destroyed in the struggle.

In Zeno's case, he gives up both his travels and his dangerous writings, even his real name, to live in obscurity and treat the sick at a monastery in Bruges, a city he had left in his youth. Involved in continuing discussions with his friend and primary patient, the Prior, who is his soul mate (although one who has kept his faith), and, in spite of himself, with the Angels, a group of young monks who have discovered the flesh and will pay for their sins at the stake, Zeno still has time to rethink his life and round it out. Wrongly accused of complicity with the Angels' revels, Zeno argues his often heretical opinions before a board of accusers whose attitudes mirror those of the times. His suicide, despite efforts of his first teacher and priest to save him, affirms his right to decide his own fate and meet death with dignity.

In Yourcenar's historical novels the characters are shaped by their times in a way that is plausible and convincing. The ways in which she has crafted these poetic and scholarly re-creations, as well as the major influences on her writing, are explained in notes appended to the novels and in articles, especially "Jeux de miroirs et feux follets" (Mirror Games and Will-o'-the-wisps) and in "Ton et langage dans le roman historique" (Tone and Language in the Historical Novel), both collected in *Le Temps, ce grand sculpteur* (1983; translated as *That Mighty Sculptor, Time,* 1987). Together these articles elucidate her self-imposed criteria for the historical novel. The relevance of such work for the twentieth century—encouragement in the case of *Mémoires d'Hadrien*

Yourcenar at the Temple de l'Emeraude in Thailand, 1983
(courtesy of Mme Yourcenar)

and warning in *L'Œuvre au noir*–is clear, although the author does not allow her voice to intrude in the novels.

During the 1970s Yourcenar lived in Maine the immobile life that Zeno experienced in Bruges, also caring for the sick, in this case Grace Frick, who had been seriously ill at intervals since about 1958. During this time she began to receive honors in increasing number. In 1961, 1968, and 1972 she received honorary doctorates from Smith, Bowdoin, and Colby Colleges. She was elected in 1970 to the Académie Royale Belge de Langue et Littérature Françaises; she was named to the Légion d'Honneur (1971) and received the Prix Littéraire de Monaco (1972), the Grand Prix National de la Culture (1974), and the Grand Prix de l'Académie Française (1977); in March 1980, three months after Frick's death, she was elected to the Académie Française.

Counterbalancing her relatively static physical life, her imagination ranged more widely, in both time and space, as she composed her semi-autobiographical work under the general title "Le Labyrinthe du monde" (The World's Labyrinth). Her translations of Greek poetry, *La Couronne et la lyre* (1979), show its progression through twelve centuries. This volume, which includes critical introductions to periods and authors, is highly regarded by scholars of Greek and continued Yourcenar's interest with the ancient world.

Her major works of the 1970s are the first two volumes of "Le Labyrinthe du monde." The first, *Souvenirs pieux* (Dear Departed, 1973), takes its somewhat ironical title from leaflets that used to be printed to commemorate deceased family members and is devoted to her mother's family. Some fifty pages describe the author's birth and her mother's death ten days later. Yourcenar then goes back to the earliest references to the family and progresses toward the "present" of the book's beginning. A part of the work's interest centers around the ways by which a writer, already near seventy, tries to gain an understanding of, and perhaps a belated bond with, a mother who died at thirty-one.

The scenes of *Souvenirs pieux* are, to a large extent, colored with the gray of landscapes on rainy days. Yourcenar describes her mother's childhood, repressed by an unapproachable father to whom his children must write their New Year's greetings; a young cousin, Rémo, with whom Yourcenar feels kinship and who, for political reasons, commits suicide at age twenty-eight to the strains of Wagner; and an "uncle," Octave Primez, a successful author, who can tame wild animals, is attached to nature, tries to present only elevated sentiments in his writings, and is haunted all his life by what he calls his brother's "fatal accident."

Archives du Nord (The Archives of Nord, 1977), the second volume of "Le Labyrinthe du Monde," deals with her father's family and is enlivened by the wit, irony, and sure touch familiar to readers of Yourcenar's work. The two most memorable characters in this volume are Yourcenar's father, Michel, soldier, humanist, gambler, and lover, whom the author greatly admires, and her grandmother, Noémi, whom she detests.

In both of these volumes Yourcenar uses techniques developed for her historical novels. Pictures and objects speak to her; travel supplies the backdrop; a "sympathetic participation" breathes life into the long-dead or the frankly imagined characters; and centuries of scholarship are combined to lend authenticity to the whole. Of three of her characters, two real and one fictional, Yourcenar says, "Mes rapports avec ces trois hommes sont bien simples. J'ai pour Rémo une brûlante estime. 'L'oncle Octave' tantôt m'émeut et tantôt m'irrite. Mais j'aime Zénon comme un frère" (My relations with these three men are quite simple. I have great admiration for Rémo. "Uncle Octave" is alternately moving and annoying. But I love Zeno like a brother). The genre of the books has been debated, but it is generally agreed that they cross generic lines, particularly in those parts dealing with generations beyond the author's grandparents, which are the province of only a novelist.

Following the death of Grace Frick, Yourcenar embarked once more on her world travels, this time accompanied by Jerry Wilson, an American whom she had met while collecting material for *Fleuve profonde, sombre rivière*. She was setting out on the first of these–a tour of the Caribbean–when she learned of her election to the Académie Française. In 1980 she received an honorary degree from Harvard, and in subsequent years she traveled often: to France, England, the Low Countries, Denmark, North Africa, Spain and Portugal, Italy, Egypt, Greece, Canada, Japan, Thailand, India, and Kenya, visiting some more than once.

During these trips Yourcenar continued to work on the projects at hand. On some of them she revisited sites that were important to her when she was writing earlier books; in Antinopolis (Egypt) she recalled Hadrian; in Alexandria, Cavafy; several trips to Bruges were like visits to Zeno. On one trip she admired the birds on the island of Texel; on another she visited the barrier islands of Virginia. At her early childhood home, Mont-Noir, she was present in 1982 at the opening of a small game preserve named in her honor. Still other travels established contacts for new projects: in Japan she began her translation of five modern Nô plays with her collaborator Jun Shiragi; in Saint-Paul-de-Vence she visited James Baldwin, whose play *The Amen Corner* she was translating; all these travels contributed to her work in progress "Le Tour de la prison."

Her production in the 1980s surpassed even that of the 1930s. Much of it was the result of many years of preparation; some of it breaks new ground. *Comme l'eau qui coule* (1982; translated as *Two Lives and a Dream*, 1987) is the only original fiction of the first half of the decade. It contains three novelettes based, as was *L'Œuvre au noir,* on stories from *La Mort conduit l'attelage. Anna Soror . . .* , published separately in 1981 before collection in *Comme l'eau qui coule,* is set in sixteenth-century Naples, at that time a kingdom belonging to Spain. It is the passionate love story of a sister and brother, Anna and Miguel de la Cerna y los Herreros, who are raised in an atmosphere of piety, but who exultantly consummate their love with no remorse and seek salvation afterward: he by dying while repelling pirates, she in a life of duty in marriage and widowhood during which she never forgets her only love.

In "Un Homme obscur" (A Common Man) Nathanaël, the humblest of all Yourcenar's protagonists, accepts life as it comes, adjusting to different places, people, and jobs as circumstances change, recoiling instinctively from the kinds of problems that might be countered with action or articulate arguments. The novelette is set in Greenwich, England, in Jamaica, on islands off the coast of Maine, and in Holland; Nathanaël finds exile and love, marries twice, and acts as father to a child, perhaps his own by a prostitute who is hanged; his occupations range from sailor to proofreader to servant. The themes of love, marriage and the family, God, relations with one's neighbor, and others common to many of Yourcenar's novels appear in "Un Homme obscur," but seen "from below." Comparisons and contrasts with both events and ideas found in *L'Œuvre au noir,* for example, underscore the limitations in life as it is lived by the underprivileged and indeed, to varying degrees, by all humankind.

"Une Belle Matinée" (A Lovely Morning), drawn, like "Un Homme commun," from "D'après Rembrandt," relates how Nathanaël's son, Lazare, runs away with a troupe of actors, thus enlarging his experience through travel and through the plays in which he is by turns hero and villain, king and subject, man and woman. Theater images, common in Yourcenar's work as a way of conveying the hidden side of her characters, are here used explicitly to show the variety and multiplicity of human endeavors and potential that reside in one boy.

Many of her books in the 1980s have been devoted to making authors and works from other literature known to French readers: *Le Coin des "Amen,"* her translation of Baldwin, appeared in 1982, followed two years later by *Blues et gospels,* which features translations by Yourcenar of American black songs accompanied by photographs by Jerry Wilson. *Mishima, ou la vision du vide* (1980;

translated as *Mishima: A Vision of the Void,* 1986) is a long study of the life, values, and works of the Japanese playwright who died by ritual suicide (*seppuku*) in 1969. *Cinq Nô modernes* (Five Modern Nô Plays, 1984), a translation of Mishima's theater, gives readers additional insight into his art and into a Japanese literary form. Yourcenar also produced translations from Indian sources. "Amrita Pritam: Poèmes," a 1983 article, written in collaboration with Rajesh Sharma and Charles Brasch, in the *Nouvelle Revue Française,* offers a sampling of the poetry of a woman from the Punjab. In her 1985 work, *Le Cheval noir à tête blanche* (The Black Horse with the White Head), Yourcenar presents a collection of tales told and illustrated by children of the Abenaki tribes in Maine. In 1984 a revised and enlarged edition of *Les Charités d'Alcippe* appeared. It gives an overall view of her early poetry, most of it in standard verse form, and includes additional poems from several later periods. *Le Temps, ce grand sculpteur* contains some of the best of her essays that appeared earlier in journals as well as previously unpublished materials. Especially noteworthy are discussions of problems Yourcenar encountered while writing her novels and comments on her methods of reading, her views of time, religions (Oriental and Occidental), suicide, art, current issues, and the eternal problem of being.

During a stop in Nairobi in 1983, the year after Yourcenar was elected to the American Academy of Arts and Letters, she and Wilson were hit by a police car recklessly driven. The next year the flu interrupted her work for a considerable time. In 1985 Wilson was diagnosed as having tuberculosis and, in September, Yourcenar suffered a heart attack, necessitating open-heart surgery. She recovered, but Wilson died of viral meningitis in February 1986, a loss that could not be compensated by the medals bestowed on her later the same month by the Légion d'Honneur and the National Institute of Arts and Letters in the United States.

She continued to work, especially on "Quoi? l'Eternité," the third volume of "Le Labyrinthe du monde," but the book posed enormous technical problems for her and was never finished. The last book published in her lifetime, *La Voix des choses* (The Voices of Things, 1987), is comprised, as was *Blues et Gospels,* of photographs by Wilson and texts chosen (and sometimes translated) by Yourcenar. It may be said to represent her worldview. The photographs show the beauty she found in earth forms, birds, and plants. The texts are those which long served her as bedside or travel reading and which cull the wisdom and the poetry of thousands of years of both Oriental and Occidental cultures.

Yourcenar maintained her interests to the end. In the last three months of her life she gave two speeches, one in Canada on "superpollution" and one at Harvard on Jorge Luis Borges. She had planned to travel to Paris and from there to India and Nepal, but on 8 November 1987 she suffered a stroke, which led to her death on 17 December. Her grave, near the memorials to Grace Frick and Jerry Wilson, is in the cemetery at Somesville, Maine, close to the first house where she lived on Mount Desert Island.

Interviews:

Paul Guth, "Avec Marguerite Yourcenar à Paris," *Figaro Littéraire,* no. 702 (3 October 1959): 8;

Jean Chalon, "Pourquoi vivre à Paris quand on partage son existence avec Hadrien et Zénon," *Figaro,* 1153 (20 May 1968): 28;

Françoise Mallet-Joris, "Le Kimono blanc de Marguerite Yourcenar," *Nouvel Observateur,* no. 212 (2-8 December 1968): 44-45;

Guy Le Clec'h, "La Régression de l'humanisme," *Nouvelles Littéraires,* no. 2280 (4 June 1971): 9;

Jean-Michel Royer, "Marguerite Yourcenar," *Actualité,* no. 88 (March 1972): 64-72;

Patrick de Rosbo, *Entretiens radiophoniques avec Marguerite Yourcenar* (Paris: Mercure de France, 1972);

Matthieu Galey, *Les Yeux ouverts: Entretiens avec Matthieu Galey* (Paris: Centurion, 1980); translated by Arthur Goldhammer as *With Open Eyes: Conversations with Matthieu Galey* (Boston: Beacon Press, 1984).

References:

Jean Blot, *Marguerite Yourcenar* (Paris: Seghers, 1971); reprinted in *Bulletin de la Société Internationale d'Etudes Yourcenariennes,* 1 number to date (Tours: Université de Tours, 1987-);

Cahiers des Saisons, special section on Yourcenar, no. 38 (September 1964);

Etudes Littéraires, special issue on Yourcenar, edited by Yvon Bernier and Vincent Nadeau, 12 (April 1979);

C. Frederick Farrell, Jr., and Edith R. Farrell, *Marguerite Yourcenar in Counterpoint* (Lanham,

Md., New York & London: University Press of America, 1983);

Farrell and Farrell, "Title as Image: Le Chef rouge/La Veuve Aphrodissia," *Romanic Review,* 74 (March 1983): 233-244;

Colette Gaudin, "Marguerite Yourcenar's Prefaces: Genesis as Self-Effacement," *Studies in Twentieth-Century Literature,* 10 (Fall 1985): 31-55;

Pierre Horn, *Marguerite Yourcenar* (Boston: Twayne, 1985);

Elena Real, ed., *Actes du colloque international Valencia (Espagne), 1984,* proceedings of the 1984 colloquium sponsored by the Société Internationale d'Etudes Yourcenariennes (Valencia: Universidad de Valencia, 1986);

Harry C. Rutledge, "Marguerite Yourcenar: The Classicism of *Feux* and *Mémoires d'Hadrien,*" *Classical and Modern Literature,* 4 (Winter 1984): 87-99;

Emese Soos, "The Only Motion is Returning: The Metaphor of Alchemy in Mallet-Joris and Yourcenar," *French Forum,* 4 (January 1979): 3-16;

Geneviève Spencer-Noël, *Zénon, ou Le Thème de l'alchimie dans "L'Œuvre au noir" de Marguerite Yourcenar* (Paris: Nizet, 1981);

Sud, special section on Yourcenar, no. 55 (1984);

Helen Watson-Williams, "Hadrian's Story Recalled," *Nottingham French Studies,* 23 (October 1984): 35-48;

Janet Whatley, "*Mémories d'Hadrien:* A Manual for Princes," *University of Toronto Quarterly,* 50 (Winter 1980-1981): 221-237.

Papers:

Some of Yourcenar's correspondence with Natalie Barney is housed at the Bibliothèque Littéraire Jacques Doucet in Paris. There is a limited selection of letters, manuscripts, and memorabilia at the library of Bowdoin College, Brunswick, Maine, for which a catalogue, *The Yourcenar Collection,* edited by Robert R. Nunn and Edward J. Geary, is available. Yourcenar's remaining correspondence, both business and personal, is at the Houghton Library, Harvard University. A portion of it, as well as fragments of her journals, has been sealed until fifty years after the author's death. This collection also includes both manuscripts and typescripts, some containing annotations and corrections, including one for *Denier du rêve* with Yourcenar's sketches.

Books for Further Reading

The following list includes a number of histories of French literature and other volumes bearing on the literary trends of the first half of this century or dealing with more than one author treated in this volume. This list is necessarily very restrictive. Additional sources, both general and specific, are listed in the major bibliographies of criticism on modern French literature. Among them, in addition to the annual *MLA International Bibliography*, are Douglas W. Alden and Richard A. Brooks, *A Critical Bibliography of French Literature*, volume 6: *The Twentieth Century*, 3 parts (Syracuse: Syracuse University Press, 1979), a work indispensable for scholars; Douglas W. Alden, et al., eds., *French XX Bibliography: Critical and Biographical Reference for the Study of French Literature Since 1885* (New York: French Institute-Alliance Française, 1949-1985; Selinsgrove, Pa.: Susquehanna University Press, 1986-), which is not annotated but lists primary works and book reviews as well as critical works; Otto Klapp, *Bibliographie der französischen Literaturwissenschaft* (Frankfurt: Klosterman, 1960-), not annotated, but very thorough and particularly good for European criticism; and the bibliography in *Revue d'Histoire Littéraire de la France*, edited by René Rancœur (formerly a quarterly or annual section of the journal, now printed as issue number 3 of each volume). Major collections of manuscripts from modern French writers are at the Bibliothèque Nationale in Paris, the Bibliothèque Littéraire Jacques Doucet in Paris, and the University of Texas at Austin.

Albérès, René Marill. *L'Aventure intellectuelle du XXe siècle, 1900-1950*. Paris: Nouvelle Edition, 1950. Revised and enlarged as *L'Aventure intellectuelle du XXe siècle: Panorama des littératures européennes 1900-1959*. Paris: Albin Michel, 1959.

Albérès. *Bilan littéraire du XXe siècle*. Paris: Aubier, 1956. Revised edition, 1962. Later revised edition, Paris: Nizet, 1971.

Albérès. *Histoire du roman moderne*. Paris: Albin Michel, 1962. Revised editions, 1967-1971.

Boisdeffre, Pierre de. *Histoire de la littérature de langue française, des annéees 1930 aux années 1980*, 2 volumes. Revised edtion, Paris: Perrin, 1985.

Boisdeffre, ed. *Dictionnaire de littérature contemporaine 1900-1962*. Paris: Editions Universitaires, 1962. Revised edition, Paris: Editions Universitaires, 1963.

Brée, Germaine. *Littérature française: Le XXe siècle*, volume 2: *1920-1970*. Paris: Arthaud, 1975. Translated by Louise Guiney as *Twentieth-Century French Literature*. Chicago: University of Chicago Press, 1983.

Brée and Margaret Guiton. *An Age of Fiction: The French Novel from Gide to Camus*. New Brunswick, N.J.: Rutgers University Press, 1957. Revised as *The French Novel from Gide to Camus*. New York: Harcourt, Brace & World, 1962.

Brombert, Victor. *The Intellectual Hero: Studies in the French Novel, 1880-1955*. Philadelphia & New York: Lippincott, 1961.

Burnier, Michel. *Les Existentialistes et la politique*. Paris: Gallimard, 1966. Translated by Bernard Murchland as *Choice of Action: The French Existentialists on the Political Front Line*. New York: Random House, 1968.

Cruickshank, John, ed. *French Literature and Its Background*, volume 6: *The Twentieth Century*. New York & London: Oxford University Press, 1970.

Cryle, P. M. *The Thematics of Commitment: The Tower and the Plain*. Princeton: Princeton University Press, 1985.

Dällenbach, Lucien. *Le Récit spéculaire: Essai sur la mise en abyme*. Paris: Editions du Seuil, 1977.

Falk, Eugene H. *Types of Thematic Structure: The Nature and Function of Motifs in Gide, Camus, and Sartre*. Chicago & London: University of Chicago Press, 1967.

Fowlie, Wallace. *Climate of Violence: The French Literary Tradition from Baudelaire to the Present*. New York: Macmillan, 1967.

Fowlie. *A Guide to Contemporary French Literature: From Valéry to Sartre*. New York: Meridian, 1957.

Frohock, Wilbur M. *Style and Temper: Studies in French Fiction, 1925-1960*. Cambridge, Mass.: Harvard University Press, 1967; Oxford: Blackwell, 1967.

Genette, Gérard. *Figures I-III*. Paris: Seuil, 1966-1972. Selections from all three volumes translated by Alan Sheridan as *Figures of Literary Discourse*. New York: Columbia University Press, 1982. Part of *Figures III* translated by Jane E. Lewin as *Narrative Discourse: An Essay on Method*. Ithaca: Cornell University Press, 1980.

Knight, Everett W. *Literature Considered as Philosophy: The French Example*. London: Routledge and Kegan Paul, 1957.

Magny, Claude-Edmonde. *Histoire du roman français depuis 1918*. Paris: Editions du Seuil, 1950.

Muñoz, Maryse Bertrand de. *La Guerre civile espagnole et la littérature française*. Montreal: Didier, 1972.

Nadeau, Maurice. *Le Roman français depuis la guerre*. Paris: Gallimard, 1963.

O'Brien, Justin. *The French Literary Horizon*. New Brunswick, N.J.: Rutgers University Press, 1967.

Pasco, Allan H. *Novel Configurations: A Study of French Fiction*. Birmingham, Ala.: Summa, 1987.

Peyre, Henri. *The Contemporary French Novel*. New York: Oxford University Press, 1955. Revised as *French Novelists of Today*. New York: Oxford University Press, 1967.

Peyre. *French Literary Imagination and Dostoevsky and Other Essays*. University: University of Alabama Press, 1975.

Picon, Gaëtan. *Contemporary French Literature 1945 and After*. New York: Ungar, 1974.

Rieuneau, Maurice. *Guerre et révolution dans le roman français de 1919 à 1939*. Paris: Klincksieck, 1974.

Robert, Marthe. *Roman des origines et origines du roman*. Paris: Grasset, 1972. Translated by Sacha Rabinovitch as *The Origins of the Novel*. Bloomington: Indiana University Press, 1980.

Robinson, Christopher. *French Literature in the Twentieth Century*. Newton Abbot, U.K.: David & Charles, 1980; Towata, N.J.: Barnes & Noble, 1980.

Simon, Pierre-Henri. *Diagnostic des lettres françaises contemporaines*. Brussels: La Renaissance du Livre, 1966.

Stambolian, George, ed. *Twentieth Century French Fiction: Essays for Germaine Brée*. New Brunswick, N.J.: Rutgers University Press, 1975.

Suleiman, Susan Rubin. *Authoritarian Fictions: The Ideological Novel as a Literary Genre*. New York: Columbia University Press, 1983.

Witt, Mary Ann Frese. *Existential Prisons: Captivity in Mid-Twentieth Century French Literature*. Durham: Duke University Press, 1985.

Contributors

Konrad Bieber ....*State University of New York at Stony Brook*
Joseph Brami ....*Massachusetts Institute of Technology*
Dorothy Brodin ....*Herbert H. Lehman College, City University of New York*
Catharine Savage Brosman ....*Tulane University*
William Bush ....*University of Western Ontario*
Megan Conway ....*Tulane University*
John M. Dunaway ....*Mercer University*
C. Frederick Farrell, Jr. ....*University of Minnesota at Morris*
Edith R. Farrell ....*University of Minnesota at Morris*
John Fletcher ....*University of East Anglia*
Raymond Gay-Crosier ....*University of Florida*
Vivian Kogan ....*Dartmouth College*
Elaine Marks ....*University of Wisconsin-Madison*
Joseph H. McMahon ....*Wesleyan University*
Jeffrey Mehlman ....*Boston University*
David O'Connell ....*Georgia State University*
Alain D. Ranwez ....*Metropolitan State College*
Rima Drell Reck ....*University of New Orleans*
Walter Redfern ....*University of Reading*
Zvjezdana Rudelic ....*Duke University*
Arlette M. Smith ....*Temple University*
F. C. St. Aubyn ....*University of Pittsburgh*
Robert S. Thornberry ....*University of Alberta*

Cumulative Index

Dictionary of Literary Biography, Volumes 1-72
Dictionary of Literary Biography Yearbook, 1980-1987
Dictionary of Literary Biography Documentary Series, Volumes 1-4

Cumulative Index

DLB before number: *Dictionary of Literary Biography*, Volumes 1-72
Y before number: *Dictionary of Literary Biography Yearbook*, 1980-1987
DS before number: *Dictionary of Literary Biography Documentary Series*, Volumes 1-4

A

Abbey Press DLB-49

The Abbey Theatre and Irish
   Drama, 1900-1945 .... DLB-10

Abbot, Willis J. 1863-1934................... DLB-29

Abbott, Jacob 1803-1879 ....DLB-1

Abbott, Robert S. 1868-1940 .... DLB-29

Abelard-Schuman DLB-46

Abell, Arunah S. 1806-1888 .... DLB-43

Abercrombie, Lascelles 1881-1938............ DLB-19

Abrams, M. H. 1912- DLB-67

Abse, Dannie 1923- DLB-27

Academy Chicago Publishers DLB-46

Ace Books................................... DLB-46

Acorn, Milton 1923-1986..................... DLB-53

Actors Theatre of Louisville.................DLB-7

Adair, James 1709?-1783? DLB-30

Adamic, Louis 1898-1951......................DLB-9

Adams, Alice 1926- Y-86

Adams, Brooks 1848-1927..................... DLB-47

Adams, Charles Francis, Jr. 1835-1915 .... DLB-47

Adams, Douglas 1952- Y-83

Adams, Franklin P. 1881-1960 .... DLB-29

Adams, Henry 1838-1918 ....DLB-12, 47

Adams, Herbert Baxter 1850-1901 .... DLB-47

Adams, J. S. and C. [publishing house]....... DLB-49

Adams, James Truslow 1878-1949............. DLB-17

Adams, John 1735-1826...................... DLB-31

Adams, John Quincy 1767-1848.............. DLB-37

Adams, Léonie 1899- DLB-48

Adams, Samuel 1722-1803 ....DLB-31, 43

Adams, William Taylor 1822-1897 .... DLB-42

Adcock, Fleur 1934- DLB-40

Ade, George 1866-1944 ....DLB-11, 25

Adeler, Max (see Clark, Charles Heber)

Advance Publishing Company................. DLB-49

AE 1867-1935 .... DLB-19

Aesthetic Poetry (1873), by Walter Pater DLB-35

Afro-American Literary Critics:
   An Introduction DLB-33

Agassiz, Jean Louis Rodolphe 1807-1873........DLB-1

Agee, James 1909-1955......................DLB-2, 26

Aiken, Conrad 1889-1973 ....DLB-9, 45

Ainsworth, William Harrison 1805-1882....... DLB-21

Aitken, Robert [publishing house]............ DLB-49

Akins, Zoë 1886-1958 .... DLB-26

Alain-Fournier 1886-1914 .... DLB-65

Alba, Nanina 1915-1968..................... DLB-41

Albee, Edward 1928- DLB-7

Alcott, Amos Bronson 1799-1888...............DLB-1

Alcott, Louisa May 1832-1888 ....DLB-1, 42

Alcott, William Andrus 1798-1859...............DLB-1

Alden, Isabella 1841-1930 .... DLB-42

Alden, John B. [publishing house]............ DLB-49

Alden, Beardsley and Company DLB-49

Aldington, Richard 1892-1962.............DLB-20, 36

Aldis, Dorothy 1896-1966 .... DLB-22

Aldiss, Brian W. 1925- DLB-14

Aldrich, Thomas Bailey 1836-1907........DLB-42, 71

Alexander, Charles Wesley
   [publishing house] DLB-49

Alexander, James 1691-1756 .... DLB-24

Alexander, Lloyd 1924- DLB-52

Alger, Horatio, Jr. 1832-1899 .... DLB-42

Algonquin Books of Chapel Hill.............. DLB-46

Algren, Nelson 1909-1981 . . . . DLB-9; Y-81, 82

Allan, Ted 1916- DLB-68

Alldritt, Keith 1935- DLB-14

Allen, Ethan 1738-1789 . . . . DLB-31

Allen, George 1808-1876 . . . . DLB-59

Allen, Grant 1848-1899 . . . . DLB-70

Allen, Henry W. 1912- Y-85

Allen, Hervey 1889-1949 . . . . DLB-9, 45

Allen, James 1739-1808 . . . . DLB-31

Allen, James Lane 1849-1925 . . . . DLB-71

Allen, Jay Presson 1922- DLB-26

Allen, John, and Company DLB-49

Allen, Samuel W. 1917- DLB-41

Allen, Woody 1935- DLB-44

Allingham, William 1824-1889 . . . . DLB-35

Allison, W. L. [publishing house] DLB-49

Allott, Kenneth 1912-1973 . . . . DLB-20

Allston, Washington 1779-1843 . . . . DLB-1

Alsop, George 1636-post 1673 . . . . DLB-24

Alsop, Richard 1761-1815 . . . . DLB-37

Altemus, Henry, and Company DLB-49

Alvarez, A. 1929- DLB-14, 40

*America: or, a Poem on the Settlement of the
British Colonies* (1780?), by Timothy
Dwight DLB-37

American Conservatory Theatre DLB-7

American Fiction and the 1930s DLB-9

American Humor: A Historical Survey
East and Northeast
South and Southwest
Midwest
West DLB-11

American News Company DLB-49

The American Poets' Corner: The First
Three Years (1983-1986) Y-86

American Publishing Company DLB-49

American Stationers' Company DLB-49

American Sunday-School Union DLB-49

American Temperance Union DLB-49

American Tract Society DLB-49

The American Writers Congress
(9-12 October 1981) Y-81

The American Writers Congress: A Report
on Continuing Business Y-81

Ames, Fisher 1758-1808 . . . . DLB-37

Ames, Mary Clemmer 1831-1884 . . . . DLB-23

Amini, Johari M. 1935- DLB-41

Amis, Kingsley 1922- DLB-15, 27

Amis, Martin 1949- DLB-14

Ammons, A. R. 1926- DLB-5

Amory, Thomas 1691?-1788 . . . . DLB-39

Andersch, Alfred 1914-1980 . . . . DLB-69

Anderson, Margaret 1886-1973 . . . . DLB-4

Anderson, Maxwell 1888-1959 . . . . DLB-7

Anderson, Patrick 1915-1979 . . . . DLB-68

Anderson, Paul Y. 1893-1938 . . . . DLB-29

Anderson, Poul 1926- DLB-8

Anderson, Robert 1917- DLB-7

Anderson, Sherwood 1876-1941 . . . . . . DLB-4, 9; DS-1

Andreas-Salomé, Lou 1861-1937 . . . . DLB-66

Andres, Stefan 1906-1970 . . . . DLB-69

Andrews, Charles M. 1863-1943 . . . . DLB-17

Andrieux, Louis (see Aragon, Louis)

Andrus, Silas, and Son DLB-49

Angell, James Burrill 1829-1916 . . . . DLB-64

Angelou, Maya 1928- DLB-38

The "Angry Young Men" DLB-15

Anhalt, Edward 1914- DLB-26

Anners, Henry F. [publishing house] DLB-49

Anthony, Piers 1934- DLB-8

Anthony Burgess's *99 Novels:* An Opinion Poll Y-84

Antin, Mary 1881-1949 . . . . Y-84

Antschel, Paul (see Celan, Paul)

Appleton, D., and Company DLB-49

Appleton-Century-Crofts DLB-46

Apple-wood Books DLB-46

Aquin, Hubert 1929-1977 . . . . DLB-53

Aragon, Louis 1897-1982 . . . . DLB-72

Arbor House Publishing Company DLB-46

Arcadia House DLB-46

Archer, William 1856-1924 . . . . DLB-10

Arden, John 1930- DLB-13

Arden of Faversham DLB-62

The Arena Publishing Company DLB-49

Arena Stage ....,............................DLB-7

Arensberg, Ann 1937- Y-82

Arland, Marcel 1899-1986................... DLB-72

Arlen, Michael 1895-1956 .... DLB-36

Armed Services Editions...................... DLB-46

Arno Press.................................... DLB-46

Arnold, Edwin 1832-1904 .... DLB-35

Arnold, Matthew 1822-1888...............DLB-32, 57

Arnold, Thomas 1795-1842 .... DLB-55

Arnow, Harriette Simpson 1908-1986...........DLB-6

Arp, Bill (see Smith, Charles Henry)

Arthur, Timothy Shay 1809-1885 ....DLB-3, 42

As I See It, by Carolyn Cassady DLB-16

Asch, Nathan 1902-1964 ....DLB-4, 28

Ash, John 1948- DLB-40

Ashbery, John 1927- DLB-5; Y-81

Asher, Sandy 1942- Y-83

Ashton, Winifred (see Dane, Clemence)

Asimov, Isaac 1920- DLB-8

Atheneum Publishers....................... DLB-46

Atherton, Gertrude 1857-1948 ....DLB-9

Atkins, Josiah circa 1755-1781................ DLB-31

Atkins, Russell 1926- DLB-41

The Atlantic Monthly Press.................. DLB-46

Atwood, Margaret 1939- DLB-53

Aubert, Alvin 1930- DLB-41

Aubin, Penelope 1685-circa, 1731 .... DLB-39

Auchincloss, Louis 1917- DLB-2; Y-80

Auden, W. H. 1907-1973..................DLB-10, 20

Audio Art in America: A Personal
    Memoir Y-85

Austin, Alfred 1835-1913..................... DLB-35

Austin, Mary 1868-1934......................DLB-9

The Author's Apology for His Book
    (1684), by John Bunyan................. DLB-39

An Author's Response, by Ronald Sukenick.......Y-82

Authors and Newspapers Association......... DLB-46

Authors' Publishing Company............... DLB-49

Avalon Books............................... DLB-46

Avison, Margaret 1918- DLB-53

Avon Books DLB-46

Ayckbourn, Alan 1939- DLB-13

Aymé, Marcel 1902-1967 .... DLB-72

Aytoun, William Edmondstoune 1813-1865 ... DLB-32

B

Babbitt, Irving 1865-1933 .... DLB-63

Babbitt, Natalie 1932- DLB-52

Babcock, John [publishing house] DLB-49

Bache, Benjamin Franklin 1769-1798 .... DLB-43

Bacon, Delia 1811-1859 ....DLB-1

Bacon, Thomas circa 1700-1768............... DLB-31

Badger, Richard G., and Company........... DLB-49

Bage, Robert 1728-1801...................... DLB-39

Bagehot, Walter 1826-1877................... DLB-55

Bagnold, Enid 1889-1981.................... DLB-13

Bailey, Alfred Goldsworthy 1905- DLB-68

Bailey, Francis [publishing house] DLB-49

Bailey, Paul 1937- DLB-14

Bailey, Philip James 1816-1902............... DLB-32

Baillie, Hugh 1890-1966..................... DLB-29

Bailyn, Bernard 1922- DLB-17

Bainbridge, Beryl 1933- DLB-14

Baird, Irene 1901-1981....................... DLB-68

The Baker and Taylor Company............. DLB-49

Baker, Houston A., Jr. 1943- DLB-67

Baker, Walter H., Company
    ("Baker's Plays")......................... DLB-49

Bald, Wambly 1902- DLB-4

Balderston, John 1889-1954.................. DLB-26

Baldwin, James 1924-1987.........DLB-2, 7, 33; Y-87

Baldwin, Joseph Glover 1815-1864..........DLB-3, 11

Ballantine Books............................ DLB-46

Ballard, J. G. 1930- DLB-14

Ballou, Robert O. [publishing house]......... DLB-46

Bambara, Toni Cade 1939- DLB-38

Bancroft, A. L., and Company DLB-49

Bancroft, George 1800-1891............DLB-1, 30, 59

Bancroft, Hubert Howe 1832-1918............ DLB-47

Bangs, John Kendrick 1862-1922............. DLB-11

Bantam Books................................. DLB-46

Banville, John 1945- DLB-14

Baraka, Amiri 1934- DLB-5, 7, 16, 38

Barber, John Warner 1798-1885 .... DLB-30

Barbour, Ralph Henry 1870-1944............ DLB-22

Barbusse, Henri 1873-1935.................... DLB-65

Barclay, E. E., and Company DLB-49

Bardeen, C. W. [publishing house] DLB-49

Baring, Maurice 1874-1945................... DLB-34

Barker, A. L. 1918- DLB-14

Barker, George 1913- DLB-20

Barker, Harley Granville 1877-1946........... DLB-10

Barker, Howard 1946- DLB-13

Barker, James Nelson 1784-1858............. DLB-37

Barker, Jane 1652-1727? DLB-39

Barks, Coleman 1937- DLB-5

Barlach, Ernst 1870-1938..................... DLB-56

Barlow, Joel 1754-1812...................... DLB-37

Barnard, John 1681-1770 .... DLB-24

Barnes, A. S., and Company................. DLB-49

Barnes, Djuna 1892-1982............... DLB-4, 9, 45

Barnes, Margaret Ayer 1886-1967...............DLB-9

Barnes, Peter 1931- DLB-13

Barnes, William 1801-1886 .... DLB-32

Barnes and Noble Books DLB-46

Barney, Natalie 1876-1972 ....DLB-4

Baron, Richard W., Publishing Company...... DLB-46

Barr, Robert 1850-1912 .... DLB-70

Barrax, Gerald William 1933- DLB-41

Barrie, James M. 1860-1937................. DLB-10

Barry, Philip 1896-1949 ....DLB-7

Barse and Hopkins........................... DLB-46

Barstow, Stan 1928- DLB-14

Barth, John 1930- DLB-2

Barthelme, Donald 1931- DLB-2; Y-80

Barthelme, Frederick 1943- Y-85

Bartlett, John 1820-1905 ....DLB-1

Bartol, Cyrus Augustus 1813-1900 ....DLB-1

Bartram, John 1699-1777 .... DLB-31

Bartram, William 1739-1823.................. DLB-37

Basic Books.................................. DLB-46

Bass, T. J. 1932- Y-81

Bassett, John Spencer 1867-1928............. DLB-17

Bassler, Thomas Joseph (see Bass, T. J.)

Bate, Walter Jackson 1918- DLB-67

Bates, Katharine Lee 1859-1929............... DLB-71

Baum, L. Frank 1856-1919.................... DLB-22

Baumbach, Jonathan 1933-....................Y-80

Bawden, Nina 1925- DLB-14

Bax, Clifford 1886-1962...................... DLB-10

Bayer, Eleanor (see Perry, Eleanor)

Beach, Sylvia 1887-1962.....................DLB-4

Beacon Press DLB-49

Beadle and Adams DLB-49

Beagle, Peter S. 1939- Y-80

Beal, M. F. 1937- Y-81

Beale, Howard K. 1899-1959................. DLB-17

Beard, Charles A. 1874-1948................. DLB-17

A Beat Chronology: The First Twenty-five
    Years, 1944-1969......................... DLB-16

Beattie, Ann 1947- Y-82

Beauchemin, Yves 1941- DLB-60

Beaulieu, Victor-Lévy 1945- DLB-53

Beaumont, Francis circa 1584-1616
    and Fletcher, John 1579-1625............. DLB-58

Beauvoir, Simone de 1908-1986......... Y-86, DLB-72

Becher, Ulrich 1910- DLB-69

Becker, Carl 1873-1945....................... DLB-17

Beckett, Samuel 1906- DLB-13, 15

Beckford, William 1760-1844................. DLB-39

Beckham, Barry 1944- DLB-33

Beecher, Catharine Esther 1800-1878 ....DLB-1

Beecher, Henry Ward 1813-1887...........DLB-3, 43

Beer, George L. 1872-1920................... DLB-47

Beer, Patricia 1919- DLB-40

Beerbohm, Max 1872-1956................... DLB-34

Beers, Henry A. 1847-1926................... DLB-71

Behan, Brendan 1923-1964 .... DLB-13

Behn, Aphra 1640?-1689..................... DLB-39

Behn, Harry 1898-1973 .... DLB-61

Behrman, S. N. 1893-1973 ....DLB-7, 44

Belasco, David 1853-1931 ....DLB-7

Belford, Clarke and Company............... DLB-49

Belitt, Ben 1911- DLB-5

Belknap, Jeremy 1744-1798 ....DLB-30, 37

Bell, James Madison 1826-1902 .... DLB-50

Bell, Marvin 1937- DLB-5

Bell, Robert [publishing house]............... DLB-49

Bellamy, Edward 1850-1898.................. DLB-12

Bellamy, Joseph 1719-1790................... DLB-31

Belloc, Hilaire 1870-1953..................... DLB-19

Bellow, Saul 1915- DLB-2, 28; Y-82; DS-3

Belmont Productions DLB-46

Bemelmans, Ludwig 1898-1962 .... DLB-22

Bemis, Samuel Flagg 1891-1973.............. DLB-17

Benchley, Robert 1889-1945.................. DLB-11

Benedictus, David 1938- DLB-14

Benedikt, Michael 1935- DLB-5

Benét, Stephen Vincent 1898-1943.........DLB-4, 48

Benét, William Rose 1886-1950............... DLB-45

Benford, Gregory 1941- Y-82

Benjamin, Park 1809-1864 ....DLB-3, 59

Benn, Gottfried 1886-1956 .... DLB-56

Bennett, Arnold 1867-1931.................DLB-10, 34

Bennett, Charles 1899- DLB-44

Bennett, Gwendolyn 1902- DLB-51

Bennett, Hal 1930- DLB-33

Bennett, James Gordon 1795-1872 .... DLB-43

Bennett, James Gordon, Jr. 1841-1918 .... DLB-23

Bennett, John 1865-1956.................... DLB-42

Benoit, Jacques 1941- DLB-60

Benson, Stella 1892-1933 .... DLB-36

Bentley, E. C. 1875-1956 .... DLB-70

Benton, Robert 1932- and Newman,
   David 1937- DLB-44

Benziger Brothers DLB-49

Beresford, Anne 1929- DLB-40

Berford, R. G., Company.................... DLB-49

Berg, Stephen 1934- DLB-5

Bergengruen, Werner 1892-1964............. DLB-56

Berger, John 1926- DLB-14

Berger, Meyer 1898-1959 .... DLB-29

Berger, Thomas 1924- DLB-2; Y-80

Berkeley, George 1685-1753.................. DLB-31

The Berkley Publishing Corporation DLB-46

Bernanos, Georges 1888-1948................ DLB-72

Bernard, John 1756-1828 .... DLB-37

Berrigan, Daniel 1921- DLB-5

Berrigan, Ted 1934-1983......................DLB-5

Berry, Wendell 1934- DLB-5, 6

Berryman, John 1914-1972................... DLB-48

Bersianik, Louky 1930- DLB-60

Berton, Pierre 1920- DLB-68

Bessette, Gerard 1920- DLB-53

Bessie, Alvah 1904-1985..................... DLB-26

Bester, Alfred 1913- DLB-8

The Bestseller Lists: An Assessment..............Y-84

Betjeman, John 1906-1984 .... DLB-20; Y-84

Betts, Doris 1932- Y-82

Beveridge, Albert J. 1862-1927............... DLB-17

Beverley, Robert circa 1673-1722..........DLB-24, 30

Biddle, Drexel [publishing house] DLB-49

Bierbaum, Otto Julius 1865-1910.............. DLB-66

Bierce, Ambrose 1842-1914? DLB-11, 12, 23, 71

Biggle, Lloyd, Jr. 1923- DLB-8

Biglow, Hosea (see Lowell, James Russell)

Billings, Josh (see Shaw, Henry Wheeler)

Binding, Rudolf G. 1867-1938................ DLB-66

Bingham, Caleb 1757-1817 .... DLB-42

Binyon, Laurence 1869-1943 .... DLB-19

Biographical Documents I Y-84

Biographical Documents II Y-85

Bioren, John [publishing house]............... DLB-49

Bird, William 1888-1963........................DLB-4

Bishop, Elizabeth 1911-1979....................DLB-5

Bishop, John Peale 1892-1944........... DLB-4, 9, 45

Bissett, Bill 1939- DLB-53

Black, David (D. M.) 1941- DLB-40

Black, Walter J. [publishing house] DLB-46

Black, Winifred 1863-1936 .... DLB-25

The Black Arts Movement, by Larry Neal..... DLB-38

Black Theaters and Theater Organizations in
  America, 1961-1982: A Research List..... DLB-38

Black Theatre: A Forum [excerpts]........... DLB-38

Blackamore, Arthur 1679-? DLB-24, 39

Blackburn, Alexander L. 1929- Y-85

Blackburn, Paul 1926-1971 .... DLB-16; Y-81

Blackburn, Thomas 1916-1977 .... DLB-27

Blackmore, R. D. 1825-1900 .... DLB-18

Blackmur, R. P. 1904-1965 .... DLB-63

Blackwood, Caroline 1931- DLB-14

Blair, Eric Arthur (see Orwell, George)

Blair, Francis Preston 1791-1876 .... DLB-43

Blair, James circa 1655-1743 .... DLB-24

Blair, John Durburrow 1759-1823............. DLB-37

Blais, Marie-Claire 1939- DLB-53

Blaise, Clark 1940- DLB-53

The Blakiston Company...................... DLB-49

Blanchot, Maurice 1907- DLB-72

Bledsoe, Albert Taylor 1809-1877..............DLB-3

Blelock and Company DLB-49

Blish, James 1921-1975......................DLB-8

Bliss, E., and E. White [publishing house]..... DLB-49

Bloch, Robert 1917- DLB-44

Block, Rudolph (see Lessing, Bruno)

Bloom, Harold 1930- DLB-67

Blume, Judy 1938- DLB-52

Blunck, Hans Friedrich 1888-1961 .... DLB-66

Blunden, Edmund 1896-1974 .... DLB-20

Blunt, Wilfrid Scawen 1840-1922............. DLB-19

Bly, Nellie (see Cochrane, Elizabeth)

Bly, Robert 1926- DLB-5

The Bobbs-Merrill Company DLB-46

Bodenheim, Maxwell 1892-1954.............DLB-9, 45

Bodkin, M. McDonnell 1850-1933............. DLB-70

Bodsworth, Fred 1918- DLB-68

Boehm, Sydney 1908- DLB-44

Boer, Charles 1939- DLB-5

Bogan, Louise 1897-1970................... DLB-45

Bogarde, Dirk 1921- DLB-14

Boland, Eavan 1944- DLB-40

Böll, Heinrich 1917-1985................ Y-85, DLB-69

Bolling, Robert 1738-1775.................... DLB-31

Bolt, Carol 1941- DLB-60

Bolt, Robert 1924- DLB-13

Bolton, Herbert E. 1870-1953 .... DLB-17

Bond, Edward 1934- DLB-13

Boni, Albert and Charles [publishing house] .. DLB-46

Boni and Liveright DLB-46

Robert Bonner's Sons....................... DLB-49

Bontemps, Arna 1902-1973 ....DLB-48, 51

The Book League of America DLB-46

Book Reviewing in America: I...................Y-87

Book Supply Company DLB-49

The Booker Prize
  Address by Anthony Thwaite, Chairman
    of the Booker Prize Judges
  Comments from Former Booker Prize
    Winners Y-86

Boorstin, Daniel J. 1914- DLB-17

Booth, Philip 1925- Y-82

Booth, Wayne C. 1921- DLB-67

Borchardt, Rudolf 1877-1945 .... DLB-66

Borchert, Wolfgang 1921-1947............... DLB-69

Borges, Jorge Luis 1899-1986 ....Y-86

Borrow, George 1803-1881................DLB-21, 55

Bosco, Henri 1888-1976...................... DLB-72

Bosco, Monique 1927- DLB-53

Botta, Anne C. Lynch 1815-1891...............DLB-3

Bottomley, Gordon 1874-1948................. DLB-10

Bottoms, David 1949- Y-83

Bottrall, Ronald 1906- DLB-20

Boucher, Anthony 1911-1968 ....DLB-8

Boucher, Jonathan 1738-1804 .... DLB-31

Bourjaily, Vance Nye 1922- DLB-2

Bourne, Edward Gaylord 1860-1908 .... DLB-47

Bourne, Randolph 1886-1918 .... DLB-63

Bousquet, Joë 1897-1950 .... DLB-72

Bova, Ben 1932- Y-81

Bove, Emmanuel 1898-1945.................. DLB-72

Bovard, Oliver K. 1872-1945 .... DLB-25

Bowen, Elizabeth 1899-1973 .... DLB-15

Bowen, Francis 1811-1890 .... DLB-1, 59

Bowen, John 1924- DLB-13

Bowen-Merrill Company DLB-49

Bowering, George 1935- DLB-53

Bowers, Claude G. 1878-1958 .... DLB-17

Bowers, Edgar 1924- DLB-5

Bowles, Paul 1910- DLB-5, 6

Bowles, Samuel III 1826-1878 .... DLB-43

Bowman, Louise Morey 1882-1944 .... DLB-68

Boyd, James 1888-1944 .... DLB-9

Boyd, John 1919- DLB-8

Boyd, Thomas 1898-1935 .... DLB-9

Boyesen, Hjalmar Hjorth 1848-1895 .... DLB-12, 71

Boyle, Kay 1902- DLB-4, 9, 48

Boyle, T. Coraghessan 1948- Y-86

Brackenbury, Alison 1953- DLB-40

Brackenridge, Hugh Henry 1748-1816 .... DLB-11, 37

Brackett, Charles 1892-1969 .... DLB-26

Brackett, Leigh 1915-1978 .... DLB-8, 26

Bradburn, John [publishing house] DLB-49

Bradbury, Malcolm 1932- DLB-14

Bradbury, Ray 1920- DLB-2, 8

Braddon, Mary Elizabeth 1835-1915 .... DLB-18, 70

Bradford, Andrew 1686-1742 .... DLB-43

Bradford, Gamaliel 1863-1932 .... DLB-17

Bradford, John 1749-1830 .... DLB-43

Bradford, William 1590-1657 .... DLB-24, 30

Bradford, William III 1719-1791 .... DLB-43

Bradlaugh, Charles 1833-1891 .... DLB-57

Bradley, David 1950- DLB-33

Bradley, Ira, and Company DLB-49

Bradley, J. W., and Company DLB-49

Bradley, Marion Zimmer 1930- DLB-8

Bradley, William Aspenwall 1878-1939 .... DLB-4

Bradstreet, Anne 1612 or 1613-1672 .... DLB-24

Brady, Frederic A. [publishing house] DLB-49

Bragg, Melvyn 1939- DLB-14

Brainard, Charles H. [publishing house] DLB-49

Braine, John 1922-1986 .... DLB-15; Y-86

Braithwaite, William Stanley
1878-1962 .... DLB-50, 54

Bramah, Ernest 1868-1942 .... DLB-70

Branagan, Thomas 1774-1843 .... DLB-37

Branden Press DLB-46

Brault, Jacques 1933- DLB-53

Brautigan, Richard 1935-1984 ...... DLB-2, 5; Y-80, 84

Braxton, Joanne M. 1950- DLB-41

Bray, Thomas 1656-1730 .... DLB-24

Braziller, George [publishing house] DLB-46

The Bread Loaf Writers' Conference 1983 .... Y-84

The Break-Up of the Novel (1922),
by John Middleton Murry DLB-36

Breasted, James Henry 1865-1935 .... DLB-47

Brecht, Bertolt 1898-1956 .... DLB-56

Bredel, Willi 1901-1964 .... DLB-56

Bremser, Bonnie 1939- DLB-16

Bremser, Ray 1934- DLB-16

Brentano, Bernard von 1901-1964 .... DLB-56

Brentano's DLB-49

Brenton, Howard 1942- DLB-13

Breton, André 1896-1966 .... DLB-65

Brewer, Warren and Putnam DLB-46

Brewster, Elizabeth 1922- DLB-60

Bridgers, Sue Ellen 1942- DLB-52

Bridges, Robert 1844-1930 .... DLB-19

Bridie, James 1888-1951 .... DLB-10

Briggs, Charles Frederick 1804-1877 .... DLB-3

Brighouse, Harold 1882-1958 .... DLB-10

Brimmer, B. J., Company DLB-46

Brinnin, John Malcolm 1916- DLB-48

Brisbane, Albert 1809-1890 .... DLB-3

Brisbane, Arthur 1864-1936 .... DLB-25

Broadway Publishing Company DLB-46

Brochu, André 1942- DLB-53

Brock, Edwin 1927- DLB-40

Brodhead, John R. 1814-1873 .... DLB-30

Brome, Richard circa 1590-1652 .... DLB-58

Bromfield, Louis 1896-1956 .... DLB-4, 9

Broner, E. M. 1930- DLB-28

Brontë, Anne 1820-1849 .... DLB-21

Brontë, Charlotte 1816-1855 .... DLB-21

Brontë, Emily 1818-1848 .... DLB-21, 32

Brooke, Frances 1724-1789.................. DLB-39

Brooke, Henry 1703?-1783 .... DLB-39

Brooke, Rupert 1887-1915 .... DLB-19

Brooke-Rose, Christine 1926- DLB-14

Brookner, Anita 1928- Y-87

Brooks, Charles Timothy 1813-1883 .... DLB-1

Brooks, Cleanth 1906- DLB-63

Brooks, Gwendolyn 1917- DLB-5

Brooks, Jeremy 1926- DLB-14

Brooks, Mel 1926- DLB-26

Brooks, Noah 1830-1903 .... DLB-42

Brooks, Richard 1912- DLB-44

Brooks, Van Wyck 1886-1963 .... DLB-45, 63

Brophy, Brigid 1929- DLB-14

Brossard, Chandler 1922- DLB-16

Brossard, Nicole 1943- DLB-53

Brother Antoninus (see Everson, William)

Brougham, John 1810-1880 .... DLB-11

Broughton, James 1913- DLB-5

Broughton, Rhoda 1840-1920 .... DLB-18

Broun, Heywood 1888-1939.................. DLB-29

Brown, Bob 1886-1959 .... DLB-4, 45

Brown, Cecil 1943- DLB-33

Brown, Charles Brockden 1771-1810...... DLB-37, 59

Brown, Christy 1932-1981.................... DLB-14

Brown, Dee 1908- Y-80

Brown, Fredric 1906-1972..................... DLB-8

Brown, George Mackay 1921- DLB-14, 27

Brown, Harry 1917-1986.................... DLB-26

Brown, Marcia 1918- DLB-61

Brown, Margaret Wise 1910-1952 .... DLB-22

Brown, Oliver Madox 1855-1874 .... DLB-21

Brown, Sterling 1901- DLB-48, 51, 63

Brown, T. E. 1830-1897 .... DLB-35

Brown, William Hill 1765-1793............... DLB-37

Brown, William Wells 1814-1884 .... DLB-3, 50

Browne, Charles Farrar 1834-1867 .... DLB-11

Browne, Michael Dennis 1940- DLB-40

Browne, Wynyard 1911-1964................. DLB-13

Brownell, W. C. 1851-1928.................... DLB-71

Browning, Elizabeth Barrett 1806-1861 .... DLB-32

Browning, Robert 1812-1889................. DLB-32

Brownjohn, Allan 1931- DLB-40

Brownson, Orestes Augustus 1803-1876..... DLB-1, 59

Bruce, Charles 1906-1971 .... DLB-68

Bruce, Philip Alexander 1856-1933 .... DLB-47

Bruce Humphries [publishing house] DLB-46

Bruckman, Clyde 1894-1955 .... DLB-26

Brundage, John Herbert (see Herbert, John)

Bryant, William Cullen 1794-1878....... DLB-3, 43, 59

Buchan, John 1875-1940 ....DLB-34, 70

Buchanan, Robert 1841-1901...............DLB-18, 35

Buchman, Sidney 1902-1975 .... DLB-26

Buck, Pearl S. 1892-1973..................... DLB-9

Buckler, Ernest 1908-1984 .... DLB-68

Buckley, William F., Jr. 1925- Y-80

Buckminster, Joseph Stevens 1784-1812....... DLB-37

Buckner, Robert 1906- DLB-26

Budd, Thomas ?-1698....................... DLB-24

Budrys, A. J. 1931- DLB-8

Buechner, Frederick 1926- Y-80

Buell, John 1927- DLB-53

Buffum, Job [publishing house] DLB-49

Bukowski, Charles 1920- DLB-5

Bullins, Ed 1935- DLB-7, 38

Bulwer-Lytton, Edward (also Edward Bulwer) 1803-1873................................ DLB-21

Bumpus, Jerry 1937- Y-81

Bunce and Brother.......................... DLB-49

Bunting, Basil 1900-1985.................... DLB-20

Bunyan, John 1628-1688 .... DLB-39

Burch, Robert 1925- DLB-52

Burgess, Anthony 1917- DLB-14

Burgess, Gelett 1866-1951.................... DLB-11

Burgess, John W. 1844-1931 .... DLB-47

Burgess, Thornton W. 1874-1965 .... DLB-22

Burgess, Stringer and Company.............. DLB-49

Burk, John Daly circa 1772-1808 .... DLB-37

Burke, Kenneth 1897- DLB-45, 63

Burnett, Frances Hodgson 1849-1924 .... DLB-42

Burnett, W. R. 1899-1982 ....DLB-9

Burney, Fanny 1752-1840 .... DLB-39

Burns, Alan 1929- DLB-14

Burns, John Horne 1916-1953 ....Y-85

Burnshaw, Stanley 1906- DLB-48

Burroughs, Edgar Rice 1875-1950..............DLB-8

Burroughs, John 1837-1921 .... DLB-64

Burroughs, Margaret T. G. 1917- DLB-41

Burroughs, William S., Jr. 1947-1981 .... DLB-16

Burroughs, William Seward 1914-
.............................DLB-2, 8, 16; Y-81

Burroway, Janet 1936- DLB-6

Burt, A. L., and Company.................... DLB-49

Burton, Richard F. 1821-1890................ DLB-55

Burton, Virginia Lee 1909-1968.............. DLB-22

Busch, Frederick 1941- DLB-6

Busch, Niven 1903- DLB-44

Butler, E. H., and Company.................. DLB-49

Butler, Juan 1942-1981...................... DLB-53

Butler, Octavia E. 1947- DLB-33

Butler, Samuel 1835-1902.................DLB-18, 57

Butterworth, Hezekiah 1839-1905............. DLB-42

B. V. (see Thomson, James)

Byars, Betsy 1928- DLB-52

Byatt, A. S. 1936- DLB-14

Byles, Mather 1707-1788 .... DLB-24

Bynner, Witter 1881-1968.................... DLB-54

Byrd, William II 1674-1744 .... DLB-24

Byrne, John Keyes (see Leonard, Hugh)

C

Cabell, James Branch 1879-1958 ....DLB-9

Cable, George Washington 1844-1925........ DLB-12

Cahan, Abraham 1860-1951.............DLB-9, 25, 28

Cain, George 1943- DLB-33

Caldwell, Ben 1937- DLB-38

Caldwell, Erskine 1903-1987.....................DLB-9

Caldwell, H. M., Company DLB-49

Calhoun, John C. 1782-1850 ....DLB-3

Calisher, Hortense 1911- DLB-2

Callaghan, Morley 1903- DLB-68

Callaloo..Y-87

Calmer, Edgar 1907- DLB-4

Calverley, C. S. 1831-1884.................... DLB-35

Calvert, George Henry 1803-1889..........DLB-1, 64

Cambridge Press............................. DLB-49

Cameron, Eleanor 1912- DLB-52

Camm, John 1718-1778 .... DLB-31

Campbell, Gabrielle Margaret Vere
(see Shearing, Joseph)

Campbell, James Edwin 1867-1896............ DLB-50

Campbell, John 1653-1728 .... DLB-43

Campbell, John W., Jr. 1910-1971..............DLB-8

Campbell, Roy 1901-1957 .... DLB-20

Campion, Thomas 1567-1620 .... DLB-58

Camus, Albert 1913-1960..................... DLB-72

Candour in English Fiction (1890),
by Thomas Hardy........................ DLB-18

Cannan, Gilbert 1884-1955 .... DLB-10

Cannell, Kathleen 1891-1974...................DLB-4

Cannell, Skipwith 1887-1957 .... DLB-45

Cantwell, Robert 1908-1978 ....DLB-9

Cape, Jonathan, and Harrison Smith
[publishing house] DLB-46

Capen, Joseph 1658-1725 .... DLB-24

Capote, Truman 1924-1984 .... DLB-2; Y-80, 84

Carey, M., and Company..................... DLB-49

Carey, Mathew 1760-1839.................... DLB-37

Carey and Hart............................. DLB-49

Carlell, Lodowick 1602-1675 .... DLB-58

Carleton, G. W. [publishing house]........... DLB-49

Carossa, Hans 1878-1956..................... DLB-66

Carr, Emily 1871-1945 .... DLB-68

Carrier, Roch 1937- DLB-53

Carlyle, Jane Welsh 1801-1866 .... DLB-55

Carlyle, Thomas 1795-1881 .... DLB-55

Carroll, Gladys Hasty 1904- DLB-9

Carroll, John 1735-1815 .... DLB-37

Carroll, Lewis 1832-1898 .... DLB-18

Carroll, Paul 1927- DLB-16

Carroll, Paul Vincent 1900-1968.............. DLB-10

Carroll and Graf Publishers DLB-46

Carruth, Hayden 1921- DLB-5

Carryl, Charles E. 1841-1920 .... DLB-42

Carswell, Catherine 1879-1946 .... DLB-36

Carter, Angela 1940- DLB-14

Carter, Henry (see Leslie, Frank)

Carter, Landon 1710-1778 .... DLB-31

Carter, Lin 1930- Y-81

Carter, Robert, and Brothers................. DLB-49

Carter and Hendee........................... DLB-49

Caruthers, William Alexander 1802-1846 ....DLB-3

Carver, Jonathan 1710-1780.................. DLB-31

Carver, Raymond 1938- Y-84

Cary, Joyce 1888-1957....................... DLB-15

Casey, Juanita 1925- DLB-14

Casey, Michael 1947- DLB-5

Cassady, Carolyn 1923- DLB-16

Cassady, Neal 1926-1968 .... DLB-16

Cassell Publishing Company.................. DLB-49

Cassill, R. V. 1919- DLB-6

Castlemon, Harry (see Fosdick, Charles Austin)

Caswall, Edward 1814-1878 .... DLB-32

Cather, Willa 1873-1947.............. DLB-9, 54; DS-1

Catton, Bruce 1899-1978 .... DLB-17

Causley, Charles 1917- DLB-27

Caute, David 1936- DLB-14

Cawein, Madison 1865-1914.................. DLB-54

The Caxton Printers, Limited DLB-46

Celan, Paul 1920-1970....................... DLB-69

Céline, Louis-Ferdinand 1894-1961 .... DLB-72

Center for the Book Research...................Y-84

The Century Company....................... DLB-49

Challans, Eileen Mary (see Renault, Mary)

Chalmers, George 1742-1825................. DLB-30

Chamberlain, Samuel S. 1851-1916........... DLB-25

Chamberland, Paul 1939- DLB-60

Chamberlin, William Henry 1897-1969........ DLB-29

Chambers, Charles Haddon 1860-1921........ DLB-10

Chandler, Harry 1864-1944 .... DLB-29

Channing, Edward 1856-1931................. DLB-17

Channing, Edward Tyrrell 1790-1856.......DLB-1, 59

Channing, William Ellery 1780-1842 ....DLB-1, 59

Channing, William Ellery II 1817-1901.........DLB-1

Channing, William Henry 1810-1884........DLB-1, 59

Chaplin, Charlie 1889-1977 .... DLB-44

Chapman, George 1559 or 1560-1634........ DLB-62

Chappell, Fred 1936- DLB-6

Charbonneau, Robert 1911-1967 .... DLB-68

Charles, Gerda 1914- DLB-14

Charles, William [publishing house] DLB-49

The Charles Wood Affair:
        A Playwright Revived Y-83

Charlotte Forten: Pages from her Diary....... DLB-50

Charyn, Jerome 1937- Y-83

Chase, Borden 1900-1971 .... DLB-26

Chase-Riboud, Barbara 1936- DLB-33

Chauncy, Charles 1705-1787 .... DLB-24

Chayefsky, Paddy 1923-1981 .... DLB-7, 44; Y-81

Cheever, Ezekiel 1615-1708 .... DLB-24

Cheever, George Barrell 1807-1890 .... DLB-59

Cheever, John 1912-1982............ DLB-2; Y-80, 82

Cheever, Susan 1943- Y-82

Chelsea House............................... DLB-46

Cheney, Ednah Dow (Littlehale) 1824-1904 .....DLB-1

Cherry, Kelly 1940 ....Y-83

Cherryh, C. J. 1942- Y-80

Chesnutt, Charles Waddell 1858-1932......DLB-12, 50

Chesterton, G. K. 1874-1936 ....DLB-10, 19, 34, 70

Cheyney, Edward P. 1861-1947 .... DLB-47

Child, Francis James 1825-1896 ....DLB-1, 64

Child, Lydia Maria 1802-1880.................DLB-1

Child, Philip 1898-1978 .... DLB-68

Childers, Erskine 1870-1922.................. DLB-70

Children's Book Awards and Prizes DLB-61

Childress, Alice 1920- DLB-7, 38

Childs, George W. 1829-1894 .... DLB-23

Chilton Book Company........................ DLB-46

Chittenden, Hiram Martin 1858-1917 .... DLB-47

Chivers, Thomas Holley 1809-1858 ....DLB-3

Chopin, Kate 1850 or 1851-1904 .... DLB-12

Choquette, Adrienne 1915-1973............... DLB-68

Choquette, Robert 1905- DLB-68

The Christian Publishing Company DLB-49

Christie, Agatha 1890-1976................... DLB-13

Church, Benjamin 1734-1778 .... DLB-31

Churchill, Caryl 1938- DLB-13

Ciardi, John 1916-1986.................. DLB-5; Y-86

City Lights Books............................. DLB-46

Clapper, Raymond 1892-1944................. DLB-29

Clare, John 1793-1864........................ DLB-55

Clark, Ann Nolan 1896- DLB-52

Clark, C. M., Publishing Company DLB-46

Clark, Catherine Anthony 1892-1977......... DLB-68

Clark, Charles Heber 1841-1915 .... DLB-11

Clark, Eleanor 1913- DLB-6

Clark, Lewis Gaylord 1808-1873.............DLB-3, 64

Clark, Walter Van Tilburg 1909-1971 ....DLB-9

Clarke, Austin 1896-1974...................DLB-10, 20

Clarke, Austin C. 1934- DLB-53

Clarke, Gillian 1937- DLB-40

Clarke, James Freeman 1810-1888 ....DLB-1, 59

Clarke, Rebecca Sophia 1833-1906 .... DLB-42

Clarke, Robert, and Company................ DLB-49

Clausen, Andy 1943- DLB-16

Claxton, Remsen and Haffelfinger DLB-49

Clay, Cassius Marcellus 1810-1903............. DLB-43

Cleary, Beverly 1916- DLB-52

Cleaver, Vera 1919-   and
      Cleaver, Bill 1920-1981 .... DLB-52

Cleland, John 1710-1789 .... DLB-39

Clemens, Samuel Langhorne
      1835-1910....................DLB-11, 12, 23, 64

Clement, Hal 1922- DLB-8

Clemo, Jack 1916- DLB-27

Clifton, Lucille 1936- DLB-5, 41

Clode, Edward J. [publishing house] DLB-46

Clough, Arthur Hugh 1819-1861............. DLB-32

Cloutier, Cécile 1930- DLB-60

Coates, Robert M. 1897-1973................DLB-4, 9

Coatsworth, Elizabeth 1893- DLB-22

Cobb, Jr., Charles E. 1943- DLB-41

Cobb, Frank I. 1869-1923 .... DLB-25

Cobb, Irvin S. 1876-1944...................DLB-11, 25

Cobbett, William 1762-1835 .... DLB-43

Cochran, Thomas C. 1902- DLB-17

Cochrane, Elizabeth 1867-1922............... DLB-25

Cockerill, John A. 1845-1896.................. DLB-23

Cocteau, Jean 1889-1963 .... DLB-65

Coffee, Lenore J. 1900?-1984 .... DLB-44

Coffin, Robert P. Tristram 1892-1955......... DLB-45

Cogswell, Fred 1917- DLB-60

Cogswell, Mason Fitch 1761-1830 .... DLB-37

Cohen, Arthur A. 1928-1986.................. DLB-28

Cohen, Leonard 1934- DLB-53

Cohen, Matt 1942- DLB-53

Colden, Cadwallader 1688-1776............DLB-24, 30

Cole, Barry 1936- DLB-14

Colegate, Isabel 1931- DLB-14

Coleman, Emily Holmes 1899-1974 ....DLB-4

Coleridge, Mary 1861-1907................... DLB-19

Colette 1873-1954 .... DLB-65

Colette, Sidonie Gabrielle (see Colette)

Collier, P. F. [publishing house] DLB-49

Collin and Small............................. DLB-49

Collins, Isaac [publishing house].............. DLB-49

Collins, Mortimer 1827-1876...............DLB-21, 35

Collins, Wilkie 1824-1889..................DLB-18, 70

Collyer, Mary 1716?-1763? DLB-39

Colman, Benjamin 1673-1747 .... DLB-24

Colman, S. [publishing house]................. DLB-49

Colombo, John Robert 1936- DLB-53

Colter, Cyrus 1910- DLB-33

Colum, Padraic 1881-1972................... DLB-19

Colwin, Laurie 1944- Y-80

Comden, Betty 1919-   and Green,
      Adolph 1918- DLB-44

The Comic Tradition Continued
      [in the British Novel]..................... DLB-15

Commager, Henry Steele 1902- DLB-17

The Commercialization of the Image of
Revolt, by Kenneth Rexroth DLB-16

Community and Commentators: Black
Theatre and Its Critics DLB-38

Compton-Burnett, Ivy 1884?-1969 .... DLB-36

Conference on Modern Biography Y-85

Congreve, William 1670-1729 .... DLB-39

Conkey, W. B., Company DLB-49

Connell, Evan S., Jr. 1924- DLB-2; Y-81

Connelly, Marc 1890-1980 .... DLB-7; Y-80

Connor, Tony 1930- DLB-40

Conquest, Robert 1917- DLB-27

Conrad, John, and Company DLB-49

Conrad, Joseph 1857-1924 ....DLB-10, 34

Conroy, Jack 1899- Y-81

Conroy, Pat 1945- DLB-6

The Consolidation of Opinion: Critical
Responses to the Modernists DLB-36

Constantine, David 1944- DLB-40

Contempo Caravan: Kites in a Windstorm Y-85

A Contemporary Flourescence of Chicano
Literature Y-84

The Continental Publishing Company DLB-49

A Conversation with Chaim Potok Y-84

Conversations with Publishers I: An Interview
with Patrick O'Connor Y-84

Conway, Moncure Daniel 1832-1907 ....DLB-1

Cook, David C., Publishing Company DLB-49

Cook, Ebenezer circa 1667-circa 1732 .... DLB-24

Cook, Michael 1933- DLB-53

Cooke, George Willis 1848-1923 .... DLB-71

Cooke, Increase, and Company DLB-49

Cooke, John Esten 1830-1886 ....DLB-3

Cooke, Philip Pendleton 1816-1850 ....DLB-3, 59

Cooke, Rose Terry 1827-1892 .... DLB-12

Coolbrith, Ina 1841-1928 .... DLB-54

Coolidge, George [publishing house] DLB-49

Coolidge, Susan (see Woolsey, Sarah Chauncy)

Cooper, Giles 1918-1966 .... DLB-13

Cooper, James Fenimore 1789-1851 ....DLB-3

Cooper, Kent 1880-1965 .... DLB-29

Coover, Robert 1932- DLB-2; Y-81

Copeland and Day DLB-49

Coppel, Alfred 1921- Y-83

Coppola, Francis Ford 1939- DLB-44

Corcoran, Barbara 1911- DLB-52

Corelli, Marie 1855-1924 .... DLB-34

Corle, Edwin 1906-1956 .... Y-85

Corman, Cid 1924- DLB-5

Cormier, Robert 1925- DLB-52

Corn, Alfred 1943- Y-80

Cornish, Sam 1935- DLB-41

Corrington, John William 1932- DLB-6

Corrothers, James D. 1869-1917 .... DLB-50

Corso, Gregory 1930- DLB-5, 16

Cortez, Jayne 1936- DLB-41

Corvo, Baron (see Rolfe, Frederick William)

Cory, William Johnson 1823-1892 .... DLB-35

Cosmopolitan Book Corporation DLB-46

Costain, Thomas B. 1885-1965 ....DLB-9

Cotter, Joseph Seamon, Sr.
1861-1949 .... DLB-50

Cotter, Joseph Seamon, Jr.
1895-1919 .... DLB-50

Cotton, John 1584-1652 .... DLB-24

Coulter, John 1888-1980 .... DLB-68

Cournos, John 1881-1966 .... DLB-54

Coventry, Francis 1725-1754 .... DLB-39

Coverly, N. [publishing house] DLB-49

Covici-Friede DLB-46

Coward, Noel 1899-1973 .... DLB-10

Coward, McCann and Geoghegan DLB-46

Cowles, Gardner 1861-1946 .... DLB-29

Cowley, Malcolm 1898- DLB-4, 48; Y-81

Cox, Palmer 1840-1924 .... DLB-42

Coxe, Louis 1918- DLB-5

Coxe, Tench 1755-1824 .... DLB-37

Cozzens, James Gould 1903-1978...DLB-9; Y-84; DS-2

Craddock, Charles Egbert (see Murfree, Mary N.)

Cradock, Thomas 1718-1770 .... DLB-31

Craig, Daniel H. 1811-1895 .... DLB-43

Craik, Dinah Maria 1826-1887 .... DLB-35

Cranch, Christopher Pearse 1813-1892......DLB-1, 42

Crane, Hart 1899-1932.....................DLB-4, 48

Crane, R. S. 1886-1967....................... DLB-63

Crane, Stephen 1871-1900 ....DLB-12, 54

Crapsey, Adelaide 1878-1914.................. DLB-54

Craven, Avery 1885-1980..................... DLB-17

Crawford, Charles 1752-circa 1815 .... DLB-31

Crawford, F. Marion 1854-1909.............. DLB-71

Crawley, Alan 1887-1975.................... DLB-68

Crayon, Geoffrey (see Irving, Washington)

Creative Age Press........................... DLB-46

Creel, George 1876-1953 .... DLB-25

Creeley, Robert 1926- DLB-5, 16

Creelman, James 1859-1915.................. DLB-23

Cregan, David 1931- DLB-13

Crèvecoeur, Michel Guillaume Jean de
    1735-1813................................ DLB-37

Crews, Harry 1935- DLB-6

Crichton, Michael 1942- Y-81

A Crisis of Culture: The Changing Role
    of Religion in the New Republic DLB-37

Cristofer, Michael 1946- DLB-7

"The Critic as Artist" (1891), by Oscar Wilde.. DLB-57

Criticism In Relation To Novels (1863),
    by G. H. Lewes........................... DLB-21

Crockett, David (Davy) 1786-1836..........DLB-3, 11

Croly, Jane Cunningham 1829-1901.......... DLB-23

Crosby, Caresse 1892-1970 .... DLB-48

Crosby, Caresse 1892-1970 and Crosby,
    Harry 1898-1929..........................DLB-4

Crosby, Harry 1898-1929.................... DLB-48

Crossley-Holland, Kevin 1941- DLB-40

Crothers, Rachel 1878-1958 ....DLB-7

Crowell, Thomas Y., Company DLB-49

Crowley, John 1942- Y-82

Crowley, Mart 1935- DLB-7

Crown Publishers........................... DLB-46

Croy, Homer 1883-1965.......................DLB-4

Crumley, James 1939- Y-84

Cruz, Victor Hernández 1949- DLB-41

Cullen, Countee 1903-1946..............DLB-4, 48, 51

Culler, Jonathan D. 1944- DLB-67

The Cult of Biography
    Excerpts from the Second Folio Debate:
      "Biographies are generally a disease of
      English Literature"—Germaine Greer,
      Victoria Glendinning, Auberon Waugh,
      and Richard Holmes Y-86

Cummings, E. E. 1894-1962 ....DLB-4, 48

Cummings, Ray 1887-1957 ....DLB-8

Cummings and Hilliard DLB-49

Cummins, Maria Susanna 1827-1866......... DLB-42

Cuney, Waring 1906-1976.................... DLB-51

Cuney-Hare, Maude 1874-1936 .... DLB-52

Cunningham, J. V. 1911- DLB-5

Cunningham, Peter F. [publishing house] DLB-49

Cuomo, George 1929- Y-80

Cupples and Leon DLB-46

Cupples, Upham and Company DLB-49

Cuppy, Will 1884-1949 .... DLB-11

Currie, Mary Montgomerie Lamb Singleton,
    Lady Currie (see Fane, Violet)

Curti, Merle E. 1897- DLB-17

Curtis, George William 1824-1892..........DLB-1, 43

D

D. M. Thomas: The Plagiarism Controversy.......Y-82

Dabit, Eugène 1898-1936..................... DLB-65

Daborne, Robert circa 1580-1628.............. DLB-58

Dahlberg, Edward 1900-1977.................. DLB-48

Dale, Peter 1938- DLB-40

Dall, Caroline Wells (Healey) 1822-1912.........DLB-1

Dallas, E. S. 1828-1879 .... DLB-55

The Dallas Theater Center DLB-7

D'Alton, Louis 1900-1951 .... DLB-10

Daly, T. A. 1871-1948....................... DLB-11

Damon, S. Foster 1893-1971................. DLB-45

Damrell, William S. [publishing house]........ DLB-49

Dana, Charles A. 1819-1897.................DLB-3, 23

Dana, Richard Henry, Jr. 1815-1882 ....DLB-1

Dandridge, Ray Garfield..................... DLB-51

Dane, Clemence 1887-1965................... DLB-10

Danforth, John 1660-1730................... DLB-24

Danforth, Samuel I 1626-1674 .... DLB-24

Danforth, Samuel II 1666-1727 .... DLB-24

Dangerous Years: London Theater,
    1939-1945............................. DLB-10

Daniel, John M. 1825-1865.................. DLB-43

Daniel, Samuel 1562 or 1563-1619 .... DLB-62

Daniells, Roy 1902-1979..................... DLB-68

Daniels, Josephus 1862-1948 .... DLB-29

Danner, Margaret Esse 1915- DLB-41

Darwin, Charles 1809-1882.................. DLB-57

Daryush, Elizabeth 1887-1977 .... DLB-20

Dashwood, Edmée Elizabeth Monica
    de la Pasture (see Delafield, E. M.)

d'Aulaire, Edgar Parin 1898- and
    d'Aulaire, Ingri 1904- DLB-22

Davenant, Sir William 1606-1668............. DLB-58

Davenport, Robert ?-? DLB-58

Daves, Delmer 1904-1977 .... DLB-26

Davey, Frank 1940- DLB-53

Davidson, Avram 1923- DLB-8

Davidson, Donald 1893-1968 .... DLB-45

Davidson, John 1857-1909.................... DLB-19

Davidson, Lionel 1922- DLB-14

Davie, Donald 1922- DLB-27

Davies, Robertson 1913- DLB-68

Davies, Samuel 1723-1761.................... DLB-31

Davies, W. H. 1871-1940 .... DLB-19

Daviot, Gordon 1896-1952 .... DLB-10

Davis, Charles A. 1795-1867................. DLB-11

Davis, Clyde Brion 1894-1962 ....DLB-9

Davis, Dick 1945- DLB-40

Davis, Frank Marshall 1905-?................ DLB-51

Davis, H. L. 1894-1960 ....DLB-9

Davis, John 1774-1854....................... DLB-37

Davis, Margaret Thomson 1926- DLB-14

Davis, Ossie 1917- DLB-7, 38

Davis, Richard Harding 1864-1916........DLB-12, 23

Davis, Samuel Cole 1764-1809............... DLB-37

Davison, Peter 1928- DLB-5

Davys, Mary 1674-1732....................... DLB-39

DAW Books DLB-46

Dawson, William 1704-1752 .... DLB-31

Day, Benjamin Henry 1810-1889.............. DLB-43

Day, Clarence 1874-1935..................... DLB-11

Day, Dorothy 1897-1980...................... DLB-29

Day, John circa 1574-circa 1640 .... DLB-62

Day, The John, Company DLB-46

Day Lewis, C. 1904-1972 ....DLB-15, 20

Day, Mahlon [publishing house].............. DLB-49

Day, Thomas 1748-1789...................... DLB-39

Deacon, William Arthur 1890-1977........... DLB-68

Deal, Borden 1922-1985.......................DLB-6

de Angeli, Marguerite 1889-1987.............. DLB-22

De Bow, James D. B. 1820-1867.................DLB-3

de Camp, L. Sprague 1907- DLB-8

The Decay of Lying (1889),
    by Oscar Wilde [excerpt].................. DLB-18

Dedication, *Ferdinand Count Fathom* (1753),
    by Tobias Smollett DLB-39

Dedication, *Lasselia* (1723), by Eliza
    Haywood [excerpt]....................... DLB-39

Dedication, *The History of Pompey the
    Little* (1751), by Francis Coventry DLB-39

Dedication, *The Wanderer* (1814),
    by Fanny Burney......................... DLB-39

Defense of *Amelia* (1752), by Henry Fielding .. DLB-39

Defoe, Daniel 1660-1731 .... DLB-39

de Fontaińe, Felix Gregory 1834-1896........ DLB-43

De Forest, John William 1826-1906 .... DLB-12

de Graff, Robert 1895-1981 ....Y-81

DeJong, Meindert 1906- DLB-52

Dekker, Thomas circa 1572-1632.............. DLB-62

Delafield, E. M. 1890-1943 .... DLB-34

de la Mare, Walter 1873-1956................. DLB-19

de la Roche, Mazo 1879-1961 .... DLB-68

Delaney, Shelagh 1939- DLB-13

Delany, Martin Robinson 1812-1885.......... DLB-50

Delany, Samuel R. 1942- DLB-8, 33

Delbanco, Nicholas 1942- DLB-6

DeLillo, Don 1936- DLB-6

Dell, Floyd 1887-1969 ....DLB-9

Dell Publishing Company..................... DLB-46

del Rey, Lester 1915- DLB-8

de Man, Paul 1919-1983.................... DLB-67

Demby, William 1922- DLB-33

Denham, Sir John 1615-1669....:.......... DLB-58

Denison, T. S., and Company DLB-49

Dennie, Joseph 1768-1812..............DLB-37, 43, 59

Dennis, Nigel 1912- DLB-13, 15

Dent, Tom 1932- DLB-38

Denton, Daniel circa 1626-1703 .... DLB-24

DePaola, Tomie 1934- DLB-61

Derby, George Horatio 1823-1861............. DLB-11

Derby, J. C., and Company.................. DLB-49

Derby and Miller DLB-49

Derleth, August 1909-1971....................DLB-9

The Derrydale Press......................... DLB-46

Desbiens, Jean-Paul 1927- DLB-53

DesRochers, Alfred 1901-1978 .... DLB-68

Desrosiers, Léo-Paul 1896-1967 .... DLB-68

Destouches, Louis-Ferdinand (see Céline, Louis-Ferdinand)

De Tabley, Lord 1835-1895 .... DLB-35

Deutsch, Babette 1895-1982 .... DLB-45

Deveaux, Alexis 1948- DLB-38

The Development of Lighting in the Staging
    of Drama, 1900-1945 [in Great Britain]... DLB-10

de Vere, Aubrey 1814-1902 .... DLB-35

The Devin-Adair Company.................... DLB-46

De Voto, Bernard 1897-1955....................DLB-9

De Vries, Peter 1910- DLB-6; Y-82

Dewdney, Christopher 1951- DLB-60

Dewdney, Selwyn 1909-1979 .... DLB-68

DeWitt, Robert M., Publisher................. DLB-49

DeWolfe, Fiske and Company................. DLB-49

de Young, M. H. 1849-1925 .... DLB-25

The Dial Press............................... DLB-46

Diamond, I. A. L. 1920- DLB-26

Di Cicco, Pier Giorgio 1949- DLB-60

Dick, Philip K. 1928- DLB-8

Dick and Fitzgerald........................... DLB-49

Dickens, Charles 1812-1870 ....DLB-21, 55, 70

Dickey, James 1923- DLB-5; Y-82

Dickey, William 1928- DLB-5

Dickinson, Emily 1830-1886 ....DLB-1

Dickinson, John 1732-1808................... DLB-31

Dickinson, Jonathan 1688-1747................ DLB-24

Dickinson, Patric 1914- DLB-27

Dickson, Gordon R. 1923- DLB-8

Didion, Joan 1934- DLB-2; Y-81, 86

Di Donato, Pietro 1911- DLB-9

Dillard, Annie 1945- Y-80

Dillard, R. H. W. 1937- DLB-5

Dillingham, Charles T., Company DLB-49

The G. W. Dillingham Company DLB-49

Dintenfass, Mark 1941- Y-84

Diogenes, Jr. (see Brougham, John)

DiPrima, Diane 1934- DLB-5, 16

Disch, Thomas M. 1940- DLB-8

Disney, Walt 1901-1966 .... DLB-22

Disraeli, Benjamin 1804-1881 ....DLB-21, 55

Ditzen, Rudolf (see Fallada, Hans)

Dix, Dorothea Lynde 1802-1887.................DLB-1

Dix, Dorothy (see Gilmer, Elizabeth Meriwether)

Dix, Edwards and Company................... DLB-49

Dixon, Paige (see Corcoran, Barbara)

Dixon, Richard Watson 1833-1900 .... DLB-19

Dobell, Sydney 1824-1874 .... DLB-32

Döblin, Alfred 1878-1957 .... DLB-66

Dobson, Austin 1840-1921.................... DLB-35

Doctorow, E. L. 1931- DLB-2, 28; Y-80

Dodd, William E. 1869-1940................. DLB-17

Dodd, Mead and Company.................... DLB-49

Dodge, B. W., and Company DLB-46

Dodge, Mary Mapes 1831?-1905.............. DLB-42

Dodge Publishing Company DLB-49

Dodgson, Charles Lutwidge (see Carroll, Lewis)

Doesticks, Q. K. Philander, P. B. (see Thomson,
    Mortimer)

Donahoe, Patrick [publishing house] DLB-49

Donald, David H. 1920- DLB-17

Donleavy, J. P. 1926- DLB-6

Donnelley, R. R., and Sons Company......... DLB-49

Donnelly, Ignatius 1831-1901 .... DLB-12

Donohue and Henneberry.................... DLB-49

Doolady, M. [publishing house]............... DLB-49

Dooley, Ebon (see Ebon)

Doolittle, Hilda 1886-1961.................DLB-4, 45

Doran, George H., Company................. DLB-46

Dorgelès, Roland 1886-1973.................. DLB-65

Dorn, Edward 1929- DLB-5

Dorr, Rheta Childe 1866-1948................. DLB-25

Dos Passos, John 1896-1970 ....DLB-4, 9; DS-1

Doubleday and Company.................... DLB-49

Doughty, Charles M. 1843-1926...........DLB-19, 57

Douglas, Keith 1920-1944 .... DLB-27

Douglas, Norman 1868-1952 .... DLB-34

Douglass, Frederick 1817?-1895 ....DLB-1, 43, 50

Douglass, William circa 1691-1752............. DLB-24

Dover Publications........................... DLB-46

Dowden, Edward 1843-1913................. DLB-35

Downing, J., Major (see Davis, Charles A.)

Downing, Major Jack (see Smith, Seba)

Dowson, Ernest 1867-1900 .... DLB-19

Doxey, William [publishing house] DLB-49

Doyle, Sir Arthur Conan 1859-1930.......DLB-18, 70

Doyle, Kirby 1932- DLB-16

Drabble, Margaret 1939- DLB-14

The Dramatic Publishing Company DLB-49

Dramatists Play Service DLB-46

Draper, John W. 1811-1882 .... DLB-30

Draper, Lyman C. 1815-1891................. DLB-30

Dreiser, Theodore 1871-1945 .... DLB-9, 12; DS-1

Drieu La Rochelle, Pierre 1893-1945 .... DLB-72

Drinkwater, John 1882-1937 ....DLB-10, 19

The Drue Heinz Literature Prize
  Excerpt from "Excerpts from a Report
    of the Commission," in David
    Bosworth's *The Death of Descartes*
    An Interview with David Bosworth Y-82

Duane, William 1760-1835 .... DLB-43

Dubé, Marcel 1930- DLB-53

Dubé, Rodolphe (see Hertel, François)

Du Bois, W. E. B. 1868-1963 ....DLB-47, 50

Du Bois, William Pène 1916- DLB-61

Ducharme, Réjean 1941- DLB-60

Duell, Sloan and Pearce DLB-46

Duffield and Green........................... DLB-46

Duffy, Maureen 1933- DLB-14

Dugan, Alan 1923- DLB-5

Duhamel, Georges 1884-1966 .... DLB-65

Dukes, Ashley 1885-1959..................... DLB-10

Dumas, Henry 1934-1968 .... DLB-41

Dunbar, Paul Laurence 1872-1906 ....DLB-50, 54

Duncan, Robert 1919- DLB-5, 16

Duncan, Ronald 1914-1982................... DLB-13

Dunigan, Edward, and Brother................ DLB-49

Dunlap, John 1747-1812 .... DLB-43

Dunlap, William 1766-1839............DLB-30, 37, 59

Dunn, Douglas 1942- DLB-40

Dunne, Finley Peter 1867-1936............DLB-11, 23

Dunne, John Gregory 1932- Y-80

Dunne, Philip 1908- DLB-26

Dunning, Ralph Cheever 1878-1930.............DLB-4

Dunning, William A. 1857-1922.............. DLB-17

Plunkett, Edward John Moreton Drax,
    Lord Dunsany 1878-1957 .... DLB-10

Durand, Lucile (see Bersianik, Louky)

Duranty, Walter 1884-1957.................... DLB-29

Durrell, Lawrence 1912- DLB-15, 27

Durrell, William [publishing house] DLB-49

Dürrenmatt, Friedrich 1921- DLB-69

Dutton, E. P., and Company................. DLB-49

Duvoisin, Roger 1904-1980.................... DLB-61

Duyckinck, Evert Augustus 1816-1878 ......DLB-3, 64

Duyckinck, George L. 1823-1863...............DLB-3

Duyckinck and Company..................... DLB-49

Dwight, John Sullivan 1813-1893...............DLB-1

Dwight, Timothy 1752-1817................. DLB-37

Dyer, Charles 1928- DLB-13

Dylan, Bob 1941- DLB-16

E

Eager, Edward 1911-1964 .... DLB-22

Earle, James H., and Company DLB-49

Early American Book Illustration,
    by Sinclair Hamilton DLB-49

Eastlake, William 1917- DLB-6

Eastman, Carol ?- DLB-44

Eberhart, Richard 1904- DLB-48

Ebon 1942- DLB-41

Ecco Press DLB-46

Edes, Benjamin 1732-1803 .... DLB-43

Edgar, David 1948- DLB-13

The Editor Publishing Company DLB-49

Edmonds, Randolph 1900- DLB-51

Edmonds, Walter D. 1903- DLB-9

Edschmid, Kasimir 1890-1966 .... DLB-56

Edwards, Jonathan 1703-1758 .... DLB-24

Edwards, Jonathan, Jr. 1745-1801 .... DLB-37

Edwards, Junius 1929- DLB-33

Edwards, Richard 1524-1566 .... DLB-62

Effinger, George Alec 1947- DLB-8

Eggleston, Edward 1837-1902 .... DLB-12

Eich, Günter 1907-1972 .... DLB-69

1873 Publishers' Catalogues DLB-49

Eighteenth-Century Aesthetic Theories DLB-31

Eighteenth-Century Philosophical
    Background DLB-31

Eigner, Larry 1927- DLB-5

Eisner, Kurt 1867-1919 .... DLB-66

Eklund, Gordon 1945- Y-83

Elder, Lonne III 1931- DLB-7, 38, 44

Elder, Paul, and Company DLB-49

Elements of Rhetoric (1828; revised, 1846),
    by Richard Whately [excerpt] DLB-57

Eliot, George 1819-1880 ....DLB-21, 35, 55

Eliot, John 1604-1690 .... DLB-24

Eliot, T. S. 1888-1965 .... DLB-7, 10, 45, 63

Elkin, Stanley 1930- DLB-2, 28; Y-80

Ellet, Elizabeth F. 1818?-1877 .... DLB-30

Elliott, George 1923- DLB-68

Elliott, Janice 1931- DLB-14

Elliott, William 1788-1863 ....DLB-3

Elliott, Thomes and Talbot DLB-49

Ellis, Edward S. 1840-1916 .... DLB-42

The George H. Ellis Company DLB-49

Ellison, Harlan 1934- DLB-8

Ellison, Ralph 1914- DLB-2

Ellmann, Richard 1918-1987 ....Y-87

The Elmer Holmes Bobst Awards
    in Arts and Letters Y-87

Emanuel, James Andrew 1921- DLB-41

Emerson, Ralph Waldo 1803-1882 ....DLB-1, 59

Emerson, William 1769-1811 .... DLB-37

Empson, William 1906-1984 .... DLB-20

The End of English Stage Censorship,
    1945-1968 .... DLB-13

Engel, Marian 1933-1985 .... DLB-53

Engle, Paul 1908- DLB-48

English Composition and Rhetoric (1866),
    by Alexander Bain [excerpt] DLB-57

The English Renaissance of Art (1908),
    by Oscar Wilde DLB-35

Enright, D. J. 1920- DLB-27

Enright, Elizabeth 1909-1968 .... DLB-22

L'Envoi (1882), by Oscar Wilde DLB-35

Epps, Bernard 1936- DLB-53

Epstein, Julius 1909- and
    Epstein, Philip 1909-1952 .... DLB-26

Equiano, Olaudah circa 1745-1797 ....DLB-37, 50

Ernst, Paul 1866-1933 .... DLB-66

Erskine, John 1879-1951 ....DLB-9

Ervine, St. John Greer 1883-1971 .... DLB-10

Eshleman, Clayton 1935- DLB-5

Ess Ess Publishing Company DLB-49

Essay on Chatterton (1842),
    by Robert Browning DLB-32

Estes, Eleanor 1906- DLB-22

Estes and Lauriat DLB-49

Ets, Marie Hall 1893- DLB-22

Eudora Welty: Eye of the Storyteller Y-87

Eugene O'Neill Memorial Theater Center DLB-7

Evans, Donald 1884-1921.....................DLB-54

Evans, George Henry 1805-1856..............DLB-43

Evans, M., and Company.....................DLB-46

Evans, Mari 1923- DLB-41

Evans, Mary Ann (see Eliot, George)

Evans, Nathaniel 1742-1767..................DLB-31

Evans, Sebastian 1830-1909..................DLB-35

Everett, Alexander Hill 1790-1847............DLB-59

Everett, Edward 1794-1865..................DLB-1, 59

Everson, William 1912- DLB-5, 16

Every Man His Own Poet; or, The
    Inspired Singer's Recipe Book (1877),
    by W. H. Mallock DLB-35

Ewart, Gavin 1916- DLB-40

Ewing, Juliana Horatia 1841-1885............DLB-21

Exley, Frederick 1929- Y-81

Experiment in the Novel (1929),
    by John D. Beresford DLB-36

F

"F. Scott Fitzgerald: St. Paul's Native Son
    and Distinguished American Writer":
    University of Minnesota Conference,
    29-31 October 1982........................Y-82

Faber, Frederick William 1814-1863..........DLB-32

Fair, Ronald L. 1932- DLB-33

Fairfax, Beatrice (see Manning, Marie)

Fallada, Hans 1893-1947....................DLB-56

Fancher, Betsy 1928- Y-83

Fane, Violet 1843-1905......................DLB-35

Fantasy Press Publishers....................DLB-46

Fante, John 1909-1983 ....Y-83

Farber, Norma 1909-1984...................DLB-61

Farigoule, Louis (see Romains, Jules)

Farley, Walter 1920- DLB-22

Farmer, Philip José 1918- DLB-8

Farquharson, Martha (see Finley, Martha)

Farrar and Rinehart.........................DLB-46

Farrar, Straus and Giroux...................DLB-46

Farrell, James T. 1904-1979...........DLB-4, 9; DS-2

Farrell, J. G. 1935-1979.....................DLB-14

Fast, Howard 1914- DLB-9

Faulkner, William 1897-1962
    ....DLB-9, 11, 44; DS-2; Y-86

Fauset, Jessie Redmon 1882-1961 ....DLB-51

Faust, Irvin 1924- DLB-2, 28; Y-80

Fawcett Books..............................DLB-46

Fearing, Kenneth 1902-1961 ....DLB-9

Federal Writers' Project.....................DLB-46

Federman, Raymond 1928- Y-80

Feiffer, Jules 1929- DLB-7, 44

Feinstein, Elaine 1930- DLB-14, 40

Fell, Frederick, Publishers...................DLB-46

Felton, Cornelius Conway 1807-1862..........DLB-1

Fennario, David 1947- DLB-60

Fenno, John 1751-1798......................DLB-43

Fenno, R. F., and Company DLB-49

Fenton, James 1949- DLB-40

Ferber, Edna 1885-1968....................DLB-9, 28

Ferdinand, Vallery III (see Salaam, Kalamu ya)

Ferguson, Sir Samuel 1810-1886 ....DLB-32

Ferguson, William Scott 1875-1954............DLB-47

Ferlinghetti, Lawrence 1919- DLB-5, 16

Fern, Fanny (see Parton, Sara
    Payson Willis)

Ferret, E., and Company DLB-49

Ferrini, Vincent 1913- DLB-48

Ferron, Jacques 1921-1985 ....DLB-60

Ferron, Madeleine 1922- DLB-53

Fetridge and Company.......................DLB-49

Feuchtwanger, Lion 1884-1958...............DLB-66

Ficke, Arthur Davison 1883-1945.............DLB-54

Fiction Best-Sellers, 1910-1945 ....DLB-9

Fiction into Film, 1928-1975: A List of Movies
    Based on the Works of Authors in
    British Novelists, 1930-1959 ....DLB-15

Fiedler, Leslie A. 1917- DLB-28, 67

Field, Eugene 1850-1895 ....DLB-23, 42

Field, Nathan 1587-1619 or 1620.............DLB-58

Field, Rachel 1894-1942.....................DLB-9, 22

A Field Guide to Recent Schools of
    American Poetry...........................Y-86

Fielding, Henry 1707-1754 .... DLB-39

Fielding, Sarah 1710-1768.................... DLB-39

Fields, James Thomas 1817-1881 ....DLB-1

Fields, Julia 1938- DLB-41

Fields, W. C. 1880-1946 .... DLB-44

Fields, Osgood and Company DLB-49

Fifty Penguin Years Y-85

Figes, Eva 1932- DLB-14

Filson, John circa 1753-1788 .... DLB-37

Findley, Timothy 1930- DLB-53

Finlay, Ian Hamilton 1925- DLB-40

Finley, Martha 1828-1909 .... DLB-42

Finney, Jack 1911- DLB-8

Finney, Walter Braden (see Finney, Jack)

Firbank, Ronald 1886-1926................... DLB-36

Firmin, Giles 1615-1697 .... DLB-24

First Strauss "Livings" Awarded to Cynthia
    Ozick and Raymond Carver
    An Interview with Cynthia Ozick
    An Interview with Raymond Carver Y-83

Fish, Stanley 1938- DLB-67

Fisher, Clay (see Allen, Henry W.)

Fisher, Dorothy Canfield 1879-1958.............DLB-9

Fisher, Leonard Everett 1924- DLB-61

Fisher, Roy 1930- DLB-40

Fisher, Rudolph 1897-1934................... DLB-51

Fisher, Sydney George 1856-1927 .... DLB-47

Fisher, Vardis 1895-1968 ....DLB-9

Fiske, John 1608-1677....................... DLB-24

Fiske, John 1842-1901.....................DLB-47, 64

Fitch, Thomas circa 1700-1774 .... DLB-31

Fitch, William Clyde 1865-1909 ....DLB-7

FitzGerald, Edward 1809-1883 .... DLB-32

Fitzgerald, F. Scott 1896-1940 ... DLB-4, 9; Y-81; DS-1

Fitzgerald, Penelope 1916- DLB-14

Fitzgerald, Robert 1910-1985.....................Y-80

Fitzgerald, Thomas 1819-1891 .... DLB-23

Fitzgerald, Zelda Sayre 1900-1948.................Y-84

Fitzhugh, Louise 1928-1974 .... DLB-52

Fitzhugh, William circa 1651-1701............ DLB-24

Flanagan, Thomas 1923- Y-80

Flanner, Hildegarde 1899-1987 .... DLB-48

Flanner, Janet 1892-1978.......................DLB-4

Flavin, Martin 1883-1967.......................DLB-9

Flecker, James Elroy 1884-1915 ....DLB-10, 19

Fleeson, Doris 1901-1970.................... DLB-29

Fleißer, Marieluise 1901-1974 .... DLB-56

The Fleshly School of Poetry and Other
    Phenomena of the Day (1872), by Robert
    Buchanan DLB-35

The Fleshly School of Poetry: Mr. D. G.
    Rossetti (1871), by Thomas Maitland
    (Robert Buchanan)....................... DLB-35

Fletcher, J. S. 1863-1935 .... DLB-70

Fletcher, John (see Beaumont, Francis)

Fletcher, John Gould 1886-1950.............DLB-4, 45

Flieg, Helmut (see Heym, Stefan)

Flint, F. S. 1885-1960......................... DLB-19

Follen, Eliza Lee (Cabot) 1787-1860 ....DLB-1

Follett, Ken 1949- Y-81

Follett Publishing Company DLB-46

Folsom, John West [publishing house]........ DLB-49

Foote, Horton 1916- DLB-26

Foote, Shelby 1916- DLB-2, 17

Forbes, Calvin 1945- DLB-41

Forbes, Ester 1891-1967..................... DLB-22

Forbes and Company......................... DLB-49

Force, Peter 1790-1868...................... DLB-30

Forché, Carolyn 1950- DLB-5

Ford, Charles Henri 1913- DLB-4, 48

Ford, Corey 1902-1969...................... DLB-11

Ford, Ford Madox 1873-1939 .... DLB-34

Ford, J. B., and Company DLB-49

Ford, Jesse Hill 1928- DLB-6

Ford, John 1586-? DLB-58

Ford, Worthington C. 1858-1941.............. DLB-47

Fords, Howard, and Hulbert DLB-49

Foreman, Carl 1914-1984 .... DLB-26

Fornés, María Irene 1930- DLB-7

Forrest, Leon 1937- DLB-33

Forster, E. M. 1879-1970 .... DLB-34

Forten, Charlotte L. 1837-1914............... DLB-50

Fortune, T. Thomas 1856-1928 .... DLB-23

Fosdick, Charles Austin 1842-1915 .... DLB-42

Foster, Genevieve 1893-1979 .... DLB-61

Foster, Hannah Webster 1758-1840 .... DLB-37

Foster, John 1648-1681 .... DLB-24

Foster, Michael 1904-1956 .... DLB-9

Four Essays on the Beat Generation,
     by John Clellon Holmes DLB-16

Four Seas Company DLB-46

Four Winds Press DLB-46

Fournier, Henri Alban (see Alain-Fournier)

Fowler and Wells Company DLB-49

Fowles, John 1926- DLB-14

Fox, John, Jr. 1862 or 1863-1919 .... DLB-9

Fox, Paula 1923- DLB-52

Fox, Richard K. [publishing house] DLB-49

Fox, William Price 1926- DLB-2; Y-81

Fraenkel, Michael 1896-1957 .... DLB-4

France, Richard 1938- DLB-7

Francis, C. S. [publishing house] DLB-49

Francis, Convers 1795-1863 .... DLB-1

Francke, Kuno 1855-1930 .... DLB-71

Frank, Leonhard 1882-1961 .... DLB-56

Frank, Melvin (see Panama, Norman)

Frank, Waldo 1889-1967 .... DLB-9, 63

Franken, Rose 1895?- Y-84

Franklin, Benjamin 1706-1790 .... DLB-24, 43

Franklin, James 1697-1735 .... DLB-43

Franklin Library DLB-46

Frantz, Ralph Jules 1902-1979 .... DLB-4

Fraser, G. S. 1915-1980 .... DLB-27

Frayn, Michael 1933- DLB-13, 14

Frederic, Harold 1856-1898 .... DLB-12, 23

Freeman, Douglas Southall 1886-1953 .... DLB-17

Freeman, Legh Richmond 1842-1915 .... DLB-23

Freeman, Mary Wilkins 1852-1930 .... DLB-12

Freeman, R. Austin 1862-1943 .... DLB-70

French, David 1939- DLB-53

French, James [publishing house] DLB-49

French, Samuel [publishing house] DLB-49

Freneau, Philip 1752-1832 .... DLB-37, 43

Friedman, Bruce Jay 1930- DLB-2, 28

Friel, Brian 1929- DLB-13

Friend, Krebs 1895?-1967? DLB-4

Fringe and Alternative Theater
     in Great Britain DLB-13

Frisch, Max 1911- DLB-69

Fritz, Jean 1915- DLB-52

Frost, Robert 1874-1963 .... DLB-54

Frothingham, Octavius Brooks 1822-1895 .... DLB-1

Froude, James Anthony 1818-1894 .... DLB-18, 57

Fry, Christopher 1907- DLB-13

Frye, Northrop 1912- DLB-67, 68

Fuchs, Daniel 1909- DLB-9, 26, 28

The Fugitives and the Agrarians:
     The First Exhibition Y-85

Fuller, Charles H., Jr. 1939- DLB-38

Fuller, Henry Blake 1857-1929 .... DLB-12

Fuller, John 1937- DLB-40

Fuller, Roy 1912- DLB-15, 20

Fuller, Samuel 1912- DLB-26

Fuller, Sarah Margaret, Marchesa
     D'Ossoli 1810-1850 .... DLB-1, 59

Fulton, Len 1934- Y-86

Fulton, Robin 1937- DLB-40

Furman, Laura 1945- Y-86

Furness, Horace Howard 1833-1912 .... DLB-64

Furness, William Henry 1802-1896 .... DLB-1

Furthman, Jules 1888-1966 .... DLB-26

The Future of the Novel (1899),
     by Henry James DLB-18

G

Gaddis, William 1922- DLB-2

Gág, Wanda 1893-1946 .... DLB-22

Gagnon, Madeleine 1938- DLB-60

Gaine, Hugh 1726-1807 .... DLB-43

Gaine, Hugh [publishing house] DLB-49

Gaines, Ernest J. 1933- DLB-2, 33; Y-80

Gaiser, Gerd 1908-1976 .... DLB-69

Galaxy Science Fiction Novels DLB-46

Gale, Zona 1874-1938 ....DLB-9

Gallant, Mavis 1922- DLB-53

Gallico, Paul 1897-1976.........................DLB-9

Galsworthy, John 1867-1933................DLB-10, 34

Galvin, Brendan 1938- DLB-5

Gambit DLB-46

Gammer Gurton's Needle.........................DLB-62

Gannett, Frank E. 1876-1957................... DLB-29

Gardam, Jane 1928- DLB-14

Garden, Alexander circa 1685-1756 .... DLB-31

Gardner, John 1933-1982 .... DLB-2; Y-82

Garis, Howard R. 1873-1962 .... DLB-22

Garland, Hamlin 1860-1940...............DLB-12, 71

Garneau, Michel 1939- DLB-53

Garner, Hugh 1913-1979..................... DLB-68

Garnett, David 1892-1981 .... DLB-34

Garraty, John A. 1920- DLB-17

Garrett, George 1929- DLB-2, 5; Y-83

Garrison, William Lloyd 1805-1879..........DLB-1, 43

Gascoyne, David 1916- DLB-20

Gaskell, Elizabeth Cleghorn 1810-1865........ DLB-21

Gass, William Howard 1924- DLB-2

Gates, Doris 1901- DLB-22

Gates, Henry Louis, Jr. 1950- DLB-67

Gates, Lewis E. 1860-1924.................... DLB-71

Gay, Ebenezer 1696-1787.................... DLB-24

The Gay Science (1866),
  by E. S. Dallas [excerpt]................... DLB-21

Gayarré, Charles E. A. 1805-1895 .... DLB-30

Gaylord, Charles [publishing house].......... DLB-49

Geddes, Gary 1940- DLB-60

Geddes, Virgil 1897- DLB-4

Geis, Bernard, Associates.................... DLB-46

Geisel, Theodor Seuss 1904- DLB-61

Gelber, Jack 1932- DLB-7

Gellhorn, Martha 1908- Y-82

Gems, Pam 1925- DLB-13

A General Idea of the College of Mirania (1753),
  by William Smith [excerpts].............. DLB-31

Genet, Jean 1910-1986 .... Y-86, DLB-72

Genevoix, Maurice 1890-1980 .... DLB-65

Genovese, Eugene D. 1930- DLB-17

Gent, Peter 1942- Y-82

George, Henry 1839-1897..................... DLB-23

George, Jean Craighead 1919- DLB-52

Gerhardie, William 1895-1977................. DLB-36

Gernsback, Hugo 1884-1967 ....DLB-8

Gerrish, Samuel [publishing house]........... DLB-49

Gerrold, David 1944- DLB-8

Geston, Mark S. 1946- DLB-8

Gibbon, Lewis Grassic (see Mitchell, James Leslie)

Gibbons, Floyd 1887-1939.................... DLB-25

Gibson, Graeme 1934- DLB-53

Gibson, Wilfrid 1878-1962.................... DLB-19

Gibson, William 1914- DLB-7

Gide, André 1869-1951....................... DLB-65

Giguère, Diane 1937- DLB-53

Giguère, Roland 1929- DLB-60

Gilder, Richard Watson 1844-1909............ DLB-64

Gildersleeve, Basil 1831-1924................. DLB-71

Giles, Henry 1809-1882 .... DLB-64

Gill, William F., Company DLB-49

Gillespie, A. Lincoln, Jr. 1895-1950 ....DLB-4

Gilliam, Florence ?-?...........................DLB-4

Gilliatt, Penelope 1932- DLB-14

Gillott, Jacky 1939-1980 .... DLB-14

Gilman, Caroline H. 1794-1888 ....DLB-3

Gilman, W. and J. [publishing house] DLB-49

Gilmer, Elizabeth Meriwether 1861-1951 ...... DLB-29

Gilmer, Francis Walker 1790-1826 .... DLB-37

Gilroy, Frank D. 1925- DLB-7

Ginsberg, Allen 1926- DLB-5, 16

Giono, Jean 1895-1970 .... DLB-72

Giovanni, Nikki 1943- DLB-5, 41

Gipson, Lawrence Henry 1880-1971........... DLB-17

Giraudoux, Jean 1882-1944 .... DLB-65

Gissing, George 1857-1903 .... DLB-18

Gladstone, William Ewart 1809-1898 .... DLB-57

Glaeser, Ernst 1902-1963..................... DLB-69

Glanville, Brian 1931- DLB-15

Glapthorne, Henry 1610-1643?............... DLB-58

Glasgow, Ellen 1873-1945 .... DLB-9, 12

Glaspell, Susan 1882-1948.................. DLB-7, 9

Glass, Montague 1877-1934 .... DLB-11

Glassco, John 1909-1981.................... DLB-68

Glauser, Friedrich 1896-1938................ DLB-56

F. Gleason's Publishing Hall DLB-49

Glück, Louise 1943- DLB-5

Godbout, Jacques 1933- DLB-53

Goddard, Morrill 1865-1937................. DLB-25

Goddard, William 1740-1817................ DLB-43

Godey and McMichael....................... DLB-49

Godfrey, Dave 1938- DLB-60

Godfrey, Thomas 1736-1763 .... DLB-31

Godine, David R., Publisher DLB-46

Godwin, Gail 1937- DLB-6

Godwin, Parke 1816-1904 ....DLB-3, 64

Godwin, William 1756-1836 .... DLB-39

Goes, Albrecht 1908- DLB-69

Goffe, Thomas circa 1592-1629 .... DLB-58

Goffstein, M. B. 1940- DLB-61

Gogarty, Oliver St. John 1878-1957 ....DLB-15, 19

Goines, Donald 1937-1974.................. DLB-33

Gold, Herbert 1924- DLB-2; Y-81

Gold, Michael 1893-1967 ....DLB-9, 28

Goldberg, Dick 1947- DLB-7

Golding, William 1911- DLB-15

Goldman, William 1931- DLB-44

Goldsmith, Oliver 1730 or 1731-1774 .... DLB-39

Goldsmith Publishing Company DLB-46

Gomme, Laurence James
    [publishing house] DLB-46

The Goodman Theatre........................DLB-7

Goodrich, Frances 1891-1984 and
    Hackett, Albert 1900- DLB-26

Goodrich, S. G. [publishing house] DLB-49

Goodrich, Samuel Griswold 1793-1860 .....DLB-1, 42

Goodspeed, C. E., and Company............. DLB-49

Goodwin, Stephen 1943- Y-82

Gookin, Daniel 1612-1687................... DLB-24

Gordon, Caroline 1895-1981 ....DLB-4, 9; Y-81

Gordon, Giles 1940- DLB-14

Gordon, Mary 1949- DLB-6; Y-81

Gordone, Charles 1925- DLB-7

Gorey, Edward 1925- DLB-61

Gosse, Edmund 1849-1928 .... DLB-57

Gould, Wallace 1882-1940.................... DLB-54

Goyen, William 1915-1983................ DLB-2; Y-83

Grady, Henry W. 1850-1889 .... DLB-23

Graf, Oskar Maria 1894-1967 .... DLB-56

Graham, W. S. 1918- DLB-20

Graham, William H. [publishing house] DLB-49

Grahame, Kenneth 1859-1932................. DLB-34

Gramatky, Hardie 1907-1979................. DLB-22

Granich, Irwin (see Gold, Michael)

Grant, Harry J. 1881-1963 .... DLB-29

Grant, James Edward 1905-1966 .... DLB-26

Grasty, Charles H. 1863-1924 .... DLB-25

Grau, Shirley Ann 1929- DLB-2

Graves, John 1920- Y-83

Graves, Richard 1715-1804.................... DLB-39

Graves, Robert 1895-1985 .... DLB-20; Y-85

Gray, Asa 1810-1888 ....DLB-1

Gray, David 1838-1861 .... DLB-32

Gray, Simon 1936- DLB-13

Grayson, William J. 1788-1863 ....DLB-3, 64

The Great War and the Theater, 1914-1918
    [Great Britain] DLB-10

Greeley, Horace 1811-1872..................DLB-3, 43

Green, Adolph (see Comden, Betty)

Green, Duff 1791-1875...................... DLB-43

Green, Gerald 1922- DLB-28

Green, Henry 1905-1973 .... DLB-15

Green, Jonas 1712-1767 .... DLB-31

Green, Joseph 1706-1780.................... DLB-31

Green, Julien 1900- DLB-4, 72

Green, Paul 1894-1981 ....DLB-7, 9; Y-81

Green, T. and S. [publishing house].......... DLB-49

Green, Timothy [publishing house]........... DLB-49

Greenberg: Publisher........................ DLB-46

Green Tiger Press DLB-46

Greene, Asa 1789-1838........................ DLB-11

Greene, Benjamin H. [publishing house] DLB-49

Greene, Graham 1904- DLB-13, 15; Y-85

Greene, Robert 1558-1592..................... DLB-62

Greenhow, Robert 1800-1854 .... DLB-30

Greenough, Horatio 1805-1852 ....DLB-1

Greenwell, Dora 1821-1882.................... DLB-35

Greenwillow Books DLB-46

Greenwood, Grace (see Lippincott, Sara Jane Clarke)

Greenwood, Walter 1903-1974 .... DLB-10

Greer, Ben 1948- DLB-6

Greg, W. R. 1809-1881 .... DLB-55

Gregg Press.................................. DLB-46

Persse, Isabella Augusta,
     Lady Gregory 1852-1932................. DLB-10

Gregory, Horace 1898-1982 .... DLB-48

Greville, Fulke, First Lord Brooke
     1554-1628................................ DLB-62

Grey, Zane 1872-1939 ....DLB-9

Grieve, C. M. (see MacDiarmid, Hugh)

Griffith, Elizabeth 1727?-1793................. DLB-39

Griffiths, Trevor 1935- DLB-13

Griggs, S. C., and Company DLB-49

Griggs, Sutton Elbert 1872-1930.............. DLB-50

Grignon, Claude-Henri 1894-1976 .... DLB-68

Grigson, Geoffrey 1905- DLB-27

Grimké, Angelina Weld 1880-1958........DLB-50, 54

Grimm, Hans 1875-1959 .... DLB-66

Griswold, Rufus Wilmot 1815-1857.........DLB-3, 59

Gross, Milt 1895-1953 .... DLB-11

Grosset and Dunlap DLB-49

Grossman Publishers DLB-46

Groulx, Lionel 1878-1967 .... DLB-68

Grove Press................................. DLB-46

Grubb, Davis 1919-1980......................DLB-6

Gruelle, Johnny 1880-1938 .... DLB-22

Guare, John 1938- DLB-7

Guest, Barbara 1920- DLB-5

Guèvremont, Germaine 1893-1968 .... DLB-68

Guilloux, Louis 1899-1980.................... DLB-72

Guiney, Louise Imogen 1861-1920 .... DLB-54

Guiterman, Arthur 1871-1943................. DLB-11

Gunn, Bill 1934- DLB-38

Gunn, James E. 1923- DLB-8

Gunn, Neil M. 1891-1973 .... DLB-15

Gunn, Thom 1929- DLB-27

Gunnars, Kristjana 1948- DLB-60

Gurik, Robert 1932- DLB-60

Guthrie, A. B., Jr. 1901- DLB-6

Guthrie, Ramon 1896-1973....................DLB-4

The Guthrie Theater..........................DLB-7

Guy, Ray 1939- DLB-60

Guy, Rosa 1925- DLB-33

Gwynne, Erskine 1898-1948....................DLB-4

Gysin, Brion 1916- DLB-16

H

H. D. (see Doolittle, Hilda)

Hackett, Albert (see Goodrich, Frances)

Hagelstange, Rudolf 1912-1984 .... DLB-69

Haggard, H. Rider 1856-1925................ DLB-70

Hailey, Arthur 1920- Y-82

Haines, John 1924- DLB-5

Hake, Thomas Gordon 1809-1895 .... DLB-32

Haldeman, Joe 1943- DLB-8

Haldeman-Julius Company.................... DLB-46

Hale, E. J., and Son DLB-49

Hale, Edward Everett 1822-1909 ....DLB-1, 42

Hale, Leo Thomas (see Ebon)

Hale, Lucretia Peabody 1820-1900 .... DLB-42

Hale, Nancy 1908- Y-80

Hale, Sarah Josepha (Buell) 1788-1879......DLB-1, 42

Haley, Alex 1921- DLB-38

Haliburton, Thomas Chandler 1796-1865..... DLB-11

Hall, Donald 1928- DLB-5

Hall, Samuel [publishing house].............. DLB-49

Hallam, Arthur Henry 1811-1833............. DLB-32

Halleck, Fitz-Greene 1790-1867 ....DLB-3

Hallmark Editions DLB-46

Halper, Albert 1904-1984 ....DLB-9

Halstead, Murat 1829-1908................... DLB-23

Hamburger, Michael 1924- DLB-27

Hamilton, Alexander 1712-1756.............. DLB-31

Hamilton, Alexander 1755?-1804.............. DLB-37

Hamilton, Cicely 1872-1952 .... DLB-10

Hamilton, Edmond 1904-1977 ....DLB-8

Hamilton, Gail (see Corcoran, Barbara)

Hamilton, Ian 1938- DLB-40

Hamilton, Patrick 1904-1962 .... DLB-10

Hamilton, Virginia 1936- DLB-33, 52

Hammon, Jupiter 1711-died between
    1790 and 1806 ....DLB-31, 50

Hammond, John ?-1663 .... DLB-24

Hamner, Earl 1923- DLB-6

Hampton, Christopher 1946- DLB-13

Handlin, Oscar 1915- DLB-17

Hankin, St. John 1869-1909 .... DLB-10

Hanley, Clifford 1922- DLB-14

Hannah, Barry 1942- DLB-6

Hannay, James 1827-1873 .... DLB-21

Hansberry, Lorraine 1930-1965 ....DLB-7, 38

Harcourt Brace Jovanovich.................... DLB-46

Hardwick, Elizabeth 1916- DLB-6

Hardy, Thomas 1840-1928 ....DLB-18, 19

Hare, David 1947- DLB-13

Hargrove, Marion 1919- DLB-11

Harlow, Robert 1923- DLB-60

Harness, Charles L. 1915- DLB-8

Harper, Frances Ellen Watkins
    1825-1911.............................. DLB-50

Harper, Michael S. 1938- DLB-41

Harper and Brothers........................ DLB-49

Harris, Benjamin ?-circa 1720 ....DLB-42, 43

Harris, George Washington 1814-1869......DLB-3, 11

Harris, Joel Chandler 1848-1908 ....DLB-11, 23, 42

Harris, Mark 1922- DLB-2; Y-80

Harrison, Charles Yale 1898-1954............. DLB-68

Harrison, Frederic 1831-1923 .... DLB-57

Harrison, Harry 1925- DLB-8

Harrison, James P., Company DLB-49

Harrison, Jim 1937- Y-82

Harrison, Paul Carter 1936- DLB-38

Harrison, Tony 1937- DLB-40

Harrisse, Henry 1829-1910.................... DLB-47

Harsent, David 1942- DLB-40

Hart, Albert Bushnell 1854-1943.............. DLB-17

Hart, Moss 1904-1961 ....DLB-7

Hart, Oliver 1723-1795....................... DLB-31

Harte, Bret 1836-1902.....................DLB-12, 64

Hartlaub, Felix 1913-1945.................... DLB-56

Hartley, L. P. 1895-1972 .... DLB-15

Hartley, Marsden 1877-1943 .... DLB-54

Hartman, Geoffrey H. 1929- DLB-67

Hartmann, Sadakichi 1867-1944.............. DLB-54

Harwood, Lee 1939- DLB-40

Harwood, Ronald 1934- DLB-13

Haskins, Charles Homer 1870-1937 .... DLB-47

A Haughty and Proud Generation (1922),
    by Ford Madox Hueffer DLB-36

Hauptmann, Carl 1858-1921 .... DLB-66

Hauptmann, Gerhart 1862-1946 .... DLB-66

Hauser, Marianne 1910- Y-83

Hawker, Robert Stephen 1803-1875.......... DLB-32

Hawkes, John 1925- DLB-2, 7; Y-80

Hawkins, Walter Everette 1883-?.............. DLB-50

Hawthorne, Nathaniel 1804-1864 ....DLB-1

Hay, John 1838-1905.....................DLB-12, 47

Hayden, Robert 1913-1980....................DLB-5

Hayes, John Michael 1919- DLB-26

Hayne, Paul Hamilton 1830-1886 ....DLB-3, 64

Haywood, Eliza 1693?-1756 .... DLB-39

Hazard, Willis P. [publishing house].......... DLB-49

Hazzard, Shirley 1931- Y-82

Headley, Joel T. 1813-1897 .... DLB-30

Heaney, Seamus 1939- DLB-40

Heard, Nathan C. 1936- DLB-33

Hearn, Lafcadio 1850-1904.................... DLB-12

Hearst, William Randolph 1863-1951 .... DLB-25

Heath, Catherine 1924- DLB-14

Heath-Stubbs, John 1918- DLB-27

Hébert, Anne 1916- DLB-68

Hébert, Jacques 1923- DLB-53

Hecht, Anthony 1923- DLB-5

Hecht, Ben 1894-1964........... DLB-7, 9, 25, 26, 28

Hecker, Isaac Thomas 1819-1888 ....DLB-1

Hedge, Frederic Henry 1805-1890 ....DLB-1, 59

Heidish, Marcy 1947- Y-82

Heinlein, Robert A. 1907- DLB-8

Heller, Joseph 1923- DLB-2, 28; Y-80

Hellman, Lillian 1906-1984............... DLB-7; Y-84

Helprin, Mark 1947- Y-85

Helwig, David 1938- DLB-60

Hemingway, Ernest
     1899-1961.............. DLB-4, 9; Y-81, 87; DS-1

Hemingway: Twenty-Five Years Later............Y-85

Hemphill, Paul 1936- Y-87

Henchman, Daniel 1689-1761 .... DLB-24

Henderson, Alice Corbin 1881-1949.......... DLB-54

Henderson, David 1942- DLB-41

Henderson, George Wylie 1904- DLB-51

Henderson, Zenna 1917- DLB-8

Henley, Beth 1952- Y-86

Henley, William Ernest 1849-1903 .... DLB-19

Henry, Buck 1930- DLB-26

Henry, Marguerite 1902- DLB-22

Henry, Robert Selph 1889-1970.............. DLB-17

Henry, Will (see Allen, Henry W.)

Henschke, Alfred (see Klabund)

Henty, G. A. 1832-1902 .... DLB-18

Hentz, Caroline Lee 1800-1856.................DLB-3

Herbert, Alan Patrick 1890-1971 .... DLB-10

Herbert, Frank 1920-1986.....................DLB-8

Herbert, Henry William 1807-1858.............DLB-3

Herbert, John 1926- DLB-53

Herbst, Josephine 1892-1969...................DLB-9

Hercules, Frank E. M. 1917- DLB-33

Herder, B., Book Company DLB-49

Hergesheimer, Joseph 1880-1954 ....DLB-9

Heritage Press................................ DLB-46

Hermlin, Stephan 1915- DLB-69

Hernton, Calvin C. 1932- DLB-38

"The Hero as Man of Letters: Johnson,
     Rousseau, Burns" (1841), by Thomas
     Carlyle [excerpt] DLB-57

The Hero as Poet. Dante; Shakspeare (1841),
     by Thomas Carlyle...................... DLB-32

Herrick, E. R., and Company................. DLB-49

Herrick, Robert 1868-1938 ....DLB-9, 12

Herrick, William 1915- Y-83

Herrmann, John 1900-1959 ....DLB-4

Hersey, John 1914- DLB-6

Hertel, François 1905-1985.................... DLB-68

Herzog, Emile Salomon Wilhelm (see Maurois, André)

Hesse, Hermann 1877-1962 .... DLB-66

Hewat, Alexander circa 1743-circa 1824....... DLB-30

Hewitt, John 1907- DLB-27

Hewlett, Maurice 1861-1923.................. DLB-34

Heyen, William 1940- DLB-5

Heym, Stefan 1913- DLB-69

Heyward, Dorothy 1890-1961 and
     Heyward, DuBose 1885-1940 ....DLB-7

Heyward, DuBose 1885-1940............ DLB-7, 9, 45

Heywood, Thomas 1573 or 1574-1641 .... DLB-62

Hiebert, Paul 1892-1987...................... DLB-68

Higgins, Aidan 1927- DLB-14

Higgins, Colin 1941- DLB-26

Higgins, George V. 1939- DLB-2; Y-81

Higginson, Thomas Wentworth 1823-1911..DLB-1, 64

Highwater, Jamake 1942?- DLB-52; Y-85

Hildesheimer, Wolfgang 1916- DLB-69

Hildreth, Richard 1807-1865 ....DLB-1, 30, 59

Hill, Geoffrey 1932- DLB-40

Hill, George M., Company DLB-49

Hill, "Sir" John 1714?-1775.................... DLB-39

Hill, Lawrence, and Company, Publishers DLB-46

Hill, Leslie 1880-1960 .... DLB-51

Hill, Susan 1942- DLB-14

Hill, Walter 1942- DLB-44

Hill and Wang................................ DLB-46

Hilliard, Gray and Company DLB-49

Hillyer, Robert 1895-1961.................... DLB-54

Hilton, James 1900-1954 .... DLB-34

Hilton and Company DLB-49

Himes, Chester 1909-1984...................DLB-2

Hine, Daryl 1936- DLB-60

The History of the Adventures of Joseph Andrews (1742), by Henry Fielding [excerpt]...... DLB-39

Hirsch, E. D., Jr. 1928- DLB-67

Hoagland, Edward 1932- DLB-6

Hoagland, Everett H. III 1942- DLB-41

Hoban, Russell 1925- DLB-52

Hobsbaum, Philip 1932- DLB-40

Hobson, Laura Z. 1900- DLB-28

Hochman, Sandra 1936- DLB-5

Hodgins, Jack 1938- DLB-60

Hodgman, Helen 1945- DLB-14

Hodgson, Ralph 1871-1962.................. DLB-19

Hodgson, William Hope 1877-1918 .... DLB-70

Hoffenstein, Samuel 1890-1947 .... DLB-11

Hoffman, Charles Fenno 1806-1884...........DLB-3

Hoffman, Daniel 1923- DLB-5

Hofmann, Michael 1957- DLB-40

Hofstadter, Richard 1916-1970............... DLB-17

Hogan, Desmond 1950- DLB-14

Hogan and Thompson DLB-49

Hohl, Ludwig 1904-1980 .... DLB-56

Holbrook, David 1923- DLB-14, 40

Holcroft, Thomas 1745-1809................ DLB-39

Holden, Molly 1927-1981................... DLB-40

Holiday House DLB-46

Holland, Norman N. 1927- DLB-67

Hollander, John 1929- DLB-5

Holley, Marietta 1836-1926................. DLB-11

Hollingsworth, Margaret 1940- DLB-60

Hollo, Anselm 1934- DLB-40

Holloway, John 1920- DLB-27

Holloway House Publishing Company........ DLB-46

Holme, Constance 1880-1955................ DLB-34

Holmes, Oliver Wendell 1809-1894...........DLB-1

Holmes, John Clellon 1926- DLB-16

Holst, Hermann E. von 1841-1904 .... DLB-47

Holt, Henry, and Company DLB-49

Holt, John 1721-1784 .... DLB-43

Holt, Rinehart and Winston DLB-46

Holthusen, Hans Egon 1913- DLB-69

Home, Henry, Lord Kames 1696-1782....... DLB-31

Home Publishing Company DLB-49

Home, William Douglas 1912- DLB-13

Homes, Geoffrey (see Mainwaring, Daniel)

Honig, Edwin 1919- DLB-5

Hood, Hugh 1928- DLB-53

Hooker, Jeremy 1941- DLB-40

Hooker, Thomas 1586-1647.................. DLB-24

Hooper, Johnson Jones 1815-1862 ....DLB-3, 11

Hopkins, Gerard Manley 1844-1889.......DLB-35, 57

Hopkins, John H., and Son................. DLB-46

Hopkins, Lemuel 1750-1801................. DLB-37

Hopkins, Pauline Elizabeth 1859-1930........ DLB-50

Hopkins, Samuel 1721-1803................. DLB-31

Hopkinson, Francis 1737-1791 .... DLB-31

Horgan, Paul 1903- Y-85

Horizon Press DLB-46

Horne, Frank 1899-1974 .... DLB-51

Horne, Richard Henry (Hengist) 1802 or 1803-1884............................ DLB-32

Hornung, E. W. 1866-1921.................. DLB-70

Horovitz, Israel 1939- DLB-7

Horton, George Moses 1797?-1883?........... DLB-50

Horwood, Harold 1923- DLB-60

Hosford, E. and E. [publishing house]........ DLB-49

Hotchkiss and Company.................... DLB-49

Hough, Emerson 1857-1923..................DLB-9

Houghton Mifflin Company................. DLB-49

Houghton, Stanley 1881-1913 .... DLB-10

Housman, A. E. 1859-1936.................. DLB-19

Housman, Laurence 1865-1959 .... DLB-10

Hovey, Richard 1864-1900 .... DLB-54

Howard, Maureen 1930- Y-83

Howard, Richard 1929- DLB-5

Howard, Roy W. 1883-1964 .... DLB-29

Howard, Sidney 1891-1939.................DLB-7, 26

Howe, E. W. 1853-1937 ....DLB-12, 25

Howe, Henry 1816-1893 .... DLB-30

Howe, Irving 1920- DLB-67

Howe, Julia Ward 1819-1910 ....DLB-1

Howell, Clark, Sr. 1863-1936 .... DLB-25

Howell, Evan P. 1839-1905 .... DLB-23

Howell, Soskin and Company DLB-46

Howells, William Dean 1837-1920 ....DLB-12, 64

Hoyem, Andrew 1935- DLB-5

Hoyt, Henry [publishing house] DLB-49

Hubbard, Kin 1868-1930 .... DLB-11

Hubbard, William circa 1621-1704 .... DLB-24

Huch, Friedrich 1873-1913 .... DLB-66

Huch, Ricarda 1864-1947 .... DLB-66

Huck at 100: How Old Is
    Huckleberry Finn? Y-85

Hudson, Henry Norman 1814-1886 .... DLB-64

Hudson and Goodwin DLB-49

Huebsch, B. W. [publishing house] DLB-46

Hughes, David 1930- DLB-14

Hughes, Langston 1902-1967 .... DLB-4, 7, 48, 51

Hughes, Richard 1900-1976 .... DLB-15

Hughes, Ted 1930- DLB-40

Hughes, Thomas 1822-1896 .... DLB-18

Hugo, Richard 1923-1982 ....DLB-5

Hugo Awards and Nebula Awards DLB-8

Hulme, T. E. 1883-1917 .... DLB-19

Hume, Fergus 1859-1932 .... DLB-70

Humorous Book Illustration DLB-11

Humphrey, William 1924- DLB-6

Humphreys, David 1752-1818 .... DLB-37

Humphreys, Emyr 1919- DLB-15

Huncke, Herbert 1915- DLB-16

Huneker, James Gibbons 1857-1921 .... DLB-71

Hunt, Irene 1907- DLB-52

Hunter, Evan 1926- Y-82

Hunter, Jim 1939- DLB-14

Hunter, Kristin 1931- DLB-33

Hunter, N. C. 1908-1971 .... DLB-10

Hurd and Houghton DLB-49

Hurst and Company DLB-49

Hurston, Zora Neale 1891-1960 .... DLB-51

Huston, John 1906- DLB-26

Hutcheson, Francis 1694-1746 .... DLB-31

Hutchinson, Thomas 1711-1780 ....DLB-30, 31

Hutton, Richard Holt 1826-1897 .... DLB-57

Huxley, Aldous 1894-1963 .... DLB-36

Huxley, T. H. 1825-1895 .... DLB-57

Hyman, Trina Schart 1939- DLB-61

I

The Iconography of Science-Fiction Art DLB-8

Ignatow, David 1914- DLB-5

Imbs, Bravig 1904-1946 ....DLB-4

Inchbald, Elizabeth 1753-1821 .... DLB-39

Inge, William 1913-1973 ....DLB-7

Ingelow, Jean 1820-1897 .... DLB-35

The Ingersoll Prizes Y-84

Ingraham, Joseph Holt 1809-1860 ....DLB-3

International Publishers Company DLB-46

An Interview with Peter S. Prescott Y-86

An Interview with Tom Jenks Y-86

Introduction to Paul Laurence Dunbar,
    Lyrics of Lowly Life (1896),
    by William Dean Howells DLB-50

Introductory Essay: *Letters of Percy Bysshe
    Shelley* (1852), by Robert Browning DLB-32

Introductory Letters from the Second Edition
    of *Pamela* (1741), by Samuel Richardson .. DLB-39

Irving, John 1942- DLB-6; Y-82

Irving, Washington 1783-1859 ...... DLB-3, 11, 30, 59

Irwin, Grace 1907- DLB-68

Irwin, Will 1873-1948 .... DLB-25

Isherwood, Christopher 1904-1986 ...... DLB-15; Y-86

The Island Trees Case: A Symposium on School
        Library Censorship
    An Interview with Judith Krug
    An Interview with Phyllis Schlafly
    An Interview with Edward B. Jenkinson
    An Interview with Lamarr Mooneyham
    An Interview with Harriet Bernstein Y-82

Ivers, M. J., and Company DLB-49

J

Jackmon, Marvin E. (see Marvin X)

Jackson, Angela 1951- DLB-41

Jackson, Helen Hunt 1830-1885...........DLB-42, 47

Jackson, Laura Riding 1901- DLB-48

Jackson, Shirley 1919-1965 ....DLB-6

Jacob, Piers Anthony Dillingham (see Anthony, Piers)

Jacobs, George W., and Company............. DLB-49

Jacobson, Dan 1929- DLB-14

Jahnn, Hans Henny 1894-1959............... DLB-56

Jakes, John 1932- Y-83

James, Henry 1843-1916 ....DLB-12, 71

James, John circa 1633-1729 .... DLB-24

James Joyce Centenary: Dublin, 1982 ....Y-82

James Joyce Conference........................Y-85

James, U. P. [publishing house] DLB-49

Jameson, Fredric 1934- DLB-67

Jameson, J. Franklin 1859-1937 .... DLB-17

Jameson, Storm 1891-1986 .... DLB-36

Jarrell, Randall 1914-1965.................DLB-48, 52

Jasmin, Claude 1930- DLB-60

Jay, John 1745-1829.......................... DLB-31

Jeffers, Lance 1919-1985 .... DLB-41

Jeffers, Robinson 1887-1962.................. DLB-45

Jefferson, Thomas 1743-1826 .... DLB-31

Jellicoe, Ann 1927- DLB-13

Jenkins, Robin 1912- DLB-14

Jenkins, William Fitzgerald (see Leinster, Murray)

Jennings, Elizabeth 1926- DLB-27

Jens, Walter 1923- DLB-69

Jensen, Merrill 1905-1980 .... DLB-17

Jerome, Jerome K. 1859-1927..............DLB-10, 34

Jewett, John P., and Company................ DLB-49

Jewett, Sarah Orne 1849-1909................ DLB-12

The Jewish Publication Society DLB-49

Jewsbury, Geraldine 1812-1880................ DLB-21

Joans, Ted 1928- DLB-16, 41

John Edward Bruce: Three Documents DLB-50

John Steinbeck Research Center..................Y-85

John Webster: The Melbourne Manuscript.......Y-86

Johnson, B. S. 1933-1973..................DLB-14, 40

Johnson, Benjamin [publishing house] DLB-49

Johnson, Benjamin, Jacob, and Robert [publishing house]................. DLB-49

Johnson, Charles R. 1948- DLB-33

Johnson, Charles S. 1893-1956 .... DLB-51

Johnson, Diane 1934- Y-80

Johnson, Edward 1598-1672................... DLB-24

Johnson, Fenton 1888-1958 ....DLB-45, 50

Johnson, Georgia Douglas 1886-1966 .... DLB-51

Johnson, Gerald W. 1890-1980................ DLB-29

Johnson, Helene 1907- DLB-51

Johnson, Jacob, and Company................. DLB-49

Johnson, James Weldon 1871-1938........... DLB-51

Johnson, Lionel 1867-1902 .... DLB-19

Johnson, Nunnally 1897-1977 .... DLB-26

Johnson, Owen 1878-1952........................Y-87

Johnson, Pamela Hansford 1912- DLB-15

Johnson, Samuel 1696-1772 .... DLB-24

Johnson, Samuel 1709-1784 .... DLB-39

Johnson, Samuel 1822-1882 ....DLB-1

Johnston, Annie Fellows 1863-1931 .... DLB-42

Johnston, Basil H. 1929- DLB-60

Johnston, Denis 1901-1984 .... DLB-10

Johnston, Jennifer 1930- DLB-14

Johnston, Mary 1870-1936 ....DLB-9

Johnstone, Charles 1719?-1800?............... DLB-39

Jolas, Eugene 1894-1952 ....DLB-4, 45

Jones, Charles C., Jr. 1831-1893.............. DLB-30

Jones, D. G. 1929- DLB-53

Jones, David 1895-1974 .... DLB-20

Jones, Ebenezer 1820-1860................... DLB-32

Jones, Ernest 1819-1868....................... DLB-32

Jones, Gayl 1949- DLB-33

Jones, Glyn 1905- DLB-15

Jones, Gwyn 1907- DLB-15

Jones, Henry Arthur 1851-1929.............. DLB-10

Jones, Hugh circa 1692-1760................. DLB-24

Jones, James 1921-1977 ....DLB-2

Jones, LeRoi (see Baraka, Amiri)

Jones, Lewis 1897-1939......................DLB-15

Jones, Major Joseph (see Thompson, William Tappan)

Jones, Preston 1936-1979......................DLB-7

Jones, William Alfred 1817-1900..............DLB-59

Jones's Publishing House.....................DLB-49

Jong, Erica 1942- DLB-2, 5, 28

Jonson, Ben 1572?-1637.....................DLB-62

Jordan, June 1936- DLB-38

Joseph, Jenny 1932- DLB-40

Josephson, Matthew 1899-1978.................DLB-4

Josiah Allen's Wife (see Holley, Marietta)

Josipovici, Gabriel 1940- DLB-14

Josselyn, John ?-1675.......................DLB-24

Joyce, Adrien (see Eastman, Carol)

Joyce, James 1882-1941 ....DLB-10, 19, 36

Judd, Orange, Publishing Company..........DLB-49

Judd, Sylvester 1813-1853.....................DLB-1

June, Jennie (see Croly, Jane Cunningham)

Jünger, Ernst 1895- DLB-56

Justice, Donald 1925- Y-83

K

Kalechofsky, Roberta 1931- DLB-28

Kaler, James Otis 1848-1912 ....DLB-12

Kandel, Lenore 1932- DLB-16

Kanin, Garson 1912- DLB-7

Kantor, Mackinlay 1904-1977 ....DLB-9

Kaplan, Johanna 1942- DLB-28

Kasack, Hermann 1896-1966.................DLB-69

Kaschnitz, Marie Luise 1901-1974............DLB-69

Kästner, Erich 1899-1974....................DLB-56

Kattan, Naim 1928- DLB-53

Katz, Steve 1935- Y-83

Kauffman, Janet 1945- Y-86

Kaufman, Bob 1925- DLB-16, 41

Kaufman, George S. 1889-1961 ....DLB-7

Kavanagh, Patrick 1904-1967..............DLB-15, 20

Kavanagh, P. J. 1931- DLB-40

Kaye-Smith, Sheila 1887-1956 ....DLB-36

Kazin, Alfred 1915- DLB-67

Keane, John B. 1928- DLB-13

Keats, Ezra Jack 1916-1983...................DLB-61

Keble, John 1792-1866 ....DLB-32, 55

Keeble, John 1944- Y-83

Keeffe, Barrie 1945- DLB-13

Keeley, James 1867-1934.....................DLB-25

W. B. Keen, Cooke and Company.............DLB-49

Keillor, Garrison 1942- Y-87

Kelley, Edith Summers 1884-1956..............DLB-9

Kelley, William Melvin 1937- DLB-33

Kellogg, Ansel Nash 1832-1886 ....DLB-23

Kellogg, Steven 1941- DLB-61

Kelly, George 1887-1974 ....DLB-7

Kelly, Piet and Company DLB-49

Kelly, Robert 1935- DLB-5

Kemble, Fanny 1809-1893....................DLB-32

Kemelman, Harry 1908- DLB-28

Kendall, Claude [publishing company] DLB-46

Kendell, George 1809-1867....................DLB-43

Kenedy, P. J., and Sons......................DLB-49

Kennedy, Adrienne 1931- DLB-38

Kennedy, John Pendleton 1795-1870...........DLB-3

Kennedy, Margaret 1896-1967 ....DLB-36

Kennedy, William 1928- Y-85

Kennedy, X. J. 1929- DLB-5

Kennelly, Brendan 1936- DLB-40

Kenner, Hugh 1923- DLB-67

Kennerley, Mitchell [publishing house]........DLB-46

Kent, Frank R. 1877-1958 ....DLB-29

Keppler and Schwartzmann DLB-49

Kerouac, Jack 1922-1969 ....DLB-2, 16; DS-3

Kerouac, Jan 1952- DLB-16

Kerr, Charles H., and Company..............DLB-49

Kerr, Orpheus C. (see Newell, Robert Henry)

Kesey, Ken 1935- DLB-2, 16

Kessel, Joseph 1898-1979....................DLB-72

Kessel, Martin 1901- DLB-56

Kesten, Hermann 1900- DLB-56

Keun, Irmgard 1905-1982.................... DLB-69

Key and Biddle............................... DLB-49

Keyserling, Eduard von 1855-1918........... DLB-66

Kiely, Benedict 1919- DLB-15

Kiggins and Kellogg......................... DLB-49

Kiley, Jed 1889-1962 ....DLB-4

Killens, John Oliver 1916- DLB-33

Killigrew, Thomas 1612-1683 .... DLB-58

Kilmer, Joyce 1886-1918 .... DLB-45

King, Clarence 1842-1901 .... DLB-12

King, Florence 1936............................Y-85

King, Francis 1923- DLB-15

King, Grace 1852-1932 .... DLB-12

King, Solomon [publishing house]............ DLB-49

King, Stephen 1947- Y-80

King, Woodie, Jr. 1937- DLB-38

Kinglake, Alexander William 1809-1891....... DLB-55

Kingsley, Charles 1819-1875...............DLB-21, 32

Kingsley, Henry 1830-1876................... DLB-21

Kingsley, Sidney 1906- DLB-7

Kingston, Maxine Hong 1940- Y-80

Kinnell, Galway 1927- DLB-5; Y-87

Kinsella, Thomas 1928- DLB-27

Kipling, Rudyard 1865-1936 ....DLB-19, 34

Kirkconnell, Watson 1895-1977 .... DLB-68

Kirkland, Caroline 1801-1864 ....DLB-3

Kirkland, Joseph 1830-1893................. DLB-12

Kirkup, James 1918- DLB-27

Kirst, Hans Hellmut 1914- DLB-69

Kizer, Carolyn 1925- DLB-5

Klabund 1890-1928.......................... DLB-66

Klappert, Peter 1942- DLB-5

Klass, Philip (see Tenn, William)

Klein, A. M. 1909-1972...................... DLB-68

Knapp, Samuel Lorenzo 1783-1838 .... DLB-59

Knickerbocker, Diedrich (see Irving, Washington)

Knight, Damon 1922- DLB-8

Knight, Etheridge 1931- DLB-41

Knight, John S. 1894-1981 .... DLB-29

Knight, Sarah Kemble 1666-1727 .... DLB-24

Knister, Raymond 1899-1932................. DLB-68

Knoblock, Edward 1874-1945 .... DLB-10

Knopf, Alfred A. 1892-1984....................Y-84

Knopf, Alfred A. [publishing house] DLB-46

Knowles, John 1926- DLB-6

Knox, Frank 1874-1944 .... DLB-29

Knox, John Armoy 1850-1906................. DLB-23

Kober, Arthur 1900-1975 .... DLB-11

Koch, Howard 1902- DLB-26

Koch, Kenneth 1925- DLB-5

Koenigsberg, Moses 1879-1945............... DLB-25

Koeppen, Wolfgang 1906- DLB-69

Koestler, Arthur 1905-1983 ....Y-83

Kolb, Annette 1870-1967 .... DLB-66

Kolbenheyer, Erwin Guido 1878-1962........ DLB-66

Kolodny, Annette 1941- DLB-67

Komroff, Manuel 1890-1974 ....DLB-4

Konigsburg, E. L. 1930- DLB-52

Kopit, Arthur 1937- DLB-7

Kops, Bernard 1926?- DLB-13

Kornbluth, C. M. 1923-1958....................DLB-8

Kosinski, Jerzy 1933- DLB-2; Y-82

Kraf, Elaine 1946- Y-81

Krasna, Norman 1909-1984 .... DLB-26

Krauss, Ruth 1911- DLB-52

Kreuder, Ernst 1903-1972.................... DLB-69

Kreymborg, Alfred 1883-1966...............DLB-4, 54

Krieger, Murray 1923- DLB-67

Krim, Seymour 1922- DLB-16

Krock, Arthur 1886-1974..................... DLB-29

Kroetsch, Robert 1927- DLB-53

Krutch, Joseph Wood 1893-1970.............. DLB-63

Kubrick, Stanley 1928- DLB-26

Kumin, Maxine 1925- DLB-5

Kunitz, Stanley 1905- DLB-48

Kunjufu, Johari M. (see Amini, Johari M.)

Kupferberg, Tuli 1923- DLB-16

Kurz, Isolde 1853-1944...................... DLB-66

Kusenberg, Kurt 1904-1983 .... DLB-69

Kuttner, Henry 1915-1958 ....DLB-8

Kyd, Thomas 1558-1594 .... DLB-62

Kyger, Joanne 1934- DLB-16

L

Laberge, Albert 1871-1960 .... DLB-68

Laberge, Marie 1950- DLB-60

Lacretelle, Jacques de 1888-1985 .... DLB-65

Ladd, Joseph Brown 1764-1786 .... DLB-37

La Farge, Oliver 1901-1963 ....DLB-9

Lafferty, R. A. 1914- DLB-8

Laird, Carobeth 1895- Y-82

Laird and Lee DLB-49

Lalonde, Michèle 1937- DLB-60

Lamantia, Philip 1927- DLB-16

Lambert, Betty 1933-1983 .... DLB-60

L'Amour, Louis 1908?- Y-80

Lamson, Wolffe and Company DLB-49

Lancer Books................................ DLB-46

Landesman, Jay 1919- and
    Landesman, Fran 1927- DLB-16

Lane, Charles 1800-1870 ....DLB-1

The John Lane Company DLB-49

Lane, M. Travis 1934- DLB-60

Lane, Patrick 1939- DLB-53

Lane, Pinkie Gordon 1923- DLB-41

Laney, Al 1896- DLB-4

Langevin, André 1927- DLB-60

Langgässer, Elisabeth 1899-1950 .... DLB-69

Lanham, Edwin 1904-1979 ....DLB-4

Lanier, Sidney 1842-1881 .... DLB-64

Lardner, Ring 1885-1933.................DLB-11, 25

Lardner, Ring, Jr. 1915- DLB-26

Lardner 100: Ring Lardner
    Centennial Symposium.......................Y-85

Larkin, Philip 1922-1985 .... DLB-27

La Rocque, Gilbert 1943-1984................ DLB-60

Laroque de Roquebrune, Robert
    (see Roquebrune, Robert de)

Larrick, Nancy 1910- DLB-61

Larsen, Nella 1893-1964..................... DLB-51

Lasker-Schüler, Else 1869-1945............... DLB-66

Lathrop, Dorothy P. 1891-1980 .... DLB-22

Lathrop, George Parsons 1851-1898.......... DLB-71

Lathrop, John, Jr. 1772-1820................. DLB-37

Latimore, Jewel Christine McLawler (see Amini,
    Johari M.)

Laughlin, James 1914- DLB-48

Laumer, Keith 1925- DLB-8

Laurence, Margaret 1926-1987................ DLB-53

Laurents, Arthur 1918- DLB-26

Laurie, Annie (see Black, Winifred)

Lavin, Mary 1912- DLB-15

Lawrence, David 1888-1973 .... DLB-29

Lawrence, D. H. 1885-1930 ....DLB-10, 19, 36

Lawson, John ?-1711 .... DLB-24

Lawson, Robert 1892-1957 .... DLB-22

Lawson, Victor F. 1850-1925 .... DLB-25

Lea, Henry Charles 1825-1909 .... DLB-47

Lea, Tom 1907- DLB-6

Leacock, John 1729-1802..................... DLB-31

Lear, Edward 1812-1888 .... DLB-32

Leary, Timothy 1920- DLB-16

Leary, W. A., and Company.................. DLB-49

Léautaud, Paul 1872-1956.................... DLB-65

Leavitt and Allen............................ DLB-49

Lécavelé, Roland (see Dorgelès, Roland)

Lechlitner, Ruth 1901- DLB-48

Leclerc, Félix 1914- DLB-60

Lectures on Rhetoric and Belles Lettres (1783),
    by Hugh Blair [excerpts].................. DLB-31

Leder, Rudolf (see Hermlin, Stephan)

Lederer, Charles 1910-1976.................. DLB-26

Ledwidge, Francis 1887-1917................. DLB-20

Lee, Dennis 1939- DLB-53

Lee, Don L. (see Madhubuti, Haki R.)

Lee, George W. 1894-1976 .... DLB-51

Lee, Harper 1926- DLB-6

Lee, Harriet (1757-1851) and
    Lee, Sophia (1750-1824) DLB-39

Lee, Laurie 1914- DLB-27

Lee, Vernon 1856-1935 .... DLB-57

Lee and Shepard DLB-49

Le Fanu, Joseph Sheridan 1814-1873 ......DLB-21, 70

Leffland, Ella 1931- Y-84

le Fort, Gertrud von 1876-1971 .... DLB-66

Le Gallienne, Richard 1866-1947................DLB-4

Legaré, Hugh Swinton 1797-1843...........DLB-3, 59

Legaré, James M. 1823-1859 ....DLB-3

Le Guin, Ursula K. 1929- DLB-8, 52

Lehman, Ernest 1920- DLB-44

Lehmann, John 1907- DLB-27

Lehmann, Rosamond 1901- DLB-15

Lehmann, Wilhelm 1882-1968................. DLB-56

Leiber, Fritz 1910- DLB-8

Leinster, Murray 1896-1975...................DLB-8

Leitch, Maurice 1933- DLB-14

Leland, Charles G. 1824-1903 .... DLB-11

L'Engle, Madeleine 1918- DLB-52

Lennart, Isobel 1915-1971.................... DLB-44

Lennox, Charlotte 1729 or 1730-1804........ DLB-39

Lenski, Lois 1893-1974...................... DLB-22

Lenz, Hermann 1913- DLB-69

Leonard, Hugh 1926- DLB-13

Leonard, William Ellery 1876-1944........... DLB-54

Le Queux, William 1864-1927................. DLB-70

Lerner, Max 1902- DLB-29

LeSieg, Theo. (see Geisel, Theodor Seuss)

Leslie, Frank 1821-1880 .... DLB-43

The Frank Leslie Publishing House DLB-49

Lessing, Bruno 1870-1940.................... DLB-28

Lessing, Doris 1919- DLB-15; Y-85

Letter to [Samuel] Richardson on *Clarissa*
    (1748), by Henry Fielding................ DLB-39

Lever, Charles 1806-1872 .... DLB-21

Levertov, Denise 1923- DLB-5

Levi, Peter 1931- DLB-40

Levien, Sonya 1888-1960..................... DLB-44

Levin, Meyer 1905-1981.............. DLB-9, 28; Y-81

Levine, Philip 1928- DLB-5

Levy, Benn Wolfe 1900-1973............DLB-13; Y-81

Lewes, George Henry 1817-1878.............. DLB-55

Lewis, Alfred H. 1857-1914 .... DLB-25

Lewis, Alun 1915-1944 .... DLB-20

Lewis, C. Day (see Day Lewis, C.)

Lewis, Charles B. 1842-1924.................. DLB-11

Lewis, C. S. 1898-1963 .... DLB-15

Lewis, Henry Clay 1825-1850 ....DLB-3

Lewis, Janet 1899- Y-87

Lewis, Matthew Gregory 1775-1818 .... DLB-39

Lewis, Richard circa 1700-1734................ DLB-24

Lewis, Sinclair 1885-1951................. DLB-9; DS-1

Lewis, Wyndham 1882-1957................... DLB-15

Lewisohn, Ludwig 1882-1955............. DLB-4, 9, 28

The Library of America DLB-46

Liebling, A. J. 1904-1963......................DLB-4

Lilly, Wait and Company DLB-49

Limited Editions Club DLB-46

Lincoln and Edmands DLB-49

Lindsay, Jack 1900- Y-84

Lindsay, Vachel 1879-1931 .... DLB-54

Linebarger, Paul Myron Anthony (see
    Smith, Cordwainer)

Link, Arthur S. 1920- DLB-17

Linn, John Blair 1777-1804 .... DLB-37

Linton, Eliza Lynn 1822-1898 .... DLB-18

Linton, William James 1812-1897 .... DLB-32

Lion Books DLB-46

Lionni, Leo 1910- DLB-61

Lippincott, J. B., Company DLB-49

Lippincott, Sara Jane Clarke 1823-1904 .... DLB-43

Lippmann, Walter 1889-1974 .... DLB-29

Lipton, Lawrence 1898-1975 .... DLB-16

Literary Documents: William Faulkner
    and the People-to-People Program............Y-86

Literary Documents II: *Library Journal*—
    Statements and Questionnaires from
    First Novelists...............................Y-87

Literary Effects of World War II
    [British novel]............................ DLB-15

Literary Prizes [British]...................... DLB-15

Literary Research Archives: The Humanities
Research Center, University of Texas.........Y-82

Literary Research Archives II: Berg
Collection of English and American Literature
of the New York Public Library...............Y-83

Literary Research Archives III:
The Lilly Library.............................Y-84

Literary Research Archives IV:
The John Carter Brown Library..............Y-85

Literary Research Archives V:
Kent State Special Collections................Y-86

Literary Research Archives VI: The Modern
Literary Manuscripts Collection in the
Special Collections of the Washington
University Libraries.........................Y-87

"Literary Style" (1857), by William
Forsyth [excerpt]......................... DLB-57

Literature at Nurse, or Circulating Morals (1885),
by George Moore DLB-18

Little, Brown and Company DLB-49

Littlewood, Joan 1914- DLB-13

Lively, Penelope 1933- DLB-14

Livesay, Dorothy 1909- DLB-68

Livings, Henry 1929- DLB-13

Livingston, Anne Howe 1763-1841 .... DLB-37

Livingston, Myra Cohn 1926- DLB-61

Livingston, William 1723-1790 .... DLB-31

Llewellyn, Richard 1906-1983 .... DLB-15

Lobel, Arnold 1933- DLB-61

Lochridge, Betsy Hopkins (see Fancher, Betsy)

Locke, David Ross 1833-1888..............DLB-11, 23

Locke, John 1632-1704...................... DLB-31

Locke, Richard Adams 1800-1871............ DLB-43

Locker-Lampson, Frederick 1821-1895........ DLB-35

Lockridge, Ross, Jr. 1914-1948 ....Y-80

Locrine and *Selimus*........................... DLB-62

Lodge, David 1935- DLB-14

Lodge, George Cabot 1873-1909 .... DLB-54

Lodge, Henry Cabot 1850-1924 .... DLB-47

Loeb, Harold 1891-1974.....................DLB-4

Logan, James 1674-1751 .... DLB-24

Logan, John 1923- DLB-5

Logue, Christopher 1926- DLB-27

London, Jack 1876-1916....................DLB-8, 12

Long, H., and Brother DLB-49

Long, Haniel 1888-1956...................... DLB-45

Longfellow, Henry Wadsworth 1807-1882...DLB-1, 59

Longfellow, Samuel 1819-1892 ....DLB-1

Longley, Michael 1939- DLB-40

Longmans, Green and Company DLB-49

Longstreet, Augustus Baldwin 1790-1870 ...DLB-3, 11

Longworth, D. [publishing house]............ DLB-49

Lonsdale, Frederick 1881-1954............... DLB-10

A Look at the Contemporary Black Theatre
Movement............................... DLB-38

Loos, Anita 1893-1981.............. DLB-11, 26; Y-81

Lopate, Phillip 1943- Y-80

The Lord Chamberlain's Office and Stage
Censorship in England................... DLB-10

Lorde, Audre 1934- DLB-41

Loring, A. K. [publishing house] DLB-49

Loring and Mussey DLB-46

Lossing, Benson J. 1813-1891 .... DLB-30

Lothrop, D., and Company................... DLB-49

Lothrop, Harriet M. 1844-1924 .... DLB-42

The Lounger, no. 20 (1785), by Henry
Mackenzie............................... DLB-39

Lounsbury, Thomas R. 1838-1915............. DLB-71

Lovell, John W., Company DLB-49

Lovell, Coryell and Company.................. DLB-49

Lovingood, Sut (see Harris, George Washington)

Low, Samuel 1765-? DLB-37

Lowell, Amy 1874-1925 .... DLB-54

Lowell, James Russell 1819-1891 ....DLB-1, 11, 64

Lowell, Robert 1917-1977 ....DLB-5

Lowenfels, Walter 1897-1976...................DLB-4

Lowndes, Marie Belloc 1868-1947............ DLB-70

Lowry, Lois 1937- DLB-52

Lowry, Malcolm 1909-1957................... DLB-15

Lowther, Pat 1935-1975 .... DLB-53

Loy, Mina 1882-1966......................DLB-4, 54

Lucas, Fielding, Jr. [publishing house]........ DLB-49

Luce, John W., and Company DLB-46

Lucie-Smith, Edward 1933- DLB-40

Ludlum, Robert 1927- Y-82

Ludwig, Jack 1922- DLB-60

Luke, Peter 1919- DLB-13

The F. M. Lupton Publishing Company DLB-49

Lurie, Alison 1926- DLB-2

Lyly, John circa 1554-1606 .... DLB-62

Lyon, Matthew 1749-1822 .... DLB-43

Lytle, Andrew 1902- DLB-6

Lytton, Edward (see Bulwer-Lytton, Edward)

Lytton, Edward Robert Bulwer 1831-1891 .... DLB-32

M

Maass, Joachim 1901-1972.................... DLB-69

Mabie, Hamilton Wright 1845-1916 .... DLB-71

Mac A'Ghobhainn, Iain (see Smith, Iain Crichton)

MacArthur, Charles 1895-1956......... DLB-7, 25, 44

Macaulay, David 1945- DLB-61

Macaulay, Rose 1881-1958.................... DLB-36

Macaulay, Thomas Babington 1800-1859...DLB-32, 55

Macaulay Company........................... DLB-46

MacBeth, George 1932- DLB-40

MacCaig, Norman 1910- DLB-27

MacDiarmid, Hugh 1892-1978 .... DLB-20

MacDonald, George 1824-1905............... DLB-18

MacDonald, John D. 1916-1986 .... DLB-8; Y-86

MacEwen, Gwendolyn 1941- DLB-53

Macfadden, Bernarr 1868-1955 .... DLB-25

Machen, Arthur Llewelyn Jones 1863-1947 ... DLB-36

MacInnes, Colin 1914-1976.................... DLB-14

MacKaye, Percy 1875-1956 .... DLB-54

Macken, Walter 1915-1967 .... DLB-13

Mackenzie, Compton 1883-1972............... DLB-34

Mackenzie, Henry 1745-1831.................. DLB-39

Mackey, William Wellington 1937- DLB-38

MacLean, Katherine Anne 1925- DLB-8

MacLeish, Archibald 1892-1982 ....DLB-4, 7, 45; Y-82

MacLennan, Hugh 1907- DLB-68

MacLeod, Alistair 1936- DLB-60

Macleod, Norman 1906- DLB-4

The Macmillan Company..................... DLB-49

MacNamara, Brinsley 1890-1963 .... DLB-10

MacNeice, Louis 1907-1963 ....DLB-10, 20

Macpherson, Jay 1931- DLB-53

Macpherson, Jeanie 1884-1946 .... DLB-44

Macrae Smith Company DLB-46

Macy-Masius................................ DLB-46

Madden, David 1933- DLB-6

Maddow, Ben 1909- DLB-44

Madhubuti, Haki R. 1942- DLB-5, 41

Madison, James 1751-1836 .... DLB-37

Mahan, Alfred Thayer 1840-1914............. DLB-47

Maheux-Forcier, Louise 1929- DLB-60

Mahin, John Lee 1902-1984.................... DLB-44

Mahon, Derek 1941- DLB-40

Mailer, Norman 1923-
.... DLB-2, 16, 28; Y-80, 83; DS-3

Maillet, Adrienne 1885-1963 .... DLB-68

Maillet, Antonine 1929- DLB-60

Main Selections of the Book-of-the-Month Club,
   1926-1945.................................DLB-9

Main Trends in Twentieth-Century
   Book Clubs.............................. DLB-46

Mainwaring, Daniel 1902-1977 .... DLB-44

Major, André 1942- DLB-60

Major, Clarence 1936- DLB-33

Major, Kevin 1949- DLB-60

Major Books................................ DLB-46

Makemie, Francis circa 1658-1708............. DLB-24

Malamud, Bernard 1914-1986.....DLB-2, 28; Y-80, 86

Mallock, W. H. 1849-1923.................DLB-18, 57

Malone, Dumas 1892-1986 .... DLB-17

Malraux, André 1901-1976.................... DLB-72

Malzberg, Barry N. 1939- DLB-8

Mamet, David 1947- DLB-7

Mandel, Eli 1922- DLB-53

Manfred, Frederick 1912- DLB-6

Mangan, Sherry 1904-1961.....................DLB-4

Mankiewicz, Herman 1897-1953............... DLB-26

Mankiewicz, Joseph L. 1909- DLB-44

Mankowitz, Wolf 1924- DLB-15

Manley, Delarivière 1672?-1724 .... DLB-39

Mann, Abby 1927- DLB-44

Mann, Heinrich 1871-1950 .... DLB-66

Mann, Horace 1796-1859 ....DLB-1

Mann, Klaus 1906-1949 .... DLB-56

Mann, Thomas 1875-1955 .... DLB-66

Manning, Marie 1873?-1945 .... DLB-29

Manning and Loring DLB-49

Mano, D. Keith 1942- DLB-6

Manor Books DLB-46

March, William 1893-1954 ....DLB-9

Marchessault, Jovette 1938- DLB-60

Marcus, Frank 1928- DLB-13

Marek, Richard, Books DLB-46

Marion, Frances 1886-1973 .... DLB-44

Marius, Richard C. 1933- Y-85

The Mark Taper Forum DLB-7

Markfield, Wallace 1926- DLB-2, 28

Markham, Edwin 1852-1940 .... DLB-54

Markle, Fletcher 1921- DLB-68

Marlatt, Daphne 1942- DLB-60

Marlowe, Christopher 1564-1593 .... DLB-62

Marmion, Shakerley 1603-1639 .... DLB-58

Marquand, John P. 1893-1960 ....DLB-9

Marquis, Don 1878-1937 ....DLB-11, 25

Marriott, Anne 1913- DLB-68

Marryat, Frederick 1792-1848 .... DLB-21

Marsh, George Perkins 1801-1882 ....DLB-1, 64

Marsh, James 1794-1842 ....DLB-1, 59

Marsh, Capen, Lyon and Webb DLB-49

Marshall, Edward 1932- DLB-16

Marshall, James 1942- DLB-61

Marshall, Paule 1929- DLB-33

Marshall, Tom 1938- DLB-60

Marston, John 1576-1634 .... DLB-58

Marston, Philip Bourke 1850-1887 .... DLB-35

Martens, Kurt 1870-1945 .... DLB-66

Martien, William S. [publishing house] DLB-49

Martin, Abe (see Hubbard, Kin)

Martin, Claire 1914- DLB-60

Martin du Gard, Roger 1881-1958 .... DLB-65

Martineau, Harriet 1802-1876 ....DLB-21, 55

Martyn, Edward 1859-1923 .... DLB-10

Marvin X 1944- DLB-38

Marzials, Theo 1850-1920 .... DLB-35

Masefield, John 1878-1967 ....DLB-10, 19

Mason, A. E. W. 1865-1948 .... DLB-70

Mason, Bobbie Ann 1940- Y-87

Mason Brothers DLB-49

Massey, Gerald 1828-1907 .... DLB-32

Massinger, Philip 1583-1640 .... DLB-58

Masters, Edgar Lee 1868-1950 .... DLB-54

Mather, Cotton 1663-1728 ....DLB-24, 30

Mather, Increase 1639-1723 .... DLB-24

Mather, Richard 1596-1669 .... DLB-24

Matheson, Richard 1926- DLB-8, 44

Matheus, John F. 1887- DLB-51

Mathews, Cornelius 1817?-1889 ....DLB-3, 64

Mathias, Roland 1915- DLB-27

Mathis, June 1892-1927 .... DLB-44

Mathis, Sharon Bell 1937- DLB-33

Matthews, Brander 1852-1929 .... DLB-71

Matthews, Jack 1925- DLB-6

Matthews, William 1942- DLB-5

Matthiessen, F. O. 1902-1950 .... DLB-63

Matthiessen, Peter 1927- DLB-6

Maugham, W. Somerset 1874-1965 ....DLB-10, 36

Mauriac, François 1885-1970 .... DLB-65

Maurice, Frederick Denison 1805-1872 .... DLB-55

Maurois, André 1885-1967 .... DLB-65

Maury, James 1718-1769 .... DLB-31

Mavor, Elizabeth 1927- DLB-14

Mavor, Osborne Henry (see Bridie, James)

Maxwell, H. [publishing house] DLB-49

Maxwell, William 1908- Y-80

May, Elaine 1932- DLB-44

May, Thomas 1595 or 1596-1650 .... DLB-58

Mayer, Mercer 1943- DLB-61

Mayer, O. B. 1818-1891 ....DLB-3

Mayes, Wendell 1919- DLB-26

Mayfield, Julian 1928-1984 .... DLB-33; Y-84

Mayhew, Henry 1812-1887 ....DLB-18, 55

Mayhew, Jonathan 1720-1766 .... DLB-31

Mayne, Seymour 1944- DLB-60

Mayor, Flora Macdonald 1872-1932 .... DLB-36

Mazursky, Paul 1930- DLB-44

McÁlmon, Robert 1896-1956 ....DLB-4, 45

McBride, Robert M., and Company DLB-46

McCaffrey, Anne 1926- DLB-8

McCarthy, Cormac 1933- DLB-6

McCarthy, Mary 1912- DLB-2; Y-81

McCay, Winsor 1871-1934.................... DLB-22

McClatchy, C. K. 1858-1936................. DLB-25

McClellan, George Marion 1860-1934 .... DLB-50

McCloskey, Robert 1914- DLB-22

McClure, Joanna 1930- DLB-16

McClure, Michael 1932- DLB-16

McClure, Phillips and Company.............. DLB-46

McClurg, A. C., and Company DLB-49

McCluskey, John A., Jr. 1944- DLB-33

McCollum, Michael A. 1946 ....Y-87

McCord, David 1897- DLB-61

McCorkle, Jill 1958- Y-87

McCorkle, Samuel Eusebius 1746-1811 .... DLB-37

McCormick, Anne O'Hare 1880-1954 .... DLB-29

McCormick, Robert R. 1880-1955 .... DLB-29

McCoy, Horace 1897-1955 ....DLB-9

McCullagh, Joseph B. 1842-1896............. DLB-23

McCullers, Carson 1917-1967 .... DLB-2, 7

McDonald, Forrest 1927- DLB-17

McDougall, Colin 1917-1984 .... DLB-68

McDowell, Obolensky........................ DLB-46

McEwan, Ian 1948- DLB-14

McFadden, David 1940- DLB-60

McGahern, John 1934- DLB-14

McGeehan, W. O. 1879-1933 .... DLB-25

McGill, Ralph 1898-1969 .... DLB-29

McGinley, Phyllis 1905-1978...............DLB-11, 48

McGirt, James E. 1874-1930................. DLB-50

McGough, Roger 1937- DLB-40

McGraw-Hill................................. DLB-46

McGuane, Thomas 1939- DLB-2; Y-80

McGuckian, Medbh 1950- DLB-40

McGuffey, William Holmes 1800-1873 .... DLB-42

McIlvanney, William 1936- DLB-14

McIntyre, O. O. 1884-1938.................. DLB-25

McKay, Claude 1889-1948..............DLB-4, 45, 51

The David McKay Company DLB-49

McKean, William V. 1820-1903................ DLB-23

McKinley, Robin 1952- DLB-52

McLaren, Floris Clark 1904-1978............ DLB-68

McLaverty, Michael 1907- DLB-15

McLean, John R. 1848-1916.................. DLB-23

McLean, William L. 1852-1931 .... DLB-25

McLoughlin Brothers........................ DLB-49

McMaster, John Bach 1852-1932 .... DLB-47

McMurtry, Larry 1936- DLB-2; Y-80, 87

McNally, Terrence 1939- DLB-7

McNeil, Florence 1937- DLB-60

McPherson, James Alan 1943- DLB-38

McPherson, Sandra 1943- Y-86

McWhirter, George 1939- DLB-60

Mead, Matthew 1924- DLB-40

Mead, Taylor ?- DLB-16

Medill, Joseph 1823-1899................... DLB-43

Medoff, Mark 1940- DLB-7

Meek, Alexander Beaufort 1814-1865..........DLB-3

Meinke, Peter 1932- DLB-5

Melançon, Robert 1947- DLB-60

Meltzer, David 1937- DLB-16

Meltzer, Milton 1915- DLB-61

Melville, Herman 1819-1891 ....DLB-3

Memoirs of Life and Literature (1920),
     by W. H. Mallock [excerpt]............... DLB-57

Mencken, H. L. 1880-1956 ....DLB-11, 29, 63

Mercer, David 1928-1980.................... DLB-13

Mercer, John 1704-1768..................... DLB-31

Meredith, George 1828-1909 ....DLB-18, 35, 57

Meredith, Owen (see Lytton, Edward Robert Bulwer)

Meredith, William 1919- DLB-5

Meriwether, Louise 1923- DLB-33

Merriam, Eve 1916- DLB-61

The Merriam Company DLB-49

Merrill, James 1926- DLB-5; Y-85

Merrill and Baker DLB-49

The Mershon Company DLB-49

Merton, Thomas 1915-1968 .... DLB-48; Y-81

Merwin, W. S. 1927- DLB-5

Messner, Julian [publishing house] DLB-46

Metcalf, J. [publishing house]................. DLB-49

Metcalf, John 1938- DLB-60

The Methodist Book Concern DLB-49

Mew, Charlotte 1869-1928.................... DLB-19

Mewshaw, Michael 1943- Y-80

Meyer, Eugene 1875-1959.................... DLB-29

Meynell, Alice 1847-1922..................... DLB-19

Micheaux, Oscar 1884-1951 .... DLB-50

Micheline, Jack 1929- DLB-16

Michener, James A. 1907?- DLB-6

Micklejohn, George circa 1717-1818.......... DLB-31

Middleton, Christopher 1926- DLB-40

Middleton, Stanley 1919- DLB-14

Middleton, Thomas 1580-1627 .... DLB-58

Miegel, Agnes 1879-1964..................... DLB-56

Miles, Josephine 1911-1985................... DLB-48

Milius, John 1944- DLB-44

Mill, John Stuart 1806-1873 .... DLB-55

Millar, Kenneth 1915-1983 .... DLB-2; Y-83

Millay, Edna St. Vincent 1892-1950 .... DLB-45

Miller, Arthur 1915- DLB-7

Miller, Caroline 1903- DLB-9

Miller, Eugene Ethelbert 1950- DLB-41

Miller, Henry 1891-1980 ....DLB-4, 9; Y-80

Miller, J. Hillis 1928- DLB-67

Miller, James [publishing house].............. DLB-49

Miller, Jason 1939- DLB-7

Miller, May 1899- DLB-41

Miller, Perry 1905-1963 ....DLB-17, 63

Miller, Walter M., Jr. 1923- DLB-8

Miller, Webb 1892-1940..................... DLB-29

Millhauser, Steven 1943- DLB-2

Millican, Arthenia J. Bates 1920- DLB-38

Milne, A. A. 1882-1956....................... DLB-10

Milner, Ron 1938- DLB-38

Milnes, Richard Monckton (Lord Houghton)
     1809-1885............................. DLB-32

Minton, Balch and Company DLB-46

Miron, Gaston 1928- DLB-60

Mitchel, Jonathan 1624-1668 .... DLB-24

Mitchell, Adrian 1932- DLB-40

Mitchell, Donald Grant 1822-1908..............DLB-1

Mitchell, James Leslie 1901-1935 .... DLB-15

Mitchell, John (see Slater, Patrick)

Mitchell, Julian 1935- DLB-14

Mitchell, Ken 1940- DLB-60

Mitchell, Langdon 1862-1935...................DLB-7

Mitchell, Loften 1919- DLB-38

Mitchell, Margaret 1900-1949 ....DLB-9

Modern Age Books........................... DLB-46

"Modern English Prose" (1876),
     by George Saintsbury DLB-57

The Modern Language Association of America
     Celebrates Its Centennial.....................Y-84

The Modern Library DLB-46

Modern Novelists—Great and Small (1855), by
     Margaret Oliphant....................... DLB-21

"Modern Style" (1857), by Cockburn
     Thomson [excerpt]....................... DLB-57

The Modernists (1932), by Joseph Warren
     Beach DLB-36

Moffat, Yard and Company DLB-46

Monkhouse, Allan 1858-1936.................. DLB-10

Monro, Harold 1879-1932..................... DLB-19

Monroe, Harriet 1860-1936 .... DLB-54

Monsarrat, Nicholas 1910-1979................ DLB-15

Montague, John 1929- DLB-40

Montgomery, John 1919- DLB-16

Montgomery, Marion 1925- DLB-6

Montherlant, Henry de 1896-1972 .... DLB-72

Moody, Joshua circa 1633-1697 .... DLB-24

Moody, William Vaughn 1869-1910.........DLB-7, 54

Moorcock, Michael 1939- DLB-14

Cumulative Index

Moore, Catherine L. 1911- DLB-8

Moore, Clement Clarke 1779-1863 .... DLB-42

Moore, George 1852-1933.............DLB-10, 18, 57

Moore, Marianne 1887-1972 .... DLB-45

Moore, T. Sturge 1870-1944 .... DLB-19

Moore, Ward 1903-1978.......................DLB-8

Moore, Wilstach, Keys and Company......... DLB-49

Morency, Pierre 1942- DLB-60

Morgan, Berry 1919- DLB-6

Morgan, Charles 1894-1958 .... DLB-34

Morgan, Edmund S. 1916- DLB-17

Morgan, Edwin 1920- DLB-27

Morison, Samuel Eliot 1887-1976............. DLB-17

Morley, Christopher 1890-1957 ....DLB-9

Morley, John 1838-1923....................... DLB-57

Morris, Lewis 1833-1907 .... DLB-35

Morris, Richard B. 1904- DLB-17

Morris, William 1834-1896 ....DLB-18, 35, 57

Morris, Willie 1934- Y-80

Morris, Wright 1910- DLB-2; Y-81

Morrison, Arthur 1863-1945 .... DLB-70

Morrison, Toni 1931- DLB-6, 33; Y-81

Morrow, William, and Company.............. DLB-46

Morse, James Herbert 1841-1923............. DLB-71

Morse, Jedidiah 1761-1826 .... DLB-37

Morse, John T., Jr. 1840-1937................ DLB-47

Mortimer, John 1923- DLB-13

Morton, John P., and Company DLB-49

Morton, Nathaniel 1613-1685 .... DLB-24

Morton, Sarah Wentworth 1759-1846 .... DLB-37

Morton, Thomas circa 1579-circa 1647....... DLB-24

Mosley, Nicholas 1923- DLB-14

Moss, Arthur 1889-1969.......................DLB-4

Moss, Howard 1922- DLB-5

The Most Powerful Book Review in America
    [*New York Times Book Review*].................Y-82

Motion, Andrew 1952- DLB-40

Motley, John Lothrop 1814-1877........DLB-1, 30, 59

Mottram, R. H. 1883-1971.................... DLB-36

Mouré, Erin 1955- DLB-60

Movies from Books, 1920-1974.................DLB-9

Mowat, Farley 1921- DLB-68

Mowrer, Edgar Ansel 1892-1977 .... DLB-29

Mowrer, Paul Scott 1887-1971................ DLB-29

Mucedorus................................... DLB-62

Muhajir, El (see Marvin X)

Muhajir, Nazzam Al Fitnah (see Marvin X)

Muir, Edwin 1887-1959 .... DLB-20

Muir, Helen 1937- DLB-14

Mukherjee, Bharati 1940- DLB-60

Muldoon, Paul 1951- DLB-40

Mumford, Lewis 1895- DLB-63

Munby, Arthur Joseph 1828-1910............. DLB-35

Munday, Anthony 1560-1633.................. DLB-62

Munford, Robert circa 1737-1783 .... DLB-31

Munro, Alice 1931- DLB-53

Munro, George [publishing house] DLB-49

Munro, H. H. 1870-1916..................... DLB-34

Munro, Norman L. [publishing house] DLB-49

Munroe, James, and Company DLB-49

Munroe, Kirk 1850-1930 .... DLB-42

Munroe and Francis......................... DLB-49

Munsell, Joel [publishing house].............. DLB-49

Munsey, Frank A. 1854-1925................. DLB-25

Munsey, Frank A., and Company DLB-49

Murdoch, Iris 1919- DLB-14

Murfree, Mary N. 1850-1922................. DLB-12

Murphy, John, and Company DLB-49

Murphy, Richard 1927- DLB-40

Murray, Albert L. 1916- DLB-38

Murray, Gilbert 1866-1957 .... DLB-10

Murray, Judith Sargent 1751-1820 .... DLB-37

Murray, Pauli 1910-1985 .... DLB-41

Mussey, Benjamin B., and Company DLB-49

Myers, Gustavus 1872-1942.................. DLB-47

Myers, L. H. 1881-1944 .... DLB-15

Myers, Walter Dean 1937- DLB-33

N

Nabbes, Thomas circa 1605-1641............. DLB-58

Nabokov, Vladimir 1899-1977......DLB-2; Y-80; DS-3

Nabokov Festival at Cornell Y-83

Nafis and Cornish DLB-49

Naipaul, Shiva 1945-1985 ....Y-85

Naipaul, V. S. 1932- Y-85

Nancrede, Joseph [publishing house].......... DLB-49

Nasby, Petroleum Vesuvius (see Locke, David Ross)

Nash, Ogden 1902-1971...................... DLB-11

Nathan, Robert 1894-1985 ....DLB-9

The National Jewish Book Awards Y-85

The National Theatre and the Royal Shakespeare
    Company: The National Companies DLB-13

Naughton, Bill 1910- DLB-13

Neagoe, Peter 1881-1960......................DLB-4

Neal, John 1793-1876 ....DLB-1, 59

Neal, Joseph C. 1807-1847 .... DLB-11

Neal, Larry 1937-1981....................... DLB-38

The Neale Publishing Company.............. DLB-49

Neely, F. Tennyson [publishing house]....... DLB-49

"The Negro as a Writer," by
    G. M. McClellan......................... DLB-50

"Negro Poets and Their Poetry," by
    Wallace Thurman........................ DLB-50

Neihardt, John G. 1881-1973...............DLB-9, 54

Nelson, Alice Moore Dunbar
    1875-1935.............................. DLB-50

Nelson, Thomas, and Sons DLB-49

Nelson, William Rockhill 1841-1915.......... DLB-23

Nemerov, Howard 1920- DLB-5, 6; Y-83

Ness, Evaline 1911-1986..................... DLB-61

Neugeboren, Jay 1938- DLB-28

Neumann, Alfred 1895-1952 .... DLB-56

Nevins, Allan 1890-1971..................... DLB-17

The New American Library DLB-46

New Directions Publishing Corporation DLB-46

A New Edition of *Huck Finn*....................Y-85

New Forces at Work in the American Theatre:
    1915-1925...............................DLB-7

New Literary Periodicals: A Report
    for 1987...................................Y-87

The New *Ulysses* Y-84

The New Variorum Shakespeare.................Y-85

A New Voice: The Center for the Book's First
    Five Years..................................Y-83

The New Wave [Science Fiction] DLB-8

Newbolt, Henry 1862-1938.................... DLB-19

Newbound, Bernard Slade (see Slade, Bernard)

Newby, P. H. 1918- DLB-15

Newcomb, Charles King 1820-1894 ....DLB-1

Newell, Peter 1862-1924...................... DLB-42

Newell, Robert Henry 1836-1901.............. DLB-11

Newman, David (see Benton, Robert)

Newman, Frances 1883-1928 ....Y-80

Newman, John Henry 1801-1890.......DLB-18, 32, 55

Newman, Mark [publishing house]........... DLB-49

Newspaper Syndication of American Humor.. DLB-11

Nichol, B. P. 1944- DLB-53

Nichols, Dudley 1895-1960 .... DLB-26

Nichols, John 1940- Y-82

Nichols, Mary Sargeant (Neal) Gove
    1810-1884................................DLB-1

Nichols, Peter 1927- DLB-13

Nichols, Roy F. 1896-1973.................... DLB-17

Nichols, Ruth 1948- DLB-60

Nicholson, Norman 1914- DLB-27

Ní Chuilleanáin, Eiléan 1942- DLB-40

Nicol, Eric 1919- DLB-68

Nicolay, John G. 1832-1901 and
    Hay, John 1838-1905 .... DLB-47

Niebuhr, Reinhold 1892-1971 .... DLB-17

Niedecker, Lorine 1903-1970.................. DLB-48

Nieman, Lucius W. 1857-1935................. DLB-25

Niggli, Josefina 1910- Y-80

Niles, Hezekiah 1777-1839 .... DLB-43

Nims, John Frederick 1913- DLB-5

Nin, Anaïs 1903-1977 ....DLB-2, 4

1985: The Year of the Mystery:
    A Symposium Y-85

Nissenson, Hugh 1933- DLB-28

Niven, Larry 1938- DLB-8

Nizan, Paul 1905-1940........................ DLB-72

Nobel Peace Prize
  The 1986 Nobel Peace Prize
    Nobel Lecture 1986: Hope, Despair
      and Memory
    Tributes from Abraham Bernstein,
      Norman Lamm, and John R. Silber Y-86

Nobel Prize in Literature
  The 1982 Nobel Prize in Literature
    Announcement by the Swedish Academy
      of the Nobel Prize
    Nobel Lecture 1982: The Solitude of Latin
      America
    Excerpt from *One Hundred Years
      of Solitude*
    The Magical World of Macondo
    A Tribute to Gabriel García Márquez Y-82
  The 1983 Nobel Prize in Literature
    Announcement by the Swedish
      Academy
    Nobel Lecture 1983
    The Stature of William Golding Y-83
  The 1984 Nobel Prize in Literature
    Announcement by the Swedish
      Academy
    Jaroslav Seifert Through the Eyes of the
      English-Speaking Reader
    Three Poems by Jaroslav Seifert Y-84
  The 1985 Nobel Prize in Literature
    Announcement by the Swedish
      Academy
    Nobel Lecture 1985 ....Y-85
  The 1986 Nobel Prize in Literature
    Nobel Lecture 1986: This Past Must
      Address Its Present....................Y-86
  The 1987 Nobel Prize in Literature
    Nobel Lecture 1987 ....Y-87

Noel, Roden 1834-1894 .... DLB-35

Nolan, William F. 1928- DLB-8

Noland, C. F. M. 1810?-1858 .... DLB-11

Noonday Press............................. DLB-46

Noone, John 1936- DLB-14

Nordhoff, Charles 1887-1947 ....DLB-9

Norman, Marsha 1947- Y-84

Norris, Charles G. 1881-1945..................DLB-9

Norris, Frank 1870-1902 .... DLB-12

Norris, Leslie 1921- DLB-27

Norse, Harold 1916- DLB-16

North Point Press............................ DLB-46

Norton, Alice Mary (see Norton, Andre)

Norton, Andre 1912- DLB-8, 52

Norton, Andrews 1786-1853 ....DLB-1

Norton, Caroline 1808-1877................... DLB-21

Norton, Charles Eliot 1827-1908 ....DLB-1, 64

Norton, John 1606-1663....................... DLB-24

Norton, Thomas (see Sackville, Thomas)

Norton, W. W., and Company................. DLB-46

Nossack, Hans Erich 1901-1977 .... DLB-69

A Note on Technique (1926), by Elizabeth
  A. Drew [excerpts] DLB-36

Nourse, Alan E. 1928- DLB-8

The Novel in [Robert Browning's] "The Ring
  and the Book" (1912), by Henry James ... DLB-32

Novel-Reading: *The Works of Charles Dickens,
  The Works of W. Makepeace Thackeray* (1879),
  by Anthony Trollope..................... DLB-21

The Novels of Dorothy Richardson (1918), by
  May Sinclair............................. DLB-36

Novels with a Purpose (1864),
  by Justin M'Carthy....................... DLB-21

Nowlan, Alden 1933-1983 .... DLB-53

Noyes, Alfred 1880-1958 .... DLB-20

Noyes, Crosby S. 1825-1908 .... DLB-23

Noyes, Nicholas 1647-1717 .... DLB-24

Noyes, Theodore W. 1858-1946............... DLB-29

Nugent, Frank 1908-1965 .... DLB-44

Nye, Edgar Wilson (Bill) 1850-1896 ....DLB-11, 23

Nye, Robert 1939- DLB-14

O

Oakes, Urian circa 1631-1681 .... DLB-24

Oates, Joyce Carol 1938- DLB-2, 5; Y-81

Oberholtzer, Ellis Paxson 1868-1936 .... DLB-47

O'Brien, Edna 1932- DLB-14

O'Brien, Kate 1897-1974 .... DLB-15

O'Brien, Tim 1946- Y-80

O'Casey, Sean 1880-1964 .... DLB-10

Ochs, Adolph S. 1858-1935.................... DLB-25

O'Connor, Flannery 1925-1964.......... DLB-2; Y-80

O'Dell, Scott 1903- DLB-52

Odell, Jonathan 1737-1818 .... DLB-31

Odets, Clifford 1906-1963 .... DLB-7, 26

O'Faolain, Julia 1932- DLB-14

O'Faolain, Sean 1900- DLB-15

O'Flaherty, Liam 1896-1984 .... DLB-36; Y-84

Off Broadway and Off-Off-Broadway DLB-7

Off-Loop Theatres DLB-7

Ogilvie, J. S., and Company DLB-49

O'Grady, Desmond 1935- DLB-40

O'Hagan, Howard 1902-1982 .... DLB-68

O'Hara, Frank 1926-1966 .... DLB-5, 16

O'Hara, John 1905-1970 .... DLB-9; DS-2

O. Henry (see Porter, William S.)

Old Franklin Publishing House DLB-49

Older, Fremont 1856-1935 .... DLB-25

Oliphant, Laurence 1829?-1888 .... DLB-18

Oliphant, Margaret 1828-1897 .... DLB-18

Oliver, Chad 1928- DLB-8

Oliver, Mary 1935- DLB-5

Olsen, Tillie 1913?- DLB-28; Y-80

Olson, Charles 1910-1970 .... DLB-5, 16

Olson, Elder 1909- DLB-48, 63

On Art in Fiction (1838), by
    Edward Bulwer DLB-21

On Some of the Characteristics of Modern
    Poetry and On the Lyrical Poems of Alfred
    Tennyson (1831), by Arthur Henry
    Hallam DLB-32

"On Style in English Prose" (1898), by Frederic
    Harrison DLB-57

"On Style in Literature: Its Technical Elements"
    (1885), by Robert Louis Stevenson DLB-57

"On the Writing of Essays" (1862),
    by Alexander Smith DLB-57

Ondaatje, Michael 1943- DLB-60

O'Neill, Eugene 1888-1953 ....DLB-7

Oppen, George 1908-1984 ....DLB-5

Oppenheim, E. Phillips 1866-1946 .... DLB-70

Oppenheim, James 1882-1932 .... DLB-28

Oppenheimer, Joel 1930- DLB-5

Optic, Oliver (see Adams, William Taylor)

Orczy, Emma, Baroness 1865-1947 .... DLB-70

Orlovitz, Gil 1918-1973 .... DLB-2, 5

Orlovsky, Peter 1933- DLB-16

Ormond, John 1923- DLB-27

Ornitz, Samuel 1890-1957 .... DLB-28, 44

Orton, Joe 1933-1967 .... DLB-13

Orwell, George 1903-1950 .... DLB-15

The Orwell Year Y-84

Osbon, B. S. 1827-1912 .... DLB-43

Osborne, John 1929- DLB-13

Osgood, Herbert L. 1855-1918 .... DLB-47

Osgood, James R., and Company DLB-49

O'Shaughnessy, Arthur 1844-1881 .... DLB-35

O'Shea, Patrick [publishing house] DLB-49

Oswald, Eleazer 1755-1795 .... DLB-43

Otis, James (see Kaler, James Otis)

Otis, James, Jr. 1725-1783 .... DLB-31

Otis, Broaders and Company DLB-49

Ottendorfer, Oswald 1826-1900 .... DLB-23

Ouellette, Fernand 1930- DLB-60

Ouida 1839-1908 .... DLB-18

Outing Publishing Company DLB-46

Outlaw Days, by Joyce Johnson DLB-16

The Overlook Press DLB-46

Overview of U.S. Book Publishing, 1910-1945 ...DLB-9

Owen, Guy 1925- DLB-5

Owen, John [publishing house] DLB-49

Owen, Wilfred 1893-1918 .... DLB-20

Owsley, Frank L. 1890-1956 .... DLB-17

Ozick, Cynthia 1928- DLB-28; Y-82

P

Pack, Robert 1929- DLB-5

Packaging Papa: *The Garden of Eden* Y-86

Padell Publishing Company DLB-46

Padgett, Ron 1942- DLB-5

Page, L. C., and Company DLB-49

Page, P. K. 1916- DLB-68

Page, Thomas Nelson 1853-1922 .... DLB-12

Page, Walter Hines 1855-1918 .... DLB-71

Paget, Violet (see Lee, Vernon)

Pain, Philip ?-circa 1666 .... DLB-24

Paine, Robert Treat, Jr. 1773-1811 .... DLB-37

Paine, Thomas 1737-1809 .... DLB-31, 43

Paley, Grace 1922- DLB-28

Palfrey, John Gorham 1796-1881 .... DLB-1, 30

Palgrave, Francis Turner 1824-1897 .... DLB-35

Paltock, Robert 1697-1767 .... DLB-39

Panama, Norman 1914- and
    Frank, Melvin 1913- DLB-26

Pangborn, Edgar 1909-1976 .... DLB-8

"Panic Among the Philistines": A Postscript,
    An Interview with Bryan Griffin Y-81

Panneton, Philippe (see Ringuet)

Panshin, Alexei 1940- DLB-8

Pansy (see Alden, Isabella)

Pantheon Books DLB-46

Paperback Library DLB-46

Paperback Science Fiction DLB-8

Paquet, Alfons 1881-1944 .... DLB-66

Paradis, Suzanne 1936- DLB-53

Parents' Magazine Press DLB-46

Parisian Theater, Fall 1984: Toward
    A New Baroque Y-85

Parizeau, Alice 1930- DLB-60

Parke, John 1754-1789 .... DLB-31

Parker, Dorothy 1893-1967 .... DLB-11, 45

Parker, James 1714-1770 .... DLB-43

Parker, Theodore 1810-1860 .... DLB-1

Parkman, Francis, Jr. 1823-1893 .... DLB-1, 30

Parks, Gordon 1912- DLB-33

Parks, William 1698-1750 .... DLB-43

Parks, William [publishing house] DLB-49

Parley, Peter (see Goodrich, Samuel Griswold)

Parrington, Vernon L. 1871-1929 .... DLB-17, 63

Parton, James 1822-1891 .... DLB-30

Parton, Sara Payson Willis 1811-1872 .... DLB-43

Pastan, Linda 1932- DLB-5

Pastorius, Francis Daniel 1651-circa 1720 ...... DLB-24

Patchen, Kenneth 1911-1972 .... DLB-16, 48

Pater, Walter 1839-1894 .... DLB-57

Paterson, Katherine 1932- DLB-52

Patmore, Coventry 1823-1896 .... DLB-35

Paton, Joseph Noel 1821-1901 .... DLB-35

Patrick, John 1906- DLB-7

Pattee, Fred Lewis 1863-1950 .... DLB-71

Patterson, Eleanor Medill 1881-1948 .... DLB-29

Patterson, Joseph Medill 1879-1946 .... DLB-29

Pattillo, Henry 1726-1801 .... DLB-37

Paul, Elliot 1891-1958 .... DLB-4

Paul, Peter, Book Company DLB-49

Paulding, James Kirke 1778-1860 .... DLB-3, 59

Paulin, Tom 1949- DLB-40

Pauper, Peter, Press DLB-46

Paxton, John 1911-1985 .... DLB-44

Payn, James 1830-1898 .... DLB-18

Payne, John 1842-1916 .... DLB-35

Payne, John Howard 1791-1852 .... DLB-37

Payson and Clarke DLB-46

Peabody, Elizabeth Palmer 1804-1894 .... DLB-1

Peabody, Elizabeth Palmer [publishing
    house] DLB-49

Peabody, Oliver William Bourn 1799-1848 .... DLB-59

Peachtree Publishers, Limited DLB-46

Pead, Deuel ?-1727 .... DLB-24

Peake, Mervyn 1911-1968 .... DLB-15

Pearson, H. B. [publishing house] DLB-49

Peck, George W. 1840-1916 .... DLB-23, 42

Peck, H. C., and Theo. Bliss [publishing
    house] DLB-49

Peck, Harry Thurston 1856-1914 .... DLB-71

Peele, George 1556-1596 .... DLB-62

Pellegrini and Cudahy DLB-46

Pemberton, Sir Max 1863-1950 .... DLB-70

Penguin Books DLB-46

Penn Publishing Company DLB-49

Penn, William 1644-1718 .... DLB-24

Penner, Jonathan 1940- Y-83

Pennington, Lee 1939- Y-82

Percy, Walker 1916- DLB-2; Y-80

Perelman, S. J. 1904-1979 .... DLB-11, 44

Periodicals of the Beat Generation DLB-16

Perkins, Eugene 1932- DLB-41

Perkoff, Stuart Z. 1930-1974 .... DLB-16

Permabooks DLB-46

Perry, Bliss 1860-1954...................... DLB-71

Perry, Eleanor 1915-1981 .... DLB-44

"Personal Style" (1890), by John Addington
    Symonds DLB-57

Peter, Laurence J. 1919- DLB-53

Peterkin, Julia 1880-1961....................DLB-9

Petersham, Maud 1889-1971 and
    Petersham, Miska 1888-1960............. DLB-22

Peterson, T. B., and Brothers DLB-49

Pharr, Robert Deane 1916- DLB-33

Philippe, Charles-Louis 1874-1909 .... DLB-65

Phillips, David Graham 1867-1911 ....DLB-9, 12

Phillips, Jayne Anne 1952- Y-80

Phillips, Stephen 1864-1915 .... DLB-10

Phillips, Ulrich B. 1877-1934 .... DLB-17

Phillips, Willard 1784-1873................... DLB-59

Phillips, Sampson and Company.............. DLB-49

Phillpotts, Eden 1862-1960 ....DLB-10, 70

Philosophical Library DLB-46

"The Philosophy of Style" (1852), by
    Herbert Spencer DLB-57

Phinney, Elihu [publishing house]............ DLB-49

Phoenix, John (see Derby, George Horatio)

Pickard, Tom 1946- DLB-40

Pictorial Printing Company................... DLB-49

Pilon, Jean-Guy 1930- DLB-60

Pinckney, Josephine 1895-1957.................DLB-6

Pinero, Arthur Wing 1855-1934.............. DLB-10

Pinnacle Books DLB-46

Pinsky, Robert 1940- Y-82

Pinter, Harold 1930- DLB-13

Piper, H. Beam 1904-1964 ....DLB-8

Piper, Watty DLB-22

Pisar, Samuel 1929- Y-83

Pitkin, Timothy 1766-1847 .... DLB-30

The Pitt Poetry Series: Poetry
    Publishing Today Y-85

Pitter, Ruth 1897- DLB-20

The Place of Realism in Fiction (1895), by
    George Gissing........................... DLB-18

Plante, David 1940- Y-83

Plath, Sylvia 1932-1963......................DLB-5, 6

Platt and Munk Company DLB-46

Playboy Press............................... DLB-46

Playwrights and Professors, by Tom
    Stoppard................................ DLB-13

Plievier, Theodor 1892-1955 .... DLB-69

Plomer, William 1903-1973................... DLB-20

Plumly, Stanley 1939- DLB-5

Plumpp, Sterling D. 1940- DLB-41

Plunkett, James 1920- DLB-14

Plymell, Charles 1935- DLB-16

Pocket Books DLB-46

Poe, Edgar Allan 1809-1849.................DLB-3, 59

Poe, James 1921-1980 .... DLB-44

The Poet Laureate of the United States
    Statements from Former Consultants
    in Poetry...................................Y-86

Pohl, Frederik 1919- DLB-8

Poliakoff, Stephen 1952- DLB-13

Polite, Carlene Hatcher 1932- DLB-33

Pollard, Edward A. 1832-1872................ DLB-30

Pollard, Percival 1869-1911.................. DLB-71

Pollard and Moss DLB-49

Pollock, Sharon 1936- DLB-60

Polonsky, Abraham 1910- DLB-26

Poole, Ernest 1880-1950......................DLB-9

Poore, Benjamin Perley 1820-1887 .... DLB-23

Popular Library DLB-46

Porter, Eleanor H. 1868-1920 ....DLB-9

Porter, Henry ?-? DLB-62

Porter, Katherine Anne 1890-1980.....DLB-4, 9; Y-80

Porter, Peter 1929- DLB-40

Porter, William S. 1862-1910 .... DLB-12

Porter, William T. 1809-1858................DLB-3, 43

Porter and Coates DLB-49

Portis, Charles 1933- DLB-6

Poston, Ted 1906-1974...................... DLB-51

Postscript to [the Third Edition of] *Clarissa*
(1751), by Samuel Richardson............ DLB-39

Potok, Chaim 1929- DLB-28; Y-84

Potter, David M. 1910-1971 .... DLB-17

Potter, John E., and Company................ DLB-49

Pottle, Frederick A. 1897-1987 ....Y-87

Poulin, Jacques 1937- DLB-60

Pound, Ezra 1885-1972.................DLB-4, 45, 63

Powell, Anthony 1905- DLB-15

Pownall, David 1938- DLB-14

Powys, John Cowper 1872-1963 .... DLB-15

Powys, T. F. 1875-1953...................... DLB-36

The Practice of Biography: An Interview with
Stanley Weintraub Y-82

The Practice of Biography II: An Interview with
B. L. Reid...................................Y-83

The Practice of Biography III: An Interview with
Humphrey Carpenter........................Y-84

The Practice of Biography IV: An Interview with
William Manchester.........................Y-85

The Practice of Biography V: An Interview with
Justin Kaplan Y-86

The Practice of Biography VI: An Interview with
David Herbert Donald Y-87

Praeger Publishers............................ DLB-46

Pratt, Samuel Jackson 1749-1814.............. DLB-39

Preface to *Alwyn* (1780), by Thomas
Holcroft.................................. DLB-39

Preface to *Colonel Jack* (1722), by Daniel
Defoe DLB-39

Preface to *Evelina* (1778), by Fanny Burney ... DLB-39

Preface to *Ferdinand Count Fathom* (1753), by
Tobias Smollett DLB-39

Preface to *Incognita* (1692), by William
Congreve.................................. DLB-39

Preface to *Joseph Andrews* (1742), by
Henry Fielding............................ DLB-39

Preface to *Moll Flanders* (1722), by Daniel
Defoe DLB-39

Preface to *Poems* (1853), by Matthew
Arnold DLB-32

Preface to *Robinson Crusoe* (1719), by Daniel
Defoe DLB-39

Preface to *Roderick Random* (1748), by Tobias
Smollett DLB-39

Preface to *Roxana* (1724), by Daniel Defoe DLB-39

Preface to *St. Leon* (1799),
by William Godwin........................ DLB-39

Preface to Sarah Fielding's *Familiar Letters*
(1747), by Henry Fielding [excerpt]....... DLB-39

Preface to Sarah Fielding's *The Adventures of
David Simple* (1744), by Henry Fielding ... DLB-39

Preface to *The Cry* (1754), by Sarah Fielding... DLB-39

Preface to *The Delicate Distress* (1769), by
Elizabeth Griffin DLB-39

Preface to *The Disguis'd Prince* (1733), by Eliza
Haywood [excerpt]....................... DLB-39

Preface to *The Farther Adventures of Robinson
Crusoe* (1719), by Daniel Defoe........... DLB-39

Preface to the First Edition of *Pamela* (1740), by
Samuel Richardson....................... DLB-39

Preface to the First Edition of *The Castle of
Otranto* (1764), by Horace Walpole........ DLB-39

Preface to *The History of Romances* (1715), by
Pierre Daniel Huet [excerpts]............. DLB-39

Preface to *The Life of Charlotta du Pont* (1723),
by Penelope Aubin....................... DLB-39

Preface to *The Old English Baron* (1778), by
Clara Reeve DLB-39

Preface to the Second Edition of *The Castle of
Otranto* (1765), by Horace Walpole........ DLB-39

Preface to *The Secret History, of Queen Zarah, and
the Zarazians* (1705), by Delarivière
Manley.................................. DLB-39

Preface to the Third Edition of *Clarissa* (1751),
by Samuel Richardson [excerpt]........... DLB-39

Preface to *The Works of Mrs. Davys* (1725), by
Mary Davys DLB-39

Preface to Volume 1 of *Clarissa* (1747), by
Samuel Richardson....................... DLB-39

Preface to Volume 3 of *Clarissa* (1748), by
Samuel Richardson....................... DLB-39

Préfontaine, Yves 1937- DLB-53

Prelutsky, Jack 1940- DLB-61

Prentice, George D. 1802-1870 .... DLB-43

Prentice-Hall DLB-46

Prescott, William Hickling 1796-1859....DLB-1, 30, 59

The Present State of the English Novel (1892),
    by George Saintsbury DLB-18

Preston, Thomas 1537-1598 .... DLB-62

Price, Reynolds 1933- DLB-2

Price, Richard 1949- Y-81

Priest, Christopher 1943- DLB-14

Priestley, J. B. 1894-1984 .... DLB-10, 34; Y-84

Prime, Benjamin Young 1733-1791 .... DLB-31

Prince, F. T. 1912- DLB-20

Prince, Thomas 1687-1758 .... DLB-24

The Principles of Success in Literature (1865), by
    George Henry Lewes [excerpt]........... DLB-57

Pritchett, V. S. 1900- DLB-15

Procter, Adelaide Anne 1825-1864 .... DLB-32

The Progress of Romance (1785), by Clara Reeve
    [excerpt] DLB-39

Prokosch, Frederic 1906- DLB-48

The Proletarian Novel........................DLB-9

Propper, Dan 1937- DLB-16

The Prospect of Peace (1778), by Joel Barlow.... DLB-37

Proud, Robert 1728-1813.................... DLB-30

Proust, Marcel 1871-1922 .... DLB-65

Prynne, J. H. 1936- DLB-40

Przybyszewski, Stanislaw 1868-1927 .... DLB-66

The Public Lending Right in America
    Statement by Sen. Charles McC. Mathias, Jr.
    PLR and the Meaning of Literary Property
    Statements on PLR by American Writers Y-83

The Public Lending Right in the United Kingdom
    Public Lending Right: The First Year in the
    United Kingdom..........................Y-83

The Publication of English Renaissance
    Plays DLB-62

Publications and Social Movements
    [Transcendentalism] DLB-1

Publishers and Agents: The Columbia
    Connection..................................Y-87

Publishing Fiction at LSU Press Y-87

Pugin, A. Welby 1812-1852.................... DLB-55

Pulitzer, Joseph 1847-1911 .... DLB-23

Pulitzer, Joseph, Jr. 1885-1955 .... DLB-29

Pulitzer Prizes for the Novel, 1917-1945........DLB-9

Purdy, James 1923- DLB-2

Pusey, Edward Bouverie 1800-1882 .... DLB-55

Putnam, George Palmer 1814-1872..............DLB-3

Putnam, Samuel 1892-1950.....................DLB-4

G. P. Putnam's Sons DLB-49

Puzo, Mario 1920- DLB-6

Pyle, Ernie 1900-1945 .... DLB-29

Pyle, Howard 1853-1911 .... DLB-42

Pym, Barbara 1913-1980 .... DLB-14; Y-87

Pynchon, Thomas 1937- DLB-2

Pyramid Books DLB-46

Pyrnelle, Louise-Clarke 1850-1907 .... DLB-42

Q

Quad, M. (see Lewis, Charles B.)

The Queen City Publishing House DLB-49

Queneau, Raymond 1903-1976................ DLB-72

The Question of American Copyright
    in the Nineteenth Century
        Headnote
        Preface, by George Haven Putnam
        The Evolution of Copyright, by Brander
            Matthews
        Summary of Copyright Legislation in the
            United States, by R. R. Bowker
        Analysis of the Provisions of the Copyright
            Law of 1891, by George Haven Putnam
        The Contest for International Copyright,
            by George Haven Putnam
        Cheap Books and Good Books,
            by Brander Matthews DLB-49

Quin, Ann 1936-1973 .... DLB-14

Quincy, Samuel of Georgia ?-? DLB-31

Quincy, Samuel of Massachusetts 1734-1789 .. DLB-31

Quist, Harlin, Books......................... DLB-46

R

Rabe, David 1940- DLB-7

Radcliffe, Ann 1764-1823 .... DLB-39

Raddall, Thomas 1903- DLB-68

Radiguet, Raymond 1903-1923............... DLB-65

Radványi, Netty Reiling (see Seghers, Anna)

Raine, Craig 1944- DLB-40

Raine, Kathleen 1908- DLB-20

Ralph, Julian 1853-1903...................... DLB-23

Ralph Waldo Emerson in 1982 .... Y-82

Rambler, no. 4 (1750), by Samuel Johnson
[excerpt] DLB-39

Ramée, Marie Louise de la (see Ouida)

Ramsay, David 1749-1815 .... DLB-30

Rand, Avery and Company................... DLB-49

Rand McNally and Company................. DLB-49

Randall, Dudley 1914- DLB-41

Randall, Henry S. 1811-1876................. DLB-30

Randall, James G. 1881-1953................. DLB-17

The Randall Jarrell Symposium: A Small
Collection of Randall Jarrells
Excerpts From Papers Delivered at
the Randall Jarrell Symposium Y-86

Randolph, Anson D. F. [publishing house] DLB-49

Randolph, Thomas 1605-1635................ DLB-58

Random House............................... DLB-46

Ranlet, Henry [publishing house]............. DLB-49

Ransom, John Crowe 1888-1974 ....DLB-45, 63

Raphael, Frederic 1931- DLB-14

Raphaelson, Samson 1896-1983 .... DLB-44

Raskin, Ellen 1928-1984..................... DLB-52

Rattigan, Terence 1911-1977 .... DLB-13

Rawlings, Marjorie Kinnan 1896-1953.......DLB-9, 22

Raworth, Tom 1938- DLB-40

Ray, David 1932- DLB-5

Ray, Henrietta Cordelia 1849-1916............ DLB-50

Raymond, Henry 1820-1869.................. DLB-43

Reach, Angus 1821-1856 .... DLB-70

Read, Herbert 1893-1968..................... DLB-20

Read, Opie 1852-1939........................ DLB-23

Read, Piers Paul 1941- DLB-14

Reade, Charles 1814-1884.................... DLB-21

Reader's Digest Condensed Books............. DLB-46

Reading, Peter 1946- DLB-40

Reaney, James 1926- DLB-68

Rechy, John 1934- Y-82

Redding, J. Saunders 1906- DLB-63

Redfield, J. S. [publishing house].............. DLB-49

Redgrove, Peter 1932- DLB-40

Redmon, Anne 1943- Y-86

Redmond, Eugene B. 1937- DLB-41

Redpath, James [publishing house]........... DLB-49

Reed, Henry 1808-1854 .... DLB-59

Reed, Henry 1914- DLB-27

Reed, Ishmael 1938- DLB-2, 5, 33

Reed, Sampson 1800-1880.....................DLB-1

Reese, Lizette Woodworth 1856-1935 .... DLB-54

Reese, Thomas 1742-1796..................... DLB-37

Reeve, Clara 1729-1807 .... DLB-39

Regnery, Henry, Company DLB-46

Reid, Alastair 1926- DLB-27

Reid, Christopher 1949- DLB-40

Reid, Helen Rogers 1882-1970 .... DLB-29

Reid, James ?-? DLB-31

Reid, Mayne 1818-1883 .... DLB-21

Reid, Thomas 1710-1796..................... DLB-31

Reid, Whitelaw 1837-1912.................... DLB-23

Reilly and Lee Publishing Company DLB-46

Reisch, Walter 1903-1983.................... DLB-44

Remarque, Erich Maria 1898-1970 .... DLB-56

"Re-meeting of Old Friends": The Jack Kerouac
Conference..................................Y-82

Remington, Frederic 1861-1909 .... DLB-12

Renaud, Jacques 1943- DLB-60

Renault, Mary 1905-1983........................Y-83

Representative Men and Women: A Historical
Perspective on the British Novel,
1930-1960................................ DLB-15

(Re-)Publishing Orwell...........................Y-86

Reuter, Gabriele 1859-1941 .... DLB-66

Revell, Fleming H., Company DLB-49

Reventlow, Franziska Gräfin zu
1871-1918................................ DLB-66

Review of [Samuel Richardson's] *Clarissa* (1748),
by Henry Fielding......................... DLB-39

The Revolt (1937), by Mary
Colum [excerpts]......................... DLB-36

Rexroth, Kenneth 1905-1982........ DLB-16, 48; Y-82

Rey, H. A. 1898-1977......................... DLB-22

Reynal and Hitchcock DLB-46

Reynolds, G. W. M. 1814-1879 .... DLB-21

Reynolds, Mack 1917- DLB-8

Reznikoff, Charles 1894-1976 ....DLB-28, 45

"Rhetoric" (1828; revised, 1859), by
     Thomas de Quincey [excerpt]............ DLB-57

Rhett, Robert Barnwell 1800-1876............. DLB-43

Rhodes, James Ford 1848-1927................ DLB-47

Rhys, Jean 1890-1979 .... DLB-36

Rice, Elmer 1892-1967 .... DLB-4, 7

Rice, Grantland 1880-1954 .... DLB-29

Rich, Adrienne 1929- DLB-5, 67

Richards, David Adams 1950- DLB-53

Richards, George circa 1760-1814............. DLB-37

Richards, I. A. 1893-1979 .... DLB-27

Richards, Laura E. 1850-1943 .... DLB-42

Richardson, Charles F. 1851-1913............. DLB-71

Richardson, Dorothy M. 1873-1957 .... DLB-36

Richardson, Jack 1935- DLB-7

Richardson, Samuel 1689-1761 .... DLB-39

Richardson, Willis 1889-1977................. DLB-51

Richler, Mordecai 1931- DLB-53

Richter, Conrad 1890-1968....................DLB-9

Richter, Hans Werner 1908- DLB-69

Rickword, Edgell 1898-1982.................. DLB-20

Riddell, John (see Ford, Corey)

Ridge, Lola 1873-1941........................ DLB-54

Ridler, Anne 1912- DLB-27

Riffaterre, Michael 1924- DLB-67

Riis, Jacob 1849-1914........................ DLB-23

Riker, John C. [publishing house] DLB-49

Riley, John 1938-1978........................ DLB-40

Rinehart and Company........................ DLB-46

Ringuet 1895-1960 .... DLB-68

Rinser, Luise 1911- DLB-69

Ripley, Arthur 1895-1961 .... DLB-44

Ripley, George 1802-1880 ....DLB-1, 64

The Rising Glory of America: Three Poems... DLB-37

The Rising Glory of America: Written in 1771
     (1786), by Hugh Henry Brackenridge and
     Philip Freneau DLB-37

Riskin, Robert 1897-1955..................... DLB-26

Risse, Heinz 1898- DLB-69

Ritchie, Anna Mowatt 1819-1870...............DLB-3

Ritchie, Anne Thackeray 1837-1919.......... DLB-18

Ritchie, Thomas 1778-1854................... DLB-43

Rites of Passage [on William Saroyan].............Y-83

The Ritz Paris Hemingway Award.................Y-85

Rivers, Conrad Kent 1933-1968 .... DLB-41

Riverside Press DLB-49

Rivington, James circa 1724-1802 .... DLB-43

Rivkin, Allen 1903- DLB-26

Robbins, Tom 1936- Y-80

Roberts, Elizabeth Madox 1881-1941.......DLB-9, 54

Roberts, Kenneth 1885-1957 ....DLB-9

Roberts Brothers DLB-49

Robertson, A. M., and Company DLB-49

Robinson, Casey 1903-1979.................... DLB-44

Robinson, Edwin Arlington 1869-1935 .... DLB-54

Robinson, James Harvey 1863-1936.......... DLB-47

Robinson, Lennox 1886-1958.................. DLB-10

Robinson, Mabel Louise 1874-1962........... DLB-22

Robinson, Therese 1797-1870 .... DLB-59

Rodgers, Carolyn M. 1945- DLB-41

Rodgers, W. R. 1909-1969.................... DLB-20

Roethke, Theodore 1908-1963 ....DLB-5

Rogers, Will 1879-1935...................... DLB-11

Rohmer, Sax 1883-1959 .... DLB-70

Roiphe, Anne 1935- Y-80

Rolfe, Frederick William 1860-1913 .... DLB-34

Rolland, Romain 1866-1944 .... DLB-65

Rolvaag, O. E. 1876-1931......................DLB-9

Romains, Jules 1885-1972 .... DLB-65

Roman, A., and Company.................... DLB-49

Roosevelt, Theodore 1858-1919.............. DLB-47

Root, Waverley 1903-1982.....................DLB-4

Roquebrune, Robert de 1889-1978 .... DLB-68

Rose, Reginald 1920- DLB-26

Rosen, Norma 1925- DLB-28

Rosenberg, Isaac 1890-1918 .... DLB-20

Rosenfeld, Isaac 1918-1956................... DLB-28

Rosenthal, M. L. 1917- DLB-5

Ross, Leonard Q. (see Rosten, Leo)

Rossen, Robert 1908-1966 .... DLB-26

Rossetti, Christina 1830-1894 .... DLB-35

Rossetti, Dante Gabriel 1828-1882 .... DLB-35

Rossner, Judith 1935- DLB-6

Rosten, Leo 1908- DLB-11

Roth, Henry 1906?- DLB-28

Roth, Philip 1933- DLB-2, 28; Y-82

Rothenberg, Jerome 1931- DLB-5

Rowe, Elizabeth 1674-1737 .... DLB-39

Rowlandson, Mary circa 1635-circa 1678 ...... DLB-24

Rowley, William circa 1585-1626 .... DLB-58

Rowson, Susanna Haswell circa 1762-1824 .... DLB-37

Roy, Gabrielle 1909-1983 .... DLB-68

The Royal Court Theatre and the English
    Stage Company DLB-13

The Royal Court Theatre and the New
    Drama DLB-10

Royall, Anne 1769-1854 .... DLB-43

The Roycroft Printing Shop DLB-49

Rubens, Bernice 1928- DLB-14

Rudd and Carleton DLB-49

Rudkin, David 1936- DLB-13

Ruggles, Henry Joseph 1813-1906 .... DLB-64

Rukeyser, Muriel 1913-1980 .... DLB-48

Rule, Jane 1931- DLB-60

Rumaker, Michael 1932- DLB-16

Rumens, Carol 1944- DLB-40

Runyon, Damon 1880-1946 .... DLB-11

Rush, Benjamin 1746-1813 .... DLB-37

Ruskin, John 1819-1900 .... DLB-55

Russ, Joanna 1937- DLB-8

Russell, B. B., and Company DLB-49

Russell, Benjamin 1761-1845 .... DLB-43

Russell, Charles Edward 1860-1941 .... DLB-25

Russell, George William (see AE)

Russell, R. H., and Son DLB-49

Rutherford, Mark 1831-1913 .... DLB-18

Ryan, Michael 1946- Y-82

Ryan, Oscar 1904- DLB-68

Ryga, George 1932- DLB-60

Ryskind, Morrie 1895-1985 .... DLB-26

S

The Saalfield Publishing Company DLB-46

Saberhagen, Fred 1930- DLB-8

Sackler, Howard 1929-1982 ....DLB-7

Sackville, Thomas 1536-1608
    and Norton, Thomas 1532-1584 .... DLB-62

Sackville-West, V. 1892-1962 .... DLB-34

Sadlier, D. and J., and Company DLB-49

Saffin, John circa 1626-1710 .... DLB-24

Sage, Robert 1899-1962 ....DLB-4

Sahkomaapii, Piitai (see Highwater, Jamake)

Sahl, Hans 1902- DLB-69

Said, Edward W. 1935- DLB-67

St. Johns, Adela Rogers 1894- DLB-29

St. Martin's Press DLB-46

Saint-Exupéry, Antoine de 1900-1944 .... DLB-72

Saintsbury, George 1845-1933 .... DLB-57

Saki (see Munro, H. H.)

Salaam, Kalamu ya 1947- DLB-38

Salemson, Harold J. 1910- DLB-4

Salinger, J. D. 1919- DLB-2

Salt, Waldo 1914- DLB-44

Sanborn, Franklin Benjamin 1831-1917 ....DLB-1

Sanchez, Sonia 1934- DLB-41

Sandburg, Carl 1878-1967 ....DLB-17, 54

Sanders, Ed 1939- DLB-16

Sandoz, Mari 1896-1966 ....DLB-9

Sandys, George 1578-1644 .... DLB-24

Santayana, George 1863-1952 ....DLB-54, 71

Santmyer, Helen Hooven 1895-1986 ....Y-84

Sargent, Pamela 1948- DLB-8

Saroyan, William 1908-1981 ....DLB-7, 9; Y-81

Sarton, May 1912- DLB-48; Y-81

Sartre, Jean-Paul 1905-1980 .... DLB-72

Sassoon, Siegfried 1886-1967 .... DLB-20

Saturday Review Press DLB-46

Saunders, James 1925- DLB-13

Saunders, John Monk 1897-1940............. DLB-26

Savage, James 1784-1873.................... DLB-30

Savage, Marmion W. 1803?-1872............. DLB-21

Savard, Félix-Antoine 1896-1982............. DLB-68

Sawyer, Ruth 1880-1970..................... DLB-22

Sayers, Dorothy L. 1893-1957 ....DLB-10, 36

Sayles, John Thomas 1950- DLB-44

Scannell, Vernon 1922- DLB-27

Scarry, Richard 1919- DLB-61

Schaeffer, Albrecht 1885-1950 .... DLB-66

Schaeffer, Susan Fromberg 1941- DLB-28

Schaper, Edzard 1908-1984 .... DLB-69

Scharf, J. Thomas 1843-1898................. DLB-47

Schickele, René 1883-1940 .... DLB-66

Schlesinger, Arthur M., Jr. 1917- DLB-17

Schlumberger, Jean 1877-1968 .... DLB-65

Schmid, Eduard Hermann Wilhelm
  (see Edschmid, Kasimir)

Schmidt, Arno 1914-1979 .... DLB-69

Schmidt, Michael 1947- DLB-40

Schmitz, James H. 1911- DLB-8

Schnurre, Wolfdietrich 1920- DLB-69

Schocken Books DLB-46

Schouler, James 1839-1920.................. DLB-47

Schrader, Paul 1946- DLB-44

Schreiner, Olive 1855-1920................. DLB-18

Schroeder, Andreas 1946- DLB-53

Schulberg, Budd 1914- DLB-6, 26, 28; Y-81

Schulte, F. J., and Company................. DLB-49

Schurz, Carl 1829-1906..................... DLB-23

Schuyler, George S. 1895-1977 ....DLB-29, 51

Schuyler, James 1923- DLB-5

Schwartz, Delmore 1913-1966 ....DLB-28, 48

Schwartz, Jonathan 1938- Y-82

Science Fantasy.............................DLB-8

Science-Fiction Fandom and Conventions DLB-8

Science-Fiction Fanzines: The Time Binders DLB-8

Science-Fiction Films DLB-8

Science Fiction Writers of America and the
  Nebula Awards...........................DLB-8

Scott, Evelyn 1893-1963 ....DLB-9, 48

Scott, Harvey W. 1838-1910.................. DLB-23

Scott, Paul 1920-1978........................ DLB-14

Scott, Sarah 1723-1795 .... DLB-39

Scott, Tom 1918- DLB-27

Scott, William Bell 1811-1890 .... DLB-32

Scott, William R. [publishing house].......... DLB-46

Scott-Heron, Gil 1949- DLB-41

Charles Scribner's Sons....................... DLB-49

Scripps, E. W. 1854-1926.................... DLB-25

Scudder, Horace Elisha 1838-1902 ....DLB-42, 71

Scudder, Vida Dutton 1861-1954.............. DLB-71

Scupham, Peter 1933- DLB-40

Seabrook, William 1886-1945.................DLB-4

Seabury, Samuel 1729-1796 .... DLB-31

Sears Publishing Company DLB-46

Seaton, George 1911-1979.................... DLB-44

Seaton, William Winston 1785-1866.......... DLB-43

Sedgwick, Arthur George 1844-1915 .... DLB-64

Sedgwick, Catharine Maria 1789-1867..........DLB-1

Seeger, Alan 1888-1916 .... DLB-45

Segal, Erich 1937- Y-86

Seghers, Anna 1900-1983 .... DLB-69

Seid, Ruth (see Sinclair, Jo)

Seidel, Frederick Lewis 1936- Y-84

Seidel, Ina 1885-1974 .... DLB-56

Séjour, Victor 1817-1874.................... DLB-50

Séjour Marcou et Ferrand,
  Juan Victor (see Séjour, Victor)

Selby, Hubert, Jr. 1928- DLB-2

Selden, George 1929- DLB-52

Selected English-Language Little Magazines and
  Newspapers [France, 1920-1939]...........DLB-4

Selected Humorous Magazines (1820-1950) ... DLB-11

Selected Science-Fiction Magazines and
  Anthologies DLB-8

Seligman, Edwin R. A. 1861-1939............. DLB-47

Seltzer, Thomas [publishing house].......... DLB-46

Sendak, Maurice 1928- DLB-61

Sensation Novels (1863), by H. L. Manse...... DLB-21

Seredy, Kate 1899-1975 .... DLB-22

Serling, Rod 1924-1975......................DLB-26

Settle, Mary Lee 1918- DLB-6

Seuss, Dr. (see Geisel, Theodor Seuss)

Sewall, Joseph 1688-1769.....................DLB-24

Sewell, Samuel 1652-1730 ....DLB-24

Sex, Class, Politics, and Religion [in the British
        Novel, 1930-1959].......................DLB-15

Sexton, Anne 1928-1974 ....DLB-5

Shaara, Michael 1929- Y-83

Shaffer, Anthony 1926- DLB-13

Shaffer, Peter 1926- DLB-13

Shairp, Mordaunt 1887-1939..................DLB-10

Shakespeare, William 1564-1616 ....DLB-62

Shange, Ntozake 1948- DLB-38

Shapiro, Karl 1913- DLB-48

Sharon Publications............................DLB-46

Sharpe, Tom 1928- DLB-14

Shaw, Bernard 1856-1950.................DLB-10, 57

Shaw, Henry Wheeler 1818-1885..............DLB-11

Shaw, Irwin 1913-1984 ....DLB-6; Y-84

Shaw, Robert 1927-1978..................DLB-13, 14

Shay, Frank [publishing house]...............DLB-46

Shea, John Gilmary 1824-1892 ....DLB-30

Shearing, Joseph 1886-1952 ....DLB-70

Shebbeare, John 1709-1788 ....DLB-39

Sheckley, Robert 1928- DLB-8

Shedd, William G. T. 1820-1894 ....DLB-64

Sheed, Wilfred 1930- DLB-6

Sheed and Ward..............................DLB-46

Sheldon, Alice B. (see Tiptree, James, Jr.)

Sheldon, Edward 1886-1946....................DLB-7

Sheldon and Company DLB-49

Shepard, Sam 1943- DLB-7

Shepard, Thomas I 1604 or 1605-1649........DLB-24

Shepard, Thomas II 1635-1677 ....DLB-24

Shepard, Clark and Brown DLB-49

Sheridan, Frances 1724-1766 ....DLB-39

Sherriff, R. C. 1896-1975.....................DLB-10

Sherwood, Robert 1896-1955...............DLB-7, 26

Shiels, George 1886-1949..................... DLB-10

Shillaber, B.[enjamin] P.[enhallow]
        1814-1890.............................DLB-1, 11

Shine, Ted 1931- DLB-38

Shirer, William L. 1904- DLB-4

Shirley, James 1596-1666.....................DLB-58

Shockley, Ann Allen 1927- DLB-33

Shorthouse, Joseph Henry 1834-1903 .... DLB-18

Showalter, Elaine 1941- DLB-67

Shulevitz, Uri 1935- DLB-61

Shulman, Max 1919- DLB-11

Shute, Henry A. 1856-1943 ....DLB-9

Shuttle, Penelope 1947- DLB-14, 40

Sidney, Margaret (see Lothrop, Harriet M.)

Sidney's Press................................DLB-49

Siegfried Loraine Sassoon: A Centenary Essay
        Tributes from Vivien F. Clarke and
        Michael Thorpe..........................Y-86

Sierra Club Books DLB-49

Sigourney, Lydia Howard (Huntley)
        1791-1865.............................DLB-1, 42

Silkin, Jon 1930- DLB-27

Silliphant, Stirling 1918- DLB-26

Sillitoe, Alan 1928- DLB-14

Silman, Roberta 1934- DLB-28

Silverberg, Robert 1935- DLB-8

Simak, Clifford D. 1904- DLB-8

Simcox, George Augustus 1841-1905.......... DLB-35

Simenon, Georges 1903- DLB-72

Simmel, Johannes Mario 1924- DLB-69

Simmons, Herbert Alfred 1930- DLB-33

Simmons, James 1933- DLB-40

Simms, William Gilmore 1806-1870 ..... DLB-3, 30, 59

Simon, Neil 1927- DLB-7

Simon and Schuster DLB-46

Simons, Katherine Drayton Mayrant 1890-1969...Y-83

Simpson, Louis 1923- DLB-5

Simpson, N. F. 1919- DLB-13

Sims, George R. 1847-1922.................DLB-35, 70

Sinclair, Andrew 1935- DLB-14

Sinclair, Jo 1913- DLB-28

Sinclair Lewis Centennial Conference Y-85

Sinclair, May 1863-1946 .... DLB-36

Sinclair, Upton 1878-1968 .... DLB-9

Sinclair, Upton [publishing house] DLB-46

Singer, Isaac Basheyis 1904- DLB-6, 28, 52

Singmaster, Elsie 1879-1958 .... DLB-9

Siodmak, Curt 1902- DLB-44

Sissman, L. E. 1928-1976 .... DLB-5

Sisson, C. H. 1914- DLB-27

Sitwell, Edith 1887-1964 .... DLB-20

Skelton, Robin 1925- DLB-27, 53

Skipsey, Joseph 1832-1903 .... DLB-35

Slade, Bernard 1930- DLB-53

Slater, Patrick 1880-1951 .... DLB-68

Slavitt, David 1935- DLB-5, 6

A Slender Thread of Hope: The Kennedy
    Center Black Theatre Project DLB-38

Slick, Sam (see Haliburton, Thomas Chandler)

Sloane, William, Associates DLB-46

Small, Maynard and Company DLB-49

Small Presses in Great Britain and Ireland,
    1960-1985 .... DLB-40

Small Presses I: Jargon Society Y-84

Small Presses II: The Spirit That
    Moves Us Press Y-85

Small Presses III: Pushcart Press Y-87

Smiles, Samuel 1812-1904 .... DLB-55

Smith, Alexander 1829-1867 .... DLB-32, 55

Smith, Betty 1896-1972 .... Y-82

Smith, Carol Sturm 1938- Y-81

Smith, Charles Henry 1826-1903 .... DLB-11

Smith, Charlotte 1749-1806 .... DLB-39

Smith, Cordwainer 1913-1966 .... DLB-8

Smith, Dave 1942- DLB-5

Smith, Dodie 1896- DLB-10

Smith, Doris Buchanan 1934- DLB-52

Smith, E. E. 1890-1965 .... DLB-8

Smith, Elihu Hubbard 1771-1798 .... DLB-37

Smith, Elizabeth Oakes (Prince) 1806-1893 ...... DLB-1

Smith, George O. 1911-1981 .... DLB-8

Smith, H. Allen 1907-1976 .... DLB-11, 29

Smith, Harrison, and Robert Haas
    [publishing house] DLB-46

Smith, Iain Crichten 1928- DLB-40

Smith, J. Allen 1860-1924 .... DLB-47

Smith, J. Stilman, and Company DLB-49

Smith, John 1580-1631 .... DLB-24, 30

Smith, Josiah 1704-1781 .... DLB-24

Smith, Ken 1938- DLB-40

Smith, Lee 1944- Y-83

Smith, Mark 1935- Y-82

Smith, Michael 1698-circa 1771 .... DLB-31

Smith, Red 1905-1982 .... DLB-29

Smith, Samuel Harrison 1772-1845 .... DLB-43

Smith, Samuel Stanhope 1751-1819 .... DLB-37

Smith, Seba 1792-1868 .... DLB-1, 11

Smith, Stevie 1902-1971 .... DLB-20

Smith, Sydney Goodsir 1915-1975 .... DLB-27

Smith, W. B., and Company DLB-49

Smith, William 1727-1803 .... DLB-31

Smith, William 1728-1793 .... DLB-30

Smith, William Jay 1918- DLB-5

Smollett, Tobias 1721-1771 .... DLB-39

Snellings, Rolland (see Touré, Askia Muhammad)

Snodgrass, W. D. 1926- DLB-5

Snow, C. P. 1905-1980 .... DLB-15

Snyder, Gary 1930- DLB-5, 16

Sobiloff, Hy 1912-1970 .... DLB-48

The Society for Textual Scholarship
    and *TEXT* Y-87

Solano, Solita 1888-1975 .... DLB-4

Solomon, Carl 1928- DLB-16

Solway, David 1941- DLB-53

Solzhenitsyn and America Y-85

Sontag, Susan 1933- DLB-2, 67

Sorrentino, Gilbert 1929- DLB-5; Y-80

Sources for the Study of Tudor
    and Stuart Drama DLB-62

Southerland, Ellease 1943- DLB-33

Southern, Terry 1924- DLB-2

Southern Writers Between the Wars DLB-9

Spark, Muriel 1918- DLB-15

Sparks, Jared 1789-1866 .... DLB-1, 30

Sparshott, Francis 1926- DLB-60

Spellman, A. B. 1935- DLB-41

Spencer, Anne 1882-1975 .... DLB-51, 54

Spencer, Elizabeth 1921- DLB-6

Spencer, Herbert 1820-1903.................. DLB-57

Spencer, Scott 1945- Y-86

Spender, Stephen 1909-...................... DLB-20

Spicer, Jack 1925-1965 .... DLB-5, 16

Spielberg, Peter 1929- Y-81

Spier, Peter 1927- DLB-61

Spinrad, Norman 1940- DLB-8

Squibob (see Derby, George Horatio)

Stafford, Jean 1915-1979....................... DLB-2

Stafford, William 1914- DLB-5

Stage Censorship: "The Rejected Statement"
    (1911), by Bernard Shaw [excerpts]....... DLB-10

Stallings, Laurence 1894-1968.............. DLB-7, 44

Stallworthy, Jon 1935- DLB-40

Stampp, Kenneth M. 1912- DLB-17

Stanford, Ann 1916- DLB-5

Stanton, Frank L. 1857-1927 .... DLB-25

Stapledon, Olaf 1886-1950 .... DLB-15

Star Spangled Banner Office DLB-49

Starkweather, David 1935-.................... DLB-7

Statements on the Art of Poetry.............. DLB-54

Steadman, Mark 1930- DLB-6

The Stealthy School of Criticism (1871), by
    Dante Gabriel Rossetti DLB-35

Stearns, Harold E. 1891-1943 .... DLB-4

Stedman, Edmund Clarence 1833-1908 .... DLB-64

Steele, Max 1922- Y-80

Steere, Richard circa 1643-1721 .... DLB-24

Stegner, Wallace 1909-........................ DLB-9

Stehr, Hermann 1864-1940................... DLB-66

Steig, William 1907- DLB-61

Stein, Gertrude 1874-1946 .... DLB-4, 54

Stein, Leo 1872-1947.......................... DLB-4

Stein and Day Publishers DLB-46

Steinbeck, John 1902-1968 .... DLB-7, 9; DS-2

Steiner, George 1929- DLB-67

Stephen, Leslie 1832-1904.................... DLB-57

Stephens, Alexander H. 1812-1883............ DLB-47

Stephens, Ann 1813-1886 .... DLB-3

Stephens, Charles Asbury 1844?-1931........ DLB-42

Stephens, James 1882?-1950................... DLB-19

Sterling, George 1869-1926................... DLB-54

Sterling, James 1701-1763.................... DLB-24

Stern, Richard 1928- Y-87

Stern, Stewart 1922- DLB-26

Sterne, Laurence 1713-1768.................. DLB-39

Sternheim, Carl 1878-1942 .... DLB-56

Stevens, Wallace 1879-1955................... DLB-54

Stevenson, Anne 1933- DLB-40

Stevenson, Robert Louis 1850-1894 .... DLB-18, 57

Stewart, Donald Ogden 1894-1980 ..... DLB-4, 11, 26

Stewart, Dugald 1753-1828................... DLB-31

Stewart, George R. 1895-1980.................. DLB-8

Stewart and Kidd Company DLB-46

Stickney, Trumbull 1874-1904................ DLB-54

Stiles, Ezra 1727-1795 .... DLB-31

Still, James 1906- DLB-9

Stith, William 1707-1755 .... DLB-31

Stockton, Frank R. 1834-1902 .... DLB-42

Stoddard, Ashbel [publishing house] DLB-49

Stoddard, Richard Henry 1825-1903........ DLB-3, 64

Stoddard, Solomon 1643-1729................ DLB-24

Stoker, Bram 1847-1912.................... DLB-36, 70

Stokes, Frederick A., Company................ DLB-49

Stokes, Thomas L. 1898-1958 .... DLB-29

Stone, Herbert S., and Company DLB-49

Stone, Melville 1848-1929 .... DLB-25

Stone, Samuel 1602-1663..................... DLB-24

Stone and Kimball............................ DLB-49

Stoppard, Tom 1937- DLB-13; Y-85

Storey, Anthony 1928- DLB-14

Storey, David 1933- DLB-13, 14

Story, Thomas circa 1670-1742............... DLB-31

Story, William Wetmore 1819-1895............. DLB-1

Storytelling: A Contemporary Renaissance Y-84

Stoughton, William 1631-1701................ DLB-24

Stowe, Harriet Beecher 1811-1896 ...... DLB-1, 12, 42

Stowe, Leland 1899- DLB-29

Strand, Mark 1934- DLB-5

Stratemeyer, Edward 1862-1930.............. DLB-42

Stratton and Barnard........................ DLB-49

Straub, Peter 1943- Y-84

Street and Smith............................ DLB-49

Streeter, Edward 1891-1976.................. DLB-11

Stribling, T. S. 1881-1965 ....DLB-9

Stringer and Townsend DLB-49

Strittmatter, Erwin 1912- DLB-69

Strother, David Hunter 1816-1888 ....DLB-3

Stuart, Jesse 1906-1984.............. DLB-9, 48; Y-84

Stuart, Lyle [publishing house] DLB-46

Stubbs, Harry Clement (see Clement, Hal)

The Study of Poetry (1880), by Matthew
    Arnold DLB-35

Sturgeon, Theodore 1918-1985 .... DLB-8; Y-85

Sturges, Preston 1898-1959................... DLB-26

"Style" (1840; revised, 1859), by Thomas
    de Quincey [excerpt]..................... DLB-57

"Style" (1888), by Walter Pater DLB-57

Style (1897), by Walter Raleigh [excerpt]....... DLB-57

"Style" (1877), by T. H. Wright [excerpt]...... DLB-57

"Le Style c'est l'homme" (1892),
    by W. H. Mallock DLB-57

Styron, William 1925- DLB-2; Y-80

Such, Peter 1939- DLB-60

Suckling, Sir John 1609-1642................. DLB-58

Suckow, Ruth 1892-1960 ....DLB-9

Suggs, Simon (see Hooper, Johnson Jones)

Sukenick, Ronald 1932- Y-81

Suknaski, Andrew 1942- DLB-53

Sullivan, C. Gardner 1886-1965 .... DLB-26

Sullivan, Frank 1892-1976................... DLB-11

Summers, Hollis 1916- DLB-6

Sumner, Henry A. [publishing house]........ DLB-49

Surtees, Robert Smith 1803-1864.............. DLB-21

A Survey of Poetry
    Anthologies, 1879-1960 .... DLB-54

Surveys of the Year's Biography
    A Transit of Poets and Others: American
        Biography in 1982 ....Y-82

The Year in Literary Biography Y-83

The Year in Literary Biography Y-84

The Year in Literary Biography Y-85

The Year in Literary Biography Y-86

The Year in Literary Biography Y-87

Surveys of the Year's Book Publishing
    The Year in Book Publishing...............Y-86

Surveys of the Year's Drama
    The Year in Drama Y-82

The Year in Drama Y-83

The Year in Drama Y-84

The Year in Drama Y-85

The Year in Drama Y-87

Surveys of the Year's Fiction
    The Year's Work in Fiction: A Survey Y-82

The Year in Fiction: A Biased View Y-83

The Year in Fiction Y-84

The Year in Fiction Y-85

The Year in Fiction Y-86

The Year in the Novel Y-87

The Year in Short Stories....................Y-87

Surveys of the Year's Poetry
    The Year's Work in American Poetry.........Y-82

The Year in Poetry Y-83

The Year in Poetry Y-84

The Year in Poetry Y-85

The Year in Poetry Y-86

The Year in Poetry Y-87

Sutherland, John 1919-1956................... DLB-68

Sutro, Alfred 1863-1933..................... DLB-10

Swados, Harvey 1920-1972 ....DLB-2

Swain, Charles 1801-1874 .... DLB-32

Swallow Press................................ DLB-46

Swenson, May 1919- DLB-5

Swerling, Jo 1897- DLB-44

Swift, Jonathan 1667-1745................... DLB-39

Swinburne, A. C. 1837-1909...............DLB-35, 57

Swinnerton, Frank 1884-1982 .... DLB-34

Swisshelm, Jane Grey 1815-1884 .... DLB-43

Swope, Herbert Bayard 1882-1958............ DLB-25

Swords, T. and J., and Company.............. DLB-49

Symonds, John Addington 1840-1893........ DLB-57

Symons, Arthur 1865-1945................DLB-19, 57

Symons, Scott 1933- DLB-53

Synge, John Millington 1871-1909.........DLB-10, 19

T

Taggard, Genevieve 1894-1948............... DLB-45

Tait, J. Selwin, and Sons..................... DLB-49

Talvj or Talvi (see Robinson, Therese)

Taradash, Daniel 1913- DLB-44

Tarbell, Ida M. 1857-1944.................... DLB-47

Tarkington, Booth 1869-1946................... DLB-9

Tashlin, Frank 1913-1972 .... DLB-44

Tate, Allen 1899-1979.................. DLB-4, 45, 63

Tate, James 1943- DLB-5

Taylor, Bayard 1825-1878..................... DLB-3

Taylor, Bert Leston 1866-1921 .... DLB-25

Taylor, Charles H. 1846-1921 .... DLB-25

Taylor, Edward circa 1642-1729............... DLB-24

Taylor, Henry 1942- DLB-5

Taylor, Sir Henry 1800-1886................ DLB-32

Taylor, Mildred D. ?- DLB-52

Taylor, Peter 1917- Y-81

Taylor, William, and Company................ DLB-49

Taylor-Made Shakespeare? Or Is
    "Shall I Die?" the Long-Lost Text
    of Bottom's Dream?........................ Y-85

Teasdale, Sara 1884-1933 .... DLB-45

The Tea-Table (1725), by Eliza Haywood
    [excerpt] DLB-39

Tenn, William 1919- DLB-8

Tennant, Emma 1937- DLB-14

Tenney, Tabitha Gilman 1762-1837.......... DLB-37

Tennyson, Alfred 1809-1892 .... DLB-32

Tennyson, Frederick 1807-1898.............. DLB-32

Terhune, Albert Payson 1872-1942............ DLB-9

Terry, Megan 1932- DLB-7

Terson, Peter 1932- DLB-13

Tesich, Steve 1943- Y-83

Thacher, James 1754-1844 .... DLB-37

Thackeray, William Makepeace
    1811-1863........................... DLB-21, 55

The Theater in Shakespeare's Time.......... DLB-62

The Theatre Guild DLB-7

Thério, Adrien 1925- DLB-53

Theroux, Paul 1941- DLB-2

Thoma, Ludwig 1867-1921.................... DLB-66

Thoma, Richard 1902- DLB-4

Thomas, Audrey 1935- DLB-60

Thomas, D. M. 1935- DLB-40

Thomas, Dylan 1914-1953................. DLB-13, 20

Thomas, Edward 1878-1917................. DLB-19

Thomas, Gwyn 1913-1981................. DLB-15

Thomas, Isaiah 1750-1831.................... DLB-43

Thomas, Isaiah [publishing house] DLB-49

Thomas, John 1900-1932...................... DLB-4

Thomas, Joyce Carol 1938- DLB-33

Thomas, Lorenzo 1944- DLB-41

Thomas, R. S. 1915- DLB-27

Thompson, Dorothy 1893-1961 .... DLB-29

Thompson, Francis 1859-1907 .... DLB-19

Thompson, George Selden (see Selden, George)

Thompson, John 1938-1976.................. DLB-60

Thompson, John R. 1823-1873................ DLB-3

Thompson, Maurice 1844-1901 .... DLB-71

Thompson, Ruth Plumly 1891-1976.......... DLB-22

Thompson, William Tappan 1812-1882.....DLB-3, 11

Thomson, James 1834-1882 .... DLB-35

Thomson, Mortimer 1831-1875 .... DLB-11

Thoreau, Henry David 1817-1862.............. DLB-1

Thorpe, Thomas Bangs 1815-1878..........DLB-3, 11

Thoughts on Poetry and Its Varieties (1833),
    by John Stuart Mill...................... DLB-32

Thurber, James 1894-1961 ....DLB-4, 11, 22

Thurman, Wallace 1902-1934 .... DLB-51

Thwaite, Anthony 1930- DLB-40

Thwaites, Reuben Gold 1853-1913 .... DLB-47

Ticknor, George 1791-1871 ....DLB-1, 59

Ticknor and Fields DLB-49

Ticknor and Fields (revived)................. DLB-46

Tietjens, Eunice 1884-1944................... DLB-54

Tilton, J. E., and Company................... DLB-49

Time and Western Man (1927), by Wyndham
  Lewis [excerpts] DLB-36

Time-Life Books DLB-46

Times Books DLB-46

Timothy, Peter circa 1725-1782 .... DLB-43

Timrod, Henry 1828-1867 .... DLB-3

Tiptree, James, Jr. 1915- DLB-8

Titus, Edward William 1870-1952 .... DLB-4

Toklas, Alice B. 1877-1967 .... DLB-4

Tolkien, J. R. R. 1892-1973 .... DLB-15

Tolson, Melvin B. 1898-1966 .... DLB-48

Tom Jones (1749), by Henry
  Fielding [excerpt] DLB-39

Tomlinson, Charles 1927- DLB-40

Tomlinson, Henry Major 1873-1958 .... DLB-36

Tompkins, Abel [publishing house] DLB-49

Tompson, Benjamin 1642-1714 .... DLB-24

Tonks, Rosemary 1932- DLB-14

Toole, John Kennedy 1937-1969 .... Y-81

Toomer, Jean 1894-1967 .... DLB-45, 51

Tor Books DLB-46

Torrence, Ridgely 1874-1950 .... DLB-54

Toth, Susan Allen 1940- Y-86

Tough-Guy Literature DLB-9

Touré, Askia Muhammad 1938- DLB-41

Tourneur, Cyril circa 1580-1626 .... DLB-58

Tousey, Frank [publishing house] DLB-49

Tower Publications DLB-46

Towne, Benjamin circa 1740-1793 .... DLB-43

Towne, Robert 1936- DLB-44

Tracy, Honor 1913- DLB-15

The Transatlantic Publishing Company DLB-49

Traven, B. 1882? or 1890?-1969? DLB-9, 56

Travers, Ben 1886-1980 .... DLB-10

Tremain, Rose 1943- DLB-14

Tremblay, Michel 1942- DLB-60

Trends in Twentieth-Century
  Mass Market Publishing DLB-46

Trent, William P. 1862-1939 .... DLB-47

Trescot, William Henry 1822-1898 .... DLB-30

Trevor, William 1928- DLB-14

Trilling, Lionel 1905-1975 .... DLB-28, 63

Triolet, Elsa 1896-1970 .... DLB-72

Tripp, John 1927- DLB-40

Trocchi, Alexander 1925- DLB-15

Trollope, Anthony 1815-1882 .... DLB-21, 57

Trollope, Frances 1779-1863 .... DLB-21

Troop, Elizabeth 1931- DLB-14

Trotti, Lamar 1898-1952 .... DLB-44

Trottier, Pierre 1925- DLB-60

Troupe, Quincy Thomas, Jr. 1943- DLB-41

Trow, John F., and Company DLB-49

Trumbo, Dalton 1905-1976 .... DLB-26

Trumbull, Benjamin 1735-1820 .... DLB-30

Trumbull, John 1750-1831 .... DLB-31

Tucholsky, Kurt 1890-1935 .... DLB-56

Tucker, George 1775-1861 .... DLB-3, 30

Tucker, Nathaniel Beverley 1784-1851 .... DLB-3

Tucker, St. George 1752-1827 .... DLB-37

Tuckerman, Henry Theodore 1813-1871 ...... DLB-64

Tunis, John R. 1889-1975 .... DLB-22

Tuohy, Frank 1925- DLB-14

Tupper, Martin F. 1810-1889 .... DLB-32

Turbyfill, Mark 1896- DLB-45

Turco, Lewis 1934- Y-84

Turnbull, Gael 1928- DLB-40

Turner, Charles (Tennyson) 1808-1879 .... DLB-32

Turner, Frederick 1943- DLB-40

Turner, Frederick Jackson 1861-1932 .... DLB-17

Turpin, Waters Edward 1910-1968 .... DLB-51

Twain, Mark (see Clemens, Samuel Langhorne)

Tyler, Anne 1941- DLB-6; Y-82

Tyler, Moses Coit 1835-1900 .... DLB-47, 64

Tyler, Royall 1757-1826 .... DLB-37

Tylor, Edward Burnett 1832-1917 .... DLB-57

U

Udall, Nicholas 1504-1556................... DLB-62

Uhse, Bodo 1904-1963 .... DLB-69

Under the Microscope (1872), by A. C.
   Swinburne DLB-35

United States Book Company DLB-49

Universal Publishing and Distributing
   Corporation........................... DLB-46

The University of Iowa Writers'
   Workshop Golden Jubilee.................Y-86

"The Unknown Public" (1858), by
   Wilkie Collins [excerpt] DLB-57

Unruh, Fritz von 1885-1970................. DLB-56

Upchurch, Boyd B. (see Boyd, John)

Updike, John 1932- DLB-2, 5; Y-80, 82; DS-3

Upton, Charles 1948- DLB-16

Upward, Allen 1863-1926 .... DLB-36

Ustinov, Peter 1921- DLB-13

V

Vail, Laurence 1891-1968 ....DLB-4

Vajda, Ernest 1887-1954 .... DLB-44

Valgardson, W. D. 1939- DLB-60

Van Allsburg, Chris 1949- DLB-61

Van Anda, Carr 1864-1945................... DLB-25

Vance, Jack 1916?- DLB-8

Van Doran, Mark 1894-1972 .... DLB-45

van Druten, John 1901-1957 .... DLB-10

Van Duyn, Mona 1921- DLB-5

Van Dyke, Henry 1852-1933 .... DLB-71

Van Dyke, Henry 1928- DLB-33

Vane, Sutton 1888-1963..................... DLB-10

Vanguard Press............................. DLB-46

van Itallie, Jean-Claude 1936- DLB-7

Vann, Robert L. 1879-1940.................. DLB-29

Van Rensselaer, Mariana Griswold
   1851-1934............................. DLB-47

Van Rensselaer, Mrs. Schuyler (see Van
   Rensselaer, Mariana Griswold)

Van Vechten, Carl 1880-1964 .... DLB-4, 9

van Vogt, A. E. 1912- DLB-8

Varley, John 1947- Y-81

Vassa, Gustavus (see Equiano, Olaudah)

Vega, Janine Pommy 1942- DLB-16

Veiller, Anthony 1903-1965 .... DLB-44

Verplanck, Gulian C. 1786-1870.............. DLB-59

Very, Jones 1813-1880 ....DLB-1

Vian, Boris 1920-1959....................... DLB-72

Victoria 1819-1901 .... DLB-55

Vidal, Gore 1925- DLB-6

Viebig, Clara 1860-1952 .... DLB-66

Viereck, George Sylvester 1884-1962......... DLB-54

Viereck, Peter 1916- DLB-5

Viewpoint: Politics and Performance, by David
   Edgar DLB-13

Vigneault, Gilles 1928- DLB-60

The Viking Press DLB-46

Villard, Henry 1835-1900 .... DLB-23

Villard, Oswald Garrison 1872-1949.......... DLB-25

Villemaire, Yolande 1949- DLB-60

Viorst, Judith ?- DLB-52

Volland, P. F., Company DLB-46

Vonnegut, Kurt 1922- DLB-2, 8; Y-80; DS-3

Vroman, Mary Elizabeth circa 1924-1967...... DLB-33

W

Waddington, Miriam 1917- DLB-68

Wagoner, David 1926- DLB-5

Wah, Fred 1939- DLB-60

Wain, John 1925- DLB-15, 27

Wainwright, Jeffrey 1944- DLB-40

Waite, Peirce and Company DLB-49

Wakoski, Diane 1937- DLB-5

Walck, Henry Z.............................. DLB-46

Walcott, Derek 1930- Y-81

Waldman, Anne 1945- DLB-16

Walker, Alice 1944- DLB-6, 33

Walker, George F. 1947- DLB-60

Walker, Joseph A. 1935- DLB-38

Walker, Ted 1934- DLB-40

Walker and Company DLB-49

Walker, Evans and Cogswell Company DLB-49

Wallace, Edgar 1875-1932 .... DLB-70

Wallant, Edward Lewis 1926-1962 .... DLB-2, 28

Walpole, Horace 1717-1797 .... DLB-39

Walpole, Hugh 1884-1941 .... DLB-34

Walrond, Eric 1898-1966 .... DLB-51

Walser, Robert 1878-1956 .... DLB-66

Walsh, Ernest 1895-1926 .... DLB-4, 45

Walsh, Robert 1784-1859 .... DLB-59

Wambaugh, Joseph 1937- DLB-6; Y-83

Ward, Artemus (see Browne, Charles Farrar)

Ward, Arthur Henry Sarsfield
    (see Rohmer, Sax)

Ward, Douglas Turner 1930- DLB-7, 38

Ward, Lynd 1905-1985 .... DLB-22

Ward, Mrs. Humphry 1851-1920 .... DLB-18

Ward, Nathaniel circa 1578-1652 .... DLB-24

Ware, William 1797-1852 .... DLB-1

Warne, Frederick, and Company DLB-49

Warner, Charles Dudley 1829-1900 .... DLB-64

Warner, Rex 1905- DLB-15

Warner, Susan Bogert 1819-1885 .... DLB-3, 42

Warner, Sylvia Townsend 1893-1978 .... DLB-34

Warner Books DLB-46

Warren, John Byrne Leicester (see De Tabley, Lord)

Warren, Lella 1899-1982 .... Y-83

Warren, Mercy Otis 1728-1814 .... DLB-31

Warren, Robert Penn 1905- DLB-2, 48; Y-80

Washington, George 1732-1799 .... DLB-31

Wassermann, Jakob 1873-1934 .... DLB-66

Wasson, David Atwood 1823-1887 .... DLB-1

Waterhouse, Keith 1929- DLB-13, 15

Waterman, Andrew 1940- DLB-40

Waters, Frank 1902- Y-86

Watkins, Vernon 1906-1967 .... DLB-20

Watmough, David 1926- DLB-53

Watson, Sheila 1909- DLB-60

Watson, Wilfred 1911- DLB-60

Watt, W. J., and Company DLB-46

Watterson, Henry 1840-1921 .... DLB-25

Watts, Alan 1915-1973 .... DLB-16

Watts, Franklin [publishing house] DLB-46

Waugh, Auberon 1939- DLB-14

Waugh, Evelyn 1903-1966 .... DLB-15

Way and Williams DLB-49

Wayman, Tom 1945- DLB-53

Weatherly, Tom 1942- DLB-41

Webb, Frank J. ?-? DLB-50

Webb, James Watson 1802-1884 .... DLB-43

Webb, Mary 1881-1927 .... DLB-34

Webb, Phyllis 1927- DLB-53

Webb, Walter Prescott 1888-1963 .... DLB-17

Webster, Augusta 1837-1894 .... DLB-35

Webster, Charles L., and Company DLB-49

Webster, John 1579 or 1580-1634? DLB-58

Webster, Noah 1758-1843 .... DLB-1, 37, 42, 43

Weems, Mason Locke 1759-1825 .... DLB-30, 37, 42

Weidman, Jerome 1913- DLB-28

Weinbaum, Stanley Grauman 1902-1935 .... DLB-8

Weisenborn, Günther 1902-1969 .... DLB-69

Weiss, John 1818-1879 .... DLB-1

Weiss, Peter 1916-1982 .... DLB-69

Weiss, Theodore 1916- DLB-5

Welch, Lew 1926-1971? DLB-16

Weldon, Fay 1931- DLB-14

Wellek, René 1903- DLB-63

Wells, Carolyn 1862-1942 .... DLB-11

Wells, Charles Jeremiah circa 1800-1879 ..... DLB-32

Wells, H. G. 1866-1946 .... DLB-34, 70

Wells, Robert 1947- DLB-40

Wells-Barnett, Ida B. 1862-1931 .... DLB-23

Welty, Eudora 1909- DLB-2; Y-87

Wendell, Barrett 1855-1921 .... DLB-71

The Werner Company DLB-49

Wersba, Barbara 1932- DLB-52

Wescott, Glenway 1901- DLB-4, 9

Wesker, Arnold 1932- DLB-13

Wesley, Richard 1945- DLB-38

Wessels, A., and Company.................... DLB-46

West, Anthony 1914- DLB-15

West, Jessamyn 1902-1984................ DLB-6; Y-84

West, Mae 1892-1980........................ DLB-44

West, Nathanael 1903-1940.............. DLB-4, 9, 28

West, Paul 1930- DLB-14

West, Rebecca 1892-1983............... DLB-36; Y-83

West and Johnson........................... DLB-49

Western Publishing Company DLB-46

Wetherell, Elizabeth (see Warner, Susan Bogert)

Whalen, Philip 1923- DLB-16

Wharton, Edith 1862-1937 .... DLB-4, 9, 12

Wharton, William 1920s?- Y-80

What's Really Wrong With Bestseller Lists........Y-84

Wheatley, Phillis circa 1754-1784..........DLB-31, 50

Wheeler, Charles Stearns 1816-1843 ....DLB-1

Wheeler, Monroe 1900- DLB-4

Wheelock, John Hall 1886-1978.............. DLB-45

Wheelwright, John circa 1592-1679 .... DLB-24

Wheelwright, J. B. 1897-1940 .... DLB-45

Whetstone, Colonel Pete (see Noland, C. F. M.)

Whipple, Edwin Percy 1819-1886 ....DLB-1, 64

Whitaker, Alexander 1585-1617.............. DLB-24

Whitcher, Frances Miriam 1814-1852 .... DLB-11

White, Andrew 1579-1656.................... DLB-24

White, Andrew Dickson 1832-1918........... DLB-47

White, E. B. 1899-1985.....................DLB-11, 22

White, Edgar B. 1947- DLB-38

White, Horace 1834-1916 .... DLB-23

White, Richard Grant 1821-1885 .... DLB-64

White, Walter 1893-1955 .... DLB-51

White, William, and Company................ DLB-49

White, William Allen 1868-1944............DLB-9, 25

White, William Anthony Parker (see Boucher, Anthony)

White, William Hale (see Rutherford, Mark)

Whitechurch, Victor L. 1868-1933............ DLB-70

Whitehead, James 1936- Y-81

Whitfield, James Monroe 1822-1871.......... DLB-50

Whiting, John 1917-1963..................... DLB-13

Whiting, Samuel 1597-1679 .... DLB-24

Whitlock, Brand 1869-1934 .... DLB-12

Whitman, Albert, and Company............... DLB-46

Whitman, Albery Allson 1851-1901 .... DLB-50

Whitman, Sarah Helen (Power) 1803-1878......DLB-1

Whitman, Walt 1819-1892...................DLB-3, 64

Whitman Publishing Company DLB-46

Whittemore, Reed 1919- DLB-5

Whittier, John Greenleaf 1807-1892............DLB-1

Whittlesey House............................ DLB-46

Wideman, John Edgar 1941- DLB-33

Wiebe, Rudy 1934- DLB-60

Wiechert, Ernst 1887-1950 .... DLB-56

Wieners, John 1934- DLB-16

Wier, Ester 1910- DLB-52

Wiesel, Elie 1928- Y-87

Wiggin, Kate Douglas 1856-1923.............. DLB-42

Wigglesworth, Michael 1631-1705.............. DLB-24

Wilbur, Richard 1921- DLB-5

Wild, Peter 1940- DLB-5

Wilde, Oscar 1854-1900 ....DLB-10, 19, 34, 57

Wilde, Richard Henry 1789-1847............DLB-3, 59

Wilde, W. A., Company DLB-49

Wilder, Billy 1906- DLB-26

Wilder, Laura Ingalls 1867-1957 .... DLB-22

Wilder, Thornton 1897-1975.............. DLB-4, 7, 9

Wiley, Bell Irvin 1906-1980 .... DLB-17

Wiley, John, and Sons........................ DLB-49

Wilhelm, Kate 1928- DLB-8

Wilkinson, Sylvia 1940- Y-86

Wilkinson, William Cleaver 1833-1920 .... DLB-71

Willard, L. [publishing house]................. DLB-49

Willard, Nancy 1936- DLB-5, 52

Willard, Samuel 1640-1707 .... DLB-24

Williams, A., and Company................... DLB-49

Williams, C. K. 1936- DLB-5

Williams, Emlyn 1905- DLB-10

Williams, Garth 1912- DLB-22

Williams, George Washington 1849-1891 ...... DLB-47

Williams, Heathcote 1941- DLB-13

Williams, Hugo 1942- DLB-40

Williams, Isaac 1802-1865 .... DLB-32

Williams, Joan 1928- DLB-6

Williams, John A. 1925- DLB-2, 33

Williams, John E. 1922- DLB-6

Williams, Jonathan 1929- DLB-5

Williams, Raymond 1921- DLB-14

Williams, Roger circa 1603-1683.............. DLB-24

Williams, Samm-Art 1946- DLB-38

Williams, Sherley Anne 1944- DLB-41

Williams, T. Harry 1909-1979................ DLB-17

Williams, Tennessee 1911-1983.....DLB-7; Y-83; DS-4

Williams, William Appleman 1921- DLB-17

Williams, William Carlos 1883-1963 ..... DLB-4, 16, 54

Williams, Wirt 1921- DLB-6

Williams Brothers DLB-49

Williamson, Jack 1908- DLB-8

Willingham, Calder Baynard, Jr. 1922- DLB-2, 44

Willis, Nathaniel Parker 1806-1867.........DLB-3, 59

Wilmer, Clive 1945- DLB-40

Wilson, A. N. 1950- DLB-14

Wilson, Angus 1913- DLB-15

Wilson, Arthur 1595-1652.................... DLB-58

Wilson, Augusta Jane Evans 1835-1909 .... DLB-42

Wilson, Colin 1931- DLB-14

Wilson, Edmund 1895-1972 .... DLB-63

Wilson, Ethel 1888-1980..................... DLB-68

Wilson, Harriet E. Adams 1828?-1863?........ DLB-50

Wilson, Harry Leon 1867-1939.................DLB-9

Wilson, John 1588-1667 .... DLB-24

Wilson, Lanford 1937- DLB-7

Wilson, Margaret 1882-1973...................DLB-9

Wilson, Michael 1914-1978 .... DLB-44

Wilson, Woodrow 1856-1924 .... DLB-47

Wimsatt, William K., Jr. 1907-1975........... DLB-63

Winchell, Walter 1897-1972 .... DLB-29

Winchester, J. [publishing house]............. DLB-49

Windham, Donald 1920- DLB-6

Winsor, Justin 1831-1897..................... DLB-47

John C. Winston Company DLB-49

Winters, Yvor 1900-1968 .... DLB-48

Winthrop, John 1588-1649 ....DLB-24, 30

Winthrop, John, Jr. 1606-1676 .... DLB-24

Wirt, William 1772-1834...................... DLB-37

Wise, John 1652-1725 .... DLB-24

Wisner, George 1812-1849 .... DLB-43

Wister, Owen 1860-1938 ....DLB-9

Witherspoon, John 1723-1794................. DLB-31

Wodehouse, P. G. 1881-1975................. DLB-34

Woiwode, Larry 1941- DLB-6

Wolcott, Roger 1679-1767 .... DLB-24

Wolfe, Gene 1931- DLB-8

Wolfe, Thomas 1900-1938.........DLB-9; DS-2; Y-85

Wollstonecraft, Mary 1759-1797.............. DLB-39

Wood, Benjamin 1820-1900 .... DLB-23

Wood, Charles 1932- DLB-13

Wood, Mrs. Henry 1814-1887................. DLB-18

Wood, Samuel [publishing house] DLB-49

Wood, William ?-? DLB-24

Woodberry, George Edward 1855-1930 .... DLB-71

Woodbridge, Benjamin 1622-1684 .... DLB-24

Woodmason, Charles circa 1720-? DLB-31

Woodson, Carter G. 1875-1950................ DLB-17

Woodward, C. Vann 1908- DLB-17

Woolf, David (see Maddow, Ben)

Woolf, Virginia 1882-1941 .... DLB-36

Woollcott, Alexander 1887-1943............... DLB-29

Woolman, John 1720-1772 .... DLB-31

Woolner, Thomas 1825-1892................. DLB-35

Woolsey, Sarah Chauncy 1835-1905.......... DLB-42

Woolson, Constance Fenimore 1840-1894 ..... DLB-12

Worcester, Joseph Emerson 1784-1865.........DLB-1

The Works of the Rev. John Witherspoon
(1800-1801) [excerpts] DLB-31

A World Chronology of Important Science
Fiction Works (1818-1979) DLB-8

World Publishing Company DLB-46

Worthington, R., and Company DLB-49

Wouk, Herman 1915- Y-82

Wright, Charles 1935- Y-82

Wright, Charles Stevenson 1932- DLB-33

Wright, Harold Bell 1872-1944.................DLB-9

Wright, James 1927-1980......................DLB-5

Wright, Jay 1935- DLB-41

Wright, Louis B. 1899-1984 .... DLB-17

Wright, Richard 1908-1960......................DS-2

Wright, Richard B. 1937- DLB-53

Wright, Sarah Elizabeth 1928- DLB-33

Writers' Forum Y-85

Writing for the Theatre, by Harold Pinter DLB-13

Wylie, Elinor 1885-1928....................DLB-9, 45

Wylie, Philip 1902-1971 ....DLB-9

Young, Stark 1881-1963.........................DLB-9

Young, Waldeman 1880-1938 .... DLB-26

Young, William [publishing house]........... DLB-49

Yourcenar, Marguerite 1903-1987............. DLB-72

"You've Never Had It So Good," Gusted by
    "Winds of Change": British Fiction in the
    1950s, 1960s, and After................... DLB-14

Y

Yates, J. Michael 1938- DLB-60

Yates, Richard 1926- DLB-2; Y-81

Yeats, William Butler 1865-1939 ....DLB-10, 19

Yep, Laurence 1948- DLB-52

Yezierska, Anzia 1885-1970 .... DLB-28

Yolen, Jane 1939- DLB-52

Yonge, Charlotte Mary 1823-1901............ DLB-18

A Yorkshire Tragedy........................... DLB-58

Yoseloff, Thomas [publishing house].......... DLB-46

Young, Al 1939- DLB-33

Z

Zangwill, Israel 1864-1926.................... DLB-10

Zebra Books DLB-46

Zebrowski, George 1945- DLB-8

Zech, Paul 1881-1946......................... DLB-56

Zelazny, Roger 1937- DLB-8

Zenger, John Peter 1697-1746.............DLB-24, 43

Zieber, G. B., and Company................... DLB-49

Zieroth, Dale 1946- DLB-60

Zimmer, Paul 1934- DLB-5

Zindel, Paul 1936- DLB-7, 52

Zolotow, Charlotte 1915- DLB-52

Zubly, John Joachim 1724-1781 .... DLB-31

Zu-Bolton II, Ahmos 1936- DLB-41

Zuckmayer, Carl 1896-1977 .... DLB-56

Zukofsky, Louis 1904-1978 ....DLB-5

zur Mühlen, Hermynia 1883-1951............. DLB-56

Zweig, Arnold 1887-1968..................... DLB-66

Dictionary of Literary Biography

1: *The American Renaissance in New England*, edited by Joel Myerson (1978)

2: *American Novelists Since World War II*, edited by Jeffrey Helterman and Richard Layman (1978)

3: *Antebellum Writers in New York and the South*, edited by Joel Myerson (1979)

4: *American Writers in Paris, 1920-1939*, edited by Karen Lane Rood (1980)

5: *American Poets Since World War II*, 2 parts, edited by Donald J. Greiner (1980)

6: *American Novelists Since World War II*, Second Series, edited by James E. Kibler, Jr. (1980)

7: *Twentieth-Century American Dramatists*, 2 parts, edited by John MacNicholas (1981)

8: *Twentieth-Century American Science-Fiction Writers*, 2 parts, edited by David Cowart and Thomas L. Wymer (1981)

9: *American Novelists, 1910-1945*, 3 parts, edited by James J. Martine (1981)

10: *Modern British Dramatists, 1900-1945*, 2 parts, edited by Stanley Weintraub (1982)

11: *American Humorists, 1800-1950*, 2 parts, edited by Stanley Trachtenberg (1982)

12: *American Realists and Naturalists*, edited by Donald Pizer and Earl N. Harbert (1982)

13: *British Dramatists Since World War II*, 2 parts, edited by Stanley Weintraub (1982)

14: *British Novelists Since 1960*, 2 parts, edited by Jay L. Halio (1983)

15: *British Novelists, 1930-1959*, 2 parts, edited by Bernard Oldsey (1983)

16: *The Beats: Literary Bohemians in Postwar America*, 2 parts, edited by Ann Charters (1983)

17: *Twentieth-Century American Historians*, edited by Clyde N. Wilson (1983)

18: *Victorian Novelists After 1885*, edited by Ira B. Nadel and William E. Fredeman (1983)

19: *British Poets, 1880-1914*, edited by Donald E. Stanford (1983)

20: *British Poets, 1914-1945*, edited by Donald E. Stanford (1983)

21: *Victorian Novelists Before 1885*, edited by Ira B. Nadel and William E. Fredeman (1983)

22: *American Writers for Children, 1900-1960*, edited by John Cech (1983)

23: *American Newspaper Journalists, 1873-1900*, edited by Perry J. Ashley (1983)

24: *American Colonial Writers, 1606-1734*, edited by Emory Elliott (1984)

25: *American Newspaper Journalists, 1901-1925*, edited by Perry J. Ashley (1984)

26: *American Screenwriters*, edited by Robert E. Morsberger, Stephen O. Lesser, and Randall Clark (1984)

27: *Poets of Great Britain and Ireland, 1945-1960*, edited by Vincent B. Sherry, Jr. (1984)

28: *Twentieth-Century American-Jewish Fiction Writers*, edited by Daniel Walden (1984)

29: *American Newspaper Journalists, 1926-1950*, edited by Perry J. Ashley (1984)

30: *American Historians, 1607-1865*, edited by Clyde N. Wilson (1984)

31: *American Colonial Writers, 1735-1781*, edited by Emory Elliott (1984)

32: *Victorian Poets Before 1850*, edited by William E. Fredeman and Ira B. Nadel (1984)

33: *Afro-American Fiction Writers After 1955*, edited by Thadious M. Davis and Trudier Harris (1984)

34: *British Novelists, 1890-1929: Traditionalists*, edited by Thomas F. Staley (1985)

35: *Victorian Poets After 1850*, edited by William E. Fredeman and Ira B. Nadel (1985)

36: *British Novelists, 1890-1929: Modernists*, edited by Thomas F. Staley (1985)

37: *American Writers of the Early Republic*, edited by Emory Elliott (1985)

38: *Afro-American Writers After 1955: Dramatists and Prose Writers*, edited by Thadious M. Davis and Trudier Harris (1985)

39: *British Novelists, 1660-1800*, 2 parts, edited by Martin C. Battestin (1985)

40: *Poets of Great Britain and Ireland Since 1960*, 2 parts, edited by Vincent B. Sherry, Jr. (1985)

41: *Afro-American Poets Since 1955*, edited by Trudier Harris and Thadious M. Davis (1985)

42: *American Writers for Children Before 1900*, edited by Glenn E. Estes (1985)

43: *American Newspaper Journalists, 1690-1872*, edited by Perry J. Ashley (1986)

44: *American Screenwriters*, Second Series, edited by Randall Clark, Robert E. Morsberger, and Stephen O. Lesser (1986)

45: *American Poets, 1880-1945*, First Series, edited by Peter Quartermain (1986)

46: *American Literary Publishing Houses, 1900-1980: Trade and Paperback*, edited by Peter Dzwonkoski (1986)

47: *American Historians, 1866-1912*, edited by Clyde N. Wilson (1986)